D0208833

Finland

Andy Symington

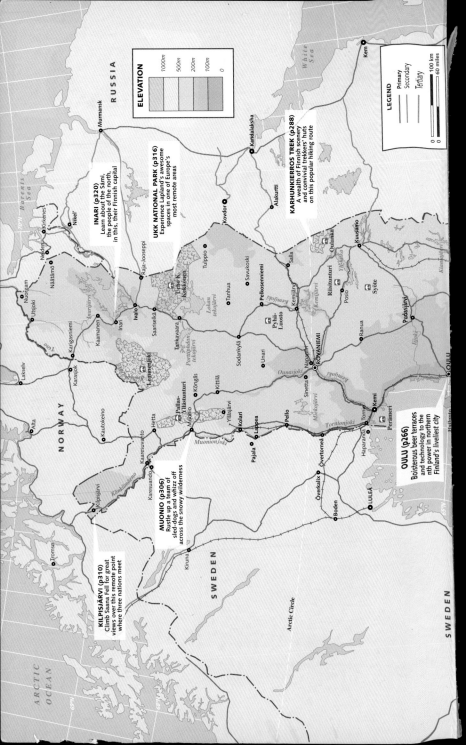

ELEVATION

	1000m
	500m
	200m
	100m
	0

RUSSIA

INARI (p320)
Learn about the Sámi, the people of the north, in this, their Finnish capital

UKK NATIONAL PARK (p316)
Experience Lapland's awesome spaces in one of Europe's most remote areas

KARHUNKIERROS TREK (p288)
A wealth of Finnish scenery and convivial trekkers' huts on this popular hiking route

LEGEND
Primary
Secondary
Tertiary

0   100 km
0   60 miles

OULU (p266)
Boisterous beer terraces and technology to the nth power in northern Finland's liveliest city

MUONIO (p306)
Rustle up a team of sledgedogs and whizz off across the snowy wilderness

KILPISJÄRVI (p310)
Climb Saana Fell for great views over this remote point where three nations meet

NORWAY

SWEDEN

ARCTIC OCEAN

Barents Sea

White Sea

Murmansk

Kem

Kandalaksha

Alakurtti

Salla

Kovdor

Kuusamo

Oulanka

Nikel'

Neiden

Kirkenes

Näätämö

Nuorgam

Utsjoki

Karigasniemi

Raja-Jooseppi

Tulppio

Kessouoen

Lake K

Ukko K

Savukoski

Tankua

Pelkosenniemi

Kemijärvi

Posio

Riisitunturi

Syöte

Pudasjärvi

Ranua

Syöte

Laksely

Alta

Kautokeino

Karasjok

Kaamanen

Inari

Ivalo

Saariselkä

Tankavaara

Pyhä-Luosto

Sodankylä

Unari

ROVANIEMI

Napapiiri

Kemijoki

Lemmenjoki

Inarijärvi

Lokan tekojärvi

Porttipahdan tekojärvi

Ounasjoki

Kemijoki

Pyhäjoki

Kaaresuvanto

Hetta

Pallas-Yllästunturi

Muonio

Köngäs

Kittilä

Kolari

Lappea

Pajala

Ylläsjärvi

Pello

Sinetta

Muonionjoki

Ounasjoki

Mikkeljärvi

Tornionjoki

Tornio

Kemi

Perämeri

Haparanda

Överkalix

Övertorneå

Boden

LULEÅ

Kiruna

Arctic Circle

OULU

Kalajoki

Kivalo

Tromsø

Karlebotn

Kilpisjärvi

Kaldoaivi

Muonionjoki

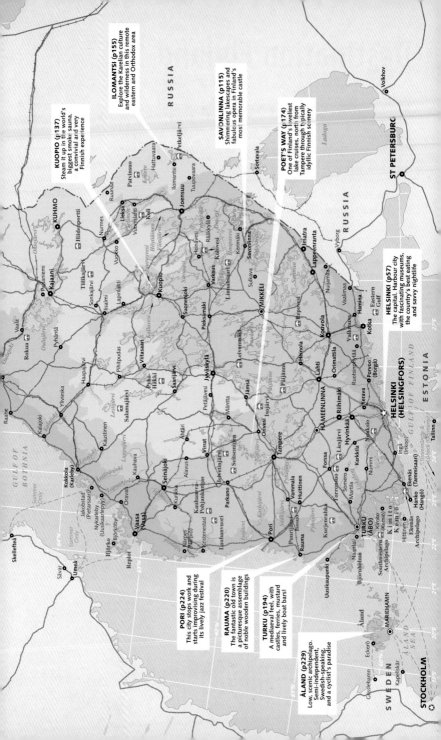

KUOPIO (p137)
Steam up in the world's biggest smoke sauna, a convivial and very Finnish experience

ILOMANTSI (p155)
Explore the Karelian culture and wilderness in this remote eastern and Orthodox area

SAVONLINNA (p115)
Shimmering lakescapes and fabulous opera in Finland's most memorable castle

POET'S WAY (p174)
One of Finland's liveliest lake cruises, north from Tampere through typically idyllic Finnish scenery

HELSINKI (p57)
The capital. Harbour city with fascinating museums, the country's best eating and savvy nightlife

PORI (p224)
This city stops work and starts improvising during its lively jazz festival

RAUMA (p220)
The fantastic old town is a picturesque assemblage of noble wooden buildings

TURKU (p194)
A mediaeval feel, with castles, ferries, mustard and lively boat bars!

ÅLAND (p229)
Low, scenic archipelago. Semi-independent, Swedish-speaking, and a cyclist's paradise

Destination Finland

There's something pure in the Finnish air and spirit that's incredibly vital and exciting. Although socially and economically it is in the vanguard of nations, parts of the country remain gloriously remote; with the trendsetting modern capital of Helsinki counterbalanced by vast forested wildernesses in the north and east. These wilds are perfect for treks among the pines and lakes in summer. And who'd have thought that so far north you could have such a summer? It's a golden, sunny season when Finland bursts into life with an explosion of festivals, good cheer and optimism. It's a time when the towns are buzzing, but it's also a time to head for the lakelands. Sit on the veranda of a waterside wooden cottage and watch the summer sun shining low over the trees, and you'll have experienced one of Finland's ultimate treats; a real Nordic peace that eases the soul.

Winter, too, has a special charm here, and the best way of banishing those scary subzero temperatures is to get active. Every type of skiing and more goes on for months, but how about chartering a team of dogs or a snowmobile and heading out on a trek across the snowy wastes, lit by a beautiful, pale, winter sun? Catch the aurora borealis after your wood-fired sauna and you'll feel blessed by the universe. The Sámi, many of whom still make a living from the reindeer roaming the awesome Lapland expanses, once believed the northern lights to be the snow beaten from the tail of a giant fox spirit.

Finnish towns, too, have much to offer. Whether cosy wooden churches, avant-garde design, quirky museums or passionate Finnish rock music are your thing, you'll find them in abundance, as well as cafés warm with the smell of baking cinnamon, and boisterous nightlife – the latter particularly in chic, cultural Helsinki.

Best of all, Finland is full of Finns, who tend to do their own thing and are much the better for it. Independent, loyal, warm and welcoming – they are a memorable people in an inspirational country.

JOHN BORTH

Highlights

Get close to some of Finland's amazing wildlife (p41)

DAVID TIPLING

JOHN MCLEAN

Learn about life up north at the Arktikum (p298), Rovaniemi

Experience the bustle of Helsinki's waterfront market (p82)

WAYNE WALTON

Turku (p194) offers old- and new-world delights for you to enjoy

Lose yourself in Lapland's wilderness (p295)

See what today's Finnish artists are up to at the Kiasma Museum of Contemporary Art (p62), Helsinki

Remember to breathe during the stunning aurora borealis (p307)

One of the 230,000-odd reindeer (p42) that roam around Finland

Spot the difference, Rovaniemi (p296)

DAVID TIPLING

Set your sights on a snowmobile safari (p298)

Cross the Finnish line in Kemijärvi (p311)

CRAIG PERSHOUSE

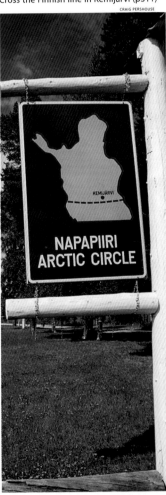

JOHN BORTHWICK

About 600 steel pipes make the Sibelius Monument (p70) in Helsinki a must-see

Contents

Regional Map Contents

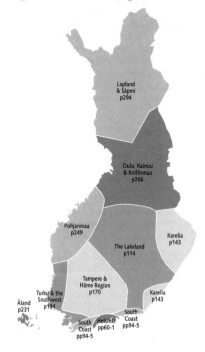

Lapland
& Sápmi
p294

Oulu, Kainuu
& Koillismaa
p266

Pohjanmaa
p249

Karelia
p143

The Lakeland
p114

Tampere &
Häme Region
p170

Karelia
p143

Åland
p231

Turku & the
Southwest
p194

South
Coast
pp94-5

Helsinki
pp60-1

South
Coast
pp94-5

The Author

ANDY SYMINGTON

Andy, a professional travel writer, first visited Finland over a decade ago by accident, and it made a deep impression on him. It was winter, and walking on frozen lakes with the midday sun low in the sky seemed very romantic, until the temperature dropped below -30°C! Everyone told him he must see Finland in summer, so he returned a couple of years later, having in the meantime made many Finnish friends. Since then, they haven't been able to keep him away. Fuelled by a love of the *Kalevala*, huskies, saunas, Finnish mustard, moody *Suomi* rock and metal, but above all of Finnish people and their country, he has spent a lot of time in the country and travelled extensively around it.

MY FAVOURITE TRIP...

Starting off in buzzy Tampere (p169) puts me right in the mood for Finland, with its unusual museums, heartwarming vanilla coffee, and cracker of a brewery-pub. From here it's a boat on the lake or a ride up Route 66 to Ruovesi (p180), where I'll spend a relaxing couple of days in a wooden cottage by a lake, fishing and taking saunas. Then on to Jyväskylä (p129) – I used to sneer at modern architecture but now I'm a big fan – and then Kuopio (p135), where a session in the fantastic communal smoke sauna ends up with a dip in the lake and a slice of *kalakukko* (little lake-fish baked inside a loaf of rye bread). Up to Kuhmo (p280) to renew my love affair with the *Kalevala* and then to Juuma (p291) and the Karhunkierros trek for a dose of Finnish forest. I never miss the Arktikum Museum in Rovaniemi (p296) but prefer smaller places, so (as it's summer) it's up to Pyhä (p312) for a relaxing cottage stay. If it were winter I might have chosen Levi (p295) for its great skiing. On to Muonio (p306) to pat my favourite huskies, and then the peaceful Sámi town of Hetta (p308) – I won't be stopping here though – then on to reach the utter north at Kilpisjärvi (p310) for a hike up Saana Fell.

Getting Started

Travel in Finland is a pleasure. Buses and trains run on time, tourist offices are eager to please and full of at-your-fingertips information, and you can get by easily enough without even dipping into a Finnish dictionary. It's not a cheap destination, but neither are prices as elevated as sometimes imagined, and accommodation in particular can be excellent value, with hotels chopping their prices in summer and at weekends.

WHEN TO GO

The tourist season in southern Finland and the Lakeland is from early June to late August. This is when all attractions and summer accommodation options are open, steamboats and ferries ply the lakes and rivers and festivals are in full swing. Things are at their busiest during Finnish holidays, typically from the summer high season in late June until the end of July. This is the time of long, light nights, when Finland doesn't seem to sleep.

See Climate Charts (p331) for more information.

The tourist season in northern Finland, including Lapland, is different. Mosquitoes can be unbearably annoying in July, but September is delightful with its *ruska* (autumn) colours. October and February/March are good times to visit Lapland to view the aurora borealis (northern lights) and enjoy winter activities such as skiing and dog-sledding. The Christmas holiday period is also prime time in Lapland – after all, this is the 'official' home of Santa Claus. Helsinki is popular year-round.

You can find everything about Finland's weather on the **Finnish Meteorological Institute** (www.fmi.fi) website.

COSTS & MONEY

Finland is an expensive country, but not quite as much as its reputation would suggest. Summer in particular can offer exceptional value, with hotel prices slashed and seasonal restaurants open. With a bit of planning, you can have a great time here on almost any budget.

A couple using public transport, travelling in summer, staying in good midrange hotels and eating out, will spend €100 to €130 per day per person, a little more if spending a lot of time in Helsinki, which is substantially pricier than the rest of Finland, particularly on the accommodation front. As bus and train travel is expensive, this figure would not be inflated

---

DON'T LEAVE HOME WITHOUT...

You can buy virtually anything you need in Finland, but be sure to carry these:

- Insect repellent (double the strength and double the quantity)
- A sleeping sheet and a pillowcase for cabins or hostels
- Eye-mask; if daylight at midnight will keep you from sleeping
- Seriously warm clothing for winter or a water- and windproof jacket for summer
- A Russian visa if you'll be tempted across the border
- A swimsuit; even if it's winter, there are great water parks and ice-holes for post-sauna dips in the lakes
- A mobile phone; it's cheap and easy to get a prepaid SIM card and be on the local network

TOP TENS

Books & Films

See p35 and p38 for more on Finnish literature and cinema.

- *Kalevala* by Elias Lönnrot, translation by Keith Bosley, is Finland's epic, compiled from the songs of bards. It tells everything from the history of the world to how to make decent home-brew.

- *Drifting Clouds*, directed by Aki Kaurismäki is a marvellous film about a couple forced to seek new jobs. It's full of awkward, stilted emotions. *Man Without a Past* is another excellent work from the same director.

- *The Year of the Hare* by Arto Paasilinna tells how a Finnish journalist revolutionizes his life and sees things in a new way while travelling around with a hare.

- *The Canine Kalevala* is a take on the Kalevala by Mauri Kunnas, successful and much-loved children's author and illustrator.

- *Popular Music* by Mikael Niemi is not strictly about Finland, but it could well be. A great read.

- *Finn Family Moomintroll* by Tove Jansson is one of the earliest and best of the loveable Moomin books!

- *Seven Brothers* by Aleksis Kivi is a classic novel. Very readable, with some memorable dialogue.

- *Tuntematon Sotilas* (Unknown Soldier), directed by Rauni Mollberg, is a good film about the Continuation war, based on the book by Väinö Linna. *The Winter War* is another good film about the fight against the Russians.

- *A Short History of Finland* by Fred Singleton is a dry but thorough history, written with affection and a leftist slant.

- *Pahat Pojat* (Bad Boys), directed by Aleksi Mäkelä. Finland does a gang film, with this take on four infamous brothers who terrorized the nation robbing petrol stations pumps and worse.

CDs

What to listen to to get you up to speed on the best recent Finnish music. Download a sample MP3 or two and you'll be able to sing along in bars once you get to Finland! See p39 for more details.

- Ulla Pirttijärvi, *Máttaráhku Askái* (In Our Foremothers' Arms) – marvellous Sámi *yoiks* (see p40 for more information on yoiks) with modern synthesizing.

- The Rasmus, *Dead Letters – In the Shadows* was a huge worldwide hit.

- Maija Vilkkumaa, *Ei* – a Finnish Alanis with plenty of attitude.

- Apulanta, *Plastik* – kicking guitar rock.

- Husky Rescue, *Country Falls* – bright, breezy and very likeable up-and-comers.

- Verenpisara, *Irtileikattu* – Excellent new hard-rock band.

- Trio Töykeät, *Wake* – new album from this successful jazz outfit.

- Vilddas, self titled – another top Sámi offering.

- Zen Café, *Laiksa, Tyhmä, ja Saamaton* – the thinking Finn's rock band with down-to-earth Finnish lyrics.

- Neljä Ruusua, *Karelia Express* – one of many good albums by this downbeat technopop group.

hugely by hiring a car, particularly if you can nab a decent deal over the Internet.

Two people travelling backpacker-style, using hostels and cabins and mostly self-catering could get by comfortably on €50 each per day, less if sleeping in dorms and not taking too many long trips.

A week in Helsinki for a couple spending €250 or more per day each will see a room in one of the best hotels, memorable meals in Finland's best restaurants, and few expenses spared.

There are numerous ways to reduce the amount you spend on holiday in Finland. Nearly all hotels and hostels will put extra beds in a room for little extra charge – great value for families and groups. There's a discount on buses for groups of four or more booking tickets together, and most attractions offer a good-value family ticket. Camp sites nearly always have some sort of cabin accommodation sleeping four or more. These range from simple huts with bunks to luxurious wooden houses, and are always excellent value.

It's much cheaper to eat in restaurants at lunchtime, when there are daily specials and often a groaning buffet table.

Students with valid ID and seniors can receive substantial discounts on museum admission prices quoted in this book, as well as on transportation.

TRAVEL LITERATURE

Michael Palin describes, in characteristically humorous style, his journey from the North to South Poles in *Pole to Pole*. He passes through a good slice of Finland along the way.

Detailing an awesome road trip through Finland, taking an icon of Elvis to the North Pole, is Bill Drummond and Mark Manning's *Bad Wisdom*. If it were a film, it'd cop an X-rating for sexual content, violence and substance abuse.

Philip Ward's *Finnish Cities*, though dated and written in a very dry style, is full of information about Finland's three main cities, as well as Rovaniemi. Strong on architecture.

INTERNET RESOURCES

Finnish Tourist Board (www.visitfinland.com) Official site, and full of excellent information from the practical to the whimsical.

Forest and Park Service (www.outdoors.fi) An excellent resource, with detailed information on all Finland's national parks and protected areas, as well as activities listings.

Helsingin Sanomat (www.helsinginsanomat.fi/english/) International edition of Finland's best daily newspaper.

LonelyPlanet.com (www.lonelyplanet.com) Check recent postings for the very latest recommendations and tips on travelling in Finland.

Virtual Finland (virtual.finland.fi) Maintained by the Finnish Ministry of Foreign Affairs, this is an excellent, informative, and entertaining website.

HOW MUCH?

Bus ride (200km) €28

Sauna free–€10

Bottle of cheap red in a restaurant €25

Day's bike hire €10

Simple log cabin for 2 €30

See also Lonely Planet Index, inside front cover.

Itineraries

CLASSIC ROUTES

ESSENTIAL SUOMI
Helsinki to Rovaniemi/Three weeks

Start in **Helsinki** (p57), a European city *par excellence*. Be sure to see the harbour – get a boat to **Suomenlinna** (p84) or eat at an island restaurant – before heading to **Porvoo** (p88), with its enchanting wooden buildings.

Head inland to **Lappeenranta** (p143) in Karelia and try the local food specialities at a waterfront stall or the beach sauna.

Pretty **Savonlinna** (p115) is next. Its stunning castle is the setting for the famous Savonlinna Opera Festival. Even if your visit doesn't coincide with the festival, it's a memorable town with plenty to do in the area.

Because you are in 'Lakeland', it would be a crime not to jump on a boat. You can take a day cruise to **Kuopio** (p135), where you'll find a tower with superb views, and a convivial smoke sauna. On your way north from here, drop in on **Sonkajärvi** for a spot of wife-carrying (see boxed text p141).

Once you get to **Oulu** (p266), you can really 'feel' the latitude – depending on the time of year, the sun will either barely set or barely rise! It's one of Finland's liveliest towns and has a great summer marketplace.

From Oulu, head to **Kemi** (p273) to see the Snow Castle in winter or, in summer, play midnight golf at **Tornio** (p275). Finally, check out **Rovaniemi** (p296), the Lappish capital and base for any number of activities.

This classic itinerary takes in the capital and a wide selection of Finnish landscapes and towns, from the pretty southern lakelands right up to Lapland's Arctic climes. A journey from south to north of about 1200km.

LAPP GOLD
Rovaniemi Loop/One to two weeks

In Rovaniemi, capital of Lapland, visit the excellent **Arktikum museum** (p298) to learn about these northern latitudes. At **Ranua Zoo** (p302), you can see some of the region's fauna.

Cut eastwards to **Ruka** (p286), a lively ski resort in winter, and a trailhead of the **Karhunkierros** (p288), one of Finland's best trekking routes.

From here, go via **Kemijärvi** (p311) to **Sodankylä** (p312), a village by most standards, but a metropolis in these parts. Don't miss the attractive old wooden church.

Heading northwards, you'll reach **Urho K Kekkonen National Park** (p316), where you can try gold panning before striking out on a trek across the spectacular fells in this vast wilderness. Nearby **Saariselkä** (p314) is a good spot for all manner of summer and winter activities.

One of the most intriguing towns in this region is **Inari** (p320), the main community centre of Finland's Sámi population. It's a handicrafts centre and home to the memorable Siida museum.

Next it's **Lemmenjoki National Park** (p322), yet another place for great trekking. Continue the loop towards northwest Finland, ending up at **Hetta** (p308), a good place to spend a night or two for its Sámi culture and local walks. From here, if you have time, you should head up the 'arm' of Finland to remote **Kilpisjärvi** (p310), overlooked by fearsome Norwegian mountains and the smaller bulk of Saana Fell, which is well worth climbing.

Retrace your steps and head to **Muonio** (p306). In winter you can go husky-sledding, but even in summer it's worth meeting the dogs. From here, return to Rovaniemi, perhaps stopping to ski or rent a summer cottage at busy **Levi** (p305) or peaceful **Pyhä** (p312).

Kilpisjärvi

Inari

Lemmenjoki
National Park

Hetta

Saariselkä

UKK National
Park

Muonio

Levi

Sodankylä

Pyhä

Kemijärvi

Rovaniemi

Ruka

Ranua

A thorough exploration of the wonders of Lapland and its landscapes, with plenty of opportunity for trekking, skiing or sledding as well as learning about Sámi culture and the Arctic environment. Around 1600km.

ROADS LESS TRAVELLED

THE WEST COAST   Helsinki to Oulu/One to two weeks

Popular with locals, the west coast of Finland doesn't attract many foreign visitors, who prefer the charms of the lakes and reindeer.

After Helsinki, stop at **Lohja** (p93) for its church and mining museum. The industrial theme continues with the pretty **ironworks** at Fagervik (p96) and **Fiskars** (p99) which are near the family-friendly seaside town, **Ekenäs** (p194). Then head southwest to the noble wooden villas of **Hanko** (p100), where St Petersburg society once summered.

Turku (p194) has many drawcards, as does the surrounding archipelago (p216) and the picturesque **Naantali** (p212).

Uusikaupunki (p218) has a museum that deserves a prize for ironic humour, while **Rauma's Old Town** (p220) features charming wooden buildings. Moving north, busy **Pori** (p224) is home to a pumping jazz festival.

The next bit of coast is known as 'Parallel Sweden' by some: **Kristinestad** (p254) is one of several places with a Swedish-speaking majority. **Kaskinen** (p256) or **Närpes** (p256) are other tranquil stops. **Vaasa** (p249) has an excellent museum, and is popular for its spa complex and adventure park.

Nykarleby (p256), famous for waffles and its painted church, is a good stop on the way to **Jakobstad** (p257), whose old town rivals Rauma's for beauty. Meanwhile, at **Kokkola** (p259), with its boat bar and fascinating mineral museum, you'll definitely feel back in Finnish Finland. Beyond here, a stretch of beautiful coastline runs north to **Oulu** (p266), with **Kalajoki** (p261), one of the world's most northerly beach resorts, on the way.

This coastal trip is an excellent way to appreciate the differences between the Swedish- and Finnish-speaking communities, not to mention a chance to see picture-perfect wooden towns, sparkling blue water and several more-than-decent beaches. About 1100km.

BORDERLANDS
Helsinki to Kuusamo/Two weeks

Russia's presence looms large in Finnish history and consciousness. This trip takes in areas that have been affected by this relationship.

From Helsinki, head first to little **Ruotsinpyhtää** (p106), an attractive village whose river once marked the boundary between the Swedish Empire and Russia. Then move on to **Kotka** (p107), a busy port near one of the tsar's favourite fishing spots. Heading towards the modern-day border, the fortress at **Hamina** (p110) was erected by the Swedes to halt the Russian advance in the early 18th century. This plan singularly failed!

Lappeenranta (p143) suffered a similar fate, with the Russians adding the finishing touches to the fortress that had been designed to keep them out. This is the beginning of Karelia, an area where a lot of the bitterest fighting of the Winter War took place; you'll see numerous memorials on this route.

Heading north, you'll pass through cities that were largely destroyed during the war. At **Imatra** (p149), whose 'rapids shows' are something to behold, you can actually see Russia from the top floor of the Imatran Valtionhotelli, while at **Joensuu** (p151), visit Carelicum museum to learn more about the area.

From **Ilomantsi** (p155), in deepest Karelia, head out to **Hattuvaara** (p157), a very Orthodox area. You can drive to the border from here – the easternmost point of the EU!

Lieksa (p159) and **Nurmes** (p165) are good bases for exploring the wilderness. Further north, **Kuhmo** (p280) was where artists and writers set out from, seeking inspiration in the deep forest wildernesses further east, which are now part of Russia and much mourned by the Finns. Shadow the border up to **Kuusamo** (p283), from where you can fly back to Helsinki.

An exploration of Finland's eastern zone, shadowing the border with Russia, whose influence has always been very important. This heads through the heartland of divided Karelia, a symbol for Finnish independence, wilderness and loss. About 1000km.

TAILORED TRIPS

WINTER FINLAND

It's cold – Finnish thermometers have more numbers below the line than above – and it's dark, but a Finnish winter is something quite magical, with snow and ice in abundance and incredible scope for activity.

The capital **Helsinki** (p57) is a memorable sight in winter, with the giant Baltic ferries sailing through channels gouged by the country's impressive icebreakers, and ice-skating in the Kallio district among other places.

But you won't want to linger in the capital's comparatively tropical winter temperatures, for the north calls! On your way there, it's highly recommended to test your mettle at the giant smoke sauna in **Kuopio** (p135). After steaming it up, a jump in the lake is required – don't worry, they've cut a hole in the ice for your convenience! Some Finns, however, prefer to sit by a hole in the ice with a hot drink and a fishing line. There are many good places to try your hand at ice fishing, including **Ruovesi** (p180). If you're good enough, you could enter the Ice-Angling Marathon at **Oulu** (p269).

Karelian forests and lakes are gorgeous when the winter sun bathes the snow in an orange light. **Nurmes** (p165) and **Lieksa** (p159) are popular places to try snowmobiling and other winter activities; you can also try something typically Finnish: taking a short cut by driving across a frozen lake!

Northwest of here, **Kemi** (p273) comes to life during winter with its magnificent Snow Castle (you can sleep inside) and the chance to sail on an icebreaker, a fascinating experience.

Lapland is a fantastic winter destination. The crisp, snowy wilderness and low, distant sun are mesmerising. There are many destinations where you can arrange exciting outdoor pursuits. In **Rovaniemi** (p296) there's the Arktikum museum and the Santa Claus post office, where hundreds of thousands of letters arrive every Christmas from all over the world.

Muonio (p306) is one of the best places to arrange husky-sledding. This memorable mode of transport can be experienced on a two-hour jaunt, or a multi-day safari, sleeping in wilderness cabins, all with their own wood sauna, and cooking over campfires.

At **Saariselkä** (p314), you can have a similar experience or choose to be pulled by reindeer, those loveably goofy-looking creatures. This is also a place to do treks on snowmobiles if you've got a valid driving licence.

At **Inari** (p320), the Sámi capital, things get busy with reindeer racing. The reindeer pull standing jockeys on sleds and have their antlers removed to prevent things getting too gladiatorial.

Then there's skiing. While Finland doesn't have huge mountains, there are some excellent resorts, including **Levi** (p305), which has great facilities and accommodation, and **Ruka** (p286), an enduringly popular family centre. At these places, and indeed almost everywhere in Finland, there are marked cross-country skiing trails, many of which are illuminated so the short hours of daylight prove no handicap.

The icing on the cake for lucky visitors is a glimpse of the **northern lights** (see boxed text, p307), an awe-inspiring natural phenomenon best seen in the north of the country. It's a humbling and memorable sight when in full flow.

NATIONAL PARKS

The word Finland conjures up images of vast expanses of pine forest dotted with hundreds – no, hundreds of thousands – of lakes. In large part, these images are very accurate. The spectacular swathes of forest are home to elk, bears and wolves, and include some of Europe's most remote wildernesses.

Some 9% of Finland is under some kind of nature protection, and there are 35 national parks. Superbly run, with comprehensive visitor information and clearly labelled short- and long-distance paths, they are some of the nation's most attractive destinations.

You can start with a taste of things to come while you are still in Helsinki. In Espoo, a short trip from the capital, is the **Nuuksio National Park** (p87), a haven for several rare bird species and a great place to go for a stroll in the woods.

While you are in the south of the country, you should also investigate one of the four maritime parks, such as the **Southwestern Archipelago National Park** (p216). You can visit the archipelago on regular boat trips from Turku or Hanko, but to really explore it you should charter a boat.

The central belt of Finland is dotted with a couple of dozen small parks, often conserving some of the country's typical Lakeland habitat. Motor boats are prohibited on many Finnish lakes, so a great way to explore them is to hire a canoe for a couple of hours, or do a full-blown journey of a week. The adjacent **Kolovesi** (p124) and **Linnansaari National Parks** (p124) are two of the best zones to take to the water in this way. If you are lucky, you may even glimpse the rare Saimaa ringed seal, which adapted to a freshwater environment after being cut off from the sea by the rising land.

The heavyweights of Finland's park system all lie further north. With three parks weighing in at over 1000 sq km each, Lapland is blessed with wide expanses to explore. One of the most important and popular is the **Urho K Kekkonen (UKK) National Park** (p316), an area of classic Lappish fells that is a magnet for trekkers of all abilities. Although the well-known routes get busy in summer, there's some awesome wilderness here where few people venture.

Finland's most popular single trek, the Karhunkierros (Bear's Ring), is located south of here, in the **Oulanka National Park** (p288). While to do it in its entirety will take you up to five days, you can easily shorten it to three days, or just try the Little Bear's Ring day walk.

Within striking distance of Rovaniemi, the newly-enlarged **Pyhä-Luosto National Park** (p313) has good walking over the forested fells that connect two low-key ski resorts. This is a peaceful area to stay with the family in summer too.

In the northwest is the lovely **Pallas-Yllästunturi National Park** (p308), with comparatively easy trekking southwards from the Sámi town of Hetta. You have to be taken by boat to the starting point, so it feels like you're kissing civilization goodbye for good, but the trek ends happily at a very hospitable hotel.

Finland's northernmost park is **Lemmenjoki** (p322), not too far from Inari. This has an excellent network of trails, some decent places to stay, and the chance to make your fortune (or at least dirty your clothes) panning for gold.

Lemmenjoki
Pallas-Yll stunturi
Urho K Kekkonen
Pyh -Luosto
Oulanka
Kolovesi
Linnansaari
Southwestern Archipelago
Nuuksio

FESTIVALS OF FINLAND

The Finnish love their short summers, and an amazing network of festivals takes place across the country. Some are highbrow, world-famous cultural events drawing international performers, while others are plain daft – mobile phone throwing, anyone? At **Savonlinna** (p115), high-quality **opera performances** are held in its romantically set castle throughout July. A separate **ballet festival** in August adds to the cultural air, but here you'll also see the latest Nokia flying through the air.

Pori (p226) has a cracking jazz event, while little **Seinäjoki** (p262) throbs to both rock music and Finnish tango. In **Kaustinen** (p264) you'll hear folk music in the middle of nowhere, while **Kuopio** (p135) has a famous dance festival. **Jyväskylä's** (p129) summer knees-up is a multi-disciplinary arts extravaganza.

Other festivals celebrate cultural differences. The Praasniekka in places like **Ilomantsi** (p155) are traditional Orthodox religious festivals and celebrations of Karelian culture, while on **Åland** (p229), Midsummer revelries (celebrated throughout the country) have a distinctly local character. In the north, **Rovaniemi** (p296) hosts an important Sámi festival.

The realm of the bizarre is vast. Honourable mentions go to Sonkajärvi for **Wife-Carrying** (p141), **Oulu** (p269) for the Air Guitar World Championships, and Naantali for **Sleepyhead Day** (p212), when the laziest citizen gets dragged out of bed and chucked in the sea!

WRITERS & ARTISTS

The decades leading up to independence were exciting times. A growing sense of Finnishness was explored by writers, artists and composers, many travelling to the wildernesses of Karelia for inspiration.

Start in Helsinki, where the **Ateneum** (p63) will acquaint you with some of these fascinating characters' work. Grab a copy of the *Kalevala* while you're in town, and have a drink at the **Hotel Kämp** (p74), where artists thrashed out the meaning of Finland during epic piss-ups!

Porvoo (p88), home to many artists, and Espoo's **Gallen-Kallela Museum** (p87) are musts, as is the journey to **Sibelius' home** (p88) near Järvenpää.

Sibelius' birthplace in Hämeenlinna (p183) is now a museum with a resident pianist; on the way (sort of) is **Lohja** (p93), near which is the rustic cottage where Lönnrot, creator of the *Kalevala,* was born.

Beyond Hämeenlinna, you should definitely investigate **Visavuori** (p186) and **Kalela** (p180), studios of sculptor Emil Wickström and painter Akseli Gallen-Kallela respectively.

Then on to Karelia, where all these women and men drew inspiration. From **Nurmes** (p165) you can plan expeditions of your own, exploring the wildernesses by foot, canoe, or husky-drawn sled. Nearby **Koli Hill** (p164) enchanted Sibelius, while further north, **Kuhmo** (p280) is the place to learn more about the *Kalevala* and its massive impact on Finnish history.

Snapshot

Although most people who aren't avid sports fans would struggle to name more Finns than they have fingers, the country is very much a quiet achiever. It's not a nation to trumpet its success stories – plenty of folk think Nokia is Japanese – and the national tendency towards irony prevents too much bigheadedness anyway.

The fact remains that for a remote, cold, sparsely-populated forest nation, Finland does extremely well. It has a strong economy, great standard of living, and is considered the least corrupt country in the world. Neighbouring Sweden, who has traditionally looked down somewhat on Finland, has been startled to find Finnish companies acquiring stakes in Swedish institutions, and Finland is one of the world's leaders in technological research.

So what are the hot issues being talked about on the streets and in the cafés? Unsurprisingly, one of them is something that's been a constant topic for at least eight centuries: Russia. Finland's entire eastern border abuts the world's largest country, and it's natural that there are a number of positive and negative implications.

Since WWII, Finland has had close relations with Russia, sometimes more by necessity than choice. This experience has seen Finnish companies use their proximity, knowledge, and expertise in dealing with Russia to gain a head start on some of their competitors in the post–Cold War period. Trade is healthy, and many Finnish firms subcontract much of their business to Russia, where wages and overheads are lower.

But there are other sides to the Bear's proximity. The Finland–Russia border has one of the biggest differences in standard of living of any international frontier, and it's no surprise that Russian crime syndicates have seen peaceful Finland as fertile ground for various operations. Finns grumble about this, and also about the fact that Russian customs seem to keep Finnish trucks waiting for a day at the borders, while Russian trucks are waved straight through. The result is that Russian companies control most of the cross-border trade.

Finns, understandably given the difficult century history as backdrop, are still nervous that a radical shift in Russian domestic politics could spell trouble. National service and the army in general are taken seriously, and the soldiers who fought in the Winter and Continuation Wars are still revered as heroes.

Since 2000, Finland's President has been Tarja Halonen of the Social Democratic party. She has proved incredibly popular and is well loved by Finns, who often affectionately refer to her as Moominmamma, the mother Moomin from the Tove Jansson books.

The Finnish parliament is currently governed by a coalition of two of the three major parties, the Centre Party, and the Social Democrats. The conservative National Coalition Party is in opposition along with the Greens, who had quit the previous governing coalition over Finland's continuing policy of nuclear energy. The Prime Minister is Matti Vanhanen, who took over shortly after the election when Anneli Jäätteenmäki was forced to resign over a document scandal. Ongoing parliamentary issues include immigration and refugee policy, and establishment of close relations with the Baltic states, fledgling members of the EU. Estonia in particular, with its proximity and linguistic ties to Finland, often features on the agenda.

FAST FACTS

Population: 5,236,611

Size: 338,145 sq km

Percentage of water: 10%

GDP per capita: €28,646

Unemployment rate: 8.8%

Number of mobile phones: 4.9 million

Number of reindeer: 230,000

Number of days of no sun in Nuorgam: 51

Number of days of constant sun in Nuorgam: 72

Another issue in recent times has been in the north. Sámi herders have complained that fences constructed by forestry firms are impeding the moving of reindeer between pasture grounds. The forestry firms claim that an insignificant proportion of the reindeer pasturing area is affected. Legislation will hopefully resolve the issue, but it's a regrettable clash between an important ethnic minority and one of Finland's major industries.

Finland has enthusiastically embraced membership of the EU and, unlike Sweden or Denmark, has taken the euro onboard too. It's been a fairly happy relationship, although people have been surprised by the fairly cutthroat nature of European politics compared to domestic affairs, and by the constant jockeying for position within the EU. When both Silvio Berlusconi and Jacques Chirac unfairly criticized Finnish food as being the worst in the EU on separate occasions recently, some Finns reacted with hurt bemusement – why would their European 'brothers' say such things?

For the truth is that Finns are very interested in what other people think of them. This is a famous national stereotype, and a run-on from this is that Finns are immensely proud of any locals who make an international success of themselves; there's no 'tall poppy' syndrome to be found here. Even elderly jazz fans will brighten up if a visitor tells them they like the heavy, dark music of bands like Nightwish or HIM, two standard-bearers of what has been an incredibly successful period for Finnish music. And any Finnish sporting success is celebrated with gusto. At the rain-plagued 2005 World Athletic Championships in Helsinki, long-jumper Tommi Evilä grabbed bronze, Finland's only medal of the games, and the nation celebrated.

Racism is a more serious issue. There is significant hostility from a small segment of society towards refugee groups, of whom the Somali community is one of the largest. This rarely manifests itself in much more than general unpleasantness, but there have been several high-profile racist attacks in recent years, with Kajaani and Joensuu named the two worst towns for race-related crimes. It's a familiar story: the culprits usually young males, typically unemployed and in a small town. Beer and flawed racist politics are involved, and suddenly irrational hatred overflows into mindless violence. Still, it wouldn't be fair to speak of a significant 'neo-Nazi movement'; violent racism is rare in Finland, but shocking when it occurs, as the country as a whole is extremely peaceful. More common are antiquated attitudes towards non-white faces, typically from the older generation and partly explained by lack of contact with other nationalities until relatively recently.

A perennial stereotype of Finns is that of moody binge-drinkers, depressed by long winters without sunlight. There is a certain amount of truth to the image, although lack of sun is too simplistic an explanation. A notoriously problematic statistic, the Finnish suicide rate is high: double that of Sweden, and around four times that in the UK, for example. The rate in Lithuania, however, is double Finland's and in general eastern Europe and the former Soviet Union feature very highly on this sombre chart.

On alcohol consumption, Finland makes the top 20, but is well behind most EU countries in consumption per capita. The manner of drinking, however, can seem fairly self-destructive at times, with the 'number of people who passed out hammered last Friday night' per capita doubtlessly giving Finland a higher ranking! Some Finns argue that the high taxes on alcohol are responsible, with many people preferring to buy a bottle of cheap vodka to down quickly at home before heading out dancing rather than having a couple of pints at the local pub. Others blame a macho 'binge-drinking' culture. But, as ever, once moralizing enters the debate, any prospect of useful answers or even a decent definition of the problem disappears.

History

Finnish history is the story of a people who for centuries were a wrestling mat between two heavyweights on either side: Sweden and Russia. The unfortunate thing about this history is that the earliest chronicles were written by Swedes, and much of ethnic Finnish culture and events before and well after the Swedish crusades has escaped written record altogether.

PREHISTORY

Little is known of the earliest human settlement in Finland. As the glaciers receded at the end of the last Ice Age, the first permanent inhabitants of what is now Finland probably began arriving around 10,000 to 12,000 years ago. Around this time the Baltic Sea formed, flooding what was a large freshwater lake. To this day, it's one of the least saline of the major seas.

But Finland was almost certainly inhabited long before this period. Recent finds of worked flint tools in a cave at Kristinestad suggest sporadic human presence as far back as 100,000 years ago, between Ice Ages.

The first settlers in Finland came from Russia and present-day Estonia. These people hunted elk and beaver using stone tools and weapons and gradually spread out into the whole of the region. Sites have been found in southern Finland dating from around the eighth millennium BC.

Pottery appears in archaeological records in the late sixth millennium BC, marking the beginning of the Late Stone Age, or Neolithic period. The discovery of ceramics makes it easier to identify broad groups of people, and it is clear that a new group arrived in southern Finland in 3000 BC or thereabouts. From this point on, we can see the development of definable Finno-Ugrian cultures. The central/northern culture, who had least cultural contact with the newcomers, have been labelled as proto-Sámi.

The Bronze Age, from around 1700 BC to 600 BC, is characterised by strong trade contacts between southern Finland and other groups around the Baltic Sea, and the use of stone cairns for burials.

WHY FINLAND?

The Finns call their country *Suomi* (*swom*-ee), so why is it generally known as Finland?

French may provide a clue. *Fin* means 'end', and *fin de lande* could easily be, if not 'the end of the world', the northern end of the European land mass.

The early Romans called this land Fennia. In English the word *fen* describes a swampy land, and is mostly used to refer to the low, flat water-logged land in eastern England. But Romans went to England too, and Finland is exactly such a swampy land, and swamp in Finnish is *suo*. A Finn in Finnish is *suomalainen,* whereas *suomaalainen* (with double a) means an inhabitant of a swampy land.

The resemblance of the word *suo* to Suomi is too close to be ignored, but the derivation of the name of the long-time inhabitants of Lapland, the Sámi, offers another explanation. Finland is called *Somija* in Latvian, *Suomija* in Lithuanian and *Soome* in Estonian.

Unimpressed by all these references to inferior interior swampy ground, many Finns would like their country to be called *Finlandia* or *Fennia* (in Latin) because it sounds more respectable.

Of course, Swedish-speaking Finns have always called Finland, Finland.

100,000 BC	AD 100
Sporadic human presence between Ice Ages in what is now Finland	Tacitus refers to the 'Fenni', perhaps the Sámi, in the first known historical record of the area

EARLY FINNISH SOCIETY

In the first century AD, the Roman historian Tacitus mentioned a tribe called the Fenni, whom he basically described as wild savages who had neither homes nor horses. He might have been referring to the Sámi or their forebears, whose nomadic existence better fits the description than the agricultural peoples of the south. Nomadic cultures leave little archaeological evidence, but proto-Sámi sites do occur from roughly this period on, and it seems the Sámi migrated gradually northwards, probably displaced by the southerners. Verses of the *Kalevala* (see boxed text on p36), derived from ancient oral tradition, seem to refer to this conflictual relationship.

In the south, the two main Finnish tribes, Hämenites (Swedish: Tavastians) and Karelians, lived separately, in the west and the east respectively, but were constantly at war with each other.

There were trading contacts with Estonians and Swedish Vikings and there were trading posts in present-day Hämeenlinna, Turku and Halikko. Many burial grounds and hill defences remain. It is probable that there was friendly contact between fortresses, despite each having its own social system. A common law and judicial system existed in each region.

For more details, http://virtual.finland.fi has excellent essays on Finnish history written by experts.

The Åland Islands and coastal regions southeast of Turku were frequented by Viking sailors. Six hill fortresses on Åland date back to the Viking era and indicate the former importance of these islands.

SWEDISH RULE

To the Swedes, Finland was a natural direction of expansion, on a promising eastern route towards Russia and the Black Sea. The Swedish chapter of Finland's history starts in 1155, when Bishop Henry, an Englishman, arrived in Kalanti under orders of the Swedish king. An aggressive period of colonisation and enforced baptism ensued, and Bishop Henry was infamously murdered by a disgruntled local peasant, Lalli. At the time of the Swedish arrival, the population of Finland has been estimated at 50,000.

Swedish crusaders manned Finnish fortresses to repel Russian attacks and protect its Christianisation efforts from Orthodox influence. Swedish settlement began in earnest in 1249 when Birger Jarl established fortifications in Tavastia and on the northern coast of the Gulf of Finland.

It took more than 200 years to define the border between Sweden and Novgorod (Russia). In 1323 the first such border was drawn in a conference at Nöteborg (Finnish: Pähkinäsaari) on Lake Ladoga. Sweden gained control of southwest Finland, much of the northwest coast and, in the east, the strategic town of Vyborg (Finnish: Viipuri), with its magnificent castle. Suzerainty was established over Karelia by Novgorod, and it was controlled from a castle at Käkisalmi (Russian: Priodzorsk) that was founded in the 13th century. Novgorod spread the Russian Orthodox faith in the Karelia region, which became influenced by Byzantine culture.

To attract Swedish settlers to the unknown land, a number of incentives were created such as giving away large tracts of land and tax concessions. These privileges were given to many soldiers of the Royal Swedish Army.

In 1527 King Gustav Vasa of Sweden adopted the Lutheran faith and confiscated much of the property of the Catholic Church. Finland had its own supporters of the Reformation: Mikael Agricola, born in Pernå (Finnish: Pernaja) in 1510, studied with Martin Luther in Germany, and returned

1155	1323
First crusade launched from Sweden against pagan Finns	Finland is divided up between Sweden and Novgorod at the Treaty of Pähkinäsaari

to Finland in 1539 to translate parts of the Bible into Finnish. He was also the first person to properly record the traditions and animist religious rites of ethnic Finns. A hardliner, Agricola ushered in the Finnish Reformation. Most of the frescoes in medieval churches were whitewashed (only to be rediscovered some 400 years later in relatively good condition).

Sweden was not satisfied with its share of power in the east. In 1546 King Gustav Vasa founded Ekenäs (Finnish: Tammisaari) and in 1550, Helsinki. Using his Finnish subjects as agents of expansion, Gustav Vasa told them to 'sweat and suffer' as pioneers in Savo and Kainuu, territories well beyond those set down in treaties with Russia. Alarmed, the Russians attempted to throw the intruders out. The bloody Kainuu War raged on and off between 1574 and 1584, and most new settlements were destroyed by fire.

GOLDEN AGE OF SWEDEN

The golden age of Sweden was the 17th century, and during this period it controlled Finland, Estonia and parts of present-day Latvia, Denmark, Germany and Russia.

Finally, after 65 years of Lutheranism, the Catholic Sigismund (grandson of King Gustav Vasa) succeeded to the Swedish throne. Karl IX, Sigismund's uncle, was given control over Finland. Karl IX didn't care much for the family business. He encouraged peasants in western Finland to mutiny in 1596, and they attacked Turku Castle in 1597 and defeated Sigismund in 1598 to bring all of Finland under his reign.

While Gustav II Adolf (son of Karl IX and king from 1611 to 1632) was busily involved in the Thirty Year's War in Europe, political power in Finland was exercised by General Governor Count Per Brahe, who resided at the Castle of Turku, capital of Finland. Count Per Brahe, a legendary figure of the local Swedish administration, travelled around the country at this time and founded many towns. He cut quite a figure; as well as being the biggest landowner in Sweden, he was a gourmet and wrote his own cookbook, which he used to take with him and insist it was followed to the letter! Once censured for having illegally bagged an elk, he responded curtly that it had been on its last legs and he had killed it out of mercy!

After Gustav II Adolf, Sweden was ruled from 1644 to 1654 by the eccentric Queen Kristina, namesake for such Finnish towns as Kristinestad and Ristiina. The Queen's conversion to Catholicism and subsequent move to Rome marked the end of the Swedish Vasa dynasty.

The German royal family of Pfalz-Zweibrücken ruled Sweden (including Finland) after the Vasa family folded. By Swedish decree, Finland grew. A chain of castle defences was built to protect against Russian attacks and new factory areas were founded. The *bruk* (early ironworks precinct) was often a self-contained society which harvested the power of water, built ironworks and transport systems for firewood. Social institutions, such as schools and churches, were also established.

Ethnic Finns didn't fare particularly well during this time. The burgher class was dominated by Swedish settlers, as very few Finns engaged in industrial enterprises. Some of the successful industrialists were central Europeans, who settled in Finland via Sweden. Furthermore the Swedish 'caste system', the House of Four Estates, was firmly established in Finland. The Swedish and Finnish nobility maintained their status in the

'Count Per Brahe…once censured for having illegally bagged an elk, responded curtly that it had been on its last legs and he had killed it out of mercy!'

1527

The Finnish Reformation gets underway

1637

Per Brahe becomes Governor of Finland and founds many towns; Finnish cavalry earn a fearsome reputation in the Thirty Years' War

Swedish Riksdagen until 1866 and in the Finnish parliament until 1906. Although Finland never experienced feudal serfdom to the extent seen in Russia, ethnic Finns were largely peasant farmers who were forced to lease land from Swedish landlords.

In 1697 the Swede Karl XII ascended the throne. Within three years he was drawn into the Great Northern War (1700–21), which marked the beginning of the end of the Swedish Empire.

THE TURBULENT 18TH CENTURY

While King Karl XII was busy fighting for his empire elsewhere, the Russians under Peter the Great seized the moment. The Great Northern War resulted in Vyborg being defeated in 1710 and much of Finland conquered, including the Swedish-dominated west coast.

From 1714 to 1721 Russia occupied Finland, a time still referred to as the Great Wrath. The Russians destroyed almost everything they could, particularly in Åland and western Finland. The 1721 Treaty of Uusikaupunki (Swedish: Nystad) brought peace at a cost – Sweden lost south Karelia to Russia. To regain its lost territories, Sweden attacked Russia in 1741–3, but with little success. Russia again occupied Finland, for a period called the Lesser Wrath, and the border was pushed further west. The Treaty of Turku in 1743 ended the conflict by ceding parts of Savo to Russia.

Only after the 1740s did the Swedish government try to improve Finland's socioeconomic situation. Defences were strengthened by building fortresses off Helsinki's coast (Sveaborg, now Suomenlinna) and at Loviisa, and new towns were founded. Later, Sweden and Russia were to clash repeatedly under King Gustav III, until he was murdered by a group of aristocrats in 1792. Gustav IV Adolf, who reigned from 1796, was drawn into the disastrous Napoleonic Wars and lost his crown in 1809.

RUSSIAN RULE

After the Treaty of Tilsit was signed by Tsar Alexander I and Napoleon, Russia attacked Finland in 1808. Following a bloody war, Sweden ceded Finland to Russia in 1809 as an autonomous grand duchy with its own senate and the Diet of the Four Estates, but all major decisions had to be approved by the tsar. At first, Finland benefited from the annexation and was loyal to the tsar, who encouraged Finns to develop the country in many ways. The Finnish capital was transferred to Helsinki in 1812, as Russians felt that the former capital, Turku, was too close to Sweden.

Early in the 19th century, the first stirring of indigenous Finnish nationalism occurred. One of the first to encourage independence during the 1820s was Al Radisson, who uttered the much-quoted sentence: 'Swedes we are not, Russians we will not become, so let us be Finns'. His views were not widely supported and he was advised to move to Sweden in 1823.

As a Russian annexation, Finland was involved in the Crimean War (1853–6), with British troops destroying fortifications at Loviisa, Helsinki and Bomarsund. Following the Crimean War, the Finnish independence movement gained credibility. While still a part of Russia, Finland issued its first postage stamps in 1856 and its own currency, the markka, in 1860.

In 1905 the Eduskunta, a unicameral parliament, was introduced in Finland with universal and equal suffrage (Finland was the first country

TK Derry's *The History of Scandinavia* is a good account of Finland's status in the Swedish Empire.

1640	1809
University of Turku is founded	Finland is occupied by Russia and becomes a grand duchy of the Russian Empire

LENIN IN FINLAND

One man who spent plenty of time in Finland was none other than Vladimir Ilyich Lenin, father of the Russian Revolution. Having had a Finn cellmate during his exile in Siberia, he then regularly visited Finland for conferences of the Social Democratic Party. At one of these, in 1905, he met Stalin for the first time. Lenin then lived near Helsinki for a period in 1907 before he was forced to flee the Russian Empire. In a Hollywood-style escape, he jumped off a moving train to avoid tsarist agents, and was then sheltered in Turku, before being moved to the remote island communities of the southwest. Lenin was on Parainen, and, fearing capture, he walked across thin ice with a local guide to Nauvo (there's a famous painting of this in the Hermitage in St Petersburg), from where he finally jumped on a steamer to Stockholm.

Lenin entered Finland again via Tornio in 1917. He returned pretty sharply after the abortive first revolution, living in a tent for a while in Iljitsevo, before going back to Russia and destiny.

Lenin, even before having visited Finland, had always agitated for Finnish independence from Russia, a conviction which he maintained. In December 1917, he signed the declaration of Finnish independence, and, without his support, it is doubtful that the nation would have been born at that time. The Lenin Museum in Tampere (p171) is the place to visit to learn more about Lenin in Finland.

in Europe to grant women full political rights). Despite these many advances, life under Russian rule continued to be harsh. Many artists, notably the composer Jean Sibelius, were inspired by this oppression, which made Finns emotionally ripe for independence.

INDEPENDENCE

The Communist revolution of October 1917 enabled the Finnish senate to declare independence on 6 December 1917. Independent Finland was first recognised by the Soviets one month later. Nevertheless, the Russian-armed Finnish Reds attacked the Finnish civil guards in Vyborg the following year, sparking the Finnish Civil War.

On 28 January 1918, the Civil War flared in two separate locations. The Reds attempted to foment revolution in Helsinki; the Whites (as the government troops were now called), led by CGE Mannerheim, clashed with Russian-backed troops near Vaasa. During the 108 days of heavy fighting in these two locations, approximately 30,000 Finns were killed. The Reds, comprising the rising working class, aspired to a Russian-style socialist revolution while retaining independence. The nationalist Whites dreamed of monarchy and sought to emulate Germany.

Mannerheim had a fascinating life divided into several distinct phases. Check out www .mannerheim.fi for an online biography.

The Whites, with Germany's help, eventually gained victory and the war ended in May 1918. Friedrich Karl, Prince of Hessen, was elected king of Finland by the Eduskunta on 9 October 1918, but the German monarchy collapsed one month later, following Germany's defeat in WWI.

BUILDING A NATION

The defeat of imperial Germany made Finland choose a republican state model, and the first president was KJ Ståhlberg. Relations with the Soviets were normalised by the Treaty of Tartu in 1920, which saw Finnish territory grow to its largest ever, including the other 'arm', the Petsamo region in the far northeast. But more trouble awaited.

1905	1917
Finland becomes the first country in Europe to grant women full political rights	Finland declares independence from the Soviet Union

Following WWI, heated exchanges between Finnish and Swedish speakers shook the administration, universities and cultural circles. Civil War skirmishes continued, mostly with illegal massacres of Reds by Whites. Despite its internal troubles, Finland at this time gained fame internationally as a brave new nation, as the only country to pay its debts to the USA, and as a sporting nation. Paavo Nurmi, the most distinguished of Finnish long-distance runners, won nine gold medals in three Olympic Games and became an enduring national hero (see p34). With continuing Finnish success in athletics, Helsinki was chosen to host the 1940 Olympic Games (these were postponed until 1952 due to WWII).

THE WINTER WAR & ITS CONTINUATION

The Winter War directed by Pekka Parikka is a memorable film about the bleak fighting in unspeakably bad conditions.

Diplomatic manoeuvrings in Europe in the 1930s meant that Finland had a few difficult choices to make. The security threat posed by the Soviet Union meant that some factions were in favour of developing closer ties with Nazi Germany, while others favoured rapprochement with Moscow. On 23 August 1939, the Soviet and German foreign ministers, Molotov and Ribbentrop, stunned the world by signing a nonaggression pact. A secret protocol stated that they would divide Poland between them in any future rearrangement; Germany would have a free hand in Lithuania, the Soviet Union in Finland, Estonia, Latvia and Bessarabia. The Red Army was moving towards the earmarked territories less than three weeks later.

The Soviet Union made more territorial claims, arguing its security required a slice of southeastern Karelia. JK Paasikivi (later to become president) visited Moscow for negotiations on the ceding of the Karelian Isthmus to the Soviet Union. The negotiations failed. On 30 November 1939, the Winter War between Finland and the Soviet Union began.

This was a harsh winter – temperatures reached -40°C and soldiers died in their thousands. After 100 days of bitter and courageous fighting Finnish forces were defeated. In the Treaty of Moscow (March 1940), Finland ceded part of Karelia and some nearby islands. About 500,000 Karelian refugees flooded across the new border.

In the following months, the Soviet Union pressured Finland for more territory. Isolated from Western allies, Finland turned to Germany for help and allowed the transit of German troops. When hostilities broke out between Germany and the Soviets in June 1941, German troops were already on Finnish soil, and the Continuation War between Finland and the Red Army began. In the fighting that followed, the Finns began to resettle Karelia. When Soviet forces staged a huge comeback in the summer of 1944, President Risto Ryti resigned and Mannerheim took his place. Mannerheim negotiated an armistice with the Russians and ordered the evacuation of German troops. Finland waged a bitter war to oust the Germans from Lapland until the general peace in the spring of 1945. Finland remained independent, but at a price: it was forced to cede territory and (the ultimate irony) pay heavy war reparations to the Soviet Union. The Treaty of Paris (February 1947) dictated that the Karelian Isthmus be ceded to the Soviet Union, together with the eastern Salla and Kuusamo regions, and the 'left arm' of Finland in the Kola Peninsula. Many Finns are still bitter about the loss of these territories. Nevertheless,

The website www .winterwar.com has a good overview of the battle-lines and forces deployed in that conflict.

the resistance against the might of the Red Army is something that Finns are still justifiably proud of.

THE COLD WAR

Finland's reparations to the Soviets were chiefly paid in machinery and ships. Thus reparations played a central role in laying the foundations for the heavy engineering industry that stabilised the Finnish economy following WWII. Finland had suffered greatly in the late 1940s, with almost everything rationed and poverty widespread. The vast majority of the population was still engaged in agriculture at that time.

Things changed quickly in the following decades, with domestic migration to southern Finland especially strong in the 1960s and 1970s. New suburbs appeared almost overnight around Helsinki. Areas in the north and east lost most of their young people, often half their population.

Urho K Kekkonen, Finnish president from 1956 to 1981, a master of diplomacy and one of the great leaders of his age, was responsible for steering Finland through the Cold War and its relationship with the Soviet Union. Often this meant bowing to the wishes of the USSR who, using veiled threats, influenced Finnish politics. Political nominations were submitted to Moscow for approval within a framework of 'friendly coexistence'.

As recently as the late 1980s, the Soviet Communist Party exercised Cold War tactics by infiltrating Finnish politics, with the aim of reducing US influence in Finland and preventing Finnish membership of the European Community (today's European Union, or EU).

Relations with Scandinavia were also extremely important in the decades following WWII. Finland was a founding member of the Nordic Council (along with the Scandinavian countries), pursuing a similar social welfare programme to Scandinavia and enjoying the benefits of free movement of labour and joint projects with its Western neighbours.

MODERN FINLAND

In the 1990s Finland's overheated economy, like many in the Western world, went through a cooling off period. The bubble economy of the 1980s had burst, the Soviet Union disappeared with debts unpaid, the markka was devalued, unemployment jumped from 3% to 20% and the tax burden grew alarmingly.

Things began to change for the better after a national referendum on 16 October 1994, when 57% of voters gave the go-ahead to join the EU. Since January 1995, Finland has prospered, and was one of the countries to adopt the new euro currency in 2002.

In 2000, Finland elected its first woman president, Tarja Halonen, who has been a popular figure. Briefly in 2003, Finland was the only country in Europe to have a woman as both president and prime minister; Anneli Jäätteenmäki, leader of the Centre Party, won a narrow victory in elections but barely two months later was forced to resign over having lied to parliament. She was replaced by Matti Vanhanen, the current incumbent.

Finland consistently ranks highly in quality of life indexes, and with a strong independent streak, a booming technology sector and a growing tourism industry, it is one of the success stories of the new Europe.

Blood, Sweat and Bears by Lasse Lehtinen is a parody of a war novel, and deals with Finland/ Soviet relations.

Did you know that Nokia started out making a whole range of things, including rubber boots and cable insulation, before getting interested in the cables themselves and telecommunications?

1995	2000
Finland joins the EU	Finland elects Tarja Halonen as its first woman president

The Culture

THE NATIONAL PSYCHE

Finnish-speaking Finns do not consider themselves Scandinavian, nor do they see themselves as part of Russia; nevertheless, Finnish tradition owes something to both cultures. The Finns' long struggle for emancipation, together with their ongoing struggle to survive in a harsh environment, has led to an ordered society that solves its problems in its own way. It has also engendered the Finnish trait of *sisu*, often translated as 'guts', or the resilience to survive prolonged hardship. Even if all looks lost, until the final defeat, a Finn with *sisu* will fight – or swim, or run, or work – valiantly. This trait is valued highly, with the country's heroic resistance against the Red Army during WWII usually thought of as the ultimate example.

While the 'silent Finn' stereotype has been exaggerated over the years, it's certainly true that nobody gets nervous if there's a gap in a conversation. Sitting in the sauna for 20 minutes with your best friend, saying nothing, is considered perfectly normal. Finns tend to consider their words, appreciate a well-timed, dry sense of humour, and be attentive listeners.

There's a depressive streak in Finns, more so than in Swedes or Norwegians. Even Finnish summer pop hits can sound like the singer's just backed over their dog or worse, and themes of lost love and general melancholy are favoured. While Finns aren't among Europe's biggest drinkers (take a bow Luxembourg and Dublin!), alcoholism is high. What this doesn't make the Finns is gruff or impolite. They are an exceptionally courteous and welcoming people. It can take a while for politeness to become friendship, but once it does, it is lasting.

The Finnish haven't traditionally been big travellers. Part of the reason for this is that in July Finland is one of the world's most relaxing and joyful places. After struggling through winter, why would they want to miss the best their country has to offer?! Finns head en-masse to their *mökki* (summer cottage; see the boxed text on p41) from Midsummer until the end of the July holidays. There, you'll find even the most urbanised Euro-executives chopping wood, lighting the sauna fire and DIY-ing.

Finns have a deep and abiding love of their forests and lakes. Most could forage in a forest for an hour at the right time of year and emerge with a feast of fresh berries, several types of wild mushroom, and probably a fish or two; city-dwelling Finns are far more knowledgeable and in touch with nature than any of their European counterparts.

LIFESTYLE

Finland is the model of a successful Northern European state and conforms, statistically speaking, to many of the tendencies that one would expect. Average income is good, there is little poverty, and Finland occupies a high position on the UN's Human Development Index. Finns are among the world's most educated people and the least regularly seen at church.

> 'Sitting in the sauna for 20 minutes with your best friend, saying nothing, is considered perfectly normal.'

LITTLE SATURDAY

Finns love the weekend, when they can get away to their cottages, play sport and party in the evening. But the working week is also broken up in the middle. On Wednesday nights restaurants are busy, music is playing at all the nightspots, bars are full – Finns are celebrating *pikku lauantai,* or 'little Saturday'.

While the economic recession in the 1990s ensured the partial decline of the welfare state, Finns still enjoy a high level of support, getting five weeks' holiday a year, as well as more-or-less free education and childcare, and generous paternity and maternity allowances. The health system, too, is excellent.

Empowerment of women is high, and they are well represented at all levels in all spheres. The divorce rate is also extremely high, with some 53 divorces per 100 marriages, perhaps reflective of the Finns' tendency towards pragmatism rather than dogmatism. The birth rate, as in much of the EU, is low. Gay and lesbian marriages are not permitted, but there is a special status afforded to same-sex relationships that confers similar rights.

POPULATION

Finland is comparatively sparsely populated with some 16 people per square kilometre, which is five times less than Spain, and one-fifteenth that of the UK. By far the majority of Finns live in the south with the Greater Helsinki area, Tampere and Turku accounting for a quarter of

SAUNA – STEAMY BUT NO SEX

The ancient Romans had their steam and hot-air baths, the Turks and Persians had their *hammams,* and the Finns gave the world the sauna (pronounced *sah*-oo-nah, not *saw*-nuh). It's one of the most essential elements of Finnish culture. Finns will prescribe a sauna session to cure all ills, from a head cold to sunburn.

The earliest written description of the Finnish sauna dates from the chronicles of Ukrainian historian Nestor in 1113. There are also numerous references to sauna-going in the Finnish national epic, the *Kalevala*. Saunas were traditionally used to smoke meats, and even to give birth.

Today there are 1.6 million saunas in Finland, which means that practically all Finns have access to one. Most are private, situated in Finnish homes. An invitation to bathe in a family's sauna is an honour, just as it is to be invited to a person's home for a meal. The sauna is taken in the nude, a fact that some people find uncomfortable and confronting, but Finns consider perfectly natural. While a Finnish family will often take the sauna together, in mixed gatherings it is usual for the men and women to go separately.

There are also public saunas, usually with separate sections for men and women, and if there is just one sauna, the hours are different for men and women. In unisex saunas you will be given some sort of wrap or covering to wear. Indeed, Finns are strict about the nonsexual character of the sauna and this point should be respected. The sauna was originally a place to bathe and meditate. It's not, as many foreigners would believe, a place for sex.

There are three principal types of sauna around these days. The most common is the electric sauna stove, which produces a fairly dry harsh heat compared with the much-loved chimney sauna, driven by a log fire and the staple of life at Finnish summer cottages. Even rarer is the true *savusauna,* or smoke sauna, without a chimney. The smoke is let out just before entry, and the soot-blackened walls are part of the experience. Although the top of a sauna can get to well over 120°C, many Finns consider the most satisfying temperature for a sauna to be around 80°C.

Proper sauna etiquette dictates that you use a *kauha* (ladle) to throw water on the *kiuas* (sauna stove), which then gives off the *löyly* (sauna steam). At this point, at least in summer in the countryside, you might take the *vihta* or *vasta* (a bunch of fresh, leafy birch twigs) and lightly strike yourself. This improves circulation, has cleansing properties and gives your skin a pleasant smell. When you are sufficiently warmed, you'll jump in the sea, a lake, river or pool, then return to the sauna to warm up and repeat the cycle several times. If you're indoors, a cold shower will do. The swim and hot-cold aspect is such an integral part of the sauna experience that in the dead of winter, Finns cut a hole in the ice and jump right in! The final essential ingredient is the sauna beer, which always tastes heavenly.

the population. Generally speaking, the population thins out dramatically inland and further north. In remote municipalities in Lapland, settlement is very sparse indeed.

Apart from the Finnish-speaking Finns, there are three other significant minority groups. Some 5.5% of Finns speak Swedish as their first language. While historically this has caused tensions, these seem to have largely eased into the odd grumble from either side. The main Swedish-speaking areas are in the southwest – where the semi-autonomous Åland islands are almost completely Swedish speaking – and in the Pohjanmaa/Ostrobotten region on the west coast.

The Sámi, who have traditionally lived in the north of the country, are another important minority (see boxed text, p324).

In the east, the Karelians, few of whom speak a Karelian language as their first language, are another distinct ethnolinguistic group, sundered from much of their homeland by the Finland/Russia border. Karelia feels different. It has distinct local character and traditions and a particularly strong Orthodox Church.

One of Finland's most famous footballers is Aki Riihilahti, famous not so much for his exploits on the pitch with Crystal Palace as his fabulously offbeat web diaries. Hit the News pages at www.akiriihilahti.com

SPORT

Ice hockey is Finland's number one national passion. The season starts in late September and finishes in March. The best places to see a quality match in the national league are Tampere (home of the ice-hockey museum), Oulu (home of the current champions) and Helsinki. Turku and Rovaniemi also have major teams. Ticket prices are reasonable (from about €15), and the atmosphere at big games can be electric. The best way to find out when and where games are on is to ask at the tourist office, or contact the national ticketing outlet **Lippupalvelu** (www.ticketservicefinland.fi).

Skiing events don't have the same intensity as team sports, but national (and international) competitions provide a thrill worth experiencing. You can watch flying Finns at the ski-jumping centres in Lahti, Kuopio and Jyväskylä. Even practice sessions can be fascinating and can be seen in summer on the dry slopes at Lahti.

In summer, football (soccer) has a national league, and is widely supported, but not as obsessively as in most European countries. Europe's major leagues are followed with interest, particularly when a successful Finn is playing. The likes of Sami Hyypiä, Mikael Forssell and Antti Niemi have been particularly successful playing in England's Premiership.

DRIVIN' WHEELS

Few nationalities have such an obsession with cars (and motorbikes) as the Finns. It's an interest that goes right down the scale from watching Formula One racing, to changing the oil on the old Datsun parked outside.

You won't be in a Finnish town for long before you'll hear a baritone bellow and see a glint of fins and whitewall tyres as some American classic car rolls by, immaculately polished and tuned. You probably never knew that so many Ford Mustangs, Dodge Chargers or Pontiac Firebirds existed on this side of the Atlantic! Even non-classics that have long since died out elsewhere are kept alive here with loyal home maintenance.

Rally driving sends Finns wild; the exploits of legends like Tommi Mäkinen and Marcus Grönholm are just the latest in a sport in which Finland excels. In Formula One, too, Finland punches well above its weight, with Keke Rosberg and Mika Häkkinen previous world champions, and Kimi Räikkönen sure to follow one day. In small towns, often the only entertainment for the local youths is trying to emulate them by doing blockies around the *kauppatori* (market square).

Outside big cities, Finnish baseball, called *pesäpallo* or simply *pesis*, is the most popular team sport in summer, with men's and women's teams enthusiastically supported. It was brought back and 'improved' from the USA in the 1920s. Check out www.pesis.fi for more details.

Athletics (track and field) is very popular in Finland, as a result of the country's many successful long-distance runners and javelin-throwers. Paavo Nurmi's nine Olympic golds place him at the top of the Finnish pantheon. Helsinki hosted the 2005 World Athletics Championships.

MULTICULTURALISM

Only 2% of all Finnish residents are foreigners – the lowest percentage of any country in Europe – and the majority of these are Russian (almost 23,000), followed by Estonian, Swedish, former Yugoslavian and Somalian. Finland is fast becoming more multicultural, as former refugees spread their wings and contract workers are brought in by Finland's booming technology companies. Overt racism is rare, although some disturbing instances have occurred in smaller towns in central Finland (see p23).

MEDIA

Newspapers

Finns are among the world's most voracious readers of broadsheets and tabloids. *Helsingin Sanomat,* the largest daily in Finland with a circulation of nearly half a million, is highly regarded, while *Ilta-Sanomat* and *Ilta-Lehti* compete with lurid 'pop star in sex and drugs shocker' type headlines. Turku's *Turun Sanomat* and Tampere's *Aamulehti* are other important regional papers. Freedom of the press is sacrosanct.

There's an excellent index of Finnish and other Nordic authors at www .kirjasto.sci.fi

Radio & TV

There are four national (noncommercial) radio stations. A summary of world news is broadcast in English daily at 10.55pm on the national radio stations YLE 3 and YLE 4. In Helsinki, YLE X plays Finnish and international rock, while Radio Nova is more poppy and Kiss FM fairly cheesy.

There are four free-to-air TV stations: the government-run YLE 1 and YLE 2, and the private MTV 3 and Nelonen 4. Cable and satellite connections are widespread. Foreign programmes are broadcast in the original language with subtitles.

Government radio and TV stations have Swedish-language equivalents.

RELIGION

About 84% of Finns describe themselves as Lutherans, 1.1% are Russian Orthodox and most of the remainder are unaffiliated. Minority churches, including the Roman Catholic Church, make up only about 1%. Only 4% of Finns are weekly churchgoers, one of the lowest rates in the world.

ARTS

Literature

Written Finnish was created by Mikael Agricola (1510–57), who wrote the first Finnish alphabet. Because Finnish remained a spoken more than written language (although it was emerging in schools), the earliest fiction was written in Swedish.

The most famous of all 19th-century writers is Elias Lönnrot, who penned the *Kalevala* (see p36). Other notable 19th-century writers include JL Runeberg *(Tales of the Ensign Ståhl),* fairy-tale writer Zacharias Topelius, and Aleksis Kivi, who founded modern Finnish literature with

Seven Brothers, a story of brothers who try to escape education and civilisation in the forest.

In the 20th century, Mika Waltari gained fame with *The Egyptian,* and FE Sillanpää received the Nobel Prize for literature in 1939. The national bestseller during the postwar period was *The Unknown Soldier* by Väinö Linna. The seemingly endless series of autobiographical novels by Kalle Päätalo and the witty short stories by Veikko Huovinen are also very popular in Finland. Another internationally famous author is the late Tove Jansson (see boxed text on p214), whose books about the Moomin family captured the hearts and imaginations of Finnish children, and adults.

One of the most popular contemporary Finnish novelists is the prolific, bizarre and whimsical Arto Paasilinna, whose best-known translated book is *The Year of the Hare.*

One book that is well worth reading is Mikael Niemi's *Popular Music,* set in Niemi's hometown in an area of Swedish Lapland with a very Finnish character and humour!

Architecture

The high standard of Finnish architecture was established by the works of Alvar Aalto (1898–1976) and Eliel Saarinen (1873–1950). People interested in architecture make pilgrimages to Finland to see superb examples of modern building.

Wood has long been the dominant building material in Finland. Some of the best early examples of wooden architecture are churches on Finland's southern and western coasts such as those at Kerimäki, Keuruu and Ruotsinpyhtää.

Eastern influences date back to 1812 when Helsinki was made the new capital under Russian rule. The magnificent city centre was created by CL Engel, a German-born architect, who combined neoclassical and St Petersburg features in designing the cathedral, the university and other buildings around Senate Square. Engel also designed a huge number of churches and town halls throughout Finland. After the 1850s National Romanticism emerged in response to pressure from the Russians.

THE *KALEVALA*

Elias Lönnrot was an adventurous country doctor who trekked in eastern Finland during the first half of the 19th century in order to collect traditional poems, oral runes, folk stories and legends. Lönnrot undertook 11 long tours, by foot and on reindeer, to complete his research. He compiled the material together with some of his own writing to form the *Kalevala,* which came to be regarded as the national epic of Finland.

The first version of the *Kalevala* appeared in 1833, another version in 1835 and yet another, the final version, *Uusi-Kalevala* (New Kalevala), in 1849. It had a huge influence on generations of Finnish artists, writers and composers, with painter Akseli Gallen-Kallela and composer Jean Sibelius, in particular, basing much work on it. See p22 for some destinations in Finland related to the *Kalevala.*

Kalevala is an epic mythology that includes creation stories and tales of the fight between good and evil. Although there are heroes and villains, there are also more nuanced characters. The main storyline concentrates on events in two imaginary countries, *Kalevala* (southern Finland, often identified as Karelia) and *Pohjola* (the north). Many commentators feel that the epic echoes ancient territorial conflicts between the Finns and the Sámi. Although it is impossible to accurately reproduce the *Kalevala,* the memorable characters are particularly well brought to life in poet Keith Bosley's English translation, which is a fantastic and lyrical read.

Equally important was Lönnrot's work in creating a standard Finnish grammar and vocabulary by adopting words and expressions from various dialects. Finnish has remained very much the same ever since, at least in written form.

The Art Nouveau period, which reached its apogee at the turn of the 20th century, combined Karelian ideals with rich ornamentation. Materials used were wood and grey granite. After independence in 1917, rationalism and functionalism emerged, as exemplified by some of Alvar Aalto's work.

Emerging regional schools of architecture include the Oulu School, featuring small towers, porticoes and combinations of various elements, most evident in the region around Oulu. Erkki Helasvuo, who died in 1995, did plenty of work in North Karelia, providing the province with several public buildings which hint at modern Karelianism. The most famous of these is Nurmes Talo, the cultural centre in Nurmes.

Design

The products of some early designers, such as Louis Sparre, Gallen-Kallela and Eliel Saarinen, reflected the ideas of Karelianism, National Romanticism and Art Nouveau. In the 1930s architect Alvar Aalto designed wooden furniture made of bent laminated wood, as well as his famous Savoy vases. Aalto won a prize for his furniture in the Milan Triennale of 1933.

After WWII, the 'Golden Age of Applied Art' began, and in Milan in 1951 Finland received 25 prizes for various designer products. Tapio Wirkkala, Kaj Franck, Timo Sarpaneva, Eero Aarnio and Yrjö Kukkapuro were the most notable designers of the time.

Iittala, Nuutajärvi and Arabia are some of the best brands of Finnish glassware and porcelain, and Pentik is a more recent brand. Aarikka is famous for wooden products, and Kalevala Koru for silver designs. The biggest name in the current Finnish design scene is Stefan Lindfors, whose reptile– and insect-inspired work has been described as a warped updating of Aalto's own nature-influenced work. Helsinki's Museum of Art & Design is a good place to see the latest in Finnish design.

JRR Tolkien based significant parts of his mythos on the Kalevala, and part of the language of Elves on Finnish.

Painting & Sculpture

Of the many prehistoric rock paintings discovered across Finland, those at Hossa (p283) and Ristiina (p127) are the most famous. Medieval churches in Åland, such as Sankt Mikael Church (in Finström), Sankta Maria Church (in Saltvik) and Sankta Birgitta Church (in Lemland), and in Southern Finland have enchanting frescoes. Modern art is alive and well in Finland, with most towns having a gallery showing exhibitions of contemporary work, headed up by Helsinki's Kiasma.

Finnish modern art and sculpture often seems to portray disaffectation with the technological society; the number of mistreated Nokias that form part of exhibits around the country is always high. The contrast of this with the output of the designers couldn't be starker; some have seen a reflection in this of the decreasing Finnishness of Helsinki, and a fear of losing some essential characteristic or soul.

GOLDEN AGE

Although contemporary art enjoys a high profile in Finland, it is works by National Romantic painters that have been bestowed with golden age status. The main features of these artworks are virgin forests and pastoral landscapes. The most comprehensive collections are displayed by the Ateneum and National Museum in Helsinki, and the Turku Art Museum. The following list contains some of the most famous names from the Finnish Golden Age.

Akseli Gallen-Kallela (1865–1931), probably the most famous Finnish painter, had a distinguished and prolific career as creator of *Kalevala*-inspired paintings.

Albert Edelfelt (1854–1905), one of the most appreciated of Finnish artists, was educated in Paris, and a number of his paintings date from this period. Many paintings are photo-like depictions of rural life.

The brothers von Wright – Magnus (1805–68), Wilhelm (1810–87) and Ferdinand (1822–1902) – are considered the first Finnish painters of the Golden Age, most famous for their paintings of birds. They worked in their home near Kuopio and in Porvoo.

Helene Schjerfbeck (1862–1946), probably the most famous female painter of her age, is known for her self-portraits, which reflect the situation of Finnish women 100 years ago; Helene didn't live a happy life, but is considered Finland's greatest artist by many contemporary observers. Fanny Churberg (1845–92), another very famous female painter, created landscapes, self-portraits and still lifes.

Hugo Simberg (1873–1917) is famous for his series of watercolours, which draw on folk tales and employ a kind of rustic symbolism.

Juho Rissanen (1873–1950) depicted life among ordinary Finns, and his much-loved paintings are displayed at the Ateneum and Turku Art Museum.

Eero Järnefelt (1863–1937) was a keen visitor to Koli, where he created more than 50 paintings of the 'national landscape'. His sister married Jean Sibelius, the composer. Pekka Halonen (1865–1933) was a popular artist of the National Romantic era. His work, mostly devoted to typical winter scenery, is largely privately owned. Victor Westerholm (1860–1919) most famous for his large Åland landscapes, had his summer studio in Önningeby (see p238) but there are landscapes from other locations too.

Emil Wickström (1864–1942), was to sculpture what Gallen-Kallela was to painting, and sculpted the memorial to Elias Lönnrot in Helsinki. Many of his works are at his studio in Visavuori.

Theatre & Dance

Dance is nurtured in Finland. The Finnish National Opera has its own ballet school, and there are a handful of small dance groups in Helsinki and other large towns. Attend the annual Kuopio Dance Festival to catch the latest trends.

Few traditional *kansan-tanssit* (folk dances) remain, but they can be seen on ceremonial occasions or at certain festivals. Old-style dancing in general remains very popular, though, with every town having a hall where *humppa* or melancholy Finnish *tango* accompanies twirling couples.

Helsinki is the home of the National Theatre. Finnish theatre is very well attended and heavily subsidised. The most famous dramatist is perhaps Aleksis Kivi, who wrote plays as well as novels.

Jim Jarmusch is a friend of the Finnish film industry and part of his film *Night on Earth* is set in Helsinki.

Cinema

Finnish cinema is alive and well, and several films are produced in Finland annually, although few make it to screens beyond the Nordic countries. Funding is a vexed issue due to the government's reluctant to over-subsidise an industry with, in the majority of cases, a limited domestic audience.

The daddy of Finnish cinema is Aki Kaurismäki, who won the Grand Prix at the 2002 Cannes Film Festival for *The Man Without a Past*, a story about a man who is so badly beaten up he loses his memory and becomes homeless. It confirmed the reputation Kaurismäki established in film noir with his brother Mika with such films as the downbeat but quintessentially Finnish *Drifting Clouds* (1997). They also collaborated with the wacky Leningrad Cowboys on two road movies.

The most successful Finn in Hollywood, Renny Harlin (real name Lauri Harjola), directed the strongly anticommunist action movie *Born American* in the 1980s, portraying an imaginary Soviet prison camp. When the film was banned in Finland and Harlin accused of presenting a 'foreign nation in a hostile manner', the young director found himself directing box-office hits for Hollywood, including *Die Hard II, Cliffhanger, Deep Blue Sea* and the recent *Exorcist: The Beginning*. A far cry from Kaurismäki.

Music

Music is a big part of Finnish culture, particularly in summer when music festivals are staged all over the country. As well as traditional dance bands, you'll find plenty of rock, jazz, folk, classical and modern electronic music playing in a variety of venues.

CLASSICAL MUSIC

Composer Jean Sibelius' (see boxed text, p184) work dominates the musical identity of Finland. His most famous composition, *Finlandia,* became a strong expression of Finnish patriotism. Sibelius can be said to have composed the music for the *Kalevala* saga, while Gallen-Kallela painted it.

Sibelius' inheritance has been taken up over the years by a string of talented musicians. Finnish musical education is perhaps the best in the world, and Finnish conductors, in particular, are in high demand. There are some excellent classical music festivals in Finland. See p334 for some of them.

POPULAR MUSIC

In recent years Finnish bands, mostly from the heavier side of the rock spectrum, have taken the world by storm. Indeed, Finland has one of the liveliest heavy and darkwave scenes around. Catchy light-metal rockers The Rasmus won international recognition with their album *Dead Letters* and have continued to build on that success. Meanwhile, Nightwish, from the little eastern town of Kitee, have risen to stardom on the blend of dark metal music and the soaring vocals of opera singer Tarja Turunen. Perhaps bigger than either are HIM (His Infernal Majesty), whose melodic 'love metal' has propelled them perhaps further than any Finnish band. Blind Guardian, with very heavy metal, much based on Tolkien's *Silmarillion,* are also big, as are Stratovarius. Other bands to look out for in this genre include gothic The 69 Eyes, classical/metal combo Apocalyptica, and the heavy Children of Bodom.

Legendary rock bands Hanoi Rocks, The Hurriganes, and the Leningrad Cowboys continue to be popular, with Hanoi Rocks on a slightly shambolic comeback trail. There are also numerous excellent groups that sing in Finnish only. Check out Zen Café, Don Huonot, Apulanta and Verenpisara (in roughly ascending order of heaviness), or Maija Vilkkumaa, often described as a Finnish Alanis. Husky Rescue have already had success in Britain with their happy, breezy approach.

The best rock festivals are Provinssirock at Seinäjoki, Ankkarock at Vantaa, Ruisrock in Turku and Ilosaarirock at Joensuu, while Tavastia is a legendary Helsinki rock club.

Finns are big fans of jazz, as can be seen by the huge jazz festivals at Pori, Espoo and Kajaani and the many jazz clubs in major cities. Notable Finnish jazz musicians include Raoul Björkenheim, and the late Edward Vesala, a visionary of the Finnish free jazz scene. Trio

The Finnish Film Archive has a good overview of Finnish cinema on its website, www.sea.fi.

www.fimic.fi is an excellent resource for finding out about Finnish music, while www.more music.fi is a good place to order hard-to-get Finnish CDs online.

Töykeät is an excellent modern jazz ensemble that has had notable worldwide success.

Electronic music is also big business in Finland. Techno and trance artist Darude has had huge successes, and the Bomfunk MCs are big in the hip-hop scene. Other names to look for in the Finnish music business include Pan Sonic, known for abstract, minimalist and experimental electronica; Laika & the Cosmonauts, who built a big reputation as surf instrumentalists (believe it or not) and Jori Hulkkonen, a house producer and DJ.

Several Finnish Sámi groups and artists have created excellent modern music with the traditional *yoik* form. The *yoik* is the basis of most Sámi music and is classically an unaccompanied and complex vocal solo often describing a person, and with immense spiritual importance in Sámi culture. In recent times it has been used with musical accompaniment and in a variety of forms. Wimme is a big name in this sphere, and Angelit produce popular, dancefloor-style Sámi music. One of their former members, Ulla Pirttijärvi, has released a particularly haunting solo album, while Vilddas are on the trancey side of Sámi music, combining it with other influences.

Environment

THE LAND

Finland, measuring in at 338,000 sq km, is the seventh-largest country in Europe, and its southernmost point is equivalent in latitude to Anchorage, Alaska, or southern Greenland.

It's often described as a country of 'forests and lakes', but is this the case? Absolutely! Ten percent of the country's surface area is taken up by its 187,888 lakes, other wetlands and countless other smaller bodies of water, and nearly seventy percent is forested. Finland has almost as many islands as it does lakes; some 180,000 of them, mostly tiny.

Much of the curious geography that we see today is a result of the last Ice Age, and its end around 10,000 years ago. The powerful moving ice masses produced classic glacial features such as *eskers* (sand/gravel ridges), formed by streams of meltwater under the main body of the glacier, and kettle holes, lumps of ice left behind in depressions by the retreating glacier that became lakes. The predominant flow of Finland's waterways is northwest to southeast, mirroring the path of the glaciers' retreat.

Without the massive weight of the ice, the Earth's crust in this area began to slowly spring back, a process that is still continuing at a rate of 6mm per year. The Baltic, which was itself a lake until the saltwater came pouring in via Denmark at about the same period, is decreasing in size as land rises from the sea.

Despite what a Monty Python song claimed, Finland has no 'mountains so lofty'; they were probably thinking of Norway. There are no real mountains; rather, the *eskers* and wooded hills dominate. The highest hills, or *tunturit* (fells) are in Lapland, which borders the mountainous areas of northern Norway and Sweden. Finland's highest point, the Halti, in the northwest corner of the country, rises only 1328m above sea level.

WILDLIFE
Animals

There are quite a few mammals in Finnish forests. The largest (and one of the rarest) is the brown bear. Other mammals include elk (moose), foxes, lynx, wolves and wolverines. There are also plenty of small animals such as lemmings, hedgehogs, muskrats, martens, beavers, otters and hares. The *hirvi* (elk) is a solitary, shy animal – to see one is a real treat, unless it's crashing into your car windscreen. There are plenty of elk about, so keep your eyes out, especially in the early morning or evening. There are around 2000 road accidents a year involving elk. *Poro* (reindeer), on

Lemmings are not really suicidal! While they do migrate in large numbers in years of overpopulation, the image of them jumping en masse over a cliff comes from the Disney film *Wild Wilderness*, when the lemmings were sacrificed for better cinema.

SUMMER COTTAGES

About 25% of the population of Finland owns a *kesämökki* or summer cottage, and the majority of Finns at least have access to one. The *mökki* is where Finns retreat to nature and should ideally be on the shores of a lake and surrounded by forest. A genuine *mökki* has only basic amenities – many have no electricity or running water – but always comes equipped with a (wood-burning) sauna and a rowing boat. These days, however, you can rent a *mökki* with a fridge, TV and even a phone. Grilling sausages over the barbecue, swimming and fishing in the lake, playing darts and gathering berries and mushrooms are typical *mökki* activities, not to mention enjoying a post-sauna beer by the lake! Getting invited to a summer cottage is a great honour and an experience not to be missed, perhaps the ultimate in Nordic peace and relaxation.

the other hand, abound in north Finland, with some 230,000 animals. These are all in semidomesticated herds owned by the Sámi. *Ilves* (lynx) used to be very rare but numbers are increasing. There are only 150 or so wolves, but they, too, are on the up. Hatred for, and fear of, the *susi* (wolf) is deep-rooted in eastern Finland, where they traditionally have been hunted and killed. Wolverines, too, have traditionally been hunted, both for their fur, and their depredations on the reindeer population, particularly in winter. Unless you head out with specialist guides or are very lucky, you are unlikely to see bears, wolves, lynx or wolverines on a trip to Finland.

The brown bear was once so feared in Finland that even mentioning its name *(karhu)* was taboo; numerous synonyms, such as *mesikämmen*, 'honeypaw', exist in Finnish.

Other interesting mammals include the rare Saimaa ringed seal, a freshwater dweller who lost its saltwater cousins as the land rose, the flying squirrel, a resident of the taiga, and the famous lemming, an Arctic resident.

There are more than 300 bird species in Finland (see p51 for more information). Large species include black grouse, capercaillies, whooper swans and birds of prey such as the osprey. Chaffinches and willow warblers are the two most common forest species, and their songs are almost synonymous with the Finnish summer. Sparrows are quite common in inhabited areas. Crested-tits, black woodpeckers, black-throated divers, ravens and many owls are common throughout the country; the glorious red-throated diver (*kaakkuri*) is also present, as are many other waterbirds. The Siberian jay is a common sight in Lapland because it follows people. There are numerous migrating birds present in spring and summer, including the common crane, a spectacular sight in the fields. Finns who watch migratory birds arrive from the south have a saying for how to determine when summer will come: it is one month from sighting a skylark, half a month from a chaffinch, just a little from a white wagtail and not a single day from a swift. Less popular creatures include the viper (*kyy*), which is the most common poisonous snake.

REINDEER ROADBLOCKS

For many travellers a highlight of a visit to Finland is the chance to glimpse some Finnish wildlife, such as bear or elk. If you are travelling in the far north you'll definitely see reindeer, and you won't have to go trekking in the wild to find them.

Reindeer are not wild animals. Reindeer herding has been an essential part of the Sámi culture for centuries, and reindeer are semidomesticated but wander freely. With some 230,000 reindeer wandering around Lapland, it's inevitable that some will find their way onto the roads and they are unfortunately very blasé about traffic. Some 3000 to 4500 reindeer die annually on Finnish roads, and trains kill an additional 600.

The worst months for reindeer-related accidents are November and December, when hours of daylight are few and road visibility is extremely poor. Also bad are July and August, when the poor animals run amok trying to escape insects. The roads to take extra precautions on are in the far north – anywhere beyond Oulu basically.

The best way to avoid an accident is to slow down immediately when you spot a reindeer, regardless of its location, direction or speed. Reindeer move slowly and do not respond to car horns. Nor do they seem to feel that vehicles deserve right of way. If a calf is on one side of the road and its mother on the other, it will almost always try and dash across.

Elk are not as common but are much larger animals and tend to dart onto the road if panicked by traffic. There are around 2000 accidents each year involving elk and generally neither the vehicle nor the animal come out of it looking too good. Be particularly vigilant when driving in the morning or evening, particularly in autumn, when elk accidents are a very real and potentially fatal danger. Respect the warning signs!

Plants

Finnish plant life has developed relatively recently, having been wiped out by the last Ice Age, and is specially adapted either to survive the harsh winters, or to take advantage of the short summers.

Although coastal areas support a more diverse tree population, nearly all of Finland's forest cover is made up of pines, spruces and birches. Pine grows generally on dryish ground and sandy soils, conditions which don't foster undergrowth. Spruce forests are dark and dense, while birch is the typical tree in deciduous forests. Most forests in Finland are logged every 80 years or so and forestry management is something of an art form here.

Finnish flora sparkles during the dynamic period between late May and September. Flowers bloom and berries are gathered; you'll see cars all over the place and families filling buckets with blueberries, wild strawberries, crowberries, and in the north, the delicious Arctic cloudberries.

Lappajärvi, northeast of Seinäjoki, is one of Europe's biggest meteorite impact sites. The crater measures 23km in diameter and was created some 70 to 80 million years ago.

NATIONAL PARKS

While much of Finland's forest covering is private land cultivated by forestry companies, Metsähallitus, the Finnish Forest and Park Service maintains an excellent series of national parks. At last count, there were 35 of them (including Koli, managed by METLA, the independent Finnish Forest Research Institute), with a total area of over 8000 sq km. A similar amount of territory is protected under other categories, while further swathes of land are designated wilderness reserves. In total, over 30,000 sq km, some 9% of the total area, is in some way protected.

Metsähallitus publishes *Finland's National Parks,* a comprehensive booklet listing all national parks, with information on trails and accommodation as well as notes on flora and fauna. This is an extremely helpful resource if you are planning to visit several parks or are particularly interested in the Finnish wilderness. This can be obtained at any Metsähallitus office, including the Helsinki **headquarters** (Map p64; ☎ 09-270 5221, 0203-44112; www.metsa .fi; Eteläesplanadi 20; ☉ 10am-6pm Mon-Fri, 10am-3pm Sat). Most of this information is online at the excellent website www.outdoors.fi, which goes into some

NATIONAL PARKS

Great National Parks	Features	Activities	Best Time to Visit
Lemmenjoki (p322)	Broad rivers and old-growth forests; golden eagles, reindeer	Trekking, boating, gold-panning	Aug-Sep
Linnansaari & Kolovesi (p124)	Luscious lakes and freshwater seals	Canoeing	May-Sep
Oulanka (p288)	Pine forests and river valleys; elk, white-tailed eagles; calypso flowers	Trekking the Bear's Ring	late Jun-Sep
Urho K Kekkonen (p316)	Fells, mires and old Sámi settlements; reindeer, flying squirrels	Trekking, cross-country skiing, fishing	Jul-Sep & Nov-Apr
Southwestern Archipelago (p99)	Strings of islets and skerries; seals, eider ducks, greylag geese	Boating, fishing	May-Sep
Nuuksio (p87)	Forest within striking distance of Helsinki; woodpeckers, elk, divers	Nature trails	May-Oct
Patvinsuo (p160)	Broad boglands and old forest; bears, beavers, cranes	Hiking	Jun-Oct
Pallas-Yllästunturi (p308)	Undulating fells; bears, snow buntings, ptarmigans	Hiking, trekking, skiing	Jul-Sep, Nov-Apr

detail about each park. Pamphlets describing individual parks are available at the national park information centres throughout the country.

The largest and most pristine national parks are in northern Finland, particularly Lapland, where vast swathes of wilderness invite trekking, cross-country skiing, fishing, and canoeing.

Linnansaari and Kolovesi National Parks, near Savonlinna, are the best parks in the Lakeland area and home to the extremely endangered Saimaa ringed seal. To see larger mammals – such as the shy and elusive elk – it's best to visit one of the national parks in the northeast, such as Oulanka National Park, or further north in Lapland, such as Lemmenjoki, Pallas-Ounastunturi and Urho Kekkonen National Parks. These parks are vast and services and facilities are few; to make the most of a visit you should be prepared to spend several days trekking and camping. See opposite for trail recommendations and more information about trekking.

ENVIRONMENTAL ISSUES

In Finland, forestry products are a huge source of income and employment, and generate some 35% of the country's total export revenue. It is also the main cause of pollution and the main topic of environmental debate. Paper and pulp industries provide work for thousands but also cause environmental hazards, which are easily seen in areas surrounding factories.

Finland is the second largest exporter of paper products in the world and is dependent on paper manufacturing. Around 70% of the country is forest – the highest percentage in the world – and most of this land is managed forest that is harvested for cutting. While this is very well-managed, it has an unavoidable impact on local ecosystems, with ecological diversity lowered. However, the main problem in Finland is water pollution, especially from use of fertilizers on the forest areas.

While Finland may look idyllic and pristine, things are not always as they seem. In the most recent government survey, published in 2005, only 43% of the country's rivers were rated 'good' or better while about 80% of lakes were given the nod of approval. Worryingly, however, Finland's sea areas had markedly declined in water quality in the early years of the 21st century. While massive emissions from Russian St Petersburg and Vyborg contribute heavily to this, it's a worrying trend.

The forestry industry is also fighting battles up in the north, where Sámi reindeer herders have complained that the companies are erecting fences that jeopardize traditional movement between pasturing areas. The Sámi are seeking legislation to prevent this, while the forestry companies claim that only a minimal area is affected and the reindeer have more than enough space anyway.

Domestic conservation efforts are spearheaded by the Finnish Forest and Park Service, which oversees 120,000 sq km of land. This organisation also works to protect endangered species and promote biodiversity on forest lands that are used for commercial purposes. For more information about the National Park Service and protected wilderness areas, see p43.

The Finnish branch of the World Wide Fund for Nature runs week-long volunteer programs every summer where you participate in a work-camp on some conservation project. Email info@wwf.fi for details of upcoming camps.

The Great Outdoors

Finland's beauty and appeal lies in its fantastic natural environment, with vast forests, long waterways and numerous lakes to explore, as well as the harsh Arctic wilderness in the north. It's the best way to experience the country and Finland is remarkably well set-up for any type of activity, from all-included safari-style packages to map-and-compass do-it-yourself adventures. There's almost unlimited scope in both summer and winter. Fishing is popular year-round; in winter you just need something to drill a hole in the ice, and a warm drink while you wait for a bite!

HIKING

The superb system of national parks offers memorable trekking throughout Finland in the summer months. The routes are backed up with resources for camping and sleeping, so it's easy to organize a multiday wilderness adventure.

The terrain is generally flat and easy-going, and pristine wilderness covers much of the country. National parks offer excellent marked trails, and most wilderness areas are crisscrossed by locally-used walking paths. Nights are short or nonexistent in summer, so you can walk for as long as your heart desires or your feet will permit.

It's important to remember what the Finnish landscape does and doesn't offer. You will get scented pine and birch forest, low hills, jewel-like lakes and brisk powerful rivers. Don't expect epic mountains, fjords, cliffs and valleys; that's not Finland.

The trekking season runs from late May to September in most parts of the country. In Lapland and the north the ground is not dry enough for hiking until late June, and mosquitoes are a serious irritation during July.

If heading off trekking on your own, always advise someone of your route and intended arrival date, or note these details in the trekkers' books.

RIGHT OF PUBLIC ACCESS

The *jokamiehenoikeus*, literally 'everyman's right', is an ancient Finnish code that gives people the right to walk, ski or cycle anywhere in forests and other wilderness areas, and even across private land as long as they behave responsibly. Canoeing, rowing and kayaking on lakes and rivers is also unrestricted. Travel by motorboat or snowmobile, though, is heavily restricted.

You can rest and swim anywhere in the Finnish countryside, and camp for one night *almost* anywhere. To camp on private property you will need the owner's permission. Try and camp on already-used sites to preserve the environment. Camping is not permitted in town parks or on beaches.

Watch out for stricter regulations regarding access in nature reserves and national parks. In these places, camping may be forbidden and travel confined to marked paths. Some areas are equipped with compost bins or toilets, and even rubbish bins and recycling containers. Many areas are not, however, and you should take out any rubbish you bring with you.

MAKING CAMPFIRES

Under the right of public access, you may not make a campfire on private land unless you have the owner's permission. In national parks, look for designated campfire areas, called *nuotiopaikka* in Finnish, and watch for fire warning signs – *metsäpalovaroitus* means the fire risk is very high.

Felling trees or cutting brush to make a campfire is forbidden; use fallen wood instead.

GATHERING BERRIES & MUSHROOMS

It's permissible to pick berries and mushrooms – but not other kinds of plants – under Finland's right of public access. Blueberries come into season in late July and wild strawberries are another gem.

Orange cloudberries are so appreciated by Finns that you may not have a chance to sample this slightly sour, creamy berry in the wild. In some parts of Lapland, cloudberries are protected. Edible mushrooms are numerous in Finnish forests, as are poisonous ones; make sure you have a mushroom guide or know what you are doing!

WHAT TO BRING
Food

You will have to carry all food when you walk in wilderness areas. If you plan to walk between wilderness huts, you generally won't need cooking equipment, but it's best to have a camp stove in case of fire bans. The most common fuels in Finland are *petroli* or *palo̊ljy* (kerosene), *spriitä* (methylated spirits) and *lamppuöljy* (paraffin). Camping Gaz and other butane cartridges are available from petrol stations and adventure sports stores.

Insect Repellent

Mosquitoes are a big problem in Finland, particularly in summer and particularly in Lapland. They are accompanied by phalanxes of other biting creatures from midges to horseflies. Skimp on protection at your own peril. Some trekkers even use a head net; they may look comical, but so does a nose swollen with bites.

ACCOMMODATION

The Metsähallitus (Forest and Park Service) maintains most of Finland's wilderness huts. Finland has one of the world's most extensive networks of free, properly-maintained wilderness huts. Some huts require advance booking, or they have a separate, lockable section that must be reserved in advance for a fee (usually €9). This is called a *varaustupa*.

Huts typically have basic bunks, cooking facilities, a pile of dry firewood and even a wilderness telephone. You are required to leave the hut as it was – ie replenish the firewood and carry away your rubbish. The Finns' 'wilderness rule' states that the last one to arrive will be given the best place to sleep, but, on busy treks in peak season, it's good to have a tent, because someone usually ends up sleeping outside.

Outside of Lapland, trekking routes generally have no free cabins, but you may be able to find a simple log shelter (*laavu*); you can pitch your tent inside or just roll out your sleeping bag. A 1:50,000 trekking map is recommended for finding wilderness huts and these cost €14 from tourist offices, national park visitor centres or map shops.

WHERE TO TREK

You can trek anywhere in Finland, but national parks and reserves will have marked routes, designated campfire places, well-maintained wilderness huts and boardwalks over the boggy bits.

Lapland is the main trekking region, with huge national parks that have well-equipped wilderness huts and good trekking routes. See p295 for details. There are other classic trekking areas at Oulanka National Park near Kuusamo, and in North Karelia.

'Orange cloudberries are so appreciated by Finns that you may not have a chance to sample this slightly sour, creamy berry in the wild.'

FORGET YOUR SKIS, DID YA?

Finland is proud of having invented the burgeoning sport of Nordic Walking, originally devised as a training method for cross-country skiers during the summer months. Basically, it involves using two specially-designed poles while briskly walking; it may look a little weird at first, but involves the upper body in the activity and results in a 20-45% increase in energy consumption, and an increase in heart rate, substantially adding to the exercise value of walking.

Nordic Blading is a speedier version, using poles while on inline skates – some pretty scary velocities can be reached!

Some recommended treks are described here. Excellent trekking maps are available in Finland for all of these routes.

Karhunkierros (Bear's Ring) The most famous of all Finnish trekking routes, this circular trail in northern Finland covers 75km of rugged cliffs, gorges and suspension bridges. See p288.

Karhunpolku (Bear's Path) This 133km marked hiking trail of medium difficulty leads north from Lieksa through a string of stunning national parks and nature reserves. See p158.

Susitaival (Wolf's Trail) Running along the border with Russia, this 100km trail stretches from the marshlands of Patvinsuo National Park, north of Ilomantsi, to the forests of Petkeljärvi National Park. See p158.

UKK Route The nation's longest trekking route is this 240km route through northern Finland. It starts at Koli Hill, continues along the western side of Lake Pielinen and ends at Iso-Syöte Hill. Farther east, there are more sections of the UKK Route, including the Kuhmo to Peurajärvi leg (connections from Nurmes) and the Kuhmo to Iso-Palonen leg. See p282 for a brief description of this trek.

CYCLING

Riding a bike in Finland is one of the best ways to explore parts of the country in summer. What sets Finland apart from both Sweden and Norway is the almost total lack of mountains. Main roads are in good condition and traffic is very light compared to elsewhere in Europe. Bicycle tours are further facilitated by the liberal camping regulations, excellent cabin accommodation at official camp sites, and the long hours of daylight in June and July.

The drawback is this: distances in Finland are vast. And let's face it, a lot of the Finnish scenery can get repetitive at a bicycle's pace. It's best to look at planning shorter explorations in particular areas, combining cycling with bus and train trips – Finnish buses and trains are very bike-friendly.

Even if your time is limited, don't skip a few quick jaunts in the countryside. There are very good networks of cycling paths in and around most major cities and holiday destinations (for instance, the networks around Oulu and Turku).

In most towns bicycles can be hired from sports shops, tourist offices, camping grounds or hostels for around €8 to €15 per day, or €45 to €60 a week.

BRINGING YOUR BICYCLE

Most airlines (but not the budget ones) will carry a bike free of charge, so long as the bike and panniers don't exceed the weight allowance per passenger. Inform the airline that you will be bringing your bike when you book your ticket. You will usually have to dismantle it.

Bikes can be carried on long-distance buses for around €3 if there is space available (and there usually is). Sometimes they can go on for free. Just advise the driver prior to departure.

Bikes can accompany passengers on most normal train journeys, with a surcharge of up to €9. Inter-City (IC) trains have spaces for bikes, which should be booked in advance; you'll have to take your bike to the appropriate space in the double-decker wagon – you can lock it in with a 50-cent coin. You can take your bike on regional trains that have a suitcase or bicycle symbol on the timetable; put it in the luggage van.

WHERE TO CYCLE

You can cycle on all public roads except motorways. Many public roads in southern Finland have a dedicated cycling track running alongside.

Åland

The Åland islands are the most bicycle-friendly region in Finland, and (not surprisingly) are the most popular region for bicycle tours.

Southern Finland

Southern Finland has more traffic than other parts of the country, but with careful planning you can find quiet roads that offer pleasant scenery. The Ox Road runs through rural areas from Turku to Hämeenlinna (see p187). There are also some good shorter rides around Turku.

The Lakeland/Karelia

Two theme routes cover the whole eastern frontier, from the south to Kuusamo in the north. *Runon ja rajan tie* (Road of the Poem and Frontier) consists of secondary sealed roads which pass several great Karelian villages and ends in northern Lieksa. Some of the smallest and most remote villages along the easternmost roads have been lumped together to create the *Korpikylien tie* (Road of Wilderness Villages). This route starts at Saramo village in northern Nurmes and ends at Hossa in northeast Suomussalmi.

A recommended loop takes you around Lake Pielinen, and may include a ferry trip across the lake. Another good loop is around Viinijärvi west of Joensuu.

Western Finland

This flat region, known as Pohjanmaa, is generally good for cycling, except that distances are long and scenery away from the coast is almost oppressively dull. The 'Swedish Coast' around Vaasa and north to Kokkola, is the most scenic part of this region.

'With snow cover in the south from November to April, and even longer in the north, Finns are very much at home on white surfaces, whether on skis, snowmobiles or reindeer-racing!'

WINTER SPORTS

There's loads to do in Finland in winter, and of course a long season in which to do it! With snow cover in the south from November to April, and even longer in the north, Finns are very much at home on white surfaces, whether on skis, snowmobiles or reindeer-racing!

One of the most popular and romantic of winter journeys is a sled safari pulled by reindeer or, even better, enthusiastic husky teams. You can head out for an hour, or go on a epic week-long adventure, looking after your own dog-team. Lapland (see p295) is the best place to do this, but it's also available further south in places like Nurmes (p165) and Lieksa (p160).

Similar excursions can be made on snowmobiles (skidoos). Operators in the same locations offer these trips. You'll need a valid drivers' licence to use one. The basic prices are increased for more powerful machines, or if everyone is on their own vehicle.

DOWNHILL SKIING & SNOWBOARDING

Finnish slopes are generally quite low and so are well-suited to beginners and families. The best resorts are in Lapland, where the vertical drop averages 250m over 3km. In central and southern Finland, ski runs are much shorter, averaging about 1km in length. For steeper, longer and more challenging slopes head across the border to Sweden or Norway.

The ski season in Finland runs from late November to early May and slightly longer in the north, where it's possible to ski from October to summer high season. Beware of the busy winter and spring (February and April) holiday periods, especially around Christmas and Easter – they can get very crowded, and accommodation prices go through the roof.

You can rent all skiing or snowboarding equipment at major ski resorts for about €25/110 a day/week. A one-day lift pass costs around €28/140 a day/week (slightly less in the shoulder and off-peak seasons), although it is possible to pay separately for each ride. Skiing lessons are also available from around €30 a day.

The best resorts are Levi (p305), Ruka (p286), Pyhä-Luosto (p312), and Ylläs (p302), but Syöte, Koli, Pallas, Ounasvaara, and Saariselkä are also good.

CROSS-COUNTRY SKIING

Cross-country skiing is one of the simplest and most pleasant things to do outdoors in winter in Finland. It's the ideal way to explore the beautiful, silent winter countryside of lakes, fells, fields and forests, and is widely used by Finns for fitness and as a means of transport.

Practically every town and village maintains ski tracks (*latu* or *ladut*) around the urban centre, in many cases illuminated (*valaistu*). The one drawback to using these tracks is that you'll need to bring your own equipment (or purchase some), as rentals usually aren't possible.

Cross-country skiing at one of Finland's many ski resorts is another option. Tracks get much longer but also are better maintained. Ski resorts offer excellent instruction and rent out equipment. The best cross-country skiing is in Lapland, where resorts offer hundreds of kilometres of trails. Keep in mind that there are only about five hours of daylight each day in northern Lapland during winter – if you're planning on a longer trek, spring is the best time. Cross-country skiing is best during January and February in southern Finland, and from December to April in the north.

> 'Practically every town and village maintains ski tracks around the urban centre.'

WATER SPORTS

ROWING, CANOEING & RAFTING

For independent travel on waterways, you will need to rent your own rowing boat, canoe or kayak. The typical Finnish rowing boat is available at camping grounds and some tourist offices, usually for less than €20 per day, and hourly rentals are possible. Hostels and rental cottages may have rowing boats that you'll be allowed to use for free. Use them on lakes, especially for visits to nearby islands.

Canoes and kayaks are suitable for trips that last several days or weeks. For longer trips you'll need a plastic barrel for your gear, a life-jacket and waterproof route maps. Route maps and guides may be purchased at local or regional tourist offices and at **Karttakeskus Aleksi** (see p59) map shop: you can also order via its website. Canoe and kayak rentals range in price from €15 to €30 per day, and €80 to €200 per week. You'll pay more if you need overland transportation to the start or end point of your trip or if you need to rent extra gear such as tents and sleeping bags. See the relevant sections of the guide for the names of rental outfitters.

WHERE TO ROW & PADDLE

The sheltered bays and islands around the Turku archipelago and Åland in southwest Finland are good for canoeing in summer.

Finland's system of rivers, canals and linked waterways means there are some extensive canoeing routes. In the Lakeland, the Kolovesi and Linnansaari National Parks (p124) are excellent waters for canoeing, and offer plenty of exploration opportunities. North Karelia, particularly around Lieksa and Ruunaa, also offers good paddling. Rivers further north, in the Kuusamo area and in Lapland, are very steep and fast-flowing, with tricky rapids, making them suitable for experienced paddlers only.

Rapids are classified according to a scale from I to VI. I is very simple, II will make your heart beat faster, III is dangerous for your canoe, IV may be fatal for the inexperienced. Rapids classified as VI are just short of Niagara Falls and will probably kill you. Unless you're an experienced paddler you shouldn't negotiate anything above a class I rapid on your own. Always be prepared to carry your canoe or kayak around an unsafe stretch of river.

Ivalojoki Route (Easy) A 70km route along the Ivalojoki, in northeast Lapland, that starts at the village of Kuttura and finishes in Ivalo, crossing 30 rapids along the way.

Kyrönjoki Routes (Easy-Medium) In western Finland the Kyrönjoki totals 205km, but you can do short trips down the river from Kauhajoki, Kurikka or Ilmajoki.

Lakeland Trail (Easy-Medium) This 350km route travels through the heart of the lake district (Kangaslampi, Enonkoski, Savonranta, Kerimäki, Punkaharju, Savonlinna and Rantasalmi) and takes 14 to 18 days.

Naarajoki Trail (Easy) A 100km route in the Mikkeli area, recommended for families.

Oravareitti (Squirrel Route, Easy-Medium) In the heart of the Lakeland, this is a 52km trip from Juva to Sulkava.

Savonselkä Circuit (Easy-Hard) The circuit, near Lahti, has three trails that are 360km, 220km and 180km in length. There are many sections that can be done as day trips and that are suitable for novice paddlers.

Seal Trail (Easy) From Kolovesi to Linnansaari, this is a 120km route that takes one to seven days.

Väliväylä Trail (Medium) This Lakeland trail goes from Kouvola to either Lappeenranta (90km) or Luumäki (60km) and includes some class I to class III rapids.

Plenty of operators offer white-water rafting expeditions in canoes or rubber rafts. The Ruunaa area (p161) is one of the best of many choices for this adrenalin-packed activity.

FISHING

The website www.fishing.fi has plenty of useful information in English on fishing throughout the country.

Finnish waters are teeming with fish – and with people trying to catch them. Finland has at least one million enthusiastic domestic anglers. Commonly caught fish include salmon (both river and landlocked), trout, grayling, perch, pike, whitefish, break and Arctic char.

With so many bodies of water there are no shortage of places to cast a line. In winter, when most water surfaces are frozen over, ice-fishing is all the craze. You simply cut a hole in the ice, drop in a line and wait for a bite. Lapland has the greatest concentration of quality fishing spots, but the number of designated places in southern Finland is also increasing. Some of the most popular fishing areas are the Tenojoki in the furthest north, the Torniojoki, the Kainuu region around Kajaani, Ruovesi, Hossa, Ruunaa, Lake Saimaa around Mikkeli, Lake Inari, and the Kymijoki near Kotka.

Local tourist offices can direct you to the best fishing spots in the area, and usually can provide some sort of regional fishing map. An annual guide to fishing the entire country is available from the **Metsähallitus** (Forest & Park Service; ☎ 09-270 5221; fax 644 421; www.outdoors.fi; Tikankontti, Eteläesplanadi 20, Helsinki). Their website also details fishing regulations in each protected area.

Permits

Several permits are required of foreigners (between the ages of 18 and 64) who wish to go fishing in Finland. Simple angling with hook and line requires no permit; neither does ice-fishing, unless you are doing these at rapids or other salmon waterways.

For other types of fishing, first, you will need a national fishing permit, known as a 'fishing management fee'. A one-week permit is €6 and an annual permit €20; they're payable at any bank or post office and shortly via the Internet (www.mmm.fi). Second, fishing with a lure always requires a special regional permit, also available at banks and post offices. Finally, you will need to pick up a local permit which has time and catch limits (say, two salmon per day and an unrestricted amount of other species). The local permit can be purchased for one day, one week or even for just a few hours. Typically these cost around €8 per day or €30 per week and are available on the spot, from the location where you're planning to fish. There are often automatic permit machines; tourist offices, sports shops and camping grounds can also supply permits. The waters in Åland are regulated separately and require a separate regional permit.

Check out www.birdlife.fi for a good introduction and links for bird-watching in Finland.

Equipment Rental

Many camping grounds and tourist offices rent out fishing gear in summer. To go ice-fishing in winter, however, you'll either need to buy your own gear or join an organised tour – nobody rents out ice-fishing tackle in Finland because every Finn has this!

OTHER ACTIVITIES

BIRD-WATCHING

Bird-watching is extremely popular in Finland, in no small part because many bird species migrate to northern Finland in summer to take advantage of the almost continuous daylight for breeding and rearing their young. Look carefully when in Finnish forests and you'll see that bird-mad locals have filled the trees with birdhouses to encourage visits by their favourite species. The best months for watching birds are May to June or mid-July, and late August to September or early October.

For information on Finnish golf courses, contact the Finnish Golf Union (Suomen Golfliitto; ☎ 09-3481 2244; www.golf.fi).

Liminganlahti (Liminka Bay), near Oulu, is a wetlands bird sanctuary and probably the best bird-watching spot in Finland. Other good areas include Puurijärvi-Isosuo National Park in Western Finland, Siikalahti in the Lakeland, Oulanka National Park near Kuusamo, the Porvoo area east of Helsinki and the Kemiö Islands. An excellent guide is *Birds* by Peter Holden. The version available within the country is in Finnish, so you will need to purchase an English-language version before you go.

GOLF

You need a green card (or handicap certificate) to play the best Finnish courses, but many courses are open to the public for €20 to €30 per round. At last count, there were around 100 uncrowded golf courses throughout Finland, typically open from late April to mid-October. The most unusual golf course in Finland is the Green Zone golf course in Tornio (see p277) – it crosses the boundary between Finland and Sweden.

Food & Drink

Finnish food was contemptuously described in 2005, by both Jacques Chirac and Silvio Berlusconi, as the worst in the EU. Now, just a moment please! There are two very distinct sides to Finnish cuisine. In winter, heavy, fatty foods have traditionally been eaten, originally designed to nourish a peasant population living in an extremely cold climate. In summer, however, Finland's fields, forests and gardens come to life, and produce some of the tastiest fresh produce imaginable. A meal of fresh salmon, the tenderest of new potatoes with home-grown dill from a Finnish garden and wild mushrooms and berries picked from the wood down the road is quite a meal, memorable for taste and freshness. Considering that Finland is north of the 60° latitude line, it's amazing, in fact.

STAPLES & SPECIALITIES

If you're seduced by all the delicious pastries in cafés here, *The Great Scandinavian Baking Book*, by Beatrice A Ojakangas, will help you reproduce some of them at home.

Finnish cuisine has been influenced by both Sweden and Russia and has drawn on what was available; fish, game, meat, milk and potatoes. Dark rye was used to make bread and porridge. Few spices were employed.

These basics remain constant, although inevitably added to by the broader choice in today's society. Restaurants have created a gourmet-Finnish cuisine, with delicate use of berries, wild mushrooms and other traditional ingredients.

Soups are a Finnish favourite, and are common in homes and restaurants. The heavy pea, meat, or cabbage soups are traditional workers' fare, while creamier fish soups have a more delicate flavour.

One light snack that you'll see everywhere is the rice-filled savoury pastry from Karelia, the *karjalanpiirakka*. These are tasty cold, heated, toasted, or with egg butter, and have several variations.

Understandably, a lot of fish is eaten in Finland. Salmon *(lohi)* is ubiquitous, both fresh and smoked, and often served with a creamy wild-mushroom sauce. *Silli* is pickled herring and comes in jars with a variety of sauces. The favourite sauce is sweet mustard, delicious with new potatoes, a traditional summer dish. Other traditional fish dishes include small deep-fried lakefish *(muikku)*, and, in the north, the Arctic char.

Two much-loved staples that you'll see in many places are grilled liver, served with mashed potatoes and bacon, and meatballs. Finns have been known to fight over whose granny cooks the best ones.

Reindeer is a domesticated animal, and has always been a staple food for the Sámi. The traditional way to eat it is sautéed with lingonberries; many restaurants also offer it on pizzas or as sausages. It also comes in fillet steaks, which, though expensive, is the tastiest way to try this meat.

Elk is also eaten, mostly in hunting season, and you can even get a bear steak in some places, although the latter is very expensive, as only a small number are hunted every year.

In summer, barbecues are the thing to do, particularly at the summer cottage. The number of sausage varieties in Finnish supermarkets has to be seen to be believed. Sausages are eaten with processed mustard; the traditional Turun Sinappi is the most loved, but has been boycotted by many since the multinational that owns it has moved production from Turku to Sweden. The equally good Auran mustard is bought in its place.

In summer too, fresh berries and wild mushrooms are delicious and ubiquitous. Many people pick them themselves and store them over the winter in the form of jams or cordials or simply frozen. Arctic cloudberries are the deliciously creamy king of berries, and feature on the Finnish €2 coin.

With your coffee, it's traditional to have a *pulla*, a sweet cardamom or cinnamon-flavoured bun with rock-sugar on top. Other delicious pastries, and there are many, include *korvapuusti* (cinnamon roll).

Finns love their sweets, although some of them make the unsuspecting visitor feel like the victim of a novelty shop joke. Salty liquorice, fiery 'Turkish peppers', and tar-flavoured gumdrops may sound like punishments rather than rewards, but are delicious after the first few times. Finnish chocolates, particularly those made by Fazer, are also excellent.

Finns tend to eat their biggest meal of the day at lunchtime, so many restaurants put on an all-you-can-eat buffet lunch, usually between 11am and 3pm Monday to Friday. This costs approximately €6 to €10 and may include soups, salad, bread, cold fish dishes, hot meat dishes, coffee and possibly even dessert. All hotels offer a free buffet breakfast, which includes bread, cheese, pastries, fruit, cereals, more fish, sausages, eggs and lots of coffee. Finns have dinner as early as 5pm, often just a light meal.

Back home and pining for decent rye bread and Finnish mustard? Never fear, www.finnishfood .net will deliver it for you!

DRINKS

Finns drink a mountain of coffee, some 10 kilos each per year, placing them first or second in the world (Norway is the other competitor). Teas are available in smarter cafés, as are bottled juices. Finnish tapwater is delicious, so still bottled water hasn't really taken on.

Strong beers, wines and spirits are sold by the state network, the beautifully named Alko. There are Alko stores in every town and they're generally open 10am to 6pm Monday to Thursday, until 8pm on Friday and 9am to 6pm Saturday. Go to www.alko.fi to survey its wares and prices online. Drinks containing more than 20% alcohol are not sold to those aged under 20; for beer and wine purchases the age limit is 18. Beer and cider under 4.7% alcohol are readily available in supermarkets. The selection of wine at Alko is good, and reasonably-priced. Restaurants, however, add around €20 per bottle on top of this.

What is served in Finland as *olut* (beer) is generally light-coloured, lager-type beer, although Guinness stout and other dark brews have gained in popularity in recent years (along with a proliferation of Irish pubs). Major brands of lager include Lapin Kulta, Olvi and Koff. There's also a growing number of microbreweries in Finland (look for the word *panimo* or *panimo-ravintola*), and these make excellent light and dark beers. Such places worthy of a visit include Huvila in Savonlinna, Plevna in Tampere, Koulu and Herman in Turku and Beer Hunters in Pori.

The strongest beer is called *A-olut*, or *nelos olut*, with more than 5% alcohol. More popular is III-beer (called *keskiolut* or *kolmonen*) and I-beer (called *mieto olut* or *pilsneri*), with less than 2% alcohol. A half-litre of beer or cider (the latter is made from apple or pear) in a bar or restaurant costs €4 to €6. Alcohol is taxed by content, so the stronger it is, the more expensive.

Another classic is *lonkero*, or 'gin long drink', a premixed blend of gin and grapefruit juice, popular after a sauna. It's fairly light and refreshing.

The Finnish spirit of choice is the traditional Koskenkorva, a vodka-like grain spirit often affectionately known as *kossu*. A favourite Finnish habit is to dissolve salty liquorice sweets into a bottle of the stuff, creating *salmiakkikossu*, which has an evil black colour but a surprisingly smooth, if understandably salty, taste. You can also buy it ready-made.

Also look out for *sahti*, a sweet, high-alcohol beer traditionally made at home on the farm – you can find it in a couple of pubs in Lahti and Savonlinna at certain times of year, and *Lakka*, a tasty cloudberry liqueur. At Christmas time, *glögi* is a heart-warming mulled wine.

Finlandia vodka is a multinational-owned Finnish vodka. Look out for the souvenir T-shirts involving an elk drinking the stuff and filling a bottle of Swedish Absolut from the other end!

If you buy cans or bottles, you pay a small deposit (about €0.15). This can be redeemed by returning them to the recycling section next time you visit a supermarket.

CELEBRATIONS

Finns celebrate Christmas enthusiastically, with Santa often making a doorstop appearance on Christmas Eve to ask awestruck children if they have been good that year. The most important Christmas food is the delicious salted and baked ham, while *rosolli*, a salad of potato, carrot and pickle, and porridge are also iconic. The person who gets the lucky almond in their porridge usually sings a song or similar.

At Midsummer, everyone gets a few days off and people tend to head into the country. On Midsummer night there are big bonfires and copious consumption of beer and *kossu*, often followed by a precarious rowboat journey to visit friends on the other side of the lake.

New Flavours from Finland, by Eero Mäkelä, is a good recipe book compiled by three of the brightest lights of the new wave of gourmet Finnish cuisine.

Later in the summer, it's a tradition to have crayfish parties, where the succulent little creatures are consumed by the dozen.

WHERE TO EAT & DRINK

Finns have a well-established café culture, particularly in cities like Helsinki, Tampere, Turku and Oulu, but also in many smaller towns. In summer, chairs and tables appear outdoors. Most cafés in Finland serve snacks, light meals and desserts, as well as coffee – and lots of it. A *kahvila* is a simple café, a *kahvio* is a café inside a supermarket or petrol station, and a *baari* serves snacks, beer and soft drinks, and probably also coffee. A refill of coffee is often free.

Every town has a kauppatori (market square) where you can buy smoked fish, fresh produce (in season), berries, pastries and the like. Most larger towns also have a kauppahalli (covered market) where stalls sell cheap hot meals, sandwiches, meats, cheese and deli produce.

A restaurant is a *ravintola*, although, confusingly, you'll see many pubs also described as this even if they don't serve food. A Finnish institution is the *lounasravintola* (lunch restaurant) which will serve a lunch buffet and/or hot specials on weekdays between about 11am and 3pm and then shut. Most other restaurants also offer lunch specials and either stay open or reopen for evening meals.

TAKE ME IN CHAINS

Finns enjoy the informality and family-friendly atmosphere of home-grown chain restaurants, which flourish here. Every town has several, often attached to the major hotels. The cuisine is generally bland, or pepped up with flavouring agents, but long opening hours and lack of other choices in small towns means you'll likely use them at least once. We've rarely listed them in the guide, but every town will have at least two of the following:

Amarillo Tex-Mex food and a lively if expensive bar.

Fransimanni The best of the bunch. Tasty with a rustic-French theme.

Golden Rax Offers an all-you-can-eat pizza and pasta buffet.

Hesburger Finland's biggest home-grown hamburger chain.

Koti Pizza Good-value pizzas eat-in or home-delivered.

Rosso Long menu with pasta, pizza, steaks and more. Best on the basics. Good with kids.

Sevilla Fairly upmarket, Spanish-style theme restaurant.

FINLAND'S TOP FIVE

- A Helsinki classic is **Sea Horse** (p75), serving traditional Finnish staples like meatballs and grilled liver in a great 1930s atmosphere.
- In a refurbished harbourside warehouse, **Nokka** (p76) is one of the best of the smart new generation of Helsinki restaurants.
- A slice of Tampere's industrial past has been converted into a great brewery-restaurant, **Panimoravintola Plevna** (p176), with heavy Germanic food and a good beer list.
- In lovely Kuopio there's **Musta Lammas** (p139), a romantic gourmet restaurant near the water.
- Feast on traditional roast mutton in **Säräpirtti Kippurasarvi** (p148), a Karelian country restaurant.

Finns tend to eat dinner early and will often stop for a bite on the way home from work. A group of friends going out to eat, though, on a Friday night, might well dine at 10pm or later. Opening hours reflect this; more upmarket restaurants (and hotel restaurants) and chains are usually open much later than cheap diners. The exception is the classic Finnish grilli, fast-food stalls selling burgers, sausages, chips and the like that stay open for the after-pub crowd. In this guide, if opening hours aren't provided, 'lunch' is at least 11am to 3pm, and 'dinner' at least 5pm to 9pm. Restaurants tend to open slightly later and shut earlier on Sundays.

In smaller towns, it can sometimes be quite difficult to find authentic Finnish food. Italian and Mexican food is very popular in Finland and these, along with kebab/pizza joints, dominate, as do the chain restaurants (see boxed text, opposite). Finland's best eating is in the big cities and, somewhat ironically, in Lapland, where the busy tourist industry necessitates it.

Pubs, bars and nightclubs are many, and range from seedy male-dominated drinking dens to some of Europe's trendiest style bars. Finns rarely drink in rounds, and people normally buy their own; this also applies to restaurants, where waiters are used to splitting the bill.

VEGETARIANS & VEGANS

Finnish cuisine isn't overly friendly to vegetarians, but nearly all à la carte restaurants will have at least a couple of options, and ethnic restaurants such as Chinese and Thai reliably serve vegetarian meals. Finnish buffets always include soups, salads, rye bread and potatoes, and are often cheaper if you don't want the meat or fish portion. Some soups, such as the ubiquitous pea soup, use meat stock, but mushroom and other common vegetable soups tend not to.

Helpfully, many modern restaurants, including the chain restaurants mentioned, flag their menus with codes indicating which dishes are vegetarian, lactose-free and gluten-free.

There are only a handful of true vegetarian restaurants in Finland, and most of them are in Helsinki.

EATING WITH KIDS

In the main, Finnish restaurants are very child-friendly, and often have a menu of children's portions, or some sort of deal for families whereby the kids eat more or less for free. Finnish food is fairly spice-free and unlikely to upset stomachs. Some of the best places for kids are the chain restaurants (see box opposite). See p331 for more on travelling with kids in Finland.

The Finnish vegan society keeps a list of vegetarian and vegan restaurants on its website, www .vegaanliitto.fi

HABITS & CUSTOMS

Finns tend to eat their main meal at lunchtime, and will usually only eat a big dinner on a social occasion. If invited to dinner at a Finnish home, it's appropriate to take a gift. Coffee and pastries is almost a Finnish cliché: wine, flowers or chocolates always go down well. The rules when visiting a Finnish home are quite simple; take your shoes off at the door, and never refuse the offer of a sauna or a cup of coffee!

Restaurants are similar to elsewhere, except that in many you are expected to seat yourself on arrival. Tips are only added for exceptional service.

The seemingly un-promising website http://212.213.217.194 is the address for FinnPlace, which has an online translator of Finnish words to English and vice versa. It's limited but may come in handy!

EAT YOUR WORDS

Nearly all restaurants these days have a menu in English. If not, the Swedish menu may be easier to decipher than the Finnish. The following phrases will help, see the Language chapter (p358) for more details.

Useful Phrases

The bill, please.	*Saisinko laskun.*
The menu/drinks menu, please.	*Saisinko ruokalistan/juomalistan.*
Do you have ...?	*Onko teillä ...?*
I'm a vegetarian.	*Olen kasvissyöjä.*
Nothing else, thanks .	*Ei muuta, kiitos.*
I'd like ...	*Saisinko ...*
I don't eat ...	*En syö ...*
Table (for one/two/four) please?	*Saisinko pöydän (yhdelle/kahdelle/neljälle)?*
Another one, please.	*Saisinko toisen.*

Food Glossary

These forms are as you would see them on a menu. Other endings apply to use them correctly in phrases.

GENERAL

aamiainen	breakfast	*pääruoka*	main course
lounas	lunch	*jälkiruoka*	dessert
illallinen	dinner	*keitto*	soup
alkuruoka	starter	*leipä*	(some) bread

DRINKS

vesi	water	*(iso/pieni) tuoppi*	(lg/sm) tap beer
kahvi	coffee	*viini*	wine
mehu	juice	*maito*	milk
olut	beer		

MEATS

kala	fish	*liha*	meat
muikku	small whitefish	*kana*	chicken
pihvi	steak/patty of meat	*kinkku*	ham
nauta	beef	*poro/poronkäristys*	reindeer/sautéed
lammas	lamb		reindeer stew
lohi	salmon	*makkara*	sausage

OTHER

peruna	potato	*appelsiini*	orange
pippuri	pepper	*kananmuna*	egg
omena	apple	*juusto*	cheese
suola	salt	*voi*	butter

Helsinki

Helsinki is a sea-town *par excellence* and an exciting, dynamic place. Half the city seems to be water, and the tortured geography of the coastline includes any number of bays, inlets and a speckling of islands. The harbour is the heart of the city, and watching the giant ferries glide into port is a defining memory and essential Helsinki experience.

Helsinki is cool without – as yet – being self-consciously so. Unlike other capitals, you sense that people go to places because they enjoy them, not to be seen. Much modern décor is ironic and humorous, and achieves stylishness by daring to differ rather than trying too hard.

While not an ancient place, much of what is loveable in Helsinki is older. The style of its glorious Art Nouveau buildings, the spacious elegance of its cafés, the careful preservation of Finnish heritage in its dozens of museums, restaurants that have changed neither menu nor furnishings since the 1930s are all part of the city's quirky charm.

It has a very different feel to the rest of Finland, partly because before the days of the hi-tech society it was the country's sole point of contact almost with the rest of the world.

Like all of Finland, though, Helsinki has a dual nature. In winter you sometimes wonder where all the people are. In spring and summer they are back again, packing green spaces and outdoor tables to get a piece of blessed sun, whirring around on thousands of bicycles and kicking the city's nightlife into overdrive.

HIGHLIGHTS

- Listening to concerts at **Temppeliaukio** (p66), an underground church hewn from solid rock
- Appreciating Finnish art both modern and old at the **Kiasma** (p62) and **Ateneum** (p63)
- Taking the ferry to historic **Suomenlinna** (p84) and walking and picnicking among the ramparts
- Heading out on a boat for a memorable dinner at a convivial **island restaurant** (p77)
- Taking the kids to **Serena Water Park** (p87) in Espoo, one of Europe's best
- Enjoying a leisurely circuit of **Tuusulanjärvi** (p88), the lake where Sibelius lived
- Chuff-chuffing down to lovely Porvoo on the **old steam train** (p91)
- Luxuriating in the summer sun in one of the city's excellent **beer terraces** (p78)

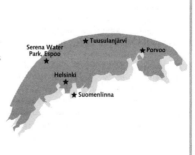

- POPULATION: 559,046
- TELEPHONE CODE: 09

HISTORY

Helsinki was founded in 1550 by King Gustav Vasa, who longed to create a rival to the Hansa trading town of Tallinn. An earlier trial at Ekenäs proved unsuccessful, so by royal decree traders from Ekenäs and a few other towns were bundled off to the newly founded Helsingfors (the Swedish name for Helsinki).

For more than 200 years Helsinki remained a backwater market town on a windy, rocky peninsula. The Swedes built a fortress named Sveaborg in 1748 to protect the eastern part of the empire against Russian attack. Following the war of 1808, the Russians succeeded in taking the fortress and a year later Russia annexed Finland as an autonomous grand duchy. A capital closer to St Petersburg was required, to keep a closer eye on Finland's domestic politics. Helsinki was chosen – in large part because of the sea fortress (now called Suomenlinna) just outside the harbour – and so in 1812 classy Turku lost its long-standing status as Finland's capital and premier town.

In the 19th and early 20th centuries, Helsinki grew rapidly in all directions. German architect CL Engel was called on to help design the city centre, which resulted in the stately, neoclassical Senaatintori (Senate Square). The city suffered heavy Russian bombing during WWII, but in the postwar period Helsinki recovered and went on to host the Summer Olympic Games in 1952.

In the 1970s and 1980s, many new suburbs were built around Helsinki and residents celebrated their 'Helsinki Spirit', a term used for Cold War détente. Since then, Helsinki has prospered as an international city with a flourishing cultural life. It is the seat of national parliament and official home to the president. Its hotels are well-stocked with conference delegates and in 2005 the city hosted the athletics World Championships, which unluckily coincided with some of the worst August rain for decades!

ORIENTATION

Helsinki is built on a peninsula surrounded by an archipelago of islets; there are links by bridge and ferry with many of them. Surrounding satellite cities include Espoo to the west and Vantaa, with the international airport, to the north – Finland's second and fourth most populous cities respectively, one reason why Helsinki feels much bigger than its population statistic indicates.

Maps

The city tourist office can supply a good free map of Helsinki, as well as walking and cycling maps and a public transport route map. *See Helsinki On Foot* is the tourist office's free walking guide, while *Helsinki*

HELSINKI IN...

Two Days

Head down to one of the cafés on the **Esplanadi** (p77) for a strong Finnish coffee before you take in the atmosphere of the kauppatori (market). A street back from here is the **Tuomiokirkko Lutheran Cathedral** (p66) which dominates Senate Square, and nearby is **Katajanokka Island** (p67), with the stunning Orthodox cathedral, beautiful buildings and tempting eating spots. In the afternoon it's gallery time; the **Ateneum** (p63) showcases the Golden Age of Finnish Art, and **Kiasma** (p62) has a contemporary slant and a great café/bar to finish up in.

Don't hit the town too hard, because the next morning you're on a boat to **Suomenlinna** (p84), perhaps with a picnic lunch if it's a nice day. When you get back, soak in some of the atmosphere of the busy shopping streets Aleksanterinkatu and Mannerheimintie and then continue the nautical theme by heading out to one of the city's excellent **island restaurants** (p77).

Four Days

With two extra days, you can delve deep into Helsinki's undulating coastline. Head past Hietaniemi Beach to pay homage to music at the **Sibelius Monument** (p70), then take in some traditional architecture at the **Seurasaari open-air museum** (p64). At night, check out what's on at **Storyville** (p81) if you're a jazz person, or **Tavastia** (p81) if you prefer it a little rockier. On your last day, take a trip to **Porvoo** (p88) for its beautiful wooden buildings and gorgeous riverside.

Your Way (also free) is a valuable booklet of events and listings.

INFORMATION
Bookshops
Akateeminen Kirjakauppa (Academic Bookshop; Map p64; ☎ 12141; Pohjoisesplanadi 39; ☺ 9am-9pm Mon-Fri, 9am-6pm Sat, noon-6pm Sun) The biggest bookshop in Finland and *the* place to go for reading matter. There's a huge travel section, maps, Finnish literature and an impressively large English section.

Hagelstams Bokhandel (Map p64; ☎ 649 291; Fredrikinkatu 35; ☺ 10am-6pm Mon-Fri, 10am-3pm Sat) Loveable antiquarian and secondhand bookshop. Rare books plus cheap English paperbacks.

Karttakeskus Aleksi (Map p64; ☎ 612 3456; Aleksanterinkatu 26; ☺ 10am-6pm Mon-Fri, 10am-4pm Sat) Map shop. Stocks atlases, road maps, topographical maps and general hiking maps.

Emergency
General Emergency (☎ 112)
Police (☎ 10022)

Internet Access
As well as those listed here, several of the cafés and bars have at least one terminal.

Ateneum (Map p64; ☎ 173 361; www.ateneum.fi; Kaivokatu 2; ☺ 9am-6pm Tue & Fri, 9am-8pm Wed & Thu, 11am-5pm Sat & Sun) The art gallery has a peaceful reading room with two free Internet terminals. Access the rear entrance off Yliopistonkatu.

Level 7 (Map p64; ☎ 673 327; Vilhonkatu 5B; per hr €4; ☺ 1-10pm) Quick access amid salvos of online gunfire.

Library 10 (Map p64; Main post office bldg; ☎ 3108 5000; Elielinkatu 2; admission free; ☺ 10am-10pm Mon-Thu, 10am-6pm Fri, noon-6pm Sat & Sun, shorter hr summer) Music and IT library on the 1st floor of the main post office, by the railway station. Several half-hour terminals and others bookable by phone.

mbar (Map p64; ☎ 6124 5420; Mannerheimintie 22; per hr €5; ☺ 9am-midnight, later at weekends) In the Lasapalatsi complex. Offers good-quality Internet access and has heaps of terminals.

Rikhardinkadun Library (Map p64; ☎ 3108 5013; Rikhardinkatu 3; ☺ 10am-8pm Mon-Thu, 10am-6pm Fri & Sat) The most central of Helsinki's public libraries has a good English-language selection and free Internet terminals.

TeleCenter (Map p64; ☎ 670 612; Vuorikatu 8; per hr €2; ☺ 9am-9pm Mon-Sat, noon-8pm Sun) Slowish but cheap and friendly.

University of Helsinki Library (☎ 1912 3196; Unioninkatu 36; Internet free; ☺ 9am-8pm Mon-Fri, 9am-4pm Sat) This impressive library is a serene place with a bank of quiet terminals on the 2nd floor.

Internet Resources
www.hel.fi Excellent Helsinki City website, with links to all the information you might need.

www.helsinkiexpert.com Sightseeing tours, accommodation bookings, tickets and events listings.

www.hkl.fi Public transportation routes and fares.

www.visitfinland.com Information pages of the Finnish Tourist Board.

Laundry
Most Helsinki hotels offer laundry service and some of the hostels have self-service facilities.

Easywash (Map pp60-1; ☎ 406 982; Topeliuksenkatu 21; per load €6-8; ☺ 10am-8pm Mon-Thu, 10am-6pm Fri & Sat) Self-service laundrette. There's a branch at Kalevankatu 45.

Left Luggage
At the bus and train station it costs €2/3 for small/large lockers – the large lockers are big enough to hold most backpacks. There are similar lockers and left-luggage counters at the ferry terminals.

Medical Services
Maria Hospital (Map pp60-1; ☎ 3106 3231; Lapinlahdenkatu 16; ☺ 24hr) For emergency medical assistance.

Töölö Health Station (Map pp60-1; ☎ 310 5015; Sibeliuksenkatu 14; ☺ 8am-6pm Mon, 8am-4pm Tue-Fri) A medical centre for non-emergencies.

Yliopiston Apteekki Mannerheimintie (Map pp60-1; ☎ 4178 0300; Mannerheimintie 96; ☺ 24hr); City Centre (Map p64; Mannerheimintie 5; ☺ 7am-midnight) The branch in the city centre is more convenient.

Money
Major banks (with international ATMs) are plentiful and easy to find throughout the city, but the best place to exchange cash or travellers cheques is at the official money-changers, who charge a lower commission. At the airport there's an exchange counter and a 24-hour exchange machine.

Forex (Map p64; Mannerheimintie 10; www.forex.fi; ☺ 8am-9pm summer, 8am-7pm Mon-Sat autumn-spring) Offers the best rates, with a flat €2 fee on travellers cheques, and no commission. There are other offices at the train station and on Pohjoisesplanadi.

Post
Main post office (Map p64; ☎ 020-451 4400; Mannerheiminaukio 1; ☺ 7am-9pm Mon-Fri, 10am-6pm Sat & Sun) The post office is in the large building between the bus and train stations. The adjacent poste restante office holds mail for a month.

HELSINKI

Map labels:
To Seta (1.3km)
To Urho Kekkonen Museum (2km); Tamminiemen Kahvila (2km); Seurasaari (3km); German Embassy (4km)
To Hartwall Arena (1.5km)
City Winter Gardens
Talvipuutarha Botanical Gardens
Linnankoskenkatu
Humalistonkatu
Eino Leinonkatu
Mäntymäentie
Helsinginkatu
Sibelius Park
Mannerheimintie
Mechelininkatu
Topeliuksenkatu
Sibeliuksenkatu
Urheilukatu
Nordenskiöldinkatu
Töölönlahti
Töölöntori
Pohjoinen Hesperiankatu
Eteläinen Hesperiankatu
Runeberginkatu
Apollonkatu
Museokatu
Hietaniemi
Töölö
Temppelikatu
Nervanderinkatu
Arkadiankatu
Runeberginkatu
Pohjoinen
Hietaniemi Cemetery
Hietaniemenkatu
Seurasaarenselkä
Hietaniemenkatu
Leppäsuonkatu
Lapinlahdenkatu
Lapinlahdenkatu
Malminkatu
Kamppi
Fredrikinkatu
Annankatu
Simonkatu
To Espoo (12km)
Länsiväylä
To Kaapelitehdas & Museums (300m)
Porkkalankatu
Ruoholahti
Hietalahdenranta
Hietalahti Flea Market
Eerikinkatu
Kalevankatu
Uudenmaankatu
Bulevardi
Albertinkatu
Menmiehenkatu
Eira
Merikatu

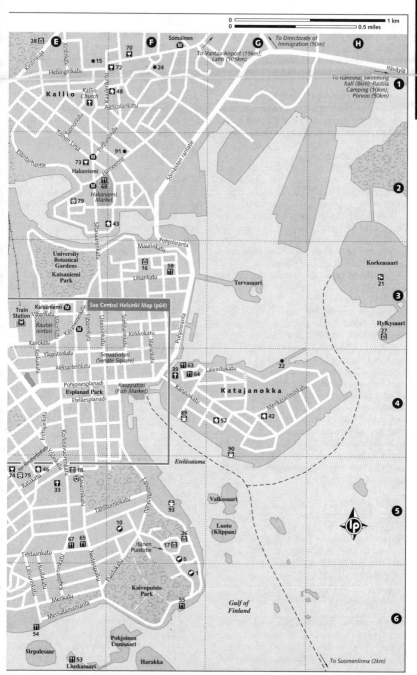

Telephone

Main telephone office (Map p64; 🕑 9am-5pm Mon-Fri) On the 2nd floor in the main post office building. You can place calls from here, but it's cheaper to call overseas using a prepaid phonecard at any public telephone, or even a mobile phone.

TeleCenter (Map p64; ☎ 670 612; Vuorikatu 8; 🕑 9am-9pm Mon-Sat, noon-8pm Sun) A call centre with cabins and cheap international rates, starting from about €0.10 per minute to other European countries.

Tourist Information

In summer you'll probably see uniformed 'Helsinki Helpers' wandering around in their green bibs – collar these useful multilinguals for any tourist information.

Apart from the tourist office publications, free tourist brochures such as *Helsinki This Week* (published monthly) and *City in English* are available at tourist offices, bookshops and other points around the city.

At **Helsinki Expert** (www.helsinkiexpert.fi) you can find up-to-date information on the Helsinki Card (see right).

Helsinki City Tourist Office (Map p64; ☎ 169 3757; www.hel.fi/tourism; Pohjoisesplanadi 19; 🕑 9am-8pm Mon-Fri, 9am-6pm Sat & Sun May-Sep, 9am-6pm Mon-Fri, 10am-4pm Sat & Sun Oct-Apr) Busy multilingual office with a great quantity of information on the city. Also here is the Helsinki Tour Expert desk where you can book hotel rooms and purchase tickets for train, bus and ferry travel around Finland and for travel to Tallinn and St Petersburg.

Tikankontti (Map p64; ☎ 270 5221, 0203-44122; www.metsa.fi; Eteläesplanadi 20; 🕑 10am-6pm Mon-Fri, 10am-3pm Sat) This is the Helsinki office of Metsähallitus, the Finnish Forest and Park Service. It has information and maps for national parks and protected hiking areas and you can buy maps and fishing licences or rent wilderness cottages around the country.

Travel Agencies

From Helsinki you can easily arrange trips to the Baltic States, Russia and beyond.

Finnsov Tours (Map pp60-1; ☎ 436 6960; Museokatu 15) One of the more established operators, providing tours, travel arrangements and help with visas.

Helsinki Expert (Map p64; ☎ 2288 1222; www .helsinkiexpert.fi) This is an agency handling travel around Finland and to Tallinn and St Petersburg. It's in the city tourist office.

Kilroy Travels (Map p64; ☎ 680 7811; www.kilroytravels .com; Kaivokatu 10C) Specializes in student and budget travel.

Traveller (Map p64; ☎ 660 002; www.traveller.fi; Kasarmikatu 26) Specializes in train routes from Helsinki to Russia and beyond on the Trans-Siberian.

SIGHTS
Museums & Galleries

It would take a good few days to get around all of Helsinki's 40 or so museums, and some, such as the **News Museum** (covering the history of Finnish newspapers) and the **Kindergarten Museum** (history of Finnish preschool strategies), are too specialized for most visitors, but there are a few stand-out attractions. For a full list, pick up the *Museums* booklet (free) from the tourist office.

KIASMA MUSEUM OF CONTEMPORARY ART

In the curvaceous, quirky chalk-white building designed by Steven Holl is **Kiasma** (Map p64; ☎ 1733 6501; www.kiasma.fi; Mannerheiminaukio 2; adult/under 18yr €5.50/free; 🕑 10am-8.30pm Wed-Sun, 9am-5pm Tue). It opened to much fanfare and controversy in 1998 and exhibits a rapidly growing collection of Finnish and international modern art from the 1960s to the present. The focus is definitely on the offbeat, and changing exhibitions feature striking visual arts and media exhibits with some bizarre themes. There's a growing permanent collection on the 3rd floor and a theatre with a changing programme (tickets usually cost extra) on the ground floor, where you can also check out the cool handwritten clock outside the good museum shop.

Kiasma is a popular local meeting point in summer – its café and beer terrace are hugely popular, locals sunbathe on the

---

HELSINKI CARD

If you intend to do some serious sightseeing, or even have a few particular places picked out, the Helsinki Card can save you money. This pass entitles you to urban travel, entry to more than 50 attractions in and around Helsinki and discounts on day tours to Porvoo and Tallinn. A card valid for 24/48/72 hours costs €25/35/45 for adults and €10/13/16 for children (7 to 16). You will need lots of planning to save money; only consider it if you are going to take the sightseeing bus tour to Suomenlinna and see several museums in a hurry. Buy the card (and a brochure outlining the discounts) at the city tourist office or at hotels, R-kiosks and transport terminals.

grassy fringes and skateboarders do their thing around the Mannerheim statue.

Behind the Kiasma is the **Sanomatalo** (Map p64), the HQ of the famous Helsinki daily, the *Helsingin Sanomat*. Designed by Sarlotta Narjus and Antti-Matti Sikula, it's a glassy, cool space that has exhibitions as well as popular shops, bars and cafés.

KANSALLISMUSEO

The impressive **Kansallismuseo** (National Museum of Finland; Map pp60-1; ☎ 4050 9544; www.kansallismuseo.fi; Mannerheimintie 34; adult/child €5.50/free; ⊗ 11am-8pm Tue-Wed, 11am-6pm Thu-Sun), just north of the mausoleum-like parliament building, looks a bit like a Gothic church with its heavy stonework and tall square tower. It was actually designed and built specifically as a museum in National Romantic style and opened in 1916, but was extensively renovated in 2000. The museum is divided into rooms covering different periods of Finnish history, including prehistoric and archaeological finds, church relics, ethnography and cultural exhibitions. The superb frescoes on the ceiling arches (by Akseli Gallen-Kallela) depict scenes from the epic *Kalevala*, including one of the hero Väinämöinen plunging a stake into the giant pike.

ATENEUM

The list of painters at the **Ateneum** (Map p64; ☎ 173 361; www.ateneum.fi; Kaivokatu 2; adult/student/child €7.50/6.50/free; ⊗ 9am-6pm Tue & Fri, 9am-8pm Wed & Thu, 11am-5pm Sat & Sun) reads like a 'who's who' of Finnish art. It houses Finnish paintings and sculptures from the 18th century to the 1950s including works by Albert Edelfelt, Akseli Gallen-Kallela, the Von Wright brothers and Pekka Halonen. Pride of place goes to the prolific Gallen-Kallela's triptych from the *Kalevala* depicting Väinämöinen's pursuit of the maiden Aino. There's also a small but interesting collection of 19th- and early-20th-century foreign art. Downstairs is a café, good bookshop and reading room. The building itself dates from 1887.

SINEBRYCHOFF MUSEUM OF FOREIGN ART

The largest collection of classic European paintings in Finland is on the premises of the old **brewery** (Map pp60-1; ☎ 1733 6460; Bulevardi 40; admission €3, with exhibitions €7; ⊗ 10am-6pm Tue & Fri, 10am-8pm Wed-Thu, 11am-5pm Sat & Sun), which also has excellent temporary exhibitions. The main collection is primarily Italian, Flemish and Swedish in origin and includes period rooms furnished in Gustavian style and collections of porcelain and crystal.

KAAPELITEHDAS

The massive **Kaapelitehdas** (Cable Factory; ☎ 4763 8305; www.kaapelitehdas.fi; Tallberginkatu 1C), off Porkkalankatu and on the way to Espoo, was once used for manufacturing sea cable and later became Nokia's main factory until the 1980s. It's now a bohemian cultural centre featuring studios, galleries, concerts, theatre and dance performances. Take tram 8, bus 15, 20, 21, 65A or 66A, or the metro to Ruoholahti stop.

There are several museums here, including the **Finnish Museum of Photography** (☎ 6866 3621; adult/child €5/free; ⊗ noon-7pm Tue-Sun), which mounts interesting temporary photographic exhibitions.

CYGNAEUS GALLERY

If you're looking for Finnish art from the 19th century, this **gallery** (Map pp60-1; ☎ 4050 9628; www.nba.fi; Kalliolinnantie 8; adult/child €3/free; ⊗ 11am-7pm Wed, 11am-4pm Thu-Sun) is a great place to go. It opened in 1882 and is one of Finland's oldest art galleries. It's in an attractive wooden building (built in 1870) in Kaivopuisto Park, close to the Mannerheim Museum.

AMOS ANDERSON ART MUSEUM

The city centre **Amos Anderson Art Museum** (Map p64; ☎ 684 4460; Yrjönkatu 27; adult/child €7/free; ⊗ 10am-6pm Mon-Fri, 11am-5pm Sat & Sun) houses the collection of publishing magnate Amos Anderson, one of the wealthiest Finns of his time. It includes Finnish and European paintings and sculptures from the 15th century to the present, furnished rooms as well as special exhibitions.

MANNERHEIM MUSEUM

This fascinating **museum** (Map pp60-1; ☎ 635 443; Kalliolinnantie 14; admission €7; ⊗ 11am-4pm Fri-Sun & by appointment) in Kaivopuisto Park was the home of CGE Mannerheim, former president, Commander in Chief of the Finnish army and Civil War victor. Among the souvenirs from Mannerheim's life are

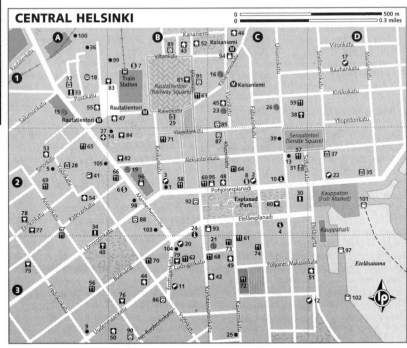

CENTRAL HELSINKI

hundreds of military medals, as well as photographs from his trip to Asia when he travelled 14,000km along the Silk Route from Samarkand to Beijing, riding the same faithful horse for two years. Entry includes a mandatory but enthusiastic guided tour (around one hour) in one of six languages, and free plastic booties to keep the hallowed floor clean.

SEURASAARI OPEN-AIR MUSEUM

West of the centre, Seurasaari is an open-air **museum** (☎ 4050 9660; adult/child €5/free; 11am-5pm mid-Sep–mid-May, 11am-7pm Wed Jun-Aug, 9am-3pm Mon-Fri, 11am-5pm Sat & Sun late May & early Sep) with 18th- and 19th-century traditional houses, manors and outbuildings from around Finland. Guides dressed in traditional costume demonstrate folk dancing and crafts such as spinning, embroidery and troll-making. There are guided tours in English at 11.30am and 3.30pm. You'll find similar sorts of museums all over Finland but this is up there with the best. It's also a venue for Helsinki's biggest Midsummer bonfires. Take bus 24 from the central train station.

URHO KEKKONEN MUSEUM

Worth visiting on a trip to Seurasaari, this large **house** (☎ 4050 9650; Seurasaarentie 15, Tamminiemi; adult/child €4/free; 11am-5pm Thu-Sun, 11am-7pm Wed, 11am-5pm Mon & Tue mid-May–mid-Aug) was a presidential residence for 30 years, right up until Urho Kekkonen's death, when it was turned into a museum. A visit includes a guided tour and the house is surrounded by a beautiful park. While here, don't miss the Tamminiementien café (see p77). From central Helsinki, take bus 24, or tram 4 and walk.

KAUPUNGINMUSEO

A group of small museums scattered around the city centre constitute the **Kaupunginmuseo** (www.helsinkicitymuseum.fi; admission per museum adult/child €3/free, free Thu). All buildings focus on an aspect of the city's past or present. Check opening hours before setting out, as these change with bewildering frequency:

Burgher's House (Ruiskumestarintalo; Map pp60-1; ☎ 135 1065; Kristianinkatu 12; 11am-4pm Sun-Thu Jun-Aug & Dec) Built in 1818, this is the oldest wooden townhouse in central Helsinki.

Hakasalmi Villa (Hakasalmenhuvila; Map pp60–1;
☎ 169 3444; Mannerheimintie 13; ☼ 11am-4pm Sun-
Thu mid-Jul–mid-Jun) Exhibition on Helsinki and thematic
temporary displays.

Helsinki City Museum (Map p64; ☎ 169 3933; Sofiankatu 4; ☼ 9am-5pm Mon-Fri, 11am-5pm Sat & Sun)
Just south of Senate Square, has a historical exhibition and
films about Helsinki.

Museum of Worker Housing (Työväenasuntomuseo;
Map pp60–1; ☎ 146 1039; Kirstinkuja 4; ☼ 11am-4pm
Sun-Thu Jun-Aug) Shows how industrial workers lived in
the early 20th century.

Sederholm House (Map p64; ☎ 169 3265; Aleksanterinkatu 18; ☼ 11am-4pm Sun-Thu Aug-Jun) Helsinki's
oldest brick building dates from 1757 and is furnished to
suit a wealthy 18th-century merchant.

Tram Museum (Raitioliikennemuseo; Map pp60–1;
☎ 169 3576; Töölönkatu 51A; ☼ 11am-4pm Sun-Thu
Aug-May) This delightful museum, in an old tram depot,
displays vintage trams and depicts daily life in Helsinki's
streets in past decades.

Tuomarinkylä Museum & Children's Museum
(Lastenmuseo; Map p85; ☎ 728 7458; Tuomarinkylä;
☼ 11am-4pm Sun-Thu mid-Mar–Jul & Sep-Dec) Not far
from the airport, this pair of museums occupies an 18th-
century manor house and shows the city through the life of
a modern family and a child. From central Helsinki take bus
64 to its terminus and walk 1km.

DESIGN MUSEUM

This **museum** (Map pp60–1; ☎ 622 0540; Korkeavuorenkatu 23; adult/child €7/free; ☼ 11am-6pm Tue-Sun,
also Mon Jun-Aug, 11am-8pm Tue Sep-May) has a permanent collection and hosts changing exhibitions, mostly focusing on contemporary
domestic and industrial design – everything
from household furniture and appliances
to tools.

HELSINKI

NATURAL HISTORY MUSEUM

The **Natural History Museum** (Luonnontieteellinen Museo; Map pp60-1; ☎ 1912 8800; Pohjoinen Rautatienkatu 13; admission €4.20; ☯ 9am-5pm Tue-Fri, 11am-4pm Sat & Sun) houses the University of Helsinki's extensive collection of mammals, birds and other creatures – about seven million specimens in all, including all Finnish species. There's a good exhibition of dinosaur skeletons too.

POSTIMUSEO

The **Post Museum** (Map p64; ☎ 020-451 4908; Asemaaukio 5; adult/child €4/free; ☯ 9am-6pm Mon-Fri, 11am-4pm Sat & Sun), in the main post office building next to the train station, may sound a bit dull, but it contains a fascinating collection of stamps, computerised data banks and other hi-tech exhibits.

SPORTS MUSEUM OF FINLAND

The **sports museum** (Map pp60-1; Urheilumuseo; ☎ 434 2250; Olympiastadion; admission €3.50; ☯ 11am-5pm Mon-Fri, noon-4pm Sat & Sun), in the 1952 Olympic Stadium, houses Finland's 'sporting hall of fame' and looks at the triumphs and defeats of its sporting heroes. Trams 3B, 3T, 4, 7A, 7B and 10 from the city centre all run past it.

Also here is the **Stadium Tower** (Stadion Torni; admission €2; ☯ 9am-8pm Mon-Fri, 9am-6pm Sat & Sun). Although the viewing platform and lift seemingly haven't been touched up since the Games, the views from the 72m-high platform are great. Don't lob coins from the top; a Lonely Planet correspondent was nearly brained recently by a misdirected rouble…

Churches

Presiding proudly over Senate Square, the chalk-white neoclassical **Tuomiokirkko** (Lutheran Cathedral; Map p64; ☎ 709 2455; Unioninkatu 29; ☯ 9am-6pm Mon-Sat, noon-6pm Sun Sep-May, 9am-midnight Jun-Aug) was designed by CL Engel but not completed until 1852, 12 years after his death. It towers high at the top of a flight of stairs, a favourite meeting place and the scene of New Year's revelry. The interior has statues of the Reformation heroes Luther, Melanchthon and Michael Agricola; true to their ideals, there is little other ornamentation under the lofty dome. There's a café in the brick-vaulted crypt.

The unmistakeable red-brick **Uspenski Cathedral** (Map pp60-1; ☎ 634 267; Kanavakatu 1; ☯ 9.30am-4pm Mon-Fri, 9.30am-2pm Sat, noon-3pm Sun, closed Mon Oct-Apr) is equally imposing on nearby Katajanokka island. The two cathedrals face each other high above the city like two queens on a theological chessboard. Built as a Russian Orthodox church in Byzantine-Slavonic style in 1868, this church features classic onion-topped domes and now serves the Finnish Orthodox congregation, many of whom are of Karelian descent. The high, square interior has a lavish iconostasis with the Evangelists flanking panels depicting the Last Supper and the Ascension. There are Orthodox services at 6pm on Saturday and 10am Sunday, well worth attending as a discreet visitor for the fabulous chorals and candlelit atmosphere.

Temppeliaukio Church (Map pp60-1; ☎ 494 698; Lutherinkatu 3; ☯ 10am-8pm Mon-Fri, 10am-6pm Sat, noon-1.45pm & 3.30-6pm Sun), designed by Timo and Tuomo Suomalainen in 1969, remains one of Helsinki's foremost attractions. Hewn into solid rock, the church symbolises the modern innovativeness of Finnish religious architecture and features a stunning 24m-diameter roof covered in 22km of copper stripping. There are regular concerts, with great acoustics; the entrance is at the northern end of Fredrikinkatu.

The oldest church in Helsinki is the white wood **Vanha Kirkko** (Map p64; Lönnrotinkatu), designed by CL Engel. Its graveyard, where once plague victims were buried, has been converted into a public park. Opposite the church is a **memorial** to Elias Lönnrot, compiler of the *Kalevala* epic. Depicting Lönnrot flanked by his most famous character, 'steady old Väinämöinen', it was sculpted by Emil Wikström.

Helsinki's largest church is the soaring twin-spired neo-Gothic **St John's Church** (Map pp60-1; St John's Park, off Korkeavuorenkatu).

Beaches & Cemeteries

Helsinki has several city beaches, of which the best is **Hietaranta**, a likeable stretch of sand just west of the centre. It's a great place to be in the afternoon and evening sun and there are those Finnish summer stalwarts nearby: a beer terrace and minigolf. The nicest way to get here is to stroll from Mechelininkatu west through the **Hietaniemi cemetery**. Finnish cemeteries are beautiful and designed to be walked in; this has Orthodox, Jewish and Muslim sections as well as the Lutheran.

Parks & Gardens

The **City Winter Gardens** (Talvipuutarha; Map pp60-1; Hammarskjöldintie 1; admission free; ☒ noon-3pm Tue-Fri, noon-4pm Sat & Sun) were founded in 1893 and are elaborate greenhouses containing cacti, palms, and other sun-loving plants foreign to Finnish soil. They are surrounded by a botanical garden, including a spectacular display of roses. Take tram 8 from Ruoholahti metro or Töölö. Closer to the centre, the **University botanical gardens** (Unioninkatu 44; admission free) comprises Finland's largest botanical collection, with classic 19th-century hothouses, a café and a park.

LINNANMÄKI

The **Linnanmäki amusement park** (Map pp60-1; ☎ 020-385 677; www.linnanmaki.fi; Tivolikuja 1; adult €26, child day pass €14-16, entry only €3.50; ☒ 11am-10pm May-early Sep), on a hill just north of Kallio suburb, has all the usual kid-pleasing rides including a rollercoaster. Its profits are donated to child welfare organizations. Day passes allow unlimited rides, or you can enter free of charge and then buy individual ride tickets (€4.50). Also here is **Sea Life** (adult/child €12.50/9.50; ☒ 10am-7pm Mon-Sat, 10am-8pm Wed, 10am-5pm Sun Jun-Sep, 10am-5pm Oct-May), a state-of-the-art aquarium. Bus 23 or trams 3B, 3T or 8 take you to Linnanmäki.

Helsinki Zoo & Maritime Museum

The spacious **Helsinki Zoo** (Map pp60-1; ☎ 169 5969; adult/child €5/3, with ferry ride €8/4.50; ☒ 10am-8pm May-Sep, 10am-4pm Oct-Feb, 10am-6pm Mar-Apr) is located on Korkeasaari – best reached by ferry from the kauppatori. Established in 1889, it has animals and birds from Finland and around the world housed in large natural enclosures, as well as a tropical house, small farm and a good café and terrace.

Ferries leave from the kauppatori and from Hakaniemi every 30 minutes or so in summer and Zoo bus 11 goes from Herttoniemi metro station. This bus also runs at weekends in winter, otherwise it's bus 16 or the metro to Kulosaari and walk 1.5km through the island of Mustikkamaa.

On the adjoining Hylkysaari, and only accessible by bridge from Korkeasaari, is the **Maritime Museum of Finland** (Suomen Merimuseo; Map pp60-1; ☎ 4050 9051; adult/child €2.50/free; ☒ 11am-5pm May-Sep). It's housed in a historic harbour building and has exhibitions on Finnish ship-building and seafaring.

Katajanokka Island

Just east of the kauppatori, this island (Map pp60-1) is divided from the mainland by a narrow canal and is one of the city's most enjoyable places to stroll. It's a paradise of upmarket Jugendstil residential buildings with extravagant turrets and curious carvings galore. While the south side of the island has two of the major ferry terminals, the other side is more peaceful, with the Engel-designed Foreign Ministry looking out over the impressively functional fleet of icebreakers. At the western end of the island, the Uspenski Cathedral looks over a leisure harbour and a series of warehouses attractively converted into enticing restaurants and bars.

The tourist office's excellent brochure *See Helsinki on Foot* (free) has a self-guided walk around Katajanokka island.

ACTIVITIES

No visit to Helsinki is complete without a sauna and swim at the **Yrjönkadun Uimahalli** (Map p64; ☎ 3108 7401; Yrjönkatu 21; admission €4-11; ☒ men 6.30am-9pm Tue, Thu, Sat, women noon-9pm Sun & Mon, 6.30am-9pm Wed & Fri). This sleek Art Deco complex was first opened in 1928 and its powerful Nordic elegance has been beautifully restored. There are separate hours for men and women and bathing suits are optional in the pool and not allowed in the saunas.

Helsinki has several public swimming pools with inexpensive admission. Most convenient is the outdoor **Olympic Swimming Stadium** (Map pp60-1; ☎ 3108 7854; Hammarskjöldintie; admission €3; ☒ May-Sep). There are also saunas here and you can rent towels and swimwear. However, the most impressive pool is the **Itäkeskus swimming hall** (☎ 3108 7202; Olavinlinnantie 6; admission €4.50; ⬤) – take the metro to Itäkeskus station, walk east for a block and turn left at Olavinlinnantie. The entirely underground complex is carved from rock and was designed to double as a bomb shelter.

Rollerblading is popular, especially in Kaivopuisto park and around Töölönlahti, the pretty bay north of the station. Skates can be hired at **Töölönlahti Recreational Centre** (Map pp60-1; ☎ 4776 9760; Mäntymäentie 1).

For information on bike rental see p83. The bike and skate route map, *Helsingin Pyöräilykartta,* is free at the city tourist office.

SOMETHING SPECIAL

One of Helsinki's most memorable experiences is the venerable **Kotiharjun Sauna** (Map pp60-1; ☎ 753 1535; Harjutorinkatu 1; admission €7; ☽ 2-8pm Tue-Fri, 1-7pm Sat, sauna time until 10pm). In a quiet street in the Kallio district, this is a historic public sauna fired by enormous wood furnaces that take four hours to warm up and then keep the heat up all day. It's a gloriously traditional place, with antique lockers, décor unchanged since it opened in 1928 and separate men's and women's sections. You can even opt to be cleaned off by a sturdy old scrubbing-woman. The wood sauna has a completely different feel and aroma to the usual electric ones; spank yourself with a birch *vihta* to massage the skin and help the cleaning process, and afterwards it's the custom to have a beer out on the street terrace – clad only in a towel of course!

In winter, **Brahen kenttä** (Map pp60-1; ☎ 753 2932; Helsinginkatu 23; admission €2, skate rental €4; ☽ Nov-Mar) is a great natural outdoor area where public skating is arranged; it feels like a nostalgic Northern European film!

HELSINKI WALKING & CYCLING TOUR

The following tour is a combination of walking and cycling – if you're on foot you'll probably want to stick to the central Helsinki area, but with a bike it's a breeze to get out to Seurasaari, west of the city.

The starting point for any tour of Helsinki is the bustling **kauppatori** (1; p82), also known as the fish market. It is surrounded by graceful 19th-century buildings – some of only a few remaining in the city after the devastation of WWII. The stone obelisk topped by a golden eagle is the **Tsarina's Stone (2)**, Helsinki's oldest monument, unveiled in 1835 in honour of a visit by Tsar Nicholas I and Tsarina Alexandra.

Havis Amanda (3), the lovely mermaid statue and fountain just west of the fish market, was designed in 1908 by one of Finland's most beloved artists, Ville Vallgren. The statue, also known as 'Manta', is commonly regarded as the symbol of Helsinki. During *Vappu* (May Day) students gather here to celebrate the coming of spring.

Across from the kauppatori is the **Presidential Palace (4)**, guarded by colourful sentries. This is the president's official Helsinki residence – at the time of writing home to Tarja Halonen, Finland's first woman president.

Heading east, cross the footbridge onto Katajanokka Island to visit the Orthodox **Uspenski Cathedral (5**; p66) on a hill above the harbour. This very photogenic red brick church is one of the most recognisable landmarks in Helsinki. **Katajanokka** itself is well worth a stroll if you have the time – many

of its narrow streets have fine Art Nouveau residential buildings.

Back on the mainland, turn right along Sofiankatu, a narrow cobbled street with interpretive boards explaining some early Helsinki history. It leads to **Senaatintori (6)**, Helsinki's 'official' centre. The **statue of Tsar Alexander II** in Senaatintori was cast in 1894 and symbolises the strong Russian influence in 19th-century Helsinki.

Engel's stately chalk-white, blue-domed **Tuomiokirkko** (Lutheran Cathedral; p66), completed in 1852, is the square's most prominent feature and Helsinki's most recognisable building. The main **University of Helsinki** building is on the west side of Senaatintori and the university's magnificent **library** is a little farther north along Unioninkatu. Two of Helsinki's museums, the **Helsinki City Museum** (p65) and **Sederholm House** (p65) are along the south side of the square.

Walking back to Pohjoisesplanadi, you're in the pleasant **Esplanad Park (7)**, with a cobbled avenue and grassy verges. It's a favourite summer spot and there's often live music here. The Esplanad leads to the city's broad main thoroughfare, Mannerheimintie. On the northeast corner is the famous **Stockmann department store (8**; p82), where seemingly every Helsinkian buys everything.

Continue two blocks north on Mannerheimintie to **Kiasma (9**; p62), the daring Museum of Contemporary Art. An **equestrian statue** of Marshal CGE Mannerheim, the most revered of Finnish leaders, dominates the square next to the museum. Protests by war veterans delayed the building of Kiasma by almost a decade because many felt that it would degrade Mannerheim's memory to build a modern art gallery on the site – ironically, the Marshal was an avid collector of avant-garde art in his day.

Detour two blocks east to the Soviet-sized Rautatientori (Railway Square), where you'll find the train station, naturally, as well as the National Gallery, **Ateneum (10**; p63). The museum building, long a work-in-progress, was completed in 1991. The train station itself is a masterpiece of the Finnish National Romantic style.

Return to Mannerheimintie and continue walking northwest. The monolithic 1931

TOUR FACTS

Start & end kauppatori
Distance 8km
Duration 3hr

Parliament House (11; ☎ 4321; Mannerheimintie 30; admission free; ☼ guided tours 11am and noon Sat, noon and 1pm Sun, also 1pm Mon-Fri Jul-Aug) dominates this stretch. A little further up Mannerheimintie, on the right, is one of Alvar Aalto's most famous works, the angular **Finlandia Talo (12**; visiting info ☎ 40241; box office ☎ 402 4400; Mannerheimintie 13; guided tours €6), a concert hall built in 1971. Opening hours depends on events, ring for information.

At this point you can detour west along Museokatu and Aurorankatu to Temppelikatu where you'll find **Temppeliaukio Church (13**; p66), a modern church hewn from solid rock.

A few blocks further north on Mannerheimintie is the 1993 **Opera House (14**; p81),

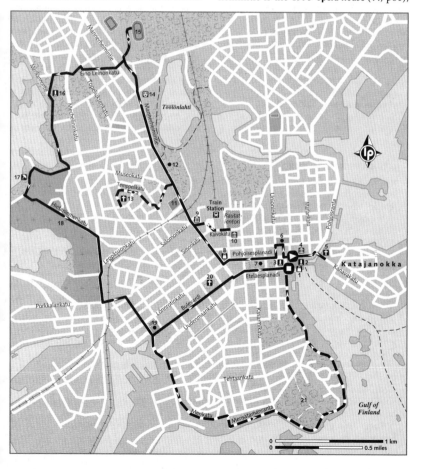

home of the Finnish National Opera. Continue a short distance north on Mannerheimintie to the 1952 **Olympic Stadium** (**15**; p66). For some of the best views of Helsinki, take a lift to the top of the 72m Stadium Tower.

From the stadium, walk or cycle west to Sibelius park and the **Sibelius monument (16)**. This kinetic sculpture was created by artist Eila Hiltunen in 1967 to honour Finland's most famous composer, Jean Sibelius. Bus 24 from the park can take you northwest to the **Seurasaari Open-Air Museum** (p64), or south to the intersection of Mannerheimintie and Pohjoisesplanadi, its terminus.

Alternatively, continue walking or riding around the coast road to **Hietaranta Beach (17**; p66), Helsinki's most popular beach. Heading back towards the city centre through the peaceful **Hietaniemi Cemetery** (**18**; p66), you'll reach **Hietalahti square (19)** which has its own kauppahalli (covered markets) and a popular flea market (p82). From here you can return to the city centre along Bulevardi, pausing in the summer park where there's a lovely church, **Vanha Kirkko** (**20**; p66).

Alternatively, continue around past the West Harbour to the south of the peninsula, following the waterfront to **Kaivopuisto park (21)**, a favourite place for Finns to picnic and laze around in summer. Note the small wooden jetties, erected for households to wash their rugs, a very typical and traditional ritual of the Finnish summer. Continuing along the waterfront you pass the Olympia ferry terminal and eventually arrive back at the kauppatori.

HELSINKI FOR CHILDREN

Helsinki is an excellent place to visit with young ones, particularly in summer when boat trips, amusement parks and outdoor events are all in operation. Finland is a child-friendly society and just about every hotel and restaurant will be keen to help out.

Nearly every accommodation choice will have either family rooms or the option of extra beds at minimal additional cost. Even the business-type hotels will cheerfully explain how the sofa in their executive-class rooms folds out into a child-size bed.

There are plenty of activities that will interest most children. The harbour ferries are an obvious attraction, with both the zoo and Suomenlinna island reached this way. Linnanmäki amusement park (p67) is a

---

GAY & LESBIAN HELSINKI

Helsinki has an active and permissive gay and lesbian scene, which, while not quite as lively as Copenhagen or Stockholm, has a number of good venues ranging from the scene-y to the relaxed. Most are in the cool Punavuori section of town, around Iso-Roobertinkatu.

The best place to start is to pick up the *Gay Guide* from the tourist office. This is updated yearly and has listings of bars, clubs, events, saunas and shops. It's also online at www.z-lehti .fi/queerguide.htm.

For more information, contact the Helsinki branch of **Seta** (☎ 681 2580; www.seta.fi; Mannerheimintie 170), the national GLB&T organization located about 4km north of the centre.

Bars & Clubs

DTM (Map pp60-1; ☎ 676 315; Iso Roobertinkatu 28; 🕑 9am-4am Mon-Sat, noon-4am Sun; 🖳) Scandinavia's biggest gay club is a multilevel complex and has an early-opening café/bar, one of the most popular spots on this busy bar street. There are a couple of club areas opening at 9pm (there's a minimum age of 22 and a Saturday cover charge) and there are regular club nights as well as drag shows or women-only sessions.

Con Hombres (Map p64; ☎ 608 826; Eerikinkatu 14; 🕑 2pm-2am) A relaxed sort of place with a terrace. It's a good spot to chat to people earlier on; the Eurovision music gets louder as the night wears on.

Hercules (Map p64; ☎ 612 1776; www.herculesgayclub.com; Lönnrotinkatu 4; 🕑 9pm-4am) A busy disco, mainly men but with some women too. Classic dancefloor hits.

Room Albert (Map pp60-1; ☎ 643 626; Kalevankatu 36; www.roombar.fi; 🕑 2pm-2am) A new, cool, bar for gay men with plenty of Eurochic style and savvy sounds.

long-standing Finnish family favourite and it now has an on-site aquarium to add to the appeal. The Serena Water Park in Espoo (see p87) is also guaranteed to please.

Many museums make a big effort to interact with children and often offer free admission. On Suomenlinna, there is a toy museum as well as a submarine to visit; the Tram Museum, Children's Museum, Sports Museum and Natural History Museum will also appeal to various ages. The Heureka Science Centre (p87) in Vantaa is also a winner.

The beaches on Suomenlinna and at Hietaniemi are particularly safe, while there are playgrounds in both Kaivopuisto park and Töölönlahti bay.

TOURS

Helsinki Expert (☎ 2288 1600; adult/child €20/10, with Helsinki Card €8; ۞ on the hour 10am-2pm in summer, 11am in winter) runs excellent 90-minute sightseeing bus tours. They depart from the Esplanad, near the tourist office, and taped commentary (in 11 languages) is via a headset. A similar route runs from the Olympic ferry terminal daily at 10.30am via the Katajanokka terminal (10.45am). The same company offers walking tours and tailored group tours.

Open Top Tours (☎ 050-430 2050; per trip €22, with Helsinki Card €10) also has hop-on hop-off tours aboard an open-top double decker bus. Tours leave from the kauppatori, follow a similar route to the Helsinki Expert and also have headphone commentary. It costs €22 or €10 with the Helsinki Card.

There are also several types of guided walking tours in summer, usually given once a week. Inquire at the city tourist office.

Cruises

Strolling through the kauppatori in summer, you won't have to look for cruises – the boat companies will find you. **Royal Line** (☎ 170 488), **Sun Lines** (☎ 727 7010; www.sunlines.fi) and a number of smaller companies offer 90-minute sea and canal **cruises** (adult/child €16/8) with regular daily departures in summer. The trip around the island of Laajasalo, run by Sun Lines, is probably the most interesting. There are also lunch and dinner cruises.

A visit to the Helsinki Zoo (p67) or Suomenlinna sea fortress (p84) is a good way to combine a scenic boat ride with other sightseeing (and they're both free with the Helsinki Card). There are also longer day-

cruises by ferry and steamer from Helsinki to the Finnish town Porvoo; see p91.

FESTIVALS & EVENTS

Vappu (May Day) The festival of students and workers is taken very seriously in Helsinki – on 30 April at 6pm people gather in the centre around the Havis Amanda statue, which receives a white 'student cap'.
Ice Hockey World Championships (www.ihwc.net) Often televised on a big screen under a tent on Rautatientori in May – there's a great atmosphere here, especially if Finland makes the finals.
Regional Fair (www.hel.fi) Held in early June, this festival spotlights a different region of Finland each year.
Helsinki Day (www.hel.fi/helsinkipaiva) Celebrating the city's anniversary brings many free and cheap activities to Esplanad Park on June 12.
Latin American Carnival (www.hel.fi) An important music festival held in mid-June.
Ankkarock (www.ankkarock.fi) Rock festival held in Vantaa in early August.
Koneisto Festival of Electronic Music and Arts (www.koneisto.com) Held in mid-August at various locations around the city.
Helsinki Festival (Helsingin Juhlaviikot; ☎ 6126 5100; www.helsinginjuhlaviikot.fi; Mannerheimintie 22-24) From late August to early September, this elaborate arts festival features chamber music, jazz, theatre, opera and more. Tickets range from €10 to €45.
Baltic Herring Market (www.hel.fi) In early October a 200-year-old tradition takes place at the kauppatori.
Etnosoi (www.globalmusic.fi) Helsinki hosts an ethnic music festival in early November.
Lucia Parade Christmas is a special time in Helsinki with the big parade starting at 6pm in Senate Square on December 13.

SLEEPING

Bookings are advisable for Helsinki hostels and hotels from mid-May to mid-August, although July is usually a quiet time for mid-range and top-end hotels. The **Hotel Booking Centre** (☎ 2288 1400; hotel@helsinkiexpert.fi; ۞ 9am-7pm Mon-Fri, 9am-6pm Sat, 10am-6pm Sun Jun-Aug, 9am-6pm Mon-Fri, 9am-5pm Sat Sep-May) in the central hall of the train station can help. There's also a branch at the city tourist office. There's a small booking fee, but room rates are often cheaper than you would get on your own.

Budget

Academica Summer Hostel (Map pp60-1; ☎ 1311 4334; www.hostelacademica.fi; Hietaniemenkatu 14; dm €18, standard s/d up to €40/60, modern s/d up to €55/75, HI discount; ۞ Jun-Aug; Ⓟ ☒ ▯ ▨) Finnish students live in luxury given the mould-ridden hovels that pass muster elsewhere in the world, which makes this a very attractive budget choice during summer. It's got friendly staff, great facilities, free parking and a swimming pool, not on offer at most of the five-star hotels around the place. All rooms are light and spacious and have their own bathroom, simple kitchen, and beds with crisp white sheets.

Eurohostel (Map pp60-1; ☎ 622 0470; www.euro hostel.fi; Linnankatu 9; dm €23-26, s €38-40, d €46-51, tr €69-76; ✗ 🖳) Right by the ferry terminals, this HI-affiliate is one of the new brand of hostels that places a premium on treating guests well and providing good conveniences. While the building is somewhat institutional, it more than makes up for it with cheery rooms that come in two categories; the Eurohostel rooms are well worth the extra couple of coins it costs to upgrade. There's also a surprisingly smart café downstairs, doing a breakfast buffet (€6.30), pizzas and cheap lunches (€7.90).

Hostel Erottajanpuisto (Map p64; ☎ 642 169; www.erottajanpuisto.com; Uudenmaankatu 9; dm €25, s/d €46/60, HI discount; ✗ 🖳) This is the most laid-back budget accommodation in Helsinki and has a good location on a lively street close to the heart of the city. It's a social sort of place with a likeably chaotic feel, and while the bunk dorms feel a little overpriced, it's worth paying if you appreciate a gregarious atmosphere more than a fistful of facilities.

Rastila (☎ 321 6551; www.hel.fi/liv; Karavaanikatu 4; tent sites €11-17, 2-person cabins €37-43, 4-person cabins €52-62, cottage with/without sauna €165/100; 🅿 ✗ 🖳) Only 20 minutes on the Metro from the heart of town, in a pretty waterside location, this camp site is an excellent choice. As well as tent and van sites, there are green wooden cabins with bunks, a microwave and a fridge, and more upmarket log cottages. There are all sorts of facilities in the complex (which gets pretty busy in July): you can hire bikes or rowboats or canoes to take out on the water.

Hostel Mekka (Map p64; ☎ 630 265; www.hostel mekka.com; Vuorikatu 8B; dm/s/d €25/47/57; 🅿) Unbeatably central, this low-key hostel is set in a stately old Helsinki building set back from the street in a courtyard. It feels more like a guesthouse, with homely, retro rooms sleeping up to four in beds. It's

pleasantly cool in summer, but the heating struggles to cope in the depths of the Helsinki winter.

Other recommendations:

Matkakoti Margarita (Map p64; ☎ 622 4261; www .matkakoti-margarita.com; Itäinen Teatterikuja 3; s/d/tr with shared bathroom €40/54/69, s/d with bathroom €55/70) Very close to the station, with a welcoming owner and a big range of rooms decorated in well-worn domestic floral.

Hostel Satakuntatalo (Map pp60-1; ☎ 6958 5233; fax 685 4245; Lapinrinne 1A; dm €19, s €36-39, d €54-58; 🕙 Jun-Aug; 🅿 ✗ 🖳) Handily located right by the bus station, this is far from flash but the rate includes a buffet breakfast. The corridors are filled with wafting curry smells from the Nepalese restaurant below.

Hostel Stadion (Map pp60-1; ☎ 477 8480; www .stadionhostel.com; Pohjoinen Stadiontie 3; dm/s/d €15/28/41; 🕙 reception 7am-2am, 7am-3am in summer; 🅿 ✗ 🖳) An easy tram ride from town, this HI hostel is actually part of the Olympic Stadium. There are no views though and it feels old-style with big dorms and shared showers.

Midrange

Accome Tölö (Map pp60-1; ☎ 251 1050; www.accome .com; Museokatu 18; studio apts €62-104, 2-bedroom apts €101-169; 🕙 reception 8am-8pm Mon-Fri; ✗) In the quiet district of Töölö, upmarket yet bohemian, and deceptively close to the centre, these furnished apartments offer excellent value. With brand-new and typical Nordic furniture, it feels like being in an upscale Finnish home; you even get your own doormat! Reception is only open on weekdays, but they will arrange a spot for you to collect a key if you will be arriving at other times.

Martta Hotelli (Map p64; ☎ 618 7400; www .marttahotelli.fi; Uudenmaankatu 24; s €103, d €130-155, weekends & Jul s €75, d €85-95; 🅿 ✗ 🕭) Don't be surprised if you are effusively greeted by name before you've even put your bags down in this ultra-welcoming hotel; the personable service here is a delight. It also wins guests over with its lavish buffet breakfast – a real Finnish homestyle treat – and for its free parking. There are two grades of rooms: those in the newer wing are much more spacious and boast shiny floors and furniture, while the older rooms are a little careworn for the price, albeit comfortable and scrubbed to an army-brass spotlessness.

Hotel Aurora (Map p64; ☎ 770 100; www.hotel aurorahelsinki.com; Helsinginkatu 50; s/d €114/138, weekends €76/98, r economy/summer €68/71; 🅿 ✗ 🖳 🕭)

This friendly charity-run hotel is significantly better than its brick exterior suggests. The modernized common areas are beautifully spacious and stylish and the rooms are decent, some with views over the bay. There are several good family suites, which are very attractively priced in the summer months, when the amusement park across the road is in operation too. As well as a pool, there are bookable squash courts, free sauna and a gym straight out of a 1980s boxing movie!

Hotel Linna (Map p64; ☎ 010-344 4100; www .palace.fi; Lönnrotinkatu 29; s/d to €162/189, weekends to €99/116; P ✗ 🖳 ⅏) This smallish hotel's name means 'castle', and the flamboyant turreted façade backs it up. Built in 1903 as the student clubhouse for the technical university opposite, it's a full-blooded Jugendstil medieval fantasy. The main part of the hotel, however, is in a quiet modern annexe behind the front building. The rooms have been recently refurbished and look very cool and handsome. There's a minimalist, even vaguely Japanese feel, all a significant contrast to the dragons-and-damsels whimsy of the façade.

Hotel Arthur (Map p64; ☎ 173 441; www.hotel arthur.fi; Vuorikatu 19; s/d €94/114, weekends €73/92; P ✗ ⅏) Always a popular choice for its combination of being very central yet located on a quiet side street right by the Kaisaniemi park, this is a decent middle-of-the-road option to rely on if your preferred choices are full. Spend the extra €15 and take a superior room; these are much larger than the standards and have been designed with plenty more verve and thought.

Gasthaus Omapohja (Map p64; ☎ 666 211; gasthaus .omapohja.oy@kolumbus.fi; Itäinen Teatterikuja 3; s with washbasin/toilet/bathroom €44/54/64, d with washbasin/ toilet/bathroom €65/75/85; ✗) Omapohja is a fine old guesthouse close to the train station but without any railway sleaze. It's located next to a theatre and the lobby is decorated with this in mind; the rooms are much simpler, but bright. If the yellow wing is a little much, ask for a room in a more subdued tone!

Other recommendations:

Hotelli Helka (Map pp60-1; ☎ 613 580; www.helka .fi; Pohjoinen Rautatiekatu 23A; s/d €117/184, weekends & summer €79/99; P ✗ 🖳 ⅏) Despite a somewhat shabby exterior, this is a smart and very central hotel handy for both bus and train stations.

Hotel Anna (Map pp60-1; ☎ 616 621; www.hotelanna .fi; Annankatu 1; s €110-125, d €150-165, junior ste €195;

✗ 🖳) This stately hotel is run by the small Finnish Free Church and will appeal to those who appreciate peace and quiet.

Hotel Finnapartments Fenno (Map pp60-1; ☎ 774 980; www.hotelfenno.fi; Kaarlenkatu 7; economy s/s/d €56/72/88, weekends €50/65/77; P ✗ 🖳) With simple, reasonably priced rooms with self-catering facilities, this is a functional sort of place.

Top End

Most of these hotels have various offers and special rates bookable with travel agents or via their websites; you rarely have to pay the full rack rate. Although it hadn't yet opened at time of research, the Klaus K hotel (www .klauskhotel.com) is destined to be a stylish addition to Helsinki's hotel scene.

Scandic Grand Marina (Map pp60-1; ☎ 16661; www.scandic-hotels.com; Katajanokanlaituri 7; s/d from €142/181, weekends €95/105, summer r for 2+ nights €81- 91; P ✗ 🖳 ⅏) A superb conversion from an early-20th-century giant brick harbour warehouse, this has bags more character than most business hotels, with cool, colourful and recently refurbished rooms. It boasts a great location on the lovable Jugendstil island of Katajanokka and is right by the ferry terminals. Service and facilities are particularly good.

Hotel Rivoli (Map p64; ☎ 681 500; www.rivoli .fi; Kasarmikatu 40; s €173-205, d €194-235, ste €335, weekend d €99-169; P ✗ 🖳) This beautiful boutique hotel is one of Helsinki's best lodgings and offers a stylish welcome. It exudes a quiet charm that begins in its fabulous lounge-and-breakfast area with charming plant-filled conservatory. The rooms are luxurious; there's a distinct design and colour scheme on each floor, all in a classic French-influenced style. It's much more romantic than most of the city's hotels and very chic without conceding anything on the comfort front. The suite is fabulous – *the* place to reserve for a memorable Helsinki honeymoon, or sumptuous short break. The hotel also has fabulous apartments round the corner, for stays of five nights or more.

Sokos Hotel Torni (Map p64; ☎ 020-1234 604; www.sokoshotels.fi; Yrjönkatu 26; s/d €189/218, weekends €94/115, summer r €98; ✗ 🖳) On a quiet, very central dog-legged street, this iconic, friendly place has been careful to preserve some of its prewar ambience, when it was famed as being Helsinki's 'skyscraper'.

The rooms in the main part of the hotel, however, have been very recently restored and feel great, with super-inviting beds and stylish moulded grey furnishings. In contrast, another part of the hotel has original, fabulously whimsical, turn-of-the-century Art Nouveau decoration. As well as a rooftop bar with great views, the Torni has an excellent restaurant and a sweet little courtyard bar.

Sokos Hotel Vaakuna (Map p64; ☎ 020-123 4610; www.sokoshotels.fi; Asema-aukio 2; s €193-220, d €218-251, summer & weekend s/d from €78/115; P ✗ 🖵) This vast central hotel was built as one of the key accommodations for the 1952 Olympics and conserves a stately elegance typical of that era. The rooms are very big – some have lovely convex doors and many have original Finnish art on the walls; a very nice change from repros of *Sunflowers*! The top-floor rooms are smaller but have balconies with fabulous views over the city. Above here is a chic restaurant and bar with similarly spectacular vistas, as well as a memorable sauna that can be booked by groups.

Palace Hotel (Map p64; ☎ 1345 6660; www.palace.fi; Eteläranta 10; r with/without view €280/235, weekends & Jul €130/165, P ✗ 🖵) Surprisingly, for a city which at times seems all water and no land, Helsinki has very few hotel rooms with watery views. The Palace however is right on the central harbour and looks straight across at where the big Baltic ferries dock. Although it looks large, it isn't; there are several classes of rooms, but, once you are staying in this level of accommodation, it'd be foolish not to pay the extra that a sea view commands.

Hotel Kämp (Map p64; ☎ 576 111; www.hotelkamp.fi; Pohjoisesplanadi 29; r €380-420, weekends from €165; P ✗ 🖵 &) This grand and stylish hotel is one of the city's finest and a Helsinki emblem, whose history includes plenty of long, animated piss-ups as the likes of composers Sibelius and Gallen-Kallela thrashed out their ideas. Eventually gutted and only recently re-converted to a hotel, it retains the original opulent façade – all balustrades and pilasters – and some interior features. Its charm nowadays lies especially in its gorgeous public areas, particularly its beautiful dark-wood bar. The rooms, while equipped to five-star levels, lack a little by comparison and all face inwards, but are very attractively furnished and comfortable.

The room prices offered are usually substantially lower than the rack rates: book online for the best offers.

Hilton Helsinki Strand (Map pp60-1; ☎ 39351; www.hilton.com; John Stenbergin ranta 4; s/d from €205/240, r weekends & summer from €125; P ✗ 🖵 🐾 &) Around the corner from the appealing Hakaniemi market, this impresses, from its quiet waterside location to its soaring lobby area and transparent lifts. The rooms are well-sized and come in a variety of standards – some rooms have a balcony. It'd be wasteful to come here and not try for a room with a view over the water, out towards where the serious business of Helsinki harbour goes on.

Scandic Simonkenttä (Map p64; ☎ 68380; www.scandic-hotels.com; Simonkatu 9; r €225-255, summer from €99, weekends from €63, ste €510-810; P ✗ 🖵 &) This giant sleek überhotel makes a stylish modern base in the heart of the action. It feels like a symbol of Finland's transformation from rural backwater to significant corporate player. The public areas feature modish couches and grand perspectives, while the air-conditioned rooms are all shiny and new, featuring particularly comfortable beds with wooden fittings. Some rooms have a sauna, so it's worth requesting one of these on the off-chance.

Radisson SAS Royal (Map pp60-1; ☎ 020-123 4701; www.radissonsas.com; Runeberginkatu 2; standard r up to €240, weekends €100, summer €95, ste €350-700; P ✗ 🖵 &) This striking modern building is right by the new bus station and offers modern contemporary rooms in a range of themed styles; Nordic rooms, for example, have no carpet and a pared-back Scandinavian feel. Business class rooms are slightly more expensive and have a few extra facilities such as free wireless Internet access. The breakfast buffet is generous and there's a good beer terrace on the forecourt.

Hotel Cumulus Seurahuone (Map p64; ☎ 69141; www.cumulus.fi; Kaivokatu 12; s/d to €195/220, weekends & summer from €99/118; P ✗ 🖵) Most Finnish towns had a *seurahuone*, which was a centre for high society to meet, a place for visiting officers, gentlemen and ladies to stay and a venue for concerts and ballroom dances; this gracious building served as Helsinki's from 1914 on. The common areas are delightful, with a fabulous restaurant, all noble furniture and sparkling chandeliers; you expect a Russian cavalry officer to dash in with an urgent message for the Tsar. The rooms are exceedingly spacious, with high ceilings and a classic feel that does justice to the building. Other rooms are in a more modern wing.

Radisson SAS Plaza (Map p64; ☎ 020-123 4703; www.radissonsas.com; Mikonkatu 23; r standard to €210, business to €250, weekends & summer €105-120; P ✕ ☐ ⚹) In a quiet but central corner of Helsinki by a park, this modern business hotel occupies a beautiful building with plenty of Art Nouveau character, some of which has been retained once you have entered through the modern glass façade. With friendly, professional service and a host of business facilities, this is a comfortable downtown choice.

AIRPORT HOTELS

There are fast transport connections from Vantaa airport to the city, but if you find yourself wanting to overnight here, there are some options.

Scandic Gateway (☎ 818 3600; www.scandic-hotels.fi; s/d from €176/209, weekend r €140; P ✕ ☐) The most convenient is this small hotel in the terminal itself. The rooms are Nordic and modern, although unfortunately they don't have windows, which makes them feel a little claustrophobic and nips planespotting plans in the bud.

A larger Hilton hotel is due to open at the airport in 2007.

EATING

Helsinki has by far the best range of restaurants in Finland, be it for fast food, authentic Finnish cuisine or international dining. It also has a fabulous café scene, good markets and some great parks to set up a summer picnic. Helsinki is notable for its excellent selection of Russian restaurants

Restaurants

BUDGET

Konstan Möljä (Map pp60-1; ☎ 694 7504; Hietalahdenkatu 14; lunch/dinner buffet €7.50/14; ☾ 11am-10pm Mon-Fri, 2-10pm Sat) This is a good place to go for hearty home-style Finnish fare in a pleasant, rustic atmosphere. Much of the maritime décor comes from an old harbour near Vyborg (once Finnish but now in Russia). The buffet includes soup, salad, bread, meat and vegetable dishes and always includes reindeer. Mains, such as fried Baltic

herring and salmon, are priced from €11 to €19. The dinner buffet starts at 4pm.

Zucchini (Map p64; ☎ 622 2907; Fabianinkatu 4; lunch €6-9; ☾ 11am-4pm Mon-Fri) This is one of the city's best vegetarian cafés and very popular with local workers for lunch. The dish of the day with various tasty components costs €8; there are also wines, cakes, a sunny back room and a small terrace out front. Snacks like quiche and soups are also on the menu.

Knossos (Map pp60-1; ☎ 621 1122; Hietalahden kauppahalli; mains €7-15; ☾ 11am-midnight Mon-Sat) This likeable and authentic Greek/Cretan restaurant is situated in the market hall at Hietalahti and is the place to take a break from fruitless bargain-hunting in the flea market. There are good lunch specials from 11am to 2pm and a sunny terrace.

Satkar (Map pp60-1; ☎ 611 077; Lönnrotinkatu 26; mains €8-18, set menus €19-21; ☾ 11am-11pm Mon-Fri, noon-11pm Sat & Sun) A Nepalese restaurant with plenty of North Indian dishes on the menu, including tandoori and thalis. There's a good range of vegetarian choices and good-value multicourse set menus.

Mt Everest (Map pp60-1; ☎ 6831 5450; Lapinlahdenkatu 17; lunch €7-9, curries €8-12; ☾ 10.30am-11pm Mon-Fri, noon-11pm Sat & Sun) Just by where the buses enter the bus station, this is a well-priced Nepalese place with friendly service and soothing velvety décor. There's a range of cheap lunch dishes, but the à la carte offers significantly better quality.

MIDRANGE

Sea Horse (☎ 628 169; Kapteeninkatu 11; mains €12-21; ☾ 10.30am-midnight) This much-loved restaurant was established in the 1930s and the décor has barely changed since then. It's frequented by people from all walks of Helsinki life, who come for its menu of home-style staples served in enormous portions. The fried herring, the meatballs, the liver and mash: all the delicious Finnish classics are there just like granny used to make them!

Kosmos (Map p64; ☎ 647 255; Kalevankatu 3; mains €15-25, lunch €25; ☾ 11.30am-1am Mon-Fri, 4pm-1am Sat, closed Jul) This Helsinki institution was originally designed by Alvar Aalto and is a great place for a smartish meal. The restaurant is decorated with Finnish art and the menu, Finnish with some Mediterranean influences, includes delicacies such as (deliciously delicate) sweetbreads in port sauce as well as excellent fish dishes and some solid vegetarian choices.

Cantina West (Map p64; ☎ 742 4210; Kasarmikatu 23; mains €10-22; ⏰ food served 11am-11pm, bar open later) This good-natured place is widely considered Helsinki's best Tex-Mex restaurant. There's an attractive dark-wood interior and a long, cheery menu with big steaks and tasty chicken fajitas. Needless to say, it's also a bar, with the tequilas and margaritas flowing freely.

Manala (Map pp60-1; ☎ 5807 7707; Dagmarinkatu 2; mains €10-22; ⏰ 11am-4am Mon-Fri, 2pm-4am Sat & Sun) Manala roughly means 'hell', but this is a paradise for those who like to eat late; this versatile place combines several dance floors and bars with a good and unpretentious Finnish restaurant which serves a full menu with proper service until around 4 in the morning! It's popular with actors refuelling after the show, and other creatures of the night.

Lappi (Map p64; ☎ 645 550; Annankatu 22; mains €15-30; ⏰ noon-10.30pm Mon-Fri, 1-10.30pm Sat & Sun) This Lapp restaurant is the place to come for a healthy dose of northern rustic décor, playing it up a little for the enjoyment of those visitors who aren't going to make it that far north. Many people come here to try the sautéed reindeer (€16), but other dishes are actually much tastier, such as the fish, or the sirloin of elk, as well as a great shared plate of mixed starters.

Kolme Kruunua (Map pp60-1; ☎ 135 4172; Liisankatu 5; mains €8-18; ⏰ food 4-11pm Mon-Sat, 2-11pm Sun, bar until 3am) A relic of the 1950s, this place is famous for its delicious *lihapullat* (meatballs; €8), which are served, along with a range of other traditional Finnish forest food, without ceremony and until late.

Kuu (Map pp60-1; ☎ 2709 0973; Töölönkatu 27; mains €13-20; ⏰ 11am-1am Mon-Fri, 1pm-1am Sat & Sun) This is a recommended place to try affordable but delicious Finnish cuisine, with readers lavish in their praises for its reindeer steaks. Not to be confused with the bohemian artists' bar called Kuu Kuu a couple of blocks away (in itself a good spot for a late bite).

Papa Giovanni (Map p64; ☎ 622 6010; Keskuskatu 7; mains €10-22; ⏰ lunch & dinner Mon-Sat, dinner Sun) This is a real favourite among Helsinki's pasta eaters. Downstairs is a spaghetteria, set within a shopping centre, with reasonably priced pasta dishes (€8 to €9) and an Italian-style café; upstairs is a stylish restaurant and wine bar with high-backed chairs and a tempting range of Italian soups, salads and mains.

Other recommendations:

Kabuki (Map p60-1; ☎ 694 9446; Lapinlahdenkatu 12; sushi €3-5, mains €10-24) Everything is as it should be at a good Japanese restaurant, with décor, service and delicate flavours all in harmony.

Maithai (Map p64; ☎ 685 6850; Annankatu 31-33; mains €10-16; ⏰ 11am-11pm Mon-Fri, noon-11pm Sat, 2-11pm Sun) Intimate and authentic Thai place. Just don't discuss state secrets; it's pretty small!

Namaskaar Bulevardi (Map p64; ☎ 6220 1155; Bulevardi 6; mains €12-18; ⏰ lunch & dinner) Best of several branches of this Indian restaurant. Food is passable, décor stylish and the terrace great. The Sunday buffet (1-6pm, €22) is popular.

Volga (Map p64; ☎ 622 1717; Rikhardinkatu 1; mains €13-23, lunch specials €9-14; ⏰ lunch & dinner) Russian restaurant with a lovely summer terrace in an enclosed courtyard. A huge serving of mixed blini is €19.90.

TOP END

Chez Dominique (Map p64; ☎ 612 7393; Ludviginkatu 3; mains €40-50, lunch menu €39, set menus €79-125; ⏰ lunch & dinner Tue-Fri, dinner Sat, closed Jul) For fine French cuisine, this is the number one choice in Helsinki and has two Michelin stars. There's a short à la carte menu featuring exquisite, rich fare, but the speciality are the set menus (prices exclude drinks). There's a fabulous list of French wines and it's served in a chic, intimate dining room.

Nokka (Map pp60-1; ☎ 687 7330; Kanavaranta 7; mains €24-29, set menus €56-60; ⏰ 11.30am-midnight Mon-Fri, 6pm-midnight Sat, dinner only Mon-Sat Jul) Atmospherically set in a restored brick warehouse on the waterfront across the canal on Katajanokka, this has rapidly created a lofty reputation for itself. You'll spot it easily with its flaming torch and huge ship's propeller backing an unbeatable summer terrace. The food is high in class and makes use of the finest Finnish produce, with tasty wild mushrooms combining memorably with delicately handled perch or salmon. The service is faultless and warm rather than formal. Interesting wine cellar.

Saslik (Map pp60-1; ☎ 7425 5500; Neitsytpolku 12; mains €16-32; ⏰ noon-midnight Mon-Sat, 4-11pm Sun) This is regarded as the city's top Russian restaurant. It offers live music nightly and seven private, themed dining rooms – all complete with plush velvet, stained-glass windows and chandeliers. Most mains are around €24 but blinis with Russian or Iranian caviar will raise your bill substantially!

Restaurant Bellevue (Map pp60-1; ☎ 636 985; Rahapajankatu 3; mains €20-30) Just down from the Uspensky Cathedral, this venerable Russian restaurant has been going since the October Revolution. It specializes in Russian and Finnish food with a French accent and has a couple of set menus. Carnivores who want to tick all the boxes will be attracted by the bear steak (€65); more moderate choices include borscht, chicken Kiev (yes it really is Russian) and a sensational baked Alaska for dessert.

Sipuli (Map pp60-1; ☎ 622 9280; Kanavaranta 7; mains €26-33; ⊙ 6pm-midnight Mon-Fri) This place, near the church on Katajanokka island, offers fine views back across the city. The speciality is gourmet Finnish food, including wild game in season. There are various dining areas; the main one is extravagantly poised under chandeliers and a large skylight with the Uspenski cathedral looming overhead.

Cafés

Tamminiementien Kahvila (☎ 481 003; Tamminiementie 8; ⊙ noon-10.30pm summer, shorter hr winter) This memorable café is set next to the City Art Museum and near the Urho Kekkonen museum in a lovely bit of parkland. It's like a cross between a Chekhov play and a flower-loving granny's country cottage and is utterly curious and charming. The coffee or tea is expensive but comes with a huge *pulla* (a typical and tasty cardamon-flavoured

bun) and can be taken on the veranda, the chairs of which fly jaunty coloured scarves. Take tram 4 or bus 24 for this beauty.

Café Esplanad (Map p64; ☎ 665 496; Pohjoisesplanadi 37; sandwiches €3-5; ⊙ 8am-10pm Mon-Fri, 9am-10pm Sat, 10am-10pm Sun) This large, busy space is a perfect spot for a variety of needs and wants. Oversized Danish pastries and excellent Finnish *pulla* are good accompaniments to coffee (bottomless) or espresso; for lunch, there are spectacular salads and a variety of wines served by the glass.

Café Strindberg (Map p64; ☎ 681 2030; Pohjoisesplanadi 33; ⊙ 9am-10pm Mon-Sat, 10am-10pm Sun) This upmarket café is a classic place to see and be seen on the Esplanad, with a terrace whose waiter-served seats are much in demand. There's a sumptuous lounge and classy bistro upstairs too.

Café Ekberg (Map p64; ☎ 6811 8660; Bulevardi 9; buffet breakfast & lunch €8; ⊙ 7.30am-7pm Mon-Fri, 8.30am-5pm Sat, 10am-5pm Sun) This is Helsinki's oldest café (opened 1861) and one of the best places for breakfast in the city. The lunch buffet is great value and they also do great loaves to take away.

Fazer (Map p64; ☎ 6159 2959; Kluuvikatu 3; ⊙ 7.30am-10pm, 9am-10pm Sat) Another historical café worth delving into, this is a huge space with character for days, classic décor and a small terrace. Founded in 1891 by the Finnish confectionary-making family (you'll see Fazer sweets and chocolate everywhere), it does amazing ice-cream sundaes and also sells cakes and tea to take away.

Café Ursula (Map pp60-1; ☎ 652 817; Ehrenströmintie 3; light mains €7-12; ⊙ 9am-7pm) Down on

---

SOMETHING SPECIAL: ISLAND RESTAURANTS

An essential summer experience for Helsinki folk is to head out for dinner to one of the small islands dotted around the harbour. There are several island restaurants, which are served by small boats that ferry diners to and from quays on the mainland opposite. The most famous is the stylish, spired Klippan, set in a villa on Luoto island, by Valkosaari.

More convivial is **Boathouse** (Map pp60-1; ☎ 6227 1070; Liuskasaari; mains €12-25; ⊙ 5pm-midnight Mon-Sat, noon-9pm Sun May-Sep), a circular two-deck restaurant on Liuskasaari, reached from a jetty on Merisatamanranta. It's only a couple of hundred metres offshore, but it already feels like an outpost, albeit a very comfortable one. The restaurant is cheerful, noisy and light, with seafood aplenty. You might choose orange-flavoured squid (€10.90) or a filling seafood platter (€27.90); it's all pretty good. Best is the atmosphere, which is very family-friendly (there's even a 'dog bar') and relaxed. Instead of the usual guestbook, visitors pin notes to the chandelier in the lobby.

Even if you're not dining at these restaurants, it's worth heading out to the islands for the city views or to have a drink watching the big ferries sliding past. The boats are around €3 to €5 return for non-diners and run every 10 to 15 minutes during eating hours.

Kaivopuisto Park, with great views over to Harakka island, this classy café is popular with locals and visitors and is a lovely, relaxing spot. When things are quiet on the diplomatic front, the British ambassador nips across for tea from the embassy opposite. Further around the peninsula (westwards), Cafe Carusel is a cheaper, more functional waterfront café with excellent focaccias.

Café Krypta (Map p64; ☎ 709 2455; Kirkkokatu 18; coffee & pastry €2; 10am-5pm Mon-Sat, 11am-5pm Sun Jun-Aug only) This welcoming, unusual café is situated in the crypt of the Lutheran cathedral and has a quiet candlelit atmosphere and good prices. You are surrounded not by creaking tombs but by vaulted brick foundations and exhibitions of modern art, and it's a good hideaway from the tour groups.

Café Engel (Map p64; ☎ 652 776; Senaatintori; 8am-10pm Mon-Fri, 9am-10pm Sat, 10am-10pm Sun) Directly opposite the cathedral, this café is popular with students popping across from the university. It's an arty place with a small gallery next door and a big notice board announcing coming events. There's a covered courtyard at the back which serves as a little cinema on summer evenings.

Limón (Map p64; ☎ 622 5992; Rikhardinkatu 4; dishes €7-18; 11.30am-11pm Mon-Fri, 11am-10pm Sat) Limón is essentially a café-bar where the beautiful people like to see and be seen, savouring finely flavoured Mediterranean-style concoctions, from light and luscious bruschettas to more substantial fare.

Quick Eats & Self-Catering

There are plenty of hamburger restaurants (such as Hesburger and Carrols), pizza shops, kebab joints, hot-dog stands and grillis in Helsinki.

The **kauppahalli** (covered market; Eteläranta; 8am-6pm Mon-Fri, 8am-4pm Sat), built in 1889, is one of the best in Finland and, although touristy, is a great place to nose around. The kauppatori, also known as the fish market, is good for salmon chowder, cheap snacks and fresh produce such as berries. Most food stalls set up plastic chairs and tables on summer afternoons.

Soppakeittiö (Map pp60-1; Hakaniemen Kauppahalli; soups €5-8; 10.30am-4pm Mon-Fri, 10.30am-3pm Sat) On the ground floor of the intriguing Hakaniemi market building north of the centre, this little soup kitchen is a great place to warm the cockles in winter. The

delicious, generously portioned soups come with bread and cheese spread; the bouillabaisse (€7) is a reader favourite.

Eatz (Map p64; ☎ 687 7240; Mikonkatu 15; sushi €3-8, mains €10-20; 9am-midnight, weekends 9am-4am) With a variety of separate eateries in one building on the east side of the Rautatientori, Eatz manages to serve up everything from Thai and Indian to Italian and even has a sushi train and Australian bar. It's also the cornerstone of Helsinki's biggest summer beer terrace.

Forum shopping centre (Mannerheimintie 20; 9am-9pm Mon-Fri, 9am-6pm Sat, noon-6pm Sun) Has an atrium-covered food court with everything from Asian noodles to burgers and kebabs. There's also a large supermarket in the basement level.

S-Market (Map p64; Kasarmikatu; 7am-9pm Mon-Sat, 7am-6pm Sat) Another well-stocked central supermarket.

DRINKING

The Finns certainly know how to party, especially in summer when open-air beer terraces spill out everywhere to take advantage of the long hours of daylight. Helsinki's biggest summer terrace is along Mikonkatu where hundreds of chairs and tables crowd the sidewalk in front of Eatz (above), and the nearby On the Rocks and Barfly. After about 4pm on a sunny day it's difficult to score a seat here, but the atmosphere is fantastic.

Another good spot to find cafés (and bars) is the pedestrian section of Iso Roobertinkatu, an animated strip just south of the centre. Popular spots include We Got Beef and Labyrinth.

The Kallio district northeast of the centre is full of downmarket character, and a stroll along Helsinginkatu will reveal many delightfully seedy bars. Just make sure you realize that 'Thai Hieronta' isn't a place to get a green curry…

Kappeli (Map p64; ☎ 681 244; Esplanad Park; 10am-midnight Mon-Sat, 10am-11pm Sun) Located in the middle of the park near the kauppatori, Kappeli has one of the most popular summer terraces. It faces a stage where various bands and musicians regularly play in summer. Inside, there's a vaulted cellar bar, which is fantastic later in the evening or when the sun's not shining. There are also restaurant and café sections.

Corona & Кафе Mockba (Map p64; ☎ 611 200; Eerikinkatu 11-15; ☼ 11am-2am) These two utterly distinct bars are run by the quirky filmmakers Aki and Mika Kaurismäki and both attract a savvy, grungy crowd. Corona has about 20 pool tables and cheap beer, while the ultra-characterful Mockba (Café Moscow in Russian) recreates a lugubrious Eastern Bloc drinking den. It's understated and ironic, with a samovar, artery-clogging salami snacks and LPs of Soviet Army hits and Brezhnev speeches. Due to open in a former cinema in the same complex is Dubrovnik, which is to be a venue for regular live jazz. Downstairs from Mockba is another bar, Superbar, a trendy little spot decorated in homage to comics.

Vltava (Map p64; ☎ 766 3650; Elielinaukio 2; bar meals €8-12; ☼ 11am-3am or later) Named for the river that runs through Prague, this new bar/restaurant is a great spot for beer lovers. Right next to the train station, it boasts a big range of draught and bottled beers, solid wooden tables and a terrace that catches the afternoon sun. There's a good bar menu and heartier Czech dishes (pork, boar, sausages…) in the bistro upstairs, which also has classy lounge seating.

Ateljee Bar (Map p64; Sokos Hotel Torni, Yrjönkatu 26; ☼ 2pm-2am Mon-Thu, noon-2am Fri & Sat, 2pm-1am Sun) This is a tiny perch on the roof of the Sokos Hotel Torni, and is worth ascending just for the views of the city. Take the lift to the 12th floor and the narrow winding staircase to the top. Downstairs, the courtyard Tornin Pivi is a cute little terrace with good wines by the glass and Coopers Stout in bottles. The rooftop bars of the Palace and the Sokos Vaakuna hotels are also notable for their great views.

Bar Tapasta (Map p64; ☎ 640 724; Uudenmaankatu 13; tapas €3-5; ☼ 11am-midnight Mon-Thu, 11am-2am Fri, 2pm-2am Sat) This is an intimate and welcoming bar with quirky Mediterranean décor, an elegant young crowd and friendly staff. The tapas are cheap and generous; there is also (how did you guess?) pasta, a selection of wines by the glass and popular sangria.

Zetor (Map p64; ☎ 666 966; Mannerheimintie 3-5; mains €10-22; ☼ 11am-4am Sat, 3pm-1am Sun & Mon, 3pm-3am Tue, 3pm-4am Wed & Thu) This is a spoofy Finnish restaurant and pub with deeply ironic tractor décor ('Zetor' is a Czech tractor manufacturer whose heyday was in the Cold War years). It's owned by film maker Aki Kaurismäki and designed by those crazy guys from the Leningrad Cowboys. It's worth going in just for a drink and a ride on a tractor, but the food is decent value too.

Kola (Map pp60-1; ☎ 694 8983; Helsinginkatu 13B; ☼ noon-2am; 🖳) Right in the heart of the intriguing Kallio district, this bar is a little classier than many of its brethren but still a relaxed, comfortable place. There's a '70s feel, a window to be seen in, and a magazine rack to browse the music press.

Carelia (Map pp60-1; ☎ 2709 0976; Mannerheimintie 56; ☼ 11am-1am Mon-Fri, 4pm-1am Sat, closed mid-Jun–early Aug) Right opposite the opera house, this former pharmacy has been beautifully converted into a wine bar and upmarket restaurant. Very atmospheric with its wooden drawers and glass bottles, it's the perfect place for a glass of something nice before or after the show.

Rytmi (Map pp60-1; ☎ 7231 5550; Toinen Linja 2; ☼ 11am-2am Mon-Sat; 🖳) Northeast of the centre, this deservedly popular bar is a favourite of musicians, actors and students, and has a stylish but bohemian feel. There are regular DJs playing on weekends and it also has a terrace.

Bar Loose (Map p64; ☎ 586 1819; Fredrikinkatu 34) The trendiest spot in the thriving Finnish rock and metal scene, this is a place where musicians hang out and black leather, vinyl and piercings are *de rigueur*. It's been voted Helsinki's favourite bar; there's also sometimes live music here.

Vanha (Map p64; Mannerheimintie 3; ⊙ 11am-midnight, later at weekends) This music bar is in the beautiful 19th-century students' house. It gets packed with students and runs various summer club nights at weekends. They also do a good lunch (€7.90) on weekdays and there's a summer terrace.

Erottaja (Map p64; ☎ 611 196; Erottajankatu 15-17) A no-frills wine bar with reasonably cheap drinks. It's well-patronised by locals in the know and is popular with students.

Roska Pankki (Map pp60-1; ☎ 735 488; Helsinginkatu 20). This is one of the classic stops on the Kallio beer trail and draws a real mix of people from muttering drunks to penny-pinching executives. It's got bags of character, a ceiling decorated with banknotes (the name means 'rubbish bank'), and beer served in plastic for the princely sum of €2.

Pub Tram Spårakoff (Map p64; ☎ 123 4600; www .koff.net, in Finnish; tickets €7, beers €5; ⊙ Tue-Sat mid-May–mid-Aug) In summer you can catch the bright red pub tram from Mikonkatu, just east of the train station, with stops at the Opera House and kauppatori. It's a bit pricey but a quaint way to do a quick tour of town. It departs from its terminus on Mikonkatu on the hour between 2pm to 3pm and between 5pm to 8pm Tuesday to Saturday.

ENTERTAINMENT

In many ways Helsinki has a typical capital-city entertainment and nightlife scene, but in recent years the city's bars, cafés and clubs have blossomed. There's a lot on offer, particularly music-wise. As well as a full range of trends, from hole-in-the-wall bars and cafés to rock and jazz clubs to dance clubs, there's generally a sophisticated but down-to-earth air about Helsinki's nightlife.

For events, concerts and performances, see *Helsinki This Week* or inquire at the city tourist office. Major rock and pop concerts by touring bands are staged at the **Hartwall Areena** (☎ 020-494 076; opposite).

Nightclubs

Lost & Found (Map p64; ☎ 680 1010; Annankatu 6; ⊙ to 4am) This popular bar has a great atmosphere and eccentric and original décor on the 'lost and found' theme. Originally a gay bar, it now is far too mixed to really be labelled as such and attracts all sorts to its relaxed upstairs and tightly packed downstairs club.

Teatteri (Map p64; ☎ 681 1130; Pohjoisesplanadi 2) The ultrachic club inside the Swedish Theatre has space for 300 people and there's a beautifully designed bar on the middle level. It doesn't feel particularly Finnish, but attracts plenty of celebrities and party people.

mbar (Map p64; ☎ 6124 5420; Mannerheimintie 22; ⊙ 9am-midnight, later at weekends) This trendy little café in the Lasipalatsi complex between the bus and train stations offers good-quality Internet access and has heaps of terminals (per hour €5). As the night draws on, it becomes a place to be seen sipping something cool and alcoholic, accompanied by some excellent DJs.

Helsinki Club (Map p64; ☎ 4332 6340; Yliopistonkatu 8; ⊙ 11pm- 4am) If you're partying late, this is a mainstream dance club popular with a youthful and trendy Helsinkian crowd. The interior is pretty tacky, with dodgy wallpaper and worse carpet; make it to the cooler back dancefloor if you can! During the week there is a variety of local acts, with big-name DJs at weekends, when the minimum age is 22.

Highlight (Map pp60-1; ☎ 734 5822; Fredrikinkatu 42; ⊙ 9pm-4am) This place atmospherically set in a former church claims to be a 'disco for demanding people' and attracts a young crowd looking for late-night dancefloor action. It's difficult to get in after 11pm on Friday and Saturday.

Arctic Icebar (Map p64; ☎ 278 1855; Yliopistonkatu 5; ⊙ 10pm-4am Wed-Sat) In the cavernous Uniq nightclub almost opposite Club Helsinki, this is a bar literally carved out of ice – tables, bar, the lot. Inside, it's minus five degrees; you get lent a suitable furry parka to enter. It's expensive (and you won't be able to ask for a glass of tap water…) but definitely worth doing once. There's an age minimum of 24. Uniq itself is popular with a slightly older, well-heeled crowd, including the occasional Finnish celebrity and at times hosts big-name live acts.

On the Rocks (Map p64; ☎ 612 2030; Mikonkatu 15; ⊙ bar from noon in summer, 4pm in winter, club from

9pm) Across the square from the train station, this cheerful bar has a great summer terrace and pool table, and a rock'n'roll theme. Downstairs is a dark, moody club, which has frequent live rock music, nightly DJs and even a fountain. Entry at weekends is €6, with a minimum age of 23.

Live Music

Tavastia (Map pp60-1; ☎ 694 8511; www.tavastiaklubi .fi; Urho Kekkosenkatu 4; ⏰ 9pm-late) One of Helsinki's legendary rock venues, this attracts both up-and-coming local acts and bigger international groups. There's a band every night of the week and the cover charge is usually around €10. Next door is another, smaller venue, Semi-Final, run by the same people.

Storyville (Map pp60-1; ☎ 408 007; Museokatu 8; ⏰ 6pm-4am Mon-Sat) This is one of Helsinki's best jazz clubs, housed in a converted coal cellar. A mature, whisky-sipping crowd enjoy the traditional, Dixieland, swing and New Orleans jazz most nights. There's also a romantic terrace here, open later than any others are allowed to be. Locals say that's because Parliament House is next door...

Juttutupa (Map pp60-1; ☎ 742 4240; Säästöpankin-ranta 6) West of Hakaniemi metro station is one of Helsinki's top live music bars, focusing on contemporary jazz and rock fusion. The best day is Wednesday, when there's nearly always a high-quality jazz act, but at any time it's a nice towering stone building looking out over a bay of the harbour, with a terrace and a couple of restaurants.

Opera, Theatre & Ballet

For concerts and performances, see *Helsinki This Week* or inquire at the tourist office. The opera and concert season is generally September to May (there are no indoor performances in summer). The Symphony Orchestra (RSO) of the Finnish Broadcasting Corporation features popular concerts in **Finlandia Talo** (Map pp60-1; ☎ 402 4400; www.finlandia.hel.fi; Mannerheiminitie 13). **Lippupiste** (☎ 0600 900 900; www.lippupiste.com) is the place to call to book tickets.

Opera House (Map pp60-1; ☎ 4030 2211; Helsinginkatu 58; tickets from €15) Opera, ballet and classical concerts are held here, but not during summer. Performances of the Finnish National Opera are subtitled in Finnish.

Kansallis Teatteri (Map p64; ☎ 1733 1331; www .kansallisteatteri.fi, in Finnish; Läntinen teatterikuja 1) The Finnish National Theatre occupies a beautiful building by the train station. Performances are in Finnish but quite an experience even if you haven't mastered the language yet.

Cinemas

There are several cinemas in Helsinki, all of which show original-version films with Finnish and Swedish subtitiles.

Diana (Map p64; ☎ 612 3622; Yrjönkatu 8) In a courtyard, this cinema offers top-grade arthouse European and world films.

Orion Theatre (Map pp60-1; ☎ 6154 0201; www .sea.fi; Eerikinkatu 15) This is where the Finnish Film Archive shows classics from their collection, with three screenings a day except Mondays. You must purchase an annual membership (€4), then admission is €3.50.

Tennispalatsi (Map pp60-1; ☎ 0600 007 007; www .finnkino.fi, in Finnish; Salomonkatu 15) This is one of Europe's largest multiplexes and screens recent blockbusters.

Forum (Map p64; ☎ 0600 007 007; Mannerheimintie 16) Another mainstream cinema, in the Forum Centre.

Sport

Sporting events in Helsinki are numerous.

Hartwall Areena (☎ 0600 10800; www.hartwall -areena.com; tickets €13-30) Between September and April ice hockey reigns supreme and the best place to see top-level matches is at this arena, about 4km north of the city centre (bus 23 or 69 or tram 7A or 7B). Built in 1997, Hartwall hosted the Ice Hockey World Championships that same year and has seating for more than 13,000 fans. It's the home of local Superleague side Jokerit Helsinki.

Helsingin Jäähalli (Map pp60-1; ☎ 477 7110; www .helsinginjaahalli.fi; Nordenskiöldinkatu 13) Ice hockey matches are also played at this indoor arena in the Olympic stadium complex.

Finnair Stadium (Map pp60-1; ☎ 0600 10800; www.lippupalvelu.fi; tickets €8-15) Next to the Olympic Stadium, this is the home ground of HJK Helsinki. The team's the closest thing Finland has to a Real Madrid or a Manchester United, having won 21 Finnish league titles and even having made a foray into the group stages of the Champions League a few years back.

SHOPPING

Helsinki is an excellent spot for shopping, particularly for Nordic fashion and, of course, the latest furniture and homewares from the avant-garde Finnish design studios. Prices are high on Pohjoisesplanadi, the main tourist street in town. Other notable shopping streets are Aleksanterinkatu and Fredrikinkatu. Mariankatu has many antiques shops and Iso Roobertinkatu is filled with funky boutiques and secondhand stores. The tourist office has a good brochure of (paid) listings of interior design shops.

Artek (Map p64; ☎ 6132 5277; www.artek.fi; Eteläesplanadi 18) As well as other Nordic homewares, this shop is especially devoted to selling the furniture and fabrics of Alvar Aalto, the Finnish architect and innovator whose designs still look modern almost a century later.

Arabia (☎ 020-439 3507; Hämeentie 135; ✆ 10am-8pm Mon-Fri, 10am-4pm Sat & Sun) The factory outlet and exhibition of this legendary Finnish ceramics company is bleakly located but worthwhile. Take tram 6 to its terminus and walk a further 200m north.

Dis 'n' Dat Records (Map p64; ☎ 680 1118; www .disndatrecords.com; Shop 18 Kaisaniemi Metro Station) Here is the place to look for CDs and other forms of music from Finland and abroad.

Marimekko (Map p64; ☎ 686 0240; Pohjoisesplanadi 31) Finland's most famous clothing and fabric label lives on with its warm floral colours loved as ever. Let Sweden sneer; Marimekko is as popular with young Nokia executives as it is with aunties and grandmas meeting over cinnamon buns.

Stockmann (Map p64; ☎ 1211; Aleksanterinkatu 52) The oldest and largest department store in Finland, this is surprisingly well priced for Finnish souvenirs and Sámi handicrafts, as well as Finnish textiles, Kalevala Koru jewellery, Lapponia jewellery, Moomintroll souvenirs and lots more. It offers an export service.

Markets

Kauppatori (✆ 6.30am-2pm winter, longer hr summer) This famous market is still an important food market for locals and well worth visiting, although it is heavy with tour groups. Fish, seasonal fruit and berries and *makkara* (sausages) are on sale and people even sell direct from boats moored at the quay. There are also plenty of stalls selling local handi-crafts and souvenirs at (sometimes) inflated prices. Nearby, the ornate indoor kauppahalli is a paradise of Finnish food stalls.

Hakaniemi kauppahalli (✆ 8am-6pm Mon-Fri, 8am-4pm Sat) This and the kauppatori at the metro stop is a traditional-style Finnish food market and is a less touristy alternative to the main one at the harbour.

Hietalahti flea market (✆ 8am-3pm Mon-Sat, 8am-8pm daily Jun-Aug) The closest secondhand centre to central Helsinki: you'll find anything from used clothes to broken accordions, but it's pretty downmarket.

Kauppahalli (✆ 10am-5pm Mon-Fri, 10am-3pm Sat) This renovated market is at the Hietalahti flea market and has a mixture of craft and antique stalls. Take tram 6.

Vallila (Aleksis Kivenkatu 17; ✆ 9am-5pm) A popular indoor flea market in Kallio. The range and quality is usually better here than at Hietalahti. Trams 1 and 1A stop opposite.

GETTING THERE & AWAY
Air

There are flights to Helsinki from the USA, Europe and Asia on many airlines. See p342 for more information on reaching Finland by air. Finnair and its subsidiaries offer international as well as domestic services, with flights to 20 Finnish cities – generally at least once a day. **Blue1** (☎ 0600 25831; www.blue1.com) has budget flights to some Finnish destinations. The **Finnair office** (Map p64; reservations ☎ 0600 140 140; www.finnair.fi; Asema-aukio 1; ✆ Mon-Sat) is in the train station complex. The airport is in Vantaa, 19km north of Helsinki.

The quickest way to Tallinn is by helicopter. **Copterline** (☎ 0200 18181; www.copterline.com; ✆ 7am-10pm) flies hourly from Helsinki to Tallinn and back. The trip takes 20 minutes one way and costs from €118 for a limited ticket (book at least two days in advance) to €228 for a guaranteed seat. At time of writing, weekend services had been suspended after a crash, but were due to resume.

Boat

International ferries travel to Stockholm and Tallinn. There is also a regular catamaran and hydrofoil service to Tallinn. See p346 for more details.

Four of the five ferry terminals are just off the central kauppatori: Kanava and Katajanokka terminals (Map pp60–1) are

TRIPPING TO TALLINN

Although Finland can seem very remote from the rest of Europe at times, Helsinki is remarkably close to the continental mainland, and a day or overnight trip to the Estonian capital of Tallinn is very easy. There's a big contrast between modern Helsinki and the turrets and spires of Tallinn's medieval Old Town.

It's 80km across the Gulf of Finland to Tallinn and the catamarans and hydrofoils do the trip several times daily in 90 minutes (p347). The ferry is cheaper, while at the other end of the price scale, you can get there by scheduled chopper (opposite). See p341 for entry requirements to Estonia.

It's a 15-minute walk from the ferry terminals to Tallinn's magnificent Old Town, with it's lofty castle and quaint, narrow lanes. The **tourist office** (☎ 645 7777; www .tourism.tallinn.ee) is in the heart of it and sells the useful Tallinn Card sightseeing pass.

served by bus 13 and trams 2, 2V and 4, and Olympia (Map pp60–1) and Makasiini (Map p64) terminals by trams 3B and 3T. The last terminal, Länsiterminaali (Map pp60–1, West Terminal), is served by bus 15.

Ferry tickets may be purchased at the terminal, from a ferry company's office in the centre or (in some cases) from the city tourist office. Book in advance during the high season (late June to mid-August).

Ferry company offices in Helsinki:

Eckerö Line (Map p64; ☎ 228 8544; Mannerheimintie 10, Länsiterminaali)
Linda Line (☎ 668 9700; Makasiini terminal)
Nordic Jet Line (☎ 681 770; Kanava terminal)
Silja Line (Map p64; ☎ 0203-74552; Mannerheimintie 2, Makasiini & Olympia terminals)
Tallink (Map p64; ☎ 2282 1222; Erottajankatu 19, Kanava Terminal)
Viking Line (Map p64; ☎ 123 577; Mannerheimintie 14, Katajanokka & Makasiini terminals)

In summer there are daily ferries between Helsinki and Porvoo, through the southeast archipelago. See p91 for more details.

Bus

Purchase long-distance and express bus tickets at the new underground **Kamppi Bus Station** (Frederikinkatu; ☺ 7am-7pm Mon-Fri, 7am-5pm Sat, 9am-6pm Sun) or on the bus itself. There's a terminal for local buses to Espoo in one wing, while longer-distance buses also depart from here to all of Finland. Destinations with several daily departures including Jyväskylä (€36.90, four to six hours), Kuopio (€49, five to seven hours), Lappeenranta (€32.30, four hours), Oulu (€77.40, 11½hrs), Savonlinna (€46.70, five to six hours), Tampere (€28.10, 2½ hours) and Turku (€28.10, 2½ hours).

Train

The *rautatieasema* (train station) is in the city centre and is linked by pedestrian tunnel with the Helsinki metro system. Helsinki is the terminus for three main railway lines, with regular trains from Turku in the west, Tampere in the north and Lahti in the northeast. There is a separate ticket counter for international trains, including the ones that go to St Petersburg and Moscow.

GETTING AROUND
To/From the Airport

Bus 615 (€3.40, 30 to 50 minutes, Helsinki Card not valid) shuttles between Vantaa airport (all international and domestic flights) and platform 10 at Rautatientori (Railway Square) next to the main train station.

Finnair buses (☎ 0307-23746) depart from the Finnair office at Asemaaukio (€5.20, 30 minutes, every 20 minutes, 5am to midnight). It also stops at several request stops including the opera house.

There are also door-to-door **airport taxis** (☎ 0600 555 555; www.airporttaxi.fi) costing from €20 for 1 or 2 persons. If leaving Helsinki, these should be booked the previous day before 6pm.

Bicycle

Helsinki is ideal for cycling: the inner city is flat and there are well-marked and high-quality bike paths. Get hold of a copy of the Helsinki cycling map at the tourist office.

The city of Helsinki provides 300 distinctive green 'City Bikes' at stands within a radius of 2km from the kauppatori – although in summer you'll be lucky to get one. The bikes are free: you deposit a €2 coin into the stand that locks them, then reclaim it when you return it to any stand.

For something more sophisticated, **Greenbike** (☎ 8502 2850; www.greenbike.fi; Mannerheimintie

13A2; ☾ 10am-6pm Mon-Fri, 10am-3pm Sat, 10am-2pm Sun) rents out quality bikes for €10 per day, €15 for 24 hours, or €50 per week (hybrid bikes €10/20/70). By the time of publication, they will have moved, so check the website or give them a ring to find the new location.

Car & Motorcycle

Cars can be rented at the airport or in the city centre. The big companies include **Avis** (☎ 441 155; www.avis.fi; Hietaniemenkatu 6); and **Hertz** (Map pp60-1; ☎ 020-555 2300; www.hertz.fi; Mannerheimintie 44) a few blocks north of the centre.

Some of the more economical rental companies include **Lacara** (☎ 719 062; Hämeentie 12) north of the centre, and **Budget** (Map pp60-1; ☎ 686 6500; Malminkatu 24) near the Radisson SAS Royal hotel. Motorcycle rental is not common in Helsinki.

Parking in Helsinki is strictly regulated and can be a big headache. Metered areas cost €0.50 to €1 per hour. There are a few free, long- or short-term parking areas around the city; for locations consult the *Parking Guide for the Inner City of Helsinki*, a free map available at the city tourist office.

Public Transport

Central Helsinki is easy to get around on foot or by bicycle and. there's also a metro line and reasonably comprehensive transport network. The city's public transport system, **Helsingin Kaupungin Liikennelaitos** (HKL; www.hkl .fi) operates buses, metro and local trains, trams and a ferry to Suomenlinna. A one-hour flat-fare ticket for any HKL transport costs €2 when purchased on board, €1.40 when purchased in advance. The ticket allows unlimited transfers but must be validated in the stamping machine on board when you first use it. A single tram ticket (no transfers) is €1.80 full fare and €1.50 concession.

Tourist tickets can be purchased at €5.40/10.80/16.20 for one/three/five days; a 24-hour group ticket (two adults and up to four children) costs €8, making it better value even for a couple. Alternatively, the Helsinki Card gives you free travel anywhere within Helsinki (see p62).

There are also regional tickets for travel by bus or train to neighbouring cities such as Vantaa and Espoo which cost €3.40 for a single ticket, €8.50/17/25.50 for one/three/ five days, and €12 for a 24-hour group ticket. Children's tickets are usually half price.

HKL offices (☾ Mon-Fri) at the Kamppi bus station and the Rautatientori and Hakaniemi metro stations sell tickets and passes, as do many of the city's R-kiosks. Metro services run daily from about 6am to 11.30pm. The metro line extends to Ruoholahti in the western part of the city and northeast to Mellunmäki and Vuosaari.

The *Helsinki Route Map,* available at HKL offices and the city tourist office, is an easily understood map of the bus, metro and tram routes.

Boat services leave from the kauppatori to Suomenlinna (see p86) and to the zoo (see p67).

Taxi

Vacant taxis are hard to come by during morning and evening rush hours. If you need one, hail one off the street or join a queue at one of the taxi stands located at the train station, bus station or Senaatintori. You can phone for a cab on ☎ 0100 0700. A trip across town from the kauppatori to somewhere like the Olympic Stadium costs about €10 to €15.

AROUND HELSINKI

SUOMENLINNA

Suomenlinna, only a 15-minute ferry ride from Helsinki kauppatori, is a very popular day or half-day trip from the city. Set on a tight cluster of islands, this Unesco World Heritage Site (the 'fortress of Finland') was the scene of a major event in Finnish history when the Russians seized it from the Swedes in 1808.

The fields around Suomenlinna's stone ramparts are a favourite picnicking destination for locals. It's not just a place to visit though – there are many residents, who are wearily accustomed to curious faces peering in their front windows.

Every evening between 5pm and 6pm people gather at Suomenlinna's main quay to wave as the ferries sail through the narrow strait – it's quite a sight.

History

The greatest fortress of the Swedish empire was founded in 1748 to protect the eastern part of the empire against Russian attack. It was named Sveaborg (Swedish fortress).

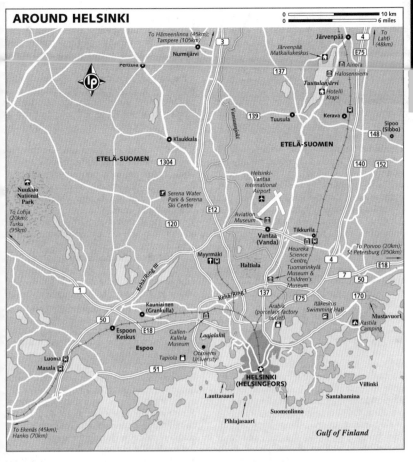

AROUND HELSINKI

Sveaborg was once the second largest town in Finland, after Turku. In 1806 it had 4600 residents whereas Helsinki had 4200.

After a prolonged attack, Sveaborg was surrendered to the Russians after the war of 1808, and renamed Viapori. Thanks in large part to the superb sea fortress, the Finnish capital was moved from Turku to Helsinki in 1812. It remained Russian until Finland gained independence in 1917, and continues to have military significance as it's still home to a naval base. During the Finnish Civil War, the Whites incarcerated many Communist prisoners here in brutal conditions. The present name was chosen in 1918, after Finland's independence.

Sights & Activities

The Helsinki Card allows free travel to Suomenlinna and admission to all the museums. Most attractions are on two main islands, Iso Mustasaari and Susisaari, connected to each other by a small bridge. At the bridge is the **Inventory Chamber Visitor Centre** (☎ 668 800) with tourist information, maps and guided walking tours in summer. In the same building is the **Suomenlinna Museum** (☎ 4050 9691; admission €5; ☽ 10am-6pm May-Sep, 10am-4pm Oct-Apr) featuring a scale model of Suomenlinna as it looked in 1808 and an illuminating 30-minute audiovisual display.

Ehrensvärd Museum (☎ 684 1850; adult/child €3/1; ☽ 10am-5pm May-Aug, 11am-4pm Sep, 11am-4pm Sat & Sun Apr & Oct) preserves an 18th-century officer's home and contains dozens of model ships, sea charts, portraits and blue-and-white tile Swedish stoves. Opposite Ehrensvärd Museum is the **shipyard** where sailmakers and other workers have been building ships since the 1750s. As many as two dozen ships are in the dry dock at any given time. They can be from 12m to 32m long and from as far away as the UK.

Three museums relating to Suomenlinna's military history can be visited with a combination ticket (€6). **Manege** (☎ 1814 5296; admission €4; 🕙 11am-6pm mid-May–Aug) commemorates WWII and displays heavy artillery. **Coast Artillery Museum** (☎ 1814 5295; admission €4; 🕙 11am-6pm Jul & Aug) displays still more heavy artillery in a bunker-style exhibition. Finland was forbidden to possess submarines by the 1947 Treaty of Paris and the WWII-era U-boat **Vesikko** (☎ 1814 6238; admission €4, 🕙 11am-6pm mid-May–Aug) is one of the few submarines remaining in the country. You can take a look inside and sympathise with its wartime crew – it's not for the claustrophobic.

The delightful **Toy Museum** (☎ 668 417; admission €4; 🕙 11am-4pm Sat & Sun Apr & Sep, 11am-5pm daily May-Aug, 11am-6pm Jul) is a private collection of hundreds of dolls – the personal achievement of Piippa Tandefelt. There's a café here serving delicious homemade apple pie. Next to the main quay, the **Jetty Barracks Gallery** (🕙 10am-5pm Tue-Sun) offers interesting temporary exhibitions.

Old bunkers, crumbling fortress walls and cannons are at the southern end of Susisaari island; poking around here gives the best impression of how the fortress once looked. Be careful with young children here, as there are some nasty drops. A torch will come in handy if you fancy exploring some of the tunnels.

The **church** on Iso Mustasaari island was built by the Russians in 1854. It's the only church in the world to double as a lighthouse – the beacon was originally gaslight but is now electric and is still in use.

Sleeping & Eating

Hostel Suomenlinna (☎ 684 7471; www.leirikoulut .com; Suomenlinna C9; dm €20, s/d/tr €40/50/75; reception 🕙 8am-9pm; ✗ 🖳) An interesting and enjoyable alternative to staying in central Helsinki is to bed down at this HI-affiliated hostel. Set in a historic building that was once a Russian primary school and later a barracks, it inevitably has a slightly dour feel, but has plenty of original character. The dormitories are high-ceilinged classrooms, while the private rooms upstairs have cosy sloping ceilings. There is a simple kitchen, as well as a laundry. It's very important to note that the warden doesn't live on the island, so you must check in during reception hours and remember to get the key code.

There are several good cafés and a couple of restaurants on Suomenlinna, or you could do as the locals do and bring a picnic (carrying enormous quantities of cider and beer will help you blend in) and find a peaceful spot among the ramparts. There's a small **supermarket** (🕙 8am-9pm Mon-Fri, 8am-6pm Sat, noon-9pm Sun) by the Suomenlinna Hostel that's open every day.

Suomenlinna Panimoravintola (☎ 228 5030; buffet lunch €11.50; 🕙 3-10pm Mon-Fri, noon-10pm Sat, noon-6pm Sun, closed Mon & Tue Jan-Mar) Further along at the main ferry quay, this is an excellent brewery-restaurant with a spectacular lunch buffet. Three types of beer are brewed here (a lager, an ale and a porter) and the enclosed courtyard terrace is a good place to enjoy one.

Walhalla (☎ 668 552; mains €26-30; 🕙 6pm-midnight Mon-Sat May–mid-Sep) This is the island's gourmet restaurant and bookings are advised. Its location on the southwest side of Susisaari offers views of passing passenger ships from its open terrace. It also has a bar and terrace open during the day.

Pizza Nikolai (pizzas €8-10; 🕙 noon-8pm Sun-Thu, noon-10pm Fri & Sat summer) Next door to Walhalla and run by it, this pizza place has a similarly memorable outlook but is cheaper and more relaxed.

Café Chapman (☎ 668 692; mains €6-12; 🕙 lunch Mon-Fri mid-Sep–Apr, lunch & dinner daily May-mid Sep) Near the dry dock on Susisaari is a pleasant café in an old stone storehouse. There's a busy terrace in summer.

Near Café Chapman, Café Piper is another good choice.

Getting There & Around

HKL ferries depart from the passenger quay at the kauppatori in Helsinki, opposite the Presidential Palace (return €3.60, 15 minutes, three times hourly, 6.20am to 2.20am). Buy tickets at the pier.

JT-Lines runs an hourly waterbus from the kauppatori to the King's Gate near the Walhalla restaurant (return €5.50, 30 minutes, mid-May to August). The first departure is from the kauppatori at 8am and the last departure is from Suomenlinna at 12.15am, except for Sunday, when the last service is at 8.30pm. Check current timetables online at www.jt-line.fi.

There's nowhere to hire bikes on the island, but they can be brought across on the ferries.

ESPOO

☎ 09 / pop 227,472

Espoo (Swedish: Esbo) is an independent municipality just west of Helsinki and while it officially ranks as the second-largest city in Finland, it is in reality a part of greater Helsinki, where much of its population works. It's a peaceful place with lots of water and green space and is very large and spread-out, with three centres and many suburbs, including Westend, with its exclusive waterside mansions. Espoo is one of the fastest-growing parts of Finland and has important technology industries of its own.

Sights & Activities

The most important sight in Espoo is **Gallen-Kallela Museum** (☎ 541 3388; www.gallen-kallela.fi; Gallen-Kallelantie 27; admission €8; � 10am-6pm mid-May–Aug, 10am-4pm Tue-Sat, 10am-5pm Sun Sep–mid-May), the pastiche studio-castle of Aleksi Gallen-Kallela, one of the most notable Finnish painters. The Art Nouveau building was designed by the artist and is now a museum of his work. Take tram 4 from central Helsinki to Munkkiniemi, then walk 2km or take bus 33 (Monday to Friday only).

Every architecturally minded person should visit **Otaniemi University** campus to see Aalto's main building and library, the Pietiläs' student building and Heikki Siren's chapel. **Tapiola** (Swedish: Hagalund), a modern shopping centre, was hailed in its day as a masterpiece of Finnish city planning.

The **Serena Water Park** (☎ 8870 5555; Tornimäentie 10; adult/child €17/13; �| 11am-8pm, closed 2 weeks in Sep) is one of Europe's best, with a cavalcade of pools, Jacuzzis, water-slides and facilities that will suit young and old. It's a great experience at any time of the year, especially during the cold winters, but in summer there are extra attractions outdoors. There's also a ski centre here in winter.

Espoo's annual **Jazz Festival** (☎ 8165 7234), held in late April, is top-notch.

NUUKSIO NATIONAL PARK

In the northwest district of Espoo, this small national park is an excellent opportunity to experience a bit of Finnish wilderness if your visit won't take you beyond the Helsinki area. Although so close to town, it's a typical slice of Finnish forest, with a multitude of lakes and ponds, and several walking trails.

You may see rare ospreys, grey-headed woodpeckers or black-throated divers on your strolls; the park is also a habitat to elk and nocturnal flying squirrels.

There's an **information centre** (☎ 020-564 4790; �| 9am-5.30pm Mon-Fri, 10am-4pm Sat & Sun mid-Apr–Sep) at the main Haukkalampi entrance to the park and an unstaffed nature exhibition in another cabin. Here or at the main national parks information centre in Helsinki you can book one of the two wilderness cabins (€9) in the park. There are also several free camping sites.

To get to Nuuksio, catch bus 85 from Espoo Centre. It drops you about 2km from the Haukkalampi centre. Helsinki Expert, in the main Helsinki tourist office, also runs regular excursions out there in summer.

Getting There & Away

You can catch buses to various parts of Espoo from the dedicated Espoo wing in the bus terminal in Helsinki. Local trains from Helsinki will drop you off at several stations, including central Espoo. Espoo also has its own bus system.

VANTAA

☎ 09 / pop 185,429

Vantaa, a large spread-out residential town that is essentially a satellite of Helsinki, is primarily of interest as the location of the Helsinki-Vantaa international airport. Vantaa is also home to **Heureka** (☎ 85799; www .heureka.fi; adult/child €18/11.50; �| 10am-5pm Mon-Wed & Fri, 10am-6pm Sat & Sun, 10am-8pm Thu), a fantastic hands-on science centre, IMAX theatre and planetarium next to the Tikkurila train station. To see the exhibitions only (without the theatre and planetarium) is €13.50/8.50.

HELSINKI

In early August, Vantaa is the venue for Ankkarock (www.ankkarock.fi), one of Finland's bigger rock festivals.

There is frequent local train and bus service between Helsinki and Vantaa, 19km to the north; see p83.

TUUSULAN RANTATIE

☎ 09

The **Tuusulan Rantatie** (Tuusula Lake Rd; www .tuusulanrantatie.com) is a narrow road along Tuusulanjärvi (Tuusula Lake), about a 30-minute drive north of Helsinki. The region attracted a number of artists during the National Romantic era of the early 20th century. Sibelius, as well as the Nobel Prize–winning novelist FE Sillanpää and the painter Pekka Halonen, worked here. A major stop along the 'museum road' is **Halosenniemi** (☎ 8718 3461; admission €5.50; ✆ 11am-5pm Tue-Sun, 11am-7pm May-Aug), the Karelian-inspired, log-built National Romantic studio of Halonen, with a walking trail through his lakeside garden.

Sibelius' home **Ainola** (☎ 287 322; www .ainola.fi; adult/child €5/1; ✆ 10am-5pm Tue-Sun May-Sep) is east of the lake near Järvenpää and is another popular stop with tour groups. The family home, designed by Lars Sonck and built on this beautiful forested site in 1904, contains original furniture, paintings, books and a piano owned by the Sibelius family. The graves of Jean Sibelius and his wife Aino are in the garden.

The main town in the area, Järvenpää, is a modern service centre with numerous restaurants and cafés but little to attract the traveller.

Sleeping & Eating

Hotelli Krapi (☎ 274 841; www.krapi.info; Rantatie 2; s/d €103/130, weekends & summer €72/90; P ✕) Thankfully this place doesn't live up to its name. It's an excellent independent hotel in what was once a cowshed; there's been a hotel here since 1883. It sits on the Tuusula Lake Road south of Halosenniemi and 30km north of Helsinki. It has great modern rooms, with bright colours and pine furnishings, three restaurants and a chance to steam up in a traditional sauna. Service and standards are excellent.

Järvenpään Matkailukeskus (☎ 7425 5200; www.matkailukeskus.com; Ståhlhanentie; tent sites €10-18, s €20, 4-person r €45, cabins €25-50; P ✕) A camp site in a great lakeside location 2.5km from Järvenpää with good-value HI-hostel and cabin accommodation.

Getting There & Away

Tuusulanjärvi is about 40km north of Helsinki. Take a local train to Kerava or Järvenpää or a bus to Hyrylä and proceed from there by bicycle.

PORVOO

☎ 019 / pop 46,793

An enduringly popular day or overnight trip from Helsinki, Porvoo (Swedish: Borgå), 50km east of Helsinki, is the second-oldest town in Finland after Turku. Officially it has been a town since 1346, but even before that Porvoo was an important trading centre.

There are three distinct sections to the city: the Old Town, the new town and the 19th-century Empire quarter, built Russian style under the rule of Tsar Nicholas I. The Old Town, with its tightly clustered wooden houses, cobbled streets and riverfront setting, is one of the most picturesque in Finland. During the day, its craft shops are bustling with visitors; if you can stay the night, you'll have it more or less to yourself. The old painted buildings are spectacular in the setting sun.

Information

North of the market square, Osuuspankki Bank has foreign exchange and an ATM.

Public library (☎ 520 2417; Papinkatu 20; ✆ 10am-8pm Mon-Fri, 10am-5pm Sat) Has free Internet terminals, which can be booked. There's also a terminal at the tourist office.

Tourist office (☎ 520 2316; www.porvoo.fi; Rihka-makatu 4; ✆ 9am-6pm Mon-Fri, 10am-4pm Sat & Sun early Jun-Aug, 9.30am-4.30pm Mon-Fri, 10am-2pm Sat Sep-early Jun) Plenty of good information including the informative and free *Porvoo* booklet.

Sights
PORVOO OLD TOWN

The Old Town district north of Mannerheiminkatu was largely built after the Great Fire of 1760. It's an alluring warren of narrow, winding cobblestone alleys and brightly coloured wooden houses. Craft boutiques and antique shops line the main roads, Välikatu and Kirkkokatu. For a glimpse of less touristed bits, head for the streets east of the cathedral; Itäinen

HELSINKI

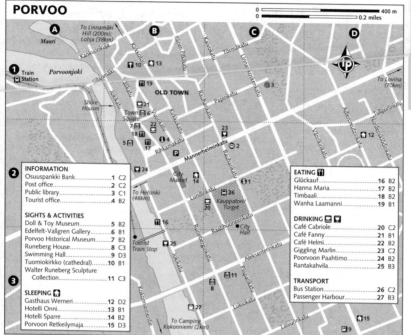

PORVOO

Pitkäkatu is one of the nicest. The distinctive row of **shore houses** along the Porvoonjoki were first painted with red ochre to impress the visiting King of Sweden, Gustavus III, in the late 18th century. They were originally used to store goods traded with German ships from the Hanseatic League, but many are now Porvoo's prime residential real estate.

The striking stone medieval **Tuomiokirkko** (cathedral; ☎ 66111; ☉ 10am-6pm Mon-Fri, 10am-2pm Sat, 2-5pm Sun May-Sep, 10am-2pm Tue-Sat, 2-4pm Sun Oct-Apr) dominates the Old Town and has an important place in Finnish history: this is where the first Diet of Finland assembled in 1809, convened by Tsar Alexander I, thus giving Finland religious freedom.

The **Porvoo Museum** (☎ 574 7500; Vanha Raatihuoneentori; combined admission adult/child €5/1; ☉ 10am-4pm Mon-Sat, 11am-4pm Sun May-Aug, 11am-4pm Wed-Sun Sep-Apr) is in two adjacent buildings on the beautiful cobbled Old Town Hall Square. The more interesting of the two is the **Edelfelt-Vallgren Museum**, with paintings by Albert Edelfelt and sculptures by Ville Vallgren, two of Porvoo's most famous artists. **Porvoo Historical Museum**, in the town hall building across the square, has old furniture and other paraphernalia. It was due to close for restoration for a period as this book went to press.

Doll & Toy Museum (☎ 582 941; Jokikatu 14; admission €2; ☉ 11am-3.30pm Mon-Thu & Sat, noon-3.30pm Sun Jun & Jul) houses over 800 dolls and other toys and is the largest museum of its kind in Finland.

There are **guided walking tours** of Old Porvoo at 2pm on Saturdays from early May to mid-September, leaving from the passenger harbour. In addition, from late June to late August, tours leave from the Porvoo Museum from Monday to Friday at 2pm. All tours last one hour, are in Finnish, Swedish and English, and cost €6.

RUNEBERG HOUSE
National poet Johan Ludvig Runeberg wrote the lyrics to the Finnish national anthem, Maamme-Laulu/Vårt Land (Our Country). His former home is a **museum** (☎ 581 330; Aleksanterinkatu 3; admission €5; ☉ 10am-4pm Mon-Sat, 11am-5pm Sun May-Aug, closed Mon & Tue Sep-Apr),

with an interior that has been preserved as it was. The **Walter Runeberg Sculpture Collection** (Aleksanterinkatu 5) has 150 sculptures by Walter Runeberg, JL Runeberg's eldest son. Opening hours are the same and admission is good for entry to both museums.

CRUISES

The M/S *Borgå* departs from the passenger harbour (€6, on the hour, 11am to 4pm, Tuesday to Sunday) and includes some historical commentary. If you have more time, archipelago cruises aboard M/S *Sandra* and M/S *Fredrika* depart on Tuesday, Wednesday, Thursday, Saturday and Sunday at noon from late June to early August (€12, four hours) and offer the chance to stop off at islands en route.

See opposite for details of Helsinki–Porvoo boat cruises.

Sleeping

Surprisingly, Porvoo is a little light on quality accommodation, perhaps because most people visit on day-trips from the capital. As well as the choices here, the tourist office can recommend a couple of one-room-only options around town.

Hotelli Onni (☎ 050-525 6446; www.hotelonni.fi; Kirkkotori 3; s/d €104/124; ⊠) With just four rooms, this boutique accommodation is Porvoo's most delightful. It's situated right opposite the cathedral in the heart of the old town, a wooden building set back from the street with an elegant terraced café. The rooms are beautifully decorated with luxuriant flair and style.

Porvoon Retkeilymaja (☎ 523 0012; www.porvoohostel.cjb.net; Linnankoskenkatu 1-3; dm/s/d €15/28/36; Ⓟ ⊠) This HI-affiliated hostel 800m southeast of Mannerheiminkatu is in a lovely old wooden house with spotless rooms, a grassy garden and a well equipped kitchen. It's a bit old school – the doors close between 10am (check-out time) and 4pm, and curfew is 11pm – but it's popular so book ahead in summer. There's a great indoor pool and sauna complex over the road.

Gasthaus Werneri (☎ 0400 494 876; gasthaus.werneri@dnainternet.net; Adlercreutzinkatu 29; s/d €35/50; ⊙ reception 10am-10pm; Ⓟ ⊠) This central guesthouse is run by a cheerful Finn and offers a variety of rooms with shared bathroom and access to kitchens. The rooms in the basement are spacious but a little

PAINTING THE TOWN RED

Colourful wooden houses are a feature of travel in Finland and other Nordic countries, but traditionally it wasn't just a matter of going down to the hardware store and picking your favourite colour. Originally, wooden buildings in Finland were uncoloured, but in the 18th century, red ochre paint began to become popular. This was mixed at home from iron and mineral extracts and protected buildings from the extreme winters for up to fifty years. It was an economical and accessible solution. Later, wealthier families began using expensive white, yellow and blue paints for their wooden houses, although this 'extravagance' was rarely extended to outbuildings.

dark; those upstairs are a better bet. There are also self-contained apartments available and a small grassy garden area.

Hotelli Sparre (☎ 584 455; www.avainhotellit.fi; Piispankatu 34; s/d €75/85, Sat, Sun & summer €70/80; ⊠) This is a central, well-kept hotel just off the main street, with friendly service and a sauna and restaurant. The rooms are done out in Finnish floral and are comfortable if not memorable.

Camping Kokonniemi (☎ 581 967; www.lomalitto.fi/kokonniemi; tent sites €11 plus €4 per person, 4-person cabins €65; ⊙ Jun-Aug) A camping ground 2km south of Porvoo town on the western side of the river, this is a good choice with plenty of greenery and a sauna, café and playground facilities.

Eating

Timbaali (☎ 523 1020; Välikatu 8; mains €11-26; ⊙ 11am-11pm, 11am-6pm Sun Sep-Apr) This is a rustic place with a summer garden, more formal interior and perfect Old Town ambience. The menu is broad but the speciality here is snails. They are done in a variety of ways and cost €10 to €12 for half a dozen. There's also a generous lunch buffet in summer.

Wanha Laamanni (☎ 523 0455; Vuorikatu 17; mains €20-26; ⊙ 10.30am-10pm) In the Old Judges' Chambers, this is the gourmet restaurant of Porvoo. It's in a splendid late-18th-century building with a fireplace for winter nights and a terrace for summer days. Game is a speciality, along with reindeer and Finnish fish dishes. There are also excellent vegetarian options, such as Jerusalem artichoke steak with mushroom risotto. There's live music at weekends in summer.

Glückauf (☎ 54761; mains €13-25; ☺ noon-11pm May-Sep) A 19th-century sailing ship moored on the eastern riverfront is the home of this boat restaurant. It specializes in seafood, and there's a cheaper 'terrace' menu (ie, you eat on the riverbank rather than the boat) from €7 to €13.

Hanna Maria (☎ 583 200; Välikatu 6; mains €5-10, steaks €9-15; ☺ 8am-5pm Mon-Sat, 10am-5pm Sun) Right in the old town, this cheap and cheerful lunchtime restaurant serves up no-nonsense Finnish food at cheap prices. It's by no means gourmet, but it more than does the job, particularly if you can nab a spot on the terrace.

CAFÉS
Quaint cafés are a speciality of Porvoo, particularly in the Old Town and on the waterfront.

Café Fanny (☎ 582 855; Välikatu 13; ☺ 10am-5pm, longer hr in summer) Try this café, on the beautiful cobbled Old Town square, for watching Porvoo drift by.

Cafe Helmi (☎ 524 5165; Välikatu 7; ☺ 10am-6pm Mon-Sat, 11am-6pm Sun, longer hr in summer) The elegant formality of this café recalls the time of the Tsars. Fittingly, it specializes in Russian-style high tea and fresh pastries.

Café Cabriole (☎ 523 2800; Piispankatu 30; ☺ 8.30am-6pm Mon-Sat) This large stylish old building on the west side of the market square is a good spot to indulge in a pastry or two. On weekdays, there's a good-value lunch buffet (€6.80) served from 11am to 2.30pm.

Drinking
Porvoon Paahtimo (☎ 617 040; Mannerheiminkatu 2) This place at the bridge is primarily a cosy bar although sandwiches and cakes are available. There's a good range of beers and a great little terrace hanging over the water.

Giggling Marlin (Mannerheiminkatu 16; ☺ 10pm-4am Wed-Sat) The liveliest of the nightclubs.

In summer, a number of terraces line the riverfront south of Mannerheimintie. One of the best is Rantakahvila (Beach Café),

with cheap drink, a range of fast food and a strangely diverse crowd.

Glory Days, in the Seurahovi Hotel on the east side of the market square, is another bar popular with young locals.

Getting There & Away
BOAT
The **M/S JL Runeberg** (☎ 524 3331; www.msjlruneberg.fi; adult one way/return €21/31, child €10/14), a former steamship, travels between Helsinki and Porvoo in summer and makes an excellent day trip. It leaves Helsinki daily (except Thursday) at 10am returning from Porvoo at 4pm, and arriving in Helsinki at 7.25pm. Since the trip takes four hours, you may want to return by bus or, on Saturdays in summer, on the vintage diesel train (adult/child combined ferry and train ticket €29/12).

An alternative is the modern, speedy M/S *King*, operated by **Royal Line** (☎ 09-612 2950; www.royalline.fi; one way/return €21/32). It travels from the Helsinki kauppatori at 10am daily bewteen late June and mid-August, returning from Porvoo at 3pm, taking three hours each way. It can be done as a day trip with an interesting archipelago cruise and two hours of sightseeing in Porvoo. The onboard lunch costs €12.

BUS
Buses depart for Porvoo from the Helsinki bus station every 30 minutes or so (€8.70, one hour) and there are frequent buses to/from towns further east, including Kotka (€12.70) and Lappeenranta (€25.40).

TRAIN
The old diesel **Porvoo Museum Train** (☎ 752 3262; one way/return €12/20) runs between Helsinki and Porvoo on Saturdays in July and August. The train departs from Helsinki at 10.16am and from Porvoo at 4.30pm and takes 1½ hours; purchase tickets at the Helsinki or Porvoo train station or on board the train. In Porvoo, the train runs to a final stop near the main bridge, about 1km past the old train station. The trip can also be combined with a cruise on the MS *JL Runeberg* (see Boat, above). It also does a trip from Porvoo to the village of Hinthaara between arrival from Helsinki and final departure.

South Coast

The southern coast of Finland extends west and east from Helsinki in two roughly equal stretches: one ending in a finger of land jutting into the Baltic towards Sweden, the other coming up short at the Russian border. For much of Finland's history it was the arena for these two powers to flex their muscles at each other, and this coastline, with its important harbours and fortresses, saw a good share of the action.

To this day the coastal settlements are a curious mixture. Kotka, an important industrial port, is near Hamina, whose quaint citadel shape gives it the feel of a quiet military museum. Hanko, on a peninsula, boasts luxurious tsarist villas, but was the scene of desperate fighting against the Russians in WWII. Nearby, you could be forgiven for thinking that the only artillery some of the peaceful Swedish-speaking seaside towns have ever seen is the starting gun for the annual regatta.

The whole coastline is a cartographer's nightmare. Speckled with thousands of islands and islets in a series of archipelagos, it is popular yachting territory and accessible by cruises from all the main towns along this coast.

The most enchanting places to visit on the south coast perhaps sound like unlikely attractions. A series of historic ironworks have been converted into beautiful rural retreats, with millstreams sparkling alongside the forge buildings, which these days are anything from museums to design shops. In the west, Fiskars and Fagervik stand out, while in the east, little Ruotsinpyhtää is equally beguiling.

This stretch of coast is the Finnish section of the Kuninkaantie, or King's Rd, a marked tourist route extending from Bergen in Norway to St Petersburg.

HIGHLIGHTS

- Staying overnight in one of Hanko's charming **Russian villas** (p102)

- Spending a summer evening at the **Mill Restaurant** (p106) in Ruotsinpyhtää

- Exploring the fascinating old ironworks at **Fiskars** (p99), where Finland's industrial age meets contemporary design

- Fly-fishing at the **Tsar's Imperial Fishing Lodge** (p110) at Langinkoski, near Kotka, or walking in the surrounding nature reserve

- Boating around the islands of Ekenäs **Archipelago National Park** (p99) or its equivalent near Kotka, the **Eastern Gulf** (p109)

History

In medieval times Sweden began exerting its influence in southwestern Finland and the signing of the Peace of Pähkinäsaari, an important peace treaty, with the rulers of Novgorod in 1323 established a border near St Petersburg that allowed for centuries of peaceful development along this coastline.

Extensive conflicts over the centuries with Russia and other Baltic powers led to various changes of the border zone and the fortification of many towns along the coast. Sweden lost part of the coast in the early 18th century, regained it again, only to lose the whole of Finland to Russia in 1809. Hanko became a popular place for the Russian aristocracy in summer, and the tsar fished at Kotka. Then came the Winter War and the Continuation War, which saw heavy fighting in the whole area. See p30 for more details.

Activities

The whole of the south coast is a boaties' paradise, with enormous numbers of islets forming chains of archipelagos. Nearly all towns offer summer cruises, good guest harbour facilities and the opportunity to charter a boat so you can find your own uninhabited spot. Alternatively, you might just fancy messing about in a hired canoe or rowboat; this can be done pretty much everywhere.

Fishing is popular here, as in many parts of Finland. The tsar did his casting on the Kymijoki river just north of Kotka. The sizeable Lohjanjärvi by the town of Lohja is a good venue for ice-fishing in winter and lake sports in summer.

The region is also good for cycling, with several marked routes along the Kuninkaantie (tourist route from Bergen to St Petersburg) both west and east from Helsinki.

Language

The south coast has a high number of Swedish speakers, who outnumber Finnish speakers in towns such as Ekenäs. This stretch of coastline is also popular with Swedish holidaymakers in summer, so it's one part of the country where you'll hear mostly Swedish spoken at that time of year.

Self-Catering Accommodation

The tourist offices and websites of most of the towns listed in this chapter have details of cottages available for rental. Another useful organization is **Suomen Eteläkarjen** (☎ 019-212 9200; www.southfinland.com) who have a portfolio of cottages in several south coast locations.

WEST OF HELSINKI

LOHJA

☎ 019 / pop 36, 218

The peaceful and friendly inland town of Lohja (Swedish: Lojo) is on the shores of Lohjanjärvi, by far the biggest lake in this southern segment of Finland. An easy daytrip from Helsinki, Lohja is well worth visiting, especially if you have a car and can explore the lakeside and the surrounding area – the stamping ground of Elias Lönnrot, compiler of the *Kalevala* epic.

Lohja, now within commuting distance from Helsinki, traditionally earned its living from two things: mining and apple-growing. Finland's oldest known iron-mining works were here, and it continues to be an important limestone extraction centre. The lime, so coveted by the building industry, also serves to enrich the soil for the growth of apples.

The **tourist office** (☎ 369 1309; www.lohja.fi; Karstuntie 4; ☉ 9am-6pm Mon-Fri, 9.30am-1.30pm Sat Jun-Aug, 9am-3pm Mon-Fri Sep-May) is near the main road junction in the centre of town. It has free Internet access. Buses stop at the station three blocks south of the tourist office on Laurinkatu.

Sights & Activities

The **Tytyri Mine Museum** (☎ 020-455 3945; admission €8; ☉ 11am-6pm daily Jun-Aug, noon-4pm Sat & Sun Sep-May) is an authentic limestone mine well worth visiting. An excellent descent into the bowels of the earth in a funicular takes you to the wide spaces below, where there are good information panels in English. Here, as elsewhere in Finland, new mine shafts were painted with tar to keep out devils. The deepest shaft measures 384m and is used to test elevators. The highlight of the visit is a short sound-and-light presentation looking into an awesomely large quarried cavern. It's cold

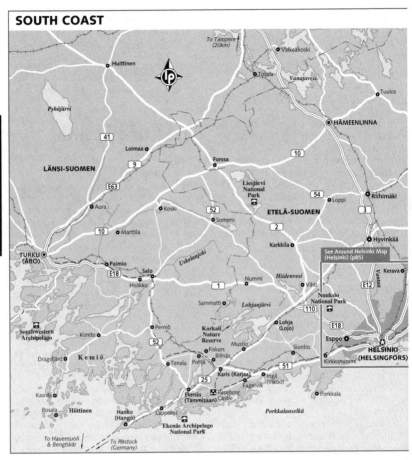

SOUTH COAST

in the mine, so take a jacket. The museum is 500m north of the town centre, past the tourist office.

Lohja's church, **Pyhän Laurin Kirkko** (☼ 9am–4pm May–mid-Aug, 10am–3pm mid-Aug–Apr) is in the heart of town. It has a great wooden belltower and some of the finest murals (not strictly frescoes) in the region. Rustic and charming in style, they sequentially depict stories from both Testaments and date from the early 16th century.

The **Lohja Museum** (☎ 369 4204; Iso-Pappila; admission €3.50; ☼ noon–4pm Tue-Sun, noon-7pm Wed) is a likeable little place with a collection of common household objects from different periods. Other buildings recreate a schoolhouse and a cowherd's cottage; there's also

an impressive range of horse-drawn carriages, including an old-style hearse. Every summer there's a different special exhibition on an aspect of local history.

There are some good nature trails around Lohja; the tourist office has maps and details. The lake is an obvious focus for sports: in summer there's canoeing and fishing, in winter ice-fishing and snowmobile safaris. Contact the tourist office for operators' details.

AROUND LOHJA

The shores of the lake in the area around Lohja are dotted with apple orchards. The tourist office has a booklet locating the orchards that produce their own apple and

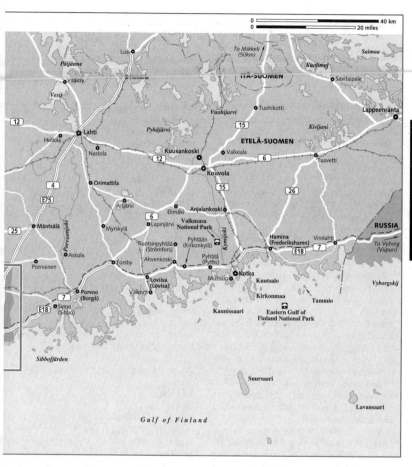

berry wines; one of the nicest is **Alitalo** (☎ 349 120; Pietiläntie 138), on Lohjansaari, which has a café and gentle farm animals for younger children.

Twenty-three kilometres west of Lohja, and 5km north of the village of Sammatti, just off Rd 104, is **Paikkarin Torppa** (☎ 356 659; admission €2.50; ☻ 11am-5pm mid-May–Aug). This pretty old wooden cottage was the birthplace of Elias Lönnrot, the compiler of the *Kalevala*. It has a large number of objects from his life, including his own *kantele* (Karelian stringed instrument). The setting (flowery meadows by a lake) is tempting picnic territory. There are many other sights on the Lönnrot 'trail' in this area.

Sleeping

Lohja is an easy day-trip from the capital, but there are a few sleeping options.

Hotelli Lohja (☎ 33221; www.personal.inet.fi/yri tys/hotellilohja; Laurinkatu 34; s/d €92/111; weekends & summer €69/89; ℗ ☒) Just across from the bus station, this hotel is Lohja's smartest option. Rooms are furnished cosily and there's friendly service.

Matkakoti Linnakangas (☎ 324 488; www.lin nakangas.com; Kauppakatu 3; s/d €32/45, d with bath €50; ☒) This comfortable and well-equipped guesthouse is in the centre of town, and has a variety of homely rooms with fridge, TV and toilet. Most rooms share a shower, while some have their own microwave; there's also a simple kitchen for guests' use.

Haikari Camping (☎ 0400 618 828; Haikarinkatu 4; s/d tent sites €10-13; ☺ Jun-Aug) This campsite is right on the lakeshore 2km southwest of town. There are kitchen facilities and a sauna, but no cabins. Next door is a summer restaurant with a great terraced garden.

Eating & Drinking

Lohja's eating choices are limited, but it boasts two memorable pubs.

Kahvila Liisa (☎ 312 581; Laurinkatu 61; ☺ 10am-4pm Mon-Fri, 9am-2pm Sat) In a pretty yellow wooden building, this café has a little outdoor terrace where you can enjoy tasty *karjalanpiirakka* (rice-filled savoury pastry) and excellent quiche. In the same building is a shop, Tuulentupa, selling attractive handicrafts and souvenirs.

Caballo Bayo (☎ 312 899; Kauppakatu 8; mains €7-20; ☺ lunch & dinner) This upstairs restaurant is one of Lohja's best and does a range of Spanish and Tex-Mex dishes. There's a charming wooden rooftop terrace, perfect at sunset. The grilled fresh fish is a favourite at €12.70.

Opus K (☎ 0500 476 632; Kauppakatu 6; ☺ 3pm-1am Tue-Thu, 4pm-2am Fri, noon-2am Sat) One of Finland's best pubs, it feels like a bibliophile's living room – lined floor to ceiling with books, which you can browse through while relaxing on the comfy chairs and sofas. Ask the owner to recommend a beer; he's always got something great on tap from an obscure Finnish microbrewery!

Kaljaasi (☎ 040-522 6612; ☺ weekends from May-end June, then daily until mid-Aug) This bar doesn't have an address, because it's on a floating platform way out in the middle of the lake and only reachable by boat. It's a stupendous spot to sit and drink . You can hire or charter boats in Lohja (ask the tourist office), or they'll pick you up from Virkkala, a village 7km southwest of town for €10 each way.

Getting There & Away

There are buses that run hourly from Helsinki to Lohja (€8.40, one hour). There are also buses from Lohja to Salo and Turku, and to Ekenäs and Hanko on the south coast.

INGÅ

☎ 019 / pop 5152

Ingå (Finnish: Inkoo) is a tiny, attractive and predominantly Swedish-speaking seaside town. There's a little marina, with a library and café, a pottery workshop, and not much else, apart from the church.

St Nicholas Church (☺ 8am-4pm Mon-Fri year-round, also 9am-6pm Sat & Sun May-Aug) was founded in the 13th century. There are beautiful frescoes over the altar, but most striking is the Dance of Death frieze opposite the entrance door. In this frieze, grinning Reapers escort various members of society to the afterlife; all are equal in death. Across the river is **Ingå Gammelgård**, the local museum.

About 8km west of Ingå is **Fagervik Ironworks** (☎ 295 151; Rd 105), one of the most attractive *bruks* (early ironworks precinct) in Finland. It was established in 1646 and helped to develop the region before anyone had thought of tourism. The Russian army destroyed the area during the Great Northern War in the 1720s, but the factory was later rebuilt before ultimately closing in 1902. The site, perfect for a bit of light strolling, features an 18th-century wooden church beautifully located by a lake, a privately owned manor, two restored blacksmith forges, the remnants of an orangery, and a resident ghost, the enigmatic Blue Lady. There's a café and an exhibition of the history of the ironworks

Ingå is southwest of Helsinki on road 51. There are several daily bus connections.

EKENÄS

☎ 019 / pop 14,521

The seaside town of Ekenäs (Finnish: Tammisaari) is a quiet resort, popular with Finnish and Swedish holidaymakers and families. It's relaxed and elegant, with avenues of wooden buildings, particularly in its well-preserved Old Town, which is delightful. Mostly Swedish-speaking, it makes a restful stop and a good place to explore parts of the adjacent Ekenäs Archipelago National Park.

It's one of Finland's oldest towns – King Gustav Vasa conceived of it in 1546 as a trading port to rival Tallinn in Estonia. The idea failed, and many local business people were soon forcibly transferred to the newly founded Helsinki. These days it makes its livelihood from tourism and fishing, and there is an army base on the edge of town.

Information

Café Carl de Mumma (☎ 241 4640; Rådhustorget; ☺ 9am-5pm) Café and bakery with Internet terminals.

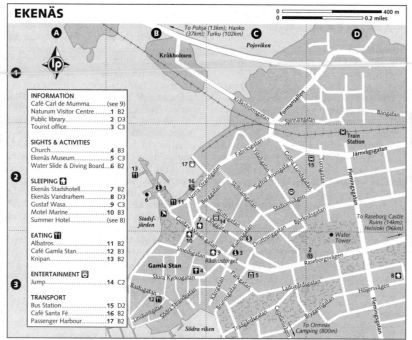

EKENÄS

INFORMATION
Café Carl de Mumma..........(see 9)
Naturum Visitor Centre........**1** B2
Public library.........................**2** D3
Tourist office.........................**3** C3

SIGHTS & ACTIVITIES
Church.................................**4** B3
Ekenäs Museum...................**5** C3
Water Slide & Diving Board...**6** B2

SLEEPING
Ekenäs Stadshotell...............**7** B2
Ekenäs Vandrarhem..............**8** D3
Gustaf Wasa.......................**9** C3
Motel Marine......................**10** B3
Summer Hotel....................(see 8)

EATING
Albatros.............................**11** B2
Café Gamla Stan.................**12** B3
Knipan...............................**13** B2

ENTERTAINMENT
Jump.................................**14** C2

TRANSPORT
Bus Station.........................**15** D2
Café Santa Fé.....................**16** B2
Passenger Harbour..............**17** B2

SOUTH COAST

Naturum Visitor Centre (☎ 241 1198; 10am-8pm May-Aug) Detailed information on Ekenäs Archipelago National Park, including a free slide show and ecoexhibits.

Public library (☎ 263 2700; Raseborgsvägen 6-8; 10am-7pm Mon-Fri, 10am-2pm Sat) Has free Internet terminals.

Tourist office (☎ 263 2100; www.ekenas.fi; Rådhustorget; 8.30am-6pm Mon-Fri, 10am-2pm Sat summer, 8.30am-5pm Mon-Fri autumn-spring) Friendly with free Internet terminal. Offers information for the entire southwest region.

Sights & Activities

The well-preserved **Gamla Stan** (Old Town) features wooden houses from the late 18th and early 19th centuries. They line narrow streets that are named after hatters, comb-makers and other artisans who once worked in the precinct. Some buildings contain artisans' shops, which are open in summer. The oldest buildings are on Linvävaregatan. Most of the buildings in Gamla Stan are named after types of fish, as this area was originally a small fishing village.

The stone **church** (10am-6pm May-Aug), in Gamla Stan has a tower that can be seen from most parts of town. It was built between 1651 and 1680, damaged in the fire of 1821, and renovated in 1990.

The main building of the **Ekenäs Museum** (☎ 020-775 2240; Gustav Wasas gatan 11; admission €2; 11am-5pm summer), built in 1802, depicts how a wealthy artisan family in the 1800s would have lived. Other buildings have temporary exhibitions of modern art and photography, and permanent displays on local history, including a re-creation of a fishing village.

Bicycles can be hired from the **marina** (☎ 241 1790) or Café Santa Fé. Rent rowing boats (€10/20 per half/full day) and bikes (€10 per day) at **Ormnäs Camping** (☎ 241 4434).

Tours

The former steamship **M/S Sunnan II** (☎ 241 1850; www.surfnet.fi/saaristoristeilyt) offers archipelago cruises daily in summer, departing from the passenger harbour. Cruises range from two hours (€10) to six hours (€45), and sometimes include meals.

The **M/S Panda** (☎ 0400 468 512) sails on Saturdays in July and August to the island of Rodjan (€15, three hours), and on Sundays

SOUTH COAST

to Jussarö (€20, five hours). Both departures are from North Harbour at 1pm.

Sleeping

The tourist office has details of numerous weekly cottage rentals or overnight home-stay accommodation in Ekenäs and the surrounding area.

Ekenäs Vandrarhem (☎ 241 6393; ekenas@vandrar hem.inet.fi; Höijersvägen 10; dm from €12.50, s/d €22/29; ✆ reception 3-9pm mid-May–mid-Aug; P ✗) An HI-affiliated summer hostel, this place offers tidy, modern apartment-style rooms (four rooms share a kitchen and bathroom). Breakfast is an extra €4.50 and sheets are €3.50 if you need them. There's a sauna and a laundry. On the same site is a **summer hotel** (s/d €32/49). The apartments are the same, but breakfast and bed linen are included.

Ekenäs Stadshotell (☎ 241 3131; www.stadsho tell.nu; Norra Strandgatan 1; s/d €67/87; P ✗ ⛽) This place is a little dated but still the top hotel in town – rates include breakfast and sauna. It's got a seaside-resort feel being very close to the beach and to most of the action. It's also pretty family-friendly. All double rooms have balconies, and suites are a fairly good deal at €114. The restaurant also has some great duck and game dishes.

Gustaf Wasa (☎ 241 3020; www.gustaf-wasa.nu; Rådhustorget; s/d from €68/86; ✗) With just 10 rooms, this is a small hotel overlooking the market square. The rooms are modern, with comfortable furnishings and small bathrooms. Breakfast is included. Rates drop by about 20% in winter. There's also a cottage available to rent in summer.

Motel Marine (☎ 241 3833; www.motelmarine.fi; Kammakaregatan 4-6; s €45-80, d €65-100; P ✗ ⛽) This is a shabby-looking weatherboard complex, but the rooms are OK and vary in price and quality. Some of them have a simple kitchen and there's also an apartment with a private sauna. It's very close to the beach and has a pretty laissez-faire management style. Breakfast is included.

Ormnäs Camping (☎ 241 4434; www.ek-camping .com; sites per person/tent €6.50/11, 2-/4-person cottages €29/47; ✆ May-Sep) At the seaside, 1km from the town centre, this camping ground is next to Ramsholmen Nature Park. There's a café, and bikes (€10 per day) and boats (€20 per day) can be rented here. The reception is only open until 6pm, so if you need a cottage, arrive before then.

Eating

There are several good cafés and restaurants around the main square, Rådhustorget, including pizzerias and Chinese restaurants. Café Carl de Mumma is a bakery and café serving inexpensive sandwiches, cakes and pastries.

Knipan (☎ 241 1169; mains €17-22; ✆ 11am-midnight Mon-Fri, noon-midnight Sat & Sun May–mid-Sep) Knipan, in the old wooden building erected in the harbour in 1867 (see Entertainment following for details), is the best summer restaurant in town. There's an excellent à la carte menu with such temptations as tournedos and salmon, and there's also a substantial lunch buffet (€10.30/17.20 with/without hot dishes). The little terrace, with water lapping all around, is a great spot.

Café Gamla Stan (☎ 241 5656; Bastugatan 5; ✆ 11am-6pm May, 11am-8pm Jun-Aug) This is a beautiful garden café in the Old Town. The small house is a bit hard to find and has just a few seats in the creeper-swathed garden, but is worth the effort. There's also a craft shop and live music in the garden during summer.

Albatros (☎ 241 2848; Stallörsparken; pasta €10-13, steaks €16-20; ✆ 10am-midnight May-Aug) By the harbour, this does a booming business in takeaway hamburgers, hot dogs and ice cream during summer. It also has a restaurant and fine sheltered terrace right opposite the kids' playground and beach, so you can keep an eye on them. They have DJs on some summer evenings.

Entertainment

Jump (☎ 246 1676; Långgatan 14) This is the main nightclub in town, and pretty lively in summer. DJs mostly play crowd-pleasers, recent hits and pop classics, to keep everyone happy.

Knipan (see Eating) becomes a dance club at night; this means elegant ballroom-style Finnish tangos and foxtrots. It was built on poles over the water because local laws allowed only one bar on town ground. There's live music on summer evenings and a floating beer terrace.

Getting There & Away

Ekenäs is 96km southwest of Helsinki on road 25. There are five to seven buses a day from Helsinki (€13.70, 1½ hours), Turku

(€16.20, two hours) or Hanko (€8.70, 30 minutes).

Trains to Ekenäs coming from Helsinki and Turku go via Karis (Finnish: Karjaa) where a change is required. Seven to nine daily trains run from Helsinki (€16.70, 1½ hours) and Turku (€19, 1½ hours), both continuing on to Hanko. Some connections from Ekenäs to Karis involve a railbus.

AROUND EKENÄS
Raseborg Castle

The Raseborg Castle ruins (Finnish: Raasepori), dating from the late 14th century, are extremely impressive, perched on a rock and towering over a grassy sward. The castle was of great strategic importance in the 15th century, when it protected the trading town of Tuna. Karl Knutsson Bonde, three times king of Sweden, was one of its most prominent residents. By the mid-16th century, Raseborg's importance had declined, and it was unoccupied for more than 300 years. The castle features in a famous Finnish children's ditty.

The **castle** (☎ 234 015; admission €1; ⌚ 10am-8pm) is 14km east of Ekenäs, and about 2km west of the wonderfully-named village of Snappertuna. It's signposted Slottsruiner/Linnanrauniot off the main road. You buy your tickets at the café (which does excellent *korvapuusti* – cinnamon rolls). You won't find a great deal of explanatory stuff, but it's great to climb up and down the levels, and patrol the ramparts; this is a proper fortress, with no soft edges. There are free tours from mid-May to August at weekends at 3pm. During July there are evening concerts at Raseborg; contact the Ekenäs tourist office for details. There are occasional buses to Snappertuna from Ekenäs or Karis.

The HI-affiliated **Snappertuna Youth Hostel** (☎ 019-234 180; Kyrkoväg 129; dm/d €17/28; P 🚫), in the village, is a quiet alternative to staying in Ekenäs. There are two simple cottages sleeping up to four each, as well as a kitchen.

Ekenäs Archipelago National Park

The beautiful archipelago that surrounds Ekenäs includes a scattering of some 1300 islands, 50 sq km of which is national park. The best way to visit the park is by boat from Ekenäs harbour.

If you visit the island of Älgö, you can see the old fishing house, use the cooking facilities or stay overnight at the camping ground. There are also camping grounds on the islands of Fladalandet and Modermagan. Visit the Naturum Visitor Centre in Ekenäs for more information about the park.

There are various cruises (see Tours p97) that visit some of the islands in the archipelago, but to really explore it, you'll need your own boat. Charter boats include the **M/S Kennedy** (☎ 0400 470 751) and **M/S Johanna** (☎ 0400 541 9480).

FISKARS
☎ 019 /pop about 200

Northeast of Ekenäs along road 111 is the village of Pohja, the centre of an area known for its historic ironworks. Several small *bruk* villages in this area can be visited in a day, but the most outstanding by far is Fiskars (Swedish: Fiskari), a beautiful riverside village where the old brick buildings have been transformed into shops, galleries, design studios and cafés. During the last few years, Fiskars has gained a reputation as a centre of modern Finnish art and design, creating an absorbing mix of the old and the new.

The *bruk* was first established on the Fiskars River in 1649, and the village grew up around it. The works mainly produced farming equipment, chiefly ploughs – more than a million horse-ploughs came out of here in the 19th century. In 1816 the mansion that housed the owner of the *bruk* was built, and this is still the centrepiece of the village. A number of other buildings were designed by German architect Carl Engel. Although manufacturing operations have long moved on, the Fiskars Company still produces its world-famous scissors and cutlery, which can be purchased in the village.

There's a **tourist information office** (☎ 277 7504; www.fiskarsvillage.net; ⌚ 10am-6pm Mon-Sat May-end Aug) located in the workers' tenement buildings, near the distinctive clock-tower building.

Sights

The best way to see Fiskars is on foot, starting from the western (Pohja) end, with the river on your right. The first building on the left is the **assembly hall**, built in 1896 as a public hall. Just beyond and opposite, encircled by a stream, is the **granary** (1902), which now hosts various art, design and history exhibitions. Behind it is the **copper Forge** (1818), with more exhibition space, a glass studio and a good restaurant with a riverside terrace. Continuing along the road, you pass the **stone house**, the mansion originally occupied by factory owner John Julin, the old **mill**, and the distinctive **clock-tower building**. It now houses shops, galleries and a café. Where the road forks is the marketplace with stalls, a café and terrace in summer. Continuing along the unpaved road towards Degersjojärvi, you pass more workers' housing and what remains of Fiskars ironworks.

Near the lake is **Fiskars Museum** (☎ 237 013; admission €2.50; ☻ 11am-4pm May-Sep, 1-4pm Sat & Sun Oct-Mar), which explains the fascinating local history of the ironworks and village. Every season there is a different exhibition, as well as a special one at Christmas.

Throughout the village are numerous design and craft shops, generally open in summer from 11am to 6pm, and at weekends during the rest of the year. The village website www.fiskarsvillage.net has a full listing.

Sleeping & Eating

Fiskars can be visited as a day trip from Helsinki, or anywhere in this section, but it also has a hotel and some boutique B&B accommodation.

Villiruusu/Wildrose B&B (☎ 237 033; villiruusu@ kolumbus.fi; Långdalintie 3; s/d €50/65; **P** ✗) This is a lovely guesthouse in a beautifully decorated wooden building. The two rooms are blissfully comfortable, one romantically kitted out in royal blue, the other in florals; they share a bathroom. If a family or group books both rooms, they get the whole upper floor at their disposal. The whole feeling is like being in one of those beautiful houses in an Ingmar Bergman film – minus the introspection of course! The breakfast is excellent. There's free use of bicycles and a rowboat on the lake nearby.

Fiskars Wärdshus (☎ 276 6510; warssy@wardshus.inet.fi; s/d from €120/150; **P** ✗) This noble old building was erected in 1836 and is the most luxurious place to stay in Fiskars. The 15 newly-renovated rooms don't quite evoke the building's history

but are undeniably comfortable, with beautiful modern fittings made from pine and elm by local craftsmen. There's also an excellent à la carte restaurant with a great terrace.

Restaurant Kuparipaja (☎ 237 045; mains €12-20; ☻ lunch & dinner) This is a good à la carte restaurant (try the bison and moose sausages if you're in carnivore mode), in one of the old copper forge buildings, as well as a café-bar dispensing filled rolls, pasta dishes and a salad buffet. There's a charming terrace overhanging the river. The lunch buffet is €16.

In the clock-tower building, **Café Antique** (☎ 237 275; ☻ 11am-6pm May-Sep) has books and is a good spot for coffee and a light meal. There's also a café set up at the market square over summer.

HANKO

☎ 019 / pop 9905

Hanko (Swedish: Hangö), on a long sandy peninsula, blossomed as a spa town in the late 19th and early 20th centuries, when it was a glamorous retreat for Russian nobles, tsars and artists. The grand seaside villas built by these wealthy summer visitors are now the town's star attraction – locals refer to them as 'the old ladies', as each has been given a woman's name. Many now operate as guesthouses; they are Finland's most unique accommodation and very popular with tourists in summer. The row of restaurants by the marina is a memorable and beautiful spot to eat in summer, with great outdoor tables and intimate interiors.

History

Even before Hanko, the southernmost town in Finland, was founded in 1874, the peninsula was an important anchorage. Hanko has also been a major point of departure from Finland. Between 1881 and 1931, about 250,000 Finns left for the USA and Canada via the Hanko docks.

At the end of the Winter War, the March 1940 peace treaty with Russia required Finland to cede to them the Hanko peninsula as a naval base. The Russians moved in with a garrison of 30,000 and constructed a huge network of fortifications. After several bloody naval engagements, Hanko eventually was abandoned in December 1941, having been isolated from the Russian frontlines. The citizens of Hanko returned to their damaged town the next spring.

Orientation

The East Harbour is the centre of the town's activity in summer, the West Harbour handling only commercial traffic. Russian villas are on Appelgrenintie, east of East Harbour. Most things are within walking distance of the adjacent bus and train stations.

Information

Park Café (☎ 248 6182; Appelgrenintie 11; ☽ May-Sep) Has a free Internet terminal.

Public library (☎ 220 3380; Vuorikatu 3-5; ☽ 11am-7pm Mon-Wed, 11am-3pm Thu, 9am-3pm Fri, also 11am-2pm Sat in winter) Has several Internet terminals.

Tourist office (☎ 220 3411; www.hanko.fi; Raatihuoneentori 5; ☽ 8am-4pm Mon-Fri Sep-May, 9am-8pm Mon-Fri, 10am-6pm Sat & Sun Jun-Jul, 9am-5pm Mon-Fri, 10am-6pm Sat & Sun Aug) In the town hall building.

Sights & Activities

Take a lift to the top of the 50m landmark **water tower** (admission €1; ☽ noon-6pm Jun-Jul, 1-3pm Aug) on Vartiovuori Hill for an excellent view across town and out to sea. The nearby neo-Gothic **Hanko Church** (☽ noon-6pm Jul-early Aug, 1-3pm rest of Aug), built in 1892, was damaged in WWII but has been thoroughly renovated.

Hanko Museum (☎ 220 3228; Nycanderinkatu 4; adult/child €2/0.50; ☽ 11am-4pm Tue-Sun & 6-7pm Thu mid-May–Aug, shorter hr winter) is the town museum housed in the brick-and-stone building near East Harbour, with a smattering of local (especially military) history and changing exhibitions.

Hanko is quite an artistic community, and there are some half a dozen **art galleries** scattered around town, including changing exhib-itions in the **town hall**. The tourist office has details of current exhibitions.

Hanko has 30km of sandy beaches. The beach from Merikatu to the Casino is the best – it even has Victorian-style changing boxes. The next beach, behind the tennis courts, is especially good for kids, with a playground, monitors and a rotary swing in the bay.

Where Bulevardi meets the beach is the **Monument of Liberty**, commemorating the landing of liberating German forces in 1918. The monument was taken down after WWII, but re-erected in 1960 with new text.

Bicycles are ideal for exploring the parkland and Russian villas east of the town centre – a ride or walk out to Neljän Tuulen Tupa on Little Pine Island is a good excursion. Bikes can be hired at **SunFun Hanko** (☎ 248 6699; www.sunfun.fi) at the East Harbour, **Café Plage** (☎ 248 2776) or **Paul Feldt's bicycle shop** (☎ 248 1860; Tarhakatu 4) in the town centre. SunFun also rents mopeds, rowboats, canoes and water-skiing gear.

At **Tennisranta**, just beyond the Casino, there are eight outdoor tennis courts available to rent.

EAST OF HANKO

Twenty kilometres east of Hanko, and just off the Ekenäs highway, the **Front Museum** (☎ 244 3068; adult/child €3/1; ☽ 11.30am-6.30pm May–mid-Sep) covers Finland's wartime involvement, specifically relating to this battlefront. There are original trenches, some foundations, a scattering of artillery and an extensive tent exhibition. Although a serious subject, the use of shop dummies gives the exhibition a mildly comic aspect.

Cruises

The most interesting short cruise from Hanko is the 1¾-hour trip to Hauensuoli. The **M/S Marina** (☎ 0400 536 930; www.hk-service.fi; fare €15) or **SunFun Charter** (☎ 248 6699) departs from East Harbour daily from May to August at 1pm and includes commentary in English, Finnish and Swedish.

From mid-June to the end of August, several boats offer day cruises to the island of Bengtskär (p104), all departing from East Harbour. The cruises include lunch and entrance to the island. **M/S Summersea** (☎ 0400 536 930; www.hk-service.fi; adult/child €46/19) sails at 10.30am, with an extra departure at 2pm in July. **M/S Anna** (☎ 469 2500; adult/child €46/20) departs at 11am. **M/Y Marilyn** (☎ 040-728 9539; per person €48, or without lunch €42) operates from July to mid-August, departing at 10am. The cruises last between four and a half (the Marilyn) and seven (the Anna) hours.

All cruises should be booked in advance with the company or the tourist office.

Festivals & Events

Since Hanko claims to have Finland's largest marina, it's hardly surprising that the most important annual event is the **Hanko Regatta** in which more than 200 boats compete. The

SOUTH COAST

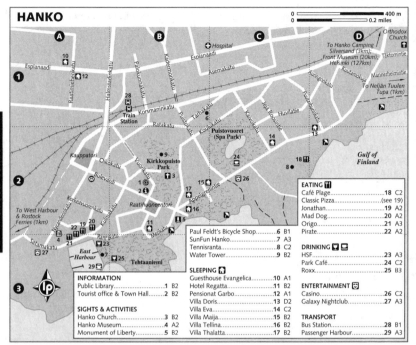

HANKO

0 ——— 400 m
0 ——— 0.2 miles

To Hanko Camping
Silversand (3km);
Front Museum (20km);
Helsinki (127km)

To Neljän Tuulen
Tupa (1km)

Orthodox
Church

Gulf of
Finland

Kauppatori

Kirkkopuisto
Park

Puistovuoret
(Spa Park)

To West Harbour
& Rostock
Ferries (1km)

East
Harbour

Tehtaaniemi

regatta takes place on the first weekend of July, attracts thousands of spectators and has a real carnival atmosphere.

Sleeping

Accommodation can be tight in the summer months, so book ahead. Prices go up during the regatta.

GUESTHOUSES & HOTELS

Pensionat Garbo (☎ 040-542 1732; fax 248 7897; Esplanaadi 84; s/d/family €30/65/100; P ☒) This quirky place is essentially a shrine to the golden age of celluloid kitsch; each room commemorates a particular Hollywood star. It has an outdoor barbecue and kitchen facilities, as well as a beautiful breakfast salon. The helpful owner also has a cottage outside Hanko available for weekly rental.

Guesthouse Evangelica (☎ 248 6923; www .evangelica.net; Esplanaadi 61; s/d from €32/51, with bathroom €46/64; P ☒ 🚴) Diagonally opposite Pensionat Garbo is this guesthouse. Part of a school complex, but open year-round, there are two buildings. The newer wing has rooms with clean, cute bathrooms, Aalto furniture

and a crisp Nordic feel. The older wing has rooms with shared bathrooms, which are also good-value. There are kitchenettes for guests' use, and breakfast is available.

Hotel Regatta (☎ 248 6491; www.surfnet.fi/regatta; Merikatu 1; s €64-80, d €81-115; P ☒) The only standard hotel in Hanko, this is a likeable place despite its somewhat shabby exterior. It's popular with tour groups and conferences. Breakfast is included in the rates and there's the obligatory sauna. You'll pay a little more for rooms with sea views. The bar gets pretty rowdy on Saturday nights.

VILLAS

A unique feature of Hanko is its selection of old Russian-style villas that have been meticulously renovated and converted into guesthouses.

Villa Maija (☎ 248 2900; www.villamaija.fi; Appelgrenintie 7; s/d from €76/96, d with shared bathroom €85; ☽ mid-Apr–mid-Oct; P ☒) This place, built in 1888, is a real beauty, with stunning French windows opening onto ornate verandahs. There's a big variety of rooms, some of which have sea views and a Jacuzzi, and there's a great little breakfast terrace and a sauna. Some of the rooms are in a couple of other villas in the same compound.

Villa Doris (☎ 248 1228; Appelgrenintie 23; s/d from €50/72; **P** ⊠) A charming *pensionat* dating from 1881, contains old furniture from various decades in all the rooms, which share bathrooms. It's homely and friendly, open all year, and the rates are much cheaper off-season. Breakfast is included.

Villa Tellina (☎ 248 6356; www.tellina.com; Appelgrenintie 2; s/d from €50/75, with bathroom from €60/90; ☺ Jun–mid-Aug; **P** ⊠) Right by the beach, this ramshackle place has basic but comfortable rooms with lots of character. The same owners run **Villa Eva** (☎ 248 6356; Kaivokatu 2) and **Villa Thalatta** (☎ 248 6356; Appelgrenintie 1), so there's a huge variety of room types and prices. Best bet for a room during busy periods.

CAMPING

Hanko Camping Silversand (☎ 248 5500; www .lomaliitto.fi; Hopeahietikko; tent sites €13.50, 2-person cabin €43-52, 4-person cabin €52-60; 6-8-person cottage €60-76; ☺ Jun-Aug) About 3km northeast of the town centre, this place is set on a long beach. There's also a **motel** (s/d €56/78; ☺ year-round; **P**) and a café and sauna.

Eating

The place to eat is at East Harbour, where a row of quaint red wooden buildings house a cluster of gourmet fish restaurants, all with crowded terraces. There are also cheaper pizza places and a grilli. The only one of these open all year is HSF (see p104).

Jonathan (☎ 248 7742; Satamakatu 15; mains €16-25; ☺ 11am-midnight May-Aug) With a maritime-themed dining room upstairs, and a terrace and bar, this restaurant (named after the seagull) is a good choice. There are small but tasty tapas portions (€3 to €4), snails in delicious garlic butter (€8.20), and great salmon and roast chicken mains. The service is good here. Adjacent and under the same management is **Classic Pizza** with reasonably priced pizzas.

Origo (☎ 248 5023; Satamakatu 7; mains €15-18; ☺ 11am-10pm mid-Apr–mid-Oct) This is a charming place and one of the best fish restaurants. It's certainly the most elegant on this strip, with a candlelit interior; its back bar is open until 3am.

Pirate (☎ 248 3006; Satamakatu 13; mains €8-18; ☺ 11am-1am Easter–mid-Sep) One of the most popular restaurants here with a dark interior and large terrace. It's a down-to-earth place with gruff service, occasional live music and big portions.

Neljän Tuulen Tupa (House of the Four Winds; ☎ 248 1455; ☺ mid-May–mid-Aug) This place on Little Pine Island, 1.5km east of the town centre, is where folks went to imbibe so-called 'hard tea' (alcohol) during the Finnish prohibition (1919–32). At the time, Field Marshal CGE Mannerheim had his summer cottage on the neighbouring island. He found the merry-making disturbing and solved the problem by buying the whole joint in 1926. He fired the chef, imported tea sets from France and ran the place himself until 1931. Little Pine Island is now connected to the mainland by a bridge and has a beautiful café and summer terrace perched over the water.

Café Plage (☎ 248 2776; Tennisranta; ☺ Jun-Aug) This is a simple café/bar right on the beach and away from the bustle of the harbour area. It does simple food, has minigolf and tennis nearby, and is on the best stretch of sand in the area for children.

For something cheap, **Mad Dog** (☎ 248 3030; Eastern Harbour; ☺ to 1am or later May-Aug) is a grilli and pub with a small terrace. It's a good spot for hamburgers and sandwiches with a beer.

Drinking & Entertainment

Casino (☎ 248 2310; www.hangoncasino.fi; Appelgrenintie 10; ☺ May-Aug) The imposing green-and-white casino, between Spa Park and the beach, is a classic seaside venue and Hanko's most famous nightspot. It has plenty of class and charm; there's music, dancing and a roulette table, and the cover charge depends on what's on. The restaurant here is good, with pepper steaks, salmon and the like for €15 to €22.

Park Café (☎ 248 6182; Appelgrenintie 11; ☺ May-Sep) This place, opposite the Casino in Spa Park, is an excellent Belgian café-bar with a casual atmosphere and free Internet access. The terrace, shaded by lofty pines, is a great place to relax.

Galaxy Nightclub (☎ 248 7700; Satamakatu 2; ☺ 10pm-3am Wed-Sun, till 4am Sat) When it gets late, the sophisticated youth of Hanko head here. The DJs are as close to cutting edge as it gets in a Finnish beach resort, with dance music usually prevailing over Europop.

Some good summertime beer terraces include **Roxx** (☎ 248 4393), which often has live music in summer, and the 2nd floor of **HSF** (☎ 248 2264), both at East Harbour. HSF, the sailing club, also has a good restaurant with large windows looking out over the marina.

Getting There & Away
BOAT
The **M/S Franz Höijer** (☎ 241 1850; www.surfnet .fi/saaristoristeilyt) travels between Hanko and Turku (then on to Uusikaupunki the next day) at 10am on Thursdays from mid-May to mid-August. (€12, eight hours one way). From Turku, the boat departs at 10am on Wednesdays, arriving in Hanko at 6pm.

Superfast Ferries has an international service to Rostock in Germany from Western Harbour (see p347).

BUS
There are regular (two to six) daily express buses to/from Helsinki (€21.30, 2¼ hours) via Ekenäs (€8.70, 30 minutes).

TRAIN
Seven to nine trains travel daily from Helsinki and Turku to Karis (Finnish: Karjaa) where they are met by connecting trains or buses to Hanko (via Ekenäs). The two-hour ride from Helsinki costs €24.40.

AROUND HANKO
Hauensuoli
The narrow strait between Tullisaari and Kobben, called Hauensuoli (Pike's Gut), is a protected natural harbour where sailing ships from countries around the Baltic Sea used to wait out storms in days of yore. Many of the sailors who passed through here paused to carve their initials or tales of bravery on the rocks, earning Hauensuoli the moniker, 'Guest Book of the Archipelago'. Some 600 rock carvings dating back to the 17th century remain. Hauensuoli can be reached by charter taxi boat or on a cruise from Hanko – see p101.

Bengtskär
Bengtskär is an islet about 25km from Hanko, at the bottom of Finland's southwestern archipelago. It's the southernmost inhabited island in Finland, chosen as a lighthouse station in 1906 to protect ships from the dangerous waters of the archipelago. At 52m the lighthouse is the tallest in Scandinavia, although it was extensively damaged during the Continuation War against the Red Army in 1941. It was restored and opened to the public in 1995 and now has a museum, café, post office and **accommodation** (☎ 02-466 7227). Day cruises to Bengtskär leave from Hanko in summer (see p101), or you can charter boats from Hanko or the village of Rosala on the island of Hiittinen. Also see p199 for cruises to Bengtskär from Turku.

EAST OF HELSINKI

LOVIISA
☎ 019 / pop 7417
Loviisa (Swedish: Lovisa) was named after the Swedish Queen Lovisa Ulrika in 1752, even though there had been a settlement at this harbour site for almost a century before that. Hurriedly fortified by the Swedes when they lost garrison towns (such as Hamina) to the east, Loviisa was finally taken easily by the Russians in 1808.

In the 18th century Loviisa was one of three towns in Finland allowed to engage in foreign trade, and by the 19th century it was a flourishing port and spa town. Loviisa was devastated by fire during the Crimean War (1853–56), so little of the original Old Town remains. These days it's very much a summer resort, when all the attractions are open and boat trips are operating from the marina – skip it out of season.

Information
Library (☎ 555 330; Kuningattarenkatu 24) Free Internet access. It's just north of Mannerheiminkatu – the entrance is via the small park.
Post office (Kuningattarenkatu 13) On the corner of the market square.
Tourist office (www.loviisa.fi) summer office (☎ 555 446; Brandensteininkatu 11B; ❧ 9am-5pm Mon-Fri, 10am-3pm Sat Jun-Aug); town hall (☎ 555 234; Mannerheiminkatu 4; ❧ 9am-4pm Mon-Fri Sep-May) Information at the town hall on the *kauppatori* (market square), or in summer in the cheerful office on the opposite side of the square.

Sights
The very small **Old Town** of Loviisa, just south of Mannerheiminkatu, is what's left of the

wooden buildings following the disastrous fire of 1855. Don't expect another Porvoo, but the narrow streets around **Degerby Gille** restaurant are the quaintest in town, and the restaurant itself is in a building that predates the town (1662).

On the market square, the impressive red-brick neo-Gothic **Loviisa Church** (10am-6pm mid-May–mid-Aug), built in 1865, is a dominant feature; guides are on hand in summer to give free tours. It was designed by Georg Theodor Chiewitz, who also designed many of the civic buildings in the wake of the blaze.

Loviisa Town Museum (☎ 555 357; Puistokatu 2; admission €2; 11am-4pm Tue-Sun Jun-Aug, noon-4pm Sun Sep-May, extended hr during exhibitions) is in an old manor house about 200m north of the market square. There are three floors of recently renovated historical exhibits, with details of Loviisa's metalwork industry, as well as period furniture and costumes, and changing local art exhibitions. There's also an exhibition on Jean Sibelius, who used to spend his summers at Sibeliuksenkatu 10. The town's biggest annual event is the **Sibelius Festival** in early June, which features a weekend of concert performances.

In summer most of the action is at **Laivasilta Marina**, 500m southeast of the centre. A cluster of old rust-coloured wooden storehouses now contains galleries, craft shops, cafés and a small maritime museum. Boats to Svartholma Sea Fortress (p106) depart from this marina.

Sleeping & Eating

Helgas Gasthaus (☎ 531 576; Sibeliuksenkatu 6; s/d €25/45;) This place is a simple, small, old-fashioned, family-run guesthouse with a range of rooms and a large, peaceful garden at the back.

Hotel Degerby (☎ 50561; www.degerby.com; Brandensteininkatu 17; s/d €81/95, Sat, Sun & summer €67/80, ste €133; P   ) This place, near the market square, is the best of the three hotels in town. The carpeted rooms have comfortable beds and standard facilities. The hotel also has a decent bar as does Styrbord Restaurant (lunch buffet for €7.50).

Casino Camping (☎ 530 244; www.casinocamping .fi; Kapteenintie 1; s/d tent sites €10/12, s/d from €35/60; lodging all year, camping early Jun-late Aug) This friendly place is in a delightful waterfront spot about 500m south of the marina. As

NUCLEAR POWER

Although Finland was one of the countries most affected by fallout from the 1986 Chernobyl disaster, it continues to use nuclear power, ironically largely in order to reduce dependency on imported energy from Russia. Reducing greenhouse-gas emissions is also an important factor.

There are four operational reactors in Finland, two of which are at the Loviisa complex, 15km from town on the island of Hästholmen. These reactors supply over a quarter of the country's energy needs. In a close and controversial parliamentary vote in 2002, the government approved construction of a fifth reactor, due to begin operation in 2009.

well as camping, there are rooms in two renovated wooden houses, most with bathrooms. Family rooms are also available.

Väherkylä (☎ 531 610; Aleksanterinkatu 2; 8am-5pm Mon-Fri, 8am-2pm Sat) This popular little bakery/café lures punters in with its wafting spicy aromas. There are a few precarious tables outside, and a spacious interior with quiches, cakes, coffee and a lunch buffet to choose from.

Saltbodan (☎ 532 572; Laivasilta 4; meals €7-16; lunch & dinner May-Aug) One of a few popular summer cafés and restaurants around the waterfront, Saltbodan serves coffee and snacks in a rustic room or on the terrace. À la carte meals and the €8 lunch buffet are served in a pleasant dining hall.

Degerby Gille (☎ 50561; Sepänkuja 4; by arrangement) Set in the oldest building in town, this is an enchanting restaurant that is usually only open for group bookings. It's worth inquiring, though, at the Hotel Degerby, as the restaurant is usually open for lunch once a week for the local Rotary Club, and the public can take advantage. There are five separate and charmingly old-fashioned dining rooms.

Getting There & Away

Loviisa is 90km east of Helsinki, reached by motorway E18 or Hwy 7. There are buses at least hourly to/from Helsinki (€16.20, 1½ to two hours), as well as a regular bus service to/from Kotka (€10, 45 minutes) and Porvoo (€9.40, 30 minutes).

AROUND LOVIISA

An interesting short trip is to the **Svartholma Sea Fortress**, on an island 10km from the town centre. It was established in 1748 soon after Sweden lost control of the eastern part of Finland and was intended to defend Finland against further Russian invasion. The fort was destroyed by the British during the Crimean War in 1855, but has since been reconstructed. From June to August boats run daily to the island from Laivasilta Marina (€9 return, 45 minutes). You can also go on **pirate and adventure cruises** (per person €11.50) leaving at 10am, which are aimed specifically at families and kids (English available by request). Guided walking tours of the fortress cost €4. There's a cheery restaurant on the island, which serves a good lunch buffet out of a rowboat.

RUOTSINPYHTÄÄ

☎ 019 / pop 2895

Combining Finland's power struggles of the past and its industrial beginnings, the tiny, peaceful village of Ruotsinpyhtää (Swedish: Strömfors) is a very worthwhile place to visit, and well worth an overnight stop if you fancy a bit of rusticity. The long name means 'Pyhtää of Sweden', as it was here, along the Kymijoki, that the Swedish-Russian border split the town of Pyhtää into two in 1743. The western, oddly-shaped section was Swedish property, while Pyhtää proper was ceded to Russia for some time.

The Kymijoki provided the power that traditionally drove a large ironworks; the old buildings and equipment are preserved. Although you could easily be forgiven for thinking Ruotsinpyhtää is a museum village, it's also a thriving community, thanks to the modern-day factory across the river. The tiny scattering of buildings includes a supermarket, bank (with ATM), library (with Internet access) and cafés.

There's a friendly and lively annual bluegrass festival, **Rootsinpyhtaa** (www.bluegrass.fi), held in early June; it's a lot of fun and the village is the perfect setting.

There's an **information office** (☎ 618 474; ☺ 8am-4pm Mon-Fri) at the end of the hostel building; across the little bridge from here, the **Forge Café** (☺ 10am-6pm May-Aug) stocks plenty of brochures and is very generous with information.

SOMETHING SPECIAL

Eating outdoors at a Finnish country restaurant in summer is a memorable experience, and one of the most enchanting places to do it is **Ravintola Ruukinmylly** (☎ 618 693; mains €10-14; ☺ 11am-7pm Mon-Thu, 11am-10pm Fri & Sat). This wonderful place is in a 17th-century former mill on a peaceful pond. In summer the restaurant has a terrace with live music and dancing. The menu includes light meals, wood-fired pizzas and some Finnish specialities – the salmon soup is something to be savoured.

Sights & Activities

Strömfors Ironworks (☺ 10am-6pm Jun–mid-Aug), founded in 1695, is one of the oldest of its kind in Finland. Today it's a picturesque open-air museum of wooden farm and industrial buildings, surrounded by forest, rivers and bridges. The rust-red-and-white wooden buildings reflected in the lake on a clear, windless day are definitely the stuff of postcards. The **Forge Museum** has two sections: one consists of an old smith's workshop and equipment, while the other has the working millwheel. There are often forging demonstrations in summer. Also in the old village are some **craft workshops** such as potters, silversmiths, textile makers and painters. One of the ironworks buildings serves as an **art gallery** in summer.

The beautiful octagonal wooden **church** dates from 1771. It's one of a handful of such-shaped churches in Finland. Its Resurrection altarpiece was painted in 1898 by the young Helene Schjerfbeck. The parish paid very little for the work, as she was unknown at the time; soon after she was to be (and still is) considered one of Finland's greatest painters.

The area is ideal for **canoeing**, and you can rent canoes from the information office or the hostel.

There's also an 8km circular **walking trail** to Kukuljärvi – the information centre has a basic trail map. The trail is well-marked and fairly easy (although there are a couple of roped scrambles); you'll see plenty of birds (species include ravens and capercaillies) and more mosquitoes. The walk starts by the sports ground at the southern entrance to town.

Sleeping & Eating

Finnhostel Krouvinmäki (☎ 618 474, 0400 492 161; fax 618 475; s/d €26/52; ◷ Jun–mid-Aug, reception 8am-4pm Mon-Fri; ✕ ⚹) This is a fabulous place to stay. It's an HI-affiliated hostel in an atmospheric clay-walled building that once served as accommodation for mill workers. The low-doored rooms are spacious and all have two cosy beds (there's one four-person room) and there's a good kitchen with VCR, and a laundry. You can stay outside the season by prior arrangement. The reception is the information office; ring ahead if you are going to arrive outside these hours.

The friendly and helpful Forge Café by the museum is a lovely old place and your best bet for a chat, snacks or a cold beer, while the grilli just behind the hostel does tasty pizzas and kebabs.

Getting There & Away

The only buses to the village itself run from Loviisa (€4, 20 minutes, three daily in summer, many more on weekdays September to May). Buses running along the main road (on the Helsinki–Loviisa–Kotka route) can drop you at **Ahvenkoski**, from where it's 5km to Ruotsinpyhtää. A taxi from Loviisa will cost €20 to €25; from Ahvenkoski about €12. Call a cab on ☎ 0400 105 465; it's also easy to hitch from Ahvenkoski.

KOTKA

☎ 05 / pop 54, 759

Kotka has been and remains Finland's most important industrial port, so don't turn up expecting a cluster of wooden houses surrounding bobbing yachts. It has massive pulp factories and large oil tanks but also some redeeming attractions, including a smart new aquarium, an excellent trattoria, a good amount of parkland, and the nearby Imperial Fishing Lodge, where the tsar used to pull on his waders and cast for salmon.

Information

Public library (☎ 212 424; Kirkkokatu 24) Near Kotka Church with a free Internet terminal as well as an Internet café inside.

Tourist office (☎ 234 4424; www.kotka.fi; Keskuskatu 6; ◷ 9am-5pm Mon-Fri Sep-May, 9am-6pm Mon-Fri, 10am-2pm Sat Jun-Aug) Helpful new tourist office. Has free Internet access.

Sights

MARETARIUM

If you've ever wondered what swims beneath the surface of Finland's many lakes, rivers and seas, the impressive **Maretarium** (☎ 234 4030; www.maretarium.fi; Sapokankatu 2; adult/child €9.50/6; ◷ 10am-8pm mid-May–mid-Aug, 10am-5pm mid-Aug–mid-May, closed late Jan) reveals all in a series of giant fish tanks, each representing a particular body of water; the Baltic tank is open to the air. It's all very informative; the usual suspects are here: perch, salmon, bream, Arctic char and herring, but there are also a few less common visitors such as the lumpsucker and the heinous-looking four-horned sculpin. Though visually not on a par with a tropical aquarium, it's a more educational experience, and there's English labelling, guided tours and a theatrette. And if all those fish are making you hungry, the town's best fish restaurant is next door.

SAPOKKA WATER PARK

Just south of Sapokka Harbour, this water park is a lovely green oasis with bridges, walking trails, gardens and the **Rose Terrace** garden, which is illuminated every evening. It's the perfect place to escape Kotka's more commercial side.

MUSEUMS & CHURCHES

Kymenlaakso Provincial Museum (Maakuntamuseo; ☎ 234 4438; Kotkankatu 13; admission €2; ◷ noon-6pm Tue-Fri, noon-4pm Sat & Sun) is the atmospherically lit museum of regional history, with exhibits from the Stone Age to the present day.

The world's oldest icebreaker, the **museumship Tarmo** (☎ 234 4405; admission €2.50; ◷ mid-May-Aug) is moored at Central Harbour. Built at Newcastle-upon-Tyne in 1907, it once kept Finnish shipping lanes open, and you can now go aboard and explore the cabins, bridge and engine room. In a hall nearby are another pair of vessels; a coastal patrolboat and a lifeboat (admission to both hall and icebreaker €3). ·

St Nicholas Orthodox Church (◷ noon-3pm Mon-Fri, noon-6pm Sat & Sun Jun-Aug), in Isopuisto Park, was completed in 1801 and is the only building in Kotka to survive the Crimean War (1853–56). It is believed to have been designed by architect Yakov Perrini, who also designed the St Petersburg Admiralty.

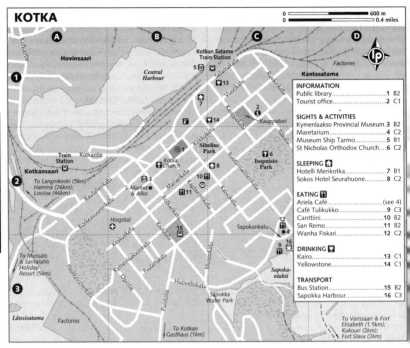

KOTKA

	0	600 m
	0	0.4 miles

INFORMATION
Public library............................1 B2
Tourist office...........................2 C1

SIGHTS & ACTIVITIES
Kymenlaakso Provincial Museum..3 B2
Maretarium..............................4 C2
Museum Ship Tarmo................5 B1
St Nicholas Orthodox Church.....6 C2

SLEEPING
Hotelli Merikotka......................7 B1
Sokos Hotel Seurahuone...........8 C2

EATING
Ariela Café.............................(see 4)
Café Tulikukko.........................9 C3
Canttiini................................10 B2
San Remo..............................11 B2
Wanha Fiskari.........................12 C2

DRINKING
Kairo.....................................13 C1
Yellowstone...........................14 C1

TRANSPORT
Bus Station............................15 B2
Sapokka Harbour....................16 C3

Activities

Archipelago cruises of all types depart from Sapokka Harbour in summer, along with scheduled ferries to the outlying islands (opposite) – the tourist office has timetables and details.

Several operators offer **white-water rafting** (also called 'rapids shooting') on the Kymijoki. A three-hour trip costs around €43/20 per adult/child, including transportation. Contact **Erämys Ky** (☎ 050-320 2559; www.eramys.fi), **Keisarin Kosket Oy** (☎ 05-210 7400; www.keisarinkosket.fi), or book at the tourist office.

Festivals & Events

Kotkan Meripäivät (Kotka Maritime Festival) is held annually in late July or early August. Events include boat racing, concerts, cruises and a market. There's also an associated wooden boat show.

Sleeping

Sokos Hotel Seurahuone (☎ 020-123 4666; www .sokoshotels.fi; Keskuskatu 21; s/d €100/116, Sat, Sun & summer r €84; P ✕ ▢) This is very much the best option in a town where quality accommodation is very thin. It's right in the thick of the action, opposite the pleasant town park. There are a couple of restaurants and a popular nightclub here.

Santalahti Holiday Resort (☎ 260 5055; www .santalahti.fi; tent sites €10, cottage from €55; ✉ May-late Sep) This is a sprawling resort on Mussalo, 5km from central Kotka. The facilities are good and some newer cottages are outstanding. There's also a small hotel and a restaurant in the same complex, and a golf course next door. There's no public transport.

Hotelli Merikotka (☎ 215 222; www.hotellimeri kotka.fi; Satamakatu 9; s/d €52/72; ✕) This friendly hotel faces Central Harbour, just opposite the Kotkan Satama train stop. The corridors are decked out in bizarre pseudo-cavern plasterwork, but the rooms are fairly standard, and not good value for singles. The breakfast is OK though; it's served early for contract workers, who make up the majority of guests. There's a café-bar downstairs, which doubles as a reception in the evenings.

Kotkan Gasthaus (☎ 225 0622; Puistotie 24; per person €30; P ☒) Catering to oil workers, this is the cheapest place to stay in town, but it's in a thoroughly depressing area near the refinery. Rooms are basic but decent value; rates include breakfast and sauna.

Eating

San Remo (☎ 212 114; Keskuskatu 29; pizza & pasta €8-10, other mains €11-16; ◷ 11am-10pm Tue-Thu, 11am-11pm Fri & Sat, noon-10pm Sun) This unpretentious but excellent upstairs restaurant was doing Italian food in Kotka long before you could even get a pizza in Helsinki. Run by an Italian-Finnish couple, it's as authentic and charming a trattoria as you could hope to find, with a great balcony space, Italian wines and Ferrari memorabilia. You come here for the fresh home-made fettuccini. There's also a café downstairs.

Wanha Fiskari (☎ 218 6585; www.wanhafiskari.fi; Ruotsinsalmenkatu 1; mains €13-24; ◷ lunch & dinner) This is an elegant and pricey restaurant renowned for its Finnish fish specialities such as Baltic herring, perch and salmon (it's no small irony that the Maretarium was built next door). There are also meat dishes, including reindeer, and a good lunchtime salad buffet.

Canttiini (☎ 214 130; Kaivokatu 15; mains €9-16; ◷ lunch & dinner) Canttiini is popular with locals and dishes up big serves of pasta and Mexican food in a casual atmosphere.

Café Tulikukko (☎ 213 925; Sapokka Harbour) is a good place for coffee and snacks, while the nearby **Ariela Café** (☎ 212 115; Maretarium) is a good lunchtime spot with filled rolls, light meals and a large terrace.

Drinking

Kairo (☎ 212 787; Satamakatu 7; ◷ 11am-11pm Sun-Tue, till 1am or later Wed-Sat) This place is something of a legendary old sailors' pub facing Central Harbour. It's a beautiful building decked with ships' flags and saucy paintings, and there's a large terrace in summer and frequent live music (often traditional Finnish dance). It's fairly upmarket these days, but still has plenty of character and is easily the best spot in town for a drink.

Yellowstone (☎ 225 0128; Ruotsinsalmenkatu 14) This popular pub has a good outdoor terrace in the centre of town. Attached is the fairly tacky disco/nightclub, Livinstone.

Getting There & Away

There are regular express buses from Helsinki (€21.30, two hours), via Porvoo, Loviisa and Pyhtää. Buses run roughly every half-hour to Hamina (€5, 20 to 45 minutes), 26km to the east.

There are between four and six local trains a day to Kouvola (€7.40, 40 minutes) from where you can catch connecting trains to all major Finnish cities. The trains stop both at Kotka Station, to the northwest of the city centre, and at Kotkan Satama, at the main harbour and very much handier for the centre.

AROUND KOTKA
Archipelago Islands

There are several interesting islands off the Kotka coast that make for good day trips during the summer months. There are daily boat connections to each from Sapokka Harbour during this season.

On **Kukouri** is Fort Slava, also called the Fortress of Honour. It was built by Russians in 1794 as part of a chain of fortresses in the Gulf of Finland. Destroyed by the British in 1855, it was partially renovated in the 1990s. There are five ferries daily from early June to mid-August (adult/child return €7/2).

On **Varissaari**, Fort Elisabeth was another of the Russian fortresses built to defend the coast against the Swedes. A fierce naval battle was fought from here in 1789, and the fortress was abandoned in the late 19th century. It is now a popular venue for open-air performances and a favourite picnic spot. There's also a restaurant here. Ferries leave Kotka hourly between 9am and 9pm from late May to late August (€5 return).

Kaunissaari is the most interesting island, with its own little community. There's a charming fishing village and a local museum, as well as a camping ground with some cabins. There are one to three regular ferries a day (€7 one way) from late May to late August. There are also evening cruises, with singing and live music, departing on Wednesdays at 7pm (€15) and returning around midnight.

On Kaunissaari is an information centre for the **Eastern Gulf of Finland National Park**, a 60km swathe of over 100 islets beginning just to the south of Kaunissaari. It's an important breeding ground for many seabirds and a habitat for grey and ringed seals. The park is best explored with your own boat, but scheduled boats do run from Kotka and Hamina to Ulko-Tammio island, which is part of the park. Here there's another information centre as well as a campsite and nature trail.

Langinkoski

The **Imperial Fishing Lodge** (☎ 228 1050; www .langinkoskimuseo.com; Koskenniskantie 5C; admission €4; ☼ 10am-7pm daily May-Aug, Sat & Sun Sep-Oct) at Langinkoski, 5km north of Kotka on the salmon-heavy Kymijoki, is worth visiting even if you're not interested in the fishing haunts of the wealthy and powerful. The surprisingly simple wooden lodge was built in 1889 for Tsar Alexander III, who visited Langinkoski frequently. Most of the furniture is original, and the rooms look much as they did at the end of the 19th century. On Sundays during summer there are (free) guided tours on the hour between 11am and 4pm.

The riverside forest setting (now a 28-hectare nature reserve) is beautiful, and there are many walking trails to soak up a few hours. **Fly-fishing** is still allowed at Langinkoski, but you will need to get a permit by contacting **Korkeakosken Kalastuskievari** (☎ 05-281 495; Kalakoski) or the tourist office in Kotka. The lodge is not well signposted – turn off road 15 at the signs (on the right if you're coming from Kotka) and drive about 1.5km to the road's end.

You can get almost all the way to Langinkoski on bus 13 or 27. Alternatively, get off at the sign at the *pikavuoro* (express) bus stop and walk 1.2km.

HAMINA

☎ 05 / pop 21,887

With its strict and unusual octagonal plan, you can really feel that Hamina (Swedish: Fredrikshamn) was once a fortress rather than a town. This pleasant harbourside spot, still home to some soldiery, seems a little empty without its garrison, and more preoccupied with invasions of Russian shoppers than the Red Army! The border is just 40km away. With a couple of good museums and a pleasant small-town atmosphere, Hamina makes an intriguing place to stop, and its network of beds in local homes is a good chance to experience Finnish hospitality.

Hamina was founded in 1653, when Finland was part of Sweden. The crumbling fortifications that surround it were begun by panicky Swedes in 1722 after Vyborg fell to Russia. Their fears were justified, but their efforts in vain – shortly afterwards the Russians marched in and took Hamina, too.

Information

Public library (Rautatienkatu 8; ☼ 1-7pm Mon-Fri, 10am-2pm Sat) Free Internet terminals.
Post office (Maariankatu 4)
Tourist office (www.hamina.fi) main office (☎ 749 2641; Raatihuoneentori 16; ☼ 9am-4pm Mon-Fri); summer office (☎ 749 2643; Lipputorni (Flagtower), kauppatori; ☼ 9am-6pm Mon-Fri, 10am-3pm Sat & Sun Jun–mid-Aug)

Sights & Activities

Restored 19th-century wooden buildings grace the eight radial streets of Hamina's octagonal town plan. From its centre – Hamina has a more literal centre than most towns, dominated by the 18th-century **town hall** – most sights are a short walk away.

Highlights of Old Hamina include the neoclassical **Hamina Church**, built in 1843 and designed by CL Engel; and directly opposite, behind the town hall, the 1837 **Orthodox Church of Saints Peter & Paul**, thought to have been created by architect Louis Visconti, who designed Napoleon's tomb in France.

Housed in Hamina's oldest building, the **Town Museum** (Kaupunginmuseo; ☎ 749 4193; Kadettikoulunkatu 2; admission €2; ☼ 11am-3pm Wed-Sat, noon-5pm Sun Sep-May, 10am-4pm Tue-Sun Jun-Aug) is the museum of local history. King Gustav III of Sweden and Catherine II (the Great) of Russia held negotiations in one of the rooms in 1783.

Shopkeeper's Museum (Kauppiaantalomuseo; ☎ 749 4196; Kasarminkatu 6; ☼ 11am-3pm Wed-Sat, noon-5pm Sun Sep-May, 10am-4pm Tue-Sun Jun-Aug) is a former merchant's store and residence, and has people dressed the part, serving customers with all manner of handmade curios and souvenirs. It's one of the best house museums in Finland. Kasarminkatu was a main shopping street in the 19th century.

Northwest of Old Hamina are remnants of the 18th-century **Hamina Fortress**, including 3km of crumbling stone walls, and the star-shaped bastions, but there really isn't much left to see.

A short walk southwest of the centre at Tervasaari harbour is the bright red former lightship SS Hyöky, a 1912 steamship completed in the same year as the Titanic. It served both Russia and Finland in its colourful career, and was the last coal-burning steamship in commercial use in Scandinavia. During summer it's now a cluttered museum, bar and hotel (p112). Moored alongside is the 1943 icebreaker and tug **M/S Merikarhu**.

Also from Tervasaari there are summer **cruises** (☎ 228 4648; www.meriset.com) offered to the fishing village on the island of Tammio (€14, three to four hours). Departures are five times a week and schedules vary significantly between mid-May and late August. You can also reach Ulko-Tammio, an island further south but still within the boundaries of the national park (see p109), on weekends from mid-June to the end of July. The **information office** (☎ 040-594 4171; 10am-4pm Mon-Fri, 10am-3pm Sat & Sun) at the harbour can provide timetables and sells tickets.

Festivals & Events

Every second (even) year in late July or early August, Hamina celebrates military music during the week-long **Hamina Tattoo** (☎ 749 2633; www.haminatattoo.com). This international event features not only Finnish and Russian military marching bands, but rock, pop, jazz and dance acts.

SOUTH COAST

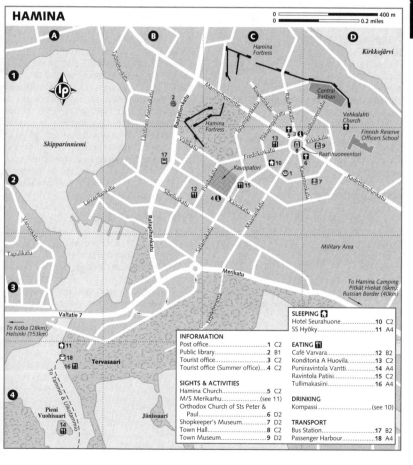

INFORMATION	
Post office.....................................1	C2
Public library...............................2	B1
Tourist office...............................3	C2
Tourist office (Summer office)....4	C2

SIGHTS & ACTIVITIES	
Hamina Church..........................5	C2
M/S Merikarhu.....................(see 11)	
Orthodox Church of Sts Peter & Paul...6	D2
Shopkeeper's Museum................7	D2
Town Hall...................................8	C2
Town Museum............................9	D2

SLEEPING	
Hotel Seurahuone....................10	C2
SS Hyöky.................................11	A4

EATING	
Café Varvara............................12	B2
Konditoria A Huovila...............13	C2
Pursiravintola Vantti................14	A4
Ravintola Patiisi.......................15	C2
Tullimakasiini...........................16	A4

DRINKING	
Kompassi..........................(see 10)	

TRANSPORT	
Bus Station..............................17	B2
Passenger Harbour...................18	A4

Sleeping

One of the best options for accommodation in and around Hamina is the local B&B network. These are rooms in private homes, some self-contained, others home-stay, and typically cost €25 to €35 per person. The tourist office can arrange these.

Hotel Seurahuone (☎ 3500 263; Pikkuympyräkatu 5; s/d €63/74) This place, in the heart of Old Hamina, is full of old-world ambience, and summer discounts are available. The subterranean Kompassi pub and restaurant is also here.

Hamina Camping Pitkät Hiekat (☎ /fax 345 9183; tent sites €10, 4-6-person cottage €40-65; 🕑 daily May-late Aug, Sat & Sun winter) This camping ground, 6km east of Hamina at Vilniemi, has a peaceful lakeside and forest setting, and you can use the rowing boats for free. It has a bar, café, sauna and laundry.

SS Hyöky (☎ 040-763 3757; s/d from €30/40; ✗) In the height of summer you can stay on this historic steamship in the tiny cabins, each with a set of bunks, plus the 'captain's cabin' above deck. It's not for the claustrophobic, but you stay here for the experience; the captain, 'Patu', is a well known local character and will make you feel part of the crew. The ship also has a bar, a cluttered museum and even a tiny sauna (free for guests). Ring ahead to check that it's open for accommodation, though.

Eating & Drinking

Some of the best places to eat are down at Tervasaari Harbour.

Pursiravintola Vantti (☎ 354 1063; mains €12-22; 🕑 food 3-9pm Tue-Sat, noon-8pm Sun, bar closes later) This is the place to be found on summer weekends – Pieni Vuohisaari, opposite Tervasaari harbour. There's drinking and dancing to live music in the friendly atmosphere of the yacht club, and good-quality seafood is available. To get to the island,

press the buzzer at the little jetty set up at Tervasaari harbour and a boat will come and pick you up for free.

Tullimakasiini (☎ 344 7470; Tervasaari harbour; mains €11-17; 🕑 lunch & dinner Tue-Sat, lunch only Sun & Mon) A quaint restaurant in an old customs house, it specialises in Finnish fish and meat dishes. It's got a good atmosphere and friendly staff, but try not to coincide with a tour group.

Konditoria A Huovila (☎ 344 0930; Fredrikinkatu 1; 🕑 9.30am-4.30pm) A *pulla's* throw from the central hub, this is one of those lovable traditional cafés in an old wooden house. It's a great place for coffee, cakes and sandwiches, and a welcome refuge in inclement weather.

Café Varvara (☎ 231 1044; Puistokatu 2; 🕑 7am-5pm Mon-Fri, 7.30am-2pm Sat) Just south of the market square, this homely café is a good spot for home-baked buns and cakes, tasty rolls, decent coffee and service with a smile.

Ravintola Patiisi (☎ 353 2444; Satamakatu 11; mains €8-15, pizzas €9; 🕑 lunch & dinner Wed-Mon) This place has a wide range of reasonably priced pizzas and Italian American–style dishes, as well as a popular 1st-floor covered terrace overlooking the market square.

Kompassi (☎ 350 0266; Pikkuympyräkatu 5) In Old Hamina, in the historic Hotel Seurahuone, is a brooding basement pub once used by visiting seafarers. There's regular live music, karaoke and a summer terrace at the side of the hotel.

Getting There & Away

You can reach Hamina by hourly bus from Kotka (€5, 20 to 45 minutes). There are express buses from Helsinki (€25.60, 2¾ hours). Buses pass through Hamina on the way to Vyborg and St Petersburg in Russia. There are no lockers at the bus station, but they'll guard your bags for a fee during business hours.

The Lakeland

All of Finland could be described as lakeland, but the prize goes to this sparkling area of the southeast, which seems to have more water than land. Any trip to Finland should take in some of this area, whose glistening lakes leave indelible impressions on any summer visitor.

Much of this region includes the Savo district, the main town of which is Savonlinna, whose majestic castle hosts the Opera Festival, a fantastic, buzzing event: it's one of Finland's most memorable festivals. High culture can also be seen in Kuopio's dance festival and Mikkeli's Classical Music Festival, but there are offbeat events, too, involving mobile-phone throwing and wife-carrying. The people of this area – the *savolaiset* – are among the most outspoken and friendly of Finns. They can laugh at themselves and are often lampooned by Finns from elsewhere due to their distinctive Savo dialect, accent and humour, but perhaps also because they are envied for their beautiful Lakeland.

Needless to say, it's a great place to get outdoors, and whether steamer-cruising or soft-paddling a canoe in search of rare seals, the lakes are the focus of any visit. It's a favoured summering place for Finns, who luxuriate in their cottages, fishing, rowing, taking saunas and generally enjoying what is almost the archetype of Finnish landscape.

The towns in the area also have much to offer. Kuopio offers fantastic lakescapes and the chance to try out a smoke sauna and the delicious things that locals create with *muikku* (whitefish). Jyväskylä is a friendly university town that draws architecture fans from the world over for its associations and buildings of Alvar Aalto, a giant of 20th-century architecture.

THE LAKELAND

HIGHLIGHTS

- Descending on **Savonlinna** (p115) for its awesome castle and bubbly opera festival

- Examining the visionary buildings of Alvar Aalto in the university town of **Jyväskylä** (p129)

- Steaming it up in the **world's largest smoke sauna** (p137) in Kuopio

- Seeking out the rare **Saimaa ringed seal** (p124) from a canoe in the national parks around Savonlinna

- Paddling the **Squirrel Route** (p125) from Juva to Sulkava, an easy two-day canoe trip

- Taking the full-day **ferry trip** (p120 and p140) between Savonlinna and Kuopio, via lakes, lochs and canals

- Spending the night at **Valamo** (p128), Finland's only Orthodox monastery

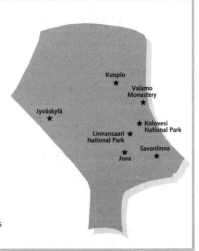

History
The Lakeland region was settled in the wake of the retreating glaciers of the last Ice Age. Various groups, coming from the east and south, eventually merged to become the Savo people. Over the centuries, the region saw much conflict as a borderland between the powers of Sweden and Russia. Tourism has been important here for well over a century: St Petersburg gentry used to travel here to admire the scenery and take rest cures.

National Parks
The Lakeland region has two excellent national parks in the Savonlinna area, Kolovesi and Linnansaari, both largely watery and habitats to the rare Saimaa inland seal. These are particularly good areas for exploring by canoe.

Activities
With so many lakes, it's no wonder that the main summer activities involve getting out on it. One of the best ways is to take a day-long lake cruise between Kuopio and Savonlinna; other cruises visit the Orthodox Monastery of Valamo or simply roam around the peaceful waters.

The more active choice is to hire a canoe, whether for a short paddle or a longer trek. In the Savonlinna area are several choices, with two national parks offering great canoeing, as well as a popular two-day route from Juva to Sulkava (p125).

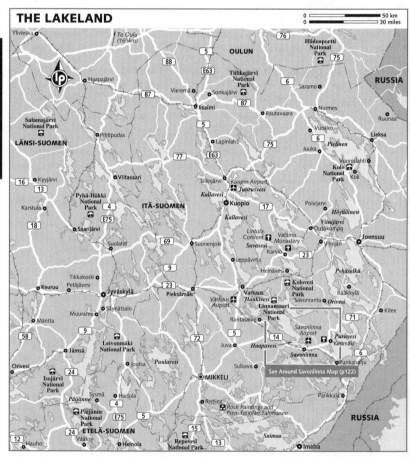

LAND OF LAKES

Lakes are the life force of southeastern Finland, with 10% of Finland consisting of water. Many of its 188,000-odd lakes (of which some 56,000 are larger than a hectare) are linked by rivers, and the towns, villages, factories and hydroelectric plants along these lakes and rivers rely on them for drinking water, and as a means of transportation. Finns cross the lakes by boat in summer and snowmobile (and car) in winter, and build summer cottages and saunas beside them.

Finnish lakes are shallow – only three are deeper than 100m. This means their waters warm quickly in summer, freeze over in winter and also makes them susceptible to pollution.

Throughout Finland you will often hear the words *järvi* (lake), *lampi* (pond), *saari* (island), *ranta* (shore), *niemi* (cape), *lahti* (bay), *koski* (rapids), *virta* (stream) and *joki* (river). All these words form some of the most common Finnish family names, especially Järvinen, Saarinen, Rantanen, Nieminen, Lahtinen, Koskinen, Virtanen and Jokinen.

Jyväskylä is the main base in the area for skiing, with a good centre northwest of town. Kuopio also sees plenty of crowds in winter.

Self-Catering Accommodation

There are numerous lakeside cottages for rent throughout the region; this is the most typically Finnish holiday you can have! See p330 for agencies who deal with rentals in this area. Local tourist offices also have extensive lists.

EASTERN LAKELAND

SAVONLINNA

☎ 015 / pop 27,463

Lorded over by one of Europe's most dramatic castles, Savonlinna is as romantic a place as you'll come by, particularly on a summer's night when its world-famous Opera Festival is in full swing. In the heart of the Lakeland, it's an incredibly rewarding place to visit and a good base for exploring this part of southeastern Finland.

Set on two islands between Lake Haapavesi and Lake Pihlajavesi, Savonlinna offers the prettiest of waterscapes. Perched on a rocky islet of its own, Olavinlinna castle seems to rise improbably out of the water itself. Whether floodlit or sunbeaten, it's a breathtaking sight.

The Opera Festival, despite high prices and crowds, is a great time to be in Savonlinna. There's a real buzz in town, and animated post-show diners and drinkers deconstruct the night's performance well into the wee hours. The performances themselves are memorably staged within the walls of the castle itself.

History

The slow growth of Savonlinna began in 1475 with the building of Olavinlinna Castle, and in 1639 it received a municipal charter at the instigation of Count Per Brahe, the founder of many towns around Finland. Despite appearances, the castle didn't prove particularly defensible, and the Russians finally grabbed the town for good in 1743. It was returned to the Finnish grand duchy in 1812; since independence it has been an important hub of Lakeland steamboat traffic; even today its passenger dock seems busier than the bus station, at least in summer.

Information

As well as the following places, there's also Internet access at the café at Hotel Seurahone.

Café Knut Posse (☎ 576 960; Olavinkatu 44; Internet free; 🕑 9am-6pm Mon-Fri, 10am-6pm Sat) Internet café, joined to the bookshop of the same name.

Main post office (Olavinkatu) Near the bus terminal.

Music library (Kirkkokatu 12; 🕑 1-7pm Mon-Thu, 10am-4pm Fri) Good collection of CDs, including opera, and a free Internet terminal.

Nestori (☎ 0205-645 929; saimaa@metsa.fi; Aino Acktén puistotie 4; 🕑 10am-6pm Jul daily, 11am-5pm Tue-Sun May, Jun, Aug & Sep) The national parks visitor centre for the Saimaa region. Art and nature exhibitions and plenty of information.

Public library (Tottinkatu; 🕑 11am-7pm Mon-Fri, 10am-2pm Sat) Free Internet terminals.

Savonlinna Tourist Service (☎ 517 510; www .savonlinnatravel.com; Puistokatu 1; 🕑 9am-5pm Jun-Aug, 8am-8pm during Opera Festival, 9am-5pm Mon-Fri Sep-May) Provides information about most places in the region, sells festival tickets, reserves accommodation and organizes tours.

THE LAKELAND

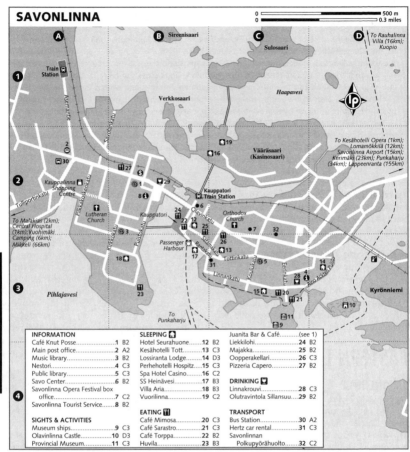

Sights

OLAVINLINNA CASTLE

Olavinlinna (☎ 531 164; admission €5; ⏱ 10am-5pm Jun–mid-Aug, 10am-3pm mid-Aug–May) is one of the most spectacular castles in northern Europe. These days it is famous as the setting for the month-long Savonlinna Opera Festival. If you visit in June you may be lucky enough to see some of the opera stars rehearsing. The venue seats 2300 in comfort.

Founded in 1475 by Erik Axelsson Tott, governor of Vyborg and the Eastern Provinces, Olavinlinna was named after Olof, an 11th-century Norwegian king and saint. The castle was meant to protect the eastern border of the Swedish empire. However, Russians occupied the castle from 1714 to

1721, and took control of it again from 1743 to the early half of the 20th century. Two exhibition rooms within the castle have exhibits on its history plus displays of Orthodox treasures.

The castle has been heavily restored, after it was gutted by fire, but is still seriously impressive, not least in the way it is built directly on the rock in the middle of the lake. To tour it, including its original towers, bastions and chambers, you have to join one of the excellent guided tours (around 45 minutes). Tours depart on the hour and guides speak English, Spanish, French, German, Japanese and Italian as well as Finnish and Swedish. The guides are quite good at bringing the castle to life and can furnish you with some interesting stories: the soldiers, for instance, were partly paid in beer – 5L a day and 7L on Sunday, which makes its frequent changes-of-hands more understandable.

PROVINCIAL MUSEUM & MUSEUM SHIPS
The **provincial museum** (☎ 571 4712; Riihisaari; adult/child €4/1; ☺ 11am-5pm Tue-Sun, 11am-5pm daily in Jul), in an old Russian warehouse near the castle, has exhibits related to local history and the importance of water transport. There are plenty of old photographs and models and upstairs is a changing art exhibition.

Moored alongside the museum are the historic ships *Salama, Mikko* and *Savonlinna,* all with exhibitions open from May to September during museum hours. The museum and ships can all be seen with a single ticket. The museum won't take your breath away like the castle, but it is worthwhile and several orders of magnitude less touristy.

RAUHALINNA VILLA
This romantic Moorish-style wooden **villa** (☎ 744 3440; Lehtiniemi; ☺ Jun-Aug) was built in 1900 by Nils Weckman, an officer in the tsar's army, as a wedding-anniversary gift for his wife. It features an intricate wooden lattice trim and has a serene lakeside setting.

These days Rauhalinna warrants a visit for its **café** (☺ 11am-early evening Mon-Sat Jun-Aug) and fine restaurant, complete with banquet hall. For a real treat, try the excellent buffet. Rauhalinna also houses a **summer hotel** (s/d €61/71). The villa is at Lehtiniemi, 16km by road north of Savonlinna. The best way to visit is by boat from Savonlinna passenger harbour (right). Alternatively, there are two to three buses (destination Lehtiniemi, 25 minutes) from the Savonlinna bus terminal to within 500m of the villa from Monday to Saturday.

Activities
The area around Savonlinna, with its quiet country lanes and gently sloping hills, is terrific for **bicycle touring**. Bikes can be carried on board local ferries for a small fee. To rent **canoes and rowing boats**, visit Vuohimäki Camping (p118).

Tours
There are numerous operators running tours that enable you to explore some of this Lakeland area. The tourist service runs many of them, from half-day to multi-day trips.

LAKE CRUISES
In summer, the Savonlinna passenger harbour is one of the busiest in Finland. There are a number of scenic cruises to choose from, with dozens of daily departures during the high season. These include cruises around the castle, to Rauhalinna villa, or through the archipelago. Most boats have café and/or bar facilities on board. Cruises include the following:

MS Ieva (www.ieva.fi) Five to seven one-hour guided lake cruises (€10) daily.

M/S Lake Star (☎ 0400 200 117; www.lakestar.info) One-hour scenic cruises in the Savonlinna area (€10) with six departures daily from June to the end of August.

SS Heinävesi (www.savonlinnanlaivat.com) To Retretti jetty in Punkaharju at 11am daily mid-June to mid-August (one way/return €19/25).

S/S Punkaharju (☎ 0500 250 075; www.vipcruise.info) Four to five lake cruises (€10) daily from late May to late August.

Festivals & Events
Savonlinna Opera Festival (☎ 476 750; www.operafestival.fi; Olavinkatu 27, 57130 Savonlinna), held throughout July, is perhaps the most famous festival in Finland, with an enviably dramatic setting; the covered courtyard of Olavinlinna Castle. It offers four weeks of high-class opera performances from early July to early August. The atmosphere in town during the festival is reason enough to come; it's buzzing, with restaurants serving post-show midnight feasts, and animated discussions and impromptu arias on all sides.

The first Opera Festival was held at Olavinlinna way back in 1912, the brainchild of Finnish soprano Aino Ackte. It was resurrected again in 1967 and has grown in stature with each passing year. The festival's excellent website details the programme of operas and concerts two years in advance and allows you to book seats in advance on the Internet.

The first three weeks have rotating performances of five operas by the Savonlinna company; the last week has a guest company performing (in 2006 it will be the Bologna Opera). Tickets cost from €31 to €201 for concerts, depending on the seats, with tickets more expensive at weekends.

Tickets for same-night performances are sold after 6pm from the booth near the bridge, and at any time from the Savonlinna Tourist Service. **Savo Center** (☎ 020-744 3447; www.savocenter.fi; Kauppatori 2), by the kauppatori, also sells tickets. If you are pressed for time, Finnair has night flights returning to Helsinki after the show during the festival, and same-day return deals including the opera ticket.

Although opera dominates the festival calendar here, there's also an important **ballet festival** (☎ 555 0020; www.savonlinnaballet .net) running for a week in early August. It wasn't held in 2005 because of internal wrangling; in 2006 it's the Hungarian National Ballet.

Less elegant, but keenly contested in late August, is the **Mobile Phone Throwing World Championships** (www.savonlinnafestivals.com)!

Sleeping

Savonlinna is notoriously expensive in summer, and prices rise pretty sharply (by between 30% and 50%) during the Opera Festival, when beds are scarce. Book accommodation well in advance – at least six months for hotels, less for hostels – if you plan to visit during opera season (any time in July).

BUDGET

Vuorilinna (☎ 73950; www.spahotelcasino.fi; Kylpylaitoksentie; dm/s/d €25/57/67; P X) An HI-affiliated hotel and hostel behind, and run by, the spa hotel on Vääräsaari, also known as Kasinosaari (Casino Island). The location is great, with access to the centre across a beautiful footbridge. The rooms are small, clean and comfortable, and share kitchen and bathroom facilities between two. The dorm rates get you the same deal. There are four different buildings, some only open in summer. Reception is very helpful.

SS Heinävesi (☎ 533 120; cabins upper/lower deck per person €25/22) During summer this boat offers cramped two-person cabin accommodation after the last cruise every afternoon/evening. There's a good chance of getting a bed here, even during the Opera Festival.

Malakias (☎ 739 5430; fax 272 524; Pihlajavedenkuja 6; s/d from €57/68; ☯ Jul-early Aug; P X) About 2km northwest of town, in a blocky complex of buildings among trees, this is another summer hotel with two-room apartments sharing a kitchen and bathroom. The décor would never be called charming, but the facilities are excellent!

Vuohimäki Camping (☎ 537 353; myyntipalvelu@ lomaliitto.fi; tent sites €11-12 plus per person €4, 4-person r from €42, 4-/6-person cabins up to €74/82; ☯ Jun-Aug) Located about 7km southwest of town, this camping ground has good facilities but fills up quickly in July. You can hire canoes and rowboats here (per hour €7, per day €25).

There's another HI hostel near Kerimäki, the Korkeamäen Majatalo (p123), which is rarely full during the week (even in July), so can make a viable alternative to staying in Savonlinna if you have a vehicle.

SOMETHING SPECIAL

Lossiranta Lodge (☎ 511 2323; www.lossiranta.net; Aino Acktén puistotie; s negotiable, d €100-140, during Opera €140-190; P X) With an inspiring location by the lake, full-frontal to the castle and a stone's throw from it, this is arguably Finland's most charming hotel, at least when the sun is shining. Five snug but perfectly-formed little nests have been created in an outbuilding of a villa; their names (garage, laundry-room, woodstore) indicate their original function but give no hint as to just how enticing they are. All are very different but decorated with love and style; they come with a small kitchen (yes, that's it in the cupboard!) and numerous personal touches. The best has its own wood sauna and Jacuzzi; a honeymoon special. Breakfast is served on the lawn or veranda if the weather allows. The grass slopes down to the water, where you can swim from a private jetty with the castle looming above. In the garden, you can graze on fresh apples and berries; it's like a summer retreat but in the middle of town. It's also attractive in winter (when the rooms are heavily discounted), as steam rises from the current cutting its way through the frozen lake. The warm personal service seals the experience. Further rooms are being readied in another building, Tavis, a couple of hundred metres beyond, but get in here if you possibly can.

MIDRANGE & TOP END

Spa Hotel Casino (☎ 73950; www.spahotelcasino.fi; Kasinosaari; s/d/large d €86/104/124, winter weekends €71/84/98; P ✕ ▯ ▣) Charmingly situated on an island across a footbridge from the *kauppatori* (market square), this is a good option. Nearly all the rooms have a balcony; those that don't, have their own sauna. In the 'small' rooms, the beds are arranged toe-to-toe. The rooms aren't luxurious for this price, but guests have unlimited access to the excellent spa facilities, and the location is fantastic. Nonresidents can use the spa for €7.

Perhehotelli Hospitz (☎ 515 661; www.hospitz .com; Linnankatu 20; s/d from €75/85; P ✕ ▯) This cosy place near the castle is a Savonlinna classic, built in the 1930s and redolent of that period's elegance, with striped wallpaper and ornate public areas. The rooms are also stylish, although the beds are a little narrow and some of the bathrooms small; there are larger rooms available for families. A balcony costs a little extra. The hotel has a pleasant terrace and garden with access to a small beach. The atmosphere during the opera festival is great, with a midnight buffet laid on, but you'll have to book rooms more than a year in advance.

Kesähotelli Tott (☎ 573 673; www.savonhotellit .fi; Satamakatu 1; s/d €77/92; ☾ Jun-Aug; P ✕ ☦) Near the kauppatori, this place will have you signing up to study in Savonlinna, for this is a student residence out of summer. Don't let that put you off; it has spacious, high-standard rooms with couch, comfortable beds, minibar, and (in some rooms) great views. The apartment-style rooms (same price) aren't quite as smart – lino floors – but have a fully-equipped kitchen. Prices during the opera festival are significantly higher, however (around €150).

Hotel Seurahuone (☎ 5731; www.savonhotellit.fi; Kauppatori 4-6; s/d from €92/107, Jul d €165; P ✕ ▯) This is a stylish high-rise hotel in the heart of town, overlooking the kauppatori. The rooms in the newer wing are best; although on the small side, they boast fantastic vistas over the lake and centre of the action. There's a good café and reasonable restaurant here.

Kesähotelli Opera (☎ 476 7515; www.savocenter .fi; Kyrönniemenkuja 9; d €75, with shared bathroom €70; ☾ mid-Jun–early Aug; P ✕) Operated as a summer hotel by the Opera Festival, this place is across the bridge from the main part of town, about 1.5km east of the centre. There are hotel and apartment-style rooms, some with kitchen.

Villa Aria (☎ 476 7515; www.savocenter.fi; Puistokatu 15; d €100-125; ☾ Jun-early Aug; P ✕) This is another festival-run summer hotel on the western side of the town centre. It's a stylish wooden hotel with 20 comfortable, modern rooms. Although these prices would be high elsewhere, this offers some of the best Opera Festival value.

Lomamökkilä (☎ 523 117; www.lomamokkila.fi; Mikonkiventie 209; s/d from €32/54, cabins €44-56, cottages €97-120; P ✕) Twelve kilometres northeast of Savonlinna, this farm makes an excellent place to stay. As well as rustic rooms in the main farmhouse, there are lakeside cabins, large upmarket cottages and various outbuildings. Room rates include a tasty breakfast.

Huvila, the brewery-restaurant, also has **boutique accommodation** (€65, €120 during Opera Festival) with two attractive attic rooms above the brewery. Similarly, Café Mimosa has comfortable guesthouse accommodation close to the castle – there are six double rooms, some with balconies facing the lake, for approximately €75.

Eating

Huvila (☎ 555 0555; www.panimoravintolahuvila.fi; Puistokatu 4; mains €14-28; ☾ lunch & dinner) This is a brewery-restaurant and one of the finest places to dine or enjoy a beer in Savonlinna. It's across the harbour from the town centre. The dining area is smart, all white linen and Riedl glasses; dishes are exquisitely presented and classy. There's also a great terrace looking over the water. Huvila also offers boutique accommodation (above).

Majakka (☎ 531 456; Satamakatu 11; lunch specials from €7, mains €12-18; ☾ 11am-11.30pm Mon-Sat, noon-11.30pm Sun) Opposite the harbour is a good restaurant with a deck-like terrace fitting the nautical theme (the name means 'lighthouse'). Local meat and fish specialities are tasty and fairly priced; the house special is medallions of wild boar served with sausage and mash. Opens late during the opera festival. Good service.

Liekkilohi (Flaming Salmon; fish mains €11-13.50) Anchored just off the kauppatori in a bright-red, covered pontoon, this place has friendly staff that serve tasty portions of flamed salmon and fried vendace (tiny lake fish). It's open until 2am during summer – perfect for a very Finnish late-night snack.

Café Mimosa (☎ 532 257; Linnankatu 12; light meals €6-12; 🕑 9am-late) This place near the castle has a fine terrace and bar shaded under the plane trees, and serves salads, cakes and light meals. They also rent boats. It's very lively after the opera performances. Mimosa also offers guesthouse accommodation (p119).

Oopperakellari (☎ 020-744 3445; www.savocenter .fi; Kalmarinkatu 10; set meals €45-55) This underground restaurant has lavish pre- and post-opera dinners, with music, and perhaps even some of the stars answering questions or knocking out a few notes. You will need to book in advance, preferably before leaving home, as tickets are usually sent by mail.

Café Sarastro (☎ 514 425; Linnankatu 10; mains €10-17; 🕑 10am-8pm May–mid-Sep) Named for the villainous cleric in Mozart's Magic Flute, Sarastro is also near the castle and is another opera festival favourite. A lovely veranda overlooks the garden, and a range of snacks and more filling fare is on hand.

Pizzeria Capero (Olavinkatu 51; pizza & pasta €6.50-8.50; 🕑 lunch & dinner) This is the best place in town for an uncomplicated and tasty feed of pizza. It's just west of the bridge by the kauppatori.

Juanita Bar & Café (☎ 514 531; Olavinkatu 44; mains €7-14; 🕑 4pm-4am Mon-Sat) This place, upstairs in an arcade off Olavinkatu, does reasonably priced burgers, fajitas and Tex-Mex, and is a popular bar later in the night.

The lively market at the lakeside kauppatori is the place to find local pastries such as *omena-lörtsy*, a tasty apple turnover (€1 to €2). Also on the kauppatori, Café Torppa is a popular kiosk for coffee and late-night snacks with a good upstairs terrace.

Drinking

With only a small student population, Savonlinna is quiet most of the year, but very lively in July, when post-opera discussions carry on late into the night.

Huvila (☎ 555 0555; www.savonniemi.com; Puistokatu 4; 🕑 until 1am) A good place for a drink is this brewery-pub, with several types of beer brewed on the premises. A pint of the deliciously hoppy Joutsen on the terrace is hard to beat; you look out across the lake to the harbour area. There's regular live music in July.

Olutravintola Sillansuu (☎ 531 451; Verkkosaarenkatu 1) This place near the main bridge is a cosy English-style pub with nearly a hundred international bottled beers and a range of whiskeys. There's a downstairs area with a pool table; during the opera festival, impromptu arias are sometimes sung as the beer kegs empty.

Juanita (☎ 514 531; Olavinkatu 44; mains €7-14; 🕑 4pm-4am Mon-Sat) Later in the night, this Tex-Mex restaurant and bar is the place to mix with young Savonlinnans – it's usually jumping until closing time.

Linnakrouvi (☎ 576 9124; Linnankatu 7; 🕑 May-Sep) Near the castle, this is an atmospheric restaurant and beer terrace open in summer only in a lovely and stylish wooden house. There's upmarket food available, but you're paying a premium for its proximity to the fort.

Shopping

Linnankatu, the quaint back street running up towards the castle, is lined with old wooden houses, some of which are craft shops and studios selling local handicrafts at hefty prices. There's some good quality here though.

The kauppatori has a particularly lively summer market with good handicrafts and souvenirs on sale alongside the fresh berries, baked treats and garden produce.

Getting There & Away

AIR

Finnair flies to Savonlinna from Helsinki, Mikkeli and Varkaus. The airport is 15km from the centre. There are night flights during the opera festival to return punters to Helsinki after the show.

BOAT

In summer there are scheduled ferry services from the Savonlinna passenger harbour to Punkaharju and to Kuopio. The SS *Heinävesi* travels to the Retretti jetty in Punkaharju daily from mid-June to mid-August. It departs from Savonlinna at 11am and from Punkaharju at 3.40pm (adult one way/return €19/25, two hours).

In summer the ferry MS *Puijo* travels to Kuopio on Monday, Wednesday and Friday at 9am (one way €75, 10½ hours), returning on Tuesday, Thursday and Saturday. The boat passes through scenic waterways, canals and locks, and stops along the way at Oravi, Heinävesi, Karvio canal and Palokki, among others. Meals are available.

BUS
There are several express buses a day from Helsinki to Savonlinna (€46.70, five to six hours), and buses run almost hourly from Mikkeli (€18.90, 1½ hours). There are also regular services to Joensuu (€22.90, three hours), Kuopio (€22.90, three hours) and Jyväskylä (€32.30, 3½ hours).

TRAIN
There are trains from Helsinki (€47.90, five hours) via Parikkala – note that you must change to a regional train or connecting bus service at Parikkala, otherwise you'll wind up in Joensuu (€24.90, 2½ hours). For Kuopio, you need to take a bus to Pieksämäki and a train from there. The main train station is a long walk from the centre of Savonlinna; get off at the kauppatori platform instead.

Getting Around
The Savonlinna airport is 15km northeast of the centre. An airport taxi shuttle meets arriving flights during the opera season; in town it picks up at the bus station and hotels on demand (☎ 040-536 9545). The 20-minute trip costs €10 one way. A normal cab to or from the airport is €20 to €25.

The city bus service costs €2.50 per ride within the Savonlinna area.

Several car rental agencies have offices in the centre and at the airport, including **Europcar** (☎ 040-306 2855; airport) and **Hertz** (☎ 020-555 2760; Rantakatu 2).

Several places in town rent bikes, among them **Savonlinnan Polkupyörähuolto** (☎ 533 977; Olavinkatu 19), which charges €10 per day.

AROUND SAVONLINNA
The area around Savonlinna, with its scenic islands, peninsulas, bays and straits, is the most beautiful part of the Lakeland. There are many opportunities for cottage rentals and farmstays; contact the Savonlinna tourist service (www.savonlinnatravel.com).

Punkaharju Region
☎ 015 / pop 4083
Between Savonlinna and Parikkala is Punkaharju, the famous pine-covered sand esker (sand or gravel ridge) that's a popular sum-

mer destination. The ridge itself is very pretty, and great for walking or cycling; there's also an innovative gallery and a forestry museum. It's an easy day-trip from Savonlinna, with good transport connections. The village of Punkaharju has a post office, bank, bus and train stations, and several shops. There's a **tourist office** (☎ 734 1011; www.punkaharju.fi; Kauppatie 20) in the village, and a small information centre in the old *vanha asema* (train station) next to Lusto Museum.

SIGHTS
Punkaharju Ridge
During the Ice Age, formations similar to this 7km-long sand ridge were created all over the country. Because the Punkaharju ridge crosses a large lake, it has always been an important travel route. Just a few hundred metres of the original unsealed road along the top of the ridge remain – this was once part of a route to Russia. To take a stroll on the famous Punkaharju Ridge, get off at the Retretti train station and walk east towards Punkaharju village. It's a spectacular walk on a sunny day, with water on both sides.

Retretti Art Centre
Retretti (☎ 775 2200; adult/senior/student/child €15/12/9/5; ☺ 10am-6pm Jun & Aug, 10am-7pm Jul) is Finland's most unusual gallery – an art exhibition inside a man-made subterranean cave. This creation features waterfalls, a concert hall and special effects, and uses the natural elements of the cave – the walls, water and the darkness – to good effect. Above the cave (at ground level) is a more conventional exhibition space displaying art exhibitions on loan from elsewhere. The entire exhibition changes each summer. Admission is steep but it's a unique look at Finnish modern art.

About 100m away is the trade-off. Most reasonable children will let you into the gallery if you treat them to the popular **Kesämaa Water Park** (☎ 739 611; admission €12-13; ☺ 10am-7pm Jun–mid-Aug), an excellent place with water slides and pools.

Lusto Forest Museum
Lusto (☎ 345 1030; admission €7; ☺ 10am-7pm Jun-Aug, 10am-5pm daily Sep, 10am-5pm Tue-Sun Oct-May) is devoted to that most Finnish of industries – forestry. It's actually very good and educational, with displays not only about

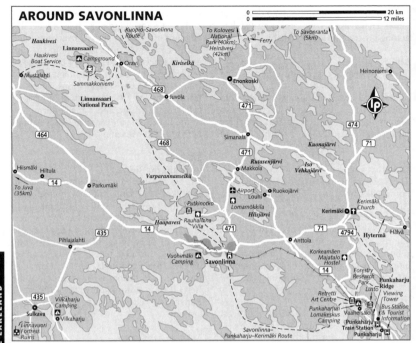

AROUND SAVONLINNA

THE LAKELAND

the industry and resource that has provided Finns with heat, power and income for many years, but also on the forest's habitats. The building itself is an interesting timber structure with the main display hall designed to represent the trunk of a tree.

SLEEPING & EATING

Gasthaus Punkaharju (☎ 441 371; www.naaranlahti.com; Palomäentie 18; s/d €45/65; P ✕ ☺) This guesthouse, in the village about 2km from the bus station, has light and cool, simply furnished rooms. You can use the sauna and pool for an additional fee. The owners also run the excellent farm-estate Naaranlahti, with 12 good apartment-rooms at the same price. This is a place where you can relax and take part in rural activities, including canoeing, fishing or gathering berries in the woods. It's about 15km from Punkaharju but transport is provided from the guesthouse.

Punkaharjun Valtionhotelli (☎ 739 611; www.lomaliitto.fi; s/d €80/106, during Savonlinna Opera Festival €97/129; P ✕) This place, on the ridge just west of the Lusto museum, is a romantic hotel dating from 1845, and one of the old-

est in Finland. As well as rooms in the lovely main house, there are two villas built for the wife of the tsar, and there's a fine restaurant attached. Rates are lower in winter.

Punkaharjun Lomakeskus Camping (☎ 739 611; www.lomaliitto.fi/punkaharjunlomakeskus; tent sites €15-16, 2-/4-person cabins €35/52, self-contained cottages €85-160) Next to the Kesämaa Water Park, this is one of the largest such complexes in Finland. It has more than 150 lakeside cottages and is very crowded in summer.

Ravintola Finlandia (☎ 644 255; Finlandiantie 98; lunch buffet €12; ☺ lunch & dinner in summer) A few hundred metres from Lusto, is this place in a beautiful house built in 1914 and surrounded by forest. The superb lunch buffet is served from 11am to 6pm daily in summer.

GETTING THERE & AWAY

All trains between Parikkala and Savonlinna stop in the village of Punkaharju, as well as at the Lusto and Retretti train stations. There are also regular buses to/from Savonlinna (€5, 20 minutes). In summer there is a ferry service from Savonlinna; see p120 for more information.

Siikalahti

Three kilometres east of the town of Parikkala, southeast of Savonlinna and accessible on the train, this bay of Simpelejärvi one of the best bird-watching spots in the country. Every summer, there are over 2000 nesting pairs of waterbirds, and it's also a busy stop on the migration routes of geese, terns and more (early May and late August are the best times to see these transients).

You'll see Siikalahti signposted off the road from Parikkala to Kaukola; from the carpark, there's a boardwalk to an observation hide. You can also camp for free here; there's an area for tents and a cooking shelter.

Kerimäki

☎ 015 / pop 5905

Kerimäki is a small farming community, yet it's dominated by the world's largest wooden church (below), which towers over the village. It's a memorable sight, and within easy range of Savonlinna.

The nearby protected island of **Hytermä** celebrates one of the weirdest of human achievements: it has a monument to Romu-Heikki (Junk Heikki), a man who built large structures with millstones. The island is also quite beautiful, and it's easily visited by hiring a rowing boat (around three to four hours €10) through the **tourist office**

(☎ 575 4211; Puruvedentie 59; ⊗ 10am-5pm Mon-Fri, 10am-1pm Sat) across from the church. The office is located in a good craft shop.

There are hourly buses along route 71 (€4, 30 minutes) between Savonlinna and Kerimäki, stopping at the bus station behind the tourist office.

SLEEPING & EATING

Gasthaus Kerihovi (☎ 541 225; Puruvedentie 28; s/d €35/60; ℗) An attractive old wooden house not far from the church (to the right of it as you face the entrance), this friendly guesthouse has spotless, comfortable rooms, each with shared bathroom. There's a popular restaurant-bar on-site and breakfast and a sauna is included in the room rate. Discounted rates apply in winter.

Korkeamäen Majatalo (☎ 544 827, 0440-544 827; www.korkeamaenmajatalo.fi; Ruokolahdentie 545; dm from €12.40, s/d €25/32; ⊗ Jun-Aug; ℗ ✗) About 8km south of Kerimäki village on the road to Punkaharju is this very friendly HI-affiliated farmhouse and cottages run by a Savonian family. As well as rooms with one to five beds, there are several cabins and cottages available. This road is not well served by public transport (two buses a day to Savonlinna), but if you have a car, this is an excellent option for cheap accommodation during the Opera Festival.

THE LAKELAND

KERIMÄKI CHURCH

Finland has plenty of notable churches, but few are as visually striking as Kerimäki's – the largest **wooden church** (☎ 578 9111; 10am-4pm mid-May–late Aug, 10am-6pm early June–mid-August, 10am-7pm in July) in the world. Built in 1847, it was designed to seat more than 3000 people and to accommodate 5000 churchgoers if all standing room was used.

The oversized church was no mistake, but was deliberately inflated from original plans by overexcited locals. At the time the church was built, the population of Kerimäki parish was around 12,000, and the reverend felt that half of the residents should be attending church on any given Sunday. Worshippers would visit the church from all around the region, crossing the lake in their *kirkkovene* (church longboat).

As stunning as the yellow-and-white church appears from the outside (it dominates tiny Kerimäki), the scale doesn't become apparent until you step inside and survey the massive interior – the height of the nave is 27m. You soon realise it would have been impossible to heat this building. It originally had eight stoves inside (now there are four) but it still wasn't enough and a smaller, 300-seat winter chapel had to be built at the rear. The main church is still used for services in summer. It's very unadorned inside apart from an altarpiece of the resurrected Christ by Aleksandra Såltin.

There's a café and gift shop in the separate bell tower in front of the church (all monies go to the maintenance of the church, an onerous burden for a small parish), and for €1.80 you can climb the bell tower on steep wooden steps for a better view.

Kahvila Kaivopirtti (Halvantie 1; ☻ 10am-8pm Mon-Sat) This place has a sunny terrace facing the church. They do reasonable coffee and pastries and very good-value grilli fare such as tasty platters of sausages, burgers, or kebabs (€2 to €6).

The Seal Lakes

Linnansaari and Kolovesi, two primarily water-based national parks in the Savonlinna area, offer fabulous lakescapes dotted with islands; it's best explored by hiring a canoe or rowing boat. There are several outfitters that offer these services, and free camping spots dotted along the lakes' shores.

This is the habitat of the Saimaa ringed seal. This endangered species (*Phoca hispida saimensis*) was separated from the Baltic ringed seal at the end of the last ice age, and is a lakebound species. After being in imminent danger of extinction due to hunting and human interference, its population levels have stabilized and are on the increase, although there remain only a precarious 300-odd of the noble silvery-grey beasts.

You are most likely to see seals in late May, when they are moulting and spend much time on rocks.

LINNANSAARI NATIONAL PARK

This scenic park consists of Lake Haukivesi and 130 uninhabited larger islands and hundreds more smaller ones; the main activity centres around the largest island, Linnansaari, which has several short hiking trails. As well as the seal population (50 to 100), rare birds, including osprey, can also be seen and heard in the park.

The best way to see the park is to pack camping gear and food, rent a rowing boat in Rantasalmi or Oravi (on the eastern shore of the lake) and spend a few days exploring. Boats, kayaks and canoes can be hired from **Saimaansydän Oravi** (☎ 647 290; www.saimaaholiday .net/wild; Oravi), who also runs guided four-day canoe trips, or **Saimaan Eräelämys** (☎ 0400-203 138; www.rantasalmi.net/eraelamys; Rantasalmi).

Oskari (☎ 0205-645 916; ☻ 10am-6pm Jun-Aug, 10am-4pm Tue-Fri, 10am-2pm Sat Feb-May & Sep-Nov) in Rantasalmi acts as a visitor information centre for the park and also has environmental displays.

On the island you can stay at the established camping areas for free, or there's a private **camping ground** (☎ 0500 275 458) with huts, tent sites and sauna. A canteen at Sammakkoniemi harbour sells provisions. Several smaller islands also have designated camping sites.

The main entrance to Linnansaari National Park is Mustalahti quay, but there is no bus stop, only boat connections. There is a boat service to the island of Linnansaari from Oravi (€7.50, 15 minutes), and from Mustalahti quay in Rantasalmi (€10, 25 minutes). If you miss a departure (there are three to four daily in summer), call a water taxi on ☎ 050-563 3257; the one-way fare from Oravi is €10.

There are regular buses to Oravi and Rantasalmi from Savonlinna. From Rantasalmi, it's an extra 3km to Mustalahti quay; you can either hitch, walk or catch a taxi. The Savonlinna–Kuopio ferry stops at Oravi.

KOLOVESI NATIONAL PARK

This fine park to the northeast of Linnansaari was founded in 1990 and covers several islands featuring well-preserved pine forests. There are high hills, rocky cliffs and caves, and even prehistoric rock paintings dating back 5000 years. There are some 30 to 40 Saimaa seals living here.

The Kolovesi park is a paradise for canoeing, the best way to explore the fantastic scenery. Motor-powered boats are prohibited in the park. There are several restricted areas within the park, and access to the islands is prohibited during winter. Check details at the small **information cabin** (☎ 015-479 040) in the village of Enonkoski, 15km south of the park, or at Savonranta (opposite). A free ferry north of Enonkoski crosses the narrows between two lakes on road 471.

There are two marked **walking trails** in the park. The 3.3km Nahkiaissalo nature trail is in the south of the park and accessible without a boat. There's a 3.9km nature trail on the northern island of Mantysalo. Just north of the park, the hill of Vierunvuori has prehistoric **rock paintings** depicting stick figures and elk.

Kolovesi Retkeily (☎ 040-558 9163; www.sealtrail .com) is the best and most experienced tour operator for the park, and specializes in canoe rental, outfitting and journeys. The office is located east of the park at Leipämäki, 15km west of Savonranta and 14km north of Enonkoski on road 471. The website www .norppateam.com lists other operators.

Inside the national park there are three **camping grounds**, one at Lohilahti near the southern access road 471; one at Lapinniemi; and the other on the island of Pitkäsaari.

Kievari Enonhovi (☎ 479431; raili.polonen@kievari-enonhovi.inet.fi; Urheilukentäntie 1; r per person €25-35; P ⊠) is an HI-affiliated hostel and hotel-restaurant in Enonkoski village, close to the national park. It's a very pleasant place, with a terrace, parkland leading down to the river and occasional live music in summer. There are two grades of rooms, all simple and likeable. The better ones have their own shower and kitchenette.

SAVONRANTA

An excellent base for exploration of the Kolovesi National Park and a quiet, attractive stop on the way north from Savonlinna, this town is east of the park on the shores of the mighty Orivesi lake.

On the shore, **Kuohu** (☎ 679 170; www.savonranta.fi; Vuokalantie 214; ⊙ 9am-9pm Sun-Thu, until midnight Fri & Sat Jun-Aug) serves as the information centre, and can also organize fishing trips on the lake. It also serves snacks, has a pleasant beer terrace and has some backpacker accommodation nearby.

The best place to stay in the Kolovesi area is in Savonranta. **Savonrannan Bed & Breakfast** (☎ 050-341 7204; http://personal.inet.fi/business/elina.gaynor; Yläsuluntie 5; r per person €35-40; ⊙ Jun-Aug; P ⊠) is a charming converted village bank. The comfortable rooms are thoughtfully and elegantly decorated, the shared bathrooms have great power showers, and the hosts lay on an excellent breakfast and will help arrange any activity. The setting is fantastic, with a garden by a small lake, the splashing of a millstream, a genuine wood sauna, and a balcony with spectacular sunsets. Guests have free use of the sauna and barbecue.

There are two daily buses from Savonlinna to Savonranta.

Sulkava

☎ 015 / pop 3257

Scenic, sleepy Sulkava, 39km southwest of Savonlinna, is known among Finns for its rowing-boat competitions (which some locals say is as much about the after-race partying as the rowing itself). It's the finishing

---

CANOEING THE SQUIRREL ROUTE

The 52km Juva to Sulkava canoeing route, known as Oravareitti ('Squirrel') route, is a highlight of this area and the perfect way for travellers to experience the lake region. Starting on Jukajärvi (at Juva Camping, see opposite), it traverses lakes, rivers and rapids on the way to Sulkava. Only one section is impassable – at Kuhakoski rapids, where canoes must be carried 50m past a broken dam. However, they should be carried at two other points along the way. Otherwise the rapids are relatively simple, though the water level drops 25m between Juva and Sulkava. Water levels vary considerably; if it's been abnormally dry, there will be more portage required.

Juva Camping provides everything you need: it rents two-person Canadian canoes (per day €25) or single kayaks (€17), gives you a waterproof map, and can arrange to pick you up (or just the canoe) at Sulkava for an additional fee. The route is signposted with information boards and there are two designated rest stops with fireplaces and toilets, as well as a midway camping area. It's also possible to start or break the route at Toivo, where there's a **hostel** (☎ 015-459 622).

It's 8km from the camping ground across the lake to the first river section, Polvijoki. Along here you must carry your canoe to the right of the dam. Passing through the small lakes, Riemiö and Souru, you come to the first rapids, the gentle 200m Voikoski, which is followed by the first rest area to the left of a small island. Continue along the canal, carrying the canoe across the road at the end, before negotiating the Karijoki.

There's a camping ground called **Oravanpesät** (☎ 0400 938 076) on the 2km long Kaitijärvi with tent sites and cottages. Next comes a series of rapids including Kissakoski and the strong currents of the Kyrsyanjoki. You continue through the Rasakanjoki and Tikanjoki before coming to the large Halmejärvi, at the end of which is another resting place. The route continues on the western shore of Lohnajärvi to the Lohnankoski, at the end of which the canoes must be carried past the broken concrete dam. From here it's a leisurely paddle down the Kuhajärvi, past a final set of rapids and into Sulkava, where you pull in at the Kulkemus Boat Centre. There's a camping ground and a café here.

point for the two-day Oravareitti canoe route leaving from Juva.

The **tourist office** (☎ 739 1210; www.sulkava.fi; Alanteentie 36; ☺ mid-Jun–mid-Aug) can provide details of some of the numerous cottages for rental in the area.

The **Sulkava Rowing Race** (www.suursoudut.net) attracts big crowds over its four days, ending on the second Sunday in July. Competitors row around Partalansaari over a 65km (one-day) course, or 75km (two-day) course, then get thoroughly hammered. There's also an 'armada race' of 12m boats.

The **Linnavuori Fortress Ruins** is probably the most interesting sight in the Sulkava area. It's well signposted. The view from the top is of idyllic Lakeland scenery and old fortifications. The site was originally a prehistoric settlement.

SLEEPING

Muikkukukko (☎ 471 651; www.muikkukukko.com; Alanteentie 40; s/d from €25/40, **P** ✗) In the centre of town, this is a small motel attached to a popular pizza restaurant and dance floor. Its 10 double rooms are simply decorated and perfectly comfortable; there are also cabins available, popular with fishermen.

Vilkaharju Camping (☎ 471 223; www.lomaliitto .fi/sulkava; tent sites €13, cottages €36-54; ☺ early Jun–mid-Aug) This place, in the Vilkaharju area 7km from Sulkava, is on a scenic headland across a pedestrian bridge (road access is possible). It's quite a village, with cottages, rooms and a dance restaurant in summer.

Juva

☎ 015 / pop 7403

The village of Juva, 60km west of Savonlinna and on the highway midway between Mikkeli and Varkaus, is mainly of interest to travellers as the starting point for the two-day Oravareitti canoeing trip. While you're here (or if you're passing through), check out the bizarre **Puutaitonäyttely** (adult/ student €7/3.50; ☺ 10am-6pm Jun-Sep) just off the highway junction. It's an exhibition space of more than 500 wooden sculptures made by 40 artists, many using chainsaws. It's Finland timber industry turned fine art.

The Juva village centre is along the main street, Juvantie, where you'll find plenty of services and the **tourist office** (☎ 755 1224; Juvantie 13; ☺ 10am-6pm Mon-Sat, 11am-2pm Sun Jun-Aug, shorter hr in winter) in the town hall building.

There's an interesting museum in the Partala manor area. **Juva Museum & Karelian Museum** (☎ 755 1297; Huttulantie 1; adult/child €2/1; ☺ 11am-5pm Tue-Sun summer) displays local history and items from Soviet Karelia.

Juva Camping (☎ 451 930; www.juvacamping .com; Hotellitie 68; tent sites €12, 2-/4-person cabins from €25/35; ☺ late May–late Aug) Just off the main road, this excellent camping ground is right beside Jukajärvi. There are various cabins available, including large ones with their own sauna (€65).

There are dozens of B&Bs in this area – contact the Juva or Mikkeli tourist offices for information.

MIKKELI & AROUND

☎ 015

Mikkeli is a sizable provincial town on Lake Saimaa and an important transport hub for eastern Lakeland. It was the headquarters of the Finnish army during WWII, and it was from here that CGE Mannerheim directed the Winter War campaign against the Soviets. Museums relating to those years are the main sights in town. It's still an important military base, and soldiers sometimes seem to outnumber civilians in town. It's a friendly place though, and although there's little to see, it often makes a convenient stopover between north and south.

For information on local attractions contact the Mikkeli **tourist office** (☎ 194 3900; Porrassalmenkatu 15; ☺ 9am-6pm Mon-Fri, 10am-3pm Sat), near the large and lively kauppatori. The office has free Internet access.

Päämajamuseo (Headquarters Museum; ☎ 194 2424; Päämajankatu 1-3; adult/child €4/free; ☺ 10am-5pm Wed-Sun Sep-Apr, 10am-5pm daily May-Aug) was the army's command centre during the war; and **Jalkaväkimuseo** (Infantry Museum; ☎ 369 666; Jääkärinkatu 6-8; adult/child €3.50/1.50) is one of the largest military museums in Finland.

The area around Mikkeli is excellent for **freshwater fishing** – its many lakes teem with perch, salmon and trout, and ice-fishing is popular in winter. The tourist office can help with information, fishing permits, guides and equipment rental.

Mikkeli Music Festival (www.mikkelimusic.net), held here in late June/early July, is a week-long classical music event featuring top Finnish and Russian conductors.

The **rock paintings** of Astuvansalmi (Astuvansalmen Kalliomaalaukset), estimated to be 3000 to 4000 years old, are some of the finest prehistoric rock paintings in Finland. They are on a steep rock cliff, 38km by road southeast of Mikkeli, reached by a walking track from the road. You'll need a vehicle or bicycle to get there.

Close to the rock paintings, the open-air **Pien-Toijolan Talomuseo** (☎ 416 103; 🕑 10am-4pm Thu-Sun) is an estate dating from 1672, and consists of over 20 old houses.

Sleeping & Eating

Hotelli Nuijamies (☎ 321 150; www.hotellinuijamies .com; Porrassalmenkatu 21; s/d €66/94; P ✕) On the market square in Mikkeli, this family-run hotel is a good choice, being in the centre and close to the bus and train stations. The rooms are bright, with big windows and good views. There are several nice touches like B&W photos of old Finland and little Persian rugs. Management are friendly and there's a good restaurant and bar downstairs.

Visulahti Camping (☎ 18281; Visuahdenkatu 1; tent sites €13.50, cabins €50-140; 🕑 late May-end Aug) This camping ground, next to the Visulahti amusement park, is the closest one to Mikkeli. It's about 5km east of the town centre and has lakeside tent sites and a wide range of cabins.

Café Sole (☎ 212 798; Porrassalmenkatu 19; lunches €7-11; 🕑 8.30am-6pm Mon-Fri, 10am-4pm Sat, 11am-4pm Sun) Facing the market square in Mikkeli, this is a good option for breakfast or lunch, when there are salads full of nice things as well as filling hot dishes. There's friendly service and a pretty terrace to watch Mikkeli march by.

Getting There & Away

Mikkeli is a transport hub between Helsinki (€32.30, 3½ hours) and eastern Lakeland or Kuopio (€25.60, 2½ to four hours) to the north, so plenty of buses pass through in all directions. The bus station is on the northern side of the kauppatori.

There are up to five trains daily from Helsinki and a similar number of connections from towns in the north. From other directions, change at Pieksämäki or Kouvola.

There are lake cruises between Mikkeli and Ristiina in summer; the Mikkeli tourist office has schedule and fare information.

RISTIINA

☎ 015

Ristiina, 18km south of Mikkeli, is one of the region's historic villages, founded by Count Per Brahe in 1649 and named after Kristina, his wife (subsequently the queen of Sweden). Little remains of the village's glorious past, though there are several places that reflect Per's aspirations.

The **tourist office** (☎ 661 750; Brahentie 53; 🕑 10am-6pm Mon-Fri, 10am-2pm Sat & Sun, shorter hr in winter), in the centre of town, 2km east of the main Mikkeli-Lappeenranta road, can provide a map, and you can rent bicycles from Gasthaus Brahe nearby.

There's a distance between the main road and Ristiina's principal attraction, the castle ruins, but most shops and places to stay and eat are on the main street, Brahentie.

Brahelinna is the castle that was built by Per Brahe; its ruin is on a hill 2km from the village. The castle's high crumbling walls and the surrounding forest make for lovely walking. A sign saying 'Dunckerin kivi' points to a stone that was erected to honour a local, Mr Duncker, who fought and died during the 1809 battles against Russia.

The only place to stay in Ristiina itself is the HI affiliated **Gasthaus Brahe** (☎ 661 078; Brahentie 54, Ristiina; beds from €12; P ✕). It's on the main street about 100m from the tourist office. It also has a decent restaurant and provides some local nightlife. The rooms are in a separate building, previously used as a school dormitory. There are bicycles, boats and canoes to rent.

VARKAUS

☎ 017 / pop 24,269

The town of Varkaus is a small transport hub in a decent location, surrounded by water and spread over several islands cut by canals. It's this location, though, that led to the arrival of the timber and pulp industry and the smoke-belching factories that blight the town. Much of the population works for the paper and pulp industries. The **tourist office** (☎ 551 555; Kauppatori 6; 🕑 9am-4.30pm Mon-Fri) is in the town centre near the market square.

If you have a vehicle, it's well worth driving the 2km from the town centre to **Mekaanisen Musiikin Museo** (Museum of Mechanical Music; ☎ 558 0643; Pelimanninkatu 8; adult/child €10/5; 🕑 Tue-Sun early Mar–mid-Dec). A Finnish-German couple runs this delightful collection of 250 unusual musical instruments, and admission includes an eccentric tour of the house and its lovingly renovated mechanical instruments from the USA and Europe. Next door is a stylish German-run restaurant, **Zeppelin** (☎ 558 0644; Pelimanninkatu 8; mains €14-20; ✆ 11am-late Tue-Sat).

There are a couple of hotels and a summer hostel in Varkaus.

There are daily flights from Helsinki to Varkaus. Keskusliikenneasema is the central station, which includes train and bus terminals. There are frequent trains to Joensuu (€14.40, 1½ hours), and regular connections to Turku (€46.40, six hours) and Helsinki (€45, 5½ hours), changing in Pieksämäki

HEINÄVESI & AROUND

☎ 017 / pop 4403

The village of Heinävesi lies amid hilly country some way off the main Lakeland routes north of Kolovesi National Park, but some of the most scenic lake routes in Finland pass through here and canals provide a means of local transport. It's not a pretty place, but the nearby monasteries are a major drawcard.

There's a huge wooden **church** on a hill at the end of Kirkkokatu. It was built in 1890, seats 2000 people, and offers good views over Kermajärvi from the tower. Nearby is the local **museum** and a **handicrafts centre**.

On the northern side of Kermajärvi, 28km by road from Heinävesi, **Karvio** has scenic rapids that are good for fishing, and the canal serves as a jetty for lake ferries. This is a stopover for the Savonlinna–Kuopio ferry and a jump-off point for the Valamo Monastery and Lintula Convent.

Sleeping

There's also accommodation at the Valamo Orthodox Monastery.

Gasthaus-Hotelli Heinävesi (☎ 562 411; Askeltie 2; s/d €55/75; ✗) This place in the village centre opposite the bus terminal is an excellent choice, with characterful rooms that are good value, and all a little different. There's friendly staff and a very good breakfast. There's a pub and restaurant here, which makes it the social heart of town.

Karvio Camping (☎ 563 603; www.lomakarvio.fi; Takunlahdentie 2; tent sites €13, cabins €25-68; ✆ May–mid-Sep) A friendly and well-run place that is beautifully located by the Karvio rapids, you can fish here to your heart's content.

There are two restaurants here, and a choice of simple cabins or upmarket, heated cottages, which are also available in the winter months by arrangement.

Uittotupa (☎ 563 603; Uitontie 1; 4–6-person cabins €60-75) This place is across the road from, and part of, Karvio Camping, but open year-round. There's a wide variety of accommodation in various cabins and cottages. There's a café here renowned for its homemade bread.

Getting There & Around

The easiest way to arrive at Heinävesi is via bus from Varkaus (€8.70, 40 minutes, up to five departures on weekdays), there are also services to Kuopio (€22.90, three hours) and two a week to Savonlinna (€12.70, 1½ hours).

In summer, the passenger ferry MS *Puijo* from Kuopio (€32, 4½ hours, leaves at 9am on Tuesday, Thursday and Saturday) or Savonlinna (€39, six hours, leaves 9am on Monday, Wednesday and Friday) calls at the Heinävesi jetty, just below the village. Bikes can be hired at the Heinävesi harbour, and boats and canoes can be hired at the Karvio or Viisalahti camping grounds.

VALAMO ORTHODOX MONASTERY

The **Valamo monastery** (☎ 017-570 111; www .valamo.fi; Valamontie 42, Uusi-Valamo) – Finland's only Orthodox monastery – is one of Savo's most popular attractions. Its history goes back 800 years to the Karelian island of Valamo on Lake Ladoga.

The original Valamo monastery was in the part of Karelia ceded to the Soviet Union after the Winter War. Its icons and treasures were packed up and brought to Finland; many of them are here.

In summer, the monastery can feel quite commercialised, with crowds flocking to buy souvenir beeswax candles, icons and CDs at the gift shop. Like any good monks, the clergy also make their own berry wine.

The two churches at the monastery contain a number of fine icons. Down at the riverside, the small chapel of St Nicholas is also worth a look. There's a **museum** (✆ 10am-5pm Mon-Sat, noon-5pm Sun mid-Jun–mid-Aug) inside the cultural centre. Guided tours are conducted regularly (€3.50), although for tours in English you may have to contact the monastery in advance for times. Services are open to the public and are given at 6am and 6pm Monday to Friday, 9am and 6pm Sunday and also at 1pm from June to August.

A good way to appreciate the monastery is to stay overnight. You can stay in the simple **Valamo Guesthouse** (dm €22, s €25; P X &) or the more comfortable **Valamo Hotel** (s/d €40/60, weekends €50/68; P X &). Also in the complex is **Trapesa**, the monastery café/restaurant. There's a lunch and dinner buffet for €11, a Russian-style 'high tea' in the evenings (€6.50, bookings required) and the usual sandwiches, coffee and monastery wine.

See below for transport information.

LINTULA ORTHODOX CONVENT

The only Orthodox convent in Finland, **Lintula** (☎ 017-563 106, ☼ 9am-6pm Jun–Aug) is much quieter than the popular Valamo monastery. It's a serene contrast that is well worth the short detour, and it's open outside the season by appointment.

Lintula was founded in Karelia in 1895 and transferred during WWII to Savo and then Häme. The nuns founded a convent at the present location in 1946. A souvenir shop on the premises sells wool and candles manufactured at the convent, and there's a pleasant coffee shop open from 10am to 6pm. The highlight is the lovely grounds, perfect for strolling. In the garden is a beautifully simple log chapel, whose icons glint in the light from the homemade candles.

Lintulan Vierasmaja (☎ 017-563 225; s/d €18/28; P X) is a small red house at the back of the convent. There are simple but clean rooms, with separate bathroom, and it's open to men and women.

Getting There & Away

There are buses direct to Valamo from Joensuu and Mikkeli, but the services aren't frequent. From Heinävesi you need to change at Karvio. For Lintula, daily buses from Kuopio stop in the nearby village of Palokki, but if you're coming from the south, the nearest bus stop is on the highway 9km away.

The most pleasant way to get to either place in summer is on a **Monastery Cruise** (adult/child €60/30) from Kuopio. The cruise uses a combination of the regular Kuopio to Savonlinna ferry and car or bus transport. The ferry departs Kuopio at 9am Tuesday, Thursday and Saturday, then there's car transport from Palokki to Lintula and Valamo, then a bus back to Kuopio. On Monday, Wednesday and Friday, and Sunday transport is reversed with a bus to Valamo at noon and a ferry back from Palokki.

There are also canal cruises on the **MS Sergei** (☎ 570 111; tickets €8-15) from Valamo to Palokki and on Joujärvi.

CENTRAL LAKELAND

JYVÄSKYLÄ
☎ 014 / pop 83,582

This bustling provincial capital of central Lakeland is a Mecca for architecture lovers around the world for its large collection of Alvar Aalto buildings, particularly the university campus. Jyväskylä (pronounced yoo-vah-skoo-lah) was founded in 1837 and its reputation as a nationalistic town goes back to the earliest days, when the first Finnish-language schools were established here. In 1966 the university was inaugurated, and Jyväskylä was to become renowned for its modern architecture. Aside from all the Aalto connections and its lakeside location, it's an enjoyable provincial city whose youthful student population and lively academic scene gives it plenty of energy and nightlife. It's also popular as a winter sports centre with some frightening ski jumps near town, and you can arrive in style by lake ferry from Lahti.

Information

Avatar (☎ 214 811; Puistokatu 1A; per hr €3; ☼ 10am-10pm) Internet café with top-notch gear and helpful staff.
Main post office (Vapaudenkatu 60; ☼ 8am-8pm Mon-Fri) In the Kauppakulma shopping centre.
Public library (☎ 624 440; Vapaudenkatu 39-41; ☼ 11am-8pm Mon-Fri, 11am-3pm Sat) Has several free Internet terminals on the 3rd floor.
Tourist office (☎ 624 903; www.jyvaskyla.fi; Asemakatu 6; ☼ 9am-6pm Mon-Fri, 10am-3pm Sat & Sun Jun-Aug, 9am-5pm Mon-Fri, 10am-3pm Sat Aug-May) This office publishes an excellent free guide to events and activities in the region, sells tickets and has a free Internet terminal.

Sights
THE ALVAR AALTO PORTFOLIO

The main reason most people visit Jyväskylä is for its modern architecture; at times the whole city centre is full of folk curiously pointing wide-angled lenses at every Aalto building. The best time to visit Jyväskylä is from Tuesday to Friday, as many buildings are closed on weekends and the Aalto Museum is closed on Monday.

Alvar Aalto (see opposite) was a giant of 20th century architecture. He was schooled here, opened his first offices here and spent his summers in nearby Muuratsalo.

The city has dozens of Aalto buildings, but your first stop should be at one of his last creations, the **Alvar Aalto Museum** (☎ 624 809; www.alvaraalto.fi; Alvar Aallon katu 7; adult/student/child €6/2/free; ☒ 11am-6pm Tue-Sun; ☐ ☒), near the university to the west of the centre. It chronicles his life and work, and has a focus on a couple of dozen of his major buildings, as well as a section on his furniture and glassware designs. It's very engaging, and you get a real feel for the man and his philosophy.

Here you can buy the *Architectural Map Guide* brochure (€2), which plots well over a hundred buildings in and around Jyväskylä designed by Aalto and other notable figures. Aalto's list includes the university's main buildings and the **city theatre** (Vapaudenkatu 36). On the corner of Kauppakatu and

Väinönkatu is the old Workers' Club building, designed by him in 1925.

Aalto fans won't want to miss Säynätsalo Town Hall (p134), where you can even sleep in a room that the man himself slept in, or his experimental summer cottage at Muuratsalo.

MUSEUMS
Jyväskylä's other museums are all free on Fridays and closed on Mondays.

Keski-Suomen Museo
The **Museum of Central Finland** (☎ 624 930; Alvar Aallon katu 7; adult/child €4/free; ☒ 11am-6pm Tue-Sun; ☒) is adjacent to the Alvar Aalto Museum and designed by him, but sees a fraction of the visitors. A pity, for it's a well-presented display. The main exhibition is an attractive overview of rural life in Central Finland from prehistoric times onwards. There's an ancient sledge-runner dated to 4000BC, and displays on hunting, fishing and logging, with English translations. It gives a good feel for traditional Finnish life and finishes in a typical old grocery store. Up-

JYVÄSKYLÄ

0   500 m
0   0.3 miles

INFORMATION		
Avatar (Internet café).........1	C2
Main post office..............2	C2
Public library................3	B3
Tourist office................4	C2

SIGHTS & ACTIVITIES		
Alvar Aalto Museum........5	B3
City Theatre................6	C2
Craft Museum of Finland..7	C2

Jyväskylä Art Museum............8 B2
Jyväskylä University Library.....9 B3
Museum of Central Finland....10 B3

SLEEPING ☐		
Hotel Yöpuu.....................11	C2
Hotelli Alba....................12	B3
Hotelli Milton..................13	C2
Kesähotelli Amis................14	B1
Pension Kampus..................15	B2
Scandic Hotel Jyväskylä.........16	C2
Sokos Hotel Alexandra...........17	C2

EATING ☐		
Figaro..........................18	C2
Karoliinan Kahvimylly...........19	C2
Katriinan Kasvisravintola.....(see 15)
Kauppahalli.....................20	C2
Kissanviikset...................21	C2
Libanon.........................22	B2
Salsa Orkidea...................23	B2

DRINKING ☐		
Jazz Bar........................24	C2
Sohwi..........................25	B3
Ye Old Brick's Inn..............26	C2

ENTERTAINMENT		
Fantasia Cinema..............(see 27)

SHOPPING ☐		
Jyväskeskus Shopping Centre..27	C3

TRANSPORT		
Bus Terminal....................28	C2
Local Bus Stop..................29	C2
Passenger harbour...............30	C3

THE LAKELAND

ALVAR AALTO

Pushing Sibelius and assorted racing drivers as most famous Finn, Alvar Aalto (1898–1976) was one of the most significant architects of the 20th century. Churches, town halls, museums and concert halls designed by Aalto can be seen across Finland from Helsinki to Rovaniemi. Aalto's buildings tread the line between the unadorned functionalism of the International Style and the people and materials orientation of the Organic Style. His designs emphasise the qualities of wood, brick and glass, the role of the building and its relationship to the people using it. It's a quintessentially democratic architecture: in previous centuries architects largely designed buildings for the wealthy few, but Aalto saw his task as 'a question of making architecture serve the well-being and prosperity of millions of citizens'.

Aalto was born in 1898 just outside Seinäjoki in the town of Kuortane. He practised in Jyväskylä, Turku and Helsinki (undoubtedly benefiting from being the first listing in the *Yellow Pages*) until gaining an international reputation for his pavilions at the World Fairs of 1937 (Paris) and 1939 (New York).

His most famous work is probably Helsinki's Finlandia Hall (1962–71), but the House of Culture (1952–58), with its convex wall of wedge-shaped bricks, and the Helsinki University of Technology in Espoo (1953–66) are also fine examples of his work. Jyväskylä is chock-a-block with Aalto-designed buildings including the Workers' Club (1952) and the Alvar Aalto Museum (1971–73). A comparison of the Civic Centre in Seinäjoki with the Church of the Three Crosses (1955–58) in Imatra highlights the range of Aalto's work. His characteristic use of rod-shaped ceramic tiles, undulated wood, woven cane, brick and marble is distinctive. Aalto's work was seminal and hugely influential; you'd guess that many of his buildings were built a couple of decades later than they were.

Aalto also achieved a reputation as an abstract painter, sculptor and furniture designer. In 1925 he married Aino Marsio, with whom he formed a dynamic team, collaborating on much of his work and on Artek furniture designs. Their work on bending and laminating wood revolutionised furniture design. The classic Aalto furniture is still a Finnish design staple.

Charmingly, the project Aalto himself loved the most was his own wooden boat, which he designed and built with great love, but little skill. It was barely seaworthy at the best of times, and regularly capsized and sank!

stairs is a history of Jyväskylä itself, with a couple of great scale models; the top floor is devoted to temporary art exhibitions, often associated with the Jyväskylä Arts Festival.

Jyväskylän Taidemuseo

Opened in 1998, the **Jyväskylä Art Museum** (☎ 626 855; Kauppakatu 23; adult/child €5/free; 🕑 11am-6pm Tue-Sun; ♿) houses exhibitions of modern art and sculpture, often arranged by the active and excellent local artists' association. This, the main gallery, is complemented by two other exhibition spaces nearby, all entered on the same ticket.

Suomen Käsityön Museo

The permanent collection at the **Craft Museum of Finland** (☎ 624 946; www.craftmuseum.fi; Kauppakatu 25; adult/child €5/free; 🕑 11am-6pm Tue-Sun) is all about Finnish handicrafts and their history. Also incorporated is the National Costume Centre, which displays regional dress from around Finland. There is a small permanent collection plus temporary exhibitions. It's an enjoyable insight into activities which, partly due to the long Finnish winters, have always been an important part of life here. There's also a good shop attached.

Activities

SKIING

Northwest of the city centre, **Laajavuori Winter Sports Centre** (☎ 624 885; www.laajavuori .com; Laajavuorentie) has six modestly sloped ski runs, 62km of cross country trails (of which 10km is illuminated) and a number of very scary ski jumps (for which it is famous). There is a good ski area for children and the resort is popular with families. Catch bus 25 from the centre; it's 6km from town.

LAKE CRUISES

Jyväskylä is a popular cruise centre in summer because of the Keitele canal route north

THE LAKELAND

of town. There are day-long excursions to Suolahti (single/return €23.50/35) on Saturdays in July; another route goes to Viitasaari via Suolahti on Thursdays (11 hours, one way/return €36/54), returning the next day.

Short cruises on northern Lake Päijänne are also available from early June to early August, with daily departures. Some of these are evening cruises with dinner and dancing. Try to catch the SS *Suomi*, one of the oldest steamers still plying the Finnish lakes, which goes at 3pm Tuesday to Sunday, and 7pm Tuesday to Saturday (€14 to €15, three to four hours).

Tickets can be purchased at the **Jyväskylä passenger harbour** (☎ 218 024; Siltakatu 4). Take buses 18, 19 or 20 from the centre.

For information about the Jyväskylä to Lahti route see p134.

Festivals & Events

In mid-July, **Jyväskylän Kesä** (Jyväskylä Arts Festival; ☎ 624 378; kesa@jkl.fi) has an international programme of concerts, exhibitions, theatre and dance. It has a strong liberal and radical tradition, having been going for over 50 years, and is one of Finland's most important arts festivals.

In early August, Jyväskylä is the centre of what many Finns regard as the most important event of the summer calendar, the **Neste Rally Finland** (www.nesterallyfinland.fi). Formerly called the Thousand Lakes Rally, this is the Finnish leg of the World Rally Championship, which Finns follow closely and have been very successful at. Head into the Torikeskus shopping centre to see the hand- and footprints of all the Finnish winners of the event, most recently Marcus Grönholm. The event goes for four days, with a big concert/party on the Thursday, Friday and Saturday nights. You can book tickets over the Internet from March onwards. To get accommodation in Jyväskylä at this time, you need to have booked well in advance (the accommodation hotline ☎ 339 8382 may be able to help place you).

Sleeping

Hotel Yöpuu (☎ 333 900; www.hotelliyopuu.fi; Yliopistonkatu 23; s/d from €87/140, ste €170, weekends r €85; P ⊠ 🖳) This exquisite boutique hotel is the pick of Jyväskylä's accommodation by several lengths. The rooms are lavishly decorated and all in markedly different styles (you

must at least see the Africa room!); there are also a couple of excellent-value suites, two fine restaurants and a little flowery terrace to enjoy a glass of wine in peace and comfort.

Hotelli Milton (☎ 337 7900; www.hotellimilton .com; Hannikaisenkatu 29; s/d €65/85, weekends €55/70; P ⊠) This family-run hotel in the heart of town has a likeably old-fashioned feel with cheery bedspreads, wooden floors and a comfy guest lounge. There's a free sauna included in the price, and it's very handy for the bus and train stations. There are no rooms for smokers.

Sokos Hotel Alexandra (☎ 123 4642; www.soko shotels.fi; Hannikaisenkatu 35; s €102-135, d €135-156, s/d weekends & summer from €65/82; P ⊠ 🖳 🖳) One of two Sokos hotels in the centre of town, this is directly across from the train and bus stations and has two separate sections with excellent modern facilities and recently refurbished rooms. There's a choice of prices based on the conveniences contained.

Scandic Hotel Jyväskylä (☎ 330 3000; www.scandic -hotels.com; Vapaudenkatu 73; s/d €123/147, weekends from €71/81; P ⊠ 🖳 🖳) The striking modern façade of this business hotel conceals a well-equipped interior, with large, light rooms that will satisfy rather than enchant. There's a small pool, saunas and use of a gymnasium as well as the expected facilities.

Retkeilyhotelli Laajari (☎ 624 885; www.laajavuori .com; Laajavuorentie 15; dm from €17-21, s/d €35/56; P ⊠) Set in the Laajavuori winter-sports complex 4km from town (bus 25), this HI-affiliated hostel is popular with winter skiing groups for its open fires, modern no-nonsense dorms, sauna and café facilities. Prices come down at weekends. It's shut on Sundays outside the summer and winter seasons.

Kesähotelli Rentukka (☎ 607 237; rentukka@co .jyu.fi; Taitoniekantie 9; s/d/tr €39/52/60; 🕒 mid-May–Aug; P ⊠) In student accommodation 2.5km northwest of town (bus 18), these are light, no-frills rooms in a self-contained campus with restaurant, shops and bar. Rooms have bathroom and kitchen facilities but no utensils. Good for families. Breakfast included.

Tuomiojärvi Camping (☎ 624 895; Taulumäentie 47; tent sites €20, cottages €45-55; 🕒 Jun-Aug) A pleasant place 2km north of town, with several four- and six-bed cottages scattered in the lakeside woods. You can rent canoes to take out on the lake, and there's a café and sauna. Take bus 8 from the centre.

Other recommendations:

Hotelli Alba (☎ 636 311; www.hotellialba.fi; Ahlmaninkatu 4; s/d €74/98, weekends & summer €57/78; P ⊠ ⊡) Right on the lake, and handy for the Aalto museum and university. Friendly staff.

Kesähotelli Amis (☎ 443 0100; www.hotelliamis.com; Sepänkatu 3; s/d/tr €46/60/69; ⊙ Jun–mid-Aug; P ⊠ ⅄) Backing onto parkland, offers new, tidy, student-style rooms with private facilities and kitchenette.

Pension Kampus (☎ 338 1400; pensionkampus@kolumbus.fi; Kauppakatu 11; s/d €55/70, Sat, Sun & summer s €45-50 d €60; P ⊠) Central and spotless 3rd-floor option with kitchen facilities. Good value if you are self-catering.

Eating

As well as the places listed, both restaurants at the Hotelli Yöpuu are worthwhile.

Karoliinan Kahvimylly (☎ 0500 627 280; Hannikaisenkatu 14; ⊙ 11am-6pm Mon-Sat) Near the station, this charming spot is part-antique furniture shop and part-café. There's an array of the most delicious quiches and cheesecakes imaginable (€3 to €4), ice-cream, and a great atmosphere.

Katriinan Kasvisravintola (☎ 449 8880; Kauppakatu 11; mains €7; ⊙ 11am-2.30pm Mon-Sat) This is a likeable, comfortable, and cool vegetarian lunch restaurant next to Pension Kampus, with veggie pasta, curries and ratatouille. For €9 you get the dish of the day and access to the scrumptious salad bar.

Figaro (☎ 212 255; Asemakatu 4; mains €13-22; ⊙ 10.30am-midnight Mon-Sat, 1-10pm Sun) This is an upmarket and intimate restaurant with a smart, drawing-room feel. The dishes are rich, with plenty of creamy sauces. There are plenty of dishes featuring local lake and sea fish, while a reindeer pasta is a more unusual choice. There are three good vegetarian mains, but what they do best are steaks; the house special comes with a mountain of fried onion.

Libanon (☎ 620 315; Kauppakatu 5; dishes €6-15; ⊙ 11am-10pm Mon-Sat, 1-8pm Sun). This small, simple, Lebanese restaurant west of the centre is a good choice. It's got only five tables, and the menu centres on kebabs for the popular vote. It's authentic and you can enjoy quality baba ganoush and tasty *foul* (broad beans stewed in oil and garlic), accompanied by belly dancing on the big screen.

Kissanviikset (☎ 618 451; Puistokatu 3; mains €13-25; ⊙ lunch & dinner) The 'cat's whiskers' is a friendly spot just off the pedestrian street.

There are two dining areas; the cellar is more atmospheric and boasts a long menu with a wide range of (particularly) meat dishes; they do a good pepper steak, and reindeer makes its customary appearance.

Salsa Orkidea (☎ 611 557; Kauppakatu 10; mains €6-14; ⊙ lunch & dinner) For big servings of pasta, salads, tortilla and kebabs, it's hard to beat this place. There's a €6 lunch buffet and most mains are under €10.

Drinking & Entertainment

Jyväskylä has the sort of animated nightlife you only find in a busy university town, and the compact nature of the centre emphasises this. Kauppakatu, the main pedestrian strip, is a great place for bar-hopping, and in summer terraces spill out along here.

Ye Old Brick's Inn (☎ 616 233; Kauppakatu 57; ⊙ 11am-2am or 3am) Right in the liveliest part of the pedestrian zone, this warm and welcoming pub has several excellent beers on tap, a cosy interior and rosy outdoor chairs and tables; the place to be on a summer evening. They also do good meals.

Sohwi (☎ 615 564; Vaasankatu 21; ⊙ noon-1am Mon-Thu, noon-3am Fri & Sat, 2-10pm Sun) A short walk from the town centre is an excellent bar with a spacious wooden terrace, a good menu of snacks and bar meals, and plenty of lively student and academic discussion lubricated by a range of good bottled and draught beers. A great place.

Jazz Bar (☎ 621 398; Puistonkatu 2; ⊙ 3pm-late) This is the place for relaxing live music, with regular jazz slots and jam sessions during the week. There are long weekend happy hours and a small terrace.

Fantasia (Jyväskeskus Shopping Centre, Kauppakatu 29) This cinema is central, in the pedestrian zone, and has six screens showing major releases.

Getting Around

BUS

For reaching areas like Aalto's summer home, the camp site or the ski centre, you'll find the network of local buses useful. Unlike intercity buses, which use the bus station, local buses all leave from Vapaudenkatu, near the tourist office. Tickets cost €2.50 to €3.60 depending on distance; a day pass is €6.50 and cheaper than a return to Säynätsalo, for example. You can buy the pass in the tourist office.

BICYCLE

Jyväskylä is a good spot to explore by bike, particularly if you plan on investigating some of the further-flung Aalto buildings. You can rent one at **Rent@Bike** (☎ 050-443 3820; Humppakuja 2; per day/week €15/50), among other places.

Getting There & Away

AIR

There are several flights from Helsinki to Jyväskylä each weekday and fewer on weekends. The Jyväskylä airport is 21km north of the town centre; Finnair buses (€6, 20 minutes) meet each arriving flight. In the centre, catch the airport bus at the bus station, where it leaves 50 minutes prior to each departure, or on Vapaudenkatu.

BOAT

There is a regular ferry service on Lake Päijänne between Jyväskylä and Lahti, operated by **Päijänne Risteilyt Hildén Oy** (☎ 783 2515; www.paijanne-risteilythilden.fi). Boats leave Lahti at 10am on Tuesday and Thursday (€45, 10½ hours) from early June to early August. The service to Lahti leaves Jyväskylä at 10am on Wednesday and Friday.

BUS

The **bus terminal** shares a building with the train station and serves the entire southern half of Finland, with many daily express buses connecting Jyväskylä to the big cities, including hourly departures to Helsinki (€36.90, four to six hours), some requiring a change.

TRAIN

The train station is between the town and the harbour, in the same building as the bus station. There are regular trains from Helsinki (€39, 5½ hours) via Tampere, and some quicker direct trains.

AROUND JYVÄSKYLÄ

Säynätsalo

The large **Säynätsalo Town Hall** (Säynätsalon Kunnantalo; ☎ 623 801; admission weekdays free, weekends €2; 🕙 8.30am-3.30pm Mon-Fri, also 1-4pm Sat & Sun Jun-Aug) is on an island 10km southeast of Jyväskylä. It's one of Aalto's most famous works, the architect winning an international competition in 1949 to design it. The building was completed in 1952. There are

two rooms (☎ 623 815; r €25-30) available to stay in here; they are furnished with Aalto chairs and stools and named after the man and his second wife, who often slept here while supervising the building's construction. The two rooms are singles (although extra beds can be put in) and share a bathroom. They have simple kitchen facilities and are very good value.

Säynätsalo can be reached from central Jyväskylä on bus 16 (€3.60, 30 minutes).

Muuratsalo

This peaceful wooded islet is connected to Säynätsalo by bridges and was Aalto's summer retreat from the early 1950s onwards. On the shores of lake Päijänne he built **Koetalo** (☎ 624 809; www.alvaraalto.fi; adult/student €15/5; 🕙 1.30-3.30pm Mon, Wed & Fri Jun–mid-Sep), a must-see for Aalto lovers, but fairly pricey if you're not. Entrance is by guided tour, and must be pre-arranged by phone or email (the Aalto Museum or tourist office can do this). The tour takes you first to see his beloved boat, named *Nemo Propheta in Patria* ('nobody is a prophet in their own land') on dry land, never having been particularly seaworthy. Then to the lakeside sauna and the house itself. It's often called the 'experimental house', because Aalto used the charming patio to try out various types and patterns of bricks and tiles to see how they looked in different seasons and how they weathered.

The interior is surprisingly small; it's cool and colourful, but doesn't particularly evoke the man's spirit. A guest wing is perched on timber and stones (another experiment), but is deemed too precarious to enter.

The setting is very Finnish, and you can well imagine Aalto looking out over the beautiful lake and pondering his designs. It's a quiet, peaceful place, but take mosquito repellent!

To get to Muuratsalo, take bus 16 from central Jyväskylä and ride it to the end, where there's a small café. The house is 500m further along this road; it's on the right, opposite a parking area. To reach the house for the 1.30pm tour, you'll need to get the bus at 12.15, as they only run every hour (€3.60, 40 minutes).

Muurame

Along the main Tampere road, about 10km south of Jyväskylä, Muurame is home to the **Sauna Village** (Saunakylä; ☎ 373 2670; Virastotie 8; admission €4; 🕙 10am-6pm Tue-Sun Jun-Aug), a very Finnish attraction. This open-air museum has a variety of old saunas with different regional styles, plus smoke saunas you can hire for private use (from €85 for at least two hours). On Wednesday evenings (6pm to 8pm) you can take a sauna for €5 – it's a pity this is only available once a week!

The white **church** (🕙 10am-6pm Jun-early Aug) was designed by Alvar Aalto during the 1920s.

Take bus 14 from Jyväskylä to Muurame (€3.60, 30 minutes).

Petäjävesi

If you're heading west from Jyväskylä, it's worth pausing at the tiny village of Petäjävesi, 35km away, to see the Unesco World Heritage–listed, cross-shaped wooden church. Built in 1765, **Petäjävesi church** (admission €4; 🕙 10am-6pm Jun-Aug) is probably the most notable example of 18th-century rustic architecture in Finland. Prior to its construction, there had been some debate about whether this village should get a church at all. While a reply to applications (sent to Stockholm for approval) was delayed, Jaakko Leppänen started the job minus permission and properly drawn instructions. The result was a marvellous, though awkward, wooden building.

Buses from Jyväskylä to Keuruu stop in Petäjävesi.

NORTHERN LAKELAND

KUOPIO

☎ 017 / pop 90,518

One of the most likeable towns in Finland, Kuopio is a very satisfying place that seems to combine several Suomi essentials – ski-jumps, forest, lakes, saunas, – in one neat package. It's a vibrant place with lots to see and do and enjoys a beautiful location, which can be surveyed from atop the famous Puijo tower. The ferry trip between Savonlinna and Kuopio also makes this a prime destination in summer. Time your visit so you can steam it up in the world's biggest smoke sauna, Jätkänkämppä!

Although not a huge place, Kuopio sprawls over a large area and manages to exude the atmosphere of a city while retaining the charm of a lake town. The university keeps things lively on the intellectual and nightlife fronts, while the annual international dance festival adds to Kuopio's sophistication.

The first Savonian people entered the area at the end of the 15th century, and in 1552 the first church was built. In 1652 Count Per Brahe founded the 'church village' of Kuopio, which had little significance until 1775, when Gustav III of Sweden incorporated Kuopio as a provincial capital. A few important figures of the National Romantic era lived here from the 1850s, but the main growth of Kuopio was in the 20th century.

Orientation

Kuopio's centre is a grid of parallel streets around the kauppatori and church. The harbour is 1km to the east of the kauppatori, while the train and bus stations are about 500m to the north. Puijo hill is to the northwest of town.

Information

Kuopio tourist office (☎ 182 585; www.kuopioinfo.fi; Haapaniemenkatu 17; 🕙 9.30am-5pm Mon-Fri, 9.30am-3pm Sat Jul, 9.30am-4.30pm Mon-Fri Aug-Jun) Has information on attractions and accommodation in the entire Kuopio region. They also sell the Kuopio Card (€11), which gives various discounts on shopping and museum entry as well as one major saving (in summer 2005 it was a free cruise).
Main post office (Tulliportinkatu) Situated just west of the market square.
Public library (☎ 182 111; Maaherrankatu 12; 🕙 10am-7pm Mon-Fri, 10am-3pm Sat) Free Internet terminals.

Sights

PUIJO HILL

In a country with few hills, Puijo Hill is the pride of Kuopio – the spectacular panoramic lake and forest views from the 75m **Puijo Tower** (adult/child €3/2) are said to represent 'the national ideal of Finnish scenery'. There's a revolving restaurant on the 12th floor, a café on the 13th and an open-air viewing deck at the very top.

Surrounding Puijo Hill is one of the best-preserved **spruce forests** in the region. It's a popular spot for walks and picnics. Also here is an all-season ski jump and chairlift. Even in summer you can see ski jumpers in training. Unfortunately there are no public buses to Puijo, but it's a nice walk through the trees, or a short drive or cab ride.

THE LAKELAND

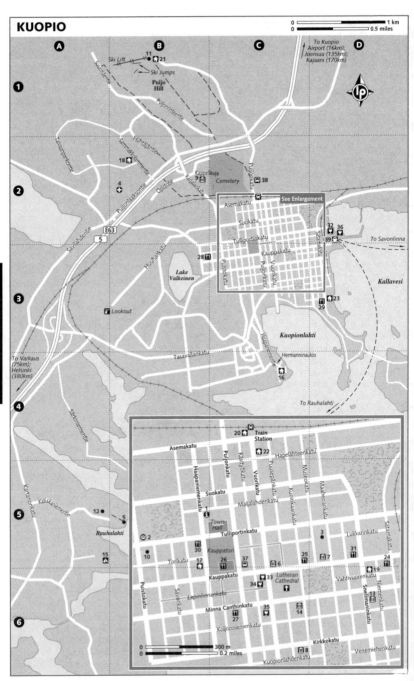

JÄTKÄNKÄMPPÄ SMOKE SAUNA

There are different types of saunas, but the smoke sauna is the original and, some say, the best. This, the largest in the world (although few other countries have attempted the record), is a memorable and sociable experience that draws locals and visitors.

The lakeside **Jätkänkämppä sauna** (☎ 473 473; admission €10; ✆ 5–10pm Tue, also Thu from Jun–mid-Sep) is at a former loggers' camp near the Rauhalahti Tourist Centre. The 60-person, mixed sauna (record capacity is 103 people) is heated 24 hours in advance with a wood fire (hence 'smoke sauna'). Guests are given towels to wear but bring a swimsuit for a dip in the lake. The technique is to sweat it out for a while, cool off in the lake, then repeat the process several times – devoted sauna-goers do so even when the lake is covered with ice. Then buy a beer and relax, looking over the lake in a Nordic peace.

There is a restaurant in the loggers' cabin serving a traditional dinner (buffet plus a hot plate €17) with accordion entertainment when the sauna is fired up, as well as a lumberjacks' show on summer evenings. Bus 7 goes every half-hour from the market square direct to just near the Rauhalahti hotel complex, from where it's a 600m walk to the sauna, or take the lake ferry from the passenger harbour in summer (see p138).

This is one of Kuopio's highlights, but it is vital to ring ahead and check the opening hours to avoid disappointment.

MUSEUMS

Kuopio has several worthwhile museums, each with discounted entry if you have a Kuopio Card.

Kuopio Museum

The beautiful Art Nouveau **'castle'** (☎ 182 603; Kauppakatu 23; admission €4; ✆ 9am–4pm Mon-Sat, to 5pm Jul, 9am–7pm Wed, 10am–5pm Sun) was built in 1907 and houses the Kuopio Museum, with interesting archaeological and cultural displays. There are also frequent special exhibitions.

Old Kuopio Museum

This block of old **town houses** (☎ 182 625; Kirkkokatu 22; adult/child €2.50/free; ✆ 10am–5pm, to 7pm Wed mid-May–mid-Sep, 10am–3pm Tue-Fri, 10am–4pm Sat & Sun mid-Sep–mid-May) forms another of Kuopio's delightful museums. Several homes – all with period furniture and décor – are very detailed and thorough and the level of information (in English) is excellent. Apteekkimuseo in building 11 contains old pharmacy paraphernalia, while in another building it's fascinating to compare photos of Kuopio from different decades.

THE LAKELAND

There is also a museum café, with coffee and the delicious *rahkapiirakka* (a local sweet pastry).

Kuopio Art Museum

The **art museum** (☎ 182 633; Kauppakatu 35; adult/child €3/free; ☺ 10am-5pm Tue, Thu & Fri, 10am-7pm Wed, 11am-5pm Sat & Sun) features mostly modern art in temporary exhibitions, but also displays permanent works. Look out for paintings by the local artist Juho Rissanen (1873–1950), whose realistic portraits of Finnish working people were a contrast to the prevalent Romanticism.

Snellman Home Museum

This **museum** (☎ 182 624; Snellmaninkatu 19; adult/student/child €1.50/1/free; ☺ 10am-5pm, 10am-7pm Wed mid-May–late Aug) is a branch of the Kuopio Museum. JV Snellman, an important cultural figure during the National Romantic era of the 19th century, used to live in this old house from 1854 to 1849.

Orthodox Church Museum

A fascinating, well-presented museum, the **Orthodox Church Museum** (☎ 287 2244; Karjalankatu 1; adult/child €5/1; ☺ 10am-4pm Tue-Sun May-Aug, noon-3pm Mon-Fri, noon-5pm Sat & Sun Sep-Apr) holds collections brought here from monasteries, churches and *tsasouni* (chapels) in USSR-occupied Karelia. Today it is the most notable collection of eastern Orthodox icons, textiles and religious objects outside Russia. The oldest artefacts date from the 10th century.

The museum is in a plain brown building about 1km west of the train station; take bus 7 from the market.

VB Photographic Centre

There are excellent exhibitions in the summer at the **Photographic Centre** (☎ 261 5599; Kuninkaankatu 14-16; admission €3, during summer exhibitions €5; ☺ 10am-7pm Mon-Fri, 11am-4pm Sat & Sun in Summer, 11am-5pm Tue-Fri, 11am-7pm Wed, 11am-3pm Sat & Sun other times), devoted to Victor Barsokevitsch, who was a local portrait photographer regarded as one of the pioneers of Finnish photography. His studio is now a photo gallery, but there are enough old cameras and photos to call this a museum. In the garden you can enjoy a cup of coffee in summer and be astounded by the camera obscura.

PIKKU-PIETARIN MARKET ALLEY

Just off Puistokatu, about 200m west of the kauppatori, **Pikku-Pietarin Torikuja** (☺ 10am-5pm Mon-Fri, 10am-2pm Sat Jun-Aug) is an atmospheric narrow lane of renovated red wooden houses converted into quirky shops stocking jewellery, clothing, handicrafts and other items. There's also a good little café with a terrace.

Activities

Rauhalahti Tourist Centre (☎ 187 718; www.rauhalahti.com) has grown around Rauhalahti Manor (Kartano Rauhalahti), an area converted into a year-round family park. The whole area is full of amusements and activities for families including boating, cycling, tennis and minigolf in summer, skating, ice-fishing, snowmobile safaris and a snow castle in winter. Take bus 7 from the town centre or a lake ferry from the passenger harbour in the town centre in summer (one way/return €5/10, 30 minutes, three to four daily).

You can rent bikes from around €10 a day, rowing boats, canoes, inline skates, and even hire Icelandic ponies for gentle trail rides.

At **Puijo Hill**, there are mountain-biking and walking tracks, including a marked nature trail. In winter there are cross-country ski trails and equipment rentals are available.

Tours

In summer there are daily departures for several different cruises. Two-hour cruises from the harbour cost €10 to €12 (half price for children) and depart hourly from 11am to 6pm. Special theme cruises include dinner and dancing, wine tasting or a trip to a local berry farm. There are also canal cruises and a monastery cruise to Valamo.

There are cruises to Rauhalahti tourist centre Tuesday to Saturday in summer (and Sunday in July); the best one is the smoke-sauna cruise on Tuesday and Thursday (single/return €5/10) at 5.45pm and 8.30pm.

Tickets for all cruises are available at the passenger harbour. Schedules are available at the harbour or from the tourist office.

Festivals & Events

Tanssii ja Soi is the **Kuopio Dance Festival** (☎ 282 1541; www.kuopiodancefestival.fi) in mid- to late June, the most international and the most interesting of Kuopio's annual events. There are open-air classical and modern dance performances, comedy and theatre gigs, and the town is generally buzzing at this time.

In addition to performances, dance lessons are also given during the festival, but you'll need to make a **booking** (☎ 368 6200) in advance.

Sleeping
BUDGET

Hermannin Salit (☎ 364 4961; www.hermannin salit.com; Hermanninaukio 3A; dm from €18, s/d €42/48; P ✂ 💻) This is the city's most central hostel, about 1.5km south of the market square. It's a small, friendly place that's very well run. There's a laundry, shop and cafeteria offering cheap breakfast and lunch. Linen is included in the rates.

Puijon Maja (☎ 255 5250, www.puijo.com; Puijontornintie; s/d €55/60; P ✂ 💻) Perched on top of Puijo Hill is this HI-affiliated place, with a great location among the trees by the tower. The rooms are spick-and-span, and there are very good facilities, including meals available. It's popular with groups, including practising ski jumpers, so book ahead. There's no public transport from the town centre.

Camping Rauhalahti (☎ 473 000; Kiviniementie; camp site per person/family €11/17, 2–4-person cabins €30–54; ⏱ mid-May–Aug) Next to the Rauhalahti spa complex, this place has a great location, plenty of facilities and is well set up for families.

MIDRANGE & TOP END

Spa Hotel Rauhalahti (☎ 473 473; www.rauhalahti .com; Katiskaniementie 8; s/d Jun-Aug €87/102, Sep-May €97/124; P ✂ 💻 🐕) This hotel at the Rauhalahti Tourist Centre, 5km south of town, is a superb place to stay. In addition to the spa facilities, the hotel has a restaurant, café and popular dance club. They offer some very attractive family packages on their website. In the same complex is the cheaper **Hostelli Rauhalahti** (s/d €61/70), with simple Nordic rooms and full use of the hotel's facilities, as well as an **Apartment Hotel** (2-/4-person apts from €124/196) with excellent brand-new modern pads with all the trimmings. Take bus 7 from town. The smoke sauna is about half a kilometre further past the hotel.

Matkustajakoti Rautatie (☎ 580 0569; fax 580 0654; Asemakatu 1 & Vuorikatu 35; s with/without bathroom €46/36, d €75/56; P ✂) Run out of the friendly grilli in the railway station, two types of very decent rooms are offered. The cheapest, across the road on Vuorikatu, are good

and light, with TV and comfortable beds but shared bathrooms. The rooms in the station itself are comfortable and surprisingly peaceful, with ensuite and family rooms available. Linen and breakfast are included.

Hotel Savonia (☎ 282 8333; Sammakkolammentie 2; s/d €88/110, weekends & summer €68/79; P ✂ 💻 🐕) On the hills northwest of the town centre, this likeable and welcoming hotel has cheery rooms with bright Marimekko florals and very good facilities, including a pool. There's a restaurant here, as well as a deli-café for lighter meals. Breakfast, sauna and swimming are included in the room rates.

Scandic Hotel Kuopio (☎ 195 111; www.scandic -hotels.com; Satamakatu 1; s/d €116/140, weekends & summer r €69-79; P ✂ 💻 🐕 ♿) This is a large hotel in an excellent location on the shores of Lake Kallavesi, about 1km from the kauppatori and near the cruise boat harbour. It has excellent facilities, including a Jacuzzi. The parquet-floored rooms are attractive; the standard rooms face the street, but it's worth paying extra for the water views.

Other recommendations:

Hotel Atlas (☎ 211 2111; www.hotelliatlas.com; Haapaniemenkatu 22; s/d €85/99, weekends & summer €63/69; P ✂ 💻) Ageing but comfortable, on the kauppatori. Popular €10 lunch special.

Hotelli Jahtihovi (☎ 264 4400; www.jahtihovi.fi; Snellmaninkatu 23; s/d €79/99, weekends & summer €65/80; P ✂ 💻) Pleasant and intimate with a good restaurant. Soft-coloured rooms with pine furnishings and small bathrooms.

Eating

The kauppahalli at the southern end of the kauppatori is a classic Finnish indoor market hall with fresh produce and food stalls. Look out for the local speciality *kalakukko*, a large rye loaf stuffed with whitefish and then baked. It's delicious hot or cold but you'll probably have to buy a whole one (around €15), enough for several picnics!

Musta Lammas (☎ 581 0458; Satamakatu 4; mains €17-24, degustation menu €48; ⏱ 5pm-midnight Mon-Sat) The 'Black Sheep' is one of the few truly gourmet restaurants in this part of Finland, set in an enchantingly romantic brick-vaulted space. The menu is mainly French in inspiration, but with some Finnish ingredients and dishes. Duck breast, roast lamb and monkfish take their places alongside oysters and some sinful chocolate desserts. The set menu is a veritable feast.

Vapaasatama Sampo (☎ 581 0458; Kauppakatu 13; muikku €10-12; ☺ lunch & dinner) This is the spot for a truly local taste. It's the town's oldest restaurant – it's been in Kuopio for almost 70 years – and is famous all over Finland for its *muikku* (small whitefish), served in various forms, especially fried. It's delicious and the restaurant is cosy and typically Finnish.

Puijon Torni (☎ 255 5255; mains €13-23; ☺ summer) This is the revolving panorama restaurant at the top of the Puijo observation tower. The cuisine at revolving restaurants isn't always commensurate with the altitude, but here it's very good, with a lot of emphasis on Finnish specialities. The Finland three-course set menu (€35) includes whitefish, reindeer, and cranberry tart, but there's equally toothsome dishes available on the à la carte menu.

Isä Camillo (☎ 581 0450; Kauppakatu 25; mains €10-22; ☺ 11am-midnight Mon-Thu, 11am-2am Fri & Sat) Set in a beautifully renovated bank – look out for the old strongroom – this spacious place is an enjoyable place to eat, with warm, elegant décor. It's reasonably informal and well-priced; the menu is international with plenty of Finnish specialities and there's a good enclosed terrace at the side.

Lounas-Salonki (☎ 281 1210; Kasarminkatu 12; lunch specials €7-8, mains €8-13, ☺ 9am-9pm Mon-Sat, noon-9pm Sun) Another good spot for lunch is this charming place in an old wooden building west of the centre. There's a salad buffet and a daily hot lunch, as well as good à la carte options. The interior is beautiful, with Empire-style horsehair chairs and other elegances.

Kummisetä (☎ 369 9889; Minna Canthinkatu 44; mains €9-16. ☺ 5-10pm Mon-Fri, 1-11pm Sat, 1-9pm Sun) This is a very popular pub-cum-restaurant, a rustic place like a little red barn. On sunny summer days its terrace gets pretty crowded. The food is good, with traditional staples like liver alongside beef madeira and woodpigeon or the big 'godfather' steak (€24).

Helmi (Kauppakatu 2; pizzas €8, panini €5; ☺ 10am-midnight or later) Located in a 19th-century stone building near the harbour, Helmi is a downmarket bar with an excellent terrace. It has no frills but does four things, and does them well: pizzas, panini, salads and seriously cheap beer!

Trube Torinkulma (☎ 263 2557; Tulliportinkatu; ☺ 7.30am-7pm Mon-Fri, 8.30am-4pm Sat) This place at the Sokos building near the kauppatori has the best pastries and cakes, as well as sandwiches and other light fare.

Drinking & Entertainment

Most of Kuopio's nightlife is conveniently strung along Kauppakatu, running east from the market square to the harbour. Here, the grungy but likeable Ale Pupi ('Sale Pub') draws people with cheap beer and karaoke, but there are many other options in this block.

Wanha Satama (☎ 197 304) Down at the harbour, this is set in a beautiful wooden building. It has pricey beer but a huge terrace, and is the place to be on a July weekend.

Albatrossi (☎ 368 8000) Across the way from Wanha Satama, this is another summer pub, set in old wooden warehouses. The massive beamed interior is something to behold, and the dance floor gets pretty lively at weekends.

Henry's Pub (Käsityökatu 17; ☺ from 7pm) This is one of the best rock music venues in town with regular live bands in its atmospheric downstairs venue, but it's a good bet at any time.

K Klubi (Vuorikatu 14; ☺ from 6pm) This is one of Kuopio's best bars, with an eclectic bunch of punters, ranging from a bohemian, arty older set to discerning students who value Finnish rock and loathe Europop. Always interesting.

Giggling Marlin (☎ 288 8100; Kauppakatu 18; ☺ 10pm-4am Tue-Wed, Fri & Sat) This is a frenetic 'Suomi pop' club with DJs, dancing on the tables, theme nights and plenty of youthful enthusiasm. There is a minimum age limit of 22 at weekends.

For good old-fashioned Finnish dancing and karaoke, the Hotel Rauhalahti has a dance-restaurant packed on Friday and Saturday nights, when there's a live dance band.

Getting There & Away
AIR

There are several daily flights from Helsinki to Kuopio, run by both Finnair and budget airline Blue1.

BOAT

Ferries and cruise boats depart from the passenger harbour, about 1km east of the kauppatori. In summer, the lake ferry MS *Puijo* departs for Savonlinna on Tuesday, Thursday and Saturday at 9am (€75, 10½ hours), going via Heinävesi and Oravi. It returns from Savonlinna on Monday, Wednesday and Friday.

SHE AIN'T HEAVY, SHE'S MY WIFE

If the thought of grabbing your wife by the legs, hurling her over your shoulder and running for your life sounds appealing, make sure you're in Sonkajärvi, 18km northeast of Iisalmi, in early July, because you won't want to miss the **Wife-Carrying World Championships**. What began as a heathenish medieval habit of pillaging neighbouring villages in search of nubile women has become one of Finland's oddest – and most publicised – events.

The championship is a race over a 253m obstacle course, where competitors must carry their 'wives' through water traps and over hurdles to achieve the fastest time. Dropping your cargo means a 150-second penalty. The winner gets the wife's weight in beer and, of course, the prestigious title of World Wife-Carrying Champion. To enter, you need only find a consenting woman – but all borrowed wives must be returned. Estonians are particularly proficient; teams from that nation had triumphed in eight consecutive events to 2005.

The championship is accompanied by a weekend of drinking, dancing and typical Finnish frivolity.

BUS

The busy bus terminal, just north of the train station, serves the entire southern half of Finland, with regular departures to all major towns and villages in the vicinity. Express services to/from Kuopio include: Helsinki (€49, five to seven hours), Joensuu (€23.20, 2½ hours), Kajaani (€25.60, 2¾ hours), Jyväskylä (€23.20, 2¼ hours) and Savonlinna (€25.60, three to four hours).

TRAIN

Five trains a day run to Kuopio from Helsinki (€47, 4½ to five hours). Kouvola, Pieksämäki, Iisalmi and Kajaani also have direct trains to/from Kuopio.

Getting Around
TO/FROM THE AIRPORT

Kuopio airport is 17km north of town. **Buses** leave from the kauppatori by the Anttila department store 55 minutes before Finnair departures (€5 one way, 30 minutes). Airport **taxis** (☎ 106 400) cost €12 for one person, or €24 for two to four people, and must be booked two hours in advance.

BIKE AND CAR HIRE

You can hire bikes for €12 to €13 a day at Hertz and Asemagrilli, both in the railway station building. Both also hire cars.

IISALMI & AROUND
☎ 017 / pop 22,639

Iisalmi, 85km north of Kuopio, is known as the home of the **Olvi Brewery** and, naturally, for its annual **beer festival**. Aside from this

and a handful of oddball festivals in the district there's not much to draw travellers here, though there's an Orthodox church and a couple of local museums.

The **tourist office** (☎ 830 3391; www.iisalmen seutu.info; Kauppakatu 22; 9am-6pm Mon-Fri, 9am-5pm in winter) is across from the bus terminal.

The **Karelian Orthodox Cultural Centre** (☎ 816 441; Kyllikinkatu 8; adult/child €2.50/1.20; 9am-6pm) displays icons, murals and models of Orthodox churches and *tsasouni* from Russian Karelia. Some icons had lain forgotten in attics and barns, and were later discovered to be valuable. The very attractive adjacent **Orthodox church** (10am-4pm Tue-Sun in summer) has beautiful illustrations painted in 1995.

Kuappi, at the harbour's edge, bills itself as the world's smallest pub – it has one table, two seats, a bar, a toilet, and an entry in the Guinness Book of Records.

Hotel Artos (☎ 812 244; hotel.artos@co.inet.fi; Kyllikinkatu 8; s/d €65/85, weekends & Jul €58/75) is the best of the town's hotels. It's run by, and adjacent to, the Orthodox church, and the modern rooms are pretty good value, with polished wooden floors and plenty of light. Some are equipped with their own sauna. The restaurant here has an €8 lunch buffet.

The many bus services include Kuopio (€12.70, 1½ hours), Joensuu (€27.40, 3½ hours), and local buses to surrounding towns and villages like Sonkajärvi (€4.60, 30 minutes).

There are five trains a day from Helsinki to Iisalmi, via Lahti, Mikkeli and Kuopio. Coming from the north, you can reach Iisalmi from Oulu or Kajaani.

THE LAKELAND

Karelia

Karelia is almost a magical word in Finland, with more connotations than can be explained. This was deep Finland, a unique zone where old traditions were maintained in isolated forest communities. When Elias Lönnrot was compiling records of Finnish folk traditions, it was here that he found the tales he wove into the *Kalevala* epic. Fuelled with enthusiasm, artists and architects headed for the Karelian wilderness in search of the 'soul' of Finnishness. Karelia became the symbol of Finnish distinctiveness and the totem of the independence movement.

Sad and ironic, then, that most of Karelia today lies over the Russian border. Much of the gruelling attrition of the Winter and Continuation Wars against the Soviet Union was in this area, and large swathes of territory were lost. In a way, Finns see Russian Karelia as a child torn from its mother, although cross-border excursions are increasingly possible and popular.

The Karelia that remains in Finland is two separate strips of territory; South Karelia, around Lappeenranta, and North Karelia, with Joensuu as its major town. It's a fantastic destination, with a different culture and distinct traditional languages. You'll see Karelian food at markets, and traditional Karelian architecture, hear Karelian music at festivals and see the scars of the Winter War along the Russian border.

Karelia is has some stunning wilderness, and is perfect for trekking and canoeing. There's a very good infrastructure of environmentally sensitive tour operators who will do anything from hire you equipment and wave you out the door, to arranging full holiday packages.

HIGHLIGHTS

- Striding out on one of North Karelia's fantastic **trekking routes** (p158) and hearing elks call
- Taking a **cruise** (p146) from Lappeenranta, perhaps along the Saimaa Canal to Vyborg in Russia
- Listening to a *kantele* performance at the **Parppeinvaara** (p155) in Ilomantsi
- Rowing across the lake to visit the **Paateri sculpture museum** (p163)
- Cycling around **Viinijärvi** (p155), with its scenic backroads, old houses and Karelian churches
- **Shooting the rapids** (p161) at Ruunaa in a rubber raft
- Snowmobiling on the frozen **Lake Pielinen** (p159) in the depths of winter

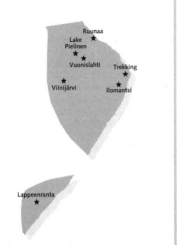

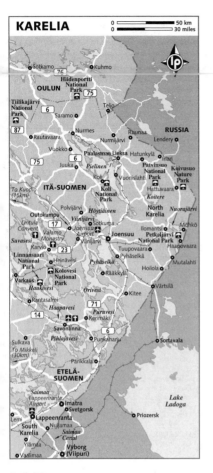

Throughout North Karelia, the best first point of contact for arranging activities and trips is the excellent **Karelia Expert** (www .kareliaexpert.fi), which functions as a tourist information service for all the major towns of North Karelia, and can sort out anything from tent hire and fishing permits to tour operators.

Self-Catering Accommodation

In North Karelia, **Karelia Expert** (www.kareliaex pert.fi) can organise cottage, cabin and apartment rental. For South Karelia, **Saimaatours** (☎ 05-411 7722; www.matka-miettinen.fi; Kirkkokatu 10, Lappeenranta) has a good selection of lakeside cottages.

SOUTH KARELIA

Just a tiny fraction of South Karelia is Finnish territory, and it's a zone where the borders have gone back and forth substantially over the centuries, as Russia and Sweden waxed and waned in power. These days, there is barely 10km between Lake Saimaa and the Russian border at the narrowest point, near Imatra. The once-busy South Karelian trade town of Vyborg (Finnish: Viipuri) and the Karelian Isthmus reaching to St Petersburg are now part of Russia.

The wars that have been a feature in this troubled region have left plenty of evidence in the form of Russian fortifications, particularly in the garrison town of Lappeenranta.

Activities

Karelia is one of the best destinations in Finland for the outdoors-lover. In North Karelia, in particular, there's a huge array of things to do. Karelia has over 1000km of marked trekking routes, some through almost untouched wilderness where you really will be alone with the elk, bears and ravening wolves (so to speak…!).

Lieksa and Nurmes are the best bases for more organized activities like whitewater rafting at the exciting Ruunaa rapids, canoeing and fishing in the remote Nurmijärvi area or, in winter, thrilling dogsled and snowmobile safaris. Located on the other side of Lake Pielinen, Koli is a major trekking trailhead and a winter ski centre.

LAPPEENRANTA

☎ 05 / pop 58,982

Set on the shore's of Finland's largest lake, Lappeenranta (Swedish: Villmanstrand), is the capital of South Karelia. It's an old spa and garrison town and a popular destination for many, including Russians, who pop across the border to shop for luxury goods. Although, like most of Karelia, the town was largely destroyed during the Winter and Continuation Wars and has few conventional sights, its lakeside location and relaxed, friendly atmosphere make it an appealing place to spend a few days.

The building of the Saimaa Canal in 1856 made this an important trading port, and

KARELIA

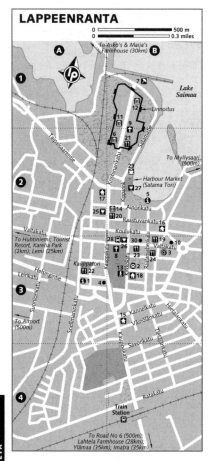

LAPPEENRANTA

Lappeenranta is now the largest inland port in Finland. The waterway from Lake Saimaa to the Gulf of Finland is 43km long and has eight lochs. A day-cruise along the Saimaa Canal to Vyborg, Russia – Finland's second-largest city until it was lost in WWII – is one of Lappeenranta's main attractions, but you'll need to book and arrange your visa in advance.

History

The early Lappeenranta area on Lake Saimaa was a busy Karelian trade centre. It was established as a town by the busy Count Per Brahe in 1649. Queen Kristina of Sweden accepted the coat of arms depicting a primitive man, after whom the Swedish 'Villmanstrand'

was unflatteringly adopted (Villmanstrand means 'Wild Man's Shore' in Swedish). Apparently jealous, Vyborg businesses lobbied against their emerging rival, and Lappeenranta lost its town status in 1683.

Following a Russian victory on 23 August 1741, and the town's complete destruction, Lappeenranta was ceded to Russia and remained part of tsarist Russia until independence in 1917. A spa was founded in 1824, but it was only after railways and industries were developed that Lappeenranta began to grow. Today the beautiful lakeside setting is marred by oversized industries, such as timber milling, that provide work and wealth to many.

Orientation

Kauppakatu and Valtakatu are the main streets. The train and bus stations are together about 1km south of their intersection, but most intercity buses stop on Valtakatu in the middle of town. Bus 9 runs between the bus and train stations and the centre of town.

Information

Main post office (Pormestarinkatu 1)
Main tourist office (☎ 667 788;
matkailuoy@lappeenranta.fi; ⏲ 8am-5pm Mon-Fri Jun-Aug, 10am-4.30pm Mon-Fri Sep-May) On the southern side of the kauppatori (market square).
Public library (☎ 616 2346; Valtakatu 47; ⏲ 10am-8pm Mon-Fri, 10am-3pm Sat) There are free bookable Internet terminals here.
Summer tourist office (⏲ 9am-8pm Jun–mid-Aug, 9am-9pm Jul) In the wooden restaurant and theatre building at the harbour. There are other summer offices at the fortress and at the Hiekkalinna (sandcastle).

Sights

LINNOITUS

The fortifications in the Linnoitus (Fortress) area of Lappeenranta above the harbour were started by the Swedes and finished by the Russians in the 18th century. It's like a separate village; some of the fortress buildings are craft shops and galleries, while others have been turned into interesting **museums** (☎ 616 226; www.lappeenranta.fi/linnoitus; adult/child combined ticket €6/free; ⏲ 10am-6pm Mon-Fri, 11am-5pm Sat & Sun Jun–late Aug, 11am-5pm Tue-Sun rest of year). There are good views from the fortress over the harbour area.

The **South Karelian Museum** (Etelä-Karjalan museo; individual ticket €5) at the northern end of the fortress has good displays on the prehistory and history of the area, as well as temporary exhibitions and a scale model of Vyborg as it looked before it fell to the Russians in 1939. Before WWII, Vyborg was the capital of Karelia and the second biggest town in Finland; it is a source of much wistful nostalgia for Finns in general and Karelians in particular.

South Karelia Art Museum (Etelä-Karjalan Taidemuseo; individual ticket €5) has a permanent collec-

tion of paintings by Finnish and Karelian artists; these are mostly modern works exhibiting not a little of the famous Finnish ironic humour. There's also a space devoted to good temporary exhibitions.

The cavalry tradition is cherished in Lappeenranta – from the 1920s to the 1940s, cavalrymen in their red trousers and skeleton jackets were a common sight on town streets (there are still regular parades mounted in summer). The town's oldest building (erected 1772), a former guardhouse, houses the small **Cavalry Museum** (Ratsuväkimuseo; individual ticket €2.50; ⏲ summer only), which exhibits portraits of commanders, uniforms, saddles and guns, as well as footage of cavalry charges, and scary-looking implements for treating wounded horses.

Other fortress buildings now house a variety of **artists' workshops** selling ceramics, paintings and hand-knitted garments during summer. The **Orthodox church** (⏲ 10am-5pm Tue-Sun Jun–mid-Aug) is Finland's oldest. It was built in 1785 by Russian soldiers. It features a glittering iconostasis and other saintly portraits.

There are walking tours of the fortress daily from late May to mid-September, leaving from the Pusupuisto kiosk opposite the Patria hotel at 2.30pm. They last an hour and cost €2.50, with children free. The tours are in Finnish and English. Some of the tours last a little longer, and have added narrative elements (€4).

CITY CENTRE

The city centre also has several attractions worth exploring.

Wolkoff Home Museum (Wolkoffin Talomuseo; ☎ 616 2258; Kauppakatu 26; adult/child €4/free; ⏲ 10am-6pm Mon-Fri, 11am-5pm Sat & Sun early Jun–mid-Aug) is the preserved home of a Russian immigrant family. The house, built in 1826, was owned by the Wolkoff family from 1872 to 1986. There are 10 rooms that have been maintained as they were; you must join one of the hourly guided tours (around 40 minutes; leave at quarter past the hour) to see them.

In the centre of town, the **Lappee Church** (⏲ 10am-6pm Jun-Aug) is a lovely wooden church (1794) built to an unusual 'double cruciform' floor plan. It's barely on speaking terms with its belltower, situated across

KARELIA

the park and housing a café. South of the church stretches the graveyard, on one side of which is the evocative **war memorial**, which commemorates those Finns who died in the Winter and Continuation Wars and whose graves are now in Russian territory.

At the start of summer, sand artists from all over Finland gather to build the **Hiekkalinna**, a giant sandcastle that uses around two and a half tons of sand. Designs change every year, but it's a seriously impressive structure before the Karelian rains take their toll.

Activities

There's a public **beach sauna** (admission €4.20) at Myllysaari, just east of the harbour area. Hours for women are 4pm to 8pm Wednesday and Friday, and the same hours Tuesday and Thursday for men.

You can hire bikes at several places in town, including the solid **Pyörä-Expert** (☎ 411 8710; Valtakatu 64), which charges €6 to €8 per day, depending on the bike.

Festivals & Events

The **Lemi-Lappeenranta Musikkijuhlat** (www.lemi .fi/musiikki) is a festival of classical music that takes place in Lappeenranta, Imatra, and Lemi in early August. Most performances are in churches, and cost €20 to €30.

Tours

Cruises on Lake Saimaa and the Saimaa Canal are popular and there are daily departures from late May to mid-September from the passenger quay at the harbour.

Saimaa Risteilyt (☎ 415 6955; www.saimaanristeilyt .fi; adult/child €10/5) at the harbour offers two-hour cruises aboard the 95-passenger M/S *El Faro*, either around the archipelago or down the Saimaa Canal. Canal cruises depart daily at noon, with an additional 3pm cruise and a 6pm archipelago cruise from early June to late August. **Karelia Lines** (☎ 453 0380; www .karelialines.fi; adult/child €11/6) has two-hour cruises on Lake Saimaa aboard the spacious MS *Camilla* at noon and 6pm from Monday to Saturday, June to late August.

The big hotels sometimes offer packages including a night's accommodation and a cruise; check their websites or ask the tourist office.

Sleeping

BUDGET

Huhtiniemi Tourist Resort (☎ 451 5555; www .huhtiniemi.com; Kuusimäenkatu 18; tent sites €14-17.50, 2-/4-person cottages €30/42, apt €34-74; ☯ mid-May–Sep) About 2km west of the centre, this is a one-stop accommodation extravaganza. It's a large, businesslike camping ground that stretches down to the lake (bring

---

CRUISING TO RUSSIA

One of the highlights of a visit to Lappeenranta is a boat trip along the Saimaa Canal, and the best way to experience it is the cruise across the border to Vyborg, 60km away in Russia. You'll need a Russian visa, so this trip requires advance planning.

The company that runs the cruises is **Saimaan Matkaverkko** (☎ 541 0100; fax 541 0140; www.saimaa travel.fi; Valtakatu 48). If you are a European Union citizen, they can organize a 'cruise visa' for you. You'll need to provide them with a copy of your passport at least four working days before departure (we recommend booking significantly in advance, as these cruises are heavily subscribed).

The return cruise aboard the M/S *Carelia* departs at 8am (three to four times weekly from late May to mid-September), arriving in Vyborg five and a half hours later. You get about 3½ hours to sightsee and shop in the Russian city before returning by bus (you can also do it the other way around). A return ticket costs adult/child €59/39 and includes a sightseeing tour in Vyborg. Meals are available on board. There are also packages involving a night in Vyborg, a trip to St Petersburg, etc. This price includes the cost of the cruise visa for EU citizens. A booking fee of €10 may apply.

If you aren't an EU citizen, you'll have to obtain a Russian tourist visa. This is best done in Helsinki (see p341), but there is a **Russian consulate** (☎ 872 0700; ☯ 9am-noon Mon, Wed & Fri) in Lappeenranta in the same building as the tourist office. They take up to six days to process a visa, although they may rush through a same-day visa if you are lucky (and pay an extremely hefty supplement).

There are also two adjacent travel agents in Lappeenranta specializing in travel to Russia that can process your visa for you. These are: **Sojuz** (☎ 453 0024; www.tourcentersojuz.inet.fi; Kauppakatu 53) and **RTT** (☎ 020-178 8130; www.rtt-matkapalvelut.fi; Kauppakatu 53).

mosquito repellent). Buses 1, 3 and 5 run past; you may also want to jump off an incoming intercity bus here, as most pass by. As well as cottages with bunks and fridge, and self-contained apartments on the mainland, there are eight upmarket cottages (for four people from €170) on an island just offshore and reached by rowboat. There are also two HI hostels at this location, with the same contact details:

Huhtiniemi Hostel (dm €10; ☺ Jun-Aug; P ☒) is two simple six-bed dorms; it books up fast.

Finnhostel Lappeenranta (s/d €52/69; ☺ all year; P ☒ ☎) is a bit flash to be called a hostel; it's really a hotel, and that's reflected in the price. Tidy rooms with bathroom include linen, breakfast and a morning swim and sauna.

Karelia Park (☎ 453 0405; fax 452 8454; Korpraalinkuja 1; dm from €17, s/d €45/54; ☺ Jun-Aug; P ☒) An HI-affiliated summer hotel 300m west of Huhtiniemi, this offers good-value budget accommodation. It's in a student apartment block – the spotless two-bed rooms each have kitchen facilities and attached bathroom. Breakfast is €2.50 if you're paying the dorm rate and there's a communal kitchen, sauna and laundry.

MIDRANGE

Kantolankulma (☎ 328 7595; www.gasthauslappeenranta.com; Kimpisenkatu 19; s/d from €50/65; ☒) Right in the centre of Lappeenranta, this place is the best value in town. Accommodation is in charming, refurbished apartments that are beautifully decorated and boast an excellent kitchen and seriously comfortable beds. There's also laundry facilities and a shared sauna.

Scandic Hotel Patria (☎ 677 511; www.scandic-hotels.com; Kauppakatu 21; s/d €109/133, d Sat, Sun & summer €79-84; P ☒ ☐ �) This place close to the harbour is Lappeenranta's best hotel. Most of the doubles have a balcony, some looking across at the park, and the rooms are nicely decorated with thoughtful art and bright colours. Superior rooms cost €10 to €15 more and have their own sauna. The service is very helpful.

Gasthaus Turistilappee (☎ 415 0800; Kauppakatu 52; s/d/tr €50/67/84; P ☒) Not far from the train station, this homely place is set behind a row of shops and offers a friendly welcome and tidy rooms with bathroom and TV. There's a kitchen and sauna available

for guests' use (small fee), and breakfast is available for €2 to €4.

Sokos Hotel Lappee (☎ 67861; www.sokoshotels.fi; Brahenkatu 1; s/d €105/125, d Sat, Sun & summer €84; P ☒ ☐ ☎ ☺) This large business hotel is convenient to the centre, and by the churchyard park. It has great facilities and rooms with attractive modern bathrooms that look either outwards or inwards onto a central atrium; the former are lighter. The sauna is free and there are gym facilities also.

FARMHOUSES

Many farmhouses in the countryside around Lappeenranta offer B&B accommodation, a unique opportunity to meet local people and observe their way of life. In some cases no English is spoken on these farms, so it may be easier to make bookings or inquiries through the tourist office at Lappeenranta.

Asko's & Maija's Farmhouse (☎/fax 454 4606; http://users.reppu.net/askomaija.saikko/; Suolahdentie 461; adult/child €28/14; ☺ mid-May–late Sep; P ☒) This friendly dairy farm is 30km northwest of Lappeenranta in the village of Peltoi in the district of Taipalsaari. Accommodation is in a traditional log outbuilding, and breakfast and sauna is included; there's also a barbecue for guests' use. There are also three cottages for daily (€70 to €80) or weekly (€380 to €450) rental. Linen costs €10 extra.

Lahtela Farmhouse (☎ 457 8034; http://matkailu.lahtela.info; Lahtelantie 120; d €60-70; P ☒) This farm, 9km from Ylämaa, south of Lappeenranta, is a dairy farm run by Hellevi and Lauri Lahtela. There's accommodation in a smart Alpine-roofed villa, as well as a simpler cottage. Rates include breakfast, sauna and use of a rowing boat on their small lake. No English is spoken.

Eating

Stalls at the kauppatori sell local Karelian specialities such as *vety* (bread roll or pie with smoked ham, sliced boiled egg, mince, and spices), rice pie, or waffles with jam and whipped cream. There are a dozen more snack stands at the harbour during summer.

Tiglio (☎ 411 8311; Raatimiehenkatu 18; pasta & pizza €9-12, other mains €12-22; ☺ lunch & dinner) A pleasant find – an authentic Italian restaurant with reasonably priced meals, including

KARELIA

a free starter buffet of fresh bread, Italian dressings, olives and vegetables. It's spacious enough to be informal but nice enough for a night out. There's a huge range of dishes; the wild salmon with shrimps is good.

Tassos (☎ 678 6565; Valtakatu 41; mains €14-25; ☺ lunch & dinner Mon-Sat) This is a fine Greek place, which is a bit pricier for dinner but has a good-value lunch special (€11.50) served 11am to 2.30pm Monday to Friday. Dishes range from traditional *mezedes* (€13) and souvlaki to Greek lamb specialities, vegetarian dishes and a few Finnish game dishes.

Café Aleksandra (☎ 887 0113; Kauppakatu 28; snacks €2.50-5; ☺ 11am-5pm Mon-Fri, 10am-1pm Sat) This lovely café is furnished with pieces that, in other countries, would have a velvet rope and a 'Keep Off' sign. It's staffed by friendly folk, has paintings on the walls, good meringues and quiches, and, in all, is a thoroughly pleasant refuge from the Karelian drizzle.

Kahvila Majurska (☎ 453 0554; Kristiinankatu 1; pastries €2-4; ☺ 10am-7pm) Formerly the Officers' Club of the fortress, this 18th-century building has lost none of its former elegance. It's a great place redolent with the aroma of raspberry jam. The plush interior features antique furniture and art exhibitions, and there's a lovely conservatory space.

Café Wolkoff (☎ 415 0320; Kauppakatu 26; mains €16-25; ☺ 11am-11pm Mon-Fri, 4.30-11pm Sat) Adjacent to the Wolkoff Museum is a plush, stylish restaurant specializing in Finnish cuisine such as whitefish, reindeer, elk and cloudberry soup.

Barut Kebab (☎ 415 0119; Valtakatu 54; ☺ 11am-10.30pm) Finland is full of reasonably good kebab-and-pizza joints, but this one merits a mention for its comfy seating and seriously good house kebab (€9), which comes on a bed of garlic potatoes, salad and chips, and smothered with yogurt and tomato sauce.

Drinking & Entertainment

Birra (Kauppakatu 19; ☺ 2pm-2am or later) This modern bar has a spacious interior and an outdoor terrace under the trees. It's usually quiet and enjoyable, but gets rowdy at weekends. There's a good range of tap beers and an excellent choice of bottled beers from around the world. There's also booth seating and cosy lounge tables.

Old Park (Valtakatu 36; ☺ noon-1am Sun-Thu, noon-3am Fri & Sat) This is a cheerful and welcoming Irish pub that gets very crowded on most nights. It's got a good balcony terrace that overlooks the heart of town. Downstairs is **Green Apple** (☺ 8am-3am), a recently opened pub which the locals have taken to their hearts. It also has a terrace, and potentially disconcerting hospital-bright lights, as well as a nightclub, **Golden Apple** (☺ 10pm-4am Wed, Fri-Sat, 10pm-3am Thu & Sun), with a popular dancefloor.

Cannibals (☎ 678 6565; www.cannibals.fi; Valtakatu 41; weekend cover charge €3; ☺ 10pm-4am) This is Lappeenranta's most popular nightclub – revellers from the preceding pubs head here after closing. There's an upstairs dance floor open at weekends.

In summer, the **S/S Suvi Saimaa** and the **Prinsessa Armaada**, at the harbour, are cheerful places to hang out. Both have terraces on shore and on the boat, and serve snacks and larger meals (€5 to €13) from noon to 8pm. The Suvi Saimaa occasionally disappears on cruises.

Nuijamies (☎ 457 0066; www.nuijamies.com; Valtakatu 39; admission €8.50) This is the town's cinema, which has screens in two adjacent buildings.

Getting There & Away

AIR
There are daily flights between Helsinki and Lappeenranta on **Finnair** (☎ 0203-140 140). Bus 4 travels the 2.5km between the city centre and the airport.

SOMETHING SPECIAL

The small village of Lemi, 25km west of Lappeenranta, is famous for its *lemin särä* (roast mutton). This traditional dish – cooked in a birch trough that adds amazing depths of flavour – has been described as 'one of the seven wonders of Finland'. And so it should – it takes nine hours to prepare and must be ordered at least two days in advance!

Säräpirtti Kippurasarvi (☎ 414 6470; www.sarapirtti.fi; Rantatie 1, Lemi) A restaurant on the lakeshore at Lemi, this is one of the best spots to try *lemin särä*. Phone ahead for a booking.

BUS

All buses along the eastern route, between Helsinki and Joensuu, stop in Lappeenranta. Bus and train tickets can be booked at the central office of **Matkahuolto** (☎ 0200 4000; ⊗ 9am-5pm Mon-Fri), opposite the church park on Valtakatu, where many intercity buses stop. Regular services include: Helsinki (€32.30, four hours), Savonlinna (€22.90, three to four hours via Parikkala), Mikkeli (€16.20, 2½ hours) and Imatra (€6.20, 45 minutes). For Kuopio change at Mikkeli.

There are local connections to smaller places in South Karelia, although some buses only run once a day, on weekdays.

TRAIN

Seven to eight trains a day between Helsinki and Joensuu will take you to Lappeenranta. There are frequent direct trains to/from Helsinki (€34.90, 2¾ hours), and to Savonlinna (€21.50, 2½ hours, change at Parikkala, sometimes to a railbus).

AROUND LAPPEENRANTA
Ylämaa
☎ 05 / pop 1511

Ylämaa, 35km south of Lappeenranta, is a rural municipality best known for the gemstone spectrolite, a marketing name given to the local labradorite. It's a beautiful, dark stone which glitters in all the colours of the spectrum. The local **tourist information office** (☎ 613 4200; www.ylamaa.fi; ⊗ Jun-Aug) is in Jewel Village.

Jewel Village (museum & shops ⊗ Jun-Aug), on the Lappeenranta-Vaalimaa road (road 387), is Ylämaa's main attraction. The village consists of a restaurant, stone grinderies, quarries, a goldsmith's workshop and gem museum. The **gem museum** (admission €2; ⊗ 10am-5pm) has a collection of spectrolites and precious minerals and fossils from around the world, many in their raw, uncut state. It's actually fascinating and beautiful; some of the gemstones are backlit, while others provide their own fluorescence. The **Gem Fair** here in early July draws plenty of international rockhounds.

Ylämaa church (Koskentie; ⊗ summer), was built in 1931 and has an unusual façade made partially of spectrolite.

Buses run from Lappeenranta in the afternoon, Monday to Friday only. You can only do a day trip on the bus during school terms, when you could catch the bus there at 1.15pm and return at 4.20pm (45 minutes).

IMATRA
☎ 05 / pop 29,728

The raging torrent of Imatra's waterfall was once the prime tourist attraction in 19th century Finland, but a legacy of wars and industrial development has removed some of the city's charm. The rapids were harnessed for hydroelectricity in 1929, but still turned on regularly in summer: a spectacular sight. Otherwise Imatra, about 40km northwest of Lappeenranta, has little to offer, though a characterful hotel and a loveable restaurant makes it a handy stop. You can also cross into Russia from here.

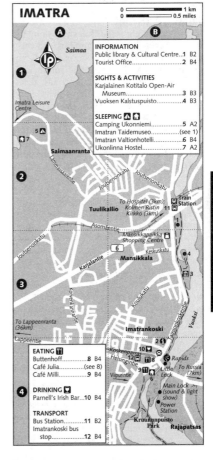

IMATRA

INFORMATION
Public library & Cultural Centre...1 B2
Tourist Office..............................2 B4

SIGHTS & ACTIVITIES
Karjalainen Kotitalo Open-Air
    Museum..................................3 B3
Vuoksen Kalastuspuisto..............4 B3

SLEEPING ⊙ ⌂
Camping Ukonniemi....................5 A2
Imatran Taidemuseo...............(see 1)
Imatran Valtionhotelli..................6 B4
Ukonlinna Hostel........................7 A2

EATING ⊙
Buttenhoff................................8 B4
Café Julia..............................(see 8)
Café Milli.................................9 B4

DRINKING ⊙
Parnell's Irish Bar....................10 B4

TRANSPORT
Bus Station............................11 B2
Imatrankoski bus
    stop.................................12 B4

Orientation & Information

Although Imatra has four dispersed 'centres', separated by highways and shopping parks, the one of most interest to travellers is Imatrankoski at the rapids, where you'll also find the best restaurants and hotels. All incoming buses make a stop here, on Olavinkatu. Three kilometres north, Mansikkala houses the bus and train station; bus 1 connects it with the centre (€2.50).

Public library (Virastokatu 1; Mansikkala) The library in the Kaupungintalo (Cultural Centre) near the bus and train stations has free Internet access.

Tourist office (☎ 020-495 2500; www.travel.imatra .fi; Heikinkatu 1; ☽ 9am-5pm Mon-Fri Jun–mid-Aug, plus 10am-4pm Sat from mid-Jul, 9am-4.30pm Mon-Fri mid-Aug–May) Exceedingly helpful and friendly; extended opening hours for Big Band Festival.

Sights & Activities

Imatra's highlight is the 3km stroll along the mighty **Vuoksi River**, from the bus and train station in Mansikkala to the power station in Imatrankoski. In spring and summer it's a haven of nesting geese, gulls and terns. Until the hydroelectric station was built and the river dammed in 1929, Imatra's **rapids** were one of the highest waterfalls in Finland. These days, the water is allowed to flow free only for the 20-minute **Rapids Shows** from May to September. There's a nightly show at 1am from early May to early July. Check the tourist office's information website for other shows between May and September (it's on, for example, at 10pm every Saturday in August, and 9pm every Saturday in September). There's an accompanying sound-and-light show. It's undeniably spectacular and definitely worth seeing if you're in town that day, but not quite memorable enough to structure your trip around.

Vuoksen Kalastuspuisto (☎ 432 3123; www.vuok senkalastuspuisto.com; Kotipolku 4; ☽ 9am-10pm May-Sep) is a fishing park on Varpasaari in Mansikkala. Pike and salmon can be caught in the river here. A kiosk sells permits (per day/week €6/10) and rents equipment and boats. You can also camp here (per tent site €13), sleep in cabins (per night €40) and hire bicycles (per day €10); and there's also a bar.

Signposted as 'Ulkomuseo', **Karjalainen Kotitalo** (Pässiniemi; admission €2; ☽ 10am-6pm Tue-Sun Jun-Aug) is an open-air museum with a dozen traditional Karelian buildings, moved here from other locations. They are typical of the region, with overlapping corner joints and overhanging eaves. The granary and the main house are particularly atmospheric; there are even real sheep in the barn.

Imatran Taidemuseo (Virastokatu 1; admission free; ☽ 11am-7pm Mon-Thu, 11am-4pm Fri Jun-Aug, 11am-8pm Mon-Fri, 11am-3pm Sat Sep-May) Just south of the bus and train stations, in the same building as the library, the town art gallery is worthwhile. Most space is taken up with good temporary exhibitions, but the permanent collection includes a pensive young violinist by Eero Järnefelt, and a Gallen-Kallela watercolour of the rapids in 1893, which gives an idea of what they were once like.

Kolmen Ristin Kirkko (Church of the Three Crosses; Ruokolahdentie 27; ☽ 9am-8pm Jun-Aug) in Vuoksenniska was designed in 1957 by Alvar Aalto; its clean white lines and soaring narrow tower are typical of the man. As an interesting detail, only two of the 103 windows of the church are identical. Take bus 1.

Festivals & Events

The **Imatra Big Band Festival** (www.ibbf.fi) takes place every year in early July and draws world-famous jazz and swing bands.

Sleeping

Imatran Valtionhotelli (☎ 625 2000; www.rantasipi .fi; Torkkelinkatu 2; castle s/d €119/144, weekends & summer €96/105, congress centre s/d €109/134, weekends & summer €89/91; P ✗ 🖥 🛋 ☝) This classic hotel is a turreted Art Nouveau gem overlooking the rapids in Imatrankoski. Built in 1902, it was a favourite spot of the St Petersburg aristocracy. The rooms are decorated in appropriate style, with replica Art Nouveau furnishings. The Tower Suite (€300) is a highlight with its own sauna and view of Russia; the best standard rooms are on the 4th floor, with curious shapes and ceilings, though they are hot in summer. Next door, the congress centre is much better than it sounds and has large, attractive rooms, some looking over the park behind.

Ukonlinna Hostel (☎ 432 1270; Leiritie 8; dm €15, f per person €22.50; P ✗) This place, alongside the camping ground, is one of the most idyllically situated HI hostels in Finland, nestled in the forest with a lake frontage and lakeside sauna. It's a small, cosy place and since it's close to a popular cross-country skiing area, it's open year-round – in winter there's ice fishing and skating on the lake.

Camping Ukonniemi (☎ 472 4055; www.loma liitto.fi; Leiritie 1; tent sites €13, 3-/4-/5-person cabins €36/42/54; ☼ early Jun–mid-Aug) This is a pleasant lakefront camping ground near the Imatra Leisure Centre. It has two saunas (for hire) and a camp kitchen. Bus 3 travels from the bus station every hour.

Also see Vuoksen Kalastuspuisto (opposite) for a further lodging option.

Eating & Drinking

Imatra's centre for cafés and restaurants is at Imatrankoski.

Buttenhoff (☎ 476 1433; Koskenparras 4; lunch €7-11, mains €14-26; ☼ lunch & dinner Mon-Sat) This is a legendary upstairs restaurant with Finnish and Karelian cuisine in a very French mould. There are fine set menus for €39 and €47 and well-priced à la carte options. Delights such as reindeer carpaccio, veal tournedos and salmon blini feature; there's also an invariably good vegetarian plate.

Café Julia (pastries €1.50-3; ☼ 8am-5pm Mon-Fri, plus 9am-3pm Sat in summer) Downstairs of Buttenhoff, this café, decorated with teddy bears, is the place for coffee and tempting cakes.

Café Milli (☎ 337 8005; Torkkelinkatu 1) Opposite Valtionhotelli, Milli is a good spot for coffee and it sells local produce and handicrafts.

Parnell's Irish Bar (☎ 476 3555; Koskenparras 5) This Irish chain pub, also on the pedestrian strip, is the pick of the pubs along here.

Getting There & Away

Imatra is served by trains (€38.70, three hours, seven daily) and buses from Helsinki, and by hourly buses from Lappeenranta (€6.20, 40 minutes). The central train station is near the river at Mansikkala; it's also the bus station and has lockers. It's dead after 5.30pm. Buses also pick up and drop off in Imatrankoski (on Olavinkatu, a small lane between Helsingintie and the pedestrian zone), a handier option.

NORTH KARELIA

This sparsely populated frontier region, where the artists found inspiration, does its best to live up to all Karelian legends. For the traveller, it is a unique place where you can meet friendly people, visit beautiful Orthodox churches and explore deep wilderness on trekking paths.

Although just outside the North Karelia province, Kuhmo (p280) is another town worth visiting if you are intrigued by Karelia and want to learn more about the *Kalevala*.

History

In 1227 a crusade from Novgorod (situated in present-day Russia) forcibly baptised Karelians into the Orthodox faith, sparking skirmishes that did not end until the Treaty of Nöteborg in 1323 established Novgorod's suzerainty over the region.

Karelians have survived repeated wars with Sweden and Russia. In 1617 Swedes annexed much of Karelia. North Karelia was constantly attacked by Russia and religious intolerance forced Orthodox believers across the border into Russia. The Treaty of Uusikaupunki in 1721 resulted in North Karelia remaining Swedish territory and South Karelia falling to Russian feudalism.

Getting Around

In the North Karelia area, a particularly useful service, given the scarcity of buses, is the *kimppakyyti* (shared taxi) system. They run several times daily along a variety of routes (eg Joensuu–Lieksa), and have a flat fare that is about the same price as the bus. You need to book a day in advance. There's a different telephone number for each route; call ☎ 0100 9986 for Joensuu–Koli, ☎ 0200 45200 for Joensuu–Lieksa or ☎ 013-525 902 for general information. As English levels vary, it may be easier to ask the local tourist office or someone at the hotel to phone for you in Finnish.

JOENSUU

☎ 013 / pop 57,558

Capital of the province of North Karelia, Joensuu is a sizeable university town at the mouth of the Pielisjoki (the name means 'river mouth'). It's the region's major travel hub and has plenty of services, a good market, and lively nocturnal life, which compensate somewhat for the lack of anything of real interest. You'll probably find yourself in Joensuu anyway if you're heading into North Karelia, as it's a base for hiking in surrounding Karelian wilderness areas.

Joensuu was founded in 1848. It soon became an important trading post and then an international port after the completion of the Saimaa Canal in the 1850s.

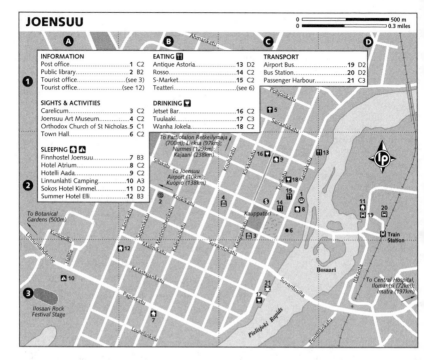

JOENSUU

INFORMATION		
Post office	1	C2
Public library	2	B2
Tourist office	(see 3)	
Tourist office	(see 12)	

SIGHTS & ACTIVITIES		
Carelicum	3	C2
Joensuu Art Museum	4	C2
Orthodox Church of St Nicholas	5	C1
Town Hall	6	C2

SLEEPING		
Finnhostel Joensuu	7	B3
Hotel Atrium	8	C2
Hotelli Aada	9	C2
Linnunlahti Camping	10	A3
Sokos Hotel Kimmel	11	D2
Summer Hotel Elli	12	B3

EATING		
Antique Astoria	13	D2
Rosso	14	C2
S-Market	15	C2
Teatteri	(see 6)	

DRINKING		
Jetset Bar	16	C2
Tuulaaki	17	C3
Wanha Jokela	18	C2

TRANSPORT		
Airport Bus	19	D2
Bus Station	20	D2
Passenger Harbour	21	C3

Orientation & Information

The gentle Pielisjoki rapids divide Joensuu into two parts. The train and bus stations are in the east; the town centre, including the market square and most accommodation, is in the west. Siltakatu and Kauppakatu are the two main streets.

Post office (☎ 0200 71000; Rantakatu 26) By the river.

Public library (☎ 267 6201; Koskikatu 25) The library near the university campus has several free Internet terminals.

Tourist service (☎ 248 5319; www.kareliaexpert .com, www.jns.fi; Koskikatu 5; ☼ 9am-5pm Mon-Fri, also 11am-4pm Sat May-Sep, 11am-4pm Sun Jul) This office is in the Carelicum, and handles tourism information and bookings for the town and region. Free Internet access.

Sights

The **Carelicum** (☎ 267 5222; Koskikatu 5; admission €4; ☼ 10am-5pm Mon-Fri, 11am-4pm Sat & Sun) is a fine conceptual museum focusing on Karelia – its history, people and customs. This is an excellent place to get acquainted with Karelia before heading further east or north. There's one main floor of pho-

tographic exhibits and static displays, an interactive area for kids modelled on part of old Joensuu, and a miniature model of Sortavala (now in Russia) upstairs. There is also a gift shop and a good café on the ground floor.

The unusual **town hall** (Rantakatu 20) dominates the town centre, between the kauppatori and the river. It was designed by Eliel Saarinen, who also designed Helsinki's train station, and was built in 1914. Part of the building now houses the local theatre and a restaurant.

Near the kauppatori, **Joensuu Art Museum** (☎ 267 5388; Kirkkokatu 23; admission €4; ☼ 11am-4pm Tue-Sun, 11am-8pm Wed) is a good display, with a diverse range of both Finnish and foreign pieces, including a good selection of Orthodox icons salvaged from the Soviets.

The most interesting church in Joensuu is the wooden **Orthodox Church of St Nicholas** (☎ 266 000; Kirkkokatu; ☼ 10am-4pm Mon-Fri mid-Jun–mid-Aug), built in 1887. The icons were painted in St Petersburg in the late 1880s. There are services at 6pm on Saturday and 10am on Sunday; worth a visit.

KARELIA

Tours

In summer there are **scenic cruises** on the Pielisjoki, a centuries-old trading route. The M/S *Vinkeri II* has day and evening cruises (€15, 2½ to three hours) on Mondays to Fridays from early June to early August, leaving from the passenger harbour south of Suvantosilta bridge. You can book and check timetables with **Saimaa Ferries** (☎ 481 244; www .saimaaferries.fi) or the city tourist office. The **M/S Satumaa** (☎ 050-5660 815, www.satumaaristeilyt.fi) also runs cruises on the Pielisjoki and nearby lakes (€15) from June to mid-August.

For ferry cruises to Koli and Lieksa, see p154.

Festivals & Events

The **Ilosaari Rock Festival** (☎ 225 550; www.ilosaari rock.fi) is a highly charged annual event held over a weekend in mid-July. The **Gospel Festival** (www.suomengospel.fi) in late July is another important music event.

Sleeping

BUDGET

Finnhostel Joensuu (☎ 267 5076; finnhostel@islo.jns .fi; Kalevankatu 8; shared r per person €28.50-31, s/d from €41/57; **P** ⊠) This excellent HI-affiliated establishment is run by a sports institute. Accommodation is in rooms within a two- or three-room apartment, with excellent kitchen facilities and plenty of space. The rooms have linen and TV, and some have balconies. There are two separate buildings, and breakfast is included. There's also a sauna and gym facilities.

Linnunlahti Camping (☎ 126 272; www.linnun lahticamping.fi; Linnunlahdentie 1; tent sites €12, 4–6-person cabins €35-42) Just south of the centre, this place has a pleasant lakeside location. It's mobbed during the rock festival.

Partiotalon Retkeilymaja (☎ 123 381; www .youthhostel-joensuu.net; Vanamokatu 25; dm €12-15, r €50; ⏲ reception 9-11am & 4-10pm Jun–Aug; ⊠) This place provides basic accommodation in the slightly run-down old scout hall, but it's certainly the cheapest in town.

MIDRANGE

Summer Hotel Elli (☎ 225 927; www.summerhotelelli.fi; Länsikatu 18; s/d €38/60; ⏲ mid-May–mid-Aug; **P** ⊠) A student apartment building that becomes a summer hotel. The facilities are excellent, including sauna and laundry, and rooms share a kitchen and bathroom between two.

Hotel Atrium (☎ 225 888; www.hotelliatrium .fi; Siltakatu 4; s/d €74/101, weekends & summer €64/75; **P** ⊠) This is a pleasant central hotel overlooking the river, with a restaurant, sauna and comfortable rooms, some with balcony. Some of the doubles have their own sauna for only a couple of euros extra. There's a cheeky pet parrot in the lobby.

Sokos Hotel Kimmel (☎ 020-123 4663; www .sokoshotels.fi; Itäranta 1; s/d €114/138, r weekends & summer €88; **P** ⊠ ▯ ▮ ⑤) The largest hotel in Joensuu is on the eastern side of the river, very close to the bus and train stations. The rooms are comfortable and stylish and some have good views. The sauna and pool are free, and there are restaurants and a nightclub. There's another Sokos hotel on Siltakatu, near the kauppatori.

Hotelli Aada (☎ 256 2200; www.hotelaada.fi; Kauppakatu 32; s/d €75/93, weekends & summer €68/76; ⊠) This is a comfortable, central hotel, recently renovated and renamed, and with a popular nightclub. They also run a nearby hostel, Aaro (single/double €39/52). During the week, the price includes breakfast and a sauna.

Eating

At the busy kauppatori look for Karelian specialities such as the classic *Karjalan piirakka*, a rice-filled savoury pastry. There are all sorts of food stalls set up here, along with cheap grillis. Joensuu is short on quality restaurants, but there are a couple of standouts.

Antique Astoria (☎ 229 766; mains €11-26; ⏲ dinner Mon-Fri, lunch & dinner Sat & Sun, closed Sun Sep-Apr) This is a stylish little restaurant with a riverfront terrace and a charming, rustic interior. It specializes in hearty Hungarian dishes, with paprika and sour cream in delicious abundance. Many of the signature dishes (goulash, for example) can only be ordered for two. There are several Hungarian wines (don't go for the cheapest one here), and a range of tempting aperitifs such as chilled slivovitz.

Teatteri (☎ 256 6900; Rantakatu 20; mains €12-29; ⏲ 9am-midnight Mon-Fri, 11.30am-midnight Sat, also noon-8pm Sun Jun-Aug) Beautifully located in the town hall, with an elegant terrace to one side, this classy restaurant showcases the best of Karelian cuisine, with everything from *muikku* (small whitefish) to hefty ox steaks.

KARELIA

Rosso (Siltakatu 8; mains €7-15; ⊗ 10am-10pm, later at weekends) While this chain is never going to hit any culinary heights, this is a branch worth considering for its excellent terrace in the centre of town.

Drinking

Joensuu's main action area is the pedestrian section of Kauppakatu, with several late-night bars and nightclubs. It's pretty boisterous at weekends, but there are a couple of more discerning places in town.

Wanha Jokela (☎ 122 891; Torikatu 26; ⊗ 10am-2am, till 3am at weekends) The oldest and best-known pub in town, this is a classic, much favoured by artists and the alternative and bohemian sets. There's cheap beer and a friendly atmosphere, as well as rooms upstairs (single/double €30/60) if you have one too many.

Tuulaaki (Rantakatu; ⊗ 11am-3am Jun-Aug) This summer café and bar is right where the passenger ferries dock. It's a great place, with a lively terrace that often features live rock. A night away from the Joensuu mainstream has to pass through here at some point.

Jetset Bar (Kauppakatu 35; ⊗ from 4pm Mon-Fri, from 11am Sat & Sun) This bar is the latest and trendiest spot in Joensuu, on a corner at the end of the pedestrian section of Kauppakatu. It would be easy to be snide about the name, but it's a cheery spot where people like to be seen, although it gets impossibly crowded at weekends.

Getting There & Away
AIR
There are several flights a day between Helsinki and Joensuu. The airport is 11km west of town; bus service one way is €5 and departs from the Sokos Hotel Kimmel 50 minutes before every departure. A taxi is €15.

BOAT
In summer the MS *Vinkeri II* operates twice weekly from Joensuu to Koli (one way/return €30/45, 6½ hours), from where you can connect with another ferry to Lieksa, across Lake Pielinen. The ferry departs at 9am on Saturday, returning from Koli at 12.10pm Sunday. You can also return the same evening from Koli to Joensuu on a bus. Book with **Saimaa Ferries** (☎ 481 244; www .saimaaferries.fi).

BUS
Joensuu is a transport hub for North Karelia so there are regular buses to all points, departing from the bus terminal east of the river. Services include Kuopio (€23.20, 2½ hours), Savonlinna (€22.90, three hours), Jyväskylä (€36.90, four hours), Helsinki (€58.50, eight hours) via Mikkeli, Ilomantsi (€11.50, one to two hours) and Nurmes (€20.50, 2½ hours). For Kuhmo, change at Nurmes or Sotkamo.

SHARED TAXI
The *kimppakyyti* system is a good way to head on from Joensuu to the Lake Pielinen area, with departures to Koli and to Lieksa. See p151 for details.

TRAIN
Direct trains run frequently to/from Helsinki (€52.70, 5¼ hours), Turku, Jyväskylä and Kajaani, as well as north to Lieksa and Nurmes. From Savonlinna you have to change at Parikkala.

AROUND JOENSUU
Outokumpu
☎ 013 / pop 7803

Outokumpu, about 50km west of Joensuu, was a wealthy copper mining town until the 1980s, when all three mining operations were permanently closed, turning this area into a shadow of its former industrial self. The abandoned **Vanha Kaivos Mine** (☎ 554 795; www.vanhakaivos.fi; Kiisukatu 6; adult/child €9/6; ⊗ 10am-6pm Jun-Aug), on a hill overlooking the town centre, is now an extensive mining museum and there's an adjacent tunnel with mining equipment. There's also an underground restaurant and a café, as well as a **summer hotel** (☎ 554 795; palvelut@vanhakaivos.fi; per person/f €20/50; ⊗ mid-Jun–early Aug; Ⓟ ✗).

One of the best bird-nesting lakes in Finland, **Sysmäjärvi Bird Sanctuary**, lies south of Outokumpu. Sysmäjärvi was declared dead in the 1950s, due to polluted mining deposits that flowed freely into the lake. It has since been rehabilitated, and the lake is now surrounded by lush vegetation, and birds have returned here in large numbers. There are several observation towers. May and June are the best months to visit. It's a half-hour walk from the carpark to the lake itself.

KARELIA

ILOMANTSI

☎ 013 / pop 6538

Ilomantsi, 72km east of Joensuu, is the centre of a charming region and Finland's most Karelian, Orthodox and eastern municipality. It is one of three regions with a non-mainstream indigenous culture (the others being Åland and the Sámi culture of northern Lapland) and indigenous Karelians see themselves as distinct from Russians and Finns.

This is the ideal place to base yourself for hiking and other activities in the Karelian wilderness. It's a very friendly region and is a good place to witness local culture in the form of Praasniekka festivals. The village centre itself is modern and quite ugly, having been trampled by the Russians, but it's the surrounding region that demands exploration, either on foot or by bicycle.

Information

Karelia Expert (☎ 248 5309; www.kareliaexpert.fi; Kalevalantie 11; ☉ 9am-4pm Mon-Fri Sep-May, 9am-5pm Mon-Fri Jun-Aug, also 10am-3pm Sat in Jul) Reservations and information. If it's shut, you can get brochures and maps by entering via the supermarket.

Library (Mantsintie; ☉ 1-7pm Mon-Thu, 10am-3pm Fri) Free Internet access.

Sights

PARPPEINVAARA

One of the most famous of Ilomantsi's historical characters was Jaakko Parppei (1792–1885), a bard and a player of the *kantele*, a traditional Karelian stringed instrument. He is the namesake of Parppeinvaara hill (where he lived), which now features a re-created **Karelian village** (☎ 881 248; adult/child €3/free; ☉ 10am-6pm Jun-Aug). It is the oldest of the Karelian theme villages in Finland and one of the most interesting. To qualify for their job, guides wearing *feresi* (traditional Karelian work dress) must know how to play the *kantele*; a highlight is the regular performance of folk music. Runonlaulajan pirtti, the main building, has exhibitions on the *Kalevala* epic and Orthodox arts.

An **Orthodox tsasouna** stands behind the Matelin *museoaitta*, a tiny museum commemorating female rune singer Mateli Kuivalatar, renowned in the 19th century for her renditions of the *Kanteletar* epic.

PELTOHERMANNI WINE TOWER & WINERY

The local water tower was reborn in 1994 as a **viinitorni** (wine tower; admission €2; ☉ noon-8pm Jun-late Aug) when some enterprising locals started a café at the top and specialized in serving their own wine. Strawberry, blackcurrant,

---

CYCLING THE VIINIJÄRVI LOOP

Roads around Viinijärvi are scenic, with beautiful churches and old houses. In August, you can find blueberries in the nearby forests. If you have a bicycle (you can hire one in Joensuu or Ilomantsi), you can bring it to Viinijärvi by train or bus from Joensuu, Varkaus or Kuopio, and ride the 60km loop between Viinijärvi, Sotkuma, Polvijärvi and Outokumpu in a day. Another option is to take a bus from Joensuu to Polvijärvi, bypassing Sotkuma.

The tiny village of **Viinijärvi**, on the southern shore of the lake, is quite famous domestically for its champion women's *pesäpallo* (baseball) team. The local field gets pretty packed on Sunday during matches. The beautiful **Orthodox church** is west of the village centre. Its 19th-century icons are copies of those in Kyiv Cathedral.

The narrow 14km road from Viinijärvi north to **Sotkuma** is scenic. The small *tsasouna* (chapel), built in 1914, also has interesting icons inside. The traditional Praasniekka Festival is held here on 20 July each year.

A further 14km, **Polvijärvi** is a larger town with an interesting background. When a canal was being constructed at the southern end of Lake Höytiäinen in 1859, the embankment collapsed and the water level sank 10m, revealing fertile land. Polvijärvi was soon incorporated as a municipality and its population soared. The **Orthodox church**, built in 1914, is not far from the village centre. Its icons are from St Petersburg and were probably painted in the early 20th century. The church has its Praasniekka Festival on 24 June.

It's another 22km along road 504 to Outokumpu. There are several buses a day from Joensuu and a few others from Kuopio and Juuka. Buses from Outokumpu run on school days only.

KARELIA

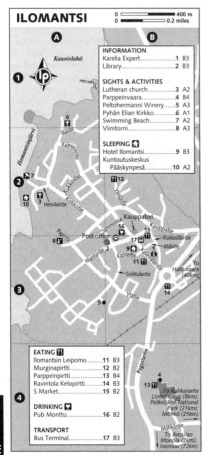

ILOMANTSI

0 _____ 400 m
0 _____ 0.2 miles

Kaunislahti

INFORMATION
Karelia Expert....................1 B3
Library...............................2 B3

SIGHTS & ACTIVITIES
Lutheran church.................3 A2
Parppeinvaara....................4 B4
Peltohermanni Winery.......5 A3
Pyhän Elian Kirkko............6 A1
Swimming Beach................7 A2
Viinitorni..........................8 A3

SLEEPING
Hotel Ilomantsi..................9 B3
Kuntoutuskeskus
Pääskynpesä.................10 A2

EATING
Ilomantsin Leipomo.........11 B3
Murginapirtti....................12 B2
Parppeinpirtti...................13 B4
Ravintola Kelopirtti..........14 B3
S Market..........................15 B2

DRINKING
Pub Monttu......................16 B2

TRANSPORT
Bus Terminal....................17 B3

To Ruhkaranta
Lomakeskus (8km);
Petkeljärvi National
Park (21km);
Möhkö (25km)

To Anssilan
Monola (2km);
Joensuu (72km)

whitecurrant, crowberry and blueberry are used as raw materials to produce the half-dozen varieties of wine sold here by the glass. The tower has a panoramic viewing deck, which is a great place to sit on a summer afternoon or evening. If you want to buy the wine by the bottle, you have to visit the **Peltohermanni winery** (☎ 882 281; www.peltohermanni.fi; ☺ 9am-5pm) about 200m down the road from the wine tower.

CHURCHES
Ilomantsi features two fabulous churches. **Pyhän Elian Kirkko** (☺ 11am-5.30pm mid-Jun–mid-Aug) is the beautiful wooden Orthodox church, 1km west of the village centre, towards Ilomantsinjärvi. The *kalmisto* (graveyard) sign

near the church points to the old graveyard at the waterfront. It is a peaceful place, where old trees give shade to a few graves.

The **Lutheran church** (☺ noon-6pm late Jun–mid-Aug), from 1796, is almost as impressive. Following the Swedish conquest, a Lutheran congregation was established in 1653 and the new religion soon overshadowed the eastern one. Colourful paintings from 1832, an achievement of Samuel Elmgren, are the highlight of this big wooden church.

Festivals & Events
As Ilomantsi has so many Orthodox believers, several Praasniekka festivals are held here. Originally, these were strictly religious events, but these days they also attract tourists. Sometimes there is dancing afterwards. Ilomantsi village celebrates **Petru Praasniekka** on 28 and 29 June and **Ilja Praasniekka** on 19 and 20 July every year.

Sleeping
Anssilan Monola (☎ 0400 881 181; anssila@ilomantsi .com; Anssilantie; s/d €28/56, 4-person cottages €112; P ✗) This is a former dairy farm on a hill 3km south of the village centre and about 500m off the main road. The friendly family rents rooms in a range of converted farmhouse buildings. Breakfast and linen are included. You can also camp in the garden here for a negotiable (but cheap) price.

Hotel Ilomantsi (☎ 683 5300; www.hotelliilomantsi .com; Kalevalantie 12; s/d €58/78, small tw €66; P ✗) In the centre of the village, the Ilomantsi is clean and comfortable. It's also a pub, restaurant, karaoke bar and local disco. This is where you should find Ilomantsi on a Saturday night.

Kuntoutuskeskus Pääskynpesä (☎ 682 1200; www.paaskynpesa.fi; Henrikintie 4; s/d €69/106; P ✗ ☝) This is an anonymous-looking spa hotel, popular with older Finns and families. It's right on Lake Ilomantsi, and facilities include saunas (naturally) and various therapy treatments.

Ruhkaranta Lomakeskus (☎ 843 161; www .ruhkaranta.fi; Ruhkarannantie 21; tent sites €9 plus €3 per person, cottages €34-85; ☺ Jun-Aug) About 9km east of Ilomantsi, in a thick pine forest, is a camping ground with spectacular views of several lakes. There's a traditional smoke sauna here for groups and an electric sauna. The restaurant is open only on weekends.

Eating & Drinking

Parppeinpirtti (☎ 881 094; lunch €10; ◷ noon-3pm) For a real *pitopöytä* (Karelian buffet) come to this place in Parppeinvaara, where there's a daily lunch buffet. Try the *vatruska* (Karelian pies of pastry and potato), and the slightly sweet *vuassa* (milk-malt drink).

Murginapirtti (☎ 881 250; Yhtiöntie; lunch buffet €6-8; ◷ 10am-3pm Mon-Fri) This is an old-style Finnish farmhouse restaurant up a dirt road near the centre of town. There's a delicious lunch buffet for around €8 served on weekdays.

Ilomantsin Leipomo (☎ 881 273; Kalevalantie 10; ◷ 6am-4pm Mon-Fri, 8.30am-2pm Sat) Opposite the tourist office, this café is great for grabbing an early coffee and a loaf of fresh picnic bread before heading out wilderness-bound. It also does lunches and is the social hub of town.

Ravintola Kelopirtti (lunch buffet €8; ◷ 10am-6pm Jun–mid-Aug) On the main-road roundabout is a log cabin with a café and an interesting Karelian craft shop.

Pub Monttu (Kalevalantie; ◷ 11am-1am Mon-Thu, to 3am Fri & Sat, noon-1am Sun) A little further along from Hotel Ilomantsi, where the nightclub action is, this is a local bar that gets busy on weekends and also serves food.

Getting There & Away

Buses run frequently between Joensuu and Ilomantsi from Monday to Friday (€11.50, one to two hours). There are fewer buses on weekends. During school term there are Monday to Friday buses from here to surrounding villages, but in summer you'll have to rely on taxi buses, which you might have to charter.

AROUND ILOMANTSI

From Ilomantsi, road 5004 heads east towards the Russian border, through a patchwork of lakes and into the start of some fine wilderness trekking country.

Petkeljärvi National Park

The turn-off to one of Finland's smallest (6.3 sq km) national parks is about 14km east of the main highway. The main reason to visit Petkeljärvi is to walk the nature trails that cover birch and pine forest and *eskers* (gravel ridges). The marked, 35km 'Taitajan Taival' trek starts here and runs northeast to the village of Mekrijärvi, about

13km north of Ilomantsi. More than one-third of the park is water, with two sizeable lakes dominating. There are also several remnants of bunkers and fortifications from the Winter War.

Petkeljärvi Nature Centre (☎ 013-844 199; s/family tent sites €7/12, lodge s/d/q €36/46/76; ◷ Jun-Aug), in the heart of the park, is an excellent retreat. As well as tent and caravan sites, there's a modern lodge building with kitchen, a café, sauna and boats and canoes for use on the lake. Park information, including maps, is also available here.

Möhkö

☎ 013

The tiny village of Möhkö, only a few kilometres from the Russian border, is at the southern end of the Wolf's Trail (see boxed text, p158).

This remote outpost was once the unlikely scene of heavy industry. An ironworks was established here in 1849 and at its peak it employed more than 2000 people and was one of the largest ore-processing works in Finland. The site included a sawmill and tar works, and a canal was dug in 1872 to transport ore and timber out of the wilderness. The small **ironworks museum** (☎ 844 111; €3.50; ◷ 10am-6pm May-Aug) explains the story.

As well as a fine lakeside camping ground location, **Möhkön Karhumajat** (☎ 844 180; beatrice.ekberg@kolumbus.fi; Jokivaarantie 4; tent sites from €9, 2-person cabins €35, cottages from €68; ◷ May-Sep) has pleasant cottages, a small beach, a couple of saunas, friendly owners and Finland's 'easternmost beer terrace'. Nearby is **Möhkön Manta** (☎ 040-861 6373; ◷ May-Aug), a café in an old, grounded canal boat. Traditional Karelian pies, soups and sweets are dished up here.

HATTUVAARA

☎ 013

Hattuvaara, about 40km northeast of Ilomantsi, is a convenient base for exploring easternmost Finland. The village is the main landmark along the little-travelled *runon ja rajan tie* ('Poem and Border Route'). Experiencing a summer night in this quaint little village is therapeutic: birds sing and cow bells tinkle.

The main attraction here is the striking wooden **Taistelijan Talo** (Heroes House; ☎ 830 111; ◷ 11am-8pm Jun–mid-Aug daily, 11am-6pm Wed-Sun

KARELIA

KARELIAN TREKS

Some of the best trekking routes in North Karelia have been linked up to create **Karjalan Kierros** (Karelian Circuit; www.karjalankierros.com), a loop of marked trails with a total length of over 1000km between Ilomantsi and Lake Pielinen. The best known are the Bear's Trail (not to be confused with the more famous Bear's Ring in Oulanka National Park) and the Wolf's Trail, which link up in Patvinsuo National Park (see p160). These can be walked in either direction, but are described here in a south-to-north direction. You'll need to arrange transport to trailheads, including Patvinsuo National Park, in advance, although there is a bus service to Möhkö village.

Although there are wilderness huts and lean-to shelters along the way, it's advisable to carry a tent. Hire of hiking equipment can be arranged at the Ilomantsi or Lieksa offices of Karelia Expert. Much of the Ilomantsi region is boggy marshland, so waterproof footwear is essential. For more information on these and other routes contact the Lieksa or Ilomantsi offices of Karelia Expert, or **Metsähallitus** (☎ 0205-645 500; Urheilukatu 3A, Lieksa), the information office for the Forest & Park Service. See also the Activities chapter (p45) for general information about trekking.

Susitaival (Wolf's Trail)

The 90km Wolf's Trail is a marked three-day trek running north from Möhkö village to the marsh-lands of Patvinsuo National Park. The terrain consists mostly of dry heath, pine forest and swampy marshland which can be wet underfoot. This trail runs close to the Russian border in places and it was here that many of the battles in the Winter War and Continuation War were fought. Early in the trek, at Lake Sysmä, you'll see a memorial and anti-tank gun. There are wilderness cabins at Sarkkajärvi, Pitkajärvi and Jorho, and farm or camping accommodation in the village of Naarva. In the Ilomantsi wilderness area there are about 100 bears and 50 wolves – chances of running into one are slim but not impossible.

Karhunpolku (Bear's Trail)

The Bear's Trail is a 133km marked hiking trail of medium difficulty leading north from Patvin-suo National Park near Lieksa, through a string of national parks and nature reserves, including Ruunaa Recreation Area, along the Russian border. Because of this accessibility, the trail can be walked in relatively short stages. The trail ends at Teljo, about 50km south of Kuhmo. You'll need to arrange transport from either end.

From Patvinsuo, the trail crosses heathland and boardwalks for 15km to the first wilderness hut at Kangas-Piilo, then another 14km to a hut and lean-to at Valkealampi. From here there's a short trail detouring to the WWII battleline of Kitsi. The trail then heads northwest to the Ruunaa Recreation Area, where there are several choices of accommodation, and opportunities for fishing canoeing and rafting.

Beyond Ruunaa it's around 42km to Änäkäinen, another WWII battlefield. The trail follows the Jongunjoki on its final leg to the Ostroskoski wilderness hut, about 6km from Teljo.

Tapios Trail (Tapion Taival)

The easternmost trekking route in Finland, Tapion Taival (Fighter's Trail) gives you the choice of a 13km wilderness track along the Koitajoki, or an 8km northern extension across the Koivusuo Nature Reserve, or yet another extension north of Koivusuo to Kivivaara. The Koitajoki section is certainly the highlight, a stunning walk through epic wilderness. The path is marked by orange paint on tree trunks.

You will need a private car and good local map to reach the trekking area, or you can negoti-ate at Taistelijan Talo in Hattuvaara about transport and price.

May & mid-Aug–Sep), designed by Joensuu architect Erkki Helasvuo to symbolise the meeting of East and West. There is a fascinating **WWII museum** (€3.50) downstairs, with a short film in several languages, multimedia, photo exhibitions, weapons and displays relating chiefly to the Winter War and Continuation War fought along the nearby border. The house is also the place to contact for accommodation in the village.

Hattuvaara has the oldest **Orthodox tsasouna** in Finland. Built in the 1720s, it has several old Russian icons inside. Its small tower was used as a watchtower during WWII. On 29 June, a wonderfully colourful **Praasniekka festival** takes place here, with a *ristinsaatto,* or Orthodox procession commemorating a saint, beginning at the *tsasouna.*

Sleeping & Eating

Arhipanpirtti (☎ 830 111, 0400 173 607; Hatunraitti 5B; s/d €22/40) This is the main place to stay in Hattuvaara and is run out of Taistelijan Talo. There are rooms available in several buildings, plus a four-person cottage at €70 a night, and the price includes linen and sauna. There are also some cottages and self-contained flats nearby for the same price. Some readers have complained about the lack of cleanliness when booking during off-season, but when we visited it was spotless.

Taistelijan Talo (buffet €10) This place serves a fabulous all-day Finnish buffet in a beautiful high wooden dining room. As well as hearty meat and fish dishes, salads, bread, cheese and Karelian pies, there's a range of desserts.

AROUND HATTUVAARA
Easternmost Point

With a vehicle you can journey east to the Finnish-Russian border crossing at **Virmajärvi**, the easternmost point of Finland and therefore of the European Union (at least until Turkey is accepted as an EU member). You need a permit from the **Border Guards Station** (☒ 8am-4pm Mon-Fri) next to Taistelijan Talo in Hattuvaara, issued free on the spot provided you have your passport details with you. It's then a 15km drive down a fairly rough gravel road, signposted by blue 'EU' markers. There's not much to see and nothing to do at the end – it's sort of a spiritual (for Karelians) and geographical pilgrimage to say you've been.

The actual border is marked by two posts on a small island in the lake. About 2km back is the **log house**, which contains nothing of interest but you can stay here overnight with permission from Taistelijan Talo, and along the way you pass several WWII *sotapaikka* (battle locations) and memorials.

LAKE PIELINEN REGION

The northernmost part of Finnish Karelia is centred around Pielinen, Finland's sixth largest lake, and impressive even in a region dominated by water features. Several attractions can be found on its shores; the Koli National Park for summer views and winter skiing, the active centres of Lieksa and Nurmes, and, nearby, the Ruunaa whitewater rafting centre. It's a place to be active; the towns offer little apart from bases for getting into the great outdoors. A main road and numerous minor roads encircle the lake, ferries cross it in several directions, and, in winter, an ice road provides a thrilling short cut across it.

LIEKSA
☎ 013 / pop 14,080

The small centre of Lieksa, on Lake Pielinen about 100km north of Joensuu, is an active place. It's known as a whitewater-rafting destination, and also has several canoeing routes of greater and lesser difficulty in the area. Operators in Lieksa can kit you out for all these. It has good transport links, including lake ferries across to Koli, accommodation and all services.

Information

Library (☎ 689 4125; Urheilukatu 4) Has free Internet access.

Karelia Expert (☎ 248 5312; kareliaexpert.lieksa@ kareliaexpert.fi; Pielisentie 7; ☒ 8am-6pm Mon-Fri, 9am-2pm Sat Jun-Aug, plus 11am-3pm Sun Jul, 8am-4pm Mon-Fri Sep-May) Loads of information on whitewater rafting, accommodation, fishing, smoke saunas and national parks, and sells trekking maps for local routes. Staff can also book tours and accommodation.

Post office (☎ 020 4511; Pielisentie 34) At the northern end of the main street.

Sights

Pielisen Museo (☎ 689 4151; Pappilantie 2; adult/child €4.50/1.50; ☒ 10am-6pm mid-May–mid-Sep) is a huge complex of almost 100 Karelian buildings and open-air exhibits, divided into several sections according to the century or the trade featured (eg, farming, milling, fire-fighting, forestry). It's certainly a comprehensive display in a relatively small area – the collection comprises some 100,000 objects and 15,000 photographs. There's a separate **indoor museum** (admission in winter €3, ☺ summer as above, plus 10am-3pm Tue-Fri winter) featuring photographs and static displays on Karelian folk history. It's open in winter when the open-air display is closed.

Activities

The most popular activity in the Lieksa area is **whitewater rafting** at the Ruunaa Recreation Area. See opposite for details; operators will pick you up from Lieksa, and trips can be booked at the tourist office at Karelia Expert.

Pony-trekking on hardy Icelandic horses can be arranged through the tourist office. It normally costs from about €12 per hour. **Ratsastustalli Ahaa** (☎ 040-525 7742; www.ahaatalli .com) has riding lessons and cross-country treks for more experienced riders.

In winter, husky-dog, cross-country skiing, and snowmobile **expeditions** along the Russian border are popular – the tourist office has a list of tour operators. These trips can largely be tailored to your own needs, with up to four hours travel per day, and lasting up to a week. **Carelian Dogsledding and Outdoor** (☎ 854 106; bear.hill@pp.inet.fi) are one of the best operators, based near Hattuvaara.

Fishing is good in Lake Pielinen, Pudasjoki River and the Ruunaa and Änäkäinen recreational fishing areas. They each require separate permits, available from local sports shops or the Lieksa tourist office.

Festivals & Events

Lieksa Brass Week (☎ /fax 689 4144; www.lieksa brass.com; Koski-Jaakonkatu 4), held during the last week in July, attracts quite a number of international musicians. There's a programme of concerts each day, with ticket prices ranging from €5 to €30.

Sleeping & Eating

There are a few places to stay in Lieksa, but it's also worth considering the surrounding options in Vuonislahti (p163), Koli (p164) and Ruunaa (p162).

Most places to eat and drink are on Lieksa's main street, Pielisentie.

Hotelli Puustelli (☎ 511 5500; www.finlandia hotels.fi; Hovileirinkatu 3; s/d €80/95, Sat, Sun & summer €65/80; Ⓟ ☒ &) This is a pleasant riverside hotel in the town centre, and rates include breakfast and sauna. There are good facilities for the disabled.

Aikuisopiston Asuntola (☎ 244 3674; Oravatie 1; dm €21; Ⓟ ☒) It may be a mouthful to pronounce, but this is basically apartment-style student accommodation with kitchen facilities. The price includes linen and a sauna; there's also a laundry available. Call ahead to book as there's no-one on site.

Timitraniemi Camping (☎ 521 780; www.timitra .com; tent sites €12, cabins €32-84; ☺ mid-May–Sep) This camping ground at the river mouth has log cabins, cottages of varying sizes, plenty of tent sites and facilities like lakeside saunas and bikes and boats for hire. There's also a café.

Café Sanna (☎ 524 921; Pielisentie 2-6; meals €6-8) This place offers reasonably priced, home-style lunches.

Tinatahti (☎ 521 914; Pielisentie 28) A lively pub that also serves meals.

Getting There & Away

Buses from Joensuu are relatively frequent (€16.20, 1¾ hours), and shared taxis (see p151) even more so. There are daily trains to Lieksa from Helsinki (€60.50, seven hours), via Joensuu (€11.20, 1¼ hours). The more scenic mode of transport is by ferry from Joensuu, via Koli; see p154 for more information.

The car ferry **MF Pielinen** (☎ 481 244; www .saimaaferries.fi) from Lieksa to Koli operates twice daily from early June to mid-August, departing from Lieksa at 9.30am and 3.30pm, and returning from Koli at 11.30am and 5.30pm. The trip takes 1¾ hours and costs per adult/child €15/8, €8 for a car, €5 for a motorcycle and €2 for a bicycle. In winter, when the ice is thick enough, there is an ice road crossing the lake from Vuonislahti to Koli, a substantial short cut.

PATVINSUO NATIONAL PARK

Patvinsuo is a large marshland area between Lieksa and Ilomantsi. Swans, cranes and other birds nest here and bears and other mammals can be seen if you're lucky. With the excellent *pitkospuu* (boardwalk) network, you can easily hike around, observing the life of a Finnish marshland.

If you have little time, go to the southern shore of Suomunjärvi. It's 3.5km from the main road to **Teretin lintutorni**, a bird-watching tower. This is a good walk through forests and wetlands, and you will see some birds.

There are three nature trails and several good hiking routes along the boardwalk path. You can walk around Lake Suomu or follow *pitkospuu* trails through the wetlands.

Suomu Park Centre (☎ 548 506) has a warden in attendance from early May to mid-September for advice, fishing permits and free maps. There is a dormitory with nine beds, including the use of a small kitchen. You can use the telephone and the sauna for a fee. There are seven camping sites and one *laavu* (an open shelter with sloping roof) within the park boundaries; all have toilets and firewood and are free of charge. You can also hire canoes and rowing boats here (per hour/day €5/20).

Getting There & Away

There is no public transport. From Lieksa, drive 18km east towards Hatunkylä, then turn right to Kontiovaara, along a narrow, very scenic road. When you reach a sealed road (Uimaharjuntie), turn left, drive a few hundred metres and turn right. If you drive along the eastern *runon ja rajan tie* route, turn west as you see the small 'Uimaharju' sign, just south of the Lieksa-Ilomantsi border. If you are trekking, the Karhunpolku (Bear's Trail) and Susitaival (Wolf's Trail) both lead here, as the park is where these trails meet.

RUUNAA RECREATION AREA

☎ 013

Ruunaa (www.ruunaa.fi), 30km northeast of Lieksa, is adventurous Finns' most sought-after destination east of Lake Pielinen, mainly for the huge variety of outdoor activities that can easily be arranged here. It boasts 38km of waterways with six white-water rapids, plus unpolluted wilderness, excellent trekking paths and good fishing. Designated camp sites (with fire rings) are also provided and maintained.

There's an observation tower situated at Huuhkajavaara. Set atop a hill, it offers a magnificent panorama over Neitijärvi. The **Ruunaa Nature Centre** (☎ 020-564 5757; 🕑 10am-5pm May, 9am-6pm Jun & Jul, 9am-5pm Aug) is near the bridge over the Naarajoki, where most boat trips start. There are exhibitions, maps, a library and a free slide show in English. This is a good stop to find out about rafting operators and hiking trails.

Activities

Ruunaa is busy all year round, as it hosts skiing and other snow sports in winter. All activities can be booked from the tourist office in Lieksa.

BOATING, CANOEING & RAFTING

There are six rapids (class II–III), and you can shoot them in wooden or rubber boats. There are several launches daily in summer from Naarajoki bridge (near the Nature Centre). A two- to four-hour trip costs €35 to €45 per adult (including lunch; most operators also offer trips without lunch for €22 to €25) and the Nature Centre or **Karelia Expert** (☎ 248 5312) in Lieksa can line you up with an operator. Transport can also be arranged from Lieksa if you book a tour. **Erästely** (☎ 0400 271 581; www.erastely.com; per person €55) organizes canoeing expeditions from the Nature Centre, and has several other self-guided routes available. You will need to book in advance. Rafting operators include the following:

Koski-Jaako (☎ 0500 366 033; www.koski-jaakko .fi; €36) Noon departure; wooden boat. Rubber boat also available.

Lieksan Koskikierros (☎ 521 645, 040-766 7148; www.lieksankoskikierros.fi; expeditions €38) Departs 11am, noon and 3.30pm; wooden boat or electric-powered boat.

Lieksan Matkakaverit (☎ 040-708 5726; www .lieksanmatkakaverit.fi; expeditions €37-45) Departures at 11am, 11.30am, noon and 12.30pm; wooden and rubber boats.

Ruunaan Matkailu (☎ 533 130, 0400 352 207; www .ruunaanmatkailu.fi; expeditions €37-45) Departs 10am, 11am, noon and 2.30pm; wooden and rubber boats.

FISHING

Ruunaa is one of the most popular fishing spots in North Karelia. The trout and salmon fishing is excellent in the numerous rapids, and good fishing spots are accessible along a long wooden walkway. One-day fishing permits cost €13 in summer and are available in Lieksa and at the Ruunaa Nature Centre. There is also a fishing-permit machine near the Neitijoki rapids. Fishing is allowed from June to early September and from mid-November to late December, and only lures and flies may be used. There are several places to hire fishing equipment, including **Lieksan Retkiaitta** (☎ 0400 172 226; Pielisentie 33) in Lieksa.

KARELIA

TREKKING

There are two trekking routes within the Ruunaa area. The **Karhunpolku** (Bear's Trail), a longer trekking route, passes through Ruunaa. You can find it just 50m north of the Naarajoki bridge. The path is marked with round orange symbols on trees. See p158 for more details.

Around the river system, and over two beautiful suspension bridges, runs **Ruunaan koskikierros**, a marked 29km loop along good *pitkospuu* paths. If you have more time, there are another 20km of side trips you can take. If you start at the Naarajoki bridge, you will have to walk 5km along the Bear's Trail to reach the Ruunaan koskikierros trail. Another 3.3km brings you to the **Neitikoski**, where you'll find commercial services. Neitikoski also has road access and a parking area.

Sleeping & Eating

There are at least 10 *laavu* shelters and another 10 designated camp sites in the area. Camping and sleeping in a *laavu* is free of charge. Get the free *Ruunaa Government Hiking Area* map and guide for accommodation information. You will need a lightweight mattress, a sleeping bag and some mosquito repellent. Lighting a fire is allowed, except during fire alerts (watch for posted signs).

Ruunaan Matkailu (☎ /fax 533 130; www.ruunaan matkailu.fi; Siikaskoskentie 47; s/d from €18.50/26, cabins €36-85; Ⓟ ✕) Five kilometres east of Naarajoki bridge, This place, has tidy accommodation, as well as a café, lakeside sauna, smoke sauna, rental boats and various snowmobile, rafting and boating tours.

Neitikoski Hiking Centre (☎ 533 170; neitikoski@ruunaa.fi; tent sites €12-18, cabins/cottages €35/95) Near the Neitikoski rapids is this centre with a large café, camping area, kitchen, sauna and luxurious four- to six-bed cottages as well as simpler cabins. There are mountain bikes, canoes and rowing boats for hire. The boardwalk to the rapids starts near here.

Lomapirtti Sillankorva (☎ /fax 533 121; Ruunantie 124; r €32-80; Ⓟ ✕) This place offers superb accommodation right at the Naarajoki bridge. You can rent the entire farmhouse if you have a large group (sleeps at least 12; a night/week €121/467), or either floor of two renovated apartments (a night/

week from €62/239), plus there's an outbuilding sleeping four (€32). Everything is extremely clean and beautifully designed. There's a smoke sauna (two hours €74) and a summer restaurant.

Getting There & Away

Infrequent minibuses make the trip from Lieksa – inquire at Karelia Expert for timetables. The best way to reach the area is on an organized rafting tour from Lieksa, by hitching or by private car.

NURMIJÄRVI AREA

☎ 013

Known for its canoeing routes, the Nurmijärvi area is wild and remote. Nurmijärvi village has enough services to get you to the Jongunjoki or Lieksajoki canoeing routes, or to the Änäkäinen area for fishing and trekking.

Activities

ÄNÄKÄINEN FISHING AREA

Änäkäinen is a government fishing area, with the Bear's Trail running through it. The Forest and Park Service controls fish quantities in three lakes in the area. Fishing is allowed year-round, except in the first three weeks of May. The Aunen Kahvila and Jongunjoen Lomapirtti (opposite) have boats and fishing permits (a day/week in summer €10/35). Permits are also available in Lieksa.

Änäkäinen experienced fierce fighting during the early weeks of the Winter War in December 1939. Finnish soldiers held their positions here, leaving a large number of Russians dead. In order to stop enemy tanks, the Finns built large rock barriers.

CANOEING THE PANKASAARI ROUTE

This is a good circular route from Nurmijärvi village, where you can rent a canoe from **Erästely** (☎ 0400 271 581; www.erastely.com, in Finnish). The paddle route starts across the road. Get yourself a free route guide, which is available at tourist offices in the area. The route follows the Lieksajoki downstream to Pankajärvi. From there, you paddle southeast under a road bridge to Pudasjärvi. Avoiding the Pankakoski power station in the south, paddle upstream to the upper part of the Lieksajoki. Heading northwest from this point, you first reach Naarajoki at Ruunaa, then round Pankasaari, before returning to Nurmijärvi. There's almost no gradient on this route and it's suitable for beginners. Only the Käpykoskis might present a problem; pull the canoes through with a rope if you're not sure.

CANOEING THE JONGUNJOKI
This beautiful wilderness river has nearly 40 small rapids, none of them very tricky. Karelia Expert in Lieksa has a good guide to the route. You can start at Jonkeri up north (in the municipality of Kuhmo), or further south at Teljo bridge, or at Aittokoski, or even at Lake Kaksinkantaja. Allow four days if you start at Jonkeri and one day from the last point. **Erästely** (☎ 0400 271 581; www.erastely.com, in Finnish) can transport you to Jonkeri, Teljo or Kaksinkantaja, and also rent canoes.

Sleeping & Eating
Erästelyn Melontakeskus (☎ 0400 271 581; www .erastely.com, in Finnish; Kivivaarantie 1, Nurmijärvi village; dm €15; P ⊠ ᴟ) The main canoe rental company, Erästely Company, also offers beds at their headquarters, in decent dormitory accommodation with good facilities. Linen is €5 extra.

Jongunjoen Lomapirtti (☎ /fax 546 531; Kivivaarantie 21, Jongunjoki; beds per person €24; P) This place is 2km from the main road towards Änäkäinen and the Russian border. There are two- to six-person rooms, cabins, tent sites, smoke saunas and bicycles, canoes and boats for rent.

Aunen Kahvila (☎ 546 503; Nurmijärventie 154) A popular roadside café in Nurmijärvi, 15km from the Russian border. There are meals, and you can buy fishing permits and pick up keys for the Änäkäinen-rented fishing boats.

VUONISLAHTI
☎ 013
Vuonislahti is a rural lakeside village, with little more than a train station and a great hostel – which is enough to justify a stay if you have the time.

There is a **war memorial** on a small hill across the road as you come from the train station. This is where Russians were stopped by Finnish soldiers in 1808. The nearby *tanssilava* (dance stage) house has dancing in summer on Saturday evenings.

The brilliant lakeside HI hostel, **Kestikievari Herranniemi** (☎ 542 110; www.herranniemi .com; Vuonislahdentie 185; dm €13, cabins €28-68, s/d B&B €50/68; P ⊠) is about 2km south of the train station. The quaint 200-year-old farm building has a restaurant, a range of comfortable accommodation, including cheap dormitories in an old *aitta* (storage) building, two lakeside saunas and rowing boats. The owners even offer a range of treatment therapies such as herbal baths and *turvesauna* (a cross between a sauna and a mud bath). To get to Herranniemi, walk straight from the Vuonislahti train station to the main road, turn left and proceed 500m.

In Vuonislahti itself, **Hotelli Pielinen** (☎ 544 144; www.hotellipielinen.com; Läpikäytäväntie 54; s/d €33/50, hotel d €64; P ⊠ ᴫ) is a modern hotel with two grades of rooms, both reasonably good value. There's also a swimming pool, restaurant, smoke sauna and a range of activities.

There are two daily trains to Vuonislahti from Joensuu (€9.40, one hour) and Lieksa (€3.40, 20 minutes). The small Vuonislahti train station keeps short hours, but you can always buy tickets on the train.

Paateri
The village of Paateri is best known for the **church and gallery** (☎ 543 223; admission €4; ⌚ 10am-6pm mid-May–mid-Sep) at the studio-home of the late Eva Ryynänen (1915–2001), a respected wood sculptor, on Vuonisjärvi. Her work became widely recognised in Finland in the 1970s, although she had been working since the 1930s. This isolated property, surrounded by pine trees, is a memorable retreat; the Paateri wilderness church was built in 1991 with walls and floor made of Russian pine, and huge doors carved from Canadian cedar. The altar was created using a stump that once belonged to the largest fir tree in Finland. The place also has a café, and is open during the February holidays.

One way to get to Paateri is to row a boat from the Herranniemi hostel, but it's a 1½-hour trip one way – not for the faint-hearted or lazy. By motor boat, also available from the hostel, it takes about 20 minutes and costs €19 return, including admission and coffee. If you are driving or cycling, follow the road signs from the main road or from the secondary road north of Vuonislahti. You can also rent a bicycle at the Herranniemi hostel.

KARELIA

KOLI NATIONAL PARK
☎ 013

The views from the top of 347m Koli Hill offer some of Finland's finest Lakeland scenery – it was these views that inspired many of the famous artists from Finland's National Romantic era, including Pekka Halonen and Eero Järnefelt.

Rising above Lake Pielinen and accessible by ferry from Lieksa, Koli has been dubbed the first-ever tourist attraction in Finland and it continues to draw holiday-makers year-round – as a winter sports resort and for hiking, boating and its unique scenery in summer. Although the lake views are panoramic and the nature trails in the national park are good, don't expect the earth – it's a beautiful hill covered in pine and birch.

Koli Hill was declared a national park in 1991 after hot debate between environmentalists and landowners. The owners agreed to sell their land and environmentalists dropped their demand that the Hotel Koli, up on the hill, be demolished. Most of the area remains relatively pristine and there are some 90km of marked walking tracks.

The hill has road access and from the lower car park there's a short funicular railcar up to the hotel (free). Also here is **Luontokeskus Ukko** (☎ 010-211 3200; www.metla koli.net; adult/child €5/2; 9am-7pm late Jun-early Aug, 10am-5pm rest of year), a modern visitor centre with exhibitions on history, nature, and geology of the park, and information on hiking. In Koli itself, **Karelia Expert** (☎ 248 2315; kareliaexpert.koli@kareliaexpert.com; Kolintie 94) is the tourist office and has a comprehensive range of information and maps.

Ukko-Koli is the highest point and 200m further is **Akka-Koli**, another peak. On the western slope of Akka-Koli is a 'Temple of Silence', an open space for contemplation with a stone altar and wooden cross mounted in the rock. The solid rock peak nearby is called **Paha-Koli**. Further south is **Mäkrävaara**, a hill that offers the best views.

In winter, Koli attracts skiers with two slalom centres (Loma-Koli and Ukko-Koli, served by a total of nine lifts) and more than 60km of cross-country trails, including 24km of lit track. If you can't make it up to Lapland, this is one of Finland's most accessible winter ski resorts. Contact the **Koli Ski Centre** (☎ 672 275, 673 141; www.koliski.fi) for lift tickets, equipment hire and more information.

Sleeping & Eating

Koli Retkeilymaja (☎ 673 131; Niinilahdentie 47; dm €12, d €24;) On a gravel road 5km from the bus stop, this family-run hostel, has a kitchen and smoke sauna; you can also sleep in a traditional Sámi hut. It's a great getaway and one of the most relaxing hostels in Finland – if you call ahead you may be able to arrange a pick-up.

Sokos Hotel Koli (☎ 020-1234 662; www.soko-sho tels.fi; Ylä-Kolintie 39; r from €72;) At the top of Koli Hill is this huge modern concrete-and-glass place dominating the hill top. Although it does nothing to enhance the scenery, the views are pretty special, and it's a very comfortable place to return after a day's skiing or hiking.

Loma-Koli Camping (☎ 673 212; tent sites €12, cabins €30-40; late Jun–mid-Aug) This camping ground, near the Hiisi Hill slopes, has excellent facilities, including cottages, and rents mountain bikes. There are also some rental tents available (€30).

Kolin Lomaranta (☎ 040-729 5030; Merilänrannan-tie 15; tent sites €10, cabins €22-40; Jun-Aug) This place has camping areas and simple 'out-buildings' for two to five people.

There are several basic huts in the national park. They each cost €9 per night and can be booked through the heritage centre or Karelia Expert.

Art-Café Kolin Ryynänen (☎ 672 160; Kolintie 1C) Opposite the supermarket in Koli village, this pleasant café serves as an exhibition space and even has an artist-in-residence living upstairs.

Getting There & Away

There are five to eight daily buses to Koli from Joensuu (€10.20, one hour and 20 minutes), Juuka (€6.20, 20 minutes), and Nurmes (€13.70, 1½ hours), including at least one a day to the top of Koli Hill. The best way to arrive in summer is by lake ferry from Joensuu (p154) or Lieksa (p160). Buses to the top of Koli Hill meet all arriving ferries.

JUUKA
☎ 013 / pop 6177

Juuka, just off the main highway about halfway between Nurmes and Koli, is known for its soapstone mining and handicrafts. It has a small **Puu-Juuka** (old town) of wooden houses, some more than 100 years old. They were preserved from demolition largely through the efforts of local individuals and have now been restored as shops, galleries and homes. There's also the **Mill Museum** and the Village Museum.

The **Suomen Kivikeskus** (Finnish Stone Centre; ☎ 681 1600; www.kivikeskus.com; Kuhnustantie 10; adult/child €5/2; ☒ 9am-7pm daily Jun–mid-Aug, 9am-7pm Mon-Fri, 10am-4pm Sat & Sun mid-Aug–May), 13 kilometres south of Juuka, is a large modern centre with displays on the geology of Finland, and the uses of stone in building and jewellery. It's an interesting, if slightly impersonal, place.

Lomakylä Piitteri (☎ 472 000; www.piitteri.fi; Piitterintie 144; tent sites €12.50, cabins €32-42; ☒ early Jun–mid-Aug), on the shore of Lake Pielinen, is a good camp site which has a marina and swimming beach. There is a typical Finnish *huvilava* (dancing stage) here, where minor Finnish celebrities sometimes sing on Saturday nights.

PAALASMAA ISLAND
☎ 013

The largest island in Lake Pielinen is connected to the mainland by a free ferry that winds through smaller islands. The island is noted for its scenery and peaceful atmosphere, and is the highest island in Finland – its tallest point is 132m above water level. There is a wooden **observation tower** on the island, 3km from the camping ground via a marked trail. If you follow the signs that say 'tornille', you will see some **old houses** that tell the long history of Paalasmaa.

The ferry terminal is 15km east of the main road and the turn-off is about 2km north of Juuka. **Paalasmaan Lomamajat** (☎ 040-592 4765; tent sites €10, cabins €25-40; ☒ Jun–mid-Aug) is a camping ground at the eastern end of the island with a nice lakeside spot.

NURMES
☎ 013 / pop 9193

Nurmes, at the northwestern tip of Lake Pielinen, has a picturesque situation, and, like Lieksa, makes an excellent base for winter activities such as dog-sledding, snowmobiling, ice-fishing and cross-country skiing tours, and canoeing and farmhouse tours in summer. It's a more pleasant town in its own right though, with a terraced Puu-Nurmes (Old Town) area of historical wooden buildings, rows of beautiful birch trees lining Kirkkokatu, and a delightful re-creation of a Karelian village. Nurmes was founded in

1876 by Tsar Alexander II of Russia and the Old Town still has the character approved of by the 19th-century Russian ruler.

Orientation & Information

The train and bus stations are in the town centre. The main street is Kirkkokatu, at the northwestern end of which is Puu-Nurmes, while the Bomba (a Karelian theme village) and best places to stay are a few kilometres southeast of the centre.

Karelia Expert (☎ 248 5316; www.nurmes.fi; kareliaexpert.nurmes@kareliaexpert.fi; ☒ 9am-6pm Mon-Fri, 9am-2pm Sat Jun-Aug, plus 11am-3pm Sun Jul, 9am-4pm Mon-Fri Sep-May)) Local information and bookings. In the ABC service station on the western edge of town. The reception at the Hyvärilä Holiday Centre 4km southeast of town also has much information.

Post office (☎ 0200 71000; Torikatu 5) In the Siwa supermarket.

Public library (☎ 689 5125; Kötsintie 2) In the Nurmes-talo building at the northeastern end of town, has free Internet access, a reading room and a collection of the *Kalevala* in various languages.

Sights & Activities

Just north of the kauppatori, the **Lutheran church** (☒ 10am-6pm summer) from 1896 is the largest in North Karelia, with 2300 seats. Inside are some miniature models of earlier Lutheran churches.

Continue northwest from the church to reach **Puu-Nurmes**, the Old Town area on the *esker* above the train station. It's a pleasant neighbourhood for a stroll among the traditional wooden houses, which are protected by law and surrounded by birch trees. The plan dates back to 1897.

Kötsi Museum (☎ 689 5149; Kötsintie 2; admission €2; ☒ 11am-5pm Mon-Fri), the local museum of history, is in the large Nurmes-talo building. Artefacts on display include some from the Stone Age. With the same ticket you can visit the **Ikola Museum**, an agricultural museum in Tuupala 1km northeast of the centre. It features an open-air exhibit of Karelian wooden buildings. Also in the Nurmes-talo building is the free **Tyko Art Gallery** (☒ 11am-5pm Mon-Fri, 10am-3pm Sat) with changing monthly exhibitions.

Nurmes' biggest tourist draw is **Bomba Village** (☎ 678 200; Suojärvenkatu), 2.5km southeast of the town centre. The imposing main building, Bomba House, – with its high roof and ornate wooden trim – is a replica of a typical

KARELIA

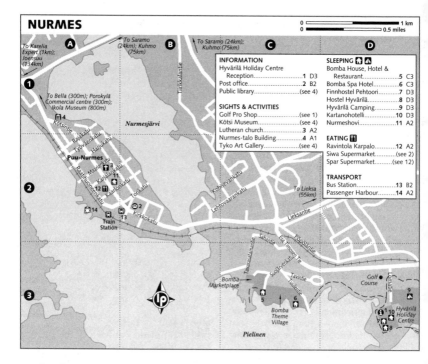

NURMES

INFORMATION
Hyvärilä Holiday Centre
Reception..........................**1** D3
Post office............................**2** B2
Public library.......................(see 4)

SIGHTS & ACTIVITIES
Golf Pro Shop.....................(see 1)
Kötsi Museum.....................(see 4)
Lutheran church..................**3** A2
Nurmes-talo Building.............**4** A1
Tyko Art Gallery..................(see 4)

SLEEPING
Bomba House, Hotel &
Restaurant.........................**5** C3
Bomba Spa Hotel................**6** C3
Finnhostel Pehtoori.............**7** D3
Hostel Hyvärilä....................**8** D3
Hyvärilä Camping................**9** D3
Kartanohotelli.....................**10** D3
Nurmeshovi........................**11** A2

EATING
Ravintola Karpalo................**12** A2
Siwa Supermarket...............(see 2)
Spar Supermarket.............(see 12)

TRANSPORT
Bus Station.........................**13** B2
Passenger Harbour.............**14** A2

Karelian family house that was built in 1855 by Jegor Bombin, a farmer from Suojärvi (now in Russian Karelia). It now houses the Bomban Talo restaurant. The surroundings include a charming re-creation of a Karelian village, with an Orthodox *tsasouna* and a summer theatre. The village also has shops, craft studios and a summer market, and you can buy locally made wines, homemade ice cream, handicrafts and more.

At the Hyvärilä Holiday Centre is a nine-hole **golf course** (☎ 687 2565; green fees €17, clubs hire per club €1; ♥ 9am-8pm May-Sep), which, while not especially challenging, has a lovely lakeside location.

Tours

Nurmes offers a well-organized schedule of tours with daily departures – dog-sledding, snowmobiling, ice-fishing and cross-country skiing from January to the end of March, and canoeing, rapids-shooting (at Ruunaa) and farmhouse tours from June to the end of August.

Contact the tourist service for an updated schedule, pricing information and other details. Bookings at least 24 hours in advance are often required for the tours.

Saimaa Ferries (☎ 481 244; www.saimaaferries.fi) has cruises (€14) on Lake Pielinen in summer from the passenger harbour near the train station.

Sleeping

Hyvärilä Holiday Centre (☎ 687 2500; www.hyvarila .com; Lomatie 12) The main choice for accommodation in Nurmes is this sprawling lakeside complex 4km southeast of town, with a camping ground, two HI-affiliated hostels, a decent hotel, restaurant and a golf course. There's also a small swimming beach, tennis courts, canoe and boat rentals and plenty of other activities. You can walk from here to Bomba Spa (1km) along marked walking routes. Not surprisingly, this is a very popular vacation destination for Finnish families and school groups, and if you're tired of travelling, it's not a bad place to pull up stumps and relax for a while. **Hyvärilä Camping** (tent sites €12-13, cabins €34-50; ♥ mid-May–mid-Sep) is a spacious area of lawn on the lake. **Hostel Hyvärilä** (dm €15, f €38; Ⓟ ✗) is a purpose-built hostel with dormitory accommodation, communal kitchen and laundry and access to all resort facilities. Breakfast and linen are €5 each. **Finnhostel Pehtoori** (dm/s/d €25/41/60; P ✗) is a better standard of hostel accommodation in a building with bunk-bedded rooms and good shared bathrooms. Breakfast and linen is included. Finally, **Kartanohotelli** (s/d €59/77, ste from €101; P ✗) is the resort's hotel, featuring comfortable rooms with TV and breakfast included.

Bomba Spa Hotel (☎ 687 200; www.bomba.fi; Suojärvenkatu 1; s/d €88/110; P ✗ 🖵 🏊) About 1km back towards town near the Karelian theme village, this is a stylish set-up where you can pamper yourself with the spa and sauna facilities, then sleep in modern hotel rooms. It's right by the lake and run by welcoming folk. Nonguests can use the spa facilities for €11. About 200m away from Bomba Spa is a group of attractive apartments in Karelian cabins decorated by local artisans. Some have their own sauna, and sleep either two to four or two to six (€135 to €185). Various special offers add in massage treatments.

Nurmeshovi (☎ 480 750; www.nurmeshovi.com; Kirkkokatu 21; s/d €58/74, Sat, Sun & summer €41/64; P ✗) In Nurmes town itself, this hotel is a bit of a travelling salesperson's joint, but it's central with a decent restaurant and functional rooms. Book in advance if you're going to be arriving on a Sunday.

Eating & Drinking

Bomban Talo (☎ 678 200; Bomba Village, Suojärvenkatu; ☎ 678 200; lunch buffet €14.50, mains €12-25; 🕒 10.30am-9pm or later, from 8am in summer) This place has a fantastic Karelian smorgasbord abounding in Karelian pies, *muikku* (fried whitefish) and varieties of *karjalanpaisti* (stew), served throughout the day in summer. The atmosphere is authentic too, it's set in an imposingly large wooden building with solid timber tables. There are good à la carte options too.

Bella (☎ 461 332; Porokylänkatu 14; mains from €7) In the commercial centre of Porokylä is a good Italian restaurant, popular with families, and with reasonably priced pizza and pasta. It becomes a fairly lively pub later on.

Ravintola Karpalo (☎ 480 651; Kirkkokatu 18; 🕒 lunch & dinner) This is an unpretentious place behind the supermarket. It serves burgers, pizzas, kebabs and steaks and has a €7 lunch buffet. It doubles as a local nightspot with karaoke and dancing nightly.

Getting There & Away

Buses run regularly to Joensuu (€18.60, two to three hours), Kajaani (€18.60, two hours), and Lieksa (€8.70, 50 minutes). For Kuhmo, change at Sotkamo.

Regional trains from Joensuu (€16, two hours) via Lieksa, stop in Nurmes.

Saimaa Ferries (☎ 481 244; www.saimaaferries .fi; Kirkkokatu 16) operate on Lake Pielinen in summer. As well as cruises, the MS *Vinkeri II* travels to and from Joensuu (via Koli) weekly, departing from Nurmes at 8.30am on Sunday (to Joensuu €50, 10½ hours, to Koli €20, 3¾ hours).

AROUND NURMES
Saramo
☎ 013

This small, remote village 24km north of Nurmes, is where the *Korpikylien tie* (Road of Wilderness Villages) begins. At the far end of the village, the **Kalastajatalo** (Fishers House; ☎ 434 066; Saramontie 77; 🕒 daily summer, Sat & Sun autumn-spring) serves as an information centre and restaurant and has accommodation options. There is a shop and a post office in Saramo.

Saramo can be used as a base for the marked 75km **Saramo Jotos Trek**. Between Saramo and Peurajärvi, there are two campfire sites in addition to Kourukoski, a spot named after rapids there. Between Peurajärvi and road 75, at Jalasjärvi, there's a *laavu*. Between road 75 and Mujejärvi, there are three *laavu* sites. South of Mujejärvi, there's a *laavu* at Markuskoski and cottages for rent at Paalikkavaara. Ask for a trail map in Nurmes or Saramo.

It is also possible to paddle the Saramojoki, starting from Peurajärvi or Mujejärvi and finishing in Saramo itself. Contact Kalastajatalo in Saramo for canoe rentals (per day €50) and transport (one-way around €15).

KARELIA

Tampere & Häme Region

The Häme (Swedish: Tavastland) region really is a place where modern and traditional Finland meet. A journey from the medieval fortress town of Hämeenlinna to corporation-driven Lahti via the 19th-century industrial boomtown of Tampere is a trip down the Finnish centuries. Here, ancient wooden churches still stand by waterlilied lakes, and steamboats take their time travelling between towns while, nearby, researchers discuss superconductivity, and Finland's finest ski-jumpers analyse the air-resistance of the latest lycra bodysuits.

In a similar pattern to other European cities, Tampere has shaken off its post-industrial hangover and become a great destination, with unusual museums, cafés and a cracker of a brewery pub. The city's important workers' movement helped bring better conditions and was bolstered Lenin himself, who spent much time in Tampere before the Russian Revolution.

The region was the scene of much of the earliest Swedish settlement in Finland's interior. In 1249 Earl Birger, on a Catholic crusade, arrived in Häme and founded the Swedish Tavastehus (Finnish: Hämeenlinna). The Swedish settlers who followed established large estates – causing irritation among locals who had traditionally been hunters and fishers.

One of the best things to do on holiday in Finland is to take a cruise on a boat; there's something about the pace of one that compels relaxation. The Poet's Way from Tampere to Virrat is a particularly fine route, and calls in at the beautiful village of Ruovesi, a tempting spot to stop for a couple of days and turn off your mobile phone.

HIGHLIGHTS

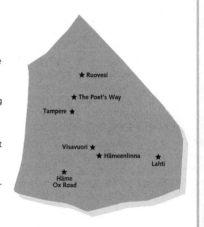

- Drinking your way down the beer list at **Panimoravintola Plevna** (p176), Tampere's memorable brewery pub
- Cruising the **Poet's Way** (p174) from Tampere to Virrat, a memorable feast of lakescapes
- Hanging out in peaceful **Ruovesi** (p180), enjoying walks in the forest and a spot of fishing
- Touring the imposing medieval **Häme Castle** (p182), pride of Hämeenlinna
- Cycling the **Häme Ox Road** (p187), an ancient trade route which once linked Turku with Hämeenlinna
- Admiring the work of Finland's greatest sculptor at peaceful **Visavuori** (p186)
- Watching ski jumpers defy gravity at Lahti's awesome **observation terrace** (p188)

Activities

In summer people tend to head for the water, and one of the best ways of experiencing the Finnish waterways is to take a cruise from Tampere or Lahti; there are several choices, some going long distances, such as the Poet's Way, a romantic journey north from Tampere.

On dry land, the little-known Häme Ox Rd, an old trade route that runs between Hämeenlinna and the coast at Turku is particularly good for exploring by bicycle.

Once the snow comes, there's also heaps to do in the region. Lahti is a prominent winter-sports centre, and while you won't be allowed to use the ski-jump, there are plenty of cross-country tracks and other options.

Fishing is popular all year round. Plenty of people fish in the rapids in the centre of Tampere, but for a more rural experience, one of the best bases in the region is Ruovesi, whose lakes teem with fish. Ice-fishing is also a fun thing to do here in winter.

Self-Catering Accommodation

For apartment, cabin and cottage rental in the region, get in touch with the Häme Tourist Service (☎ 03-621 2388; www.hameen matkailu.fi; Linnankatu 6; ☿ 8am-4pm Mon-Fri).

TAMPERE

☎ 03 / pop 202,932

Effectively Finland's second city, Tampere (Swedish: Tammerfors) is an exciting place combining Finnish sophistication with an industrious energy that is perhaps an inheritance from its days as 'the Manchester of Finland', as 19th-century cotton mills once busily churned alongside the energetic Tammerkoski (the rapids right in the middle of town). Set between two huge lakes that seem almost sea-like at times, Tampere is a great destination with good restaurants and bars and a few unusual museums.

With a large student population and a growing technology industry, Tampere is a dynamic, fast-developing place, although on a grey day the silhouettes of its brick chimneys through the misty haze can evoke a more Dickensian feel. The Finlayson mill complex, though, is the very symbol of regeneration; it is now a collection of bars, museums, shops and cinemas.

HISTORY

In the Middle Ages, the area around Tampere was inhabited by the Pirkka tribe, a devil-may-care guild of hunters and trappers which collected taxes as far north as Lapland. At that time, the 'town' consisted of a number of Swedish-run estates around the forests and the two lakes that surround Tampere. Modern Tampere was founded in 1779 during Gustav III of Sweden's reign.

In the 19th century, the Tampere Rapids, or Tammerkoski, which today supply abundant hydroelectric power, were a magnet for textile industries. Finnish and foreign investors flocked to the busy town, including the Scottish industrialist James Finlayson, who founded the cotton mill in 1820.

The Russian Revolution in 1917 increased interest in socialism among Tampere's large working-class population. It became the capital of the 'Reds' during the Civil War that followed Finnish independence.

ORIENTATION

Tampere is set between Näsijärvi and Pyhäjärvi, which are connected by the Tammerkoski. Just about everything is conveniently arranged along one street, Hämeenkatu, with the train station at its eastern end.

INFORMATION

Bookshops

Akateeminen Kirjakauppa (☎ 248 0300; Hämeenkatu 6; ☿ 9am-9pm Mon-Fri, 9am-6pm Sat, noon-6pm Sun) Extensive selection of English-language books.

Emergency

Phone ☎ 112 in any emergency. To report a crime, phone ☎ 219 5111, or visit the police station at Sorinkatu 12.

Internet Access

In addition to the places listed below, there are three free terminals in the tourist office.
Internet Café Madi (☎ 214 8513; Tuomiokirkonkatu 36; per hr €3; ☿ 10am-10pm Mon-Fri, 11am-10pm Sat) Not far from the train station.
Tampere City library (Metso; ☎ 314 614; Pirkankatu 2; ☿ 9.30am-8pm Mon-Fri, 9.30am-3pm Sat, 9.30am-7pm weekdays in summer) The library is called 'Metso' (capercaillie) by locals because of its unusual architecture. It has several Internet terminals, some of which are first-come-first-served (15 minute time limit).

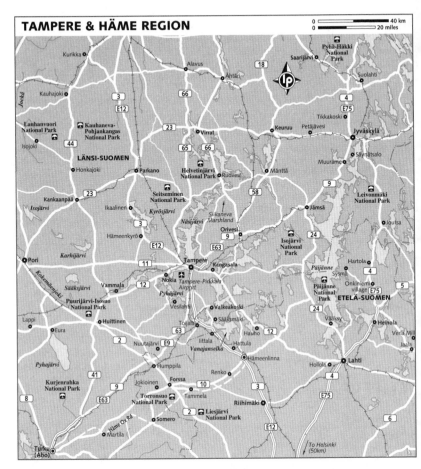

TAMPERE & HÄME REGION

Vuoltsu Internet Café (☎ 3146 6899; Vuolteenkatu 13; per hr €3; ☷ noon-6pm Mon-Fri Jun-Aug, 1-8pm Mon-Fri Sep-May) Opposite the bus station.

Laundry
Pese Itse (☎ 222 8755; Hämeenpuisto 12B) A self-service coin-operated launderette.

Left Luggage
The train station has lockers for €2 to €3, depending on size. It also has a left-luggage counter. Lockers at the bus station cost €2 for 24 hours.

Medical Services
You can dial ☎ 10023 between 7am and 10pm to get an on-call doctor.

Tampere University Hospital (☎ 247 5111) This hospital, about 2km east of the train station, deals with emergencies.

Money
Forex (☎ 020-751 2640; Hämeenkatu 14B; ☷ 9am-7pm Mon-Fri, 9am-3pm Sat) Moneychangers on the main square.

Post
Main post office (☎ 0200 7100; Rautatienkatu 21, 33100 Tampere; ☷ 9am-8pm Mon-Fri, 10am-2pm Sat) Near the train station.

Tourist Information
Tampere city tourist office (☎ 3146 6800; www.tampere.fi; Verkatehtaankatu 2; ☷ 9am-4pm Mon-Fri Oct-May, 9am-8pm Mon-Fri, 10am-5pm Sat & Sun Jun-Aug, 9am-5pm

Mon-Fri, 10am-5pm Sat & Sun Sep; 🖥) Lots of information and helpful staff. Pick up the free guide to the town. In summer, yellow-shirted cyclists act as mobile information points; just flag them down!

Travel Agencies

Kilroy Travels (☎ 020-354 5769; Tuomiokirkonkatu 34A; ☽ 10am-6pm Mon-Fri) Deals in all travel including student/discount fares.

SIGHTS
Finlayson Centre

Tampere's era as an industrial city began with the arrival of Scot James Finlayson, who established a small workshop by the Tammerkoski here in 1820. He later erected a huge cotton mill; the massive red-brick building was the first in the Nordic countries to have electric lighting, which came on in 1882. It has now been sensitively converted into a glitzy mall of cafés and shops; you'll also find a cinema here, as well as a great brewery pub and a couple of intriguing museums.

VAKOILUMUSEO

This popular but off-beat **spy museum** (☎ 212 3007; www.vakoilumuseo.fi; Satakunnankatu 18; adult/child €7/5; ☽ noon-6pm Mon-Fri, 10am-4pm Sat & Sun, from 10am daily May-Aug) under the Finlayson centre plays to the budding secret agent in all of us, with a large and well-assembled display of the devices of international espionage, mainly from the Cold War era. As well as histories of famous Finnish and foreign spies, it has numerous Bond-style gadgets and some interactive displays – write your name in invisible ink, tap a telephone call, intercept an email, or measure the microwave emissions of your mobile. There are folders with English translations, but they are slightly unsatisfying. When it's busy, there are more activities for kids, who can take a suitability test for KGB cadet school.

WERSTAS

The **Central Museum of Labour** (☎ 253 8800; www.tkm.fi; Väinö Linnan aukio 8; admission €4; ☽ 11am-6pm Tue-Sun) is dedicated to the history of working and of the workers' movement. You will find changing exhibitions covering social history and labour industries. There's a particularly good coverage of the steam engine, with the highlight one of the enormous wheels that powered up the Finlayson factory.

Other Museums
VAPRIIKKI MUSEUM CENTRE

Tampere's premier exhibition space is **Vapriikki** (☎ 3146 6966; Veturiaukio 4; www.tampere.fi/vapriikki; adult/child from €5/1 depending on exhibitions; ☽ 10am-6pm Tue & Thu-Sun, 11am-8pm Wed), a bright, modern glass and steel gallery in the renovated Tampella textile mill. As well as regularly changing art and photography exhibitions, there's a permanent display on Tampere's history from prehistoric times to the present. Also here is the small but cluttered **ice hockey museum**, with memorabilia of the players and teams that star in Finland's national sporting passion.

There's also a museum of shoes – Tampere was known for its footwear industry – and a pleasant café in the complex.

LENIN MUSEUM

Admirers of bearded revolutionaries won't want to miss the small **Lenin Museum** (☎ 276 8100; www.lenin.fi; Hämeenpuisto 28; admission €4; ☽ 9am-6pm Mon-Fri, 11am-4pm Sat & Sun), housed in the Workers' Hall where Lenin and Stalin first met at a conference in 1905 (see p29 for more on Lenin's time in Finland). In two rooms, the museum documents his life by way of photos and documents; it's a little dry but it's fascinating to see, for example, Vladimir's old school report (a straight-A student) or a threadbare couch that the man slept on. One note, penned shortly before his death in 1924, recommends that Comrade Stalin be ousted from his position as General Secretary; this unfortunately wasn't acted on. Remarkably, this claims to be the only permanent museum in the world devoted to one of the 20th century's most influential figures. There's a crazy gift shop where you can buy Lenin pens, badges, T-shirts and other souvenirs of the Soviet era.

MOOMIN VALLEY MUSEUM

Tove Jansson, the Finnish artist and writer, created her Moomin figures decades ago, but their popularity never seems to wane – at least not in Finland or Japan. The **museum** (Muumilaakso; ☎ 020-716 6578; Hämeenpuisto 20; adult/child €4/1; ☽ 9am-5pm Mon-Fri, 10am-6pm Sat & Sun, closed Mon Sep-May), in the basement of the public library building, contains original drawings, plus elaborate tableaux models depicting stories from Moomin Valley (English-language explanations available), computer

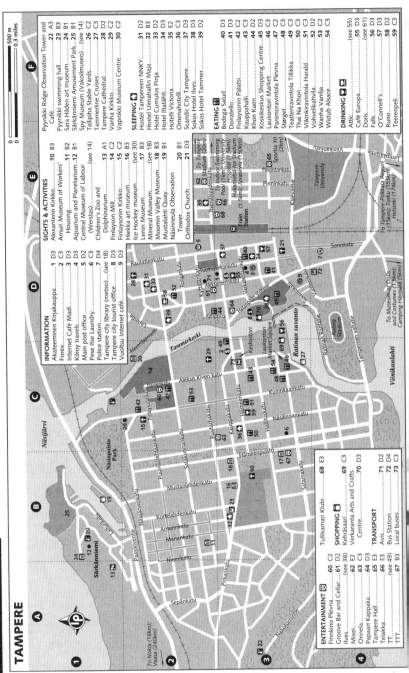

TAMPERE

TAMPERE & HÄME REGION

INFORMATION
Akateeminen Kirjakauppa	1 D3
Forex	2 C3
Internet Café Madi	3 D3
Kilroy travels	4 D3
Main post office	5 D2
Pese Itse Laundry	6 C3
Police station	7 D4
Tampere city library (metso)	(see 18)
Tampere city tourist office	8 D3
Vuoltsu Internet café	9 D3

SIGHTS & ACTIVITIES
Alexanterin Kirkko	10 B3
Amuri Museum of Workers' Housing	11 B2
Aquarium and Planetarium	12 B1
Central Museum of Labour (Werstas)	(see 14)
Children's Zoo and Dolphinarium	13 A1
Finlayson Mill	14 C2
Finlaysonin Kirkko	15 C2
Hiekka art museum	16 B3
Ice Hockey museum	(see 30)
Lenin Museum	17 B3
Mineral Museum	(see 18)
Moomin Valley Museum	18 B3
Mustalahti Quay	19 B1
Näsinneula Observation Tower	20 B1
Orthodox Church	21 D3
Pyynikki Ridge Observation Tower and Café	22 A3
Pyynikki swimming hall	23 B3
Sara Hilden art museum	24 B1
Särkänniemi Amusement Park	25 B1
Spy Museum (Vakoilumuseo)	26 C2
Tammerfine Cruises	27 C3
Tampere Cathedral	28 D2
Vanha Kirkko	29 C2
Vaprikki Museum Centre	30 C2

SLEEPING
Hostel Tampereen NNKY	31 D2
Hostel Uimahallin Maja	32 B3
Hotel Cumulus Pinja	33 D2
Hotel Iltatähti	34 D3
Hotelli Victoria	35 E2
Omenahotelli	36 C3
Scandic City Tampere	37 D3
Sokos Hotel Ilves	38 D3
Sokos Hotel Tammer	39 D2

EATING
Bodega Salud	40 D3
Donatello	41 D3
Finlaysonin Palatsi	42 C3
Kauppahalli	43 C3
Khon Kaen	44 D3
Koskikeskus Shopping Centre	45 D3
Laukontori Market	46 C3
Panimoravintola Plevna	47 C3
Storget	48 C3
Teatteriravintola Tillikka	49 C3
Thai Na Khon	50 C3
Viikinkiravintola Harald	51 C3
Vohvelikahvila	52 D2
Wanha Vanilja	53 C3
Wistub Alsace	54 C3

DRINKING
Attic	(see 55)
Café Europa	55 D3
Doris	(see 61)
Falls	56 D3
O'Connell's	57 D3
Runo	58 D2
Teerenpeli	59 C3

ENTERTAINMENT
Finnkino Plevna	60 C2
Groove Bar and Cellar	61 D2
Ilves	(see 38)
Mixei	62 E2
Onnela	63 C3
Papaari Kappaka	64 D3
Tampere Hall	65 E3
Telakka	66 E3
TT	(see 49)
TTT	67 B3

SHOPPING
Kehäsaari	68 E3
Tullikamari Klubi	69 C3
Verkaranta Arts and Crafts Centre	70 D3

TRANSPORT
Avis	71 D2
Bus Station	72 D4
Local buses	73 C3

displays, toys and other memorabilia. Naturally, there's a gift shop.

Adjacent is the small **Mineral Museum** (Kivimuseo; ☎ 3146 6046; adult/child €4/1), devoted to rare stones and fossils. There's a huge array of delicate, spectacular crystal formations and vivid colours, as well as fossils that include dinosaur eggs, but, needless to say, although it has the same hours as Moomin Valley, it doesn't have the same crowds.

HIEKKA ART MUSEUM
The collection of Kustaa Hiekka, a wealthy industrialist, is contained in the **Hiekka museum** (☎ 212 3973; Pirkankatu 6; admission €5; ⊙ 3-6pm Tue-Thu, noon-3pm Sun). There are paintings, furniture and fine old gold and silver items in the impressive building.

AMURIN TYÖLÄISMUSEOKORTTELI
An entire block of 19th-century wooden houses, including 32 apartments, a bakery, a shoemaker, two general shops and a café is preserved in the **Amuri Museum of Workers' Housing** (☎ 3146 6690; Satakunnankatu 49; adult/child €4/1; ⊙ 10am-6pm Tue-Sun May–mid-Sep). It's one of the most realistic home museums in Finland – many homes look as if the tenant had left just moments ago to go shopping.

MUSEUM OF DOLLS & COSTUMES
This fascinating **museum** (☎ 222 6261; Hatanpään puistokuja 1; adult/child €4/1; ⊙ 11am-5pm Tue-Sun mid-Apr–early Dec) at Hatanpää Manor, south of the city, has more than 4000 dolls on display. The oldest and rarest date from the 12th century. There are also temporary exhibitions on various doll-related themes.

Hatanpää Manor house is surrounded by the large **Arboretum Park** with about 350 species of flora. Buses 3, 7 and 21 run from the city centre to Hatanpää.

Särkänniemi
On the northern edge of town, this promontory **amusement park** (☎ 248 8111; www.sarkanniemi .fi; adult/child day pass up to €29/18; ⊙ rides noon-7pm mid-May–Aug) is a large complex with several attractions, including a good art gallery and an aquarium. There's a bewildering system of entry tickets and opening times depending on what your interest is. A day pass is valid for all sights and unlimited rides, while €5 will get you up the observation tower, and into the gallery and farm zoo, on days that

the rides are open. To get to Särkänniemi, take bus 4 from the train station.

Inside the amusement park are 30 **carnival rides** including the 'Tornado super rollercoaster', plus cafés and restaurants. The **aquarium** (⊙ as per amusement park, plus 10am-4pm in winter) has limited information in English and isn't especially memorable, with the Finnish fish (including some rare sturgeon relatives) more interesting than the colourful hobby-tank favourites. The **planetarium**, with daily shows, is in the same complex, above which soars the 168m high **Näsinneula Observation Tower** (⊙ 11am-11.30pm). This is the tallest such tower in these Northern lands and it alone is worth the visit, with spectacular views of the city and surrounding lakes. There's a revolving restaurant near the top.

Opposite, the **Dolphinarium** has Finland's only dolphin show. There are one to five dolphin shows in summer and an entertaining dolphin training show (in Finnish) daily at other times. Nearby is the **children's zoo**, with gentle domestic animals.

On a different note, the complex also contains the **Sara Hildén art museum** (☎ 3144 3500; ⊙ 11am-6pm, closed Mon Sep-Apr), which has a collection of international and Finnish modern art and sculpture amassed by Sara Hildén, a local businessperson and art collector. The space is normally devoted to excellent exhibitions showcasing particular artists. There are good views from the café, which has Alvar Aalto furniture.

Churches
The wonderful **Tampere Cathedral** (Tuomiokirkonkatu; ⊙ 10am-6pm) is one of the most notable examples of National Romantic architecture in Finland. It was designed by Lars Sonck and was finished in 1907. The famous artist Hugo Simberg was responsible for the frescoes and stained glass; once you've seen them you'll appreciate that they were controversial at the time. A procession of ghostly child-like apostles holds the 'garland of life', the garden of death shows graves tended by skeletal figures, while another image shows a wounded angel being stretchered off by two children. In the dome is a winged serpent with the Apple of Knowledge in its mouth. The altarpiece is by Magnus Enckell, and shows a dreamlike Resurrection in similar style. The symbolist stonework adds to the haunting feel.

TAMPERE & HÄME REGION

The small but ornate, onion-domed **Orthodox church** (10am-4pm Mon-Sat, noon-4pm Sun Jun-Aug), near the train station, is also worth a visit. During the Civil War, White troops (loyal to the government) besieged the church, which had been taken over by the Reds (Russian-backed troops).

The landmark **Vanha Kirkko** (Jun-Aug) just north of Keskustori Square is a lovely old wooden building and has occasional gospel concerts on Saturday evenings.

Other notable churches include the **Alexanterin Kirkko** (Pirkankatu; 10am-6pm), beautiful with its red brick and green spires and named for the Tsar Alexander II, and the **Finlaysonin Kirkko** (Puuvillatehtaankatu 2; 10am-6pm Jun-Aug), built for employees of the cotton mill and their families.

Other Sights

PYYNIKKI RIDGE
Rising between Tampere's two lakes, this ridge is a forested area of walking and cycling trails with fine views on both sides. It rises 85m above the shores of the lake; this is an Everest by Finnish standards and claims to be the highest gravel ridge in the world. There's a stone **observation tower** (9am-8pm; adult/child €1/0.50) on the ridge, which also has a great café serving Tampere's best doughnuts. You can easily walk or drive to the tower, or take westbound bus 15 to its terminus and walk back from there along the ridge.

TALLIPIHA STABLE YARDS
In the attractive Näsinpuisto park, **Tallipiha** (040-507 499; Kuninkaankatu 4; admission free; 10am-6pm Mon-Sat, 11am-5pm Sun Jun–mid-Aug, shorter hrs in winter) is a restored collection of 19th-century stable yards and staff cottages that now house artists and craftworkers making handicrafts, chocolates, ceramics and shoes. Traditional Midsummer and Christmas celebrations are held here and you can ride in a horse-drawn carriage or eat at the Russian-style **Café Vatruska**.

ACTIVITIES
There's an **indoor swimming pool** (215 5812; Joukahaisenkatu 7; admission €4.50; 6am-7.45pm Mon-Fri, 10am-4.45pm Sat & Sun, closed Tue morning) about 1.5km east of the train station.

The **Pyynikki swimming hall** (3146 6863; Kortelahdenkatu 26; admission €4.50; closed Wed, Thu, Sun & summer) is next to Hostel Uimahallin Maja.

To **fish** in the Tammerkoski in the town centre, you will need a daily (€4.50) or weekly (€16) permit, available from the tourist office. The tourist office also have a list of operators who run guided fishing tours in the lakes and rivers hereabouts.

You can rent **rowing boats** and **canoes** from Camping Härmälä (see Sleeping). Bikes can be had at **Sportia 10** (225 0000; Sammonkatu 60), and roller blades, skis, and kayaks from **Moto-Rent** (379 2778; www.kangasalanmotorent .fi; Lentolantie 21, Kangasala). Moto-Rent is based in Kangasala, 10km southwest of Tampere, but will deliver stuff to town

TOURS
You can get an overview of Tampere's attractions on a **bus tour** (tickets €12; 2pm Jun-Aug). The guided tours depart from the tourist office and cover the main sights, the Tammerkoski industrial area and Pyynikki Ridge. They take about two hours and have commentary in Finnish and English.

CRUISES
Lake cruises on Tampere's two magnificent lakes are extremely popular in summer and there are plenty of options. Trips on Näsijärvi leave from Mustalahti quay, while Laukontori quay serves Pyhäjärvi.

Tammerline (254 2500; www.tammerline.fi) offers short cruises on Pyhäjärvi from mid-June to mid-August, with departures from the Laukontori quay on Monday and Wednesday (adult/child €10/2). On Monday and Saturday the cruise goes further to Nokia (adult/child €15/4).

Tammerlines Cruises also has a shuttle service to nearby **Viikinsaari**, a pleasant picnic spot with a good restaurant, from Tuesday to Sunday in summer (late May to late August). Departures from Laukontori quay are every hour on the hour (adult/ child return €6/2).

The **SS Tarjanne** (212 4804; www.finnishsil verline.com; 10.45am Tue, Thu & Sat Jun-late Aug), a steam ship, departs from Mustalahti quay. The route, from Tampere to Ruovesi and Virrat, is known as the **Poet's Way** and is one of the finest lake cruises in Finland. A one-way ticket costs €33 to Ruovesi and €44 to Virrat. For €23 per person, you can sleep in this old boat before or after your trip, and get free day-use of the cabin (which is otherwise €21). Bicycles can be taken on board for a small fee. You can book a day-trip to Virrat or Ruovesi, with one of the legs made by bus (return to Virrat €50).

For information about cruises with Finnish Silverline between Tampere and Hämeenlinna see p179.

FESTIVALS & EVENTS

There are festivals and annual events in Tampere almost year-round. Usually held in early March, the **Tampere Film Festival** (www .tamperefilmfestival.fi) is a respected international festival of short films. The **Tampere Biennale** (www.tampere.fi) is a festival of new Finnish music, held in April of even-numbered years only. The **Pispala Schottische** (www.sottiisi.net), an international folk-dance festival, takes place in early June. **Tammerfest** (www.tammerfest.net) is the city's premier music festival, held over five days in mid-July and featuring rock concerts at the Ratina Stadium and smaller gigs around town. The **Tampere International Theatre Festival** (www.teatterikesa.fi), held in early August, is a showcase of international and Finnish theatre. There's also a fringe festival called **Off-Tampere** (www.teatterikesa.fi) held at the same time. October or early November brings the **Tampere Jazz Happening** (www.tampere .fi), an award-winning event featuring Finnish and international jazz musicians. Twice a year in autumn and mid-winter, the **Tampere Illuminations** (www.tampere.fi) light up the city streets with 40,000 coloured lights.

SLEEPING
Budget

Hostel Uimahallin Maja (☎ 222 9460; www.hosteltam pere.com; Pirkankatu 10-12; dm €20-23, s/d €38.50/54; ✗) Tampere's main hostel is an HI-affiliated place with large light rooms at the western end of town. The dorms are a little crowded but it's all comfy beds (no bunks) and the lino floors evoke a '70s feel. There's a basic kitchen – you have to fetch water from the bathroom – but an on-site café, sociable feel and friendly staff make it a good choice.

Hostel Tampereen NNKY (☎ 254 4020; fax 254 4044; Tuomiokirkonkatu 12A; dm €13.50-15, s/d €31/44; ✑ Jun-late Aug; ℗ ✗) Right opposite the cathedral, this HI-affiliated summer-only place is run by the Finnish YWCA. The rooms are spacious and have beds, desks, and large windows. There's a tiny kitchen, laundry sink and drying room, and good showers (the rooms near them are noisier).

Reception is open from 8am to 10am and 4pm to 11pm.

Camping Härmälä (☎ 265 1355, 6138 3210; Leirintäkatu 8; tent sites €9-11 plus per person €4, 3–5-person cabins €29-66) About 5km south of the centre (take bus 1) is this spacious camping ground on the shores of the Pyhäjärvi lake. There's a café/restaurant, saunas and rowing boats, as well as an adjacent summer hotel with self-contained rooms (single/double €36/50); open June to August.

Midrange

Hotelli Victoria (☎ 242 5111; www.hotellivictoria.fi; Itsenäisyydenkatu 1; s/d €99/134, weekends & summer €79/84; ℗ ✗ ▣ ✑) This warm family-run hotel is handy for the station and offers considerable style, colour and comfort as well as business-standard facilities. The recently renovated rooms are light and quiet despite the busy road and there's a good sauna. It's closed most of December.

Hotel Iltatähti (☎ 315 161; www.hoteliltatahti.fi; Tuomiokirkonkatu 19; s/d €40/50, with bathroom €53/60; ✑ reception 9am-7pm Mon-Fri, noon-6pm Sat & Sun; ✗) Close to the train station, this is a friendly guesthouse with a large network of rooms. Guests have use of a kitchen, and the rooms are good value. The same owners run a bed and breakfast 4km from town, which has its own pool and countryside feel.

Omenahotelli (www.omenahotelli.fi; Hämeenkatu 28; r €55; ✗) This offering from the good-value Internet-booking chain couldn't be much more central. As usual, rooms have to be booked in advance (although there is a terminal in the lobby to do it), as there is no reception staff. There are twin beds and a fold-out sofa in every modern room.

Hotel Cumulus Pinja (☎ 241 5111; www.cumulus .fi; Satakunnankatu 10; s/d €115/135, weekends & summer €94; ℗ ✗ ▣) This friendly, relatively small Art Nouveau building near the cathedral has a quiet but central location. Its charm is that it feels more intimate than most Finnish chain hotels; the rooms are somewhat small however, and lack a little light. Service is good and an evening sauna is included.

Scandic City Tampere (☎ 244 6111; www.scandic -hotels.com; Hämeenkatu 1; s/d €125/149, in summer €86/96; ℗ ✗ ▣ ✦) Opposite the train station, this hotel has just undergone a substantial renovation. It has plenty of facilities, including sauna, gym, restaurants and a cocktail bar.

The rooms are good; the superior class costs about €15 more but has wireless Internet access and a couple of other extras.

Sokos Hotel Tammer (☎ 020-1234 632; www .sokoshotels.fi; Satakunnankatu 13; s/d €116/145, weekends & summer s €81-91, d €91-97, ste €250; P X ⬜) Constructed in 1929 as the city's Grand Hotel, this magnificent building has plush public areas, with an old-fashioned elegance. The rooms are large, many with fine views over town, and have the expected facilities but feel a little tired and could do with a coat of varnish and new carpet. Parking is very limited. Good breakfast buffet and sauna included.

Top End
Sokos Hotel Ilves (☎ 020-1234 631; www.sokoshotels .fi; Hatanpäänvaltatie 1; s/d €132/162; summer & weekend r €105; ste €275-530; P X ⬜ ⬛ 🐧) This large tower hotel is Tampere's premier business hotel and popular with visitors for the excellent views from its rooms, most of which overlook the Tammerkoski just next to the tourist office. There are several restaurants, a popular nightclub and business centre. As well as the saunas, there's an enticing Jacuzzi. Superior rooms, which cost €18 extra, have marginally better facilities, including wireless Internet access.

EATING
Tampere's speciality, *mustamakkara*, is a mild sausage made with cow's blood, black-pudding style. It's normally eaten with lingonberry jam and is much tastier than it might sound. You can get it at several markets, including the kauppahalli.

Restaurants
FINNISH
Panimoravintola Plevna (☎ 260 1200, Itäinenkatu 8; mains €10-23; 🕑 food served 11am-10pm) Inside the old Finlayson textile mill is a huge brewery pub and restaurant that is the most enjoyable place to dine in Tampere. As well as Finnish-style fish and steak dishes, the speciality here is German sausages such as bratwurst and bockwurst (from €8) which can be combined in the famous sausage platter (€15.30) served in a pan with potatoes. Wash down a plate of this hearty fare with a pint of one of Plevna's nine delicious beers; the strong stout is especially good.

Finlaysonin Palatsi (☎ 260 5770; Kuninkaankatu 1; mains €17-23; 🕑 11am-midnight Tue-Fri, noon-midnight

Sat) This grand turn-of-the-20th-century residence behind the Finlayson centre has gardens and grounds and houses a classy restaurant with a relaxing terrace. The food is ambitious and delivers, with a short, quality selection of dishes such as reindeer carpaccio or lamb kidneys and tongue in port sauce.

Teatteriravintola Tillikka (☎ 254 4700; Teatter-italo; lunch from €7, mains €12-24; 🕑 lunch & dinner) This place, wedged between the river and the TT (Tampere Theatre), serves a fine buffet-style lunch. In the evenings it steps up a gear, serving a creatively prepared range of steaks and fish and also happily catering to children. The theatre also has a good café, Kivi, with a terrace overlooking the central square.

Viikinkiravintola Harald (☎ 213 8380; Hämeenkatu 23; mains €16-22; 🕑 lunch & dinner) This is a Viking-theme restaurant, which isn't really Finnish, though much of the food is, with game specialities such as reindeer. It's a lot of fun, and identical to the one in Turku, with plenty of pageantry; some meals are served on Viking shields. There's a variety of set menus starting at €24.

INTERNATIONAL
Wistub Alsace (☎ 212 0260; Laukontori 6B; mains €15-21; 🕑 5pm-midnight Tue-Fri, noon-midnight Sat). This small, intimate and softly lit place specializes in the cuisine of the Alsace region and does it well, with delicious magret (the breast of corn-fattened birds) of duck and tasty chicken with spätzle noodles perfectly accompanied by deliciously aromatic Alsatian white wines. The desserts are original and delicious.

Thai Na Khon (☎ 212 1779; Hämeenkatu 29; lunch buffet €7.10, mains €10-16; 🕑 lunch & dinner) This Thai restaurant on the main street is soothingly and tastefully decorated, with plush seats, varnished tables, and a colonial-era feel. The main dishes are pretty abundant and they come with rice, so it's good value. There's plenty of vegetarian choices.

Khon Kaen (☎ 212 1776; Koskikatu 3) A sister restaurant to Thai Na Khon, this is on the other side of the bridge. It's smaller but similar in feel.

Bodega Salud (☎ 233 4400; Tuomiokirkonkatu 19; mains €14-26; 🕑 11am-11pm Mon-Fri, noon-midnight Sat, 1-10pm Sun) This popular place is a Tampere favourite for its cosy atmosphere and good salad, fruit and cheese bar (included with main courses). It styles itself as a Spanish restaurant and certainly does a decent paella, but most dishes have a distinctly Finnish feel, with salmon, reindeer and creamy sauces all present and tasty. Adventurous types may go for the alligator or the Rocky Mountain oysters. You get a certificate if you eat the latter – shellfish are scarce in Colorado, but a few rams have been heard bleating in countertenor tones.

Donatello (Aleksanterinkatu 37; buffet €6; buffet 10.30am-5pm, kitchen 10.30am-9pm Mon-Fri, 10.30am-10pm weekends) With a lavish all-you-can-eat pizza and pasta buffet during the day, Donatello is excellent value and the food is much tastier than at the chains that offer similar fare.

Cafés

Wanha Vanilja (214 7141; Kuninkaankatu 15; 10am-6pm Tue-Fri, 10am-5pm Sat, also Sun in Jul & Aug). Tampere's best café is a treasure-trove of time-worn furniture and curios, including dozens of clocks showing different times. It has a seriously tempting array of cakes and pastries which are well accompanied by their famed vanilla coffee. There's also a good lunchtime salad bar and a range of quiches.

Størget (222 6210; Laukontori 10; sandwiches €4-8; 10am-6pm Mon-Sat) A small bright café at the quay, this specializes in spectacular Danish open sandwiches (Danwiches), as well as burgers and American-style tuna and club sandwiches. It's not cheap but the sandwiches are big.

Vohvelikahvila (214 4225; Ojakatu 2; waffles €3-6; 9am-8pm Mon-Sat, 10am-8pm Sun) This is a cosy and quaint little place specializing in Tampere's best fresh waffles, which come laden with cream and chocolate.

Quick Eats & Self Catering

Kauppahalli (Hämeenkatu 19; 8am-6pm Mon-Fri, 8am-3pm Sat) This intriguing indoor market is one of Finland's best, with picturesque wooden stalls. There are several good cafés, and, at number 50, Teivon Liha, the best place to try cheap *mustamakkara* with berry jam.

Laukontori market (8am-2pm Mon-Sat) This is a produce and fish market at Laukontori, also called *alaranta* (lower lakeside).

Koskikeskus Shopping Centre (Hatanpäänvaltatiel; 10am-7pm Mon-Fri, 10am-5pm Sat) Just south of the tourist office, this centre is good for fast food – it has pizza, kebab, taco and hamburger outlets, as well as a supermarket.

DRINKING

Café Europa (223 5526; Aleksanterinkatu 29; noon-2 or 3am) This is easily the coolest bar in Tampere. Furnished with 1930s-style horsehair couches and chairs, it is a romantic old-world European type of place complete with Belgian and German beers, board games, ornate mirrors and chandeliers, and an excellent summer terrace. Upstairs is a small dance club called Attic, with DJs playing hip-hop and funk, open from Thursday to Sunday.

Panimoravintola Plevna (260 1200; Itäinenkatu 8; 11am-1am Mon-Thu, 11am-2am Fri & Sat, noon-11pm Sun) This is a superb and spacious brewery pub in the converted Finlayson cotton mill buildings. It brews nine beers, including an award-winning strong stout, two ciders and even distils its own schnapps. Plevna is cheery without being overly boisterous and is mostly teenager-free.

Runo (213 3931; Ojakatu 3; 9am-8pm Mon-Sat, 10am-8pm Sun) This elegant but relaxed spot is the perfect place for a bit of light contemplation. The huge windows allow you to keep tabs on the weather, the coffee is good, and there's a selection of books and art to browse. Runo means 'poem' in Finnish.

O'Connell's (Rautatienkatu 24; 4pm-1am) Near the train station, this rambling and attractive Irish pub is an unpretentious place with plenty of comfy seats to sink into with a pint. It's popular with locals, travellers and expats, and has some good beers on tap as well as free Internet access.

Teerenpeli (0424 925 210; Hämeenkatu 25; noon-2am) Another good pub with home-brewed beer and cider, this has a relaxing, candle-lit interior and heaps of choice at the taps. They do some good fruit-flavoured brews and also have a terrace and a cavernous club downstairs.

Falls (Kehräsaari; noon-3am) This bar in the converted brick factory is set in a good little zone of shops and has a range of beers and ciders to choose from. The main reason to come here is for its fantastic little terrace wedged between the building and the water; a top Tampere spot!

ENTERTAINMENT
Nightclubs & Live Music

Tullikamari klubi (Tullikamarinaukio 2; nightly, to 4am Wed-Sat) This cavernous place near the train station is Tampere's main indoor venue for rock concerts. Big-name Finnish bands sometimes perform here and the cover charge varies from free to €15. This is also one of the venues for the film festival.

Telakka (☎ 225 0700; Tullikamarinaukio 3) This is a bohemian bar-theatre-restaurant in another of Tampere's restored red-brick factories. There's live music here regularly, theatre performances, art exhibitions and a brilliant summer terrace with colourful blocky wooden seats.

Paapan Kapakka (☎ 211 0037; Koskikatu 9; ⓦ noon-late) A small bar in the heart of town (across from the tourist office) with live jazz and blues every day and a swinging terrace.

Ilves (Hatanpäänvaltatie 1; ⓦ 9pm-4am Wed-Sat) In the Sokos Hotel Ilves, this is one of the town's more popular nightclubs, with fashionable folk aged 25 and over.

Groove Bar (☎ 389 9000; Aleksanterinkatu 22; ⓦ 4pm-4am Mon-Sat, 10pm-4am Sun) Just off the main drag, this dark and moody bar is a popular spot for a pre-club drink. Handily, there's a club downstairs, the Cellar, that's open from 10pm Wednesday to Saturday.

Doris (ⓦ 11pm-4am Tue-Sun) Next door to the Groove Bar, this plays classic popular rock for dancing until late.

Mixei (☎ 222 0364; Itsenäisyydenkatu 7; ⓦ to 2am nightly, to 4am weekends) Recently moved to larger premises, Tampere's premier gay venue is a café and restaurant that livens up considerably later on; it hosts regular club nights and themed parties and is a good place to meet people. The name means 'Why Not?'.

Onnela (Puutarhakatu 21; ⓦ Wed-Sun 10pm-4am) This dark building looks like a library from outside but has become one of Tampere's most popular mainstream discos, with a relaxed crowd in their 20s and 30s listening to unchallenging Europop.

Classical Music, Theatre & Cinema

Tampere is a thriving centre for the performing arts. There are several theatres in the city and a programme of what's on where is available from the tourist office.

Both the theatres listed here present major Finnish and international shows, including musicals, but as is the case elsewhere in the country, almost all performances are in Finnish.

Tampere Hall (box office ☎ 243 4500; www.tampere talo.fi; Yliopistonkatu 55) For classical concerts, this is the city's spectacular modern concert hall. It hosts classical concerts by the Tampere Philharmonic Orchestra on Friday from September to May. In addition to this it also puts on regular chamber music concerts, and visiting opera and ballet performances.

TT (Tampere Theatre; ☎ 216 0500; Keskustori) Just off Hameenkatu near the river, this is one of the two biggest theatres in town.

TTT (Tampere Workers' Theatre; ☎ 217 8222; Hameen-puisto 32) This is the other main theatre venue.

Finnkino Plevna (☎ 3138 3831; Itäinenkatu 4) In the Finlayson centre, this is one of two main cinemas in the city and has late sessions on Friday and Saturday. It's the main venue for the film festival.

Sport

Tampere has two ice-hockey teams in the national league – Ilves and Tappara – both of which are among the best in the country, and the city is generally regarded as the home of the sport. Finland's first artificial hockey rink was opened here in 1955.

Hakametsä Ice Stadium (off Hervannan Valtaväg fwy) This place, about 2km east of the train station, is the venue for matches on Thursday, Saturday and Sunday from September to March. Take eastbound bus No 25 to get there.

Tampere United (☎ 255 4454; www.tampereunited .com) The local football team is also quite successful in the national league. It plays games in summer at Tampere Stadium and sometimes at the Ratina Stadium.

Shopping

Verkaranta Arts & Crafts Centre (Verkatehtaankatu 2; ⓦ 10am-6pm Mon-Fri, 10am-4pm Sat) This is a small former factory building, located near the tourist office, which features exhibits and sells extraordinary textiles and handicrafts.

Kehräsaari (ⓦ 10am-6pm Mon-Fri, 10am-4pm Sat) Across the footbridge from Verkaranta, just east of Laukontori market square, this converted brick factory building has many boutiques selling authentic Finnish glassware, handicrafts, knitted clothing and T-shirts.

GETTING THERE & AWAY
Air

You can fly to Tampere direct from Stockholm and Copenhagen with **Blue 1** (☎ 06000-25831; www.blue1.com); all other international flights are via Helsinki. There are several daily Finnair flights to Tampere from Helsinki and other major Finnish cities.

Ryanair (www.ryanair.com) also flies to and from Tampere, using a dedicated terminal. There are daily services to London Stansted, Hahn and Riga.

Boat

You can cruise to and from Hämeenlinna by lake ferry in summer. **Suomen Hopealinja** (Finnish Silverline; ☎ 212 4804; www.finnishsilver line.com) operates cruises from Tampere's Laukontori quay daily (one way €39, 8½ hours), and north to Virrat along the Poet's Way (€44, eight hours).

Bus

The **main bus station** (Hatanpäänvaltatie 7) is a block from the Koskikeskus shopping centre. Regular express buses run from Helsinki (€28.10, 2½ hours) and Turku (€25.60, three hours) and most other major towns in Finland are served from here.

Local buses are most conveniently taken from Keskustori (central square).

Train

The train station is in the centre at the eastern end of Hämeenkatu. Express trains run hourly to/from Helsinki (€24.90, two hours). Intercity trains continue to Oulu (€52.50, five hours) and there are direct trains to Turku, Pori, Jyväskylä, Vaasa and Joensuu.

GETTING AROUND
To/From the Airport

The Tampere-Pirkkala airport is 15km southwest of the city centre. Each arriving flight is met by a bus to Tampere. Bus 61 to the airport stops at Pyynikintori and several points in the city centre (€2, 30 to 45 minutes). Another company, Tokee, serves the Ryanair flights, leaving from the railway station just under two hours before take-off (€6).

There are also shared **taxis** (☎ 10041; per person €12) carrying up to eight passengers; these must be booked at least three hours in advance from the city to the airport.

Bus

The local bus service is extensive and a one-hour ticket costs €1.40. A 24-hour Traveller's Ticket is €6. You can pick up a free bus-route map at the city tourist office.

Car Hire

There are several car hire companies at the airport and in town. These include **Avis** (☎ 231 4944; www.avis.com; Kyttälänkatu) and **Netrent** (www.netrent.fi; Tampere Airport Terminal 2).

Taxi

There are plenty of cab ranks; otherwise call ☎ 10041. For a wheelchair-friendly cab, call ☎ 10045.

NORTH OF TAMPERE

ROUTE 66
☎ 03

Road No 66, starting northeast of Tampere and winding 75km north to Virrat, is one of the oldest roads in Finland. When the famous song, first performed by Nat King Cole, was translated into Finnish, the popular rock star Jussi Raittinen adapted the lyrics to this highway. It's a good drive, through young pine forest and lakescapes. Cycling isn't such a great option, as the road is narrowish, and there are plenty of logging trucks hurtling by. There's plenty of hiking opportunities and the town of Ruovesi, by far the best base, is also a great place to try some fishing.

Orivesi

Road 66 begins in Orivesi. There's nothing spectacular in the village itself, but it is at a major crossroads. The village's silo-like modern **church** (🕑 Mon-Fri +summer) was controversial when built, one reason being the Kain Tapper woodcarving in the altar. The old bell tower remains, with its *vaivaisukko* (pauper statue).

Kallenautio Roadhouse

This beautiful wooden **roadhouse** (☎ 335 8915; 🕑 11am-6pm Sun-Fri, 11am-4pm Sat Jun-Aug) is the oldest building along Route 66 and dates from 1757. It has always been a roadside guesthouse. Around 200 years ago these were nearly as common as petrol stations are today. However, there are few such places left.

The complex has a beautiful café; you sit at long old wooden tables and imagine winter travellers huddled around the blazing fire. There are sometimes handicraft exhibitions – you can see how *päre* is made

TAMPERE & HÄME REGION

from timber. *Päre* is a thin sheet of wood once burnt to provide light in a house. It was often the cause of fires that destroyed entire towns.

Siikaneva Marshland

This large protected marshland accommodates some unusual bird species, including owls. It's a great place to walk, with duckboard paths across the peat bog alternating with stretches of peaceful stands of pine forest. There are two loops; one of 3km, and one of about 10km. No camping is allowed, but there's a simple shelter and a couple of fireplaces. The entrance is on Route 66, 20km south of Ruovesi; you pass some sinister-looking military buildings on the way to the carpark.

Kalela

The most celebrated artist of the National Romantic Era, Akseli Gallen-Kallela painted most of his famous *Kalevala* works in this **studio** (☎ 476 0623; www.kalela.net; admission depending on exhibition €5-8; ☽ 10am-5pm mid-Jun–mid-Aug), which he also designed and helped build in the forest wilderness near Ruovesi. Exhibitions are held here in summer; to get here, follow main road No 66 5km south from the village of Ruovesi, then turn east. It's 3km to Kalela along a gravel road.

Ruovesi

Once voted the most beautiful village in Finland, Ruovesi, just off Route 66, retains much of its charm and is the best place to stay along Route 66. There is not much to see or do in the village, but if you have a car it makes a good base for exploring the area's attractions and scenic lakeshores. The **local museum** (☎ 050 514 6475; €2; admission €2; ☽ 1-7pm Jun–mid-Aug) covers local history and includes a collection of 18th-century farm buildings.

The lakes around here are prime fishing country and teem with pike, perch, pikeperch (zandel) and trout. **Kalatiira** (☎ 0400 250 365; www.fishinginfinland.com/kalatiira; Haukkamaantie 93) is an excellent outfit who organize fishing excursions. They'll arrange permits and equipment; even more fun are their winter ice-fishing trips; as well as the traditional method, they've also pioneered ice netfishing. It's best to book a week or so in advance, but it's worth a try even if you didn't. They also offer guided hikes in the area.

Haapasaari Holiday Village (☎ 044-080 0290; www.ruovedenhaapasaarenmatkailu.fi; Haapasaarentie 5; tent sites €15, cabins from €40, 4-/8-person cottages €95/170) is a great place to stay on a small islet north of the village, connected by a causeway. There's water all around, and fabulous self-contained cottages available year-round; they have a sauna, barbecue and fully equipped kitchen. The cabins are simpler, but also have simple cooking facilities. It's great for kids, with a large play area. You may be able to negotiate a substantial discount when things are quiet.

The rustic organic **Ylä-Tuuhonen Farm** (☎ 472 6426; www.yla-tuuhonen.fi; Tanhuantie 105; s/d from €35/55; Ⓟ ☒) is perfect for getting away from things in the Finnish wilderness. It's run by a generous-hearted owner, who offers three pretty rooms (sharing two bathrooms) and use of an excellent kitchen and lounge. You can also sleep in one of the old log barns, converted to a cosy cottage. It's by a lake, and there's plenty to be doing, and kids will enjoy the docile animals roaming around. To get there from Ruovesi, head 9km north on the Virrat road, then turn right onto the 3481 at Mustajärvi (signposted to Innala). Continue for another 9km, and the farmhouse is signposted on the left.

Hotel Ruovesi (☎ 476 2273; Ruovedentie 44; s/d €39/61; Ⓟ ☒) The better of the two dullish hotels in the centre of Ruovesi.

Several buses a day connect Ruovesi with Tampere and other places in the region. The SS *Tarjanne*, travelling along the Poet's Way between Tampere and Virrat, stops at Ruovesi; see p174 for more information.

Helvetinjärvi National Park

The main attraction of this national park is the narrow **Helvetinkolu gorge**, probably created as the ice moved the huge rocks apart some 10,000 years ago. The scene inspired the design of the Finnish pavilion at the Sevilla World Expo in 1992. There are numerous trails to follow, including a walk to **Haukanhieta**, a sandy beach and popular camping spot on the shores of Haukkajärvi. You can pitch a tent for the night at designated camp sites in the park and there's a free hut at Helvetinkolu. To get there from Route 66, take the signposted road via Pohtio village, which heads off west from the main road a kilometre north of the northern end of Ruovesi.

Virrat

pop 7943

The town of Virrat is the end point for some ferry cruises from Tampere. It is useful to have a bicycle with you to continue exploring the region. There's a **tourist office** (☎ 485 1276; www.virrat.fi; Virtaintie 26; ☻ 9am-3pm Mon-Fri) in the town hall building, about 1km from the ferry dock. Even when it's shut, you can still grab a map and brochures from the hall.

While the harbour is pretty, the centre of Virrat brings an abrupt end to any romantic dreaming on the Poet's Way or Route 66; it's ugly and functional. The best place to stay is **Domus Virrat** (☎ 475 5600; Sipiläntie 3; dm/s/d €18/37/58; ☻ Jun–mid-Aug; Ⓟ ✕), just uphill from the harbour. It's a fairly institutional summer hotel but has good facilities including kitchen, tennis court and sauna. It also has an HI-affiliated hostel beds.

Lakari Camping (☎ 475 8639; Lakarintie; tent sites €15, cabins from €33 ☻ May-Sep), 7km east of the town centre, is a beautifully-situated camping ground between two lakes. It has tent sites, cabins and well-equipped cottages as well as a beach and plenty of trees.

Several buses a day connect Virrat to Tampere and other towns in the region. The Poet's Way cruises from Tampere end here; see p174 for more information.

Virtain Perinnekylä

About 5km northwest of Virrat along road 23, **Tradition Village** (☎ 472 8160; Herrasentie 16; admission €5; ☻ noon-6pm mid-Jun–mid-Aug) is a sprawling open-air museum featuring four main museum buildings, handicraft shops and a restaurant with a lavish buffet lunch. Most attractions are open daily from late May to late August.

The **Talomuseo** has furniture, traditional Sunday decorations from the 1840s and a smoke sauna. The **Metsäkämppämuseo** features a large house and two small huts once used by loggers. The **Sotaveteraanien museohuone**, or War Veteran Museum Room, has guns and other things that were used during WWII. The **Kanavamuseo** has an exhibition relating to the canal.

Tuulimylly is a restored windmill dating from 1828. The nature trail or the gravel road (old road No 66) will take you to **Herrasen Lintutorni**, a bird-watching tower that provides a good view of birdlife on Lake Toisvesi bay.

Kenttälinnoitusalue, the area near the canal, was used by Russian troops as a depot during the war in 1808. Today the area has renovated trenches and a bunker.

KEURUU

☎ 014 / pop 11, 260

The happy, shiny, little town of Keuruu is on the northern shore of Lake Keurusselkä and boasts one of the most interesting wooden churches in Finland. There is a **tourist office** (☎ 751 7144; Multiantie 5; ☻ 9am-4pm Mon-Fri Jun-Aug) in the town hall.

Keuruu's fascinating **wooden church** (admission €1; ☻ 11am-5pm Jun-Aug), built in 1758, has superb portraits of Bible characters (although the artist didn't complete the set, due to a pay dispute), and photos of the mummified corpses buried below the chancel. There's also a set of stocks for miscreants who didn't show up at church often enough.

It's worth noting that the fabulous wooden church at Petäjävesi (p135) is only 28km east of here.

There are **lake cruises** on the MS *Elias Lönnrot,* a paddle boat, from early June to mid-August. It has service to the town of Mänttä once weekly (single/return €13.50/20, three hours) and more frequent services to other destinations.

MÄNTTÄ

☎ 03 / pop 6578

The reason for visiting the industrial town of Mänttä, about 30km south of Keuruu, is to see the Serlachius museum, one of the best art collections in Finland. The town has a **tourist office** (☎ 474 0070; Länsitorikatu 5; ☻ 11am-6pm summer).

The private home of Gösta Serlachius, of the dynasty that owns the huge paper factory that dominates the town, is now the **Gösta Serlachius Museum of Fine Arts** (☎ 474 5511; www.serla chiusartmuseum.fi; adult/child €6/1; ☻ 11am-6pm Tue-Sun May-Aug, 2-8pm Wed, noon-5pm Thu-Sun Sep-Apr). Situated 2km east of the town centre in elegant grounds, it houses an excellent collection of Finnish art. All the names from the Golden Age are here, including seemingly dozens of Gallen-Kallelas, and plenty of Edelfelts and Schjerfbecks, as well as Wickström sculptures. Look out for a mischievous painting of Gallen-Kallela getting pissed with his mate Sibelius, and Hugo Simberg's whimsical *Entrance to Hades.* There's also a sizeable

European collection, including a fine deposition scene by Van der Weyden.

Honkahovi Art Centre (☎ 474 7005) is another mansion belonging to the Serlachius family. It's a 1938 Art Deco building containing temporary art exhibitions. You can walk between Honkahovi and the Museum of Fine Arts via a trail around Lake Melasjärvi.

In Mänttä itself, the Art Nouveau **church** (1928) was financed by the factory, and has unique woodcarvings on the altar and pulpit.

The HI-affiliated **Mänttä Hostel** (☎ 488 8641; Koulukatu 6; dm €17; ☒ Jun–mid-Aug) is in the modern dormitory building of a school, not far from the centre.

Getting There & Away

In summer, you can catch the MS *Elias Lönnrot* from Keuruu. Otherwise, there are several buses a day to Mänttä from Tampere (€14.20, 1½ to 1¾ hours). The bus station is 700m west of the centre, on the way to the gallery.

HÄME REGION

HÄMEENLINNA

☎ 03 / pop 47,178

Dominated by its namesake, the majestic Häme Castle, Hämeenlinna (Swedish: Tavastehus) is the capital of the Province of Häme and the oldest inland town in Finland, founded in 1649. However, there had been a trading settlement at this location from the 9th century. After the Swedes built the castle on a crusade to Finland in the 13th century, Hämeenlinna developed into an administrative, educational and garrison town.

Hämeenlinna's partly cobbled town centre is pleasantly small and navigable, there are enough sights to keep you busy for a day, and its location on the motorway between Helsinki and Tampere keeps it firmly on the tourist route. A great way to arrive or depart from here is by ferry from Tampere.

Information

City tourist office (☎ 621 3373; www.hameenlinna .fi; Raatihuoneenkatu 11; ☒ 9am-5pm Mon, 9am-4pm Tue-Fri, also 10am-2pm Sat May-Aug) You'll find plenty of information and a free Internet terminal here.

Häme Tourist Service (☎ 621 2388; www.hameen matkailu.fi; Linnankatu 6; ☒ 8am-4pm Mon-Fri) Sells tickets for lake cruises and books accommodation at hotels and cabins throughout the region.

Post office (Palokunnankatu 13-15, 13100 Hämeenlinna; ☒ 9am-8pm Mon-Fri) Near the bus station.

Public library (Lukiokatu 2; ☒ Mon-Sat) Has half a dozen Internet terminals at no charge, but must be prebooked.

Sights & Activities

Despite its small size, Hämeenlinna has a wealth of museums and other attractions.

HÄME CASTLE & MUSEUMS

The bulky red-brick **Häme Castle** (☎ 675 6820; admission €5; ☒ 10am-6pm May–mid-Aug, 10am-4pm mid-Aug–Apr) is the symbol of Hämeenlinna and its most significant attraction. Construction of the castle started during the 1260s by Swedes, who wanted to establish a military redoubt against the power of Novgorod. It was originally built on an island, but to the annoyance of the defenders, the lake receded and necessitated the building of new defensive walls. It never saw serious military action and, after the Russian takeover, was converted into a jail. The last prisoners left in the 1980s and extensive renovations of the castle were finally completed in 1991.

The inside has been substantially rebuilt and now houses a museum displaying period costumes, furniture and various exhibitions, some related to the castle (its history and archaeology). Free guided tours in English are given hourly from June to August; if you don't read Finnish or Swedish this is the only way you will really appreciate the structure, as the English pamphlets are uninformative.

Around the castle are three **museums** which can be visited with the castle on a combined ticket (€12).

National Prison Museum

The old prison block near the castle has been converted into a **museum** (☎ 621 2977; adult/child €4/1; ☒ 11am-5pm) where you can visit a solitary confinement cell or admire the graffiti left by former inmates. The most interesting bit is the three cells, left more or less as they were when the inmates departed, along with a brief description of their occupants' crime and lifestyle. There's also a sauna, where prisoners would sometimes violently settle disputes, as they were not accompanied by guards. The building was last used as a prison in 1993.

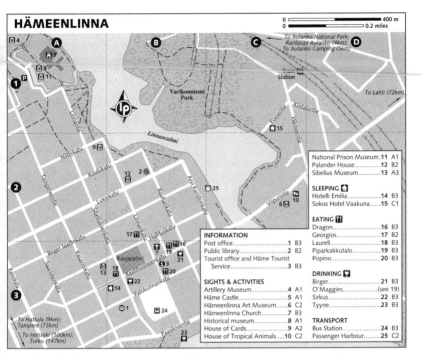

HÄMEENLINNA

To Aulanko National Park;
Rantasipi Aulanko (4km);
To Aulanko Camping (5km)

To Lahti (72km)

Varikonniemi
Park

Station

Linnansalmi

To Hattula (9km);
Tampere (73km)

To Helsinki (100km);
Turku (147km)

National Prison Museum..11	A1
Palander House...........12	B2
Sibelius Museum..........13	A3
SLEEPING 🏠	
Hotelli Emilia.............14	B3
Sokos Hotel Vaakuna......15	C1
EATING 🍴	
Dragon...................16	B3
Georgios.................17	B2
Laurell..................18	B3
Piparkakkutalo...........19	B3
Popino...................20	B3
DRINKING 🍷	
Birger...................21	B3
O'Maggies...............(see 19)
Sirkus..................22	B3
Tyyne..................23	B3
TRANSPORT	
Bus Station...............24	B3
Passenger Harbour........25	C2

INFORMATION	
Post office...................1	B3
Public library.................2	B2
Tourist office and Häme Tourist	
Service......................3	B3
SIGHTS & ACTIVITIES	
Artillery Museum.............4	A1
Häme Castle.................5	A1
Hämeenlinna Art Museum...6	C2
Hämeenlinna Church.........7	B3
Historical museum...........8	A1
House of Cards..............9	A2
House of Tropical Animals...10	C2

Historical Museum

Next to the Prison Museum, the **historical museum** (☎ 621 2979; adult/child €4/1; ⏱ 11am-5pm) is a relatively new display showcasing the local Häme area through the ages – from around the 18th century to the present – through models, photographs, costumes and bits of memorabilia. There's a replica of an early bank, and lots of pop-culture memorabilia.

Artillery Museum

There are numerous museums devoted to the Finnish involvement in WWII, but this one takes the cake. It's huge. The **museum** (☎ 682 4600; admission €6; ⏱ noon-5pm Oct-Apr, 10am-6pm May-Sep) consists of three floors packed with war memorabilia, and outside is a collection of phallic heavy artillery big enough to start a war on several fronts.

SIBELIUS MUSEUM

Johan Julius Christian (Jean) Sibelius, the most famous Finnish composer, was born in Hämeenlinna in 1865 and went to school here, but surprisingly the town makes little fuss about this fact. His childhood home has

been converted into a small and unassuming **museum** (☎ 621 2755, Hallituskatu 11; €3; ⏱ 10am-4pm May-Aug, noon-4pm Sep-Apr) with only a small plaque on the side to alert you to the fact that there's something of interest inside. The four rooms contain photographs, letters, his upright piano and some family furniture. It's a likeable place, although uninformative about his life; it's lovely if you coincide with the resident pianist, who often plays at weekends. There are also regular concert performances, free with an entry ticket.

HÄMEENLINNA ART MUSEUM

The town's pleasing **art museum** (☎ 621 3017; Viipurintie 2; admission €5-6; ⏱ noon-6pm Tue-Sun, noon-8pm Thu) is housed in a former grain store designed by CL Engel and has an interesting collection of Finnish art from the 19th and 20th centuries. Notable is Gallen-Kallela's painting of the Kalevala's final scene, with the shaman Väinämöinen leaving Finland, displaced by a Jesus-like baby that symbolizes the arrival of Christianity. Other scenes from the epic are painted on the ceiling. There are a couple of Schjerfbecks, including a *Rigoletto*

TAMPERE & HÄME REGION

JEAN SIBELIUS

Born in 1865 in Hämeenlinna, Jean Sibelius started playing piano when he was nine and composed his first notable work at age 20. During the cultural flowering that inspired Finland's independence, Sibelius provided the nation with music that complemented its literature and visual arts. Sibelius was fascinated by mythology and one of his greatest inspirations was the *Kalevala,* the Finnish epic compiled by Elias Lönnrot in 1833.

In 1892 Sibelius gained international recognition for his tone poem *En Saga,* and in 1899 composed the *Finlandia* symphony, a piece which has come to symbolise the Finnish struggle for independence.

Sibelius experimented with tonality and rejected the classical sonata form, building movements from a variety of short phrases that grow together as they develop. His work, particularly the early symphonies, is notable for its economical orchestration and melancholic mood.

In 1892 he married Aino Järnefelt (sister of the painter Eero Järnefelt) and together they had six daughters. The family moved to a new home, Ainola, north of Helsinki, in 1904; this is where Sibelius composed five of his seven symphonies. Ainola is now preserved as a museum that is open to the public in summer (p88).

Sibelius studied in Berlin and Vienna and visited the USA in 1914 as an honorary doctor at Yale University. In later life he wrote incidental music for plays and a number of choral works and songs. He died in 1957, at the age of 92.

There's a Sibelius Festival in Loviisa, where he had a summer home, and the excellent Sibelius Museum in Turku (p198) is devoted to the composer and his musical instruments, and frequently holds concerts. It's a terrific introduction to the music of Finland's greatest composer.

painted when she was just 19, and a beautiful wooden lynx and cubs by Jussi Mäntynen. The building opposite houses the temporary exhibitions, which are invariably excellent.

HOUSE OF TROPICAL ANIMALS

There's nothing like a reptile house on a winter's day, and this small **tropical zoo** (☎ 676 5773; Viipurintie 4; admission €7; ⊙ 11am-7pm), next to the art museum, is something different for Finland. It houses an interesting collection of our scaly brethren – including snakes and alligators – as well as birds and fish.

HOUSE OF CARDS

Hundreds of postcards are displayed at this small, quirky **museum of postcards** (Korttientalo; ☎ 616 9502; Niittykatu 1; admission €1.70; ⊙ 10am-5pm, closed Mon Sep-Apr). Some of the cards on display date back over a century and contain the original handwritten 'wish you were here…' messages. And people just don't have handwriting like they did in the good old days. There are also temporary thematic exhibitions. The museum gift shop sells a great range of cards, and there's also a café here.

PALANDERIN TALO

An upper middle-class home built in 1861, the historic **Palander House** (☎ 621 2967; Linnankatu 16; adult/child €4/1; ⊙ noon-3pm Jun-Aug, closed Mon-Fri Sep-May) is filled with period furnishings, including Art Nouveau furniture and copper utensils. A guided tour in English (every half hour) is included with admission.

HÄMEENLINNA CHURCH

Dating from 1798 the town **church** (⊙ 10am-6pm Jun-Aug, 11am-1pm Sep-May) was designed by Louis Jean Depréz, court painter for King Gustav III of Sweden. It is modelled on the Pantheon in Rome.

AULANKO NATIONAL PARK

This beautiful park, northeast of the town centre, was founded early in the 20th century by Hugo Standertskjöld, who dreamt of a Central European–style park with ponds, swans, pavilions and exotic trees. He spent a fortune to achieve his goal and the result was Aulanko. Although the best way to explore it is on foot, the sealed one-way road loop is accessible by private car. An observation tower in a granite, fortress-style building is open daily in summer (free) and gives superb views. There's a nature trail in the park and a lakeside golf course.

Buses 2, 13 or 17 will take you to Aulanko from Hämeenlinna centre, but it's only 6km away (turn left on Aulangontie just east of the railway tracks) and makes a pleasant bike ride. The park's **visitor centre** (☎ 621 3750; ☺ 10am-8pm Wed-Sun mid-Aug–May, daily Jun–mid-Aug) will supply you with a map.

Tours

Hämeenlinna is on Lake Vanajavesi at the southern tip of a lake network that stretches north to Tampere. See p186 for details of lake ferries.

On Friday and Saturday in summer (Midsummer to mid-August), the **MS Wanaja** (☎ 020-741 1770) cruises the lake all evening; picking up passengers from the dock at Arvi Karistonkatu 8 every two hours. It's essentially a booze cruise, but a good way to spend the evening; it costs €6 to step on board and you can stay as long as you like.

Sleeping

There are no hostels in Hämeenlinna.

Hotelli Emilia (☎ 612 2106; www.hotelliemilia.net; Raatihuoneenkatu 23; s/d €62/82, Sat, Sun & summer €57/76; ℗ ✗) This is the cheapest hotel in town and is something of a bargain. Right in the heart of things, its rooms are modern, with crisp white sheets and air-conditioning. There's a sauna, bar, friendly management and a good buffet breakfast.

Sokos Hotel Vaakuna (☎ 020-123 4636; www.sokoshotels.fi; Possentie 7; s/d €101/122, d Sat, Sun & summer €84; ℗ ✗ 🖳) Across the river from the town centre and very near the train station, this attractive modern hotel has been designed to echo Häme Castle, of which many rooms have a view across the lake. There's the usual array of restaurants and bars; the rooms have plenty of natural light and all the mod cons.

Rantasipi Aulanko (☎ 658 801; www.rantasipi.fi; s/d €120/144, d Sat, Sun & summer €89; ℗ ✗ 🖳 🐾) This lakeside place in Aulanko National Park has a long tradition and is considered one of the best hotels in the region. Its location, between the lake and the forest park, could not be better, but it's essentially just a big conference hotel with lots of facilities, including five saunas, restaurants and an adjacent golf course. There's plenty for kids to do, and large family rooms.

Aulanko Camping (☎ 675 9772; dm €10, tent & van sites €15, cabins €43-61; ☺ May-Sep) On the edge of a beautiful nature park, this is the closest camping ground to the city. There are also fully self-contained five-person cottages for

€70. It's located beyond the main body of the park, on the shores of Aulangonjärvi. It's signposted Aulangon Lomäkylä.

Eating

Piparkakkutalo (☎ 648 040; Kirkkorinne 2; pasta €10-12, mains €11-23; ☺ lunch & dinner) This place, one block east of the church, is easily the best restaurant in Hämeenlinna and everyone's favourite for a gourmet meal. Dishes range from inexpensive pasta and vegetarian to reindeer, wild boar and ostrich. The restaurant is in a historic 1906 shingled house with period décor, formerly the home of artist Albert Edelfelt. The name means 'gingerbread house'.

Georgios (☎ 682 8884; Linnankatu 3; mains €8-16; ☺ lunch & dinner Tue-Sat, lunch only Mon) Just off the kauppatori, this authentic Greek restaurant is one of the town's best places to eat. As well as the expected but comforting Acropolis 'n' Apollo décor, the food is excellent, with great Greek salads, dips and tender meat dishes.

Popino (☎ 653 2555; Raatihuoneenkatu 11; mains €8-18; ☺ 11am-10pm Mon-Sat, noon-8pm Sun) Tucked away where the steps divide Linnankatu into two levels, just behind the tourist office, is a fine pizza and pasta restaurant. As well as pizza there are meat and fish dishes and lunch specials for €7.50. It's stylish, but informal and family friendly, with a play area for young kids.

Dragon (☎ 612 1858; Raatihuoneenkatu 8A; mains €10-16; ☺ 11am-10pm Mon-Thu & Sun, 11am-11pm Fri & Sat) The best of the town's Chinese restaurants, this is in a cellar on the main street through town, with soothing décor and a couple of intimate nook-tables. Although it's not cheap, the portions are generous and the service good.

Laurell (☎ 467 7722; Sibeliuksenkatu 7; ☺ 8.30am-6pm Mon-Fri, 8.30am-4pm Sat, 11am-5pm Sun) This spacious café on the kauppatori is a popular meeting spot for locals. There's an appetizing selection of squishy cakes, rolls, pastries and pasties, and another branch in the same building as the tourist office.

Drinking & Entertainment

O'Maggie's (☎ 648 0450; Kirkkorinne 2; ☺ from 4pm) A very cosy Irish pub in the same building as Piparkakkutalo. Since there's no terrace it fills up later in the evening during summer, but it's definitely the place to be in winter when there's weekly live Irish music.

Birger (☎ 570 9777; Raatihuoneenkatu 5; ⏲ 4pm-midnight or later) This relaxed pub is typical of a certain sort of Finnish bar, with comfortable seating and a restrained, peaceful atmosphere (at least early in the night). The friendly owner stocks an excellent range of bottled beer from around the world.

Sirkus (☎ 633 6391; Sibeliuksenkatu 2; admission €5-7; ⏲ 10pm-4am Wed, Fri & Sat) This is the main live music and nightclub venue with regular rock acts. All three nights are fairly different. There's live music on Wednesdays, while Saturdays are a more sophisticated scene with a minimum age of 24.

In summer the floating boat-bar **Tyyne** (Paasikiventie; ⏲ from 11am), south of the bus station, is a fun place for a beer.

Getting There & Away
BUS
Hourly buses between Helsinki (€18.90, 1½ hours) and Tampere (€14, one hour) stop in Hämeenlinna at the central bus station. From Turku, there are eight buses daily (€23.20, two hours).

BOAT
Leaving from Hämeenlinna's passenger harbour, **Finnish Silverline** (☎ 03-212 4804; www .finnishsilverline.com) has a ferry to Tampere (€39, 8½ hours, 11.30am, June to late August). The route goes via Visavuori, where there's a one-hour stopover.

The passenger harbour is on Arvi Karistonkatu 8, just north of the Rantakasino beer terrace.

TRAIN
The train station is 1km northeast of the town centre, on the other side of the bridge. Trains between Helsinki (€16.70, one hour, hourly) and Tampere (€14.30, 40 minutes, hourly) stop at Hämeenlinna. From Turku (€20.60, 1¾ hours), change trains in Toijala.

HÄMEENLINNA TO TAMPERE
There are several interesting sights just off the main highway between Tampere and Hämeenlinna.

Pyhän Ristin Kirkko (Church of the Holy Cross; admission €2.80; ⏲ 11am-5pm Jun-Aug) in Hattula, only 9km north of Hämeenlinna, is one of Finland's oldest and most memorable churches.

Dating from the early 1400s, the interior is filled with fabulous naïve frescoes (early 16th century). They tell the main stories of the Bible as you go around the nave; the Tree of Jesse in the sacristy is particularly fine. As this was probably the nearest that most of the parishioners ever got to being able to read, it must have been an awe-inspiring place for them; it still is. The **old grain store** built in 1840, close to the old church, houses the information office and sells handicrafts.

The church is easy to reach from Hämeenlinna by public transport; take bus 5, 6 or 16. Take something warm to wear if you plan a lengthy look at the interior.

Iittala
Iittala, a village on the highway 23km northwest of Hämeenlinna, is best known for its famous glass factory, which sells its products under the same name.

Iittala Glass Centre (☎ 0204-393 512; Lasikeskus; ⏲ 9am-8pm May-Aug, 10am-6pm Sep-Apr) is opposite the bus terminal. Around the corner, the **glass museum** (☎ 0204-396 230; admission €2) exhibits objects designed and manufactured locally. It also gives an insight into the history of Finnish design. It's free to watch craftspeople blowing glassware in the back room. The shop sells second-grade products at a 35% discount.

Sääksmäki
This historical and scenic area northwest of Hämeenlinna is one of the highlights of the region.

Rapolan Linnavuori on Rapola Hill is the largest prehistoric fortress in Finland. There are fine views and you can follow a marked trail that will take you to 100 burial mounds on the western side of the hill. You can get to Rapola either by following the signs from the main road, about 25km northwest of Hämeenlinna, or by taking the narrow road, Rapolankuja, that passes by the privately owned Rapola estate.

Once the studio of Emil Wickström (1864–1942), a sculptor from the National Romantic era, **Visavuori** (☎ 03-543 6528; admission €6; ⏲ 11am-7pm Tue-Sun, 11am-5pm Mon Jun-Aug, Tue-Sun 11am-5pm Sep-May) is the best-known sight in the region and well worth a visit. Stunningly situated on a ridge with water on both sides, it consists of three houses, the oldest of which was the home of Wickström, built in 1902 in Karelian and Finnish Romantic styles and containing fantastic Art Nouveau furniture; it really brings the man to life and is worth visiting first. The beautiful studio next door, with dozens of models and sculptures, was built in 1903; the pervading smell of baking will force you to stop for a *pulla* (cardamon-flavoured bun) in the brick-vaulted café downstairs. Kari Paviljonki is dedicated to Kari Suomalainen, Emil Wickström's grandson. The best-known of Finland's political cartoonists, his long career spanned several decades and he was drawing up to his death in 1999. His cartoons are excellent; the ones that can be, are translated well. Perhaps even more amusing is the award from the US National Cartoonist Society in 1959 for his daring cartoons 'exposing the deceit of Communism'. Ferries from Hämeenlinna and Tampere stop at Visavuori in summer; Wickström was the curse of the local boatmen, who used to have to deliver to him huge slabs of marble.

Visavuori is about 4km east of the Hämeenlinna-Tampere motorway, just off Toijala road.

HÄME OX ROAD

One of the oldest roads in Finland and still partly unpaved, the Ox Rd (Härkätie) winds its way through rural landscape between Hämeenlinna and Turku. It was both trade route and path of pilgrimage; in spite of the present name, most travel was on foot, with goods carried by horses rather than oxen.

The Härkätie runs roughly parallel to, and mostly south of, Hwy 10 (which opened in 1962), passing through Renko, Porras, Somero, Marttila and Lieto. At around 160km, the route can be cycled in two or three days.

Just west of the village of Porras and on the south side of Ruostejärvi is the **Häme Visitor Centre** (☎ 0205-644 630) with information on hiking and the natural environment. For more information see www.harkatie.net.

Renko

Renko, 15km southwest of Hämeenlinna, is the first stop along the Ox Rd and is just off Hwy 10. The main attraction is the Pyhän Jaakonkirkko (church of St James), a 15th century structure with a curious octagonal shape. Next door is the local museum, **Härkätien Museo** (☎ 618 5933; free admission;

☼ 11am-2pm Sun in summer), a basic display of farming implements and clerical tools; upstairs are the carts and harnesses used for traditional transport. Although official opening hours are short, it often seems to be open at other times.

Tammela

Tammela village is on the shores of Pyhäjärvi, 11km north of Porras and the Ox Rd. It stretches along the lake and is a service centre for the summer cottages around; there's a bank, ATM, post office, pub and a couple of cafés. It's worth visiting the huge supermarket to see what Finnish summer catering is all about; count the types of sausage! The old **Tammela church** dates from the early 16th century. It was enlarged in 1785 and is of prodigious length. Some mediaeval wooden sculptures line the walls but otherwise it's fairly unadorned.

North of Tammela village, the impressive **Mustiala Manor** (☎ 03-646 5519; ☼ 10am-4pm Mon-Fri, also 11am-3pm Sat in summer) was originally owned in the 16th century by Marshal Klaus Horn, a Swede. Now the estate houses an agricultural school, a small museum devoted to farming tools, and a brewery and restaurant.

Four kilometres east of central Tammela, and 7km north of Porras, the **Venesilta** (☎ 436 0077; Portaantie 225; tent sites €15, plus per person €1; cabins €40-75) camp site is one of the best places to bed down hereabouts. It's right by the lake and very peaceful. It's open all year; phone ☎ 040-551 7025 outside of summer.

Saari Park

The scenery in **Saari Park** (☎ 03-434 1833), 4km north of Porras and 7km southeast of Tammela, inspired many painters during the National Romantic era. The attractive sand ridge is part of the estate of Saari, which includes a private manor nearby. The park allows public access to anyone any time. For the best view, climb the 20m **observation tower**. You can get the keys from the restaurant on the eastern side of the park.

Somero

The Ox Rd town of Somero was founded in the 15th century. The **kivisakasti**, a stone building on the grounds of the old **church**, dates from that time. The church dates from 1859. **Someron torpparimuseo** (🕑 summer), the local museum, which is north of the centre, includes a windmill and peasants' houses that are very old.

Jokioinen & Forssa

The town of Jokioinen, north of the Ox Rd, has a unique history. In the 16th century, King Erik XIV of Sweden (who later went insane) gave exclusive rights to the Swedish war hero Klaus Horn to establish an estate in the Jokioinen region. At the time of independence in 1917, it had grown to be the largest such estate in Finland.

The little **church** of Jokioinen (1631), 1km past the granary, is the second-oldest wooden church in Finland but renovations hide the original architecture.

Near Jokioinen, Forssa is the largest town in the region. Originally built on the cotton-spinning industry, it's not a particularly enthralling place, but has plenty of accommodation options and a tourist office.

Getting There & Away

There are regular buses from Hämeenlinna to Renko, the first village on the Ox Rd route, and to all the other towns mentioned. Local buses connect the rest of the towns, mainly coming from the large industrial town of Forssa. However, it's easiest to explore the Ox Rd by private car or bicycle.

LAHTI

☎ 03 / pop 98,281

One of Finland's major winter-sports centres, Lahti is a modern town about 100km north of Helsinki. It's a good place to go if you're interested in skiing, with a good museum on the sport, alongside the city's frighteningly high ski jumps. Lahti has hosted several world championships, most recently in 2001.

Founded in 1905, the city isn't hugely interesting in other respects, and lacks anything that could be called an 'old town'. Most of the downtown area, in fact, consists of a series of linked shopping centres. The 10,000 Karelian refugees who arrived after WWII have contributed their entrepreneurial spirit to what the locals call the 'Business City'. Lahti does make a good base for visiting nearby attractions. Its location by Vesijärvi (which is connected to Lake Päijänne) makes it the obvious place to start a ferry trip to Jyväskylä. One of the largest lakes in Finland, Päijänne provides Helsinki with tap water.

Information

Public library (☎ 812 511; Kirkkokatu 31; 🕑 10am-8pm Mon-Fri, 10am-3pm Sat) Several free Internet terminals.

Tourist information office (☎ 877 677; www .lahtitravel.fi; Aleksanterinkatu 13; 🕑 9am-5pm Mon-Fri) Free Internet terminals; also makes hotel and transport bookings. There's a summer tourist booth at the harbour.

Sights

SPORTS CENTRE

At the Sports Centre, a 10-minute walk west of town, things are dominated by three imposing ski-jumps, the biggest standing 73m high and stretching 116m. You'll often see high-level jumpers training here in summer. There's a whole complex here, including the football stadium, a summer swimming pool, ski tracks and the delightful **Ski Museum** (☎ 814 4523; admission €5; 🕑 10am-5pm Mon-Fri, 11am-5pm Sat & Sun). A history of skis includes some excavated examples from 2000 years ago, and Lahti's proud record as a winter sports centre is given plenty of treatment. In the next room the fun starts; frustrate yourself on the ski-jump simulator, then try the biathlon, skiing on Velcro before nailing five bullseyes with your rifle. A combined ticket (€7) will let you take the chairlift up to the observation terrace at the top of the ski-jump; great if there's someone practising, and good for the views in any event.

OTHER SIGHTS

The **Lahti Historical Museum** (☎ 814 4536; Lahdenkatu 4; admission €5; 🕑 10am-5pm Mon-Fri, 11am-5pm Sat & Sun) is in a beautiful old manor house. This guide was updated just before the triumphant re-opening after renovation; exhibits include the Klaus Holma collection of French and Italian furniture and medieval and Renaissance art.

In the heart of town in a modern office building, the **Art Museum & Poster Museum** (☎ 814 4547; Vesijärvenkatu 11; admission €5; 🕑 10am-5pm Mon-Fri, 11am-5pm Sat & Sun) has temporary exhibitions of sculpture and paintings, and an off-beat collection of advertising posters from yesteryear.

The **Radio & TV Museum** (☎ 814 4512; Radiomäki Hill; admission €5; 🕑 10am-5pm Mon-Fri, 11am-5pm Sat & Sun), on a hill just south of the

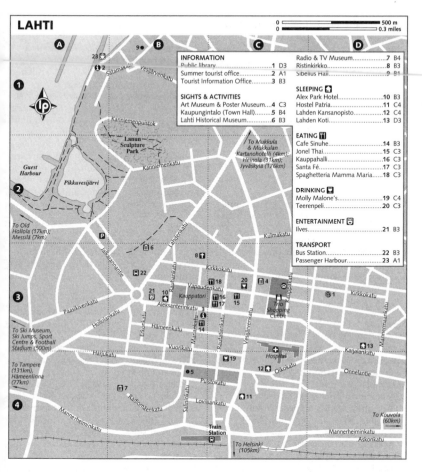

LAHTI

INFORMATION
Public library.........................1 D3
Summer tourist office..............2 A1
Tourist Information Office........3 B3

SIGHTS & ACTIVITIES
Art Museum & Poster Museum....4 C3
Kaupungintalo (Town Hall)......5 B4
Lahti Historical Museum...........6 B3

Radio & TV Museum................7 B4
Ristinkirkko.............................8 B3
Sibelius Hall...........................9 B1

SLEEPING
Alex Park Hotel.....................10 B3
Hostel Patria.........................11 C4
Lahden Kansanopisto.............12 C4
Lahden Koti..........................13 D3

EATING
Cafe Sinuhe.........................14 B3
Jonel Thai............................15 C3
Kauppahalli..........................16 C3
Santa Fé..............................17 C3
Spaghetteria Mamma Maria......18 C3

DRINKING
Molly Malone's.....................19 C4
Teerenpeli............................20 C3

ENTERTAINMENT
Ilves...................................21 B3

TRANSPORT
Bus Station..........................22 B3
Passenger Harbour................23 A1

---

centre, has a collection of old radios and a working broadcasting studio from the 1950s. You can film and appear in your own TV broadcast or radio programme, guaranteed fun for kids.

The striking **Ristinkirkko** (Church of the Cross; Kirkkokatu 4; 10am-6pm summer, 10am-3pm winter) was designed by Alvar Aalto and finished in 1978. Although the exterior is made of brown brick, the interior is typically Aalto: wooden benches, white walls and, on the ceiling, four concrete rays emanating from the cross.

The Art Nouveau **Kaupungintalo** (town hall; Harjukatu 31) was designed by another famous Finnish architect, Eliel Saarinen. There are guided tours of the building at 2pm on Fri-

day. **Sibelius Hall** (81418; www.lahti.fi/sibeliustalo; Ankkurikatu 7), near the harbour on Vesijärvi, is a huge new concert-hall creation made from wood and glass.

Activities

Although the public can't use the ski-jump at the **Sports Centre** (814 4570), there's still plenty for the average visitor to do. In winter, there is an ice-skating hall and a total of 145km of cross-country ski tracks, 35km of which are illuminated. Skiing and skating gear can be rented in the main building. In summer the centre offers bike trails and a large outdoor **swimming pool**. FC Lahti also play their home games at the stadium here.

TAMPERE & HÄME REGION

There's also plenty to do out at **Mukkula** (☎ 753 5380; Rietaniemenkatu 10; ⊙ Jun-Aug) in summer. The lakefront location, 5km from Lahti, has boat and canoe hire, tennis, mini-golf, beach volleyball and bicycles for rent.

As well as the longer lake trips mentioned on opposite, in summer there are several daily 1½-hour return **cruises** from the passenger harbour, as well as evening 3½-hour cruises to the Vääksy Canal and back on the **MS Suometar** (adult/child €14/7). Contact the tourist office for times and bookings.

Festivals & Events

Unsurprisingly, Lahti hosts several annual winter sports events including the **Ski Games** (www.lahtiskigames.com) in early March. There are also some good summer music festivals such as **Jazz at the Marketplace** (www.jazztori.com), a week-long street festival in early August, and the **Sibelius Festival** (www.sinfonialahti.fi), with performances by the Lahti Symphony Orchestra in mid-September.

Sleeping

Lahden Koti (☎ 752 2173; www.lahdenkoti.fi; Karjalankatu 6; s/d studio apt €62/73, one-room apt €67/79, 3-/4-person 2-room apt €95/124; **P** 🗙) In a renovated apartment building, this place has been converted into a very nice small hotel. All apartments are tastefully decorated and come with a well-equipped kitchen and a bathroom. There are generous family rates and plenty of choice of size and price.

Mukkulan Kartanohotelli (☎ 874 140; www.mukkulankartano.net; Ritaniemenkatu 10; s/d €70/85, simpler accommodation €45/70; **P** 🗙) In the old manor house at Mukkula, 5km north of Lahti, this is a romantic spot; the lakeside location is superb and the price very reasonable. There's an outdoor Jacuzzi and sauna a hop, skip and plunge from the water, and friendly staff. There's also a **camp site** (☎ 874 1442; www.mukkulacamping.fi; tent sites per person/2-4 people €8/14; ⊙ Jun-Aug, ring for opening at other times) and a summer HI-hostel (no dorms) in the grounds.

Lahden Kansanopisto (☎ 878 1181; www.lahdenkansanopisto.sci.fi; Harjukatu 46; dm €24, s/d €29/47, with bathroom €39/52; ⊙ Jun–mid-Aug; **P** 🗙 🖵) The local folk college is a welcoming place to stay in summer. It's friendly, HI affiliated, and has a variety of rooms with beds (linen provided), as well as a well-equipped kitchen. The rooms are good, with desks

and bedside lamps, and the shared facilities more than adequate.

Hostel Patria (☎ 782 3783; Vesijärvenjatu 3; s/d €30/44; 🗙) If Lahden Kansanopisto is not open, there's this simpler HI-affiliated guesthouse around the corner.

Alex Park Hotel (☎ 52511; www.alexpark.fi; Aleksanterinkatu 6; s/d €104/123, weekends €79/84, summer r €68; **P** 🗙 🖵 🖭 🖫) This is a central hotel that's long been a Lahti favourite. If you can find your way to the lifts through the melee of cafés, bars and nightclub downstairs, you'll discover well-appointed rooms, some of which overlook the market square. They are furnished in dark wood and are particularly good value in summer.

Eating

Being a popular winter sports centre, some restaurants and cafés in Lahti have an interesting feature – glassed-in terraces for winter dining. It's not a gourmet capital, however.

Café Sinuhe (☎ 751 1620; Mariankatu 21; ⊙ 6.30am-8pm Mon-Fri, 8am-4pm Sat, 10am-6pm Sun) Around the corner from the tourist office, this lively café is a Lahti staple. Folk stream in at all hours of the day for its mellow coffee or to buy a loaf of crusty bread. it has a few daily salads on the go and plenty of sweet things.

Spaghetteria Mamma Maria (☎ 751 6716; Vapaudenkatu 10; mains €7-15; ⊙ lunch & dinner) This is an Italian restaurant with an authentic feel and stocks of Peroni beer, located on the central square. It's got bags of variety: heaps of pastas, pizzas, veals and steaks; the quantities are generous and it's pretty tasty. To round off, there's homemade gelati.

Jonel Thai (☎ 734 2958; Vapaudenkatu 15; mains €6.50-11.50; ⊙ 11am-8.30pm Mon-Thu, 11am-9.30pm Fri & Sat, noon-8.30pm Sun) This is one of a couple of decent Thai restaurants near the centre. There's a filling lunch special for €7 as well as a take-away snack section.

Sante Fé (☎ 781 8007; Aleksanterinkatu 16; mains €8-15; ⊙ lunch & dinner) On the southeast corner of the kauppatori is a busy Tex-Mex restaurant with a comfy, friendly bar and colourful terrace downstairs and dining room on the 1st floor. The menu features the usual nachos, fajitas, steaks and pastas.

Drinking & Entertainment

Teerenpeli (☎ 042-492 5220; Vapaudenkatu 20; ⊙ noon-1 or 2am) This is a great brewery pub with a glassed-in terrace. It brews four beers on the premises, and sometimes sells *sahti*, the sweet Finnish homebrew-style beer. It's always lively with chatter and also does food.

Molly Malone's (☎ 525 2399; Vuorikatu 35; 🕑 4pm-1am) This is a laid-back Irish pub with live music on Friday and Saturday nights.

Ilves (☎ 0600 007 007; www.finnkino.fi; Aleksanterinkatu 4) Lahti's main cinema has five screens and is very central. During the week, it's evening screenings only.

Getting There & Away

BUS

There are regular daily buses along the motorway from Helsinki (€18.90, 1½ hours), and frequent services to/from Tampere (€21.30, two hours), Jyväskylä (€25.60, three hours) and Turku (€32.30, 3½ hours).

BOAT

From early June to mid-August **Päijänne Risteilyt Hildén Oy** (☎ 783 2515; www.paijanne-risteilythilden.fi) operates daily ferries from Lahti's passenger harbour to Heinola at 10am (one way/return €17/26, 4½ hours each way). The cruise goes via Vääksy and Kalkkinen canals. It also has a twice-weekly ferry to Jyväskylä at 10am on Tuesday and Thursday (€45, 10½ hours) from early June to early August.

TRAIN

There are at least 15 direct trains per day from Helsinki (€15.70, 1½ hours) and Riihimäki. Travellers from Tampere change trains at Riihimäki.

AROUND LAHTI

Hollola

☎ 03

Hollola, west of Lahti, is the most historical place in this area. It used to be the major settlement around here until Lahti's rapid growth left the venerable parish as a pleasant rural backwater. These days there are two Hollolas – the modern town centre is on the highway 7km west of Lahti, but the old village and most of the attractions are 15km to 18km northwest of Lahti on the southern shores of Vesijärvi. To get there, you can either track north from the modern Hollola, or, better, take road 2956 from Lahti and follow Vesijärvi. It's close enough for a leisurely bike tour.

SIGHTS & ACTIVITIES

Heading west along the lake from Lahti, the first place you'll reach is **Messilä**, where signposted off the road is a fine old estate with a golf course, guest harbour and winter ski slopes (see also p192). **Messilän Pajat** is a separate building featuring local craft (and a bakery).

Pirunpesä (Devil's Nest) is a steep rock cliff, near Messilä. A marked trail takes you there, or you can walk the entire 7km *luontopolku* (nature trail) that goes via a series of hills and offers some good views. One of these hills, **Tiirismaa**, is a downhill-skiing resort in winter.

Continuing along the lake road, and before reaching the old Hollola village, you'll see **Kutajärvi**, a resting place for migratory birds, on your left.

Pyhäniemi Manor (☎ 788 1466; admission €7; 🕑 11am-6pm Jun-Aug) is a wooden mansion, dubbed the 'Hollywood of Hollola' in the 1930s, when many Finnish films were shot here. It has had quite a colourful history; Swedish king Gustav III granted the estate to the Schmiedefelt family in 1780 and even visited it himself in 1783. The estate grew immensely and its industries included a sawmill, a wheel factory and a posh dairy that exported its products to St Petersburg.

On the shores of Vesijärvi, 17km northwest of Lahti, the large **Hollola church** (☎ 788 1351; free admission; 🕑 11am-6pm Jun–mid-Aug, 11am-4pm Sun mid-Aug–May) was once the heart of this parish, before Lahti grew up. It's an elegant late 15th-century structure with steep gables; the belltower was designed by the indefatigable Carl Engel in the 19th century. Mounted above the double nave are 10 fine polychrome wood sculptures of saints; also noteworthy are the elaborate coats of arms from the von Essen family and the 14th-century baptismal font and Pietà that were from the earlier, wooden church. There are English-speaking guides in summer. The church is marked 'Hollola kk' on signs and bus timetables.

Taking the first right after the church, you'll find two small local museums, both open Tuesday to Sunday. **Esinemuseo**, the large red building not far from the church, contains a collection of local paraphernalia, including a Stone Age axe. **Hentilä museum** features old buildings that have been transferred from nearby locations.

WORTH THE TRIP

A great daytrip from Heinola is a visit to the Verla Mill, a complex of beautiful brick buildings enchantingly set by a stream about 40km southeast of Heinola. Built in 1882, it operated as a ground wood and board mill until 1964 and is incredibly well preserved, so much so that Unesco have listed it. Entry to the **Verla Mill Museum** (☎ 020-415 2170; adult/child €6/2; ☻ 10am-6pm Tue-Sun early-May–mid-Sep) is by guided tour (ring ahead to arrange an English one), and make sure you bring a picnic to have in the gardens or by one of the nearby lakes. If not, there's a café and restaurant here too. To get there, head just north of Heinola to the Kouvola turnoff, and follow that to Jaala, where there's a signposted left turn to Verla.

Sleeping & Eating

Messilä Estate (☎ 86011; www.messila.fi; s/d €98/115, 4-person cottages €185; ℗ ✗ ☎) This place offers plenty of choices. There are modern hotel rooms, characterful accommodation in the 'old storehouse', plus a holiday village with self-contained cottages. The several restaurants here serve everything from gourmet cuisine to burgers and beers, and this is a popular venue in summer for live music and dancing.

Camping Messila (☎ 753 7006; www.campingmessila.fi; tent sites €15, cottage €55-185) This is a beautifully equipped holiday park next to the estate on Vesijärvi, 7km west of Lahti. There's a little swimming beach, a good café with a beer terrace, and a jetty perfect for some light strolling or fishing. It's open year-round and offers a host of summer and winter activities. They even keep a hole open in the ice for a hardy post-sauna dip!

HEINOLA

☎ 03 / pop 20,910

Heinola is today overshadowed by Lahti to the south but is a much older town. It has a scenic waterfront setting, with the Jyrängönvirta River flowing through it. In addition to summer cultural attractions, Heinola serves as a starting point for scenic summer lake cruises. There's a **tourist office** (☎ 849 3615; Kauppakatu 10-12).

Heinola Ridge has a few attractions. The 1900 Harjupaviljonki pavilion is meant to look like a Japanese temple. In summer there is an art exhibition here. Nearby, the tower offers good views. The **Heinola Bird Zoo** (☎ 715 2916; admission free; ☻ 10am-4pm) is an aviary housing more than 500 species. It also acts as a hospital for sick or injured birds.

The **Sauna World Championships** in mid-August are a test and a half of endurance, with plenty of beer consumed.

Heinäsaari Camping (☎ 0500-491 637; tent sites €12-14, cabins and cottages €34-120) on Heinäsaari, 1.5km from the town centre, is a great location with a range of simple cabins and some pretty swish cottages.

Getting There & Away

There are buses roughly every 30 minutes from Lahti (€5.50 to €8, 20 to 40 minutes). Heinola is 136km north of Helsinki. Ferries from Lahti sail to Heinola in summer; see p191 for details.

AROUND HEINOLA
Onkiniemi

Situated around 25km north of Heinola on the road to Hartola, Onkiniemi is home to **Musta & Valkea Ratsu Nukketalot** (Black & White Horse Puppet House; ☎ 03-718 6959; Onkiniementie 222; ☻ noon-4pm). *Nukketalot* (puppet houses) are extremely popular with Finnish kids, and here you can meet the puppets and even make your own. A family has created more than 350 hand puppets – some appearing regularly on TV – and give daily theatre performances (adult/child €7/5). Most people fall totally in love with the place, the people and the puppets.

Turku & the Southwest

The closest mainland area to Sweden, the southwest is Finland's most historic area. It's centred around the noble port city of Turku, the seat of Finland's oldest university. Until the 19th century Turku was the nation's capital and it is a place redolent with history as well, as an important modern city and gateway to the country for ferry travellers.

It also is the jumping-off point for exploration of the myriad islands of the southwestern archipelago, which in summer shine like a galaxy of emeralds offshore. Some are accessible by road and ferries, but for others you'll need to charter or own a boat of your own. This is one of the areas of Finland where Swedish-speaking culture is strongest, reinforced by plenty of summer visitors from across the water. These visitors now come in peace, but once were fairly unwelcome arrivals, crusading inland from coastal bases and performing forcible baptisms on the Finnish tribes.

North from Turku are a series of picture-pretty coastal towns. Naantali is a popular family destination thanks to its theme park devoted to the much-loved Moomin trolls; further north, Uusikaupunki is so laid-back as to be almost horizontal. The citizens of Rauma managed to never burn the toast and send the whole town up, meaning that it boasts the best-preserved area of old wooden buildings in Finland. Beyond here, bigger Pori shakes off its workaday feel for an excellent summer jazz event, one of Finland's best festivals.

HIGHLIGHTS

- Reliving the past in medieval **Turku Castle** (p195), with its dungeons, extensive museums and magnificent banquet halls
- **Cruising the archipelago** (p199) from Turku to Naantali or Hanko
- Browsing in Naantali's quaint **Old Town** (p213), then dining on the marina or taking the kids to **Moominworld** (p212)
- Learning about productivity duels and giant Peruvian anchovies at the hilariously ironic **Bonk Dynamo Centre** (p218) in lovely Uusikaupunki
- Meeting the ghosts of the past at **Louhisaari Manor** (p216) in Askainen village – one of Finland's grandest manors
- Taking a walking tour of historic **Vanha Rauma** (p221), a Unesco World Heritage–listed living museum
- Partying at the annual week-long **Pori Jazz Festival** (p226) in July

★ Pori
★ Rauma
★ Uusikaupunki
Askainen ★
★ Naantali
★ Turku
★ Cruising the Archipelago

History

Due to its proximity to southern Sweden, this region became the first foothold of Swedish settlement and missionary activity in Finland. As Sweden's hold on the country increased, the port of Turku became an important Baltic trading port and gateway to the interior. It was the capital of Finland and its first university town, but the region's importance declined when Finland came under Russian control, as the tsars wanted the Finnish capital a bit closer to home where they could keep an eye on it!

Activities

The various archipelagos are much beloved of yachties in summer; even tiny islands have guest harbours that are well-equipped; you can also arrange charters in Turku. The area is also very well-suited to exploration by bicycle, and can be combined into a circular route through Åland via the Korpo–Kökar and Kustavi–Brändö archipelago ferries.

Self-Catering Accommodation

The southwest is a great place to get away from it all, and there are enough islands to go around that you may even get your own if you can arrange boat transport. The Turku tourist office (opposite) has a good selection, as does **Archipelago Booking** (☎ 465 1000; www.archipelagobooking.com).

TURKU

☎ 02 / pop 174, 824

This one-time capital of Finland has a very historic feel, being the country's oldest city. While hardly any mediaeval buildings remain, a visit to the doughty castle and superb archaeological museum will stimulate your imagination into populating the riverbanks with bustling crowds of merchants receiving and dispatching Baltic cargoes. The city really has a lot to offer, with an array of museums, and lively summers when the whole city seems to head for the small armada of boat bars moored in the heart of town. For many travellers Turku is their first taste of Finland, since frequent and inexpensive ferries ply the route between here and Stockholm via the Åland islands.

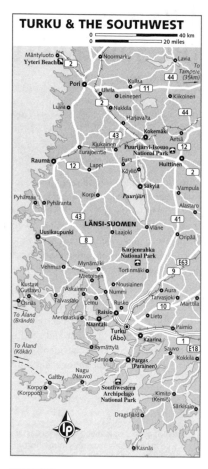

TURKU & THE SOUTHWEST

HISTORY

The region had its beginnings in 1229 when a Catholic settlement was founded at Koroinen, near the present centre of Turku. Work soon started on the new church (consecrated in 1300) and the Turku Castle. Both the early Catholic Church and the Swedish administration ran what is present-day Finland from Turku, which was at times the second-largest town in Sweden. Fire has destroyed Turku several times during the centuries.

Turku was named Åbo by Swedish settlers because it was a *bo* (settlement) on the Aura River (*å*). The Finnish name, Turku, is an archaic Russian word for 'marketplace' – the city's market has long been one of the

---

FINNISH OR SWEDISH?

Throughout this part of the country, places have two names, one Finnish, one Swedish. The official line states that, in places where there's a majority of Swedish-speaking Finns, the Swedish takes precedence. Hence, Pargas, where Swedish-speakers are more numerous, comes before the Finnish version Parainen, but Turku, which has more Finnish speakers, has its Swedish name, Åbo, in secondary position. However, be prepared to see and hear either one used!

---

largest and finest on the south coast. Turku has a thriving university – the first in Finland, founded in 1640 – a cultural spirit, and proud residents, some of whom are still irked that Helsinki took over as Finland's capital back in 1812. The longstanding joke among its loyal residents is that after Turku spread culture to the rest of Finland, it never returned. The number of art and antique shops around tend to contradict this though.

The city is also famous throughout Finland for its processed mustard; Turun Sinappi, though now controversially produced in Sweden, remains an icon of the summer barbecue.

ORIENTATION

The centre of Turku town is 3km northeast of the harbour, and is reached by bus from each arriving ferry. The city centre straddles the Aurajoki, and most things are within walking distance. The streets around the kauppatori (market square) are the heart of modern Turku and the riverbank is the scene of much of the city's lively social life.

INFORMATION
Bookshops
Akateeminen Kirjakauppa (Hansa Shopping Arcade, Yliopistonkatu) Stocks maps, English-language books and foreign newspapers.

Internet Access
Surf City (Aninkaistenkatu 3; per hr €2.40; ☼ noon-8pm Mon-Fri, 4-8pm Sat & Sun) Internet café and fax service; also sells international phone cards.
CyberCafé (Hansa Arcade; per hr €2.40; ☼ 9am-9pm Mon-Fri, 10am-9pm Sat & Sun) Automated Internet place with coin-operated computers.

Internet Resources
www.turku.fi The city website, with links to many attractions and businesses.
www.turkutouring.fi The city's tourist board website.
www.turunmuseot.fi Links to the web pages of the various museums in Turku.

Left Luggage
The train station offers a left-luggage counter and locker service, and there are more lockers (€2) located at the ferry terminal and Silja and Viking Line buildings.

Libraries
Public library (☎ 262 3611; Linnankatu 2; ☼ 11am-8pm Mon-Thu, 11am-6pm Fri, 11am-4pm Sat) Several free Internet terminals (maximum 15 minutes) and plenty of English books.

Money
Several banks located on the market square have 24-hour ATMs.
Forex (Eerikinkatu 12; ☼ 8am-7pm Mon-Fri, 9am-3pm Sat) Offering better rates than banks, this is the best place to change cash and travellers cheques.

Post
Main post office (Humalistonkatu 1; ☼ 9am-8pm Mon-Fri) Situated two blocks west of the kauppatori.

Tourist Information
Turku City Tourist Office (☎ 262 7444; www .turkutouring.fi; Aurakatu 4; ☼ 8.30am-6pm Mon-Fri, 9am-4pm Sat & Sun, 10am-3pm winter weekends) Busy, very helpful, information on entire region. Rents bikes (per day/week €10/50); free Internet access for short periods.

Travel Agencies
Citytours (☎ 251 0370; www.citytours.fi; Eerikinkatu 4) Finnair agent.
Kilroy Travels (☎ 273 7500; www.kilroytravels.com; Eerikinkatu 2; ☼ 10am-6pm Mon-Fri) Specialists in student and budget travel.

SIGHTS & ACTIVITIES
Turku Castle & Historical Museum
The mammoth **Turku Castle** (☎ 262 0300; admission €6.50, guided tours €1.50; ☼ 10am-6pm daily mid-Apr–mid-Sep, 10am-3pm Tue-Sun mid-Sep–mid-Apr), near the ferry terminals, is a must for everyone visiting the city and is one of the country's most popular tourist attractions. Founded in 1280 at the mouth of the Aurajoki, the

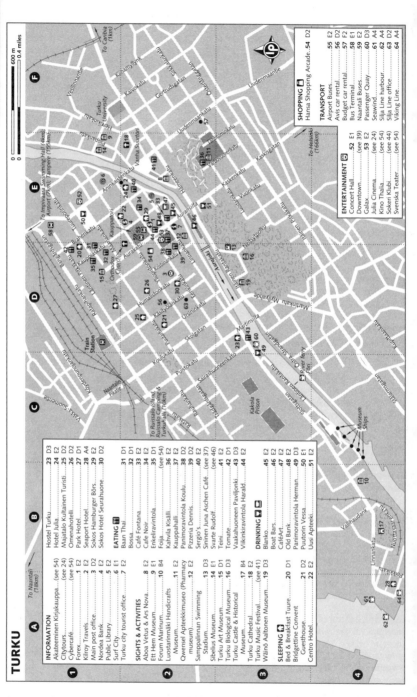

TURKU

TURKU & THE SOUTHWEST

To Naantali (18km)

0   600 m
0   0.4 miles

INFORMATION	
Akateeminen Kirjakauppa	(see 54)
Citytours	(see 54)
Cybercafé	(see 54)
Forex	1 E2
Kilroy Travels	2 E2
Main post office	3 D2
Nordea Bank	4 E2
Public Library	5 E2
Surf City	6 E1
Turku city tourist office	7 E2

SIGHTS & ACTIVITIES	
Aboa Vetus & Ars Nova	8 E2
Ett Hem Museum	9 E1
Forum Marinum	10 B4
Luostarinmäki Handicrafts Museum	11 E2
Qwensel Apteekkimuseo (Pharmacy museum)	12 E2
Samppalinnan Swimming Stadium	13 D3
Sibelius Museum	14 E1
Turku Art Museum	15 D1
Turku Biological Museum	16 D3
Turku Castle & Historical Museum	17 B4
Turku Cathedral	18 E2
Turku Music Festival	(see 41)
Wäinö Aaltonen Museum	19 D3

SLEEPING	
Bed & Breakfast Tuure	20 D1
Bridgettine Convent Guesthouse	21 D2
Centro Hotel	22 E2
Hostel Turku	23 D3
Hotel Julia	24 E2
Majatalo Kultainen Turisti	25 D2
Omenahotelli	26 D2
Park Hotel	27 D1
Seaport Hotel	28 A4
Sokos Hamburger Börs	29 E2
Sokos Hotel Seurahuone	30 D2

EATING	
Baan Thai	31 D1
Bossa	32 D1
Café Fontana	33 E2
Cafe Noir	34 E2
Enkeliravintola	35 D1
Foija	(see 54)
Kahvila Kisälli	36 E2
Kauppahalli	37 E2
Panimoravintola Koulu	38 D2
Pizzeria Dennis	39 D2
Sergio's	40 E2
Sininen Juna Aschen Café	(see 37)
Svarte Rudolf	(see 46)
Teini	41 E2
Tomate	42 D1
Vaakahuoneen Paviljonki	43 D3
Vikinkiravintola Harald	44 E2

DRINKING	
Blanko	45 E2
Boat Bars	46 E2
CaféArt	47 E2
Old Bank	48 E2
Panimoravintola Herman	49 D3
Puutori Vessa	50 E1
Uusi Apteeki	51 E2

ENTERTAINMENT	
Concert Hall	52 E1
Downtown	53 E2
Galax	(see 39)
Julia Cinema	(see 24)
Kino Thalia	(see 54)
Sokeri Klubi	(see 44)
Svenska Teater	(see 54)

SHOPPING	
Hansa Shopping Arcade	54 D2

TRANSPORT	
Airport Buses	55 E2
Avis car rental	56 D2
Budget car rental	57 F2
Bus Terminal	58 E1
Naantali Buses	59 E2
Passenger Quay	60 D3
Seawind	61 A4
Silja Line harbour	62 A4
Silja Line office	63 D2
Viking Line	64 A4

TURKU CARD

Like the Helsinki Card, the Turku Card gives admission to most museums and attractions in the region, public transport and various other discounts for a set period. The 24-hour card costs €21, the 48-hour card is €28, and a 24-hour family card (two adults and three kids) is €40. You can buy the card at the tourist office or from most participating attractions, and it's valid from the first time you use it.

castle has been growing ever since. Notable occupants have included Count Per Brahe, founder of many towns in Finland, who lived here in the 17th century, and Sweden's King Eric XIV, who was imprisoned in the castle's Round Tower in the late 16th century, having been declared insane.

Highlights include two dungeons and magnificent banqueting halls, as well as a fascinating historical museum of medieval Turku in a maze of restored rooms in the castle's old bailey. A series of models in the main part of the castle shows its growth from a simple island fortress to medieval castle.

Guided tours of the stronghold area are given hourly in English. They give a good account of the castle's history but do not visit the Renaissance rooms on the upper floor, or the extensive museums in the bailey section of the castle, so you should allow time to explore those yourself, before or after a tour.

Luostarinmäki Handicrafts museum

The name 'handicrafts museum' gives little indication of how fascinating this open-air **museum** (☎ 262 0350; admission €3.40; ⊙ 10am-6pm daily mid-Apr–mid-Sep, 10am-3pm Tue-Sun mid-Sep–mid-Apr) really is. It is made up of the only surviving 18th-century area of this medieval town – Turku has been razed by fire 30 times – and all the buildings are still in their original locations, unlike most Finnish open-air museums where the buildings are moved from elsewhere, or re-created. Carpenters, stonemasons, jewellers and other workers built homes and shops in the area, beginning in 1779. When the great fire of 1827 destroyed most of Turku, Luostarinmäki neighbourhood was one of the few that survived.

Since 1940 it has served as a museum, but doesn't feel like one: it's more like stepping back in time. There are about 30 furnished workshops altogether, including a printing press, silversmith, watchmaker, bakery and cigar shop. In summer, artisans in period costume work inside the old wooden houses and musicians stroll its paths. There are guided tours in English given roughly hourly from 10.30am to 4.30pm in the height of summer. There's also a good café, and a gift shop selling products made in the village.

Turku Cathedral

Towering over the river and town, **Turku Cathedral** (cathedral & museum ⊙ 9am-7pm mid-Sep–mid-Apr, 9am-8pm mid-Apr–mid-Sep) is one of Finland's most important churches. Consecrated in 1300, much of the building has been rebuilt over the centuries after frequent fire damage. The interior is immensely high, with towering wall arches and a lofty vaulted nave. The side chapels hold tombs of Finnish and Swedish war heroes; many of these are names that ring loud in the history of this region. In one chapel rests Catherine Mansdotter, Queen of Sweden, wife of the unfortunate Erik XIV. The retable and pulpit were designed by the famous German architect CL Engel (who also built the Orthodox church on the market square).

The **cathedral museum** (admission €2) displays models showing different stages of the cathedral's construction from the 14th century, as well as medieval sculptures and various valuable religious paraphernalia.

Most Tuesday evenings the cathedral offers live music, and English-language services are held at 4pm every Sunday.

Opposite the cathedral, the **Vanha Suurtori** was once the main town square. It's surrounded by elegant buildings; the old town hall and trading mansions. A cobbled courtyard holds a book café; a peaceful spot on a sunny day.

Forum Marinum

This excellent **maritime museum** (☎ 282 9511; www.forum-marinum.fi; Linnankatu 72; admission €7, with museum ships €12; ⊙ 11am-7pm daily May-Sep, 10am-6pm Tue-Sun Oct-Apr) is set back from the riverfront near the castle. The permanent exhibition is housed in an old granary and has a comprehensive look at different aspects of ships and shipping, including scale models, full-size vessels – check out the hydrocopter, WWII torpedoes and multimedia displays (including a puzzling account of a Crimean War naval engagement in which not very much happened!). The newer building opposite has regular exhibitions, as well as several vessels and a cabin from a luxury cruise-liner; Turku's shipyards produce some of the classiest of these. There's a good café and shop in the foyer.

Outside, anchored in the river, are four **museum ships** (☯ 11am-7pm Jun-Aug; per boat €5, all boats & museum €12) which you can climb aboard and poke around in, above and below deck. The WWII mine layer *Keihässalmi* and the corvette *Karjala* give an insight into wartime conditions at sea; the beautiful three-masted barque *Sigyn*, originally launched from Göteborg in 1887, has well preserved cabins; and the impressive 1902 sailing ship *Suomen Joutsen* (Swan of Finland), which was built in France, was used by the Finnish Navy during WWII as a mother ship for submarines and as a hospital.

Aboa Vetus & Ars Nova Museums

These twin **museums** (☎ 250 0552; Itäinen Rantakatu 4-6; admission €8; ☯ 11am-7pm, closed Mon mid-Sep–Mar) are under one roof. Ars Nova is a museum of contemporary art with temporary exhibitions, the highlight of which is the Turku Biennaali, a themed display held in summer in odd years. Aboa Vetus is an absolutely fascinating museum of archaeology. You descend into the excavated remains of medieval Turku; these are brought to life by lively commentary, plenty of information and activities for kids, and replica items that make sense of the fragments. It's an amazing achievement that deserves the highest praise. There are free guided tours in English at 11.30am in July and August. Outside, on the riverbank, is a memorial to Herman Spöring, a Turku man who sailed with Cook on his discovery of Australia; some islands off New Zealand are named after him.

Turun Taidemuseo

Recently re-opened, the excellent **Turku Art Museum** (☎ 262 7100; Aurakatu 26; adult/child €6/free; ☯ 11am-7pm Tue-Fri, 11am-5pm Sat & Sun; &) is in a striking granite building with elaborately carved pilasters, conical turrets and a polished iron hat. The majority of the art is from the last century or so; the 'Turku school' was

one of Finland's most influential art movements; look out for works by Ilmari Kaijala and Emil Rautala among others. Two famous tempera works by Akseli Gallen-Kallela, a friend of Sibelius, vividly depict scenes from the Kalevala, while pointillist landscapes by William Finch, a series of bronze Finnish animals by Jussi Mäntynen, Finnish scenes painted by Victor Westerholm and an enchanting family of pigs by Harro Koskinen are other things to look out for.

Sibelius Museum

Near the cathedral the **Sibelius Museum** (☎ 215 4494; Piispankatu 17; admission €3; ☯ 11am-4pm Tue-Sun, 11am-3pm & 6-8pm Wed) displays some 350 musical instruments from around the world in a landmark 1960s building, and exhibits memorabilia of the famous Finnish composer Jean Sibelius. It is the most extensive musical museum in Finland. You can listen to Sibelius' music on record or, better still, attend a Wednesday evening concert (every Wednesday from September to May, less often in summer).

Qwensel apteekkimuseo

On the riverfront this, the oldest surviving **wooden house** (☎ 262 0280; Läntinen Rantakatu 13; admission €3.40; ☯ 10am-6pm daily mid-Apr–mid-Sep, 10am-3pm Tue-Sun mid-Sep–mid-Apr) in Turku, was built around 1700, and now houses the small **Pharmacy Museum**. You can see an old laboratorium with aromatic herbs, fine 18th-century furnishings with hints of 'Gustavian' (Swedish) style, and an exhibition of bottles and other pharmacy items.

Other Museums

In a beautiful building, the **Turku Biological Museum** (☎ 262 0340; Neitsytpolku 1; admission €3.40; ☯ 10am-6pm mid-Apr–mid-Sep, 10am-3pm Tue-Sun mid-Sep–mid-Apr) is surprisingly interesting and superbly presented, if you don't mind staring at stuffed beasts.

Ett Hem Museum (☎ 215 4279; Piispankatu 14; admission €3; ☯ noon-3pm Tue-Sun May-Sep) preserves a wealthy turn-of-the-20th-century home, with furniture of various styles, and works by famous painters Albert Edelfelt and Helene Schjerfbeck.

The **Wäinö Aaltonen Museum** (☎ 262 0850; www.wam.fi; Itäinen Rantakatu 38; admission €4; ☯ 11am-7pm Tue-Sun) displays permanent exhibitions of this famous artist's paintings and sculptures.

Its temporary exhibitions are of contemporary art.

Cruises
Archipelago cruises are a popular activity in Turku during summer. There are day trips around the islands as well as evening dinner-and-dance cruises. Most departures are from the quay at Martinsilta bridge.

The historic steamship **SS Ukkopekka** (☎ 515 3300; www.ukkopekka.fi) cruises to Naantali (one way/return €15/20, 10am and 2pm, daily, early June to late August). The trip takes 1¾ hours and you can have lunch on board (€10 to €13). If you'd rather party on board, there's an evening dinner-dance cruise, departing at 7pm Monday to Saturday from mid-May to late August (€28 to €43). The meals (starters plus buffet) are served on dry land – on the island of Loistokari.

Less atmospheric, but good value, the **M/S Rudolfina** (☎ 250 2995; www.rudolfina.fi) runs 90-minute lunch and dinner cruises from only €19, including a buffet meal. More leisurely are the evening cruises, departing at 7pm from Monday to Saturday and taking three hours to Naantali Bay and back (€26).

The **M/S Lily** (☎ 469 2500; www.rosita.fi) cruises out to Vepsa island three times daily from mid-June to mid-August (€9.50 return, one hour each way) and as far as Maisaari on Friday and Sunday evening (€14.50, four hours total). In May and September, cruises are Friday to Sunday only. Rosita also has cruises to Bengtskär island on scheduled Saturdays in May, June and August (€45, 12 hours). The full-day return cruise includes guide fees and entry to the island.

SS *Franz Hoijer* takes off north to Uusikaupunki and south to Hanko once a week – see p211 for information.

Cycling
The city tourist office can suggest cycling routes and publishes an excellent free *pyörätiekartta* (bike route map) of the city and surrounding towns. You can rent bikes from them per day/week for €10/50; Hostel Turku (see Sleeping) is another of several places to offer this.

Swimming & Sauna
At the **Samppalinnan outdoor swimming stadium** (☎ 262 3590; Samppalinnanvuori, admission €3; late May-late Aug), the entry fee includes a sauna and use of the 50m pool with diving boards. In winter, go to the indoor **Impivaara swimming hall** (☎ 262 3588; Uimahallinpolku 4; €3.50; 10am-5pm) for swimming and sauna, north of the city centre (take bus 13 to Impivaara).

FESTIVALS & EVENTS
The **Turku Music Festival**, held during the second week of August, is a feast of classical and contemporary music and opera. Venues include the Turku Castle and the cathedral and tickets cost €10 to €30. For further information contact the **Turku Music Festival Foundation** (☎ 251 1162; www.turkumusicfestival.fi; Uudenmaankatu 1, 20500 Turku).

Quite different is **Ruisrock** (www.ruisrock.fi), Finland's oldest and largest annual rock festival, held since 1969. The festival takes place over two days in early June at the recreational park on Ruissalo island. Tickets cost from €35 to €50.

Keskiajan Turku, held over a summer weekend (variable date), is the festival of medieval Turku. It's a fantastic four days of pageantry, banqueting, fencing and outrageous costumes, with plenty of actors adding authenticity. Events take place at the market square, Turku Castle, the cathedral and Aboa Vetus museum. Inquire at the city tourist office about the festival programme and tickets.

Paavo Nurmi Marathon, named after the legendary distance runner, one of Turku's favourite sons, is a big event in late June/early July. It attracts an international field as well as hundreds of marathon-mad Finns. The course begins in the town centre and goes out to Ruissalo island. There's a statue of Nurmi on the south side of the river.

SLEEPING
Budget
Bed & Breakfast Tuure (☎ 233 0230; Tuureporinkatu 17C; s/d €37/50; P ✕ 💻) Very handy for the bus station and close to the market square, this tidy and friendly guesthouse makes an excellent place to stay. The rooms are bright and thoughtfully decorated, you get your own keys, and there's microwave, fridge, and free Internet use for guests. A well-fed cat shares the premises!

Hostel Turku (☎ 262 7680; www.turku.fi/hostel turku; Linnankatu 39; dm/s/d €14/33.50/38; reception 6-10am & 3pm-midnight; P ✕) This HI-affiliated place is well located on the river close to the town centre and is spacious and friendly. Reception is friendly, there's a decent kitchen, laundry, lockers, and bike hire (per day/week €10/50). It gets very busy with school groups and backpackers in summer, so it's worth booking ahead. Linen and breakfast each cost €4.50 extra. From the train station, it's about a 10-minute walk downhill; from the bus station and harbour take bus 1.

Omenahotelli (www.omenahotelli.fi; Humalistonkatu 7; r €55; ☎ ☒) Although the building is designed by Finnish architect Alvar Aalto, it's fair to say it wasn't one of his best. It's now part of this good-value Internet-booked chain. You get a keycode when you make a booking; there are no staff. Terminals in the lobby also allow you to book. The rooms are good, sleeping up to four as there's a fold-out sofa, as well as TV and bathroom.

Ruissalo Camping (☎ 262 5100; fax 262 5101; camp sites €10, plus per person €4, 2-/4-person r €30/55; ☼ Jun-Aug) Situated on Ruissalo island, 10km west of the city centre, this place has a variety of rooms as well as saunas, a cafeteria and nice beaches – including a nude beach. It gets packed for the Ruisrock festival and at Midsummer. Bus 8 runs from the market square in the centre to the camping ground.

Majatalo Kultainen Turisti (☎ 250 0265; Käsityöläiskatu 11; s/d €40/50) This comfortable guesthouse is handy for the train station. While the public areas are decorated in a slightly fussy style, the rooms are simpler and pleasant enough, although the welcome isn't exactly effusive. There are also higher standard, hotel-style rooms available (single/double €50/65). It's above a set of shops.

Midrange

Centro Hotel (☎ 469 0469; www.centrohotel.com; Yliopistonkatu 12; s/d €86/96, Sat, Sun, & summer €61/72; ☎ ☒ ☐) Right in the heart of town but quiet, this is a very likeable place with top-class friendly service and attention to detail. The rooms are gleaming, with polished parquetry floors and large windows. For an extra €10, you can get a 'superior' room with a few extra touches like wood panelling and extravagant bedside lamps. Best of all is the breakfast spread, which has been heartily endorsed by readers.

Bridgettine Convent Guesthouse (☎ 250 1910; birgitta.turku@kolumbus.fi; Ursininkatu 15A; s/d €42/61; ☎ ☒) Catholics are thin on the ground in Finland, but this small community of

---

nuns is well worth seeking out, for their guesthouse offers substantial comfort. The rate includes breakfast, and the rooms are spacious, with pine floorboards, phone and bedside lamps. Silence is expected around the corridors and reception areas after 10pm. It's wise to book ahead.

Sokos Hamburger Börs (☎ 337 381; www.sokosho tels.fi; Kauppiaskatu 6; economy r/r €106/146, Sat, Sun & summer €71/94; ☎ ☒ ☐ ☎ ☒) Overlooking the market square is the town's largest hotel. The rooms are spacious, with standard business facilities (including wireless Internet); ask for one close to the lifts if you have mobility difficulties – it's a big building! The annexe across the road offers the same standard of comfort at a significant saving. There are suites with their own sauna (around €300) and a huge array of restaurants and bars attached. After 6pm they offer an excellent 'last minute' rate (saving more than 50%) if there is availability; during the week there's quite a good chance of this.

Hotel Julia (☎ 336 000; www.scandic-hotels.fi; Eerikinkatu 4; s/d €93/117, Sat, Sun & summer €69/79; ☎ ☒ ☐ ☒) Just off the market square, this is one of the better hotels in Turku. As it's situated in a modern block, the wood-beamed reception is surprising, but the rooms are light, with bright bedspreads and big windows. The bathrooms are a touch small, but there's wireless Internet access and a free sauna included with the weekday rate.

Sokos Hotel Seurahuone (☎ 337 301; www.soko shotels.fi; Eerikinkatu 23; s/d €95/116, d Sat, Sun & summer €77-78, ste €220; ☎ ☒ ☐ ☒) The sister Sokos hotel is more peaceful though the rooms

(Continued on page 209)

JONATHAN SMITH

Olympic Stadium tower (p66), Helsinki

Memorial Mask, Sibelius Monument (p70), Helsinki

WAYNE WALTON

Alfresco dining at the harbour market cafés (p75), Helsinki

VERONICA GARBUTT

Kiasma Museum of Contemporary Art (p62), Helsinki

Tuomiokirkko (p66), Helsinki

Monuments to the musicians of Finland (p58), Helsinki

Kauppahalli (p70), Helsinki

WAYNE WALTON

JONATHAN SMITH

Marina, near Senaatintori (p68), Helsinki

Chess has never been so cool, Helsinki (p57)

WAYNE WALTON

204

Open-air museum (p64), Seurasaari

WAYNE WALTON

WAYNE WALTON

Residential apartments,
Suomenlinna (p84)

Shore houses (p88), Porvoo

VERONICA G

WAYNE WALTON

Olavinlinna Castle (p116), Savonlinna

CRAIG PERSHOUSE

Convent Church (p213), Naantali

Tengmalm's Owl, one of several owl species (p42) in Finland

DAVID TIPLING

JOHN BORTHWICK

Arktikum (p298), Rovaniemi

Inner city Tampere (p169)

JOHN MCLEAN

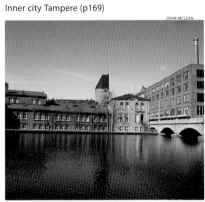

Kauppahalli, Turku (p70)

STEP

Oulanka National Park (p288)

Pine sapling, Oulu (p266)

Partly frozen river, Kuusamo (p283)

Speed sign for snowmobiles, Levi (p305)

Sámi herder, Rovaniemi (p324)

Traditional open boat on the Kemijoki, Rovaniemi (p298)

(Continued from page 200)

have similar facilities, including digital films, mini-bar, and wireless Internet; the twins are much roomier than the doubles. There's a business centre, free sauna and helpful service. Disabled access areas are limited.

Seaport Hotel (☎ 283 3000; www.hotelseaport.fi; Matkustajasatama; s/d €76/86, Sat, Sun & summer €59/69; P ✕) This is an attractive hotel in a low restored harbour warehouse, right next to the Viking Line and Silja Line terminals, perfect for early-morning departures or late arrivals. Rooms are welcoming, with pine floors and homely wooden furniture. There's also a restaurant and friendly service. Bus 1 will take you into the centre.

EATING
Restaurants
FINNISH

Enkeliravintola (☎ 231 8088; Kauppiaskatu 16; mains €13-20; ✕ dinner Tue-Fri, lunch & dinner Sat & Sun) This delightful spot is tucked away in a corner near the art museum. The name means 'angel restaurant', and you can't get away from the theme; the ethereal beings are everywhere you look, and the dishes are named for them too. The food includes steaks, duck and an excellent mutton with garlic. Child-friendly.

Vaakahuoneen Paviljonki (☎ 515 3324; Linnankatu 38; mains €7-18, fish buffet €9; ✕ food served 11am-10pm May-Aug) While the floating bars may be good for drink and socializing, this is *the* place to go for great value food and entertainment. As well as an à la carte menu of snacks, pasta, pizzas and steak, there's are daily buffets in summer, one with 'archipelago fish', and another varying Asian cuisines. On top of this it's on the riverfront and there's live music, usually traditional jazz, most days in spring and summer.

Teini (☎ 223 0203; Uudenmaankatu 1; mains €13-24; ✕ lunch & dinner) A city institution for traditional Finnish food. It has a mind-boggling array of dining halls and smaller rooms. Grilling things, be it fish or steaks, is what they do best, and it's pretty good value for the quality on offer: a fine chateaubriand, for example, comes in at €19.90.

Foija (☎ 251 8665; Aurakatu 10; mains €12-22; ✕ 11am-11pm) It's quite a surprise to descend under the Hansa shopping centre and discover this gently-lit, brick-vaulted space. It's been a restaurant for over 150 years,

and these days is a favourite for tasty steaks, but also has several elegant options.

Svarte Rudolf (☎ 250 4567; Leirikatu 7; mains €10-18; ✕ lunch & dinner) This is the fanciest of the floating restaurants moored on the south side of the Aurajoki. The speciality is seafood, which goes well with the nautical theme, and the below deck dining room is elegant. There's a daily lunch buffet which is great value at €8.90 during the week and on Saturday/Sunday €12/16.

Viikinkiravintola Harald (☎ 276 5050; Aurakatu 3; mains €16-22; ✕ lunch & dinner) A theme restaurant where you get to mix it with Norse warriors and eat with your hands. There's a variety of set meals (from €24) and all sorts of period paraphernalia on the walls. Plenty of fun; after all, in Valhalla there are no hangovers.

Panimoravintola Koulu (☎ 274 5757; Eerikinkatu 18; mains €12-20; ✕ 11am-midnight Mon-Sat) This is in an enormous former schoolhouse built in 1889, complete with desks and inkwells. Upstairs is an upmarket restaurant, downstairs a brewery pub and a large beer garden, complete with minigolf course. There are good-value lunches served here.

INTERNATIONAL

Sergio's (☎ 233 0068; Läntinen Rantakatu 27; pizzas €8-12, mains €13-20; ✕ 11am-11pm Mon-Fri, 1-11pm Sat, 1-9pm Sun; ✕) This stylish Italian restaurant and café is a cut above most of its kind. The outside tables are well poised to have a drink and do some Turku-watching. The mains are classy, the pizzas good value and there's a good selection of Italian wines.

Pizzeria Dennis (☎ 469 1191; Linnankatu 17; pizza/pasta €8-11; ✕ lunch & dinner) This place doesn't look much from the outside, but within is a warren of cosy rooms adorned with Chianti bottles and strings of garlic. There's a long and innovative range of pizzas and pasta, but you're better sticking to the tried and tested combinations: there's a good reason you don't see parmesan cheese and curry sauce together more often! Enthusiastic service.

Bossa (☎ 251 5880; Kauppiaskatu 12; mains €16-19; ✕ 4-11pm Mon-Fri, noon-11pm Sat, 2-9pm Sun) This is probably the only Brazilian restaurant in Finland. While the sleek, intimate contemporary styling doesn't exactly evoke Rio, the food is authentic. The hearty *caldo de feijão* is the broth of a black-bean stew, while main dishes are large, colourful and tasty. There's live music most Tuesdays.

Baan Thai (☎ 233 8290; Kauppiaskatu 15; dishes €6-12; ☉ 11am-9pm Mon-Thu, 11am-10pm Fri & Sat, noon-9pm Sun) This is an authentic and intimate little Thai restaurant a short walk north of the kauppatori. With a fairly down-to-earth interior (the trellised grapevine is a little out of place) and no-nonsense service, the dishes are tasty, if a little mild by Southeast Asian standards. The lunch buffet at €5.50 during the week is a bargain.

Tomate (☎ 4885 5511; Brahenkatu 20; mains €12-18; ☉ 11am-11pm Mon-Fri, noon-midnight Sat, 1-9pm Sun) This cheerful pseudo-Spanish restaurant is decorated with colourful tablecloths and cases of Iberian wine, of which there's a good selection. It's run with enthusiasm – there are regular Spanish events and wine tastings as well. The food is good, with decent steaks and tasty tapas (a selection of three €6.50). There's an outdoor summer terrace.

Cafés

Cafe Fontana (cnr Aurakatu & Linnankatu; ☉ 9am-8pm Mon-Sat, noon-6pm Sun) This place, in the heart of the city, is an Art Nouveau café with delicious pastries and pies. Inside there are large, elegant wooden tables and comfortable chairs, while outside is a terrace in the heart of things.

Sininen Juna Aschan Café (kauppahalli) This is a neat little café where you sit in a converted train carriage. The name translates as 'blue train'. It's run by a famous Turku bakery, which supplies the delicious bread, buns, and cakes

Cafe Noir (Eerikinkatu 8; meals €5-10; ☉ Tue-Sat 11am-7pm) While it's far from fancy, the Noir is a Turku institution and one of the cheapest sit-down places to eat. It's very cheap, with simple but filling plates such as meatballs or spaghetti with salad going for as little as €5.90; the eclectic menu also includes pizza, schnitzel, chicken curry and omelettes.

At the entrance to the Luostarinmäki Handicrafts Museum, Kahvila Kisälli is a large, cheery café in a historic 1851 building. It's a good spot to stop for coffee after visiting the museum; they also do tasty slices of pancake with strawberry jam.

Quick Eats

Cheap eats abound in the city centre, in the **kauppahalli** (covered market; Eerikinkatu; ☉ 7am-5.30pm

Mon-Fri, 7am-3pm Sat) and around the **kauppatori** (market square; ☉ 8am-4pm May-Sep). In particular, the outdoor market (held Monday to Saturday in summer) is superb for fresh fruit and vegetables and smoked fish. Look for kebab stands and grillis around the market square, on Aurakatu and Yliopistonkatu. Hesburger restaurants – Finland's answer to McDonald's – are everywhere in Turku, which is hardly surprising since the chain was born here.

DRINKING

In summer the heart of Turku's nightlife is along the river. The evening usually begins on many of the boats lining the south bank of the river. Although some of these also serve food, they are primarily floating beer terraces with music and lots of shipboard socializing. Hard-up young locals drink on the grassy riverbank nearby. Popular boats on the south side of the river include the upmarket *Donna*, and the down-to-earth *Papa Joe* and *Cindy*.

Uusi Apteekki (☎ 250 2595; Kaskenkatu 1; ☉ 10am-3am) South of the river is a wonderful bar in a converted old pharmacy; the antique shelving and desks have been retained, but they are filled with hundreds of old beer bottles. Bags of character.

CaféArt (Läntinen Rantakatu 5; ☉ 11am-7pm Mon-Sat, noon-7pm Sun) In a noble old waterfront building on one of Turku's most pleasant stretches, this hospitable café has tables out along the river, as well as two elegant interior salons. There's good espresso, as well as art exhibitions on the walls.

Blanko (☎ 233 3966; Aurakatu 1; ☉ bar until 1am weeknights, 3am weekends) Next to the bridge and opposite the tourist office is the ultra-chic Blanko, where Turku's gorgeous young things shake their booty to DJs on Friday and Saturday night; it's also a decent if overpriced lunch or dinner spot, with tables outside by the river, and dishes like Caesar salad (€11) and a range of pastas (€12 to €18).

Old Bank (Aurakatu 3, cnr Linnankatu; ☉ until 1am, later at weekends) This was once a bank but is now a boisterous Irish pub that attracts a slightly older drinking crowd, and has a huge range of beers to satisfy connoisseurs.

Panimoravintola Koulu (☎ 274 5757; Eerikinkatu 18) This is a great brewery pub in the town centre (see p209). There are three home-grown brews on tap including a fine stout.

Panimoravintola Herman (☎ 230 3333; Läntinen Rantakatu 37) This is another brewery pub–restaurant fronting the river near Hostel Turku. It's a lot smaller than Koulu but is part of a busy little waterfront area. As well as tasty beer, it does very posh pub grub.

Puutorin Vessa (☎ 233 8123; Puutori; ☺ noon-midnight) Near the bus terminal, this bar is unusually set in what was formerly a public loo! There's toilet humour and paraphernalia on the walls and a sunny terrace.

ENTERTAINMENT
Nightclubs

Galax (☎ 284 3300; Aurakatu 6; ☺ 9pm-3 or 4am). This giant venue is also a café and restaurant, but is of most interest for its nightclub, which covers several levels and has live music and DJs most weekends.

Sokeri Klubi (☎ 276 5700; www.sokeriklubi.com; Aurakatu 3; ☺ 10pm-4am Thu-Sat) Across the road from the Galax, this has a more cutting-edge DJ scene and fills to the brim with Turku's young, bright, and restless at weekends.

Cinema

Julia (☎ 0600 007 007; Eerikinkatu 4) Central cinema in the same building as the hotel of the same name.

Kino Thalia (☎ 237 9400, Hansa Centre) Shows more off-beat films and arthouse releases.

Music & Theatre

Concert Hall (☎ 262 0800; Aninkaistenkatu 9; tickets usually €7-16) The Turku Philharmonic Orchestra is one of the oldest in Europe – it was founded in the 1790s. The orchestra performs here.

Vaakahuoneen Pavijonki (☎ 515 3324; Linnankatu 38) There's live jazz most days at this place at the passenger quay.

Downtown (Linnankatu 17) For live rock music, this slightly down-at-heel place on the corner by Pizzeria Dennis, is an excellent choice, and open until 4am at weekends.

Svenska Teater (☎ 277 7377; Eerikinkatu 13) Next to the Hansa Shopping Arcade, this is one of the oldest theatres in Finland and it hosts well known musicals with performances in Swedish.

GETTING THERE & AWAY
Air

Finnair flies to Turku from a number of Finnish cities and some European capitals, including Stockholm. Domestic flights are generally at least once a day but more often to Helsinki, Mariehamn, Tampere, Rovaniemi and Oulu. The **Finnair office** (☎ 415 4909) is at the airport (see also Travel Agencies, p195)

Boat

Turku is a major gateway to Finland from Sweden and Åland and smaller boats ply the waters up and down the coast. The MS *Franz Höijer* (☎ 241 1850; www.surfnet.fi/saaristoristeilyt) travels from Turku to Hanko (10am, Wednesday) and to Uusikaupunki (10am, Friday) from mid-May to mid-August. Both trips take eight hours one way and cost only €12.

SWEDEN & ÅLAND

The harbour, southwest of the centre, has terminals for **Silja Line** (☎ 335 255; www.silja.com), **Viking Line** (☎ 333 1331; www.vikingline.fi) and **Seawind** (☎ 210 2800). Ferries sail to Turku from Stockholm (11 hours) and Mariehamn (six hours). Prices vary widely according to season and class of service, with deck class one-way tickets ranging from €14 to €35. Finnlink (see p215) offers a faster but pricier service from nearby Naantali.

Purchase tickets from one of the offices at the harbour, from the Viking Line office in the Hansa Shopping Arcade, or from Silja Lines on Käsityöläiskatu; you should book ahead during the high season if you plan to take a car or if you're travelling on a weekend (or Friday night). Bus 1 travels between the market square and the harbour. There are also connecting trains and buses from other cities that stop at the harbour itself.

See p346 for more details about international ferry travel.

Bus

From the bus terminal at Aninkaistentulli there are hourly express buses to Helsinki (€28.10, 2½ hours), and frequent services to Tampere (€25.60, three hours), Rauma (€13.70, 1½ hours) and other points in southern Finland. Regional buses depart from the kauppatori.

Train

Turku is the terminus for the southeastern railway line. The train station is a short walk northwest of the centre; trains also stop at the ferry harbour and at Kupittaa train station east of the centre. Bus 32 shuttles between the centre and the main train station. Express trains run frequently to and from Helsinki (€24.90, two hours), Tampere (€22.70, 1¾ hours), Oulu (€62.50, six to nine hours), Rovaniemi (€71.40, 10 to 14 hours). For Oulu and Rovaniemi there's usually a change in Tampere.

GETTING AROUND
To/From the Airport

Bus 1 runs between the kauppatori and the airport, about 8km north of the city, every 15 minutes from 5am to midnight Monday to Friday, from 5.30am to 9.30pm Saturday and from 7am to midnight Sunday (€2, 25 minutes). This same bus also goes from the kauppatori to the harbour.

Bus

City and regional buses are frequent and you pay €2 for a two-hour ticket or €4.50 for a 24-hour ticket. Important city bus routes include bus 1 (harbour-kauppatori-bus station-airport) and buses 32 and 42 (train station-kauppatori).

Car Hire

There are several car rental offices, among them **Avis** (☎ 231 1333; Käsityöläiskatu 7B) and **Budget** (☎ 233 4040; Sirkkalankatu 15).

Ferry

There's a small passenger and bike ferry that crosses the river a few blocks downstream from the last bridge. It's the last crossing point, and runs from May to September (free).

AROUND TURKU

NAANTALI
☎ 02 / pop 13, 818

With water lapping at its wooden mooring-posts in front of picturesque timber houses, Naantali (Swedish: Nådendal) is one of Finland's most idyllic port towns and makes a great, and popular, day-trip destination from Turku – it's only 18km away.

Once you get over the shock of the summertime crowds – and the fact that the majority of them are making a beeline for a children's theme park – it's difficult not to like Naantali. The compact boat-filled harbour is ringed with pleasant cafés and restaurants, the cobbled Old Town has a quaint (if slightly dressed up) old-world feel,

and there's plenty of sights and shopping to occupy an afternoon. The main attraction for all those Finnish families is Moominworld, a theme park celebrating characters from the storybooks by Tove Jansson. Out of season, Naantali is pretty quiet, and feels a little like a filmset after the actors have gone home.

History

Naantali grew around the Catholic Convent of the Order of Saint Birgitta, which was founded in 1443. After Finland became Protestant in 1527, the convent was dissolved and Naantali had to struggle for its existence; the convent had been important not only spiritually but also economically. When the pilgrims no longer came to town, people had to find other means of making a living, notably by knitting socks, which became Naantali's main export.

Orientation

Naantali sprawls on both sides of the channel Naantalinsalmi. The island of Luonnonmaa is on the southwest side of the channel, accessible by bridge, and the mainland, with the town centre, is on the northeast side. The old part of Naantali surrounds the harbour, 1km west of the bus terminal.

Information

Library Free Internet access on the 2nd floor of the post office building.

Tourist service (Naantalin Matkailu; ☎ 435 9800; info@naantalinmatkailu.fi; Kaivotori 2; ☒ 9am-6pm Mon-Fri, 10am-3pm Sat & Sun mid-Jun–mid-Aug, 9am-4.30pm Mon-Fri mid-Aug–mid-Jun) By the harbour. Internet access for 30 minutes €1.

Sights
MUUMIMAAILMA (MOOMINWORLD)

One of Finland's most popular family attractions, this island-based Disney-like theme park brings to life the characters and stories of children's writer Tove Jansson. Even kids who haven't grown up with the books (or seen the Moomin film or TV series) will warm to the whimsies of the **Muumimaailma** (☎ 511 1111; www.muumimaailma.fi; 1-/2-day pass 3yr & above €16/25; ☒ 10am-6pm early Jun-late Aug).

The main attraction is on Kailo island, accessible by bridge from the mainland at the end of the harbour. Costumed characters inhabit its Moominhouse, Pirate Fort, Snork's Pancake Factory, Whispering

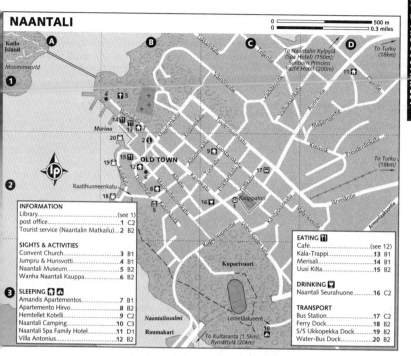

NAANTALI

Woods and more. There is a theatre, a safe swimming beach and a minigolf course.

Next door, there's also **Väski Adventure Island** (☎ 511 1111; www.vaski.fi; above/under 6yr €13/7, with Moominworld entry discount €1; ☻ 11am-7pm early Jun–mid-Aug) with pirate adventures that will suit older children.

OLD TOWN
The Old Town of Naantali is like a big open-air museum. The town grew around the convent, without any regular town plan, and new buildings were always built on the sites of older ones. The result is a delightfully photogenic district of old narrow cobbled streets and low wooden houses – many of which now house handicraft shops, art galleries and cafés. Only the old windmills and storehouses along the shore have disappeared. The main thoroughfare is Mannerheiminkatu and at number 13, **Wanha Naantali Kauppa** is a much-visited shop selling old-fashioned Finnish sweets, bottled soft drinks, stamps, postcards and souvenirs – it's a nostalgia trip, although not a cheap one.

Housed in three old wooden buildings dating from the 18th century, **Naantali Museum** (☎ 434 5321; Katinhäntä 1; admission €2; ☻ noon-7pm Tue-Sun mid-May–Aug) displays include old furniture and exhibitions on the history of Naantali as a convent settlement and as a ritzy spa town.

CONVENT CHURCH
The only building remaining from the Convent of the Order of Saint Birgitta is the massive **Convent Church** (☻ 10am-6pm May, 10am-8pm daily Jun-Aug, 11am-3pm Sun, noon-2pm Wed Sep-Apr), which towers above the harbour. The church was completed in 1462 and its fine baroque stone tower dates from 1797. The interior is surprisingly wide, with elegant vaulting and a very handsome 17th-century pulpit depicting the apostles and evangelists in a blaze of colour. Also noteworthy is the carved 15th-century polychrome wood triptych behind the altar and an evocative wooden head of Christ below it.

During summer the church offers a programme of organ music; the tourist

---

MS MOOMIN

The late Tove Jansson, creator of the much-loved Moomin children's books, was born on 9 August 1914 in Helsinki to Swedish-speaking parents. The talented young Tove was an artist from a young age, and she published her first drawings in a magazine at 14. The first book featuring Moomin trolls came out in 1945, and a new Moomin adventure followed every two years or so.

Despite almost immediate Moomin fever in Finland, it was more than 40 years before the lovable Moomin family attracted worldwide attention. The big break was a Japanese-made cartoon which has been shown on TV in several countries.

Today, the Moomin world comprises four picture books, eight novels and one short-story collection, which have been translated into many languages – including English. Apart from Naantali's Moominworld theme park, you can get acquainted with the characters at the Moomin Valley Museum in Tampere (p171) and at galleries and bookshops around Finland.

Tove lived most of her life on various islands off the Finnish south coast. Whenever she tired of the journalists who frequently visited her studio, she moved to a more isolated island. She passed away in June 2001 in Helsinki, aged 86.

---

office can provide a schedule. At 8pm on summer evenings you'll hear the 'vespers' (evensong) played by a trumpeter from the belfry of the church.

KULTARANTA

The summer residence of the president of Finland is a fanciful stone castle on Luonnonmaa island; the tower is visible from Naantali harbour across the bay. The castle, designed by Lars Sonck, was built in 1916 and is surrounded by a 56-hectare estate with beautiful, extensive rose gardens.

The **Kultaranta grounds** (Tue-Sun late Jun–mid-Aug) are visited by guided tour only. The hour-long tour costs €5 if you start from Kulturanta gate (3pm), or €8 for the bus tour from Naantali (1.55pm). Book through the tourist office.

Activities

Naantali's **spa** (445 5100; www.naantalispa.fi; 2hr €10) traditions date from 1723, when people took health-giving waters from a spring in Viluluoto. Naantalin Kylpylä (see Sleeping), the town's top-class spa hotel allows non-guests to use its fantastic facilities – including several pools and a Turkish bath – during daytime hours. There's a huge range of spa, massage and beauty treatments, including 'Cleopatra's Bath', with milk and honey (€32) or a luxury treatment package for €140. It's best to book ahead in summer.

You can rent bicycles at **Jumpru & Hunsvotti** (533 2242; per day €10), a small marine shop at the harbour near the bridge to Moominworld.

Festivals & Events

The **Naantali Music Festival** (434 5363; www.naantalimusic.com), held over two weeks from early June, features a huge variety of classical music. Most events are held in the Convent Church; performers come from all over the globe and range from string quartets to choral groups. Tickets (generally €10 to €30) are available through the tourist office, or by phone.

One of the more unusual Finnish festivals is **Sleepyhead Day** (27 July), a Naantali tradition that goes back more than 100 years. Townspeople elect a 'Sleepyhead of the Year' who is woken early in the morning by being tossed into the sea! A carnival with music, dancing and games follows.

Sleeping

Villa Antonius (435 1938; fax 435 1333; Mannerheiminkatu 9; d €85-120, ste €170) In the heart of the old town, this has a variety of rooms priced according to the size and level of decoration, which is lavish, romantic and wholly in keeping with the slightly unreal historical atmosphere of this street. Run with plenty of verve and character.

Naantali Camping (435 0855; Kuparivuori; tent sites €9.50-18, cabins €32-45, cottages €79-109) About 400m south of the town centre is this exceptional camping ground. It's open all year and has great management and good facilities, including a beachside sauna. There's a variety of cabins and cottages sleeping two to six people; some of these have heating; the best even have their own bathroom and sauna.

Naantalin Kylpylä (Spa Hotel; ☎ 44550; www
.naantalispa.fi; Matkailijantie 2; s/d €127/150; P ⊠
🖪 🖭 🖫) For the ultimate in indulgence,
look no further than this massive, upmarket spa hotel. It trades partly on Naantali's
history as a spa town but does it in style.
Guests have use of the spa, sauna and gym.
The service is excellent, and the rooms are
very spacious, almost suites, with a lounge
area and balcony or veranda; the sofa folds
out to make a family room.

Although the owners possess half of
Naantali, they were denied permission to
build any more extensions. Their solution: to park a massive cruise-ship outside! The **Sunborn Princess Yacht Hotel** (s/d
€147/170) is stationary, but at least there's
no risk of seasickness. Although the comfortable rooms are called mini-suites,
you're paying for the thrill of being on the
boat, as they are no bigger than the main
complex's doubles. Rooms with balcony
cost €20 extra, but are smaller. Luxurious, honeymoon-style suites with their
own sauna and Jacuzzi cost €520 per
night.

Naantali Spa Family Hotel (☎ 445 5660; Opintie
3; r €50, 2 connecting r €90; P ⊠) This modern
hostel-type place is across the road from
and run by the spa hotel. The functional
but comfortable rooms share kitchen and
bathroom facilities between two; families
and groups can take two adjacent rooms
and make a sort of apartment out of them.

Amandis Apartementos (☎ 430 8774; www.hotel
amandis.com; Nunnakatu 5; d €80; P ⊠) The closest
accommodation to the harbour, this friendly
spot has gleaming apartments with a shared
veranda for lolling about on summer evenings. The rooms (single/double €35/60)
are equipped with simple kitchen facilities;
there's also a pretty café. Single rates are only
available from September to May.

Other recommendations:

Apartemento Hirvo (☎ 435 1619; Mannerheiminkatu
19; d €60; ⊠) Well-placed in the Old Town, friendly staff,
quiet garden; guests can use the kitchen.

Hemtellet Kotelli (☎ 435 1419; Luostarinkatu 13; s/d
€60/65; ⊠) A fine early 19th-century villa that's well-
kept and furnished. The dining room has heaps of style and
the garden is pleasant.

Eating

Merisali (☎ 435 2451; Nunnakatu 1; buffet lunch/dinner
€9.70/11.50, Sun lunch €13.50; ⏰ lunch & dinner) If you
have an appetite, this place is without question the best on the Naantali dining scene;
indeed, many come here from Turku just
for the lunch. Once a spa pavillion, it has a
shaded terrace and a mind-blowing smorgasbord for lunch and dinner, including stagger-
ing quantities of salads and fish. If you value
your waistline, beware the Sunday spread.

Kala-Trappi (☎ 435 2477; Nunnakatu 3; pizzas
€9.70-10.50, mains €11-17; ⏰ lunch & dinner) This
child-friendly place at the harbour has a
large patio, good-value wafer-thin pizzas
and a few off-beat dishes such as chicken
with fruit salsa and pan-fried snails. They
have a daily lunch special.

Cafe Antonius (Mannerheiminkatu 9; cakes and pastries €3-6; ⏰ 10am-6pm Mon-Sat, 11am-5pm Sun) An
unbeatable café in Villa Antonius, with gingerbread and other mouth-watering sweets.
The cosy interior is an endearing combination of heavy style, kitsch and very tasty
pastries; cheap it isn't, but it's like Grand-
ma's house from a fairy tale.

Uusi Kilta (☎ 435 1066; Mannerheiminkatu 1) On
the other side of the harbour from Kala-
Trappi, Uusi Kilta has an international
menu, great outdoor seating and cold beer.

Naantalin Seurahuone (☎ 432 2165; Kaivokatu
21; ⏰ 10am-1am Mon-Sat, noon-11pm Sun) Near the
kauppatori, this is a no-frills cheap bar and
restaurant with a beer garden, and a grilli.

Getting There & Away

Buses to Naantali (routes 11 and 110) run
every 15 minutes from the market square
(opposite Hansa shopping arcade) in Turku
(€3.70, 20 minutes).

SS *Ukkopekka* sails between Turku and
Naantali in summer, arriving at the passen-
ger quay on the south side of the harbour.
For more information see p199.

Finnlink (☎ 010 436 7676; www.finnlink.fi) is a
low-key ferry service that runs three times
daily between Naantali and Kapellskär, near
Stockholm in Sweden. It takes 7½ hours
and is designed for faster transit rather than
a duty-free bonanza. One-way fares are €30
for day departures, and €40 for evenings,
plus €30 to €45 for a car. Two meals are
included as well as a berth.

RYMÄTTYLÄ

Rymättylä, a sleepy island village 20km
southwest of Naantali, is an ideal and
tranquil escape; the perfect place for some

Finnish contemplation. Worth a look is the large stone **church** which dominates the village centre and has one of the most colourful of all Finnish medieval church interiors.

Päiväkulman Kartano (☎ 252 1894; www .paivakulma.com; Kuristentie 225; bed per person €27-30; ☺ mid-May–Aug; P ✗) is in a big, old former schoolhouse on the seafront in farming country. There are rooms in the main house and two cottages, as well as a kitchen, laundry facilities and a seaside sauna. The house is on an unpaved road about 3km from the village – take the turnoff to Heinäinen then follow the signs. There are good discounts if you stay more than one night.

Buses run roughly hourly from Naantali to Rymättylä.

LOUHISAARI MANOR

The village of Askainen, 30km northwest of Turku, is the setting for stunning **Louhisaari Manor** (☎ 431 2515; admission €4; ☺ 11am-5pm mid-May–Aug). Its lavishly decorated rooms include a 'ghost room', and there's an extensive museum and gardens. The manor was built in 1655 in the Dutch Renaissance style. The five-storey pile was purchased by the Mannerheim family in 1795, and Finland's greatest military leader and president, Marshal CGE Mannerheim, was born here in 1867. It's now an attraction rivalling the castles at Turku and Savonlinna. Tours are in Finnish only unless you make a group booking.

The village and manor are located just off road No 193. There are three to four buses daily from Turku to Askainen.

NOUSIAINEN

Nousiainen, 25km north of Turku, is worth a visit for the **Nousiainen church** (☺ noon-6pm Tue-Sun). In a country with seemingly limitless medieval churches, this one is notable as the first resting place of St Henry, an Englishman and Swedish-consecrated bishop who was the first to bring Christianity to the Finns (with a bit of light war to accompany it) in the mid 12th century. His bones were taken to Turku cathedral in the 13th century. The current church post-dates this, having been largely built in the 14th century and restored in the 1960s. Hourly buses from Turku to Mynämäki stop at Nousiainen.

KUSTAVI

The island village of Kustavi (Swedish: Gustavs) offers scenic seascapes, a peaceful rural setting and a jumping-off point for the Åland islands. Its wooden **church** (☺ May–mid-Aug), built in 1783, features the votive miniature ships common in coastal churches – sailors offered these in exchange for divine blessings.

There are several places to stay and eat, as well as a summer-only **tourist service** (☎ 842 6620; www.kustavi.fi).

Kustavin Lomakeskus ja Camping (☎ 848 1200; myyntipalvelu@lomaliitto.fi; tent sites €13-14, r €43-46; ☺ early May–mid-Aug) is a large holiday village 2km south of Kustavi. It has a café-restaurant, many cottages and a host of activities.

A great place to eat is **Laura Peterzéns Studio** (☎ 877 696; ☺ noon-10pm Jun-Aug), with outdoor tables on a picturesque wooden deck.

Kustavi is on road 192, about 70km from Turku, and there are many buses. To reach Åland, continue 8.5km west to the passenger pier of Osnäs (Finnish: Vuosnainen) on Vartsala island. From there ferries depart regularly for the island of Brändö.

Most buses from Turku travel direct to Osnäs. See p246 for ferry details; bicycles and passengers travel free, but if travelling by car you'll need to book, and spend a night in the archipelago.

SOUTH OF TURKU

TURUNMAA ARCHIPELAGO
☎ 02

The Turunmaa archipelago is a tightly clustered chain of low islands that begins south of Turku at Pargas, then stretches southwest to Korpo. It's great ground to explore, and popular boating territory in summer. Free local ferries – especially for those travelling by bicycle or bus – can be taken all the way out to Galtby harbour on Korppoo island. From there, you can catch one of the frequent ferries plying the southern archipelago route to Mariehamn, Åland; see p232 for more details. Local ferries on the route between Pargas, Nagu and Korpo offer a continuous service. There's plenty of accommodation on the islands, mostly cottages for weekly rental. Contact **Archipelago Booking** (☎ 465 1000; www.archipelagobooking.com) or the tourist office in Turku for further details.

Pargas

The de facto 'capital' of the archipelago is Swedish-majority Pargas (Finnish: Parainen), about 25km south of Turku. With a population of 12,000, it's the largest town, and has all facilities. There's a **tourist office** (☎ 458 5942; Runeberinkatu 6). The **old town**, with wooden houses, is behind the church. Lenin stayed near Pargas in December 1907, fleeing Russia en route to Stockholm.

Solliden Camping (☎ 485 5955; www.solliden .fi; Norrby; tent sites €14, 4–8-person cottages €40-120; ☺ May-Sep) is the seaside camping ground of Pargas, 1.5km north of the centre. It has camp sites, cottages, saunas and a hostel **Norrdal** (dm €10) in a rustic old building with a kitchen and a TV room.

Sattmark, halfway between Parainen and the island of Nagu, is worth a stop for the Sattmark Coffee Shop, a charming 18th-century red wooden crofter's cottage serving home-made wheat buns and cakes.

Pargas is on road 180 from Turku. There are one to three buses an hour from Turku to Pargas, and five or six buses a day from Helsinki.

Nagu

Nagu (Finnish: Nauvo) is an idyllic island community between Pargas to the east and Korpo to the west. It is connected to both by free ferries. **Nagu church** (☺ Jun–late Aug) dates from the 14th century and contains the oldest Bible in Finland.

From Nagu harbour it's possible to island-hop around the Turunmaa archipelago on free local ferries.

Korpo

Korpo (Finnish: Korppoo) is the most distant island in the Turunmaa archipelago, and the final stop before entering the Åland archipelago. A highlight is the medieval **Korpo church** (☺ summer) built in the late 13th century. Treasures in this church include naïve paintings on the ceiling and a statue of St George fighting a dragon.

Korpo has plenty of B&Bs and cottages. **Faffas B&B** (☎ 464 6106; s/d €40/60; P ✗) is a comfortable and welcoming year-round guesthouse about 4km east of the Galtby harbour in Österretais. There are four very attractive rooms, some cheaper, and a discount for longer stays. The main hotel in the village centre is **Forellen** (☎ 463 1202; Kyrkbyn).

Korpo is 75km southwest of Turku on road 180 and is connected to Nagu by continuous ferry. Galtby is the passenger harbour, 4km northeast of Korpo centre. A number of free ferries depart from Galtby for Åland (cars must reserve accommodation; see p232); there are also regular ferries to smaller, nearby islands of the Turunmaa archipelago, such as Houtskär.

KIMITO/KEMIÖ ISLAND

☎ 02 / pop 3301

Kimito Island (Finnish: Kemiö) offers excellent possibilities for bicycle tours. The access point is the village of Kimito, which has a **tourist office** (☎ 423 572; Arkadiantie 13). Swedish is the predominant language here.

The village has a 14th-century **church** (☺ mid-May–mid-Aug) with a grand interior. **Sagalund Museum** (☎ 421 738; adult/child €4/free; ☺ 11am-6pm Tue-Sun), 2km west of the church, is an open-air museum with more than 20 old buildings and guided tours every hour.

Dragsfjärd

Dragsfjärd, in the southwest of Kimito Island is a quiet, rural village with a **church** dating from the 1700s. **Söderlångvik** (☎ 424 662; adult/child €3.50/free; ☺ 11am-6pm summer) is a manor house that belonged to local newspaper magnate and art collector Amos Anderson until 1961. There are paintings, furniture and special exhibitions in this beautiful manor, as well as an extensive garden and a café. The best reason to stick around in Dragsfjärd, however, is the excellent hostel.

Pensionat och Vandrarhotell (☎ 424 553; Kulla; dm from €14, s/d €22/36, with bathroom & breakfast €40/48; ☺ May-Sep), at the turn-off to Dragsfjärd, is one of the most comfortable hostels in Finland. It's beautifully furnished like a private home, has several common areas, kitchen, a big garden, sauna and bicycles and boats for rent. The sea is just steps away.

Dragsfjärd is on road 183, 18km south of Kimito village. Take a bus from Salo, Turku or Kimito village; there are several daily.

Kasnäs

The Kasnäs harbour, on a small island south of Kimito Island, is the main jumping-off point for archipelago ferries to some smaller islands. Visit **Sinisimpukka** (Naturum; ☎ 466 6290; ☺ 10am-6pm summer) for information on the

South-West Archipelago National Park. The centre organizes tours to some islands in June, July and August, depending on demand. There's also a nature trail from Sinisimpukka.

At the road's end **Hotel Kasnäs** (☎ 521 0100; www.kasnas.com; s/d €84/118, weekends €74/98; P ⊠ ▣ ▣) is a sprawling hotel at the harbour. There are plenty of facilities, including a brand-new spa complex with 25m pool. The rooms are spread over several buildings and many have good views; they are cheaper outside the summer season. There's also a good restaurant and terrace, a beach sauna and water-sports hire kiosk. Non-guests can use the spa for €6 per two-hour session.

Ferries MS *Rosala II* and MS *Aura* ferry to nearby islands, including Hitis/ Hiittinen, daily in summer. Even if you don't want to visit the islands, they make a pleasant day cruise.

There are just one or two daily bus-and-ferry connections from Dalsbruk (Taalintehdas) on Kimito Island, about 5km south of Dragsfjärd on road No 183.

NORTH OF TURKU

UUSIKAUPUNKI
☎ 02 / pop 16,260

One of Finland's more appealing spots, relaxed Uusikaupunki, 70km north of Turku, makes a great place to stop for a day or two. The name translates as 'New Town' – ironic because Uusikaupunki is now one of the oldest towns in Finland, first founded in 1617 by Gustav II Adolf, the king of Sweden.

Uusikaupunki's claim to fame is the treaty of 1721 which brought an uneasy peace between Sweden and Russia after the Great Northern War. Today, almost nobody in the town speaks Swedish and Nystad (the Swedish name) is an historical note – use Uusikaupunki (*oo-see-cow-*poonki).

Built on either side of an inlet well-stocked with boats, Uusikaupunki boasts an hilarious spoof museum, a great place to stay and eat, riverside beer terraces and a cheerful Finnish summer holiday atmosphere.

Information

Public library (☎ 8451 5382; Alinenkatu 34; ⊙ 11am-7pm Mon-Fri, 10am-2pm Sat, closed Sat in Jun & Jul) Free Internet access and a newspaper reading room.

Tourist office (☎ 8451 5443; http://uusikaupunki .fi; Rauhankatu 10; ⊙ 9am-5pm Mon-Fri, 9am-3pm Sat late Jun-early Aug, 8.30am-4pm Mon-Fri rest of year) Has free Internet terminal, rents bikes per hour/day €2/8, and produces an excellent booklet of services in the town.

Sights

The **Bonk Dynamo Centre** (☎ 841 8404; www.bonk centre.fi; Siltakatu 2; admission €5; ⊙ 10am-6pm mid-May-late Aug, 10am-4pm late Aug–mid-May) is a museum that sends-up the world of corporations and advertising: and crackles with dry, offbeat Finnish humour. The Bonk dynasty began by shipping giant Peruvian anchovies to the Baltic; the business soon diversified and these days produces a variety of 'fully dysfunctional machinery applications' and turns a tidy profit by repacking consumer goods with the Bonk label. Read about Tom of Riga, whose productivity duel with an Enochite steamdrill 'left him broken but launched a legend'. The creation of local artist Alvar Gullichsen, this is a classic and not to be missed. The humour will be over the head of small children, but they can construct their own Bonk machines in the workshop.

Three museums concentrate on the region's seafaring history and can be visited on a combined ticket (€3). **Kulttuurihistoriallinen Museo** (Museum of Cultural History; ☎ 8451 5447; Ylinenkatu 11; admission €2; ⊙ 10am-5pm Mon-Fri, noon-3pm Sat & Sun early Jun-early Sep, noon-5pm Tue-Fri rest of year) is in an old house built by a powerful shipowner and tobacco magnate. Rooms are furnished in the style of a wealthy 19th-century home and exhibit seafaring memorabilia.

Merimiehen Koti (Seaman's Home; ☎ 8451 5413; Myllykatu 18; admission €1; ⊙ 11am-3pm Tue-Fri, noon-3pm Sat & Sun early Jun–mid-Aug, weekends only in late Aug) is a home museum of a local sailor and evokes the life of a seaman and his family in the early 20th century. **Luotsimuseo** (Pilot Museum; ☎ 8451 5450; Vallimäki hill) is a small house devoted to maritime navigation. Admission and hours are the same as for the Seaman's Home.

Automuseo (☎ 484 8068; Autotehtaantie 14; admission €5; ⊙ 11am-5pm Sep-May, 10am-6pm Jun-Aug) is dedicated to old Saab cars; Saab (and Porsche) models are still manufactured in Uusikaupunki. If you're a fan of Scandinavian automobiles, you'll love it.

Vanha Kirkko (Old Church; Kirkkokatu 2; ⊙ 11am-3.30pm Mon-Sat, noon-4pm Sun Jun–mid-Aug) is worth

UUSIKAUPUNKI

INFORMATION
Public library...........................1 B2
Tourist office..........................2 B2

SIGHTS & ACTIVITIES
Bonk Dynamo Centre.............3 C3
Kulttuuristoriallinen Museo.....4 C2
Luotsimuseo...........................5 B3
Merimiehen Koti.....................6 C2
MS Kuha.................................7 B3
Vanha Kirkko..........................8 B3

SLEEPING
Gasthaus Pooki.......................9 C2
Hotelli Aquarius....................10 A3

EATING
Apteekin Krouvi....................11 C2
Captain's Makasiini.................12 B3
Juhla Pooki Restaurant....(see 9)
Pakkahuone Cafe..................13 B3

DRINKING
Orren Krouvi.........................14 B3

TRANSPORT
Bus Stop...............................15 B2
Passenger Quay.....................16 A3

---

a look. Completed in 1629, it's the town's oldest building. Its ornate barrel-vaulted roof is meant to resemble a ship's hull. Outside are the evocative graves of locals killed defending their homeland against Russia during the Winter War.

Myllymäki (Windmill Hill), northeast of the centre, is a hilltop park with four lovely windmills – the sole survivors of the dozens that used to exist in Uusikaupunki.

The village of **Kalanti**, about 7km to the east of Uusikaupunki on road 43, is where the first sizeable party of Swedes, led by King Erik, arrived on a crusade in 1155. Among the party was Henry, an Englishman who was the bishop of Uppsala. He began the process of Christianizing Finland; this incursion also marks the beginning of our knowledge of Swedish influence and rule over Finland. **Kalanti Church** dates from the late 14th century and its interior paintings depict Bishop Henry meeting a pagan on the Finnish coast. There are buses roughly hourly from Uusikaupunki to Kalanti (10 minutes); they are marked Laitila.

Activities

There are plenty of charter boats and water taxis available for archipelago cruises from the harbour in Uusikaupunki. The **M/S Marival II** (☎ 050 66 698; www.marival.fi) runs from late June to mid-August and on Thursdays and Sundays goes to the **Isokari Lighthouse,** and on Saturdays to **Katanpää fort island** (€35, both 6½ hours). The cost of this full-day cruise includes lunch and a guided walk. On Fridays the boat heads to Kustavi (€15), from where you can head out on a ferry to the nearby Åland. There are various other trips available on this boat. Cruises just to the lighthouse and back (adult/child €5/2) are also arranged in summer and it can be booked through the tourist office.

Little **MS Kuha** (☎ 8451 5443) offers hourlong archipelago cruises leaving Monday, Wednesday and Saturday in summer (€6), as well as day-cruises to the lighthouse (€25, Tuesday and Friday) and other destinations.

In summer the MS *Franz Höijer* sails to and from Turku once a week (see p211).

Sleeping

Gasthaus Pooki (☎ 847 7100; pooki@uusikaupunki.fi; Ylinenkatu 21; s/d €70/95; P ✗) This is *the* place to stay hereabouts, and has a little bit of everything. A sturdy granite building right in the centre, this was once a bank but is now a charming, welcoming inn with just four spacious, stylish rooms looking over the new church. Rates include breakfast, and there's everything from restaurants and theatre at Juhla Pooki, to bizarre indoor skiing, available. An excellent choice, but you'll need to book ahead.

Hotelli Aquarius (☎ 841 3123; www.hotelliaquarius.fi; Kullervontie 11; s/d €85/100, d Sat, Sun & summer €69-75; P ✗ 🖳 🖦) The largest and most business-like hotel in town, this good-value spot is in a park-like setting near the sea with tennis courts. The rates include breakfast and a free morning or evening sauna.

Santtioranta Camping (☎ 842 3862; Kalalokkikuja 14; tent sites €10 plus per person €1.50, cabins €30-42; ❨ mid-May–mid-Sep) An attractive seaside camping ground, 1.5km northwest of the town centre. You can rent bikes as well as rowing boats here.

Hotel Lännentie (☎ 845 6100; www.hotelli-lannentie.fi; Levysepänkatu 1; s/d from €55/65; P ✗ 🖦) East of the centre on the road to Rauma is a hotel-motel with basic but tidy rooms. There's a slight discount in summer and on weekends. There are plenty of facilities to grease the holiday wheels, like a sauna and small pool table.

Eating & Drinking

Juhla Pooki (☎ 847 7100; Ylinenkatu 21; buffet lunch €14) A cracking place to eat or drink, the Pooki does a variety of food. The best is in the Juhla, a pretty wooden building next door, which has a buffet served in a boat that offers great quality and value (noon to 6pm June to August). In the main building, bar-style lunches cost €7.50, and there are also more elaborate plates, while the big outdoor terrace buzzes with happy families in summer. There's regular entertainment in summer, including performances in an ultra-characterful wooden theatre building.

Captain's Makasiini (☎ 841 3600; Aittaranta 12; pizzas €6-8, steaks €15-16; ❨ from 5pm weekdays, from 2pm weekends) The place to dine – or just sun yourself over a drink – on a summer afternoon is at one of the red wooden shophouses lining the south bank of the *kaupunginlahti*

(town bay). All have enticing terraces and among the restaurants are some interesting craft and souvenir shops. This is the pick of these if you want to have just one big meal in Uusikaupunki. The menu basically has three things; burgers, pizzas and steaks – but you're really here to soak up the terrific nautical atmosphere. **Orren Krouvi**, next door, is a great pub with a popular terrace.

Pakkahuone Cafe (☎ 842 4822; ❨ 8.30am-8pm Mon-Sat, 9am-8pm Sun) A little west of the centre, and also on the water, this place services the visiting yachties at the guest harbour, and is the town's liveliest café, with a nice waterfront terrace. They do tasty little rolls and a good *karjalanpiirakka* (delicious rice-filled savoury pastries) with egg.

Apteekin Krouvi (☎ 844 2244; Alinenkatu 28; pizza €9-11, lunch specials €6-10; ❨ food served 11am-10pm Mon-Sat, noon-9pm Sun) A fine pub and restaurant in a historic building that was once a pharmacy. There's a great courtyard terrace at the back. Pizza is the speciality, but the daily lunch plates are a good deal. At nights, when it dubs itself the Hot Rock Café, it's one of the livelier spots in town to drink, and is open late at weekends.

The kauppatori is in full swing from Monday to Saturday in summer with snack stalls and grillis.

Getting There & Away

Uusikaupunki is 70km north of Turku and 50km south of Rauma, off the main north-south road (road 8) – take road 43 west to reach Uusikaupunki.

Buses to Turku (€10.20, 1¼ hours) run from behind the kauppatori in the centre of town once or twice per hour on weekdays, less frequently on weekends. There are five to eight buses per day from Rauma (€8.70, one hour). Buses from Helsinki run via Turku.

RAUMA

☎ 02 / pop 36,673

Rauma (Swedish: Raumo) was founded in 1442 and came of age in the 18th century, when it became famous throughout Europe for its production of beautiful hand-made lace. Locals still turn out the delicate material, and celebrate their heritage of lacemaking with an annual festival.

Although Rauma is not as attractive as many south coast seaside towns, it certainly merits a stop for its Vanha Rauma (Old Town) district. The old-town area of more than 600 low wooden houses won a spot on the Unesco World Heritage list as Finland's first entry and is the largest wooden town preserved in the Nordic countries. Refreshingly, the town doesn't live off past glories; Rauma is presently an important shipbuilding centre and has a busy port that ships Finnish paper round the world.

Information

Public library (☎ 834 4531; Ankkurikatu 1; ☽ 10am-7pm Mon-Fri, 10am-2pm Sat) Has free Internet terminals.
Tourist office (☎ 8378 7731; www.rauma.fi; Valtakatu 2; ☽ 8am-6pm Mon-Fri, 10am-3pm Sat, 11am-2pm Sun

Jun-Aug, 8am-4pm Mon-Fri Sep-May) Publishes a good self-guided walking tour through the old town.

Sights

VANHA RAUMA

Vanha Rauma, the World Heritage–listed Old Town in the heart of modern Rauma, is not a museum but a living centre, with low-key cafés, hardware shops, residences and a smattering of artisans and lacemakers working in small studios.

Most of the low wooden buildings of Vanha Rauma were erected in the 18th and 19th centuries. There are some 600 houses and 180 shops, and each building has a name – look for it on a small oval sign near the door. You can spend a pleasant half day

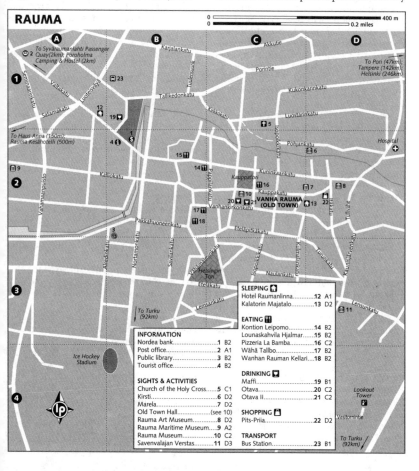

RAUMA

INFORMATION	
Nordea bank.....................1 B2	
Post office.......................2 A1	
Public library...................3 B2	
Tourist office...................4 B2	
SIGHTS & ACTIVITIES	
Church of the Holy Cross.....5 C1	
Kirsti...............................6 D2	
Marela.............................7 D2	
Old Town Hall............(see 10)	
Rauma Art Museum............8 D2	
Rauma Maritime Museum....9 A2	
Rauma Museum................10 C2	
Savenvalajan Verstas........11 D3	

SLEEPING	
Hotel Raumanlinna............12 A1	
Kalatorin Majatalo.............13 D2	
EATING	
Kontion Leipomo...............14 B2	
Lounaskahvila Hjalmar.......15 B2	
Pizzeria La Bamba............16 C2	
Wähä Tallbo....................17 B2	
Wanhan Rauman Kellari....18 B2	
DRINKING	
Maffi..............................19 B1	
Otava.............................20 C2	
Otava II..........................21 C2	
SHOPPING	
Pits-Priia........................22 D2	
TRANSPORT	
Bus Station......................23 B1	

wandering around Vanha Rauma's cobbled streets and visiting its shops and museums. The tourist office has an excellent pamphlet detailing a self-guided walk

The **kauppatori** is in the heart of Old Rauma. It's a typically lively market square teeming with food and craft stalls, buskers and tourists. On the south side is Rauma's most imposing building, the Vanha Raatihuone (old town hall), built in 1776. It now houses the **Rauma Museum** (☎ 834 3532; Kauppakatu 13; combined entry to all museums €4, when only 2 are open €2; ⊙ Tue-Sun, also Mon mid-May–Aug), with exhibits relating to seafaring and the city's lacemaking heritage, including model ships, paintings, baroque furniture and lace costumes.

North of the kauppatori is the attractive stone **Church of the Holy Cross** (Pyhän Ristin Kirkko; Luostarinkatu 1; ⊙ May-Sep), a 15th-century Franciscan monastery church set by the slim Raumanjoki. It has early-16th-century frescoes around a stained-glass window depicting the Transformation, and several beautiful painted panels, a fine Prussian triptych from the 15th century and an ornate pulpit.

Marela (☎ 834 3528; Kauppakatu 24; ⊙ Tue-Sun, also Mon mid-May–Aug) is the most interesting of Rauma's museums and one of its most elaborate buildings. The preserved home of a wealthy 18th-century shipowner is furnished with turn-of-the-century antiques, wall paintings and Swedish ceramic stoves.

Kirsti (☎ 834 3529; Pohjankatu 3; ⊙ mid-May–mid-Sep) is another loveable house museum – this has rooms from the 1930s and 1960s, as well as a stable and granary.

Savenvalajan Verstas (☎ 533 5526; Nummenkatu 2; ⊙ mid-May–mid-Aug) is a small museum of pottery, and a workshop where you can see potters at work and have a go yourself.

Rauma Art Museum (☎ 822 4346; Kuninkaankatu 37; admission €3.50; ⊙ 10am-6pm Mon-Thu, 10am-4pm Fri, also 10am-6pm Mon in summer), in the heart of Vanha Rauma, features changing exhibitions of traditional and modern art. Note the old town well in the middle of the square.

RAUMA MARITIME MUSEUM

Wandering around the wooden centre of Rauma, it's easy to forget that this is a port, so this **maritime museum** (☎ 822 4911; Kalliokatu 34; www.rmm.fi; admission €4; ⊙ noon-4pm Tue-Sun) is a good way to fill you in on Rauma's main livelihood. It's been well thought-out, with

lots of interesting old photos. The highlight is practising your navigation skills – keep that oil tanker off the rocks please!

Festivals & Events

Rauma's biggest event sounds pretty staid on paper, but it's a good time to be in town. **Rauma Lace Week**, beginning in the last week in July, celebrates the town's lacemaking heritage. Lace-trimmed caps were in vogue in Europe during the 18th century – heady days indeed for Rauma's 600 or so lacemaking women, many of whom started learning the craft when only six. Museums hold lace-related exhibitions, and lacemakers in period costume can be seen sewing in shops around Vanha Rauma. Lace Week culminates with the 'Night of Black Lace', a carnival that draws party-minded Finns. Check for details on the town website, www.rauma.fi.

There are also several music festivals worth looking out for: the **Rauma Blues Festival** (www.raumablues.com) is for two days only in mid July, but it draws a decent line-up of international and Finnish performers to the main venue at the ice hockey stadium; **Festivo** (www.raumanfestivo.fi) is a week of classical and choral music at various venues held in early August; and **Raumanmeren Juhannus** (www.raumanmerenjuhannus.com) is a three-day rock festival held during Midsummer.

Sleeping

Kalatorin Majatalo (☎ 8378 6150; www.kalatorin majatalo.com; Kalatori 4; s/d €98/130, Sat, Sun & summer €78/95; P ⊠) The only accommodation in the old town, and it's in the only building not made out of wood! Although it clashes with the plank façades all around, this Art Deco warehouse holds a very pleasant family-run hotel. The owners are very friendly and know a lot about the history and sights of the area. The rooms are spacious and decorated with a personal touch. There's also a good restaurant here.

Rauman Kesähotelli (☎ 824 0130; Satamakatu 20; s/d/tr €40/52/72; ⊙ Jun-Aug; P ⊠) A 10-minute walk from the bus station, this summer-only option houses guests in a student residence. But forget any negative connotations: the rooms are sparkling, bright and spacious, with their own bathroom (good shower), TV and kitchen (although no utensils).

Haus Anna (☎ 822 8223; www.hausanna.com; Sata-makatu 7; s/d €47/60; P ☒) This is a modern and tidy family-run B&B not far from the town centre. The rooms are a cut above most B&Bs in Finland, having their own bathroom, TV and small fridge.

Hotel Raumanlinna (☎ 83221; www.raumanlinna .fi; Valtakatu 5; s/d €105/130, ste €175; P ☒ ☐ ☒ ☒) This central hotel is one of the most popular with both tourists and business travellers. It has excellent facilities, including a small swimming pool, restaurant, and bar. For €20 more than the normal rate, you can get a 'business class' room, which are bigger and have a few small extras.

Poroholma Camping & Hostel (☎ 8388 2500; fax 8388 2502; Poroholmantie; camping per person/tent sites €4/10, dm €10, s/d €30/45, cottages €44-54; ☒ mid-May–late Aug) This place is on Otanlahti bay about 2km northwest of the town centre. It's a pleasant waterside location with plenty of boats around. The HI-affiliated hostel section is in two parts – one a cheaper, very basic building with dormitories, the other a nice old villa that also houses a café and the reception. Kitchen, sauna and laundry are available. There is no local bus service.

Eating

Wanhan Rauman Kellari (☎ 866 6700; Anundilankatu 8; mains €12-20; ☒ 11am-11pm Mon-Thu, 11am-midnight Fri & Sat, 1-11pm Sun) On the edge of Vanha Rauma, this is a very popular cellar restaurant with a terrific rooftop beer terrace open in summer. The restaurant is brightly lit; the service is good and well-accustomed to foreigners. There are good salads, including a tasty one of smoked salmon and shrimp; you can follow this up with a range of cutlets, steaks and fish dishes. Grab a booth to avoid the attractive but backbreaking leather sling seats.

Wähä Tallbo (☎ 822 6610; Vanhankirkonkatu 3; mains €11-20; ☒ 10.30am-7pm Mon-Fri, 11am-4pm Sat) In a relatively quiet street south of the kauppatori, this attractive restaurant has a refined old-world atmosphere entirely suited to its location. As well as a tasty à la carte menu, there are daily lunch specials from €6 to €9.

Kontion Leipomo (Kuninkaankatu 9; ☒ 7.30am-5.30pm Mon-Fri, 8am-3pm Sat, 11am-4pm Sun) Charming cafés are plentiful in Vanha Rauma and this is a perennial favourite. It's a great place for compassionately priced coffee, cakes or pastries, has teddy bears lounging on the seats, and a large garden at the back.

Lounaskahvila Hjalmar (Kuninkaankatu 6; specials €6.50; ☒ lunch Mon-Sat) This is a hearty home-cooking kind of place in Vanha Rauma. On the menu you'll find fare such as chicken nuggets, Wiener schnitzel, and pan pizza on the menu for a relative pittance.

Pizzeria La Bamba (Kauppatori; mains €7-11; ☒ lunch & dinner) Although its logo looks alarmingly like an extracted molar from a distance, this popular restaurant on the kauppatori serves reasonably priced pizzas and pastas and has a festive, family atmosphere, all hanging garlic and Mediterranean cheer.

Drinking & Entertainment

Rauma doesn't have the liveliest nightlife on the west coast.

Maffi (☎ 533 0857; Valikatu) The best spot in town for a few sociable beers, this is a hotel bar, but doesn't feel like it. It's warmly decorated and has a couple of levels and a terrace. Out the back are several pool tables; there's also Internet access.

Otava (Isoraastuvankatu; ☒ 9pm-3am Fri & Sat) In the old town you'll find this typical Finnish dance club, with couples of all ages twirling solemnly to tango and humppa music.

Otava II, just around the corner, is equally typical and rustic, but, as it opens at 9am, usually has a couple of paralytic customers by midday.

Shopping

Pits-Priia (Kauppakatu 29) This is the best place to buy bobbin lace, and you can see it being made.

Getting There & Away

Between Rauma and Pori, there are buses every hour or so (€8.70, 50 minutes). From the south, Turku and Uusikaupunki are connected by buses every two hours or so. There are also direct services to Helsinki and Tampere.

Get off the Tampere-to-Pori train at the Kokemäki train station, and transfer to a connecting bus. Your train pass will be valid on the bus.

AROUND RAUMA
Lappi

The small village of Lappi (Finnish for Lapland) is particularly pleasant, with the Lapinjoki running through it, and more importantly it's a base for visiting a couple of very significant prehistoric sites. In the village an old stone bridge survives, and nearby is a **church** dating from 1760. It has medieval sculpture and a separate bell tower.

Sammallahdenmäki is a Bronze Age burial complex probably dating from the late 2nd millennium BC. Spread over an area about a kilometre long are a number of stone burial cairns of different shapes and sizes. The main attraction is nearest the car park: the **Kirkonlaattia** (Church Floor), is a flat stone tableau roughly 20m x 20m in extension. While it seems that there was an associated burial, the meaning and function of this monument are shrouded in time. The site is 4km from the main road 12 – turn north to Eurajoentie and then follow the signs. Buses to Lappi from Rauma (10 a day, 15 minutes) will let you off at the turn-off.

Köyliö

This quiet hamlet was an important estate in medieval times. It is famous for being the scene of a celebrity crime in the 12th century. The crusading Bishop Henry of Uppsala, after a Swedish force had defeated the Finns in battle, set about baptizing the conquered. One of his flock, a peasant named Lalli, rebelled, and did in Henry with a club, propelling the English-born bishop to sainthood. The circumstances are unclear; some sources suggest Lalli was upset at having been excommunicated, while others suggest the bishop had helped himself to a sandwich from Lalli's larder without permission. In any event, winners write history, so the local **church** has paintings – created much later and intended to teach a lesson – that depict Lalli under the perfumed foot of a saint, his inevitable fate in the afterlife. The church and its paintings are on an island in Köyliönjärvi and are accessible by a small causeway. This is the finishing point of Catholic pilgrimages from Turku.

Köyliö is about 35km east of Rauma, south from road 12 at the town of Eura. There is no bus service beyond Eura.

PUURIJÄRVI-ISOSUO NATIONAL PARK

Puurijärvi, 65km due east of Rauma, is one of the best **bird-watching** lakes in Western Finland. The lake and surrounding marshlands have been protected since 1993 and are a favourite nesting site for migrating

waterfowl of many varieties, totalling about 500 pairs in season. The lake itself can be reached by a 800m nature trail from the main road. A boardwalk makes a loop of the open marshland, where there's an observation tower. The *näköalapaikka* (a viewing cliff) also offers a good general view. Visitors are required to stay on marked paths during breeding season, and camping is not allowed in the park at any time.

PORI

☎ 02 / pop 76,152

Pori (Swedish: Björneborg) would be a very unremarkable west coast town if it weren't for its internationally renowned Jazz Festival which sets the town ablaze for a week in July. Domestically it's one of the most important deep-water harbours in Finland, and is kept prosperous by numerous industries including brewing – you can smell the rich malty odours – and minting Finland's euro coins. Don't go robbing the factory though: they get stamped with the heads and tails elsewhere, after leaving town.

In 1558, Duke Juhana, who was then ruler of Finland, decided to establish a trading town on the eastern coast of the Gulf of Bothnia. As a result, Pori was founded at the mouth of the Kokemäenjoki. For a brief shining moment in 1726 a Professor Israel Nesselius championed Pori as the new capital of Finland – but it was not to be.

Information

There are 24-hour luggage lockers at the train and bus stations.

Public library (Gallen-Kallenkatu 12; ⊙ 10am-7pm Mon-Fri, 10am-3pm Sat) Has several free Internet terminals.

Tourist office (☎ 621 1273; www.pori.fi; Yrjönkatu 17; ⊙ 9am-5pm Mon-Fri, also 10am-3pm Sat May-Aug) The new tourist office is between the bus station and the kauppatori. There's Internet access here.

Sights

Despite being one of the oldest towns in Finland, Pori has few historic buildings or other attractions.

Satakunta Museum (☎ 621 1063; Hallituskatu 11; admission €4; ⊙ 11am-5pm Tue-Sun, 11am-8pm Wed) is a stimulating museum of regional history and archaeology – the theme is water and how the river and sea have affected life in the town over the centuries.

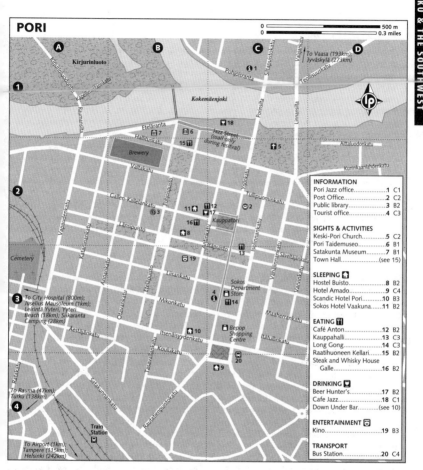

PORI

0 ———————— 500 m
0 ———————— 0.3 miles

Pori Taidemuseo (Pori Art Museum; ☎ 621 1080; Eteläranta; admission €3; ☺ 11am-6pm Tue-Sun, 11am-8pm Wed) is a fine modern art museum with a good permanent collection. Finnish and international art is exhibited in the airy, elegant space, a former warehouse, and there are various changing exhibitions.

The neo-Gothic **Keski-Pori Church** (Yrjönkatu) was built in 1863 and lovingly renovated in 1998. It has a steeple with blind arching and unusual ornate iron fretwork.

Juselius Mausoleum (Käppänä Cemetery; ☎ 623 8746; Maantiekatu; admission free; ☺ noon-3pm summer), west of the centre, is the most poignant sight in Pori. FA Juselius, a wealthy businessman, had the mausoleum built as a memorial to his daughter who died of

tuberculosis at the age of 11. The original frescoes were painted in 1898 by famous Finnish artist Akseli Gallen-Kallela (who had just lost his own daughter). The ones you see now were painted by Akseli's son, Jorma Gallen-Kallela, after his father's death.

Sleeping

If you are planning to visit Pori during the Jazz Festival it's advisable to book hotel accommodation up to a year in advance, particularly for the final weekend – and expect to pay up to double the regular rates. The tourist office also has a list of festival-only accommodation, which ranges to comfortable rooms in private homes to a mattress on

---

PORI JAZZ FESTIVAL

Running over a week in mid-July, **Pori Jazz Festival** is one of the most appreciated summer events in Finland. It's a great time to be in Pori, even if you don't attend any of the major concerts – the free jam sessions and electric atmosphere alone make it worthwhile. The festival started in 1966 when some local musicians arranged a two-day event with an audience of 1000 people. These days the Jazz Festival features more than 100 concerts held in tents, outdoors or in old warehouses. Performers – and thousands of visitors – pour in from all over the world, and hotels are fully booked up to a year in advance. Even the local football team is now called FC Jazz! Although the emphasis is on jazz, the musical styles include blues, soul and mainstream performers. The line-up in recent years has included Stevie Wonder, Lauryn Hill and the Pointer Sisters.

There are 10 or so venues; the main arena is Kirjurinluoto Concert Park, on the north side of the river, where an open-air stage is set up for an audience of up to 25,000. Jazz Street, the closed off section of Eteläranta along the riverfront, is where a lot of the action happens, with stalls, free concerts, makeshift bars and street dancing.

Tickets for the biggest concerts are €50 to €60, or €160 for a four-day pass to the main stage. Other concerts are free or cost €10 to €30. For more information and to purchase tickets contact **Pori Jazz** (☎ 626 2200; www.porijazz.fi; Pohjoisranta 11D, 28100 Pori; 🕑 8.30am-4.30pm Mon-Fri, during festival 8.30am-10pm daily), or the Pori tourist office.

---

the floor of a school classroom; this is available on a first-come, first-served basis.

Hostel Buisto (☎ 633 0646, 633 0647; www .hostelbuisto.net; Itäpuisto 13; s/d €34/48; P ✗) An enterprising new owner has completely reformed this once-shabby central guesthouse, and what a job she's done. The rooms are very appealing and welcoming, with bright cheery colours, wooden floors, and washbasin. Shared bathrooms are good, and while there's no breakfast, guests have access to a modern kitchen with free tea and coffee. Ring ahead outside summer time so the owner can arrange to be there. A top choice.

Yyterin Kylpylähotelli (☎ 628 5300; www.yyter inkylpylahotelli.fi; Sipintie 1, Yyteri; s/d €79/100; P ✗ 🔊) Situated at Yyteri beach, this is a good-value spa hotel, and more pleasant than Pori's hotels, as long as you've got transport.

Hotel Amado (☎ 631 0100; www.amado.fi; Keskusaukio 2; s/d €80/98, Sat, Sun & summer €65/75; P ✗) Right by the bus station, this is the most reasonably priced of the city's big hotels and is independently owned and perfectly comfortable, with a very good à la carte restaurant. The rooms are cool and modern with large windows.

Sokos Hotel Vaakuna (☎ 020-123 4626; www .sokoshotels.fi; Gallen-Kallelankatu 7; standard s/d €89/114, superior s/d €101/127, Sat, Sun & summer r from €65; P ✗ 🔊) This place is in the town centre and is Pori's largest hotel. The superior rooms have a few extras like bathrobes, and

the hotel is excellent value at weekends and in summer (apart from during the festival of course). It's also something of a centre for local nightlife.

Leirintä Yyteri (☎ 634 5700; leirinta.yyteri@pori .fi; Yyterinsatojentie; tent sites €9-16, 4-bed cabins €45-55, 4–6-bed cottages with sauna €65-100; 🕑 May-Aug) A fair way from Pori, but in a great location at the popular Yyteri beach, this camping ground is usually full around Jazz Festival time. There's a café and good facilities.

Scandic Hotel Pori (☎ 624 900; www.scandic-ho tels.com; Itsenäisyydenkatu 41; s/d €99/123, Sat, Sun & summer r from €79, ste from €175; P ✗ 🔊) This is a stylish hotel within walking distance of the centre. It's a fairly sober place kitted out for business travellers, and has two classes of rooms. Downstairs, however, is a little slice of the Australian outback, the Down Under Bar (see Drinking & Entertainment).

Siikaranta Camping (☎ 638 4120; www.siikaran tacamping.fi; camp sites €10 plus per person €3.50, cabins €35-40; 🕑 Jun–mid-Aug) This peaceful camp site is on Reposaari, just northwest of Yyteri beach. The island is linked to the mainland by bridge. Take bus 30 or 40 from the centre.

Eating

Grillis around town sell the local speciality, *Porilainen* (Pori burger), best enjoyed late at night after a few pints of Porin Karhu (Bear of Pori) beer.

Kauppahalli (Isolinnankatu; 🕑 9am-5pm Mon-Fri, 8am-2pm Sat) There's food aplenty; look for another local specialty here, smoked river lamprey (a fish that looks like an eel and killed Henry I of England when he ate too many one day).

Raatihuoneen Kellari (☎ 633 4804; Hallituskatu 9; starters €8-10, mains €15-23, lunch from €9) This is an elegant cellar restaurant in the old town hall and by far the best dining experience in town. There's a superb weekday buffet luncheon, and Finnish cuisine is the speciality in the evenings, when you can enjoy such exquisite plates as salmon tournedos with morel mushroom sauce, or roast reindeer with sea buckthorn. Delicious.

Steak & Whisky House Galle (☎ 648 2170; Gallen-Kallelakatu 6; mains €12-20; ☽ lunch & dinner) This is a lot classier than it sounds. The interior is stylish and elegant, with intimate tables and a decent Finnish-continental menu of steaks, fish and salads. The lunch specials are the most worthwhile. Attached is a sophisticated bar with frequent live jazz; it's open fairly late most nights.

Long Gong (☎ 633 0088; Yrjönkatu 20; mains €8-13, lunch from €6.50; ☽ lunch & dinner). In an arcade across the road from the tourist office, this is a reliable Chinese restaurant with welcoming management. As well as the traditional choices, which are tasty enough, there are also a few fried reindeer dishes, which work well with a bottle of Tsingtao beer.

Café Anton (☎ 641 4144; Antinkatu 11; ☽ lunch & bar food until 9pm) On the corner of the market square, this place is more pub than café but it has a €7 lunch special and bar snacks such as nachos, wedges or pizza from €3 to €8.

Drinking & Entertainment

Pori is pumping around the time of the Jazz Festival, with the eastern section of Eteläranta being converted into 'Jazz Street', a pulsating and infectious strip of makeshift bars and food stalls.

Beer Hunter's (cnr Gallen-Kallelankatu & Antinkatu; ☽ 11am-2am) A great brewery pub and one of the most popular drinking spots in town. Its interior is low-lit and moody, with a maze of wooden booths. Of the beers brewed on the premises, the dark lager, Mufloni IV, is a (sweetish) taste sensation, but all are seriously good, and they also have a connoisseur's range of bottled ales and lagers from around Europe.

Café Jazz (☎ 641 1344; Eteläranta; ☽ noon-midnight Sun-Thu, noon-2am Fri & Sat) This is the most dynamic venue along Jazz Street. It has a perfect location on the river, a warm ambience and regular jazz slots and jam sessions. There's a good summer terrace to discuss what you've seen during the festival and reasonable food is served here.

Down Under Bar (Scandic Hotel Pori; Itsenäisyydenkatu 41; ☽ 9pm-4am) A little piece of Australiana up near the Arctic. Along with the shockin' pseudo-Aboriginal murals and the crocodile-and-Kombi-van décor, there are some 'Aussie' cocktails with more bite than a Great White shark, and plenty of music and dancing.

Kino (Itäpuisto 10; ☽ Wed-Sat) Formerly a cinema, this spacious venue is now a popular club for the young, cheerful and mortgageless. The music is far from groundbreaking, treading a line between disco, Eurodance and bubblehead pop, but it's a happy place to be.

Getting There & Away

AIR

There are two to four daily flights between Pori and Helsinki (45 minutes). The airport is a couple of kilometres southeast of the centre.

BUS

There are frequent daily buses between Pori and Helsinki (€34.70, four hours), Rauma (€8.70, 50 to 70 minutes), Turku (€23.20, 2¼ hours) and Tampere (€18.90, 1¾ hours). Some Tampere-bound buses require a change at Huittinen and take considerably longer, so avoid those. There are also direct connections with Vaasa, Oulu and Jyväskylä.

TRAIN

All trains to Pori go via Tampere, where you usually have to change. There are frequent daily trains (regional and Intercity) between Tampere and Pori (€19.90, 1½ hours), all of which have good connections with trains from Helsinki (€35.80, three to four hours).

Getting Around

Local buses run from the kauppatori; route maps are available from the tourist office. These are handy to reach the attractions around the city (see p228) but won't be necessary within the town, which is compact.

AROUND PORI
Yteri Beach

Yteri beach, 18km northwest of Pori town centre, is still something of a playground in summer, though like many Finnish beach resorts, it has been in a decline ever since charter flights to Spain were invented. This is the nation's best beach for windsurfing: you can hire equipment in summer, and the long white-sand strip offers plenty of scope for strolling. There is a good camping ground and a spa hotel here; see p226.

Beyond Yteri, **Reposaari**, linked by a causeway to the mainland, has a pretty, if slightly over-spruced, wooden harbour village which is a great place to wander around. There are a few choice spots for a beer in the sun if things turn thirsty.

Leineperi

This fine village received the Europe Nostra award in 1993 for careful preservation of 18th-century buildings. The area was first developed in 1771 by the Swedish as a *bruk* (early ironworks precinct) for making household items, and was in operation for about a century. Today it is a lively place, at least on summer weekends. Attractions along the scenic Kullaanjoki riverside include **Masuuni ironworks**, now renovated, a blacksmith's shop, now a **museum**, and some **artisans' workshops**. **Museo Kangasniemi** is devoted to Kaarlo Kangasniemi, the 1968 Olympic weight-lifting champion (he is Finnish, of course). On weekends you may be lucky enough to meet the champion. Most of these museums charge a €1 admission and are open on summer weekends. Free town maps are available at most attractions.

Leineperi is on an unpaved road that runs parallel to the Tampere–Pori road 11. Buses between Pori and Kullaa stop at Leineperi; there are usually two daily.

Åland

Little known beyond the Baltic, this sweeping archipelago is a curious geopolitical entity that belongs to Finland, speaks Swedish, but has its own parliament, flies its own flag proudly from every pole, and issues its own national stamps.

There are over 6000 islands, although many of these are small mounds of granite rising centimetres above the sea. Indeed, the islands are all so flat that few eminences top 100m above sea level; Ålanders won't be voting for global warming at the next elections.

This flatness, however, makes the islands ideal for exploration by bike. The main island (Åland) is connected with those around it by bridge and cable ferry, while, northeast and southeast of here, the archipelago islands are even more rural and remote: on places like Kökar you could easily think you have stepped back in time to a Viking village. Throughout Åland, traditions such as the Midsummer celebration bear a marked local character.

More than elsewhere in Finland, Åland has a very defined holiday season. From Midsummer until the end of July, the islands are full of Swedes and Finns enjoying the summer break cycling and camping. Consider visiting in May or September, when you'll have the islands to yourself. Outside these months, very little is open; the winters are wet and gusty.

Åland is easily accessed from both Sweden and Finland, and Mariehamn, its spread-out and tranquil capital, makes a convenient stop between the two.

HIGHLIGHTS

- Island-hopping by bike around the ideally flat archipelago. You can rent a bike right by the ferry terminal in Mariehamn or **Eckerö** (p242).

- Enjoying the slow pace of island life and the Swedish-speaking culture. Things don't get much more relaxed than at the camp site on **Vårdö** island (p241).

- Touring the **Kastelholms Slott** (p239) in Sund, then a **snail safari** (p240) nearby

- Visiting the southern archipelago, perhaps staying on fascinating, remote **Kökar** (p247)

- Returning to 'city' life in **Mariehamn** (p232), with its maritime history and bustling harbour

- **Midsummer celebrations** (p235), when the colourful Midsummer poles are erected

- Summer cruises on the schooner **Linden** (p235)

| ■ TELEPHONE: 018 | ■ POPULATION: 26,200 |

ÅLAND

History

The first settlers set foot on Åland 6000 years ago, and more than a hundred Bronze and Iron Age *fornminne* (burial sites) have been discovered. These are all clearly signposted, though they are in a fairly ruinous state. Åland was an important harbour and trading centre during the Viking era, and evidence has been found of six fortresses from that time.

During the Great Northern War of 1700–21 (nicknamed the 'Great Wrath'), most of the population fled to Sweden to escape the Russians, who were bent on destroying Åland. The Russians returned during the 1740s (a period known as the 'Lesser Wrath') and again in 1809.

When Finland gained independence in 1917, Ålanders were all too familiar with Russians and feared occupation by Bolsheviks. There were strong moves for Åland to be incorporated into Sweden, which was not only the Ålanders' former mother country but also their source of language and cultural identity But Finland refused to give up its island province. The Swedish-Finnish dispute only came to an end in 1921, when Åland was given its status as an autonomous, demilitarized and neutral province within the Republic of Finland by a decision of the League of Nations. Today Åland is almost a Little Sweden, and locals are more aware of events in Stockholm than Helsinki.

Although Åland joined the EU along with Finland in 1995, it was granted a number of exemptions, including duty-free tax laws that allowed the essential ferry services between the islands and mainland Finland and Sweden to continue operating profitably.

Information

Åland shares the same time zone as Finland; one hour ahead of Sweden, and two ahead of GMT.

While the euro is the currency, most places also accept the Swedish krona.

The main tourist information office is in the capital, Mariehamn; there are smaller, summer-only, offices in Godby, Eckerö, and Föglö. The website www.visitaland .com is very helpful, and www.alandsresor .fi lets you book much of the islands' accommodation online.

Finnish telephone cards can be used on Åland, but there are also local cards. Åland uses the Finnish mobile phone network but DNA service (mobile network provider) is sketchy. Mail sent in Åland must have Åland postage stamps – Finnish ones won't work.

The general emergency number is ☎ 112; for the police call ☎ 10022, for medical services ☎ 10023 and for a dental emergency ☎ 14600.

Activities

Åland's manageable size, flat landscape and great network of trails make it a cyclist's paradise. There are heaps of places to rent bikes, and great facilities. In summer there are more bikes on the road than cars.

The water is an obvious attraction; sailing boats from all around the Baltic pull in at the archipelago's secluded islands in summer. You can do anything: from charter a yacht for a week's cruising to renting a kayak for a couple of hours' splashing about.

Fishing is popular, both from boats and the shore. In winter, Åland is many Swedes' destination of choice for ice-fishing.

Self-Catering Accommodation

There's a wealth of cottages for rent on Åland. Both Eckerö and Viking ferry lines (see p238) have a comprehensive list of bookable places, as does **Destination Åland** (☎ 040-300 8001; www.destinationaland.com; Elverksgatan 5, Mariehamn).

Dangers & Annoyances

Ticks carrying infectious diseases that may cause rash and fever are a concern in rural areas of Åland. The simplest way to deal with this problem is to take proper precautions – do not walk barefoot outside, wear trousers or long pants when hiking, and always conduct a swift 'tick check' after spending time outdoors. For more information, see p356.

Getting There & Away

AIR

The airport is 4km northwest of Mariehamn and there is a bus into the centre. A taxi to the centre costs about €14. **Finnair** (☎ 634 500; www.finnair.fi) has a daily service from Helsinki. There's a Finnair office in **Hotell Arkipelag** (Strandgatan 31, Mariehamn).

ÅLAND

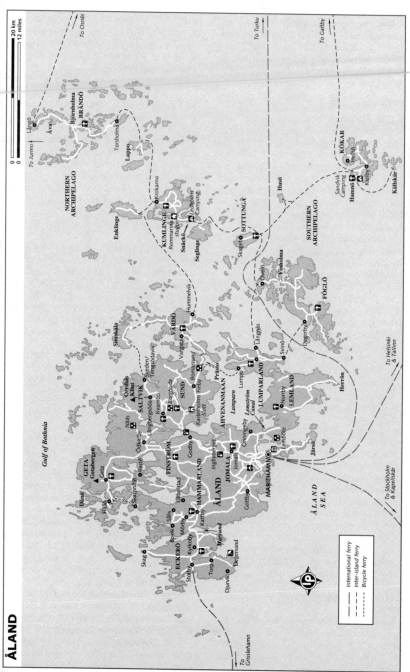

Executive Express European (☎ 02-415 4957; www.european.se) flies three times a day Monday to Friday between Turku and Mariehamn and twice daily between Mariehamn and Stockholm Arlanda. It suspends flights between mid-June and late July.

BOAT

Viking and Silja lines have year-round daily ferries to Mariehamn from Turku as part of their links with Stockholm (see p238); you can stop off 'between' countries or sail return from either. Viking also sails to Mariehamn from Helsinki and from Kapellskär (north of Stockholm) in Sweden. Birka Cruises sails only between Stockholm and Mariehamn. **Tallink** (www.tallink.com) runs a new route from Stockholm to Tallinn via Mariehamn.

Eckerö Linjen (☎ 28000; www.eckerolinjen.fi; Torggatan 2, Mariehamn) sails from Grisslehamn in Sweden to Eckerö – this is the cheapest and quickest route from Sweden to Åland. There are three to five connections a day from Grisslehamn during the high season and two or three during the low season. The trips have a bus connection to/from Stockholm and Mariehamn. The boat trip takes two hours (remember the time difference!), and a combined boat and bus trip from Stockholm to Mariehamn takes five hours.

Ferry fares vary widely by season and class of travel. As a rule, they are very cheap: off-season, these ferries make their money on sprightly pensioners buying duty free with the grey krona. The passenger fare from Grisslehamn to Eckerö is €8.90 in high season (€5.50 off season).

Free travel for pedestrians and cyclists on the archipelago ferries all the way to the central Åland islands is possible from mainland Finland via Korpo (southern route, from Galtby passenger harbour) or Kustavi (northern route, from Osnäs passenger harbour), but you usually have to break your outward journey in the archipelago; car drivers are required to do this.

Getting Around

BICYCLE

Cycling is a great way to tour these flat, rural islands. The most scenic roads have separate bike lanes that are clearly marked. Ro-No Rent has bicycles available at Mariehamn (p238) and Eckerö harbours.

BUS

Five main bus lines depart from Mariehamn's regional bus terminal on Torggatan in front of the library. Bus 1 goes to Hammarland and Eckerö; route 2 to Godby and Geta; route 3 to Godby and Saltvik; route 4 to Godby, Sund and Vårdö (Hummelvik); and route 5 to Lemland and Lumparland (Långnäs). Bus 6 runs from Godby Monday to Friday, servicing other destinations in Finström. The one-way fare from Mariehamn to Storby (Eckerö) is €4.90; from Mariehamn to Långnäs is €4.70. Bicycles can be carried on buses (space permitting) for €4.

If you plan to use the bus a lot, you can buy a bus pass valid for the whole island (24-hour/three days €12/24).

FERRY

There are three kinds of inter-island ferry. For short trips across straits, simple vehicle ferries ply nonstop and are free. For longer routes, ferries run according to schedule, and take cars, bicycles and pedestrians. There are also three bicycle ferries in summer – a ride is €7 to €9 per person with a bicycle. The bike ferry routes are Hammarland–Geta, Lumparland–Sund and Vårdö–Saltvik.

Timetables for all inter-island ferries are available at the main tourist office in Mariehamn and online at www.alandstrafiken .aland.fi.

MARIEHAMN

pop 10,712

Pretty Mariehamn will seem a bustling metropolis if you've arrived from some of the other entry points in Åland or have spent some time in the archipelago. It's by far the largest settlement hereabouts and is spread-out and elegant, with stately wooden houses looking over broad tree-lined streets – it has been dubbed the 'town of a thousand linden trees'. Built on a peninsula, it is framed on either side by marinas full of gleaming sailing boats. It is hectic here in summer but outside the peak season Mariehamn reverts to its somnolent, local self.

Mariehamn was founded in 1861 by Tsar Alexander II, who named the town after his wife, Tsarina Maria. Mariehamn is the administrative and economic centre of Åland. It is the seat of the *lagting* and *landskapsstyrelse,* the legislative and executive bodies of Åland, and has several good museums.

Orientation

Mariehamn is situated on a long, narrow peninsula and has two harbours – Västerhamn (West Harbour) and Österhamn (East Harbour). Ferries from Sweden and mainland Finland dock at Västerhamn, but just about everything else is at Österhamn, a stone's throw from the city centre. Torggatan is the colourful pedestrian street, while the long, broad, tree-lined Storagatan is the main thoroughfare connecting the two harbours. The airport is 4km northwest of the centre.

Information

You can store luggage in the lockers (€2) at the ferry terminal for up to 24 hours.

Ålands Turistinformation (☎ 24000; www.visitaland .com; Storagatan 8; ☺ 9am-6pm daily mid-Jun–mid-Aug, 9am-5pm Mon-Fri 9am-4pm Sat & Sun early–mid-Jun & mid-late Aug, 9am-4pm Mon-Fri 10am-3pm Sat Apr, May & Sep) Heaps of information on Åland and books tours. Internet for 15 minutes €1. Very helpful.

Ålandsresor (☎ 28040; www.alandsresor.fi; Torggatan 2; ☺ 8.30am-5pm Mon-Fri, also 9am-2pm Sat Jun & Jul) Eckerö Linjen's travel-agent arm handles hotel, guesthouse and cottage bookings for the entire island. Often the *only* way to secure accommodation other than camping grounds. Viking Line offers a similar service.

Ålandstrafiken (☎ 25155; Strandgatan 25; ☺ 9am-5pm Mon-Fri, also 9am-3pm Sat Jun & Jul) Will store backpacks for longer periods.

Cycle Info (☺ 9am-7pm Jun-Aug) Two-wheeled summer tourist information units: just flag them down and ask a question.

Main hospital (☎ 5355; Norragatan 17)

Main post office (☎ 6360; Torggatan 4; ☺ Mon-Sat). Sells the collectable Åland stamps; Finnish stamps won't work here.

Mariehamn library (☎ 531 441, Strandgatan 8; ☺ 10am-8pm Mon-Fri, 11am-4pm Sat, noon-3pm Sun) Several free Internet terminals; maximum 15 minutes at a time if you don't book ahead.

Tourist information booth (☎ 531 214; ☺ daily Jul, Mon-Sat Jun & Aug) At the Västerhamn ferry terminal.

Sights & Activities
MUSEUMS

The Åland Museum Card allows entry to any four museums for €8.50. If you choose your visits wisely, this can garner a big saving. Buy it at the tourist office or at most museums.

In the centre of town, the **Ålands Museum & Ålands Konstmuseum** (Ålands Museum & Art Museum; ☎ 25426; Stadhusparken; admission €3; ☺ 10am-4pm Wed-Mon, 10am-7pm Tue Jun & Aug, 10am-7pm daily Jul, 10am-4pm Wed-Sun 10am-8pm Tue Sep-May; ☒) are housed in the same building and should definitely head your list of things to see in Mariehamn. The lively and well-presented museum gives an absorbing insight into the complete history of the islands and includes a Stone-Age replica boat made of sealskin, and a reconstructed traditional pharmacy. The panels don't have English, so take an information leaflet on entry.

The gallery has changing exhibitions as well as a handful of paintings by local artists. Perhaps most interesting among them are the canvases of Joel Pettersson (1892–1937). You really sense the elemental forces at work behind the Åland treescapes and behind his furrowed brow in a self-portrait; he's something of an Åland Van Gogh.

The stalwarts of Åland are mariners and the **Sjöfartsmuseum** (Maritime Museum; ☎ 19930; Hamngatan 2; admission €5, joint ticket with Pommern €8; ☺ 9am-5pm May-Aug, 9am-7pm Jul, 10am-4pm Sep-Apr), an enjoyably kitschy museum of sailing and maritime commerce, is devoted to them. There are heaps of items from old boats, including figureheads that once graced local ships, model ships, ships in bottles, sea chests and nautical equipment. The central part of the museum is a re-creation of a ship with mast, saloon, galley and cabins, but to see the real thing, go outside.

The **museum ship Pommern** (☎ 531423; admission €5, with Sjöfartsmuseum €8; ☺ 9am-5pm May-Aug, 9am-7pm Jul, 10am-4pm Sep & Oct), anchored behind the Sjöfartsmuseum, is a beautifully preserved four-masted merchant ship and a symbol of Mariehamn. The four-masted barque was built in 1903 in Glasgow, Scotland, and once carried tons of cargo and a 26-man crew on the trade route between Australia and England; its record run was a very creditable 110 days. An audio guide (available in English; €3.50) can help bring the old ship to life.

On the opposite side of the peninsula, at the northern end of Österhamn, is **Sjökvarteret** (Maritime Quarter; ☎ 16033; www.sjokvarteret .com; adult/child €4/free; ☺ 10am-6pm daily mid-Jun–mid-Aug, 9-11am Mon-Fri mid-Aug–mid-Jun), where you can see the modern-day approach to boat-building, along with traditional wooden boats. There's also a museum with exhibitions on shipbuilding, several craft workshops and a café.

ÅLAND

ÅLAND

MARIEHAMN

0 — 500 m
0 — 0.3 miles

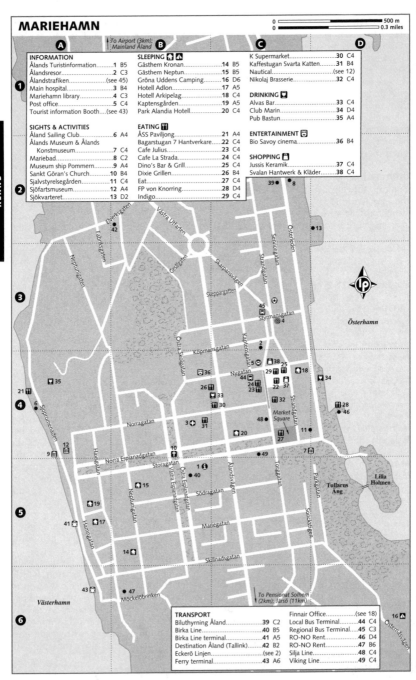

INFORMATION
Ålands Turistinformation..........**1** B5
Ålandsresor....................................**2** C3
Ålandstrafiken........................(see 45)
Main hospital............................**3** B4
Mariehamn library......................**4** C3
Post office..................................**5** C4
Tourist information Booth....(see 43)

SIGHTS & ACTIVITIES
Åland Sailing Club.......................**6** A4
Ålands Museum & Ålands
Konstmuseum........................**7** C4
Mariebad....................................**8** C2
Museum ship Pommern.............**9** A4
Sankt Göran's Church..............**10** B4
Sjalvstyrelsegården..................**11** C4
Sjöfartsmuseum........................**12** A4
Sjökvarteret..............................**13** D2

SLEEPING
Gästhem Kronan.......................**14** B5
Gästhem Neptun.......................**15** B5
Gröna Uddens Camping...........**16** D6
Hotell Adlon.............................**17** A5
Hotell Arkipelag.......................**18** C4
Kaptensgården.........................**19** A5
Park Alandia Hotell..................**20** C4

EATING
ÅSS Paviljong..........................**21** A4
Bagarstugan 7 Hantverkare....**22** C4
Cafe Julius................................**23** C4
Cafe La Strada..........................**24** C4
Dino's Bar & Grill.....................**25** C4
Dixie Grillen.............................**26** B4
Eat...**27** C4
FP von Knorring........................**28** D4
Indigo......................................**29** C4

K Supermarket........................**30** C4
Kaffestugan Svarta Katten......**31** B4
Nautical................................(see 12)
Nikolaj Brasserie......................**32** C4

DRINKING
Alvas Bar..................................**33** C4
Club Marin................................**34** D4
Pub Bastun...............................**35** A4

ENTERTAINMENT
Bio Savoy cinema.....................**36** B4

SHOPPING
Jussis Keramik..........................**37** C4
Svalan Hantwerk & Kläder........**38** C4

TRANSPORT
Biluthyrning Åland....................**39** C2
Birka Line.................................**40** B5
Birka Line terminal...................**41** A5
Destination Åland (Tallink).......**42** B2
Eckerö Linjen........................(see 2)
Ferry terminal..........................**43** A6

Finnair Office..........................(see 18)
Local Bus Terminal...................**44** C4
Regional Bus Terminal.............**45** C3
RO-NO Rent.............................**46** D4
RO-NO Rent.............................**47** B6
Silja Line..................................**48** C4
Viking Line...............................**49** C4

OTHER ATTRACTIONS

The 1927 copper-roofed **Sankt Göran's Church** (St George's Church; ☼ 10am-3pm Mon-Fri) in the town centre is not as interesting as the medieval treasure-trove churches in Åland's villages. The design is Art Nouveau, by Lars Sonck, and the church was donated to the town by a wealthy shipowner.

Sjalvstyrelsegården (Self-Government Bldg; ☎ 25000; cnr Österleden & Storagatan) is home of the Åland parliament. Free guided tours (available in English) are given at 10am every Friday from June to mid-August. The tour ends with a slide show about Åland.

South of Österhamn is **Tullarns Äng**, a small park that is prized for its spring wildflowers. **Lilla Holmen** island, connected to Tullarns Äng by a bridge, has a summer café, a decent swimming beach and peacocks strolling through the grounds.

The **Järsö** recreational area, 12km south of Mariehamn at the tip of the peninsula, is a good place for short bicycle and walking tours. The area is at its most beautiful in spring and early summer, when wildflowers cover the ground.

ACTIVITIES

In addition to bicycles, Ro-No Rent (☎ 12820; www.goaland.net/rono; ☼ 10-11am & 4-5pm May, 10am-6pm Jun-Aug) rents all kinds of fun outdoor equipment. You can rent fishing rods per day/week for €7/15; canoes per hour/day for €10/20; boats seating six with outboard motor per two hours/day for €60/102; and beach buggies per two hours/day for €25/45. Scooters can be had per two hours/day from €17/45, with free mileage and a full tank.

With so many boats packed into Mariehamn's harbours it's tempting to try your hand at sailing. **Åland Sailing Club** (☎ 040-724 5797; Västra Hamnen) runs sailing courses and private lessons, while **Midnight Sun Sailing** (☎ 57500; www.midnightsunsailing.fi) rents out yachts for charter or cruises.

On the eastern harbour, **Mariebad** (☎ 531 650; Österleden; www.mariebad.net; adult/child €7/4) is one of those fun Northern European waterparks, excellent for the whole family. There's a serious pool for lengths, as well as a warm pool, waterslide, saunas, Jacuzzi and café.

Tours

From mid-June to mid-August a novel sightseeing tour is operated by **Röde Orm** (☎ 0457-548 3554). Leaving from the market square in Mariehamn, a red London double-decker bus does a 45-minute tour to Järsö and back, (€7, 11.15am, 1.15pm and 2.15pm Monday to Friday, from mid-June to mid-August).

In July to early August there are cruises aboard the traditional wooden schooner **Linden** (☎ 12055; www.linden.aland.fi). There's a four-hour lunch cruise at noon (per person €39) and a four-hour dinner cruise at 6pm (per person €49) every day. The lunch one leaves from Sjökvarteret and arrives at Västerhamn; the dinner one vice versa.

Festivals and Events

The decoration and raising of the Midsummer poles (see below) and the subsequent dancing is memorable; you might also want to check out the **Viking Market** (www.visitaland.com) at Kvarnbo at the end of July, or the **Organ Festival** (www.alfest.org) in late June. The harvest festival in mid-September sees a variety of traditional events organized across the island. On a less traditional note, the

---

MIDSUMMER POLES

The most striking manmade feature in the Åland landscape is the Midsummer pole. It's a long flagpole decorated with leaves, miniature flags, small boats and other symbols, whose nature and symbolism varies from village to village. Each village usually has one or more poles, decorated in a public gathering the day before Midsummer. The pole then stands until the next Midsummer.

Although some theorists feel that the pole is a development of an ancient fertility rite, its origins on Åland itself are probably more recent. The poles often resemble ships' masts, with cross spars and cords resembling the rigging. Atop the poles there is usually a figure, the Fäktargubbe, who represents toil and diligence. Below him may come a streamer bearing the year of the Midsummer pole. Other motifs may include sailing boats, ears of corn representing the harvest, a wreath of love, a sun symbol facing east and symbols of community togetherness.

Rockoff (www.rockoff.nu) rock festival takes place in late July and draws some big Swedish, if not international, acts. It runs for a week in the evenings only.

Sleeping

Mariehamn's hotels generally raise their rates between mid-June and the end of August. It pays to book ahead, as the islands are popular destinations.

BUDGET

Mariehamn has no youth hostels.

Gröna Uddens Camping (☎ 21121; www.gron audden.com; per site €4-5 plus per adult €4-5, 2-/4-person cabins €55/85, r €50; ☒ mid-May–Aug) Just a 15-minute walk south of the centre, this seaside camping ground is a great place to stay. The beach is good for swimming, and, while the tent spaces can be a bit cramped, the brand new cabins are very cute and cosy. There are also simple rooms sleeping one to three, a sauna and minigolf. You can walk back into town through the seaside parkland.

Pensionat Solhem (☎ 16322; fax 16350; Ytternäs; s/d €41/61; ⓟ ☒) This is one of the more peaceful places to stay in Mariehamn. It's pleasantly situated near an inlet, 3km south of the centre. The rooms are simply but caringly decorated, the shared bathrooms are good, and guests can use the rowing boats and sauna. The local bus (routes B and D) stops nearby.

Gästhem Kronan (☎ 12617; kronan@aland.net; Neptunigatan 52; s/d €41/62; ⓟ ☒) This guesthouse is handily close to the Västerhamn ferry port but a bit of a hike from the centre. The rooms are spacious if a little austere, and the shared bathrooms tiny, but the management is helpful and it's not a bad deal, at least out of season (singles/doubles without breakfast €26/47). It also runs the summer-only **Gästhem Neptun** (Neptunigatan 41; s/d €46/67; ☒ mid-May–mid-Aug; ⓟ ☒), which is newer. Breakfast and linen are included at both.

MIDRANGE

Hotell Arkipelag (☎ 24020; www.hotellarkipelag.com; Strandgatan 31; s/d €110/135, ste from €185; ⓟ ☒ ⯐ ☎) Overlooking Österhamn, this hotel is large but friendly. It has all sorts of facilities: sauna, indoor and outdoor pools, casino, nightclub and more; the rooms are polished if unexciting. It's well worth shelling out an extra €12 to get a (magnificent)

view over the water; you can sit out on the balcony and toast it.

Park Alandia Hotell (☎ 14130; www.parkhotel .vikingline.fi; Norra Esplanadgatan 3; s/d €78/98; ⓟ ☒ ⯐ ⓕ) This place is on the main boulevard. The rooms feel particularly Scandinavian with their polished pine floors; they are spacious and light. The hotel also has a popular sunny public terrace. Rates are significantly cheaper on Sunday nights.

Hotell Adlon (☎ 15300; www.alandhotels.fi; Hamngatan 7; s/d €109/121; ☒ May-Oct; ⓟ ☒ ⯐) This modern hotel close to the ferry terminal is pretty ugly from outside but has light and comfy rooms as well as a restaurant, sports bar, and indoor pool. The décor veers towards the maritime. It has a cheaper annexe across the road, the Kaptensgården (doubles with/without bathroom €91/73); rates include use of the Adlon's facilities.

Eating

The best dining on the islands is found in Mariehamn. Many cafés in town serve the local speciality, *Ålandspannkaka* (Åland pancakes), for around €3 to €4. They're fluffy square puddings made with semolina and served with stewed prunes and whipped cream. Another tasty local speciality, *Ålands svartbröd* (Åland dark bread), is available at local markets – this fruity creation takes four days to make and is cracking with *sill* (pickled herring).

RESTAURANTS

ÅSS Paviljong (☎ 19141; Västhamn; lunch €13, mains €24-29; ☒ lunch & dinner May-Aug; ☒) Don't worry about the acronym: this boat-owners' favourite is the oldest restaurant in town, and also one of the most atmospheric. It's in a lovely old wooden building on the water's edge. The speciality is seafood and the set lunch buffet is good value.

FP von Knorring (☎ 16500; Österhamn; mains €15-27; ☒ lunch & dinner May-Aug; ☒) This beautiful boat restaurant has classy seafood meals served in intimate surroundings below deck, plus a busy beer terrace on the deck. It tends to use local ingredients prepared in fairly traditional ways.

Indigo (☎ 16550; www.indigo.ax; Nygatan 1; mains €20-30; ☒ restaurant 11am-3pm & 5-11pm, bar until 3am weekends; ☒) This spot is an intriguing mix of the old and the new. Set in an elegant historic stone building, the interior is warm and cosy. The kitchen has a more contemporary slant, turning out smart, tasty fare like carpaccio of beef. There's a cheaper bistro menu on the terrace, and it fills up after dinner with a trendy drinking crowd.

Nautical (☎ 19931; Hamngatan 2; mains €22-28; 🕑 lunch & dinner Mon-Fri, dinner Sat; ✗) Above the maritime museum, this classy spot has great views over the western harbour and the *Pommern*. The décor is, unsurprisingly, nautical (ahem); the food is classy, with small, elaborate portions of such fare as medallions of venison, as well as fine seafood.

CAFÉS

Bagarstugan 7 Hantverkare (☎ 19881; Ekonomiegatan 2; light meals €3-8; 🕑 10am-5pm Tue-Fri, 10am-3pm Sat; ✗) Just off Torggatan, this is one of Mariehamn's more charming cafés. Its homemade soups and sandwiches come with a smile and have a strong local following; there are also local crafts for sale.

Nikolaj Brasserie (☎ 22560; Torggatan; mains €8-14; 🕑 9am-8pm Mon-Fri, 9am-7pm Sat, 11am-1pm Sun; ✗) Set in the Galleria shopping arcade on Torggatan, this makes a filling stop for lunch or dinner. There's a tasty daily soup and huge pizzas, vegetarian dishes and more elaborate plates. Eat on the terrace if you can find a table.

Kaffestugan Svarta Katten (☎ 21599; Norragatan 15; 🕑 10am-5pm Mon-Fri, 11am-4pm Sat) This cosy place is a smart but homely café and stands out as one of the best places to try *Ålandspannkaka* (though not the cheapest). There are a few classic metal garden chairs if you fancy sitting out.

Eat (☎ 19999; Torget; meals €4-9; 🕑 11am-6pm Mon-Fri, 11.30am-3.30pm Sat) This place at the market square is an incredibly popular lunchtime spot, particularly with Åland's parliamentarians. There's an open and enclosed terrace.

Also recommended:

Café Julius (☎ 14211; Torggatan 10; 🕑 7am-5pm Mon-Sat, 9am-5pm Sun) Early opener with plenty of cheap sandwiches, pastries and snacks.

Café La Strada (☎ 13270; Torggatan; pizzas & pasta from €7-10; 🕑 10am-6pm Mon-Fri, 10am-4pm Sat) As well as pizza and pasta, they do a dish of the day for €8 to €10.

QUICK EATS

Dino's Bar & Grill (☎ 13939; Strandgatan 12; mains €9-23; 🕑 food 10.30am-9pm Mon-Sat, 2-9pm Sun) This bar is a popular meeting spot, with enormous hamburgers, pasta and pizza and a great outdoor deck. The mains, such as a mixed kebab, are tasty if a touch overpriced and come with chips and salad.

Dixie Grillen (☎ 19743; Ålandsvägen 40; burgers €4-5; 🕑 until 10pm) While the décor is nothing to put on your postcard home, this is an established spot for cheap snacks; burgers (including a veggie one), pizza and the like.

SELF-CATERING

There are several minimarkets all over town, but the largest supermarket is **K** (cnr Ålandsvägen and Norragatan).

Drinking

Mariehamn is busy with holidaying people of all ages in summer, so there's a reasonably varied nightlife on offer. As well as these places, see the previously mentioned Indigo and FP von Knorring restaurants, and the Park Alandia Hotell.

Club Marin (Österhamn; 🕑 11am-1am daily May-Jul, lunch and dinner Aug-Apr) This is an attractive, slightly upmarket harbour pavilion serving beer and meals, and is very popular on weekend nights in summer when there's dancing and live music.

Pub Bastun (Hamngatan) This down-to-earth place near the maritime museum has a small terrace and a grassy bank to lie back on with a beer. It has loud live music most weekends in summer; some surprisingly well-known Swedish and Finnish rock groups have played here.

Dino's Bar and Grill (☎ 13939; Strandgatan 12; 🕑 10am-1am or later Mon-Sat, 2-11pm Sun) This is a popular central pub with live entertainment in summer. The terrace on the enclosed square is a great place to relax.

Hotell Arkipelag (☎ 24020; Strandgatan 31; 🕑 bar 11am-midnight, disco 10pm-3am Thu-Sat) An evening hotspot, especially for the big-spending boat-owners. It has a lively disco and a casino.

Alvas Bar (☎ 16141; Ålandsvägen 42; 🕑 10pm-4am) The most popular late-night bar and disco with the younger crowd, particularly on weekends.

Entertainment

Bio Savoy cinema (cnr Nygatan & Ålandsvägen) This cinema, west of the centre, usually shows films in English, with Swedish subtitles.

Shopping

Mariehamn is a great place to shop for quality handicrafts – pick up a map of craft shops in Mariehamn and around mainland Åland at the tourist office.

Jussis Keramik (☎ 13606; Nygatan 1) This place sells interesting ceramics and glassware, and you can watch the objects being made.

Bagarstugan 7 Hantverkare (☎ 19881; Ekonomi-egatan 2) This is a crafts collective representing nearly a dozen artists. It also has a lovely café of the same name.

Sjökvarteret (Maritime Quarter; ☎ 16033; www.sjokvarteret.com) There are several craft workshops in this boat-building complex, see p233.

Svalan Hantverk & Kläder (☎ 13470, Torggatan 5). This shop sells handicrafts, materials and handmade clothing.

Getting There & Away

See p230 for information on travelling to and from Mariehamn by plane or ferry.

Viking, Tallink and Silja ferries depart from the ferry terminal at Västerhamn. Just north of it is a smaller terminal used only by Birka Line.

All ferry lines have offices in Mariehamn:

Birka Line (☎ 27027; www.birkaline.com; Östra Esplanadgatan 7).

Eckerö Linjen (☎ 28000; www.eckerolinjen.fi; Torggatan 2)

Silja Line (☎ 16711; www.silja.com; Torggatan 14)

Tallink (c/o Destination Åland; ☎ 040-300 8000; www.tallink.com)

Viking Line (☎ 26211; www.vikingline.fi; Storagatan 2)

Regional buses depart from the terminal in front of the library; for route and fare information see p232, or get a timetable from the tourist office.

Getting Around

There are four local bus routes running around two circular routes. A and C serve the northern parts of town, while B and D serve the south. They run half-hourly in winter and hourly in summer and are free.

For bicycles, **Ro-No Rent** (☎ 12820; www.goaland.net/rono; ⏰ 10-11am & 4-5pm May, 10am-6pm Jun-end Aug) is the main rental firm and it has outlets at Mariehamn's Österhamn and Västerhamn. There are daily/weekly rates for standard bicycles (€7/35), three-speed models (€9/45) and mountain bikes

(€13/65), as well as tandem bikes (€17/85) and motor scooters (€45/135). When its office isn't open, arrangements can be made by phone.

Hiring a car is a good way to see Åland. The best place is friendly **Biluthyrning Åland** (☎ 525 505) at the Esso petrol station opposite the Sjökvarteret. Rates for a small car start at €63 for a day, but there's often a 24-hour special for €55. There's a minimum of fuss involved, and they'll deliver it for free within Mariehamn.

MAINLAND ÅLAND & AROUND

The largest islands of the archipelago form a core group, which is the most popular destination in the province. This is where many of the oldest historical landmarks in Finland are found. Eckerö is particularly loved by Swedish families, given its proximity by ferry to Sweden, while Saltvik and Sund have the most well-known sights.

Bicycle tours around this part of Åland are very popular in summer because there are marked paths, distances are not too great and bridges or ferries connect the various islands to make up an area large enough for an interesting week of touring.

JOMALA
pop 3508

The Jomala region, just north of Mariehamn, has two main centres: Kyrkby, with a range of facilities, and the smaller Gottby.

The famous landscape painter Victor Westerholm had his summer house in Önnin-geby, a tiny village in eastern Jomala. Other artists followed him there, and for two decades around the turn of the 20th century, the area was known as the 'Önningeby colony'. There's an interesting **museum** (☎ 33710; admission €3; ⏰ noon-3pm Sun May-Aug, 10am-4pm Tue-Sun late Jun-early Aug) here that is dedicated to the artist and the village, with local historical memorabilia on display. The building itself was once a stone cowshed. The art collection and exhibitions include works by many of the artists influenced by the Önningeby School, but none by Westerholm himself. The area around the museum forms a photogenic scene of red wooden farm buildings, windmills and Midsummer poles.

Two kilometres west beyond Gottby, and 4km from the main road, the peaceful hamlet of Djurvik overlooks a gentle bay. Right by the water, **Djurviks Gästgård** (☎ 32433; www .goaland.net/djurviks; d €42, 2-/4-person cabins €45/57; P ✗) has an apartment with a kitchen, good cabins, simple double rooms and a garden; it's a remote spot and great for a relaxing stay with kids.

From Mariehamn, catch bus 5 to near Önnin-geby or bus 1 to Gottby. From Tuesday to Thursday in July, a special taxi leaves for the Önningeby museum from Mariehamn, allowing a couple of hours at the museum. A return ticket including museum entry is €6; cheaper than the bus.

FINSTRÖM
pop 2399

Finström is the central municipality in Åland. Godby is the island's second-biggest town and offers all facilities, including a **tourist office** (☎ 41890; ☉ 10am-8pm Mon-Fri, 10am-4pm Sat, noon-4pm Sun mid-Jun–mid-Aug) in the main shopping centre.

The medieval **Sankt Mikael Church** (☉ Mon-Fri May-Sep), with a wealth of frescoes and sculptures, is in a small village 5km north of Godby along a picturesque secondary road and is perfect for a stopover on a bicycle tour.

Just outside Godby, the Café Uffe på Berget, just south of the bridge to Sund, has a 30m-high **observation tower** with superb views of the archipelago. Across the road is **Godby Arboretum**, a tiny park with native and exotic trees along a short, marked nature trail.

Sleeping & Eating
Bastö Hotell & Stugby (☎ 42382; www.basto.aland .fi; s/d €72/91; ☉ May-Sep; P ✗ ☐) This largish holiday complex is set on a headland at Bastö, 12km northwest of Godby. Its hotel rooms are fairly simple, but come with en suite; all have a fridge, and some have simple cooking facilities. Large cottages sleep four to six people. There are saunas, minigolf, restaurant and all the other Finnish holiday essentials.

Café Uffe på Berget (☎ 41190; ☉ 10am-8pm Mon-Sat, 11am-8pm Sun May-Aug) Just outside Godby, this sits right on the bridge on the Mariehamn–Sund road. It's a popular stopover, as much for its viewing tower and outdoor terrace as for its pancakes and coffees (espresso machine!).

Getting There & Away
Road 2 from Mariehamn takes you to Godby. Bus 2, 3 and 4 from Mariehamn all go via Godby (€3). Bus 6 services other parts of Finström, leaving Godby three times a day, Monday to Friday only.

SUND
pop 1024

Sund, just east of the main island group and connected by bridge to Saltvik, is one of the most interesting municipalities in Åland. As well as a muscular medieval castle and large open-air museum, its attractions include a snail-tasting tour and the ruins of a formidable Russian stronghold. Sund is just 30km from Mariehamn, which makes it an ideal first overnight stop on a slow-paced bicycle tour. Finby, in the centre of Sund, is the largest town, with all services.

Sights & Activities
One of Åland's premier sights, **Kastelholms Slott** (☎ 432 156; admission €5; ☉ 10am-4pm Mon-Fri May, 10am-5pm daily Jun & Aug, 10am-6pm daily Jul, 10am-4pm Mon-Fri early–mid-Sep) is a smallish but perfectly formed castle picturesquely set by a little inlet. It has experienced several building phases, the earliest of which was in the 14th century. The most impressive part is the keep, which towers 15m high in parts; the walls are 3m thick; there was no escape for Eric XIV, a Swedish king imprisoned here for a time. The hall, a later construction, ended up being used as a grain storehouse and has an exhibition of items found by archaeologists. Entry is by regular guided tour; while English tours are rare (2pm Saturday and Sunday from late June to early August), there are plenty of information panels. The castle is just off the main road number 2, clearly signposted and visible to the right (when heading east), after passing Kastelholm village.

Next to the castle is **Jan Karlsgårdens Friluftsmuseum** (admission free; ☉ 10am-4pm May–mid-Sep, 10am-5pm Jun-Aug, closed weekends in Sep), a delightful open-air museum. Stroll around examining a variety of traditional Åland buildings, including windmills and a smoke sauna. It's worth purchasing the guidebook

ÅLAND

(€1) from the Vita Björn museum before entering. Central to all is a Midsummer pole; this is a great place to be when it's erected at the Midsummer festival.

By the entrance of the Jan Karlsgården Museum is **Fängelsemuseet Vita Björn** (☎ 432 156; admission €2; ☻ 10am-5pm May-Aug, 10am-4pm Mon-Fri early Sep), a small prison museum. The building was used as a jail until 1975, and there's a demonstration of how cell conditions evolved over the two centuries it was in use. Although it looks like a cottage, the walls and floor are of thick stone, so there was no tunnelling out.

Also near Kastelholm is Åland's oddest tourist attraction, the **snail safari** run by **Alandia Escargots** (☎ 43964; admission €5.50; ☻ 2-3 tours daily Jul, 2 tours Tue-Fri late Jun & Aug). The snail farm opens only for the one-hour tours; it's worth paying the extra (total €9) to taste one of the little critters in garlic butter, washed down by a glass of strong cider.

Åland's original **golf course** (☎ 43883), boasting 36 holes, is across the bay from Kastelholm. The Slottsbanan course is harder than the Kungsbanan.

North of Kastelholm, **Sankt Johannes Church** (☻ May-Aug) is the biggest church on Åland. It is 800 years old and is decorated with beautiful paintings. Note the stone cross with the text 'Wenni E'. According to researchers, it was erected in memory of the Hamburg bishop Wenni, who died here when on a crusade in 936.

East of Kastelholm are the ruins of the Russian fortress at **Bomarsund**. After the war of 1809, Russian troops began to build Bomarsund as a defence against the Swedes. Construction took decades, and the mammoth building was operational but not wholly complete by the time the Crimean War (1854) came around. Twenty-five British and French ships bombarded it heavily from the sea; after two days it capitulated and was demolished by the victors. The evocative honeycomb ruins can be seen on both sides of the main road at the eastern end of Sund, by the bridge leading across a beautiful sound to Prästö island. On the other side of the water is the small **Bomarsund museum** (☎ 44032; admission by donation; ☻ 10am-4pm Mon-Fri Jun-mid-Aug, also Sat & Sun in Jul) has more information and displays bits and pieces excavated from the site of the fortress ruins.

There are several **graveyards** – Greek Orthodox, Jewish, Muslim and Christian – clearly marked on the island of Prästö. All date back to the Russian occupation.

Sleeping & Eating

Kastelholms Gästhem (☎ 43841; kastelholms.gast hem@aland.net; s/d €47/65; ☻ May–mid-Oct; P ✗) This tranquil spot is a 15-minute walk from the castle in the village of Tosarby. It's a serene spot with a grassy garden, wooden deck and laundry/kitchen facilities. Accommodation is good for this price, for which reason you should really book in advance.

Puttes Camping (☎ 44040; puttes.camping@aland .net; tent sites per person €2.50 plus per tent or vehicle €2, cabins €29; ☻ May-Aug; P) Right next to the ruins of Bomarsund, this friendly place has plenty of grassy camp sites, well-priced simple four-berth powered cabins, laundry, kitchen, a beach sauna and a canoe jetty. Phone ☎ 0457-313 4177 if there's nobody about.

Prästö Stugor & Camping (☎ /fax 44045; tent sites €3, cabins €39-59; ☻ mid-Apr–mid-Sep) Located at the eastern end of Prästö, just near the ferry across to Vårdö, this location has a bit of everything. As well as small and large cabins and camping space, there are amusements including sand volleyball and a sauna, as well as a grilli that does simple hamburger 'n chips (€8.50) and the like. It's also a popular spot to sip a beer on the veranda as the sun hangs in the evening sky.

The restaurant at the Jan Karlsgården Museum serves light snacks and delicious meals. It serves surprisingly classy fare for a museum restaurant, so it makes a great lunch stop.

Getting There & Away

Road 2 and bus 4 from Mariehamn to Vårdö will take you to Sund. The bus goes via Kastelholm (€3.60, 20 minutes), Svensböle, Bomarsund and Prästö (€4.90, 30 to 45 minutes).

The bicycle ferry **Nadja** (☎ 040-553 3256; ☻ Jun–mid-Aug) operates between Prästö and Lumpo, Lumparland. There is one departure a day from Monday to Saturday from June to mid-August. It leaves Lumpo at midday, and returns from Prästö at 12.30pm (one way €7).

VÅRDÖ
pop 425

This quiet and remote spot has been chosen as a retreat by several noted Finnish and Swedish authors. Small wonder, as its rippling bays, rustling silver birches, and views over the numerous islets of the archipelago impart much inner calm.

The main settlement is Vargata, which has a bank (no ATM), a shop and a post office. The **library** (☎ 47970, ◷ 2-4.30pm & 6-9pm Tue & Thu) has free Internet access. Beyond here, the island's **church** (◷ 10am-6pm Jun-Aug) is a typically picturesque 18th-century affair with a curiously bulbous tower. Further northeast, Lövö village was the scene of a peace conference in 1718 between representatives of King Karl XII of Sweden and Tsar Peter I (Peter the Great) of Russia, during the Great Northern War. Judging by what has been dug from the earth here, the 1200 participants in this high-class event consumed French wine and oysters in frightening quantities.

On the main road between Vargata and Lövö, **Seffers Homestead Museum** (☎ 47605; adult/child €2/free; ◷ noon-3pm Tue, Thu & Sat midJun–Jul) is an old 18th-century farmhouse with a windmill, farm equipment and a Midsummer pole on display.

Sleeping

Sandösunds Camping (☎ 47750; www.sandocamping .aland.fi; tent sites per person €3, plus tent or vehicle €2, cabins from €35) This delightful spot is a great camp site. On a beach in the island's north, there are pleasant two- and four- bed cabins, a café-restaurant and canoe and bike rentals. Best of all, the enthusiastic owners have created a unique 'floating sauna' on the picture-perfect sound. While it's nominally open from May to August, you won't be turned away if you ring ahead out of season.

Bomans Gästhem (☎ 47821; Vårdöby; dm/d €22/72; ◷ May-Sep; P ✗) This HI-affiliated hostel is signposted 500m off the road between Vargata and Lövö. As well as dorm beds, there are some smart new rooms in little bungalows and simpler cabins (€50) also. There are all sorts of facilities and activities; guests have use of a kitchen and sauna, and can rent bikes. There's even a driving range in the field out the front. Breakfast and linen are included in price.

Getting There & Away

Bus 4 will take you to Vårdö from Mariehamn (€5.60, 40 to 55 minutes), crossing on the short, free car ferry from Prästö. Ferries on the northern archipelago route depart from the village of Hummelvik on Vårdö; the bus meets them. For more details see p245. For information on the bicycle ferry between Saltvik and Vårdö, see p242.

SALTVIK
pop 1723

Was the legendary 10th-century Viking capital, Birka, situated in Saltvik? Though there's no evidence – and stronger proof exists that the Viking stronghold was near the Swedish Lake Mälaren – one Ålandese archaeologist is convinced of Saltvik's former glory.

Whatever the case, many signs of Viking occupation have been unearthed around Saltvik, more so than elsewhere on the Åland archipelago. Nevertheless, a giant leap of the imagination will be required to reconstruct longhouses from the scant ruins.

East of Kvarnbo, the central village of Saltvik, is the Iron Age fortress of **Borgboda**. On the main Saltvik bicycle route, it is thought to have been built in the mid- to-late first millennium AD. Some stone outcroppings remain, but otherwise it's just a cow field with a nice view.

Kvarnbo has the large **Sankta Maria Church** that dates from the 12th century and is probably the oldest church in Finland. There are some wall paintings and sculptures from the 13th century, as well as a fine baptismal font, but most of the paintings are from the Lutheran era, in the 1500s.

Orrdals Klint & The Stone Age Village

The highest 'mountain' in Åland, 129m above sea level, is really no more than a big hill. Two short, well-marked walking tracks (1km and 2.5km long respectively) lead to the top, where there's a viewing tower and a simple four-bed camp hut.

On the road to Orrdals Klint near Långbergsöda is a Stone Age walking trail starting from a clearly-marked car park. It's more of a stroll than a hike, taking you past two excavated settlements and then to a fully reconstructed **Stone Age Village** (◷ 11am-6pm late Jun–mid-Aug), with sealskin-covered huts.

ÅLAND

In summer there are plenty of Neolithic skills to try your hand at; there are even real people living Stone Age–like lives there. There is no public transport; you'll have to make your own way from Kvarnbo.

Getting There & Away

Bus 3 runs from Mariehamn to Kvarnbo (€3.60, 35 minutes) and other villages in Saltvik.

The bicycle ferry **Kajo** (☎ 0400-783 086) runs between Tengsödavik (Saltvik) and Västra Simskäla (Vårdö) late June to early August. There is one daily departure each way, leaving Västra Simskäla at noon and Tengsödavik at 12.30pm. One way it's €9.

GETA

pop 461

The northern municipality of Geta is quiet and isolated; the main attraction is **Getabergen** – a formidable peak at 98m above sea level. One nature trail here is aimed at kids (2km), while a longer trail (5.5km) leads to Djupviksgrottan, a spacious natural grotto that is one of several striking geological features hereabouts.

Soltuna Stugor (☎ 49530; 2-/3-/4-person cabins €30/35/40; ☺ May-Aug), at the top of Getabergen, is a pleasant group of 10 cottages and a popular stop for cyclists. Soltuna restaurant at the top of Getabergen serves breakfast, lunch and dinner during summer.

Bus 2 runs from Marienhamn to Geta (€5.40, 50 minutes) via Godby.

The bicycle ferry **Silvana** (☎ 0400 229 149; ☺ Jun–mid-Aug) travels between Hällö in Geta, and Skarpnåtö in Hammarland. There is one departure daily in early June (leaving Skarpnåtö at noon and Hällö at 12.30pm) and two daily departures during the rest of the season (the second leaves Skarpnåtö at 4.30pm and Hällö at 5pm). The trip one way costs €7.

HAMMARLAND

pop 1387

The northwestern section of mainland Åland is called Hammarland. This is one of the oldest inhabited areas in Åland; almost 40 burial mound sites have been discovered. Kattby is the main village, with all facilities.

Sankta Catharina Church (☺ summer) in Kattby was probably built in the 12th century. There's an **Iron Age burial site** to the west of the church, with more than 30 burial mounds.

North of Kattby, on the road to Skarpnåtö, is **Ålands Wool Spinnery** (☎ 37810) and shop. It sells homespun yarn and handmade sweaters. Further north in Lillbolstad is a ceramics shop, **Lugnet Ceramics** (☎ 37780). All products are handmade. West of the village of Sålis, **Bovik** is a pretty little fishing harbour.

Activities in Skarpnåtö centre around **Södergård Estate** (☺ closed winter), a museum and handicrafts shop. The owners of the estate rent fishing boats.

Sleeping & Eating

Kattnäs Camping (☎ 37687; tent sites €8-13, cabins €37; ☺ May–mid-Sep) This camping ground is 3km south of the Eckerö-Mariehamn road, a bit west of Kattby. It feels delightfully remote when not too busy, and is set by sparkling blue water; it has a café, TV lounge and kitchen.

Kvarnhagens Stugor (☎ /fax 37212; 2-/3-/4-person cottages €45/50/55; ☺ May-Sep) This place at Skarpnåtö has six sturdy timber cottages. They are equipped with fridge and simple kitchen facilities, and the communal facilities include sauna, laundry, and a smoke hut in case you catch any fish!

Getting There & Away

Bus 1 from Mariehamn to Eckerö runs through Hammarland. For information on the bicycle ferry between Hammarland and Geta, see left.

ECKERÖ

pop 897

The island of Eckerö is the westernmost municipality in Finland, just a two-hour ferry ride from mainland Sweden. Eckerö has been a popular holiday spot since the 1800s. While it is very quiet in spring or autumn, vacationing Swedish families multiply the population by several times in July.

Storby (Big Village), at the ferry terminal, is the main centre, with an information point, petrol station, and bank. The distance from Mariehamn to Storby (40km) makes this a suitable day trip by bicycle.

Sights & Activities

The historic **Post och Tullhuset** (Post & Customs House; ☎ 38689) in Storby was designed by German architect Carl Ludwig Engel, designer of parts of central Helsinki. It was completed in 1828, during the era of Tsar Alexander I of Russia. As Åland was the westernmost extremity of the Russian Empire, the building was meant to be a show of might to the west and, for that reason, is far more grandiose than a post office in a small village should be. If there's something about the façade that troubles you, it may be the lack of a front door! It also now houses a café, post office, and exhibition gallery and the small **mailboat museum** (☎ 39000; admission €1.70; ⏰ 10am-3pm Jun–mid-Aug, 10am-4pm mid-Jun–Jul). The museum (and, at time of writing, the exhibition gallery) tells the story of the dedicated men whose job it was to get the mail through to mainland Sweden and Finland by boat. This gruelling system was in place for two and a half centuries, and many perished. The post office and art gallery are open daily in summer, and Monday to Friday only in winter.

Also in Storby, the **Labbas Homestead & Bank Museum** (☎ 38507; admission €1.70; ⏰ noon-4pm Wed Jul–mid-Aug) opens about as often as Halley's Comet comes around. If you do coincide, drop in; the typical archipelago houses have traditional local furniture, maritime displays and a section devoted to banking history.

Just north of Storby is the attractive **Käringsund harbour**. On summer evenings this peaceful little cove with its rustic old wooden boathouses reflected in the water is so scenic it's almost unreal. There's a nature trail and small **beach** here and canoes and rowing boats can be hired from a kiosk nearby.

At Käringsund harbour is **Ålands Jakt och Fiskemuseum** (Åland Hunting & Fishing Museum; ☎ 38299; admission €4.20; ⏰ 10am-5pm May–mid-Sep, 10am-6pm mid-Jun–mid-Aug) with photographs, stuffed animals, pearl-digging displays and the history of the hunting and fishing industries.

Viltsafari (☎ 38000), also at Käringsund harbour, is a fenced-in forest with typical Finnish fauna like red and fallow deer, swans and wild boar, as well as a few ostriches. The 45-minute tour (€4) departs from opposite the Hunting & Fishing Museum hourly in summer and by arrangement during other seasons.

In the village of Kyrkoby, about 5km east from Storby on the road to Mariehamn, the 13th-century **Sankt Lars Church of Eckerö** (⏰ 10am-6pm May-Sep; admission by donation) is a delightful little place with a cosy wooden interior, a 14th-century Madonna sculpture, and rustic murals. The altar painting is a 19th-century work depicting a Magdalene penitent.

Kyrkoby is also home to the **Kyrkoby golf course** (☎ 38370; short course €17, weekday/weekend green fees €28/35), which has a brand-new 18-hole course, a short-course, and a driving range, as well as one of Åland's best restaurants.

Degersand, about 9km south of Storby beyond the village of Torp, has a good **beach** for swimming and sunning, and it's also possible to camp right on the beach.

There's a branch of Ro-No Rent near the harbour for bicycle, scooter and canoe hire. See p238 for price details.

Sleeping

Eckerö has more cabin and cottage rentals than any other Åland province – contact **Ålandsresor** (☎ 28040; www.alandsresor.fi; Torggatan 2, Mariehamn; ⏰ 8.30am-5pm Mon-Fri, also 9am-2pm Sat Jun & Jul) for details.

GUESTHOUSES & HOTELS

Ängstorp Gästhem (☎ 38665; angstorp@aland.net; s/d 55/63; ⏰ Apr-Oct; P ✗) In an 18th-century wooden house in Storby, this is one of the best places to stay on Åland and should be booked ahead. The rustic décor is simple and beautiful; there are three upstairs rooms, with loveable sloping ceilings, that share kitchen facilities and a downstairs apartment that's great for families. There's also a sauna, garden, bike rental and a genuine welcome. It's very handy for the Grisslehamn ferry.

Hotell Havsbandet (☎ 38200; havsbandet@aland .net; s/d €78/95; ⏰ Apr-Dec; P ✗) This place, between the Post and Customs House and the sea, is a likeable place run by a sound old couple. It's good for families; on a very quiet road and opposite the gentlest of beaches. There's a grassy terrace and a good restaurant.

Österängens Hotell (☎ 38268; osterangen@aland .net; s/d €70/83; ⏰ Mar-Sep; P ✗ ✸) This place, on the quiet beach of Torp, has a good restaurant and sea views. There are all the beachside activities you could desire, and there's an indoor pool and sauna. Some of the rooms have their own sauna.

ÅLAND

ÅLAND

CAMPING

Käringsunds Camping (☎ 38309, 040-589 7230; yvonnee@aland.net; tent sites €6-9, cabins €35-55; ⏱ mid-May–Aug) At Käringsund harbour, this is a down-to-earth place with friendly management, camping and lots of cabins. There are all kinds of activities available, and the restaurant is busy at weekends with Swedes dancing to live music.

Uddens Camping (☎ 38670; fax 38547; tent sites per person & per car €1.20, cabins €54; ⏱ May-Sep) This place is in the isolated village of Skag on the northern coast. It's a good place to get away from things, although it is over-caravanned at times. There's a kiosk and café.

Eating

Restaurang Rusell (☎ 38499; lunch €12.95, mains €18-28; ⏱ lunch & dinner late Apr-Oct, no weeknight dinners until mid-May; ✗) A significant advance on the usual '19th green' concept, the Kyrkoby golf course has one of the best eateries in the whole 'nation' of Åland. Lunch is available until 3pm, but evenings see plenty of locals gossiping downstairs at the pub. There's also accommodation (doubles €62).

Jannes Bodega (Käringsund Harbour; ⏱ Jun-Aug) This little café sits on a rickety wooden dock overlooking the tiny harbour with its gently warping boathouses. It's a beautiful place to while away some time.

Café Lugn & Ro (☎ 38420; Post & Customs House; ⏱ 10am-4pm May-Sep, 10am-6pm Jul–mid-Aug) This friendly place serves sandwiches, hamburgers and delicious pastries with a Venezuelan touch. There's also accommodation available in the historic complex: singles/doubles €60/68, mid-January to December.

Getting There & Away

Road 2 runs from Mariehamn to Eckerö. If you use public transport, take bus 1 (€4.90, 40 minutes). For information on ferries between Eckerö and Grisslehamn, Sweden, see p232.

LEMLAND

pop 1694

Lemland municipality is between Lumparland and the Lemström Canal, 5km east of Mariehamn on road 3 (take bus 5). The canal was built in 1882 by prisoners of war. **Norrby** village is Lemland's centre.

In Norrby, **Sankta Birgitta Church** (⏱ Mon-Fri May-Aug) has 13th- to 14th-century wall paint-

ings that were rediscovered in 1956. **Burial mounds** from the Iron Age are nearby. At **Lemböte** on the western side of the island are the ruins of a 13th-century chapel and more ancient burial mounds. Near the crossing to Lumparland, **Skeppargården Pellas** (☎ 34001; adult/child €2.50/free; ⏱ 11am-4pm late Jun-Aug) is the homestead museum of a local shipmaster.

LUMPARLAND

pop 379

Many travellers pass through Lumparland in southeastern Åland because of its two ferry harbours, Svinö and Långnäs. Otherwise, there's little reason to visit.

Sankt Andreas Church (⏱ Jun-Aug), built in 1720, is one of the 'newer' churches of Åland. This little wooden church is in a beautiful seaside spot along the road to Lumparby village and Lumpo.

Långnäsbyn (☎ 35557; 4-/5-person cottages €42/48; ⏱ May-Aug), near the Långnäs ferry terminal, has nine reasonably priced cottages and a communal kitchen. **Svinö Stugby** (☎ 35781; cabins €29; ⏱ May-Sep) is a rustic group of 10 simple but good-value two-person cottages by the beach in Svinö.

From Mariehamn take bus 5 to Svinö and Långnäs (€4.50, 45 minutes); it meets the ferries. For information on the bicycle ferry to Prästö see p240.

NORTHERN ARCHIPELAGO

The northern group of the Åland islands consists of the archipelago municipalities of Kumlinge and Brändö. They are very quiet and offer less for the traveller than the southern group, but you're certainly away from it all exploring these far-flung islands. If you're coming to Åland from Kustavi on the Finnish mainland through Osnäs, you'll arrive at Långö in the north of the Brändö island group. You can also depart from here, but confirm ferry times in advance to avoid getting stuck.

KUMLINGE

pop 371

About 1¼ hours by ferry from Vårdö, Kumlinge municipality isn't exactly a thrumming tourist hotspot. The main island, Kumlinge, is flanked by **Enklinge** island to the north and **Seglinge** island to the south. All services can be found on Kumlinge, and a bank is on Enklinge. There is no accommodation on Seglinge and no restaurant – only a shop in the main village.

The ferry to Seglinge departs from the island of **Snäckö**, 8km from Kumlinge village. Local ferries to Enklinge from the main island depart from the village of **Krokarno**.

A marked **cycling route** runs from Snäckö north to Krokarno, with bridges between the islands. On Enklinge there is a signposted route from the harbour to the local museum.

Many consider **Sankta Anna Church** (summer) on Kumlinge island to be one of Finland's most beautiful churches, with 500-year-old Franciscan-style paintings. The church is some 2km north of Kumlinge village.

On Enklinge is the small open-air **Hermas Farm Museum** (55334; admission €2; 10am-4pm Mon-Fri Jun-Aug, 10am-7pm Jul), 3.5km from the pier, with 20 buildings that are all original to this island.

Sleeping & Eating

Remmarina Stugor (0400-529 199; 2-/3-/4-person cottages €45/50/55; P) At the guest harbour 2km from Kumlinge village, this place has 12 clean, reasonably priced cottages on a small hill, plus a wood sauna and a small canteen for snacks. It's open all year round; call if there's nobody about.

Ledholms Camping (/fax 55647; tent sites per person €2.50; Jun-Aug) This camping ground is on the island of Snäckö near the ferry pier. It also has cheap cabins and a small grocery.

Getting There & Away

Ferries on the route between Hummelvik and Torsholma on Brändö stop at both Enklinge (one hour) and Kumlinge islands (70 minutes).

One or two ferries a day go from Långnäs in Lumparland to Snäckö in Kumlinge, via Överö in the Föglö island group (1¾ hours).

BRÄNDÖ

pop 516

The municipality of Brändö consists of a group of 1180 islands, the largest and most important of which are connected by bridges. Banks and other services are on the main island and in the villages of **Lappo** and **Torsholma** on smaller islands.

The peculiar shape of the main island makes for interesting cycling – no matter where you go, you will always be riding by the sea. A signposted **bike route** runs from the harbour at Torsholma north across the main island to the harbour at Långö.

St Jakobs Church, the wooden place of worship on the main island of Brändö, dates from 1893. On Lappo island further south (and connected to the main island by ferry), **Skärgårdsmuseet** (56689; adult/child €3.50/free; 10am-noon & 2-4pm mid-Jun–mid-Aug) has exhibits of local history, boats and nature as well as a photography exhibition.

Sleeping & Eating

Hotell Gullvivan (56350; www.gullvivan.aland.fi; s/d €66/84; P) Open all year and completely nonsmoking, this comfortable hotel sits on Björnholma island not far from the central services. There's a restaurant, sauna and mini-golf as well as the opportunity to hire boats or go fishing. There are also four-person huts available (€84) with a microwave, fridge and cooking facilities.

Pellas Gästhem (040-832 4333; www.pellas.aland.fi; Lappo; 2-/4-/6-person apt up to €44/59/76; late Mar-early Dec; P) Formerly the local school, this friendly accommodation option is on Lappo, southwest of the main Brändö island complex; the Hummelvik-Kumlinge-Brändö ferry stops here. There are cabins with simple cooking facilities sleeping four (€44), and a variety of spick-and-span apartments with bathroom and kitchen facilities; they are attractively furnished in pine and some come with sauna.

Brändö Stugby (56221; http://come.to/brando.stugby; May–mid-Oct) There's a camping ground on Brändö which also has log cabins and rowing boats for hire.

Getting There & Away

From Mariehamn, take bus 4 to Hummelvik harbour on Vårdö. There are three ferry connections a day from Vårdö to Lappo and Torsholma via Kumlinge. The trip from Hummelvik to Torsholma takes about 2½ hours. It's free for passengers and bicycles, and €19 for cars.

From Turku on mainland Finland, take a bus to Kustavi, and on to Vartsala Island

ÅLAND

ARCHIPELAGO FERRIES

If travelling by car between the main part of Åland and the Finnish mainland via the northern or southern archipelago, you must spend a night en route: reservations will not be accepted on through ferries. The ferries run for the benefit of islanders, so this system ensures that the islands benefit from tourists taking advantage of the subsidized ferries. It's a blessing in disguise anyway; you may end up staying much longer!

---

to reach the harbour of Osnäs (Finnish: Vuosnainen). There are five to seven connections a day from Osnäs to Långö on the northern Brändö island of Åva. This journey is free for passengers and bicycles, and €14 for cars.

SOUTHERN ARCHIPELAGO

The southern group of Åland islands consists of the municipalities of Föglö, tiny Sottunga and remote Kökar. Kökar is the most quaint and appealing island, and is also the jumping-off point for archipelago ferries from Galtby harbour on Korpo on the Finnish mainland (see opposite). The ferry trips are worthwhile in themselves; it's quite feasible to do a day-trip from Mariehamn, spending a couple of hours in, say, Kökar or Sottunga. The views from the boat, of myriad low granite islets clung to by pine and silver birch, are memorable.

FÖGLÖ
pop 607

The Föglö island group was first mentioned in 1241 by a Danish bishop who landed here en route to Tallinn. An inn was founded in 1745 at Föglö at Enigheten Estate.

A signposted bike route runs between the settlements of **Degerby** and **Överö**, and there is a regular bus service. Both villages are served by archipelago ferries.

Degerby has a bank, post office and grocery, as well as a summer **tourist information kiosk** (☎ 0457-342 7274; 10am-7pm Mon-Fri, 10am-5pm Sat, 10am-2.30pm Sun mid-Jun–mid-Aug). The 'capital' of Föglö, Degerby is a small

village noted for its unusual **architecture**. Many Föglöites have traditionally been civil servants, not farmers, and have chosen to build their houses in Art Nouveau or Empire styles instead of the traditional archipelago style.

In the red building at the harbour you'll find the local **museum** (☎ 50348; admission €2; 10am-5pm Tue-Sun mid-Jun–mid-Aug). **Sankta Maria Magdalena Church** (Mon-Fri summer) is on an island south from Degerby, connected by a bridge. Getting there is half the fun, as the road is scenic. The simple 14th-century church is not very impressive but the way it rises from the plain rock bed is dramatic.

Sleeping & Eating
Enighetens Gästhem (☎ 50310; s/d €40/56; May-Sep;) This rustic retreat 1km from the Degerby ferry terminal is a fine place to stay. Booking is essential. It has a café and good breakfasts.

C & C Camping (☎ 51440; per tent & car €2, per person €3, cabins €30-49; Jun-Aug) This place is on the small Finholma island northeast of Degerby. It's on the Degerby–Överö cycle route and has a variety of cabins sleeping from two to four; you pay a little more for a simple kitchen. It's relaxed and family-friendly.

Seagram (☎ 51092; May-Aug) This place on the shore in Degerby is a good licensed restaurant with dancing in summer and a terrace popular with boat people.

Getting There & Away
From Mariehamn, bus 5 goes to the Svinö and Långnäs ferry harbours, both in Lumparland. A dozen or so ferries a day make the one-hour trip between Svinö and Degerby. There are six to seven ferries a day from Långnäs to Överö, some going on to Kumlinge, and others to Kökar.

SOTTUNGA
pop 131

Somnolent Sottunga island has more cows than people. Despite the small population, the island has its own bank, shop, school, health-care centre, library and church.

The wooden **Sankta Maria Magdalena Church** was built in 1661 and renovated in 1974. A short **nature trail** starts at the fishing harbour, and a marked **cycling route** runs north from the harbour to the village of Skaget.

Strandhuggets Stugor (☎ 55255; d €30; ☺ Jun-Aug; Ⓟ ⊠) right next to the harbour, has six cute pine-shaded cottages for two people available for overnight or longer stays, as well as a café/restaurant and sauna.

Ferries on the southern archipelago route from Lumparland or Föglö, as well as occasional ferries from Kumlinge, will take you to Sottunga.

KÖKAR
pop 296

The Kökar island group, with its strikingly barren landscape, is one of the most interesting in Åland. Many of the inhabitants live in and around the quaint little town of Karlby, which has a bank, post office and grocery.

Though it feels quite isolated from the rest of the world, Kökar is not difficult to reach by ferry. Its marshier areas harbour a significant number of species of waterbird.

Sights & Activities

Historic **Hamnö Island** is connected to the main island by a bridge. Since time immemorial, boats have been anchored at its shores, many of them plying the Hanseatic trade route between Germany and Turku. A very small – a dozen members at most – Franciscan community built a monastery here in the 14th century. The main building is long gone, but the present **church** (☺ daily May-Sep), from 1784, was built on the same site.

The small **Kökar Homestead Museum** (☎ 55816; admission €2; ☺ noon-5pm mid-Jun–mid-Aug) of local history is on the east side of the main island, in the village of Hellsö. A short **nature trail** starts near Hellsö.

Sleeping & Eating

Hotell Brudhäll (☎ 55955; www.goaland.net/brudhall; s/d €91/108, ste €195; Ⓟ) Right in the throbbing heart of things in tiny Karlby, this is one of the best hotels of the islands. It's a pretty red place right on the little harbour, with plenty of chairs on the terrace to relax on by the lapping water. The rooms are rustic and attractive; the suite has its own sauna, and it has a highly regarded restaurant serving traditional archipelago dishes. There's entertainment and dancing on summer evenings.

Antons Gästhem (☎ 55729; fax 55938; summer s/d €64/68) This chunky old house is 3.5km from the ferry harbour near the island of Hamno. It's friendly and open year round. There are bikes for hire, and rates are cheaper outside the June-to-August high season.

Sandvik Camping (☎ 55911; tent €5; ☺ May-Sep) This camping ground is 3.5km southwest of the harbour, near Hamno Island. If you're on foot, you can get there much quicker picking your way around the coast (to your right as you exit the ferry). There are kitchen facilities, one cabin, a sauna and a grilli (June to August) as well as a good swimming beach.

Getting There & Away

On mainland Finland, ferries depart for Kökar once or twice daily from the harbour of Galtby on Korpo Island, 75km from Turku and connected by bus. The trip from Galtby to Kökar takes 2¼ hours. It's free for passengers and bicycles, and €19 for cars.

To get to Kökar from mainland Åland, there are three to five connections a day from Långnäs (take bus 5 from Mariehamn) via Föglö and Sottunga. The ferry also stops at the tiny island of Husö. Travel time is 2½ hours from Långnäs. It's free for passengers and bicycles and €19 for cars.

See the boxed text, opposite, for important information about this ferry route.

Pohjanmaa

This coast is often referred to as Ostrobothnia (Swedish: Österbotten), for it has historically had a strong Swedish presence, and many communities are still largely Swedophone.

Stretching from Pori in the south to Kalajoki in the north, and inland to Seinäjoki, the interplay of the Finnish- and Swedish-speaking cultures is fascinating.

As well as the year-round appeal of the main town, Vaasa, with its waterside location and art galleries, and the beautiful wooden old-towns of Kokkola and Jakobstad, there are a number of events that are among Finland's best. The sunny summers here host the Folk Music Festival at Kaustinen, and two wildly different affairs at Seinäjoki – the major international Provinssirock festival, and a hugely popular fiesta of that curious subculture, Finnish tango.

Swedes first developed trading towns on the west coast in the 17th century to exploit the forests for tar. After this dried up, many Swedes remained and a farming culture emerged. Language is the distinctive feature here; a newsstand in Jakobstad will have a collection of imported Swedish papers that keep locals gossiping about Sweden's TV stars, and the radio station is more likely to be playing Stockholm's 'P3' than a Finnish station. People from Sweden treat this region with curiosity and call it *Parallelsverige,* or 'Parallel Sweden'.

While Pohjanmaa lacks the mystery of Lapland or the beauty of the Lakeland, skipping the coast here would be a mistake for anyone wanting a full picture of Finland. The inland areas, fields splashed with bright yellow canola and dotted with dozens of grey or rust-red hay barns, seem a rural idyll out of a pastoral novel, very quiet apart from the festivals.

HIGHLIGHTS

- Pitching a tent for the **Kaustinen Folk Music Festival** (p264) in July; Finland's answer to Woodstock

- Wandering the picturesque **old town** (p257) of Jakobstad

- Visiting the excellent art collection in Vaasa's **Museum of Ostrobothnia** (p250)

- Cycling around the fishing villages on the island of **Replot** (p254)

- Relaxing in lovely **Kristinestad** (p254) or peaceful **Kaskinen** (p256)

- Marvelling at the natural crystal formations in Kokkola's **Mineral Museum** (p260)

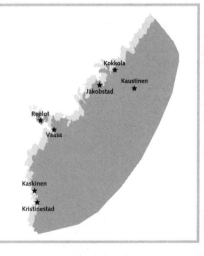

POHJANMAA

Activities

Pohjanmaa's rolling fields, unchallenging gradients, regularly-spaced towns and beautiful coastal scenery make it an appealing destination for a spot of leisurely cycling. Apart from two-wheeled activities, the water itself is an obvious and popular attraction, with boating, fishing, and swimming all popular and quite easily accessible.

Self-Catering Accommodation

Local tourist offices have details of cottages in the area. An organization that organizes self-catering packages is **FinFun Finwest** (☎ 020 1334 882; www.finfun.fi; Mannenkatu 1, Oulu).

VAASA

☎ 06 / pop 57,030

Located at the slender waist of the Gulf of Bothnia and a bare 45 nautical miles from Sweden, it's no surprise that a cultural duality exists in Vaasa (Swedish: Vasa). A quarter of the population here speak Swedish as their first language, and the city has a feel all of its own. You'll hear conversations between friends and colleagues in restaurants and bars flitting between Finnish and Swedish, often in the same sentence, but, even after centuries, it still feels a little like a border town that is torn between two masters.

We're beyond the 63rd parallel here – in the Southern Hemisphere we'd have reached bits of Antarctica – and in the minds of many southern Finns, this is already 'The North'. Thus, although Vaasa isn't huge, it feels like a metropolis compared to the much smaller settlements around. It has a lively, bustling air, and is a popular family holiday destination in summer, thanks to its waterside location and adventure park. The surrounding countryside and nearby islands are easily accessible; in spring, nesting waterbirds crowd its shorelines, and you feel the wilderness is never that far away.

The town began in the 14th century as a village called Korsholm. In 1606 Swedish King Charles IX created Vasa, named after the royal Swedish Wasa family. The original town was located 7km east of modern Vaasa but, like all respectable Finnish wooden settlements, it burned down in a Great Fire; the new city was begun in the mid-19th century. During the Civil War that followed Finnish independence, Vaasa was the scene of heavy fighting, and an important base of the Whites, monarchists loyal to the existing government fighting against the workers' rebellion.

ORIENTATION

Vaasanpuistikko is the main street through the centre of Vaasa. Vaskiluoto to the west and Palosaari to the north are two islands connected to central Vaasa by bridges.

INFORMATION

Main post office (Hovioikeudenpuistikko 23A; 10am-6pm Mon-Fri) Opposite the train station.

Public library (325 3533; Kirjastonkatu 13) Several free Internet terminals.

Tourist office (325 1145; www.vaasa.fi; Kaupungintalo; 9am-6pm Mon-Fri, 10am-6pm Sat & Sun Jun-Aug, 10am-4pm Mon-Fri Sep-May;) In the town hall building, books accommodation and rents bikes.

SIGHTS & ACTIVITIES
Pohjanmaan Museo

Vaasa is blessed with an excellent museum. The **Pohjanmaan Museo** (Ostrobothnian Museum; 325 3800; Museokatu 3; admission €4; 10am-5pm Tue-Fri, 10am-8pm Wed, noon-5pm Sat & Sun) has two sections, both worthwhile.

The art collection upstairs is extraordinary. Most of it was amassed by local doctor Karl Hedman, with the help of art-

hound Gösta Stenman. There's an excellent range of works from the 'Golden Age' of Finnish painting, with Hugo Simberg, Helene Schjerfbeck and the characteristic expressionist landscapes of Tyko Sallinen particularly well represented. Look out for the latter's famous *Dwarf*, as well as a fine head of Christ by Akseli Gallen-Kallela. More surprisingly, there's also a high-quality selection of European masters, purchased for virtually nothing in the chaos in Russia after the revolution. A Tintoretto, a pair of Luca Giordanos, a fine 15th-century Flemish Deposition by Roger van der Weyden, and a round Botticelli Madonna are some of several fine canvases. There's also a good porcelain collection, with Meissen, Delft, and Wedgwood pieces prominent.

Downstairs, Terra Nova is devoted to the ecosystem of the local environment. This part of the Gulf of Bothnia is known as the Kvarken; the land is still rising as the crust 'rebounds' after the last Ice Age weighed it down. There's a collection of local butterflies, great photos of seals, and a display of bird and animal life. A spooky 'virtual aquarium' introduces the finny tribes.

Other Sights

Tikanoja Art Gallery (325 3916; Hovioikeudenpuistikko 4; admission €5; 11am-4pm Tue-Sat, noon-5pm Sun) has a good collection of Finnish and international paintings, and regularly puts on high-quality temporary exhibitions.

The **Orthodox Church** at Kasarmintori has some old icons brought from St Petersburg; contact the tourist office to see them.

If you plan on visiting a few museums in the Vaasa region, pick up an **Art City Pass** (€5) from the tourist office. It's valid for one day and includes entry to most regional galleries and museums.

Vaskiluoto

The island of Vaskiluoto is a big holiday destination for Finnish families, with beaches, boating, a popular camping ground and **Wasalandia Amusement Park** (211 1200; www.wasalandia.fi; adult/child-under-120cm day pass €16/11; from 11am mid-May–mid-Aug, closing varies 4-7pm), the Finnish answer to Disneyland. There's a good variety of rides, none of them too hair raising; it will appeal most to kids under 14.

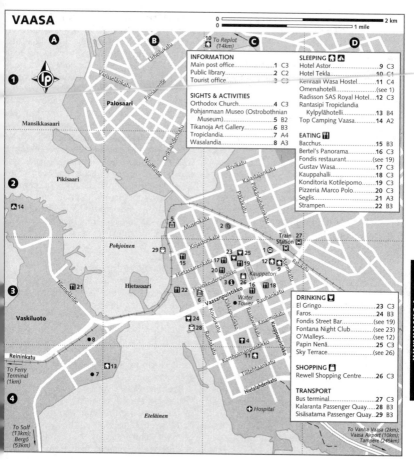

VAASA

0 — 2 km
0 — 1 mile

INFORMATION
Main post office.....................1 C3
Public library..........................2 C2
Tourist office...........................3 C3

SIGHTS & ACTIVITIES
Orthodox Church....................4 C3
Pohjanmaan Museo (Ostrobothnian
  Museum)..............................5 B2
Tikanoja Art Gallery................6 B3
Tropiclandia............................7 A4
Wasalandia.............................8 A3

SLEEPING
Hotel Astor.............................9 C3
Hotel Tekla...........................10 C1
Kenraali Wasa Hostel...........11 C4
Omenahotelli....................(see 1)
Radisson SAS Royal Hotel...12 C3
Rantasipi Tropiclandia
  Kylpylähotelli.....................13 B4
Top Camping Vaasa.............14 A2

EATING
Bacchus................................15 B3
Bertel's Panorama.................16 C3
Fondis restaurant.............(see 19)
Gustav Wasa.........................17 C3
Kauppahalli..........................18 C3
Konditoria Kotileipomo........19 C3
Pizzeria Marco Polo..............20 C3
Seglis...................................21 A3
Strampen..............................22 B3

DRINKING
El Gringo...............................23 C3
Faros....................................24 B3
Fondis Street Bar..............(see 19)
Fontana Night Club...........(see 23)
O'Malleys..........................(see 12)
Papin Nenä...........................25 C3
Sky Terrace.......................(see 26)

SHOPPING
Rewell Shopping Centre........26 C3

TRANSPORT
Bus terminal.........................27 C3
Kalaranta Passenger Quay....28 B3
Sisäsatama Passenger Quay...29 B3

To Vanha Vaasa (2km);
Vaasa Airport (10km);
Tampere (245km)

POHJANMAA

Opposite the amusement park is the excellent water park **Tropiclandia** (☎ 211 1300; www.tropiclandia.fi; adult/child €16/12; ☼ 7am-9pm Mon-Fri, 10am-9pm Sat, 10am-8pm Sun, closed most of Sep). It's got plenty to keep both kids and adults happy, with slides, Jacuzzis, restaurant and more. There's also a new outdoor section that's open from mid-June to August.

TOURS
The **MS Tiira** (☎ 315 4057; tickets €12) cruises the Vaasa archipelago from Midsummer to mid-August. It departs from the Kalaranta passenger quay at midday and 4pm, picking up passengers at the Top Camping Vaasa camp site shortly thereafter. The cruise lasts about 3½ hours, about half of which seems to be taken up by a lunch stop (food not included) at a restaurant owned by the same outfit.

FESTIVALS & EVENTS
The **Korsholm Music Festival** (☎ 322 2390; www.korsholm.fi/music), an international chamber music festival, is held in late June.

The Vaasa shoreline reverberates to **Rockperry** (www.rockperry.fi), a major summer music festival at Vaskiluoto in mid-July. It attracts top Finnish and international acts.

Vaasa Rules (www.vaasa.fi) is a big Midsummer party with music and concerts, and at the **Wasa Water Carnival** (www.topthrob.fi/water), in late

July or early August, there is dancing, music, drinking, and plenty of water-based fun.

SLEEPING

Kenraali Wasa Hostel (☎ 0400-668 521; www.kenraali wasahostel.com; Korsholmanpuistikko 6-8; s/d/tr €37/46/50; P ☒) This great place to stay is housed in part of an old military complex, and beautifully decorated in keeping with the theme. The rooms are cosy and elegant, with cable TV, a small fridge and shared bathroom. There are kitchen facilities, books, free bikes to use and plenty of peace and quiet. There's excellent value for groups sharing a room too.

Hotel Astor (☎ 326 9111; www.astorvaasa.com; Asemakatu 4; r €117, with sauna €138, Sat, Sun & summer €88; P ☒ 🖳) This stylish, intimate hotel is in a lovely old building with a classy interior. It's more personal and personable than the chain hotels; the nicest rooms are in the old wing of the building, with polished floors and dark-wood furnishings. The pricing is a little strange; as singles are normally the same price as doubles, solo travellers are better off with the latter, which are bigger. Best value are the rooms with their own sauna, which are only a little more expensive.

Radisson SAS Royal Hotel (☎ 020-123 4720; www .radissonsas.com; Hovioikeudenpuistikko 18; r €120, ste €300, s/d Sat, Sun & summer €80/85; P ☒ 🖳 🛋 🔥) This is the biggest of Vaasa's business hotels, boasting not only rooms on both sides of the street but a pub, nightclub and two restaurants. The rooms are well-equipped and guests have use of a sauna, pool and the gym next door.

Omenahotelli (www.omenahotelli.fi; Hovioikeudenpuistikko 23; r €55; ☒) This good-value chain of hotels run without reception staff, so you have to book in advance over the Internet (you can also book via a terminal in the lobby). The rooms are good, with a twin bed and a fold-out couch that can accommodate another two people for the same price.

Top Camping Vaasa (☎ 211 1255; www.topcamp ing.fi/vaasa; Niemeläntie; tent sites €8 plus per person €4, 4-person cabins €50; ☺ late Jun–mid-Aug) For happy campers there's a well-kept, family-friendly camping ground about 2km from the town centre, on the grassy tip of Vaskiluoto island. It also rents bicycles and boats, and offers discount coupons for the Tropiclandia spa and free admission to Wasalandia Amusement Park.

Hotel Tekla (☎ 327 6411; www.hoteltekla.net; Palosaarentie 58; s/d €49/69; P ☒ 🖳) This hotel on Palosaari island in northern Vaasa is kitted out for sports enthusiasts. It's a good base near a lake, and has its own gym, restaurant, sauna and badminton court. Although the corridors are a bit cellblock-like, the rooms are bright, with large windows, cane seats, fridge and a simple shared kitchen. Take bus 1 or 2 from the centre.

Rantasipi Tropiclandia Kylpylähotelli (☎ 283 8000; www.rantasipi.fi; Lemmenpolku 3; s/d €114/135, ste €220; P ☒ 🖳 🛋 🔥) This is a large spa hotel attached to Tropiclandia on Vaskiluoto island. Rates include all kinds of spa and resort activities so it's popular with families and anyone wanting a relaxing time out. The spacious, warmly furnished rooms have wireless Internet access.

EATING

Fondis (☎ 280 0400; Hovioikeudenpuistikko 15; mains €12-20; ☺ 11am-11pm Mon-Thu, 11am-midnight Fri & Sat, noon-9pm Sun) This has a restaurant and bar in adjoining doorways and is one of the best places to eat in Vaasa. The restaurant is smartly kitted out with crisp white cloths and bright red chairs; the varied menu includes good Caesar salads, plenty of grilled meat (including very tasty liver with lingonberry sauce) and top service.

Bacchus (☎ 317 3484; Rantakatu 4; mains €22-29; ☺ 3pm-1am Mon-Sat, noon-10pm Sun) This upmarket restaurant is set in a lovely wooden building near the water, at the museum end of town. The menu is short but long on quality, with delicious dishes such as partridge with lentils and artichoke sauce.

Gustav Wasa (☎ 326 9200; Raastuvankatu 24; mains €17-31; ☺ dinner Mon-Sat) Around the corner from the tourist office is a cellar restaurant with a small but gourmet menu of Finnish cuisine including wild duck, rack of lamb and butter-fried sirloin of reindeer; there are also vegetarian options. It's got an upmarket, bygone years sort of a feel and, unusually for a restaurant, there's a sauna in an adjoining building so patrons can cook themselves.

Konditoria Kotileipomo (Hovioikeudenpuistikko 13; ☺ 8am-6pm Mon-Fri, 9am-3pm Sat) This place, on the kauppatori (market square) in the city centre, is a pleasant café with a light, quiet, interior and a small terrace in summer. It serves tasty pastries in particular, and if you're planning a picnic, you can't beat one of the many types of loaves they bake fresh.

Seglis (☎ 317 2037; Niemeläntie 14; mains €12-16, light meals €6-10; ☺ May-Sep) On Vaskiluoto, and part of the local sailing club, this is a stylish but surprisingly reasonably priced restaurant. It has a terrace overlooking the marina and features dishes such as whitefish fillet in lobster sauce, and chicken in cola sauce. There's plenty of value in the steaks, and there's also a decent lunch buffet and plenty of children's choices.

Strampen (☎ 320 0355; Rantakatu 6; Sisäsatama; mains €11-18, lunch buffet €7-9.50; ☺ May-Aug) On the opposite side of the harbour to Seglis, this is a summer beer terrace in the waterfront park, with a spacious, pleasant restaurant serving a range of warming meals.

Faros (☎ 312 6411; Kalaranta; meals €9-12) This is a boat restaurant moored in Kalaranta Harbour on the southern side of the bridge. It's a good place for lunch or an evening drink and snack, with decent burgers, pasta and salads.

Pizzeria Marco Polo (☎ 317 5922; Hovioikeudenpuistikko 11; pizzas €6-10; ☺ 11am-9pm Mon-Sat, noon-9pm Sun) A traditional little Italian place serving cheap pizzas and pastas. There's a good range, and they'll even whip up a gluten-free pizza for those with dietary requirements.

Bertel's Panorama (Vaasanpuistikko 16; lunch buffet €7.40; ☺ 10am-4pm Mon-Fri) This is a great place for lunch with a view over the kauppatori. The daily buffet is not gourmet but is very generous.

There are cheap grillis, pizzerias and hamburger restaurants around the kauppatori and in the Rewell shopping centre. The **kauppahalli** (Kauppapuistikko) or covered market, has stalls selling fresh bakery products and the usual market fare.

DRINKING

Sky Terrace (☎ 212 4115; Sokos Hotel Vaakuna, Kauppatori; ☺ from 4pm) With a bird's eye view over the kauppatori and central Vaasa, this 9th floor bar is a great place to relax. With leather couches and two outdoor areas, it's popular but not too pricey. On Friday and Saturday nights, there are DJs and a cover charge.

O'Malley's (Hovioikeudenpuistikko 18) This is an Irish bar popular with visiting business people since it's part of the Radisson Hotel. With international beers and stout on tap,

booth seating and a cosy atmosphere, it's a good place to be in winter. They pour a good Guinness when it's not too busy.

El Gringo (☎ 280 0415; Raastuvankatu) Around the corner from Fondis Street Bar is a basement saloon bar that packs them in with cheap beer (€2.50). When that closes everyone heads upstairs to Fontana Night Club.

Papin Nenä (☎ 361 0557; Hietasaarenkatu 14; ☺ disco 10pm-4am Wed-Sat). This large brick building holds both this popular disco that has regular and diverse live acts, and the more sedate Munkhaus bar.

GETTING THERE & AWAY
Air
Finnair offers daily flights from Vaasa to Helsinki, Kokkola and Stockholm. The budget operator **Blue1** (www.blue1.com) also has flights to Helsinki and Stockholm

Boat
From late June to early August there are one to two daily ferries (€41, four hours) between Vaasa and the Swedish town of Umeå (Uumaja) with **RG Lines** (☎ 320 0300; www.rgline.com). It also runs once-weekly to Sundsvall (Friday, eight hours). The ferry terminal is on the western side of Vaskiluoto (take bus 10).

Bus
There are daily bus services from the terminal on Vöyrinkatu to all major western and central towns, and there are several express buses a day from Helsinki (€55.60, seven hours) and normal buses from Turku (€43.20, 5½ hours), both via Pori (€29.20, three hours). Buses run up and down the west coast pretty much hourly from Monday to Friday.

Train
Vaasa is off the main train lines, but there is a connecting line to Seinäjoki, where you can connect with trains to mainline destinations, such as Tampere (€30.30, 2½ hours) and Helsinki (€47.10, four to five hours). Trains to Seinäjoki run up to eight times a day (€8.80, 50 minutes).

GETTING AROUND
The airport is situated 12km southeast of the centre; airport buses depart from the city bus station (one way €3).

POHJANMAA

Local buses from the kauppatori come in handy if you want to reach areas outside the centre. Take bus 5 or 10 to Vaskiluoto island and bus 1 or 2 to the hostel on Palosaari island. The fare is €2.40. The Lilliputti city train runs between the kauppatori and Wasalandia (€3) daily in summer.

Bicycles can be rented at the tourist office or Top Camping Vaasa for around €3.50 for two hours.

AROUND VAASA

VANHA VAASA

The Old Town of Vaasa developed around a harbour, southeast of the modern centre, but the harbour became unsuitable for large vessels. The medieval church is now in ruins and, although the old fortress area has been protected, not much remains. Probably the most interesting sight is the **Church of Korsholm**, built in 1786. It looks very pompous; it was originally a judges' palace. **Köpmanshuset Wasasferne** (☎ 356 7578; Kauppiaankatu 10; admission €2; ☉ 11am-5pm Thu-Sun mid-May–mid-Aug) is a museum of local history with reconstructions of a 19th-century post office and some furniture salvaged from the blaze.

Bus 7, 9, 12A and 12B travel between Vanha Vaasa and the town centre.

SOLF

One of the most attractive villages in Finland, Solf (Finnish: Sulva) is best known for its **Stundars Handicraft Village** (☎ 344 2200; www.stundars.fi; admission €3.50; ☉ noon-6pm Jul–mid-Aug), an open-air museum and crafts centre boasting 60 traditional wooden buildings, progressively moved here from surrounding villages. The whole place hums with activity in summer, when artisans demonstrate crafts such as wool dyeing and wood carving. The entrance fee includes a guided tour.

Regional buses from Vaasa make the 15km trip south to Solf. There are six daily Monday to Friday, but only one on Saturday, and a late one on Sunday (€4.20, 15 minutes)

REPLOT

Replot (Finnish: Raippaluoto) is a large island that lies just off the Vaasa coast. It's easy to reach and ideal for exploring by bicycle. On the island there are several small fishing communities in addition to the main village, which is also called Replot.

Södra Vallgrund village is on the southwestern corner of the island, some 10km from the village of Replot. It has a small museum. **Klobbskat** village, at the western end of the island, is in a barren, Lappish-like setting. **Björkön** (Swedish: Björköby) is a fishing village on a smaller, northern island, accessible from Replot by bridge.

In 1997 a 1045m bridge – the longest bridge in Finland – was completed connecting Replot with the mainland.

Bulleråsin Holiday Village (☎ 352 7613; Bulleråsvägen 330; tent sites €10, cottages €42-58) in Södra Vallgrund has camping, cottages and a restaurant in a 1920s villa.

SOUTH OF VAASA

KRISTINESTAD

☎ 06 / pop 7760

Peaceful little Kristinestad (Finnish: Kristiinankaupunki) is a small, idyllic seaside town with a proud seafaring history. Once an important port shipping tar and timber to distant harbours, it's now more or less in retirement (although timber and potatoes still employ plenty of locals), and languishes gracefully on the shores of a bay, whose waters sparkle azure on a sunny summer's day.

Named after Queen Kristina of Sweden, Kristinestad is, like many other towns on this coast, bilingual – some 58% of inhabitants are Swedish-speakers. Founded in the mid 17th century by the maverick count Per Brahe, the town rapidly became an important shipbuilding and trading centre. With the arrival of steamships, Kristinestad's importance declined, and many residents moved to Sweden.

Kristinestad is quite small, with a village feel and everything except the camping ground within a block or two of the market square.

Information

Internet Café (Strandgatan 37; ☉ 5-10pm Mon-Fri; per hr €3) Charming wooden building.

Tourist office (☎ 221 2311; www.krs.fi; Sjögatan 47; ☉ 8am-4pm Mon-Fri, 10am-2pm Sat Aug-Jun, 9am-5pm Mon-Fri, 10am-2pm Sun Jul) Plenty of information and free Internet access. Very helpful.

Sights

The most interesting thing in Kristinestad is the town itself, with its rows of colourful, old, painted wooden houses and its charming small-town feel. In its heyday as a key port, every traveller entering the town had to pay customs duty, collected at the **Old Customs House** (Staketgatan), a smallish rust-wood building dating from 1720, just along from the imposing town hall.

Behind the customs house is the striking red-wood **Old Church** (Ulrika Eleonora Kyrkan; Tue-Sat mid-May–late Aug) from 1698 which retains much of its original detail. The red-brick **New Church** (Nya Kirka; Parmansgatan; 9am-4pm Mon-Fri, 9am-2pm Sat, 9am-1pm Sun), has a high wooden ceiling, the typical church-ship dedicated by mariners, and a large painting of the Crucifixion above the altar.

Sjöfartsmuseum (Maritime Museum; ☎ 221 2859; Salutorget 1; admission €3.50; noon-4pm Tue-Sun May–mid-Aug) displays marine-related items collected by an old sea captain and portrays Kristinestad's proud maritime history – the whole town seems to have pitched in to help put this place together, and they've done a fine job.

Lebell House (Lebellska Köpmansgården; ☎ 221 2159; Strandgatan 51; admission €4; 11am-5pm Mon-Fri, 11am-2pm Sat & Sun May-Aug), a block south of the market square, is a home museum that once belonged to a wealthy merchant. Dating from the mid-19th century, it's an excellent representation of upper-class life in old Kristinestad. The original Lebell certainly pulled himself up by his bootlaces; he first arrived in Kristinestad as a Polish prisoner of war before making his fortune in shipping.

About 5km north of town, **Carlsro Museum** (☎ 221 6343; Carlsrovägen 181; admission €4.50; 11am-6pm Tue-Sun Jun-late Aug) is in an old villa (1896) and is quite delightful, with a collection of bric-a-brac and toys from the Tsarist era. It's well worth the trip out there.

Three blocks south of the market square is **Kattpiskargränden** (Cat Whipper's Alley). In the 1880s the town employed a cat catcher, whose job was to kill sick cats in order to prevent the spreading of plague – hence the name of the street.

Festivals & Events

The town has three big **market fairs**; one in mid-July, another in winter (Candelmas) and the third in autumn (Michaelmas). They feature music, dancing and exhibitions as well as the usual market stalls.

Sleeping & Eating

Bed & Breakfast Jylli (☎ 0400-661 434; www.huutokauppa.biz; Östra Långgatan 47; s/d/tr €50/60/80; P) Run by a hearty auctioneer and his family, these beautiful wooden apartment/cabins are right in the heart of town. They are enchantingly rustic, but also very comfortable, and each one comes with fully-equipped kitchen, TV, phone socket and modern bathroom. One has been designed with wide entries and space to manoeuvre a wheelchair. Some are year-round, while two-level summer cabins have a blessedly dark sleeping area under the wooden roof. Despite the name, there's no breakfast.

Hotel Alma (☎ 221 3455; www.hotelalma.info; Sjögatan; s/d €69/85, weekends €59/75; P) This is a great place to stay, in a charismatic wooden building just along from the Café Alma, which is the reception for this hotel. The rooms are elegant and different, with some period furniture and elaborate bed canopies. The same people also run a summer hostel across the river about 2km east of the centre (singles/doubles €35/55). Enquire at the café in all cases.

Pukinsaari/Bockholmens Camping (☎ 221 1484; Salavägen 32; tent sites €12, cabins €32-65; late May-early Sep) This is a pleasant place at a small beach, 1.5km southwest of the town centre. There are bicycles for rent.

Café Alma (☎ 221 3455; Sjögatan 8; lunch soup & salad €6, full buffet €8.50, Sun €9.50; lunch 11am-5pm Mon-Fri, noon-5pm Sun) This fabulous place on the waterfront has a bright atrium dining area at the front and a sizeable terrace. Dominating the interior is a sizeable scale model of the ship *Alma*. There's a fine buffet lunch; the filled rolls and other snacks are also delicious.

Crazy Cat (☎ 221 3100, Östralånggatan 53-55; lunch special €7.50; 11am-9pm Mon-Fri, noon-9pm Sat & Sun) A small friendly pizzeria just off the market square. As well as the lunch special there is the usual range of pizzas.

Getting There & Away

Kristinestad is on road 662, 100km south of Vaasa. Buses between Pori (€16.20, one hour 20 minutes) and Vaasa (€18.90, 1½ hours) stop at Kristinestad. There are two daily buses from Tampere (€28.10, five hours).

POHJANMAA

KASKINEN

☎ 06 / pop 1519

Kaskinen (Swedish: Kaskö) is technically Finland's smallest town, and also the westernmost town on the Finnish coast, but in reality it's a relaxing and peaceful island village and a good place to break your journey. Finnish is spoken by the majority of people, many of whom work in the enormous pulp factory at the southern end of the town. There's also an important fish-processing plant.

Although there's not a lot to see, there's a hospitable feel, and opportunities for boating and fishing. Naturally there's a **local museum** (☎ 220 7711; Raatihuoneenkatu 48; admission €2; ☿ Jun-Aug or by appointment) which recreates a wealthy Finnish home from the 19th century, as well as a fisherman's cottage. Also in town is a small **fishing museum** (☎ 220 7711; Sjöbobacken; admission €2; ☿ Jun-Aug or by appointment) at the northern end of the island, at the Kalaranta boat dock. Set in the old salting sheds, it demonstrates the pursuit of herring, whitefish, and salmon with a range of authentic fishing objects. The 18th-century **Bladh House**, on Kaskinen Sound, is a restored burgher house and the most important building in Kaskinen. It's a solid, impressive sight with its trapezoid roof characteristic of the period.

Two bridges connect the island town to the mainland. There's a small **tourist office** (☎ 220 7310; info@kaskinen.fi; ☿ Jun–mid-Aug) down at the harbour. The **Fishing Festival** in early July is a good time to be in Kaskinen, with market stalls and plenty of activities for kids.

Sleeping & Eating

Björnträ Vandrarhem (☎ /fax 222 7007; Raatihuoneenkatu 22; r per person €18-23; ☿ Jun–mid-Aug; ⊠) This is a very friendly hostel in a low old wooden building, with six rooms almost of hotel standard. It's run by a very helpful and hospitable Swedish-speaking couple. Guests have use of a well-equipped kitchen and TV room and rooms may be available out of season by arrangement.

Hotelli Kaske (☎ 222 7771; Raatihuoneenkatu 41; s/d €61/78; Ⓟ ⊠) The only hotel in the village, this is comfy and well-equipped. The rooms have large recessed windows and come with cable TV and telephone. It's right opposite the kauppatori.

Café Kung Gustav (☎ 222 7111; Raatihuoneenkatu 39; ☿ 10am-11pm or later) This place does triple duty as the town's main central café, pub, and restaurant. There's also a restaurant at the Hotelli Kaske, as well as a bakery-café and a pizzeria in town.

Marianranta Camping (☎ 220 7311; tent sites €10, cabins €20-27; ☿ Jun-Aug) This camping ground is small, but very grassy and peaceful, and right by the seaside at the northeastern tip of the island. There are a few cottages and they rent canoes and bicycles.

NÄRPES

☎ 06 / pop 9515

Närpes (Finnish: Närpiö), 85km southwest of Vaasa, is the tomato basket of Finland. Take a few from a market stall and eat them with bread and salt, and you'll wonder what those tasteless red things are that you get in your local supermarket! It has one of the highest ratios of Swedish to Finnish speakers in the country – 93% are Swedophone, with a local accent that is hard to understand.

Some 150 *kyrkstallar*, or 'church stables' (though they were designed for the use of people not horses), surround the medieval **Närpes Church**, a few blocks south of where the bus stops. This is the only place in Finland where these temporary shelters have been preserved. In the past, people from outlying districts used these to stay overnight when visiting the church.

NORTH OF VAASA

NYKARLEBY

☎ 06 / pop 7436

Nykarleby (Finnish: Uusikaarlepyy) is a small town 20km south of Jakobstad where 91% of the population speak Swedish. The town was founded in 1620, the very same day as Karleby (Kokkola); despite the identical founding dates, this place got the name Nykarleby which means 'new Kokkola'. Today Nykarleby is a peaceful riverside town and it makes a pleasant stop on the road north from Vaasa. In summer, you can get tourist information and town maps from the **Café Kyrktuppen** (☎ 050-302 5207; Pankkikatu 4).

The yellow **Nykarleby Church** (☿ 9am-6pm summer) on the riverside was built in 1708. Its walls, pulpit and ceiling are covered with 18th-century paintings. **Nykarleby Museum**, to the north along the main street, has plenty of local flavour. It features bric-a-brac, old costumes and furniture.

Nykarleby is famous to Finns as the town of Zacharias Topelius, a writer of much-loved children's' poetry. His home, **Kuddnäs** (☎ 785 6111; 22 Jakobstadsvägen; ☼ May-Aug), is a beautiful old house but doesn't really evoke the man himself.

There are several cafés where you can try the famous local *våfflor* (waffles) with cream and strawberry jam. One of the nicest, Brostugan, is just across the river from the heart of town, opposite the church.

Several daily buses connect the two Nykarleby and Jakobstad, and northbound buses from Vaasa also stop here.

JAKOBSTAD

☎ 06 / pop 19,467

The pretty town of Jakobstad (Finnish: Pietarsaari) is distinctively Swedish (55% of the population speak Swedish), and the most interesting place to stop and sample the curious world of *Parallelsverige*. There is a well-preserved historic Old Town filled with 18th- and 19th-century wooden houses, some off-beat museums and easy access to some interesting coastal area.

Jakobstad was founded in 1652 by Ebba Brahe, wife of war hero Jacob de la Gardie. The surrounding region, Pedersöre, gave the town its Finnish name, which translates as Peter's Island. Russians sacked Jakobstad twice in 1714; despite the repeated drubbings, it became the leading shipping town in Finland during the 18th century.

Information

After Eight (Storgatan; ☼ 10am-3pm Mon-Fri) Free Internet terminals at this café and cultural centre.

Public library (☎ 785 1272; Runebergsgatan 12; ☼ 11am-7pm Mon-Thu, 11am-4pm Fri summer, 11am-8pm Mon-Fri autumn-spring) Has a couple of Internet terminals; maximum 15 minutes unless you book.

Tourist office (☎ 785 1208; www.jakobstad.fi; Köpmansgatan 12; ☼ 8am-6pm Mon-Fri, 9am-3pm Sat Jun-Aug, 8am-5pm Mon-Fri Sep-May) Very helpful; has information on all parts of Finland.

Sights
SKATA

Stretching for several blocks to the north of the new town, Skata, the old town of Jakobstad, has around 300 **wooden houses** that have

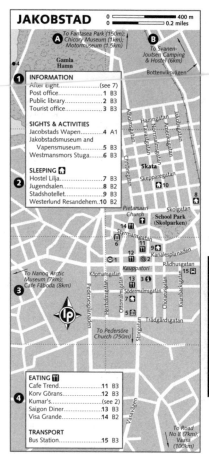

JAKOBSTAD

0 —————— 400 m
0 —————— 0.2 miles

INFORMATION	
After Eight	(see 7)
Post office	1 B3
Public library	2 B3
Tourist office	3 B3

SIGHTS & ACTIVITIES	
Jacobstads Wapen	4 A1
Jakobstadsmuseum and Vapensmuseum	5 B3
Westmansmors Stuga	6 B3

SLEEPING	
Hostel Lilja	7 B3
Jugendsalen	8 B3
Stadshotellet	9 B3
Westerlund Resandehem	10 B3

EATING	
Cafe Trend	11 B3
Korv Görans	12 B3
Kumar's	(see 2)
Saigon Diner	13 B3
Visa Grande	14 B2

TRANSPORT	
Bus Station	15 B3

To Fantasea Park (150m); Chicory Museum (1km); Motormuseum (1.5km)

To Svanen-Joutsen Camping & Hostel (6km)

To Nanoq Arctic Museum (7km); Cafe Fäboda (8km)

To Pedersöre Church (750m)

To Road No 8 (7km); Vaasa (100km)

POHJANMAA

been beautifully preserved and are the highlight of a visit. Most of them were built in the 19th century and were occupied by sailors and workers; the 18th-century houses along Hamngatan are the oldest in town. One of the prettiest streets is **Norrmalmsgatan**. The area is wholly residential; there are no trendy antique shops or quirky cafés to slake a visitor's thirst! To enter, you pass through an ornamental entranceway, with a (visually) striking clocktower bridging the street.

JACOBSTADS WAPEN

In Gamla Hamn (the old harbour area) is the pride of Jakobstad, the **Jacobstads Wapen** (admission €4; ☼ mid-May–late Aug), modelled after a 17th-century galleon. There's a small museum explaining the history of the ship and the building of the replica. Public sailings are given only a couple of times a year; inquire at the tourist office.

MUSEUMS

Jakobstad has an eclectic collection of small private museums.

Jakobstadsmuseum (☎ 758 1111; Storgatan 2; admission €2; ⏰ noon-4pm) includes the old main building (Malmska Gården, dating back to 1904) with local-history displays on the shipping industry and town itself, as well as a tobacco museum and several historic houses scattered around the town centre.

Next door is the **Vapenmuseum** (Weapons Museum; ☎ 723 2974; Storgatan 2; admission €4; ⏰ noon-5pm Tue-Sun Jun-Jul), a small private collection of Jakobstad resident Bengt Ena. There are more than 300 old guns, hunting rifles, machine guns and military pistols dating back to the 1740s.

The **Motormuseum** (☎ 724 4500; Alholmsvägen 71; admission €4; ⏰ noon-5pm Mon-Fri, noon-4pm Sat & Sun mid-May–mid-Aug), to the north of town, by the harbour, is a private museum with a fascinating collection of over 120 motorcycles – from old Harley Davidsons and Nortons to home-made, motor-powered bicycles.

Nearby, the **Chicory Museum** (☎ 020-416 1113; Alholma; admission free; ⏰ noon-5pm Tue-Sat Jun-Aug, noon-6pm Jul) is in the old chicory factory, founded in 1883 and preserved pretty much as it was when it closed in 1960. It was built by local entrepreneur Wilhelm Schauman who saw the market for making chicory into an additive for coffee, which at the time was an expensive commodity.

PEDERSÖRE CHURCH

The beautiful **Pedersöre Church** (Vasavägen 118), on the way into town from the south, was originally built in the 1400s, but the bell tower dates from the 1760s. During the reign of King Gustav III the church was greatly enlarged to become a cross-shaped structure. Thankfully, the architect thumbed his nose at the king's plan to demolish the 85m spire. It's well worth the walk out to see it.

FANTASEA PARK

This **amusement park** (☎ 785 1625; admission €2.50; ⏰ 11am-5pm early Jun-early Aug) at Gamla Hamn has water slides, arcade games, pools and a good swimming beach.

Sleeping

Westerlund Resandehem (☎ 723 0440; Norrmalmsgatan 8; s/d/tr €27/41/54; P X) Run by a friendly Swedish-speaking family, this is a charming B&B in the heart of Skata, on its most beautiful street. Spotless rooms all have shared bathrooms, but it's only a small place so book ahead.

Jugendsalen (☎ 723 1521; sandlin@multi.fi; Skolgatan 11; s/d €30/50; P X). Although in a large modern building opposite the park, this guesthouse manages to feel cosy and intimate, with the rooms nestled around a good central kitchen and lounge area. It's great value, with TV, bedside light and new furniture in the rooms, as well as a sauna, bar and pool table. Breakfast available but not included.

Stadshotellet (☎ 788 8111; www.stadshotellet.multi.fi; Kanalesplanaden 13; s/d €90/110, summer €67/84; P X 🖳) On the main pedestrian street, this is Jakobstad's top hotel, with comfortable rooms, two restaurants and a nightclub. It's in a characterful centenarian building with a charming façade. On our last visit the welcome was positively icy, but it might have just been a bad day for them!

Hostel Lilja (☎ 781 6500, 050-516 7301; www.aftereight.fi; Storgatan 6; dm/s/d €22.50/40/45; ⏰ reception 9am-4pm Mon-Fri; P X 🖳) This is a stylish new HI hostel attached to Musikcafé After Eight in the town centre. Although part of a historic building, the rooms and facilities are brand new: bunk beds meet Nordic pine-floor chic. There's a sauna and bike rental available. Outside of reception hours, phone to make contact.

Svanen/Joutsen Camping (☎ 723 0660; www.multi.fi/svanen; Larsmövägen 50; tent sites €14.50, 2-person cabins €22-28, 4-person cabins €38-65; ⏰ Jun-Aug) About 6km north of town in Nissasörn, this is a family camping ground (take a Larsmo- or Kokkola-bound bus from the city bus station) set among the birches and pines. There are plenty of cabins, minigolf and you can hire bikes, boats and canoes.

Eating

Café Trend (☎ 723 1265; Gågatan) Right in the heart of town, this café lives up to its name – Jakobstad's beautiful people crowd the terrace or read magazines over coffee inside. They do sinfully rich cakes and also a pretty good salad buffet (€7.50) at lunch time.

Visa Grande (☎ 723 4150; Storgatan 20; pizza & pasta buffet €7-9, mains €12-22; ☺ food 10.30am-10pm Mon-Sat, bar 10.30am-2am Mon-Sat & 8pm-2am Sun; ▣) The best place in town for a drink, with its large, bright terrace, and extended opening hours. This place also has some decent food, with a pizza and pasta buffet lunch as well as an à la carte menu that's mainly steaks and salmon. They're good, if a touch overpriced; best is the cool underfloor fish tank.

Saigon Diner (☎ 723 0470; Storgatan 8; lunch buffet €6; ☺ 10.30am-8pm Mon-Fri, noon-8pm Sat, noon-7pm Sun) This is an appealing and authentic Vietnamese restaurant, with a bargain lunch special. On the menu is wok-fried reindeer fillet – the Arctic meets the tropics with good results. Lunch specials are served from 11am to 3pm weekdays.

Kumar's (☎ 723 7559, Storgatan 11; mains €8-14; ☺ lunch & dinner Tue-Sun) This popular spot is an interesting restaurant combining Indian and Asian flavours with pizzas and sandwiches. It's reasonably priced and packs the locals in for its lunch buffet.

Korv Görans (Kanalesplanaden 18) On the pedestrian mall is a busy little pizza, fried food and kebab kiosk that has been in business for three decades and is a Jakobstad institution. Most options are under €6, and there are pleasant wooden seats on the mall if the weather permits.

Getting There & Away

There are regular buses to Jakobstad from Vaasa (from €13.70, 1½ to 2½ hours), Kokkola (€6.20, 40 minutes) and other towns along the west coast.

Bennäs (Finnish: Pännäinen), 11km away, is the closest railway station to Jakobstad. A shuttle bus (€3.10, 10 minutes) meets arriving trains.

The Kruunupyy/Kronoby airport (see p261) is 30km from Jakobstad and buses (€5) meet arriving flights.

The **M/S Jenny** (☎ 044-780 9140) sails between Jakobstad and Kokkola (one-way €14) on Thursdays at 5pm, from Midsummer to mid-August, arriving at Kokkola camping at 10.30pm.

AROUND JAKOBSTAD
Fäboda

About 8km west of Jakobstad, Fäboda is a small recreational area facing the Gulf of Bothnia. There are small lovely, sandy beaches, rocky inlets and forest walks, and this is a favourite spot for swimming, surfing and windsurfing. It's an easy cycle out to Fäboda along a narrow country road and with a good restaurant and intriguing museum, it's a great day out.

While the concept might seem incongruous here (the Arctic Circle is, after all, several hundred kilometres to the north), the **Nanoq Arctic Museum** (☎ 729 3679; Pörkenäsvägen 60; admission €6; ☺ noon-6pm Jun-Aug) is a little museum that is surprisingly good, and worth a detour. Housed in a model of a Greenlandic peat house, the collection is the private achievement of Pentti Kronqvist who has made several expeditions to the Arctic. There are Eskimo tools, fossils, authentic Arctic huts from Greenland and elsewhere, and various other Arctic souvenirs.

Café Fäboda (☎ 729 3510; Lillsandvägen; mains €11-19; ☺ 10am-11pm May-Aug), near the beach, is a wonderful café and restaurant and worth the trip. There's a generous lunch buffet, and international menu, sunny summer deck and children's playground. In the evenings the bar is popular and there's often entertainment in summer.

KOKKOLA
☎ 06 / pop 35,888

Not really known as a tourist town, Kokkola (Swedish: Karleby) is a charming place. It was given its town charter in 1620 to stimulate its growth as a port for the tar trade, which flourished in the 17th century. It's been chasing its port ever since; as the land continues to rise, rebounding after the last Ice Age, the sea gets further and further away. At last glimpse, the harbour was over 2km north of town.

As well as a couple of good museums and an attractive centre, Kokkola preserves a beautiful district of old wooden houses and also has plenty of parkland to stroll through down to the harbour. It makes a good stop on your way north or south; the predominantly Finnish-speaking people are tangibly proud of their town, and it feels more welcoming than Jakobstad, for example.

Orientation & Information

The centre of town is compact. The train and bus station are a couple of blocks south of the centre, while most places of interest are within walking distance of the riverside

POHJANMAA

kauppatori, at the intersection of Rantakatu and Torikatu.

Public library (☎ 828 9560; Isokatu 3; ☒ Mon-Fri, also Sat winter) Free Internet at this spectacular modern building one block north of the train station.

Tourist office (☎ 828 9402; www.kokkola.fi; Kauppatori; ☒ 8am-5pm Mon-Fri, 9am-1pm Sat Jun-Aug, 8am-4pm Mon-Fri Sep-May) Very helpful. On the northern side of the square.

Sights and Activities

NERISTAN

This delightful area of wooden houses is what remains of the working class area of Kokkola (Neristan means 'lower town') where the sailors and fishermen lived. Until relatively recently, the river was wide and navigable up to here, and fishing boats docked to unload their finny cargo and sell it in the kauppatori. It's a pleasure to wander around these streets (one of the most picturesque is **Läntinen kirkkokatu**), which have a range of antique shops as well as a couple of cafés and restaurants. The tourist office publishes a good walking tour of town.

Beyond Neristan, the Suntti stream continues down to the harbour. There is a beach here, **Halkokari**, where a British attack was repelled during the Crimean war. One of the gunboats was captured, and can be seen in the 'English Park' on the river just north of Neristan. The event is commemorated in the town's **festival** in early June, when people dress-up 1854-style, and there's a theatrical re-enactment.

MUSEUMS

On Pitkänsillankatu in the centre of town are a number of **museums** (☎ 828 9474; for 1 museum €2, for all €4; ☒ noon-3pm Tue-Fri, noon-5pm Sat & Sun Sep-May, noon-5pm Tue-Sun Jun-Aug, free on Thu in winter) that share opening hours and ticketing.

The best of them is the **Mineraalikokoelma** (mineral collection; Pitkänsillankatu 28). While it may not sound thrilling, it's an amazing assembly of natural beauty. The resident geologist will enthusiastically talk you through the exhibits, which include stunning geometrical figures, delicate crystals and fragments of meteorites. In the same building, the **Luontokokoelma Kieppi** (natural history collection) is less compelling, with a collection of stuffed animals, antlers and traps.

Across the courtyard, the **Historiallinen Museo** (historical museum) consists of two proud old wooden buildings; the old school dates from 1696, making it one of the oldest secular buildings *in situ* in the country.

A block up the street, the **Taidemuseo** (Art gallery; Pitkänsillankatu 39) is in a large 19th-century merchants' mansion. It contains the collection of the portly Karl Herman Renlund (1850–1908), a shopworker who made good and left his art collection for the benefit of 'students and the working class'. He tipped the scales at 160kg when he died, but his collection is less heavyweight, although a Victor Westerholm canvas depicting the savage beauty of the Voikkaa rapids is memorable.

ACTIVITIES

The **M/S Jenny** (☎ 044-780 9140) does day-trips to Tankar island (€12, 4½ hours, midday, Friday to Wednesday). On Thursdays, it sails down the coast to Jakobstad and returns. It leaves Kokkola at noon, and returns at 10.30pm. A one-way fare is €14.

Sleeping

Kaupunkikartano Lumitähti (☎ 0500-162 302; jorma.aspegren@kolumbus.fi; r €68; ℗ ☒) The most characterful place to stay in town is this achingly lovely 19th-century wooden house in the heart of the old town, Neristan. There are just five rooms, so it's worth booking ahead. Breakfast is €2 per head extra, and you can rent bikes.

Hotel Kokkola (☎ 824 1000; www.hotelkokkola .com; Rantakatu 14; s/d €88/108, r Jun-Aug & weekends €68; ℗ ☒ ▢) This offers the best value for money of the three major hotels that overlook the kauppatori in the heart of town. The rooms are spacious and airy, with trouser-press, movie channel, and small minibar. There are large windows and new, comfortable beds. Breakfast and sauna included.

Camping Suntinsuu (☎ 831 4006; www.kokkol acamping.com; Pikiruukki; camping per person/tent sites €5.50/12, cottages €44-68; ☒ Jun-late Aug) This is a riverside camping ground a pleasant 2km northwest of the centre; follow the river downstream from the kauppatori. There are good cabins and facilities, as well as dormitory accommodation (€18) in an HI-affiliated hostel. You can rent canoes here, and the bar gets pretty lively in summer.

EATING & DRINKING

Vanhankaupingin Ravintola (☎ 834 9030; Isokatu 28; mains €13-22; ☼ dinner Tue-Sat) This smart place is in the heart of the old town and appropriately decorated. It's a great place to eat, elegantly formal and offering well-prepared fish dishes – the grilled Arctic char *(rautu)* is delicious – and, more unusually, a starter of garlic cappuccino!

Wanha Lyhty & Kellari (☎ 868 0188; Pitkänsillankatu 24; mains €12-24) This is a café, smart restaurant (open for dinner), and beer cellar cheerfully decorated in the spirit of the Old Town. The beer cellar offers live music on weekends.

Kokkolinna (☎ 825 2025; Isokatu 1; ☼ café 11am-6pm Mon-Fri, 11am-4pm Sat) Just across the road from the station, this beautiful café has been decorated in faithful Art Nouveau style. There's a selection of salads (which can be taken away), good rolls and a terrace, as well as an adjoining restaurant (run by a highly-regarded restaurant school).

Krunni (☎ 040-516 2311; Kauppatori; ☼ May-Sep). The best spot for a drink in town is the deck of this old Danish fishing boat around and dominating the market square. There's also a terrace and indoor seating where snacks are served.

Getting There & Away

The Kruunupyy/Kronoby airport is 22km southeast of Kokkola and served by a regional bus service. Buses meet arriving flights and go to Kokkola (€6) and Jakobstad/Pietarsaari (€5). There are several flights a day to/from Helsinki, run by Finnair subsidiaries.

Regular buses run to/from all coastal towns, especially Vaasa (€21.30, three hours) and Jakobstad (€6.20, 40 minutes). The bus station is one block northwest of the train station.

There is a major train station in Kokkola and all trains using the main western line stop here. The daytime journey from Helsinki (€50.30, seven daily) takes under five hours; there are also several night trains.

If you're driving to or from Jakobstad, a scenic (and quicker) alternative to the main highway is to take road 749, which crosses the island of Luoto.

KALAJOKI

☎ 08 / pop 9152

Most Finns know Kalajoki for its long, wide, sandy beaches; it's a name that con-jures up the phrase 'seaside holiday'. The local tourist industry had to really get its backside into gear once it became cheaper to get a charter flight to Malaga than the train up here, and now there are some excellent specials offered for family holidays. There's a plethora of cottages to rent, and many services for tourists, including a huge spa and amusement park, resort-style hotels, and a new 18-hole golf course.

Things don't close down completely in winter – there are plenty of cross-country skiing trails and many of the cottages are available for rent.

Orientation & Information

The bus terminal, supermarkets, banks, a post office and a large travel and booking agency are all in Kalajoki village, on the banks of the Kalajoki just off the highway. The resort area, with the beach, airfield, and most of the accommodation, is 6km south of the village along Hwy 8.

The **Tourist office** (☎ 469 4449; www.kalajoki.fi; ☼ 9am-5pm Mon-Fri Sep-May, 9am-8pm Mon-Fri, 11am-8pm Sat & Sun Jun-Aug) is on the highway at the turn-off to the beach. Both the office and the website have a list of all the rental cottages hereabouts.

Activities

Kalajoki Särkät (Kalajoki Beach) is one of the country's most popular holiday spots for Finns. It has a lot to offer: **Jukujukumaa Amusement Park** (admission €12-14; ☼ 11am-6pm early Jun-early Aug), spa, golf course, holiday villas, beaches, restaurants and cafés, hotels and discos. It's billed as a 'Mediterranean-style holiday experience at a latitude of 64°', but it's all very Finnish – saunas, summer cottages and *humppa* music.

Sleeping & Eating

The beach, 6km south of the village, is the place to look for accommodation. Dozens of sturdy summer cottages dot the forest behind the beach, and range from the simple (a couple are on islands with no power) to the luxurious. Nearly all are also available by the day. The best place to book is through the tourist office. Look out for specials that throw in amusement park entry or a round of golf.

Tapion Tupa (☎ 466 622; www.tapiontupa.com; Hiekkasärkät; s/d €20/40, 2-/4-person apt €79/105;

POHJANMAA

(P) (X) (R)) Near the main road and close to the beach, this large complex has a range of accommodation including an HI-associated hostel, log cabins and self-contained holiday apartments.

Hotelli Rantakalla (☎ 466 642; s/d €74/103; (P) (X) (R)) This is one of many hotels at the beach. It has everything you need for a super-Finnish summer holiday; minigolf, saunas and a terrace to drink beers in the sun. Rates drop considerably outside the summer high season.

Ravintola Lokkilinna (☎ 469 6700; lunch buffet €9; (Y) lunch & dinner) This place has a fine summer terrace overlooking the beach, a big lunch buffet and a casual bar-restaurant with ocean views.

Top Camping (☎ 469 2400; www.hiekkasarkat .fi; tent sites €8-9 plus per person €4-5, cabins €30-85; (Y) Jun-Aug) This is a huge and very busy place fronting the beach and adjacent to the amusement park.

Getting There & Away
Several daily buses running between Oulu (€22.10, two hours) and Kokkola (€13.20, one hour) stop at Kalajoki and the beach. The easiest way to reach Kalajoki by train is to get off at Kokkola and catch a bus from there.

AROUND KALAJOKI
Maakalla & Ulkokalla Islets
An isolated islet that has only existed since the 15th century, Maakalla has managed to retain a genuine fishing-village feel. There are no roads, shops or electricity – in fact, there are no permanent humans – but you will find an interesting wooden **church**, abundant plant and birdlife and some old **fishing huts**. The owners of the huts hold regular meetings and vote to keep the islet exactly as it is.

For what is probably the most isolated accommodation in Finland, contact **FemE-Mare** (☎ 040-569 5896; www.fememare.fi) which has recently renovated the lighthouse keeper's house on the rocky islet of Ulkolalla and offers accommodation and board. There's no power, but fresh water for the sauna stove is brought from the mainland!

In summer (mid-June to early August) there are three-hour **cruises** (return €15) to Maakalla from the pier at Kalajoki.

CENTRAL POHJANMAA

SEINÄJOKI
☎ 06 / pop 35,918
Seinäjoki, the commercial centre of the region, is a supply and service centre for the surrounding agricultural region and a low-key conference centre. For most travellers, it is little more than a train junction. However, it hosts two of Finland's major summer festivals – the Tango Fair and Provinssirock, perhaps as far apart in the music spectrum as you can get. The town is also known for its modern centre designed by Alvar Aalto, and there's a large open-air museum area a few kilometres to the south of the centre.

Information
Public library (☎ 416 2318; Koulukatu 21; (Y) 10am-7pm Mon-Fri, 11am-3pm Sat, closed Sat Jun-Aug) The library has three Internet terminals.
Tourist office (☎ 420 9090; matkailu@epmatkailu.fi; (Y) 9am-5pm Mon-Fri) In the bus and train station complex. This is the place to book accommodation in private homes during the festivals.

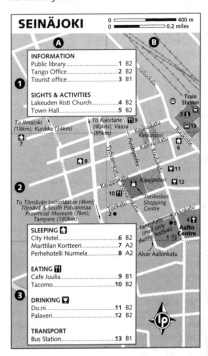

| SEINÄJOKI | 0 — 400 m |
| | 0 — 0.2 miles |

INFORMATION
Public library...............................1 B2
Tango Office................................2 B2
Tourist office...............................3 B1

SIGHTS & ACTIVITIES
Lakeuden Risti Church................4 B2
Town Hall....................................5 B2

SLEEPING
City Hotel....................................6 B2
Marttilan Kortteeri......................7 A2
Perhehotelli Nurmela..................8 A2

EATING
Cafe Juulia..................................9 B1
Tacomo......................................10 B2

DRINKING
Du:ni..11 B2
Palaveri......................................12 B2

TRANSPORT
Bus Station.................................13 B1

Sights

AALTO CENTRE

The monumental Aalto Centre (1960) is a complex consisting of several buildings covering two large city blocks. It's one of the most important works of architect Alvar Aalto (see p131), who was born in nearby Kuortane in 1898. The stark white buildings are softened in places by ridged ceramic tiles; you can see the massive influence Aalto has had and how modern his designs must have looked in the early 1960s. The complex buildings include the **town hall** and **public library**. The massive **church** (noon-6pm), with its oddly secular steeple-clock tower, is the most recognizable building. Take a lift (€1) to the top for a view of the region.

ETELÄ-POHJANMAAN MAAKUNTAMUSEO

Seven kilometres south of town, the **South Pohjanmaa Provincial Museum** (416 2642; admission €2; noon-6pm Wed, noon-4pm Thu, Fri & Sun, ring for other times) is an open-air museum in the leafy suburb of Törnävä. The wealthy Wasastjerna family first settled this area in 1806 and built a mansion that still stands. On the grounds are other wooden buildings, mostly transferred from elsewhere.

On your right, when coming from the town centre, is the **Agriculture Museum** and the **Mill Museum**. On your left in the old yellow building is the **Gunpowder Museum**. Behind is a smoke house and a smith's house from the 17th century.

Local bus 1 runs from Seinäjoki bus station to Törnävä.

Festivals & Events

Seinäjoki's two major summer festivals are both are enormously popular, so book accommodation in advance.

Provinssirock (421 2700; www.provinssirock.fi) is a classic, open-air international rock concert held mainly 4km south of town, near Törnävä, over three days in mid-June. Day passes cost €40 to €55, a three-day pass is €77. The acts are of the highest international profile, and include many of the top Finnish groups, many from the darker end of the rock/metal spectrum. The 2005 program included Marilyn Manson, Nine Inch Nails, Nightwish, Slipknot and the 69 Eyes; a heavyweight line-up indeed. There are five stages and connecting buses both from Seinäjoki itself and also from Helsinki.

Tangomarkkinat (420 1123; Torikatu; www.tangomarkkinat.fi) appeals to a generally older and almost exclusively Finnish crowd but, in terms of audience, it's one of Finland's biggest festivals. Held in early July, it opens with a huge open-air dance and party in 'Tango Street' and continues over four days with dance competitions, tango classes, and other festivities, culminating in the awarding of the 'Tango King & Queen', the best singers of the festival. Needless to say, the standard of dancing is pretty high, although perhaps not recognizable in a bar in Buenos Aires.

Sleeping

There are several chain hotels in Seinäjoki (including Sokos and Cumulus), but little reason to stay outside festival time.

Perhehotelli Nurmela (414 1771; Kalevankatu 29; s/d from €35/55;) This is a cosy, family-run guesthouse on a quiet street just west of the centre. Some rooms have private bathroom, and all rates include breakfast.

City Hotel (215 9111; www.sdr.fi; Kalevankatu 2; s/d €88/106, Sat, Sun & summer €68/76;) The homeliest of the town's hotels, this is handily situated right opposite the bus and train stations. Most of the rooms are a little on

POHJANMAA

TANGO

Seinäjoki is the undisputed tango capital of a country that is certifiably tango-mad. In the rest of the world the tango craze was swept away by Elvis, but in Finland it never died.

Argentinean musicians and dancers brought tango to Europe around 1910. A Finnish version of tango developed soon after, championed by the composer Unto Mononen and Olavi Virta, the Finnish king of tango dancing.

No other music could epitomise the melancholic Finn better. If Finns lack the electrifying tension that Latin Americans bring to the tango, they lack none of the enthusiasm. Finnish tango music is usually performed with a live band and the lyrics deal with loneliness, unrequited love and desperation. It's fair to say that it's not as popular with the younger generations.

the small side (although there are some bigger ones, so ask for one of those), but have wireless Internet, fan and minibar. There's a good restaurant, nightclub, and café. The pool needs to be booked (and paid for).

Marttilan Kortteeri (☎ 420 4800; Puskantie 38; s/d €45/65; Ⓨ Jun-early Aug; Ⓟ Ⓧ) A few blocks west of the action of central Seinäjoki, this complex is set in a quiet pine-clad residential district. The accommodation is comfortable hostel-type; there's a good café-restaurant, and rates include breakfast. You'll need to book well ahead during the festivals but at other times it's virtually empty.

Törnävän Leirintäalue (☎ 412 0784, 414 6585; Törnäväntie 29; tent sites €10, cabins €35-50; Ⓨ Jun-Aug) This camping ground is south of the centre. There is also a temporary camping area set up near the festival during Provinssirock. To pitch a tent there costs €15 per person for the weekend or €7 for one night.

Eating & Drinking
Seinäjoki isn't the gourmet capital of Finland. The hotel restaurants are the best bet for a square meal, while there are fast food stalls in the kauppatori.

Cafe Juulia (☎ 414 4544; Puistopolku 15; lunch specials €5-8; Ⓨ 8am-3pm Mon-Fri) Utterly unpretentious, this likeable little lunch spot has cane chairs, and the mustard and ketchup already in place. They do four or five daily specials which are filling and tasty.

Tacomo (☎ 414 4800; Alvar Aallonkatu 3; mains from €6; Ⓨ 11am-8pm Mon-Thu, 11am-10pm Fri & Sat, 1-8pm Sun). This trendy modern restaurant has bare, cool décor and caters to Finland's enduring love of Mexican food. There's a good range of prices, with simple tortilla or taco dishes going for as little as €5.95.

Du:ni (cnr Kauppakatu & Koulukatu) This is a loungey café-bar with a great terrace, free Internet access and a popular club downstairs. On the same block, Palaveri is another popular bar that kicks during Provinssirock. Both are open late, do tasty rolls and snacks, and have a wooden terrace.

Getting There & Away
The bus station and train station are adjacent and very central. There are buses to towns and villages throughout western Finland.

Seinäjoki is a rail hub and the fastest trains from Helsinki cover the 346km in under three hours (€46.80). There are regular connections to Vaasa (€8.80, 50 minutes), Jyväskylä and cities further north.

There are four or five commuter flights Monday to Friday from Helsinki to Seinäjoki (return from €127 to €220) and one on Sunday, run by subsidiaries of Finnair.

KAUSTINEN
☎ 06 / pop 4393
Kaustinen is a small village 47km southeast of Kokkola. There isn't much to see in the village itself, so plan your visit around the superb Kaustinen Folk Music Festival in July. Such is the renown of this festival, the Peanuts cartoon character 'Woodstock' is called 'Kaustinen' in the Finnish translation.

The small **tourist information office** (Kaustintie 1) is easy to find in the centre. Nearby is the festival office, which handles accommodation during the event. The bus station, shops and services are all easily reached on foot.

The **Kaustinen Folk Music Festival** (☎ 860 4111; www.kaustinen.net; PL 11, 69601 Kaustinen) is one of the most beloved of summer festivals in Finland, attracting huge crowds. It's *the* place to be if you're interested in Finnish folk music and dance, since some 300 Finnish bands (and many international acts) perform more than 250 concerts during the week in mid-July. At any time between 10am and 3am there are several official concerts and half a dozen impromptu jam sessions going on. Folk dance performances are also an integral part of the festival, with everything from Celtic and Latin dancing alongside Finnish dance.

Sleeping
The festival office organizes accommodation during the busy periods. Camping and dormitory beds cost around €10, accommodation in private homes is around €30 per person. Call ahead to see what's available.

Koskelan Lomatalo (☎ 861 1338; www.koskelanlomatalo.kaustinen.fi; Känsäläntie 123; per person €25) This HI-affiliated place, about 5km north of Kaustinen, offers kitchen, sauna and laundry facilities and has a café.

Getting There & Away
There are several buses daily from Kokkola (€7.80, 45 minutes), which has a railway station. There are express buses from other cities during the festival season; check the festival website.

Oulu, Kainuu & Koillismaa

In between the Lakeland and Lapland, the central strip of Finland is a transitional region comprising the province of Oulu to the west, the wilderness area of Kainuu to the east, and Koillismaa in the northeast. Administratively, the entire region is called Oulu Province.

Oulu itself is a vibrant, exciting city with a booming technology industry, lively market square, and, in summer, some memorable terraced bars and cafés. It's the undisputed capital of the region, and a great stop on the way north. Kainuu is a heavily forested wilderness traversed by the famed UKK trekking route close to the border with Russia. Koillismaa, near the Russian border, is the transitional region between the south and Lapland, and includes the rugged Kuusamo area and Oulanka National Park – one of the natural highlights of Finxland. It is an area of tumbling rivers, isolated lakes and dense forests.

Finns entered the Kainuu region in the 16th century, violating the earlier border treaty between Sweden and Russia. In the late 16th century, the region witnessed fierce frontier wars between Russians and citizens of the Swedish Empire. After these bloody wars, Swedish territory was pushed further east, to where the border stands today.

By the 19th century tar had become the salvation of the economically depressed Kainuu region, but most of the profits were sent downriver to Oulu, along with the barrels of tar. During WWII, bloody battles were fought against the Red Army in the area around Kuhmo, and soon after the war a flood of emigrants escaped poverty-stricken Kainuu for Sweden and elsewhere. The region remains sparsely populated.

HIGHLIGHTS

- Cycling on **Oulu's** (p266) bike paths, then enjoying the energetic nightlife in the city's cafés and bars
- Bird-watching in **Liminka Bay** (p273) during the 'great migration' of May, August and September
- Trekking the **Karhunkierros (Bear's Ring) route** (p288) in Oulanka National Park – some of the best wilderness scenery in Finland
- Rafting, sledding, trekking or skiing – in and around **Ruka** (p286), the adventure capital of the region
- Sailing on an icebreaker and exploring the snow castle at **Kemi** (p273)
- Experiencing high culture in remotest Finland at Kuhmo's **Chamber Music Festival** (p282)

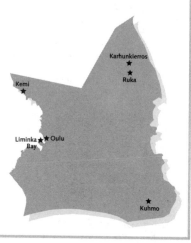

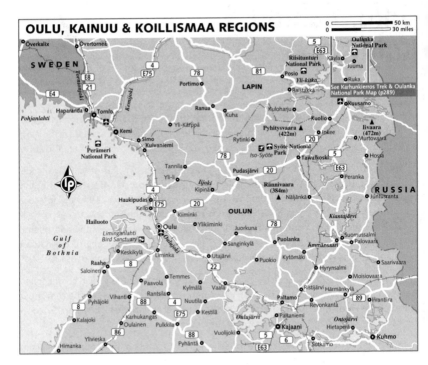

OULU, KAINUU & KOILLISMAA REGIONS

Activities

This large province covers a wide swathe of Finnish territory, from the coast to the Russian border, so it's no surprise that the scope for activity is almost endless!

In the east, the Karhunkierros (Bear's Ring) is one of Finland's most rewarding and popular trekking routes, and has a good network of huts and a variety of scenery. The longer UKK route is another memorable hike.

On the waterways, fishing and canoeing are popular, with the Oulankajoki and Kitkajoki particularly suitable for the latter. The Liminganlahti wetlands are great for bird watching, while at Tornio you can play one of the world's northernmost golf courses, which straddles two nations.

The city of Oulu and the surrounding area is a paradise for cyclists, who will seldom see a more comprehensive network of cycle paths and trails! Some hardy Finns even cycle in winter, but you might prefer to try skiing; the province has the high-profile resort of Ruka, and the more family-oriented Syöte.

Last but not least, the region boasts an unbeatable winter experience in a trip on the icebreaker *Sampo*, a memorable journey that includes a dip in the icy water – thankfully wearing a high-tech thermal suit.

Self-Catering Accommodation

Contact **FinFun** (☎ 020 1334 882; www.finfun.fi; Mannenkatu 1) for a wide selection of holiday cottages for rental. They also have a branch in Kuusamo. Local tourist offices have details of cottages in the region.

OULU REGION

OULU

☎ 08 / pop 127,226

Prosperous Oulu (Swedish: Uleåborg) is one of Finland's most enjoyable cities to visit. In summer the locals, who appreciate daylight when they get it, crowd the terraces around the marketplace, and stalls groan under the weight of Arctic berries and giant pans laden with all manner of delicious food.

The centre is spread across several islands, elegantly connected by pedestrian bridges, and the water never seems far away. This layout has made it very convenient for cycling, and Oulu's network of bike paths is one of the best in Europe.

Oulu, the largest city north of Tampere and the sixth-biggest in Finland, is also one of the world's foremost technology cities; the university turns out top-notch IT graduates and the corporate science and technology parks on the city's outskirts employ people from all over the globe. The centre of Oulu is even rigged up as a free wireless network, so you can check your emails from the terrace of the local pub.

But never fear, it's not all laptops and cycle lanes; this is Finland after all, and there's a good dollop of weirdness here, particularly in the summer season, when the World Air-Guitar Championships come to town!

History

Oulu was founded by King Karl IX of Sweden in 1605. It wasn't long before industrious and hard-working Swedish pioneers descended upon the Kainuu forests in search of tar, which was floated in barrels to Oulu – the sticky stuff was essential to the building of unsinkable wooden ships. By the late 19th century Oulu boasted the largest fleet in Finland.

In 1822 Oulu burned to the ground and was rebuilt, although very few old buildings now remain.

Orientation

Oulu is situated at the mouth of the Oulujoki, with bridges connecting the riverbanks and several islands. Although the entire city covers a very large area, you can easily walk from the train and bus stations to most places in the compact centre.

Information

Forex (☎ 020-751 2680; www.forex.fi; Kauppurienkatu 13)

Main post office (Hallituskatu 36; ◷ 9am-8pm Mon-Fri) Near the train station.

Pint Netti Baari (per 10 min €1; Rotuaari) Pub with three Internet terminals, free for customers.

Public library (☎ 558 410; Kaarlenväylä; ◷ 10am-8pm Mon-Fri, 10am-3pm Sat, noon-4pm Sun) The impressive library is on the waterfront opposite the Oulu Theatre. It has several Internet terminals.

Tourist office (☎ 5584 1330; www.oulutourism.fi; Torikatu 10; ◷ 9am-6pm Mon-Fri, 11am-3pm Sat & Sun mid-Jun–early Sep, 9am-4pm Mon-Fri early Sep–mid-Jun) Publishes the useful guide *Look at Oulu*.

Sights
KAUPPATORI

Oulu has perhaps the liveliest market square of all Finnish towns, and its position at the waterfront makes it all the more appealing. The square is bordered by several old wooden storehouses that now serve as restaurants, bars and craft shops selling woven pine baskets, carved wooden cups and other typical Finnish souvenirs. Look for the squat *Toripolliisi* statue, a humorous representation of the local police. At the southern end of the square is the **kauppahalli** (covered market; ◷ 8am-6pm Mon-Fri, 8am-3pm Sat), with fresh produce, souvenirs and food stalls.

OULU CATHEDRAL

The imposing 19th-century **cathedral** (Kirkkokatu 36; ◷ 11am-8pm Jun–Aug, 11am-9pm Jul, noon-1pm Sep-May) has Finland's oldest portrait (dating from 1611) above the door to the vestry, and a fine altarpiece of the Ascension. A much older church, built in 1777, stood here until the great fire of 1822. This version was designed by the German architect CL Engel. It got promoted to cathedral in 1900 when the bishopric moved here from Kuopio.

TIETOMAA

The mammoth **Tietomaa Science Centre** (☎ 5584 1340; www.tietomaa.fi; adult/child €12/10; ◷ 10am-6pm mid-Feb–Aug, 10am-8pm Jul; 10am-4pm Mon-Fri, 10am-6pm Sat & Sun Sep–mid-Feb), in an old factory building, is Scandinavia's oldest and largest science museum. At any given time it's mobbed with hundreds of school children bussed in from all over Finland. It's one of those places you can poke around in for half a day, and the excellent changing interactive exhibits are good for kids. As well as the UFO exhibit, hologram hall, junior science centre, 'world of sport', weather exhibition and display of the human body, you can take a lift up the tower for a view over Oulu.

TAIDEMUSEO

The **Taidemuseo** (Oulu Art Museum; ☎ 5584 7450; Kasarmintie 7; adult/child €3/1, admission free Fri; ◷ 10am-5pm Tue-Sun) is a bright gallery opposite Tietomaa. It has excellent temporary exhibitions of both international and Finnish contemporary art, and a good permanent collection. The café is an exhibit in its own right!

MERIMIEHEN KOTIMUSEO

The **Sailor's Home Museum** (☎ 5584 7185; Pikisaarentie 6; admission €1; 🕙 10am-5pm Wed-Sun Jun-Aug) on Pikisaari belonged to a local sailor. Built in 1737, it is the oldest house in Oulu and was transferred here from the town centre in 1983. The wallpaper and extendable bed are typical of 19th-century Finnish homes.

OULUNLINNA

There's not much left of Oulu Castle, although you can clearly see the remaining fort-like structure dominating the small park near the bridge. The observation tower of the castle, rebuilt in 1873, now houses a café, but you can go below and look in the cellar, which has a small interpretative display. The original castle was built in 1590 as a base for the Swedish army moving east towards Russia. The whole thing blew up in 1793 when a lightning strike hit a powder magazine.

PARKS & GARDENS

Oulu University Botanical Gardens (Kaitoväylä 5; 🕙 8am-8pm, greenhouses 🕙 8am-3pm Tue-Fri, 11am-3pm Sat & Sun), in Lineman, north of the centre, are pleasantly landscaped with thousands of exotic plants – including hardy 5m-tall cacti. A pair of greenhouses, named Romeo and Juliet, house tropical species.

Just north of the town centre and connected by small bridges, **Hupisaaret Island** is a pleasant city park with bike paths, greenhouses, a summer café and the **Ainola Park**. It's a popular place for strolling in summer.

Activities
CYCLING & ROLLERBLADING

One of Oulu's best features is the extensive network of wonderful **bicycle paths** – routinely praised as the best local cycling routes in Finland. Nowhere is the Finns' love of two-wheeled transport more obvious than here in summer. Bike paths cross bridges, waterways and islands and can take you all the way out to surrounding villages. A good easy ride is from the kauppatori (market square), across the bridge to Pikisaari and across another

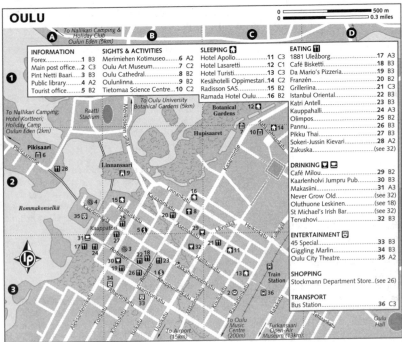

LET IT ALL OUT

As if an air-guitar festival wasn't enough, Oulu is also home to one of Finland's most unusual musical ensembles, Mieskuoro Huutajat. The name, which translates to 'The Shouters Male Choir', says, or rather yells, it all.

Under the steely gaze of conductor and composer Petri Sirtiö, the 30-odd men, dressed in very smart black suits with rubber ties, shout various complex arrangements of well-known songs and anthems. It's actually more musical than it sounds, with softly melodic barks building to stunning crescendos of red-faced bellowing. Some shouters have long cardboard tubes to add an orchestral tone to proceedings. It's a memorable display, added to by their traditionally silent, expressionless entrance and exit.

At times, the shouters have courted controversy, particularly when shouting national anthems; the Finnish embassy in Paris tried, in vain, to prevent them shouting La Marseillaise in an art gallery. A documentary film, *Screaming Men*, was even made about their tour to Japan.

Throughout, the deeply ironic Sirtiö has trodden a very Finnish line between the totally serious and the absurdly comic. Critics have raved about the primal forces at play, but be assured the Huutajat do everything with a large dose of Finnish irony. Check their website, www.huutajat .org, for upcoming dates.

bridge to Nallikari where there's a good beach facing the Gulf of Bothnia.

Bikes can be hired from the train station, and bikes and rollerblades can be hired from shop 24 at the kauppatori. Nallikari Camping (p270) rents out bikes but only to guests. An excellent cycling route map is available for free from the tourist office.

Tours

The 'Potnapekka' – a tourist trolley – travels around in summer, from Rotuaari pedestrian street to Hupisaaret island or Nallikari beach. The fare is €4/2 per adult/child to either, or €6/3 for both routes; departures are from Rotuaari every hour on the hour, daily from early June to early August.

From May to October the **MS Alexandra** (☎ 528 2190; cruises 1½hr adult/child €10/5; 4hr adult & child €15) cruises the Oulu archipelago, with daily departures from the kauppatori.

Festivals & Events

In a country that wrote the book on oddball festivals, Oulu hosts more than its fair share. Take the **World Air Guitar Championships** (www.airguitarworldchampionships.com), which is part of the **Oulu Music Video Festival** (www .omvf.net) in late August. Contestants – with no musical ability required – from all over Finland and overseas take the stage to show what they can do with their imaginary instruments.

There are two unusual winter events, both the largest of their kind anywhere in the world. The **Oulu Tar Ski Race** (www.arktisetvalot .fi), held in early March, is a 70km skiing race (40km for women) that is entering its 113th year. The **Ice-Angling Marathon** (www.oulutourism.fi) is a 48-hour contest held on the open sea in early April (when the ice is still quite thick) and draws more than 400 participants.

The biggest summer event is **Tar-Burning Week** (www.oulutourism.fi), a festival that takes place in late June, around Midsummer. **Elojazz & Blues** (www.elojazz.com) is a two-day music festival in early August.

Garlic Night (www.oulutourism.fi) is one of Oulu's strangest but most popular festivals. Held for one day and evening in mid-July, this event draws huge crowds to Rotuaari and the kauppatori. The focus is eating or tasting garlic – everything from garlic potatoes, pizzas and bread to garlic-flavoured beer and ice cream – all enhanced by festivities and live entertainment.

Sleeping

Strangely enough for a provincial capital with reasonable tourist appeal, there's a limited choice of accommodation in Oulu, and little in the budget bracket. Book ahead if you're staying in hotels on a weekday outside summer: business and conference travellers book out hotels months in advance.

Hotel Lasaretti (☎ 884 8300; www.lasaretti.com; Kasarmintie 13; s/d €112/127, weekends €80/96, summer €60/80; P ⊠ ⬛ ⬛ &) Set in a complex on a little island north of the centre, this shiny new place has all the mod cons, with rooms that are contemporary Nordic – allergy free, with no-nonsense interplay of wood and fabrics. It still has a friendly, personal feel, however, and plenty of greenery nearby; you can stroll into town through the park.

Hotel Turisti (☎ 563 6100; www.hotellituristi.fi; Rautatienkatu 9; s/d €75/90, weekends & summer €50/60; P ✗ ☺) Right opposite the train station, with reception doubling as a newsagent, this looks well seedy from outside, but actually has very pleasing rooms; spacious, modern, and bright. It's good value at weekends and summer – and for groups, with rooms sleeping up to five – and rates include sauna and breakfast. Don't leave anything in your car, as break-ins have been known to happen.

Kesähotelli Oppimestari (☎ 884 8527; fax 884 8772; Nahkatehtaankatu 3; s/d €37/55; ☺ early Jun–early Aug; P ✗ ☺) This efficient place in the north of town offers some of the cheapest summer beds around. It's a modern, well-equipped facility with spacious student-residence rooms, all equipped with kitchenettes. Disabled facilities are excellent, and a simple breakfast is included.

Nallikari Camping (☎ 5586 1350; www.nallikaricamping.fi; Hietasaari; tent sites €5-8 plus per adult/child €4/1, 2–4–bed camping cabins €32, small cottages €65-93, large cottages €123) This camping ground is a great budget option in a lovely location within easy striking distance of the heart of town. It's on Hietasaari, 5km northwest of the centre – but only 2.5km via the pedestrian bridges. Nearby is the good Nallikari beach. There are child-friendly activities in summer, and a kid-minding service.

Radisson SAS (☎ 887 7666; www.radisson.com /oulufi; Hallituskatu 1; standard/superior r €135/160, Sat, Sun & summer €83/92; P ✗ ☐ ☎ ☺) This is the highest-profile business hotel in Oulu, ideally located near the waterfront and kauppatori. The standard rooms are spacious and airy, with good bathrooms, and one has its own sauna. The suite with views is also very tempting. There are excellent facilities, and a popular nightclub and restaurant.

Ramada Hotel Oulu (☎ 883 9111; www.ramada .com; Kirkkokatu 3; s/d €141/166, weekend & summer r €82-88; P ✗ ☐ ☺) With a satisfying location overlooking the cathedral, this is one of Oulu's better choices. There are three grades of room; many with balconies; the 'business comfort' rooms cost some €35 more but come with either their own sauna or Jacuzzi. All the rooms have been recently renovated, and there's good service and a big breakfast buffet.

Hotel Apollo (☎ 52211; hotel@apollo.inet.fi; Asemakatu 31; s/d from €80/100, Sat, Sun & summer r from €60; P ✗) This hotel is an easy walk from the train station although in a bit of a dull area. It has a variety of rooms, some recently made over, and many with their own sauna (€20 extra in summer). Some of the colour schemes are a bit weird but it's a cosy and welcoming place. It also has a good café and popular karaoke bar that's open to 4am.

Holiday Club Oulun Eden (☎ 884 2000; www.holidayclub.fi; Nallikari; s/d €125/135; P ✗ ☐ ☎) This is a deluxe spa hotel on Hietasaari, near Nallikari Camping and the beach. Discounts are available for longer stays and there are various holiday packages. Accommodation prices include unlimited use of saunas, water slides and lushly landscaped indoor pools, plus you can call on the services of various massage and hydrotherapy treatments.

Eating

Oulu is the most cosmopolitan city in western Finland, and offers a good variety of restaurants in all price ranges. The best and cheapest snacks and local specialities can be found in the lively kauppatori and the classic indoor kauppahalli on the southern side of the square. In summer there are stalls selling fresh salmon, paella and Oulu specialities, such as *rieska* (flat bread), *leipäjuusto* (cheese bread), and *lohikeitto* (salmon soup).

RESTAURANTS

1881 Uleåborg (☎ 881 1188; Aittatori 4; mains €24-28; ☺ dinner Mon-Sat, lunch & dinner Sun & daily in summer) In an old warehouse near the kauppatori, this classy spot combines chic Finnish style with a traditional setting. There's a decent wine list and a range of set menus. The à la carte menu is short but high on quality, with daily fish and vegetarian specials, reindeer and grilled veal liver with gooseberry sauce, among others on offer.

Franzén (☎ 311 3224; Kirkkokatu 2; mains €16-35; ☺ 4pm-midnight Mon-Sat) Opposite the cathedral, in a building dating from 1829, this is one of Oulu's finest. The cuisine is French and Finnish, with fish (salmon, trout, perch), reindeer and willow grouse featuring on the menu. The wine list is good and the decoration impeccable, and there's also a German-style beer cellar (Johanneksen kellari). Book ahead, as they may not open otherwise.

Sokeri-Jussin Kievari (☎ 376 628; Pikisaarentie 2; mains €12-26; ☾ kitchen 11am-10pm) An Oulu classic, this timbered local on Pikisaari was once a sugar warehouse and has outdoor tables that have good views of the centre. Although the renovated interior has lost a bit of the original character, it's still very attractive and a top spot to eat.

Zakuska (☎ 379 369; Hallituskatu 13; mains €11-19; ☾ 4pm-midnight Mon-Sat) This place is one of the best-value restaurants in town and deservedly popular for its tasty Russian cuisine. The décor and music add to the 'east of Finland' atmosphere, the onion steak is good, as are the blini.

Pannu (☎ 815 1600; Kauppurienkatu 12; mains €6.50-19.50; ☾ 10.30am-10pm Mon-Thu, 10.30am-11pm Fri & Sat, noon-9pm Sun) This is an informal grill restaurant, in the basement of Stockmann department store, with a huge range of dishes including snails, ostrich, pan pizzas, and various steaks. It manages to blur the lines between informal, affordable dining and gourmet restaurant, and does it well.

Olimpos (☎ 311 3941; Pakkahuoneenkatu 7; mains €10-22; ☾ lunch & dinner) This newish restaurant has fast become popular with locals for its Greek cuisine, to which a few dishes from other Mediterranean countries are added. There's a big range of lunch options, from a €6 cheapie, to a full €21 set menu that will send you hotel-bound for a siesta.

Other recommendations:

Istanbul Oriental (☎ 311 2922; Kauppurienkatu 11; dishes €12-24; ☾ lunch & dinner) Reasonable Turkish restaurant with stylish décor, and a good range of vegetarian options, including felafels (€11 to €13).

Pikku Thai (☎ 370 889; Pakkahuoneenkatu 8; mains €10-14; ☾ 10.30am-10pm Mon-Fri, noon-11pm Sat, noon-9pm Sun) Cosy Thai restaurant with better food than exterior décor and good lunch specials.

CAFÉS

Café Bisketti (Kirkkokatu 8; ☾ 8am-10pm Mon-Thu, 8am-1am Fri & Sat, noon-10pm Sun) On the north-south section of Rotuaari is this great spot for lunch. It has filled rolls, croissants, quiche and cakes, and a terrace facing the square. At lunchtime soup, salad, coffee and a pastry are €5.50, and only €7 with a tasty hot dish.

Katri Antell (☎ 311 2182; Kirkkokatu 17; ☾ 8am-6pm Mon-Fri, 9am-3pm Sat) Opposite Bisketti, this place has been an Oulu institution for a very long time; the first Katri Antell was founded in 1880. Come for its freshly baked pastries and cakes and relax on the curious couch.

QUICK EATS

Oulu's hungry student population means there are plenty of cheap kebab and pizza places. Locals say there are more pizza shops per head of population in Oulu than any other city in the world!

Da Mario's Pizzeria (Torikatu 24; pizzas €6-8; ☾ lunch & dinner, till 4.30am Fri & Sat) One of the most popular pizza places, this is comparatively classy, and is handily open late at weekends.

Grilleriina (Asemakatu 29; ☾ 11am-5am) There are grillis, and then there's this place, a class above and a step beyond the standard. While it boasts the usual all-possible-permutations menu, it's far tastier than most, and has a spacious, Marimekko-furnished dining room to enjoy the abundant portions in. The opening hours alone inspire respect.

Drinking

There's plenty going on in Oulu at night – the number of bikes lined up outside pubs and bars on summer weekends has to be seen to be believed!

Oluthuone Leskinen (☎ 311 7993; Kirkkokatu 10; ☾ noon-2am Sun-Tue, noon-3am Wed-Sat) This bar on the central pedestrian zone has a good terrace and has an extraordinary range of Finnish and international beers, as well as malt whiskies. There's notably friendly service and a good atmosphere.

Makasiini (Kauppatori; ☾ from 6am Mon-Sat, 8am Sun) This is a classic café set in an old wooden warehouse on the kauppatori. It opens extremely early so that stallholders can get their first coffee of the day in, and in summer has a great terrace that sucks all it can get from the evening sun.

Never Grow Old (Hallituskatu 17; ☾ 2pm-2am, 2pm-3am weekends) This enduringly popular bar hits its stride after 10pm, with plenty of dancing, DJs and revelry in the tightly packed interior. The goofy décor includes some seriously comfortable and some really uncomfortable places to sit, and a log-palisade bar that seems designed to get you to wear your drink.

St Michaels (Hallituskatu 13; ☾ 2pm-2am) In the same block as Never Grow Old, St Michaels

OULU, KAINUU & KOILLISMAA

is a convivial Irish bar that pours a very acceptable Guinness, and has an excellent selection of whiskies.

Tervahovi (Hallituskatu 15; ⏰ noon-1am or later Tue-Sat, noon-10pm Sun, 4pm-midnight Mon) A more typically Finnish place than St Michaels, with leopard-skin and a vaguely French theme; they also do tasty food.

Café Milou (Asemakatu 21; ⏰ noon-2am) Named after Tin Tin's hound, this place is away from the main strip but packs in students with its relaxed vibe, bookshelves filled with comics, and service so rude it's almost comical. There's a small terrace.

Kaarlenholvi Jumpru Pub (Kauppurienkatu 6; ⏰ 11am-2am Mon-Tue, 11am-4am Wed-Sat, noon-2am Sun) This Oulu institution is a great place for meeting locals. It has an enclosed terrace, a perennial favourite, and a warren of cosy rooms inside, as well as a nightclub that opens at 10pm Wednesday to Saturday.

Entertainment
CLUBS
45 Special (☎ 881 1845; Saaristonkatu 12; ⏰ 8pm-4am) This grungy club is Oulu's best rock venue, with wall-to-wall patrons. Entry is €4 most nights.

Giggling Marlin (Torikatu 21-22; ⏰ 10pm-4am Wed-Sat) This is one of a new brand of 'Suomi pop' clubs, featuring two dance floors with contemporary Finnish pop and international music and young Finns dancing on the tables.

CLASSICAL MUSIC & THEATRE
Oulu Music Centre (Madetoja Hall; ☎ 5584 7212; Lintulammentie 1-3) The Oulu Symphony Orchestra – the world's northernmost professional symphony orchestra – holds concerts here most Thursdays.

Oulu City Theatre (☎ 5584 7600; Kaarlenväylä 2) This theatre has classical music, contemporary theatre and the occasional Shakespearian performance, almost all of it in Finnish.

SPORT
Oulu is very proud of their champion ice-hockey team, the Oulun Kärpät (the Oulu Stoats), who won successive Finnish titles in 2004 and 2005. They play their home games in the **Raksila Arena** (club ☎ 815 5700, ticketline ☎ 0600-10800; www.oulunkarpat.fi; tickets €10.50-26) in the Oulu Hall complex east of town.

Getting There & Away
AIR
Oulu airport is one of the busiest in Finland. There are several daily direct flights from Helsinki, operated by Finnair and Blue1, as well as services from Stockholm and from other Finnish cities.

BUS
The bus station, near the train station, has services connecting Oulu with all the main centres. These include Rovaniemi (€32.30, 3½ hours), Tornio (€18.60, 2½ hours); Kajaani (€28.10, 2½ hours) and Helsinki (€77.40, 11½ hours). To reach nearby villages, catch a local bus from the centre.

TRAIN
The train station is just east of the centre. Six to 10 trains a day run from Helsinki to Oulu; the fastest direct train from Helsinki takes only six hours (€68). There are also trains via Kajaani.

Getting Around
The airport is 15km south of the centre. Arriving flights are met by a Finnair bus to Oulu (€4.40). From the bus or train station you can catch local bus 19 to the airport (€2.50, 25 minutes).

There is a good network of local buses. Each ride costs about €2.50, and route maps are displayed at bus stops.

The main roads north and south from Oulu are motorways (freeways) which are off-limits to cyclists – fortunately there are many minor roads and bikeways. Pick up a bike route map at the Oulu tourist office.

AROUND OULU
Hailuoto Island
☎ 08 / pop 986

Hailuoto is the opposite of Atlantis – it rose from the sea about 2000 years ago. This flat island is 200 sq km in size, and growing. These days Hailuoto's main appeal is its sleepy fishing villages, as traffic is regulated by ferries. Grey lichen, used for reindeer food, is the main produce of Hailuoto. Most of the island can be explored only on foot.

The island is 30km long and has just one main road. Hailuoto village has shops and a bank. The **tourist information office** (☎ 810 1133) at the ferry harbour distributes free maps and can help with accommodation.

OULU, KAINUU & KOILLISMAA

The open-air **Kniivilä Museum** (admission €1; ☼ 11am-5pm Wed-Sun mid-Jun–mid-Aug), in Hailuoto village, has a collection of old houses. Marjaniemi is the westernmost point of Hailuoto, with a lighthouse and a cluster of old homes.

Ranta-Sumppu Camping (☎ 810 0690; tent sites €10, cottages €35) is at Marjaniemi, 30km west of the ferry pier. There are cottages for rent, camping and a simple lunch restaurant. There is a café at the ferry pier.

Bus 18 from Oulu crosses the 7km strait from the mainland on a free *lossi* (ferry) and continues across Hailuoto island to Marjaniemi. There are two or three buses daily. If you are coming from Oulu by car, take road 816.

Haukipudas
☎ 08 / pop 17,090

Haukipudas is 20km north of Oulu at a scenic spot along the Kiiminkijoki. The buttercup-coloured **church** is one of the most notable 'picture churches' in Finland, with superb naïve frescoes and a small, wooden *vaivaisukko* (pauper statue) outside.

Virpiniemen Retkeilyhotelli (☎ 561 4200; www .virpiniemenliikuntaopisto.com; Hiihtomajantie 27; dm €13, d €44; P ✗), at the seashore near Kello village, is 6km from the main road and 20km from Oulu. It is an HI-affiliated Finnhostel in a sports complex, with many opportunities for activities. There is a kitchen and sauna. Reception closes at 4pm from September to May, so ring ahead.

Särkyneen Pyörän Karjatila, next to the church in Haukipudas village, is a 150-year-old cowshed, now wonderfully transformed into a cosy restaurant serving 'country-style' gourmet Finnish food.

To get here take bus 1 to Kello from Oulu or bus 15 or 20 to Haukipudas.

Liminganlahti Bird Sanctuary
The bird sanctuary at Liminka Bay, near the attractive old farming village of Liminka, attracts more avian species than any other similar place in Finland. The wide bay is protected and funded by the World Wide Fund for Nature (WWF).

The 'great bird migration' is best seen in May, August and September. Several rare species of birds nest here during summer, and up to 70 species of birds can be seen in a single summer day. Prominent species include the yellow-breasted bunting, a variety of wader, and the Ural owl. There are several observation towers, boardwalks and a couple of designated camp sites.

Your first stop should be the **Liminka Bay Nature Centre** (☎ 562 0000; www.liminganlahti.net; Rantakurvi 6), about 600m from road 813 between Liminka and Lumijoki, and about 6km from Liminka village. As well as a nature display explaining the birdlife, migrations and flora, there's an observation tower, café and information desk. A guide is in attendance from 9am to 5pm daily from May to August and you can borrow a telescope to use at any of four bird-watching towers – the nearest is just 400m away.

The nature centre also has a new accommodation wing, with comfortable, modern rooms sleeping two to six people, a sauna and a guest kitchen. Cost ranges from €37 to €55.

Several daily Raahe-bound buses make the 30km trip from Oulu to Liminka and on to Lumijoki, and will stop at the turn-off to the Nature Centre.

Turkansaari Open-Air Museum
In summer you can take a boat out to the folksy **Turkansaari Open-Air Museum** (☎ 5586 7191; admission €3; ☼ 10am-7pm late May–mid-Aug, to 5pm mid-Aug–mid-Sep) on Turkansaari, 13km southeast of the city. Originally the island was a trading post for Russians and Swedes and many of the old buildings remain. There are regular displays of tar-burning, log-rolling and folk music and dancing. The MS *Sympaatti* departs from Värtto Pier in Oulu (return €17, noon, Tuesday to Sunday, June to August). Otherwise take bus 3 or 4, or drive or cycle along road 22 east in the direction of Muho.

KEMI
☎ 016 / pop 22,907

Kemi is an industrial town and important deepwater harbour. It also has a significant pulp-and-paper production, with the associated smell. Although not a hugely appealing place (in summer only the gem museum by the wide waterfront has any sort of siren song), Kemi is home to two of Finland's blockbuster winter attractions: the authentic Arctic icebreaker ship, *Sampo*, and the Lumilinna (Snow Castle), complete with ice hotel.

OULU, KAINUU & KOILLISMAA

Information

Public library (☎ 258 207; Marina Takalon katu 3; ⏱ 11am-8pm Mon-Thu, 11am-6pm Fri, 10am-4pm Sat) At the kauppatori, with free Internet access.

Tourist office (☎ 259 690; www.kemi.fi; Kauppakatu 29; ⏱ 10am-6pm late Jan–mid-Apr & mid-Jun–mid-Aug, 8am-4pm Mon-Fri rest of year) In the Gemstone Gallery at the town harbour. There's also a national park information office here. Turn left out of the bus station (right out of the train station), then left down Kauppakatu until you reach the harbour.

Sights

ICEBREAKER *SAMPO*

The highlight of a visit to Kemi in winter is a trip aboard the *Sampo*, the only Arctic icebreaker in the world that accepts passengers. The four-hour cruise includes ice swimming in special drysuits, as well as a walk on the ice – a remarkable experience. The *Sampo* sails at noon on Thursday, Friday and Saturday from mid-December to mid-April, with several Wednesday departures during busy periods, and costs €162 per person. The best time to go is when the ice is thickest, which is usually in March. Contact **Sampo Tours** (☎ 256 548; www.sampotours.com; Torikatu 2).

Departures are from Ajos Harbour, 15km south of Kemi, where you'll also find the *Sampo* out to pasture in summer, when it operates as a restaurant.

LUMILINNA

Kemi's **Snow Castle** (☎ 259 502, www.snowcastle .net; admission €5; ⏱ 10am-8pm Feb–mid-Apr), by the water near the tourist office, is another big winter drawcard. In 1996 the 'World's Largest Snow Castle' – 13,500 sq metres – was built here. It was such a success that the castle is now constructed every year and features a beautiful chapel and an **ice restaurant** (mains €12-26; ⏱ lunch & dinner Jan-Mar), with bar, ice tables covered with reindeer fur, and ice sculptures. The restaurant opens from 30 December. It's also possible to stay overnight in the **snow hotel** (d from €117; ⏱ Jan-Mar), where heavy-duty Arctic sleeping bags keep you warm in –5°C room temperature!

JALOKIVIGALLERIA

The **Gemstone Gallery** (☎ 259 690; Kauppakatu 29; €5; ⏱ 10am-6pm late Jan–mid-Apr & mid-Jun–mid-Aug, 8am-4pm Mon-Fri rest of year), in an old seaside customs house, has an internationally notable collection of over 3000 beautiful, rare stones

and jewellery, including a crown made using a design that was meant for the short-lived king of Finland. The crown was made in the 1980s by the gallery's founder, who created the crown of the king of Finland from original drawings. Sheets translated into various languages guide you in an offbeat manner around the exhibits, which include replicas of the world's most famous diamonds, and a solid dose of Finnish humour.

Nearby are a number of craft shops in old wooden buildings near the water's edge.

Festivals & Events

Every May, Kemi hosts **Arctic Comics**, an international comic festival. Check the city website (www.kemi.fi) for details.

Sleeping

The Snow Castle offers the most interesting accommodation (left) until it melts. There are four other hotels in town.

Hotelli Palomestari (☎ 257 117; www.hotelli palomestari.com; Valtakatu 12; s/d €76/105, weekends & summer r €76; P ✗) This is a friendly, worthwhile family hotel close to the bus and train stations (a block south and one west). It has a good sauna, and a convivial bar with a terrace on the street. The rooms are newly renovated with trademark Finnish furniture; some have their own sauna.

Hotel Yöpuu (☎ 232 034; www.hotelliyopuu.com; Eteläntie 227; s/d from €60/68; P ✗) Yöpuu, a little way out of town on road E4, is a pleasant guesthouse-style hotel with comfortable rooms and a good restaurant. There's also a camp site attached.

Eating & Drinking

There are plenty of grillis and pizzerias on Valtakatu and around the kauppatori.

Panorama Café (☎ 259 363; Valtakatu 26; ⏱ 8am-4pm Mon-Fri) If you like your morning coffee with a stunning view, and aren't superstitious by nature, this café on the 13th floor of the town hall is the place to be.

Orgidean Kukka (☎ 257 750; Valtakatu 7; mains €8-15; ⏱ 10.30am-8pm Mon-Thu, 10.30am-9pm Fri, noon-9pm Sat, noon-8pm Sun) This humble but attractive little place is a Vietnamese restaurant with a lunch buffet and tasty à la carte options.

Sampo (☎ 282 001; mains €15-22; ⏱ 10am-6pm Jun–mid-Aug) The icebreaker serves as an atmospheric daytime restaurant in summer, but you'll need your own transport to get to Ajos Harbour, 15km away.

Kemin Panimo (☎ 23502; Keskuspuistokatu; ☻ 2pm-1am or later) This is one of the liveliest pubs in town, brews its own beer, and also has a good range of international nectars. The large terrace doesn't have the greatest of views; it looks over the supermarket car-park, but in Kemi you can't be too picky!

Kemi's Snow Castle also features an ice restaurant (opposite).

Getting There & Away

The Kemi/Tornio airport is 6km north of town, and there are regular flights from Helsinki. A trip in a taxi will cost €10 from Kemi, or €12 from Tornio.

Half-hourly buses from Tornio (less at weekends) will take you to Kemi train station (€5 free with a train pass, 30 to 40 minutes). There are also some departures to Muonio to the north and Oulu to the south.

There are trains from Helsinki (€67, nine hours), Oulu (€14.60, 1¼ hours) and Rovaniemi (€15.70, 1½ hours)

TORNIO

☎ 016 / pop 22,204

Right on the impressive Tornionjoki, the longest free-flowing river in Northern Europe, Tornio (Swedish: Torneå) is joined to its Swedish counterpart Haparanda (Finnish: Haaparanta) by a short bridge. Although the two places bill themselves as 'the Eurocity', they are in reality service towns, not overly attractive or interesting, but useful stops on the way north. They share a tourist office and a famous golf course, where you can tee off into another country and another time zone. Nearby, the rapids at Kukkolankoski are another highlight, as is the cracking Umpitunnel pub. Tornio is a bigger place, but a couple of the better accommodation options are in Haparanda. Don't forget that Finland is one hour ahead of Sweden!

History

The area along the Tornionjoki has been inhabited since medieval times, when it was the centre for Pirkka tax collectors (who worked for the king of Sweden). The town of Tornio was founded in 1621, and the entire Tornionjoki valley was administered by Sweden until 1809, when it was incorporated into Finland, under Russian suzerainty. In 1821, Haparanda was founded as a Swedish trading town to replace the loss of Tornio to Russia.

Information

Green Line Centre (☎ 432 733; www.tornio.fi; ☻ 8am-7pm Mon-Fri, 10am-7pm Sat & Sun Jun–mid-Aug, 9am-noon & 1-4pm Mon-Fri mid-Aug–May) Near the bridge on the Tornio side of the border, acts as the tourist office for both towns. There's a free Internet terminal.

Public library (☎ 432 433; Torikatu 2; ☻ 11am-7pm Mon-Thu, 11am-5pm Fri, also 11am-3pm Sat Sep-May) Free Internet access.

Sights & Activities

Tornio church was completed in 1686 and is one of the most beautiful wooden churches in Finland. It is dedicated to the Swedish Queen Eleonora. The unusual 19th-century onion-domed **Orthodox church** in the town centre was built by order of Tsar Alexander I of Russia. Both are open from 9am to 5pm daily in summer, longer during July.

Aineen Taidemuseo (Aine Art Museum; ☎ 432 438; Torikatu 2; admission €2; ☻ 11am-6pm Tue-Thu, 11am-3pm Fri-Sun) features a private collection of Veli Aine, a local business tycoon. It features Finnish art from the 19th and 20th centuries, temporary exhibitions, and has a good café.

Historical Museum of the Tornio River Valley (☎ 432 451, Keskikatu 22; admission €2; ☻ noon-5pm noon-3pm Sun, closed Sat) has a collection of interesting old artefacts and costumes, although all displays are labelled in Finnish.

Lapin Kulta Brewery (☎ 54021; Lapinkullantie 1), founded in 1873, was the original brewery producing the ubiquitous Lappish lager. Hour-long free tours of the brewery plant begin at the front gate at 2pm on Monday and Thursday from June to August.

River-rafting trips are popular in summer on the Kukkolankoski (p277). Rafting tours are run by **Safaris Unlimited** (☎ 253 405; www .safarisunlimited.fi) and **Nordic Safaris** (☎ 040-755 1858; www.nordicsafaris.com; Koulutie 3, Keminmaa) from around €35 to €60 per person. Various trips use either inflatable rubber rafts or traditional wooden boats. Safaris Unlimited also has kayaking trips, and both companies offer winter excursions such as snowmobile, reindeer and husky safaris. The Tornio tourist office can make bookings for all trips.

The tourist office also handles **fishing** permits; there are several excellent spots along the Tornio River.

OULU, KAINUU & KOILLISMAA

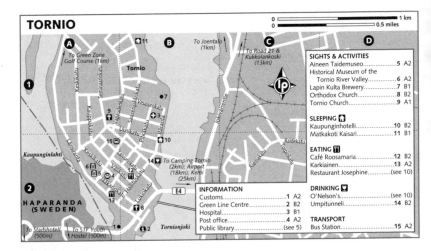

TORNIO

SIGHTS & ACTIVITIES
Aineen Taidemuseo.....................5 A2
Historical Museum of the
    Tornio River Valley................6 A2
Lapin Kulta Brewery....................7 B1
Orthodox Church..........................8 B2
Tornio Church................................9 A1

SLEEPING 🏠
Kaupunginhotelli.........................10 B2
Matkakoti Kaisari.........................11 B1

EATING 🍴
Café Roosamaria...........................12 B2
Karkiainen....................................13 A2
Restaurant Josephine.............(see 10)

DRINKING 🍷
O'Nelson's...............................(see 10)
Umpitunneli................................14 B2

TRANSPORT
Bus Station.................................15 A2

INFORMATION
Customs..1 A2
Green Line Centre.........................2 B2
Hospital...3 B1
Post office.....................................4 A2
Public library...........................(see 5)

Sleeping

The most characterful place to sleep is actually across in Haparanda; the **Stadshotell** (☎ 46 922 614 90; www.haparandastadshotell.se; d €90–140) is a lovely old building with plenty of history. There is also budget accommodation available in summer.

STF Youth Hostel (☎ 46 922 611 71; vandrarhem haparanda@telia.com; Strandgatan 26; dm €18, s/d with shower €36/52; ⏰ reception 7-10am & 4-7pm Mon-Fri, 9-10am & 4-7pm Sat & Sun; 🅿 ⊠ 💻 ♿) This is a good choice for budget accommodation, also just across the bridge in Sweden. There's a café/restaurant here, and a variety of rooms. There's a very good kitchen and lounge, and proper disabled facilities.

Joentalo (☎ 211 9244; www.ppopisto.fi; Kivirannantie 13-15; s/d €46/57; ⏰ early Jun-early Aug, reception 8am-3pm; 🅿 ⊠ 🅿 ♿) This HI-affiliated summer hotel is on the other side of the river from town, and 2.5km north; inconvenient with bags, but otherwise a pleasant riverside walk. The rooms are modern, and there are excellent facilities here. There is also a youth hostel on the same site. It was closed for renovations at time of research but due to be open again for the 2006 season.

Other options:

Matkatkoti Kaisari (☎ 480 897; www.kaisari.com; Saarenpäänkatu 39; s/d/tr €40/60/80; 🅿 ⊠) This newly renovated guesthouse north of the centre is simple in style but attractive and colourful.

Kaupunginhotelli (☎ 43311; www.tornionkaupung inhotelli.fi; Itäranta 4; s/d €99/119, Sat, Sun & summer r €84; 🅿 ⊠ 🅿) This is the only hotel in Tornio itself.

It's a huge, ageing place with a decent restaurant and a couple of pubs.

Camping Tornio (☎ 445 945; www.campingtornio .com; Matkailijantie; camp sites €10, cabins €54) This is about 3km from town on the road to Kemi. There are saunas, a tennis court and a beach. You can hire rowboats and bikes here.

Eating & Drinking

There is very little eating choice in Tornio. Haparanda has even less, although the Stadshotell has a quality restaurant.

Umpitunneli (☎ 430 360; www.umpitunneli.fi; Hallituskatu 15; mains €8-21.50; ⏰ 11am-1am or later) The Umpitunneli ('dead-end tunnel') is perhaps Tornio's biggest attraction. It's a cavernous pub and restaurant with a huge and convivial beer terrace that's a lot of fun when things are animated. The food is generously portioned and good value; later the *humppa* (a fast Finnish dance, between a waltz and a foxtrot) music gets going (€5 cover Wednesday to Saturday nights); there are sometimes live bands. It's one of the best nightspots in the north, and utterly Finnish.

Restaurant Josephine (Itäranta 4; mains €7-18, Lapp dishes €18-24; ⏰ 10am-midnight, 10am-1am Thu-Sat) For a quality sit-down meal, Josephine, in the Kaupunginhotelli, is a good choice. The menu is broad and excellent value, with tasty salmon, liver and other Finnish specialities alongside pan pizzas and pastas. There's also a 'Lapp menu', with several reindeer dishes (including boiled tongue) and a couple of set menus (€32).

MIDNIGHT AT THE GREEN ZONE GOLF COURSE

You walk up to the first hole and place your ball on the tee. The sun is hanging low on the horizon. The time is five minutes to midnight, but you know it doesn't really matter how badly you play or how long it takes to get around 18 holes: fading light won't be an issue. You're standing on one of the most unique golf courses in the world – the Green Zone Golf Course (☎ 431 711; tornio@golf.inet.fi) at Tornio-Haparanda.

This is the world's northernmost golf club, and playing at this latitude (just south of the Arctic Circle) brings with it a few advantages. For a start, in summer you can play all night. Secondly, the course straddles the border of Finland and Sweden, beautifully laid out on either side of the Tornionjoki, with nine holes in each country.

Of the 18 holes on this remarkable course, four cross the international border. Given the one-hour time difference, this technically means that if you tee off on the par 3 sixth hole, your ball remains in the air for at least an hour before it lands on the green (eight iron required here). If you tee off from the par 4 third hole at 12.30am on Saturday, you'll hit the ball into Friday (driver or 3 wood). Play a short nine-iron from the 18th onto the green at a similar time on a Sunday, and you'll have smacked the ball into next week.

All this may sound a bit trite, but golfers should note that this is a very decent course, with lush fairways and well-maintained, solid greens. How can you deny yourself this story when you're on the 19th back home?

All this golfing novelty can be yours for €33 green fees plus €10 if you need to hire a rather shoddy set of clubs. To play after 10pm (and get the full novelty benefit) you need to book in advance, since the clubhouse closes at 10pm. You'll need a Green Card or a handicap certificate from your home club to play; if you don't have that, there's a driving range and a 9-hole pitch 'n' putt course (€8). It's usually open from mid-May to late August, but snow golf is sometimes available. That's when those bright orange and yellow balls really come into their own!

Karkiainen (Länsiranta 9; ☼ 8am-5pm Mon-Fri, 9am-2.30pm Sat) This bakery-café has the best fresh pastries, cakes and doughnuts in town. There's a €6 big breakfast served before midday.

Café Roosamaria (☎ 430 953; Hallituskatu 10; ☼ 9am-8pm Mon-Fri, 11am-5pm Sat) This is a good café on the main street, with stylish crepe-paper lamps banishing the winter gloom.

O'Nelson's (Kaupunginhotelli) Then there's this lively, Irish-style pub at the Kaupunginhotelli. At weekends the €5 entry includes admission to the inaccurately-named but entertaining Paradise, a well-attended disco.

Getting There & Away

The Kemi/Tornio airport is 18km east of town, and there are regular flights to and from Helsinki. A taxi from Tornio to the airport costs around €12.

There are a few daily buses from Rovaniemi (€18.60, two hours) – although there are more connections (bus and train) via Kemi – and north to Muonio (€34.20, 4½ hours). Buses from Kemi (€5, 30 to 40 minutes) run more than hourly. Most continue to Haparanda. There are also frequent shuttle buses between Haparanda and Tornio, although the distance is so short you can walk. There are buses direct to Stockholm four times a week (Skr480/€55, 15 hours).

AROUND TORNIO
Kukkolankoski

The Kukkolankoski on the Tornionjoki, 16km north of Tornio on road 21, are the longest free-flowing rapids in Finland. The length is 3500m and the fall is just under 14m. Kukkolankoski has been a favoured fishing place since the Middle Ages and locals still catch whitefish using traditional long-handled nets. An annual whitefish festival is celebrated on the last weekend of July.

You can sample grilled *siika* (whitefish) at Café Myllypirtti.

KAINUU REGION

KAJAANI
☎ 08 / pop 35,675

The further north you get, the smaller the 'major' towns. Kajaani is the centre of the Kainuu region, and although a pleasant enough riverside town, it's no metropolis, being mainly a transport changeover and stopover between the Lakeland and the north. What little there is to see is related to Kajaani's long position as an important station on the Kainuu tar transportation route – until the 19th century this region produced more tar than anywhere else in the world.

One of Kajaani's claims to fame is that Elias Lönnrot, creator of Finland's national epic, the *Kalevala*, worked here for a period in the 19th century, using it as a base for his travels. The long-reigning president Urho Kekkonen also lived here as a student (his house stills stands at Kalliokatu 7). More disturbing, though, has been a publicized trend of racist violence, with Kajaani named the most racist city in Finland by the *Helsingin Sanomat* newspaper according to statistics on racially-motivated crime.

Information

Kajaani Info (☎ 6155 2555; www.kajaani.fi; Kauppakatu 21; 8.30am-5pm Mon-Fri, 9am-2pm Sat early Jun–mid-Aug, 8.30am-4pm Mon-Fri mid-Aug–early Jun) Tourist information and free Internet access.

Public library (☎ 6155 2422; Kauppakatu 35; 10am-8pm Mon-Fri, 10am-3pm Sat) Has free Internet access.

Sights & Activities

In town, the beautiful wooden **church** (Pohjolankatu; 10am-6pm early Jun-late Aug) from 1896 is a rare example of neo-Gothic architecture. It's typically Karelian, with lots of ornate wooden trim and a delicate, slender, Italianate belltower. The Orthodox church is nearby. See p280 for details of the Paltaniemi church, 9km north of town.

On an island in the middle of the Kajaaninjoki near the town centre is what's left of **Kajaani Castle**, built in the 17th century and thoroughly damaged by war, time and some more recent mischief. There's not much to see, admission is free and it's easily viewed from the bridge.

At the Ämmäkoski waterfall, near the castle ruins, is a **tar-boat canal**, a channel built in 1846 to enable the boats laden with tar barrels to pass the rapids. There's a small **museum** (11am-5pm Tue-Sun; admission free) in the old lock-keeper's cottage, and tar boat shows at 11am on Saturdays in July.

Kainuu Museum (☎ 6155 2407; Asemakatu 4; admission €2; noon-4pm Mon-Fri, noon-8pm Wed, noon-5pm Sun, closed Sun summer), near the train station, is a good place to get acquainted with local history, including the *Kalevala* and its author, Elias Lönnrot. There is little information in English.

Facing the small *raatihuoneentori* (town square) is the old **town hall**, designed by German architect CL Engel. Behind it is the former police station, which now serves as the **Kajaani art museum** (Linnankatu 14; admission €2; 10am-5pm Sun-Fri, 10am-8pm Wed).

Festivals & Events

Kainuun Jazzkevät in late May is a festival of international jazz, blues and rock. Stars have included Dizzy Gillespie, Mick Taylor and the Phil Woods Quintet, and many Finnish performers. For information and tickets contact the Kajaani tourist office.

Sleeping

Kartanohotelli Karolineburg (☎ 613 1291; www .karolineburg.com; Karoliinantie 4; s/d €70/80, d with sauna €100, summer s/d €50/60; P) This is easily the most romantic place to stay in Kajaani. It's an elegant 19th-century wooden manor house across the river from the centre, with rooms in the main building and two outbuildings. There are elegantly furnished public areas and spacious grounds.

Retkeilymaja Huone ja Aamiainen (☎ /fax 622 254; Pohjolankatu 4; s/d/tr €28/40/54; reception 8am-noon, 4-11pm;) This curious HI-affiliated place offers reasonably comfortable budget accommodation not far from the bus station. There's a mound of information in myriad languages, linen is included, and the owner brings breakfast to your room, as well as selling burgers, beer, toiletries and other thoughtful necessities. It grows on you.

Sokos Hotel Valjus (☎ 615 0200; www.sokoshotels .fi; Kauppakatu 20; s/d from €99/122, weekends & summer €78; P) This place is very central, situated right on the main street. The rooms are comfortable, service is good, and there's a reasonable restaurant and a popular bar and nightclub on the premises too.

Scandic Hotel Kajanus (☎ 61641; www.scandic -hotels.com; Koskikatu 3; s/d from €85/109, Fri, Sat & summer from €63/73; P) Across the river from the centre, this is one of the larger hotels in Northern Finland. It has three grades of rooms, which differ in size and a few extra conveniences; there's also a gym, squash court, large sauna complex and several restaurants.

OULU, KAINUU & KOILLISMAA

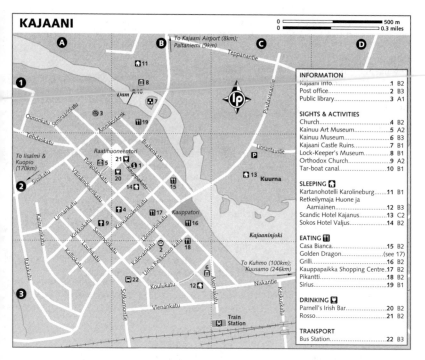

KAJAANI

Eating & Drinking

The kauppatori, at the southeast end of Kauppakatu, has stalls selling smoked fish and other goodies and a cheap grilli.

Sirius (☎ 612 2087; mains €14-21; ⏰ 11am-3pm Mon-Fri) Located above the rapids, this restaurant is set in a characterful 1940s villa built as a residence for the local paper company. It serves classy meat and fish dishes and has a good lunch buffet for €13. There's a great terrace out the back. It opens in the evenings for group bookings only.

Pikantti (☎ 628 870; Kauppakatu 10; lunch buffet €8.60; ⏰ 10am-5pm Mon-Fri, 10am-3pm Sat) This place offers a typically excellent Finnish lunch buffet until 5pm weekdays. It includes vegetable soup and a main course, salads, bread, milk, dessert and coffee. There's also a nice terrace.

Kauppapaikka Shopping Centre (Kauppakatu 18) This centre has some cheap eating options, including Golden Dragon.

Golden Dragon (☎ 627 776; Kauppakatu 18; mains €6-10; ⏰ 11am-9pm, later at weekends) A better-than-average Chinese place serving Cantonese and Szechuan and cheap lunch specials. The lunch buffet is €7.50. It's in the Kauppapaikka shopping centre; enter around the back if the centre is closed.

Casa Bianca (☎ 628 498; Koivukoskenkatu 17D; pizzas €7-9; ⏰ 11am-9pm Mon-Sat, noon-9pm Sun) This is a cosy little Italian-style pizzeria tucked away on the street corner facing the river. It's a favourite with local families.

Rosso (☎ 615 0341; Kauppakatu 21; mains from €6.50; ⏰ 11am-10pm, later at weekends) On the town hall square is a branch of the Rosso chain, with the usual unremarkable array of pizzas, pastas and steaks. However, this also has a public bar with a very pleasant terrace.

Parnell's Irish Bar (☎ 612 1306; Kauppakatu 30; ⏰ 6pm-1am Mon-Thu, to 2am Fri & Sat, noon-11pm Sun) Opposite Rosso, this is another decent place for a drink.

Getting There & Away

Finnair has two to four daily flights from Helsinki to Kajaani. The airport is 8km northwest of town; take bus 4 (€2.50).

Kajaani is the major travel hub in the Kainuu district. There are frequent departures for Kuhmo (€15.20, 1½ hours) and other towns in the region during the week, but few departures on weekends. The local bus service is useful if you want to visit Paltaniemi (same bus as to the airport).

Kajaani is on the main Helsinki to Oulu line. There are four daily trains from Helsinki (€67, seven hours), via Kouvola and Kuopio.

AROUND KAJAANI
Paltaniemi
The village of Paltaniemi 9km from Kajaani, has its own distinctive history. The first church was built here in 1599. In the centuries that followed, Paltaniemi became the regional centre for the Lutheran Church. You'll see some of the most exciting church paintings in Finland here.

The old wooden **church** (☎ 687 5334; 🕙 10am-6pm late May–mid-Aug) was built in 1726, and its bell tower dates from 1776. The church is known for its wonderful old murals and ceiling paintings (some were altered and repainted in 1940). The Hell scene has been partly covered, apparently to avoid disturbing the locals. An information tape in English is available on request.

Keisarintalli, an old wooden stable, was used as a boarding house for Tsar Alexander I when he toured Finland in 1819. This simple building (moved from Vuolijoki) was actually the best available for the exalted visitor. Ask at the church to be shown around.

Take local bus 4 (the airport bus) from Pohjolankatu in Kajaani to Paltaniemi. There are hourly departures on weekdays, less often on weekends.

KUHMO
☎ 08 / pop 10,449
Kuhmo is a curious place; although not officially part of Karelia, it is sort of the unofficial capital of Vienan Karjala, the Karelian heartland that is now in Russia. This was the region that artists explored in the Karelian movement, such a crucial part of the development of Finnish national identity. Most of their expeditions set off from Kuhmo, as did one of Elias Lönnrot's, when he headed into 'Songland' to record the verses of bards that he later wove into the *Kalevala* epic. There's a fine Kalevala resource centre in town, as well as a less informative theme park.

Kuhmo, once a major tar producer, is still a good jumping-off point for the wilderness;

it makes a natural base for hiking the UKK route, Finland's longest marked trek. The vast taiga run from here right across Siberia and harbours many 'respect' animals like wolves, bears and lynx.

Kuhmo is well known in Finland for its annual chamber music festival, and is small and very pleasant.

Information
Petola Visitor Centre (☎ 0205-646 380; petola@ metsa.fi; Lentiirantie 342; 🕙 9am-5pm daily Jul-Aug, 9am-4pm Mon-Fri Sep-May) Near the Kalevala Village theme park, this is a good national park information centre. As well as providing hiking advice, there's a good exhibition on the four major carnivores of Finland.
Kuhmo tourist office (☎ 6155 5292; www.kuhmo .fi; Kainuuntie 82; 🕙 8am-6pm Mon-Fri, 10am-4pm Sat Jun-Aug; 8am-5pm Mon-Fri Sep-May) In the town centre, this has extended hours during festival time. Very helpful. Stocks good maps and walking guides to the region. Free Internet access at time of publication.
Public library (☎ 6155 5390; Pajakkakatu 2; 🕙 10am-7pm Mon-Wed & Fri, 2-7pm Thu, plus Sat 9am-3pm Sep-May) The modern library has free Internet access

Sights
JUMINKEKO
If you are interested in the *Kalevala* or Karelian culture as a whole, you must pay a visit to the excellent **Juminkeko** (☎ 653 0670; www .juminkeko.fi; Kontionkatu 25; adult/child €4/free; 🕙 noon-6pm Sun-Thu), a beautiful building made using traditional methods and modern styling. The fantastic staff can tell you anything about Karelia or the *Kalevala* that you wish to know; there are also three to four detailed exhibitions here every year. The auditorium, whose walls were hand-worked by adze, has three worthwhile audiovisual presentations in English; also on display is Finland's largest collection of *Kalevala* books translated into over 50 languages. With the multimedia programme you can view pictures, and read and listen to extracts from the epic in anything from Japanese to Swahili.

TUUPALA MUSEUM
This charming **Karelian farmhouse** (☎ 655 6283; Tervatie 1; adult/child €3/2; 🕙 10am-4pm Tue-Sun Jun, 10am-6pm daily Jul-late Aug) has been, in its past lives, a general store, pharmacy, inn, post office and home to the town's police chief. Fittingly, it now houses the museum of local history.

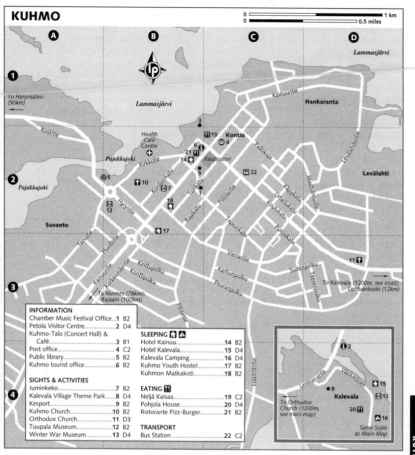

KUHMO

OULU, KAINUU & KOILLISMAA

CHURCHES

The striking 1816 wooden **Kuhmo Church** (noon-6pm summer) in the town centre is a venue for concerts during the chamber music festival. The **Orthodox Church**, 1km from the centre on the road to the theme park, is only 35 years old. It contains several 18th-century icons that were painted in the Valamo Monastery before it was annexed by the Soviet Union, plus a 300-year-old Madonna icon. The church is open on request only; inquire at the tourist office for more details.

KALEVALA VILLAGE

This **theme park** (☎ 652 0114; www.kalevalakyla.fi; adult/child €11/5.50; 10am-5pm Mon-Sat Jun-Aug, also Sun in Jul), 3km east of the centre of town, is a big drawcard but of debatable value, especially if you're not with children. Despite the name, you won't learn much about the *Kalevala*; it's basically an open-air museum of Karelian folk history and log buildings with cultural exhibitions, artisan displays and costumed staff demonstrating tar-making, woodcarving, fishing and so on. On the marked circuit, you will see a re-creation of the cabin and desk Elias Lönnrot worked at, and Pohjola House, which includes a gallery and café. From mid-December to mid-January, the site opens as a **Christmas Village**.

The adjacent **Winter War Museum** (☎ 655 6368; adult/child €3/2; 10am-4pm Tue-Sun Jun, 10am-6pm daily Jul-late Aug) displays artefacts from that bitter conflict.

Activities

There's plenty to do in and around Kuhmo. The tourist office has a full list of activities.

Whitewater rafting trips to Lentuankoski, 15km north of Kuhmo, can be arranged on weekends in June and daily during July, with a minimum of two persons. Book through the Kuhmo tourist office, but call ahead, as the trips weren't run in 2005 due to low water levels.

Fishing for perch and pike is popular at Pajakkakoski near the town centre and at Lentuankoski north of town. Check with Kainuu Nature Centre or the tourist office about permits. There's a complex series of them depending on which stretches you want to fish (per day €5 to €10, per week €10 to €22).

The tourist office also has brochures and maps describing various easy hikes in the Kuhmo region. See below for the UKK hiking route.

There are bears in the Kuhmo region, and **Wild Brown Bear** (☎ 040-546 9008; www.wild brownbear.fi) runs excursions to watch them (if you are lucky).

Bicycles can be hired from **Kesport** (Kainuntie 85) on the kauppatori for €10 a day or €45 for a week.

Festivals & Events

The **Kuhmo Chamber Music Festival** (☎ 652 0936; www.kuhmofestival.fi; Torikatu 39), held over two weeks in late July each year, attracts top musicians from around the world. It's been going since 1969 and more than 200 musicians participate in over 100 concerts each year. Most of the concerts are held at Kuhmo-Talo (Kuhmo Arts Centre), a spacious, modern concert hall. Tickets are €10 to €25, with most costing around €15. There are also a few free concerts every day. For advance bookings contact the Kuhmo tourist office or the festival office.

Sleeping

Most places charge a premium during the Chamber Music Festival (mid-July) and you'll need to book well ahead for a bed then anyway. There are other options in town at that period, and the tourist office can help find a bed.

Hotel Kalevala (☎ 655 4100; www.hotellikale vala.fi; Väinämöinen 9; s/d €77/105, Sat, Sun & summer €66/79; P ⊠ ⿴) About 4km east of the centre, near the Kalevala theme park, this is Kuhmo's top hotel – a modern, upmarket place in a lakeside location. It handles most rental services, including canoes, and can arrange tailored trips; fishing, hiking, snowmobiling, skiing, canoeing, and so on. There's a gym, sunbeds and a swimming pool.

Kalevala Camping (☎ 6155 5295; fax 655 6384; tent sites €11, 2-/4-person cabins from €26/34; ⊙ Jun-Aug), on the lake near the theme park, has good facilities including a smoke sauna and boats. There are several different cabin options, some with their own shower, and a simple dormitory building (up to six people €20).

TREKKING THE UKK

Pockets of the now-rare Finnish wilderness still exist – in pristine condition – along the eastern border of Finland. They are best seen and experienced on a trek along the Urho K Kekkonen (UKK) route. This 240km trail is the nation's longest and greatest trekking route. It was named after President Urho K Kekkonen, and it has been in development for decades, with new shelters and boardwalks regularly being constructed.

The trail starts a long way south at Koli Hill in North Karelia and continues along the western side of Lake Pielinen, ending at Iso-Syöte Hill far to the north of Kuhmo.

However, two of the finest sections of the UKK route are easily accessible from Kuhmo: the Kuhmo to Hiidenportti leg and the Kuhmo to Lentiira leg. The trek east from Kuhmo to Lentiira village via Iso-Palonen park takes at least four days and offers superb scenery.

The trail is well maintained in the Kuhmo area, with clear markings, and *laavu* (simple shelters) are spaced every 10km to 20km. Each *laavu* is near water and has an established campfire place, firewood and a pit toilet. Carry a sleeping bag and *plenty* of mosquito repellent to take advantage of this free open-air accommodation.

Pick up route maps at the Kuhmo tourist office or the **Kainuu Nature Centre** (☎ 877 6380; kaapalinna@metsa.fi), also in Kuhmo.

Other options:

Hotel Kainuu (☎ 655 1711; www.hotellikainuu.com; Kainuuntie 84; s/d €57/74, weekends €51/67; P ⊠ ⊠) Pleasant family-run hotel in the town centre, near the tourist office.

Kuhmon Matkakoti (☎ /fax 655 0271, Vienantie 3; s/d/tr €25/44/60; P ⊠) This is a friendly, good-value guesthouse near the town centre.

Youth hostel (☎ 6155 5369; dm/s/d €12/26/30; ⊗ Jul) A simple accommodation choice that's available during the Chamber Music Festival.

Eating

Try a *rönttönen* in the kauppatori; this is a curious open pastry filled with potato and lingonberry.

Hotel Kalevala (☎ 655 4100; mains €13-23; ⊗ lunch & dinner) The best restaurant around is out at this hotel, where the à la carte menu features Finnish, Lappish and international dishes.

Ristorante Pizz-Burger (☎ 652 0144; Kainuuntie 84; mains €7-15; ⊗ 10am-9pm) Despite the name (get it?), this restaurant actually serves quite a bit more than just pizza (€7 to €9) and the like. There are also decent portions of trout or steak available, as well as pasta and salad. There's a filling lunchtime buffet (10am to 2pm), booth seating and a small terrace.

Neljä Kaisaa (☎ 652 1573; Koulukatu 3; ⊗ 8am-5pm Mon-Fri, 8am-1pm Sat) Around the corner from the tourist office is a pleasant café with a range of lunch specials.

There are also good cafés at the Kuhmo-Talo and Pohjola House at the Kalevala Village.

Getting There & Away

A taxi minibus runs from Kajaani airport to the town of Kuhmo after the arrival of each flight, and there is also a regular service the other way (€27, 1½ hours).

There are numerous daily buses to/from Kajaani (€15.20, 1½ hours), where you can get connections to other towns west and south and less frequent direct buses to Joensuu (€27.10, four hours). For Nurmes, change at Sotkamo. Trains arriving in Kajaani (102km to the west) connect with buses to Kuhmo.

There are buses east on Monday, Wednesday, and Friday to the Russian Karelian town of Kostamus run by **Turistiliikenne Kyllönen** (☎ 652 0771).

HOSSA
☎ 08

Hossa, dubbed the 'fisher's paradise', is one of the most carefully maintained fishing areas in Finland. Trekking is also excellent – it's designated as a National Hiking Area – and some of the paths take you to beautiful ridges between lakes. It's very remote, near the Russian border 170km north of Kuhmo and 70km south of Kuusamo.

To visit Hossa you will need to plan in advance where to stay and where to purchase fishing permits. See p51 for more information on permits.

Hossa visitor centre (☎ 0205-646 041; Jatkonsalmentie 6; ⊗ 10am-5pm mid-Feb–May, Sep & Oct, 9am-10pm Jun-Aug) on Lake Ollori provides everything for a successful stay. It rents cottages, boats, hiking and fishing gear, sells fishing permits and hiking maps and has a café/restaurant and lakeside sauna. In winter the centre rents out cross-country skis as well.

On the road south from the information centre, **Hossan Lomakeskus** (☎ 732 322; d from €60; P ⊠) is a large hotel with double rooms and many kinds of cottages at the waterfront. Buffet lunch is available.

There are daily buses to Hossa from Kuusamo. You can reach Hossa from Kajaani by changing buses at Ämmänsaari; these buses run only on weekdays.

KOILLISMAA REGION

KUUSAMO
☎ 08 / pop 17,193

Kuusamo is a spread-out frontier town about 200km northeast of Oulu and similar in feel to the towns of Lapland, with reindeer roaming the roads in this area. There is little to see in the town itself, but it's perfectly situated as a base for planning and launching treks or canoeing trips into the surrounding area and it's close to one of Finland's most popular ski resorts. There are good services, including shops with trekking supplies, and many agencies running all manner of activities and tours.

A Lutheran parish for over 300 years, Kuusamo was incorporated as a municipality in 1868. By 1900, its population had grown to 10,000, and it had close relations with nearby Russia. During WWII, the village was a command centre for German troops, who also supervised the construction of the 'Death Railway' that operated for 242 days. When the Soviet army marched into Kuusamo on 15 September 1944, the Germans burned the town and blew up the railway. The Soviets retreated, after occupying Kuusamo for about two months, and the inhabitants of Kuusamo returned to their shattered town.

Information

Karhuntassa Tourist Centre (☎ 850 2910; www .kuusamo.fi; Torangintaival 2; ☉ 9am-5pm Jun–mid-Sep, 9am-8pm Midsummer-early Aug, 9am-5pm Mon-Fri mid-Sep–May) In the Karhuntassu (Bear's Paw) Tourist Centre on road 5 (the main highway), 2km southwest of the town centre. Excellent information and free Internet terminals. There's also a nature centre here (reduced hours).

Nettilähde (Kitkantie 42; ☉ 11.30am-6pm Mon-Fri) Free Internet access at the local sports centre.

Public library (☎ 850 6031; Kaiterantie 22; ☉ noon-8pm Mon, Wed & Thu, 10am-8pm Tue, 10am-2pm Fri, 10am-3pm Sat) Has free Internet access.

Sights

About 500m southeast of the town centre is **Porkkatörmä** (☎ 850 6027; Kitronintie 6; admission free; ☉ noon-6pm mid-Jun–mid-Aug, 9am-3pm Mon-Fri mid-late Aug), the local open-air museum, which brings together a selection of venerable farm buildings from the Kuusamo region. It's not as interesting as some of these museums can be.

The modern **water tower** (Joukamontie 32; ☉ 10am-6pm Tue-Sat Jun-Aug) has an observation platform with a good view, as well as a café. On the other side of the bus terminal, **Kuusamotalo** (☎ 850 6550; Kaarlo Hännisentie 2) is a concert hall and cultural centre – the pride of Kuusamo. Check with the tourist office or call direct for coming performances and exhibitions. The building is a sleek, elegant, Finnish creation designed by Arto Sipinen.

There are quite a few craft shops and studios in Kuusamo, which means you can pick up some good buys. **Bjarmia** (☎ 853 869; Vienantie 1) is a ceramics factory and studio right in the centre. There's a ceramics and textiles 'museum' here (€2) or you can just visit the shop and café.

Kuusamon Uistin (☎ 860 3400), north of the centre on main road 5 to Ruka, sells beautifully crafted fishing lures and sheath knives from its factory. Some of these products are exported throughout the world under the brand name Kuusamo.

Activities & Tours

See p288 for the Karhunkierros trekking route, and p290 for information on canoeing in the Kuusamo area. There are a dozen or more independent tour operators based in the Kuusamo area, offering activities as diverse as ice climbing, river rafting, mountain biking, ice fishing, snowshoe hiking and more. If you're travelling alone or in a small group, it's worth checking with the bigger agencies as they often round up individuals for trips that require a larger group.

Ruka Palvelu (☎ 860 8600; www.rukapalvelu.fi; Rukatunturintie 18, Ruka) has canoeing, whitewater rafting, quad bikes, fishing courses and bird watching. There are regular weekly programs during summer.

On the main highway at the Ruka turnoff is **Stella Polaris** (☎ 852 3122; www.stellapolaris.net; Rukanriutta 11, Ruka). It offers rafting, fishing, walking, climbing, canoeing.

There's also **Green Line Safaris** (☎ 852 3041; www.greenlinesafaris.fi; Kitkantie 38-40, Kuusamo).

Sleeping

There are numerous holiday cottages in the Kuusamo area. Contact the tourist office, or **FinFun** (☎ 0203 70021; www.finfun.fi; Huoparintie 1, Kuusamo), who have a portfolio of hundreds.

Hotelli Kuusanka (☎ 852 2240; hotellikuusanka .kuusamo@co.inet.fi; Ouluntie 2; s/d €52/68; P ⊠ ⛅) This is a small, friendly, family-run hotel that makes a pleasant place to stop. It's on the main street but there's off-street parking and a good breakfast included. There's also a gym and sauna. The twin rooms are pretty small, but nicely furnished, and there are spacious family rooms available.

Sokos Hotel Kuusamo (☎ 020-1234 693; www .sokoshotels.fi; Kirkkotie 23; s/d Mon-Fri €98/123, weekends & summer r €90; P ⊠ ⛁ ⛅) Close to the centre, this is a long, low, box-like structure topped by a glowing *kota* (Lappish hut). It has good facilities, including free use of the pool and sauna, and is family-friendly. At the back is parkland running down to the lake.

Holiday Club Kuusamon Tropiikki (☎ 859 6000; www.holidayclub.fi; Kylpyläntie; s/d €107/127, summer €68/89; P ⊠ ⛅) Some 6km north of Kuusamo is a modern hotel and spa complex in a forest setting. Rooms are plain but comfortable (apartments are also available) and you get full use of the spa, sauna, pool and other services (the spa is a plastic tropical wonder-

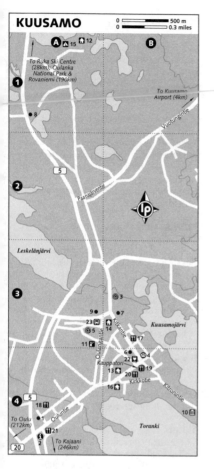

a range of rooms. There is a kitchen and a satellite TV in the common room, as well as sauna and laundry facilities. Inconveniently, you must book ahead, and collect the key during reception opening hours.

Eating

Martina (☎ 852 2051; Ouluntie 3; meals €8-22; ☺ lunch & dinner) This is one of those Finnish family restaurants that has a go at everything – pasta, steaks, fish and a salad buffet. It's a comfortable and accommodating place for an informal dinner.

Baari Martai (☎ 851 4199; Airotie; lunch €6-8; ☺ 10am-3pm Mon-Fri) This place is in an unattractive industrial area between the town centre and the tourist office, but it's a well-known workers' lunch spot, serving up an excellent spread on weekdays in summer.

Herkkusuu (Ouluntie 1; ☺ 7am-6pm Mon-Fri, 8am-3pm Sat) This early-opening café next to the kauppatori bakes excellent bread and pastries.

Ampan Pizza Bar (☎ 853 502; Kitkantie 18; pizzas €6-10; ☺ 11am-10pm) This is popular for its reasonably priced pizzas. Don't expect

land with a 45m water slide). Nonguests can use the spa for a modest fee. There are excellent family rates available in summer.

Rantatropiikki Camping (☎ 859 6404; www.holidayclub.fi; Kylpyläntie; tent sites €9; ⊗) This camping ground is 6km north of the centre, and is associated with the Holiday Club, you can take advantage of the spa and pool facilities as well as the restaurant and bar. There are also stylish cottages (2-/4-/8-person €86/124/218) with the works. There are several other camp sites in the Kuusamo area.

Kuusamon Kansanopisto (☎ 852 2132; kuusamon .kansanopisto@koillismaa.fi; Kitkantie 35; dm from €10-12, s/d €18/30, with bathroom €30/40; ☺ Midsummer-Aug, reception 8am-3.45pm Mon-Fri; ℗ ⊗) Close to the centre is a rambling summer HI hostel with any culinary masterpieces; Kuusamo ain't a gourmet town!

Bjarmia (Vienantie 1) This is a quaint little coffee shop above the ceramics factory of the same name.

Kuiske Café at the top of the water tower serves coffee, cakes and light meals with a view. Tori Grilli on the kauppatori is open past midnight.

Adjacent to the tourist office are several giant supermarkets where you can stock up on trekking supplies; there's another (open on Sundays) in the Sokos Centre next to the kauppatori.

Drinking & Entertainment

Parnell's Irish Bar (☎ 852 2051; Ouluntie 5; ⊙ 6pm-midnight Sun-Thu, 6pm-2am Fri & Sat) *The* top pub in town, with international brews on tap.

Sokos Hotel Kuusamo (☎ 85920; Kirkkotie 23) This place has a good à la carte restaurant, as well as a nightclub.

Kuukettu (Kitkantie 1; ⊙ 6pm-4am Wed-Sat, 6pm-midnight Sun) If you're up for a party, this place kicks on late and has the liveliest dance floor in town. There's a happy hour between 11pm and midnight from Wed to Sat.

Getting There & Away

Finnair flies daily from Helsinki to Kuusamo airport, which is 7km northeast of the town centre. Buses meet incoming flights (€3 to Kuusamo, €5 to Ruka) during the ski season. Local taxis can be called on ☎ 852 2290.

Buses run daily from Kajaani (€34.70, four hours), Oulu (€30.10, three hours) and Rovaniemi (€25.40, three hours). There are frequent services to the ski centre at Ruka (€5, 30 minutes). In summer (early June to mid-August) an excursion bus travels between the Karhuntassu tourist office in Kuusamo and the Oulanka Visitor Centre (€9.30, 1½ hours), stopping at the Kuusamo bus terminal, Tropiikki spa centre, Ruka and Juuma village. It departs at 8.45am from Monday to Friday, and 1.50pm Saturday. At the Juuma road junction (Käylä) you can change buses to get to Ristikallio, Hautajärvi visitor centre and Salla.

RUKA

☎ 08

Finland's major ski resort, Ruka, is just 30km north of Kuusamo, in a beautiful protected nature area, with abundant wildlife. The centre buzzes during the winter, but has plenty to offer in summer, with enough services open and people about that it doesn't feel spooky. There are good deals on accommodation, from single-night stays to longer rentals. The resort itself has the usual ensemble of ugly buildings, but there are some great views westwards over the forest.

Ruka makes a good place to start or finish the Karhunkierros trek because there are good bus connections from Kuusamo. **Valtavaara hill**, adjacent to the Ruka ski slope, is the best place in the region for bird-watching: around 100 species of birds nest here, and an annual **bird-watching competition** is held in the area in June.

Information

The turnoff to Ruka is 26km north of Kuusamo. Two kilometres down this road, you can turn right to the small centre of Itä Ruka (another 3km), or continue up the hill to the main centre of the resort. This is where most of the facilities are. The Kuusamo tourist office can also provide information on Ruka activities and accommodation.

Rukakeskus (☎ 860 0200; www.ruka.fi) is the main information centre at the ski resort. It's in the Rukaklubi building in the main village parking area. In the same area there are ski rental shops, lift ticket outlets, postal services, a supermarket and accommodation booking services.

Skiing

There are 28 downhill ski slopes and 18 lifts on **Ruka fell** (www.ruka.fi). The vertical drop is 201m and the longest run is 1300m – not bad averages at all for Finland, where hills are small and slope gently. Ruka also boasts cross-country trails totalling 250km. There are special areas for snowboarders.

The ski season runs from early November to mid-May, depending on snowfalls. During holiday periods such as Christmas, February and Easter, it seems that almost the entire population of Finland can be seen on Ruka's slopes.

A single ride up on the ski lift costs €4.50, a day/week pass is €30/140. Rates are slightly lower in the shoulder seasons. Alpine skis, including poles and boots, rent for €26.50/112.50 for one/seven days; snowboards for €31/112.50. Ski lessons are available in all disciplines.

Tours

See p284 for details of tour operators in the Kuusamo area.

Sleeping

Ruka is a very busy winter sports centre, and in season it may be difficult to find a bed, especially at reasonable prices. Book accommodation in advance, or stay in Kuusamo. In summer, rooms can be good value, though some of the village services close down completely.

There are numerous apartments available in Ruka itself, and cottages in the surrounding area. These offer great value in summer. Contact the Karhuntassa Tourist Centre (p284) or the FinFun agency (☎ 0203 70021; www.finfun.fi; Huoparintie 1, Kuusamo). For apartments and chalets also try **Ruka-ko** (☎ 866 0088; www.ruka-ko.fi; Postibaari) at the resort. You can make online accommodation bookings for cabins on www.ruka.fi.

Rukan Omena (☎ 020-39000; www.omena.com; 1–4-person r €55, May-Aug €45; P ✗) The first of the Omenahotelli chain, offering good-value accommodation at Itä Ruka. The small, self-contained apartments have four beds at a flat rate. Reservations should be made over the Internet; there's also a reservation machine in the lobby, accessed via credit card.

Hotel Rantasipi Rukahovi (☎ 85910; www.rantasipi.fi; s/d €112/140, high season €135/164, all r €74-79 May-Aug; P ✗) At the foot of the Ruka West ski slopes is the largest hotel in Ruka. It has three parts: an old wing, the new wing (built in 2001) and apartments, along with a couple of restaurants, bars, nightclubs and karaoke – in many ways it's the thumping heart of the resort.

Willi's West (☎ 868 1712; www.williswest.com; Rukanriutta 13; s/d/tr €29/39/49; P ✗) At the Ruka turnoff on the main road is this friendly motel-style set-up offering excellent value. The rooms are small apartments sleeping up to five, and have spacious bathroom and a small, equipped kitchen. There's not a lot of privacy, but it's a steal at the price. The owner will take groups of walkers to the Karhunkierros trailheads free of charge.

Klubi Apartments (☎ 860 0200; www.ruka.fi; 2-/4-/6-person apt Sep & winter €87/125/199, summer €64/98/148; P ✗) These apartments on the main square in Ruka are excellent value in summer. They are very new, with full kitchen, sauna and laundry; just the thing after a heavy trek!

Royal Hotel Ruka (☎ 868 6000; www.royalruka.fi; d €122, r Aug-Oct €90; ✷ Aug-Apr; P ✗) Down at the foot of the fell at the turn-off to Rukajärvi is a well-appointed hotel that looks somewhat like a children's fort to be populated with toy soldiers. It has a restaurant, and breakfast and sauna included. It's closed in early summer; if you are arriving in August you should call ahead to book.

Viipus Camping (☎ 868 1213; Kemijärventie; camp sites €10, 2–4-person cabins €25-54; ✷ Jun–mid-Sep) This is a very small rustic camping ground at Viipusjärvi, several kilometres north of Ruka. It's a good spot in summer, with camp sites, a few cabins, a shop, sauna and boats for hire.

There are places for caravans in Itä Ruka, with power points and toilets. It's run by **Rukakeskus** (☎ 860 0200; ✷ May-Sep).

Eating & Drinking

Riipisen Riistakauppa (☎ 868 1219; mains €14-36; ✷ noon-9pm Mon-Sat) At the Kelo ski-lift area, this is a meat-lover's dream and a classic restaurant – popular with Finnish celebrities in winter. It's speciality is pricey game dishes, including sautéed wild boar, reindeer pepper steak, and hare or woodgrouse stew.

Pizzeria Ruka (☎ 868 1445; pizzas €8-10; ✷ 11am-11pm) Nearby, this is the place for Italian-style pizzas in a family-friendly atmosphere. There are attractive special offers for the younger generation.

Piste (☎ 860 0360; mains €10-22; ✷ 10am-midnight) This cavernous wooden hall on the Ruka square has several attractive dining areas and good service. There's a pleasing range of dishes, all generously portioned, and ranging from burgers and fried fish to weightier mixed grills. The house snails are good as a starter.

Zone (☎ 860 8600; ✷ noon-4am) On the main square in the Safaritalo building, this is the liveliest nightlife spot. It's open year-round, and has karaoke, live music, a great terrace and other après-hike-or-ski delights.

Getting There & Away

Ruka is 30km north of Kuusamo on main road 5. Most regular bus services to Kuusamo continue further north to Ruka. During ski season (early November to early May) a skibus shuttles between Kuusamo and Ruka, stopping at all of the big hotels. In summer there's an excursion bus (see opposite for details).

OULU, KAINUU & KOILLISMAA

KARHUNKIERROS TREK & OULANKA NATIONAL PARK

The 80km Karhunkierros (Bear's Ring), one of the oldest and best-established trekking routes in Finland, offers up some of the country's most breathtaking scenery. It is extremely popular during the *ruska* (autumn colours) period, but it can be walked practically anytime between late May and October.

Despite the name, it's not a circuit, rather a point-to-point walk. Because the trail runs through some isolated areas within Oulanka National Park, getting there – or at least to and from the trailheads – will require some strategic planning. There are four possible starting points: the northern access point is from Hautajärvi visitor centre on the road to Salla; further south on road 950 is the Ristikallio parking area where there's another starting point; in the south you can start the walk at Ruka ski resort; or further northeast at Juuma village. The best section of the trail runs from Ristikallio to Juuma. Also at Juuma there's a short but demanding marked loop trail, the 12km Little Bear's Ring (p291).

Most people choose to walk north to south; cars and luggage can be more easily left at Ruka, and there are plenty of hotels and bars to rest weary legs on arrival.

Information

The 1:50,000 *Rukatunturi-Oulanka* map is useful for treks of any length. The new edition costs €18 and is sold at both of the park's visitor centres and at the Kuusamo tourist office. That said, the trail is so well signposted that you can easily make do with the free map.

Hautajärvi visitor centre (☎ 020-564 6870; hauta jarvi@metsa.fi; ☽ 9am-6pm Jun–mid-Aug, shorter hr mid-Aug–May) This helpful office is at the northern trailhead, right on the Arctic Circle on the Kuusamo to Salla road a kilometre north of Hautajärvi village. There's a café and wildlife exhibition here.

Oulanka visitor centre (☎ 020-564 6850; oulanka@ metsa.fi; ☽ 10am-8pm Jun–mid-Aug, shorter hr Apr-May & mid-Aug–Oct) The other tourist office, at Kiutaköngäs Rapids in the middle of Oulanka National Park, is accessible by car or by bus along a partly sealed road from Käylä on road 950. The centre has nature exhibits and a slide show, and sells trekking supplies, maps and fishing licences. There's also a café, and easy walking trails take you along the Oulankajoki to the rapids.

Trekking

The track is well marked. If you're just on a day trip, you could do it in light shoes on dry summer days, but for the full route, you'll need proper hiking boots, particularly for the Juuma to Ruka section. Prior to mid-June the ground is too soggy to make hiking enjoyable. Even if you don't intend to walk the whole route, if you have a vehicle it's possible to do relatively short return treks from parking areas. A day walk can take you from Ristikallio to Oulanka Canyon, for example. It's also possible to drive to within 1km of Oulanka Canyon along a signposted dirt road about 12km north of Ristikallio.

DAY ONE

Start your trek at the parking area at the Ristikallio parking area. After 15 minutes you will reach the national park border. You can stop at a camp site at Aventojoki or proceed further to Ristikallio, which offers some breathtaking scenery. Proceed less than one hour further to reach Puik-kokämppä hut at a small lake. Continue another kilometre and a bit past the lake to reach Taivalköngäs (near the wilderness hut of the same name), with two sets of rapids and three suspension bridges.

Northern extension

If you really enjoy hiking, begin your trek further north at the Hautajärvi visitor centre – this adds an extra 22km to the hike. The landscape is unimpressive until the path reaches the Savinajoki. The deep Oulanka Canyon is a highlight of this part of the trek. A wilderness hut, Savilampi kämppä, is at the Oulanka riverfront near Lake Savilampi, 18km south of Hautajärvi. The distance from Lake Savilampi to Taivalköngäs – where you'll join the Ristikallio trail – is 4km.

DAY TWO

The first leg is an 8km trek from Taivalköngäs through some ordinary scenery although there are a few beautiful lakes. After 4.2km, you can camp at Lake Runsu-lampi; there's dry wood available. About 4km further east, you can stay overnight at Oulanka Camping, or continue to the Oulanka visitor centre. The Kiutaköngäs, just 800m from the visitor centre, are noted for the rugged cliffs nearby. It's possible to reach Ansakämppä cabin by early evening

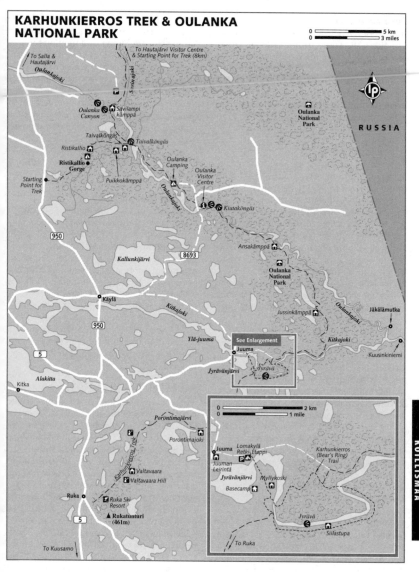

KARHUNKIERROS TREK & OULANKA
NATIONAL PARK

from here, or even Jussinkämppä wilderness hut on Kulmakkajärvi.

DAY THREE
This is tougher than the preceding days. A hike through ridges and forests (and boardwalks across wetlands) takes you to the Kitkajoki in another deep gorge. After

following the river, you can choose between several routes, either walking directly to Juuma or crossing the river at Myllykoski to see the mighty Jyrävä waterfall (3km from Juuma) that has an elevation of 12m. There's the Siilastupa hut at Jyrävä, and Basecamp lodge on the trail just outside Juuma.

Ruka extension

Juuma is a convenient end to the trek, but you can also walk 24km further to Ruka, which has an great choice of accommodation and better road connections to Kuusamo. This is much more strenuous than the previous three days, with many ascents and descents. There is one wilderness hut, Porontimajoki (often full), and several lean-to shelters.

Sleeping

WILDERNESS HUTS

There is a good network of wilderness huts along the Karhunkierros route. They are all pretty similar and tend to be crowded in the high season. Although the theory goes that there's always room for the last to arrive, it's handy to have a tent, as someone often ends up sleeping outside. Dry firewood is generally available, but you'll need to carry a lightweight mattress for sleeping. From north to south, your options are as follows:

Ristikallio 5km east of the main road, has a nice lakeside location. It sleeps 10 people and has dry firewood.

Puikkokämppä 2.5km further east, is a basic lakeside hut that sleeps 10 people.

Taivalköngäs 1.3km further east, accommodates 15 people on two floors. You can cook on the gas stove or at the campfire.

Ansakämppä 8.5km east from the visitor centre, accommodates at least 10 people.

Jussinkämppä 9km further on, sleeps 20 people.

Myllykoski 2km from Juuma, is an old mill building with few facilities but it accommodates at least 10 people. The mill is in working condition; there are sometimes demonstrations; but the stream can make for noisy sleeping.

Siilastupa 4km from Juuma just opposite the Jyrävä waterfall, sleeps 12 people. Often full.

Porontimajoki – 8km south of Juuma, accommodates four people. This is a popular last- or first-night stop, and is often full.

CAMPING

Oulanka Camping (☎ 020-564 6855; abctt1@surfeu .fi; Liikasenvaarantie 137; tent sites €10, 4-person cabins €37; ☼ Jun-Aug) The Bear's Trail runs right though this place, 500m from the park visitor centre. It rents out canoes and rowing boats, and has a café and sauna.

There are a few camping grounds in Juuma; see opposite.

LODGE

Basecamp Oulanka (☎ 0400 509 741; www.basecamp oulanka.fi; Jyräväntie 15; s/d €79/98, low season €50/70;

Ⓟ ⊠) This new wilderness lodge is just the place to rest your weary legs. It's about a kilometre from Juuma, and right on the trail itself near Myllykoski (but 4.5km by car). The snug rustic rooms smell of new pine, have a roof-space that can sleep extra bodies, and a charming balcony looking over the forest. There's a convivial bar and restaurant (lunch always on, dinner by arrangement), a sauna and even a Jacuzzi. The friendly staff organize all sorts of daily activities; rafting, fishing, husky rides and snowshoe walking among others. Off season, it's worth asking if any discounted rates are available.

Getting There & Away

There are one to three buses daily (except Sunday) along the main road between Salla and Kuusamo, departing from either town and stopping at both the Ristikallio starting point and the Hautajärvi visitor centre. In summer there is an excursion bus Monday to Saturday from Kuusamo to the Oulanka visitor centre, Oulanka Camping and Kiutaköngäs. It also goes to Juuma – see p286 for details. In winter, take the daily school bus. A **taxi** (☎ 868 1222) from Ruka can be a good option if shared between three or four people; it costs €30 to Juuma, and about €55 to Hautajärvi.

PADDLING THE KITKAJOKI

The rugged Kitkajoki offers some of the most challenging canoeing and kayaking in Finland. There are plenty of tricky rapids, including the class IV, 900m Aallokkokoski.

The village of **Käylä**, on the Kuusamo to Salla road, is a starting point for whitewater rafting along the Kitkajoki. There is a shop, a fuel station and a post office. You can also start the trip from Juuma, where it's about a 20km trip to the exit point near the Russian border. You can do this trip as an organized whitewater adventure, or hire canoes or kayaks from the operators, who will also arrange transport at either end. Most of the operators are based in Kuusamo or Ruka (p284). **Kitkan Safarit** (☎ 0400 280 569; www.kitkansafarit.fi; Juumantie 134) in Juuma also arranges trips.

Käylä to Juuma

The first 14km leg of the journey is definitely the easier of the two, suitable for families with children, and does not involve any carrying at all. You start at the Käylänkoski, and continue 3km to the easy Kiehtäjänniva, and a further kilometre to the Vähä-Käylänkoski. These are both class I rapids. After a bit more than 1km, there are three class II rapids spaced every 400m or so. A kilometre further, there's the trickiest one, the class III Harjakoski, which is 300m long. The rest of the journey, almost 7km, is mostly lakes. The road bridge between the lakes Ylä and Ala-Juumajärvi marks the end of the trip. It is 1km to Juuma from the bridge.

Juuma to the Russian Border

This 20km journey is the most dangerous river route in Finland. You should be an expert paddler, and you *must* carry your canoe at least once – around the 12m, class VI Jyrävä waterfall. Inspect the tricky rapids before you let go and ask for local advice in case the water level is unfavourable. There's a minimum age of 18 to canoe this route.

The thrill starts just 300m after Juuma, with the class II Niskakoski. From here on, there is only 1km of quiet water. Myllykoski, with a water-mill, is a tricky class IV waterfall. Right after Myllykoski, the 900m Aallokkokoski Rapids mean quick paddling for quite some time. The Jyrävä waterfall comes right after this long section. Pull aside before Jyrävä, and carry your canoe. You might want to carry it from Myllykoski to well beyond the Jyrävä waterfall, skipping the Aallokkokoski Rapids.

After Jyrävä things cool down considerably, although there are some class III rapids. After about 6km, there is a wilderness hut, the Päähkänäkallio. When you meet the Oulankajoki, 7km downriver from the hut, paddle upriver to Jäkälämutka or downriver to Kuusinkiniemi, 100m from the Russian border. At either spot you can access a 4WD forest road that will take you back to civilization. You must arrange return transport from this point in advance, as traffic is nonexistent.

PADDLING THE OULANKAJOKI

Equally impressive, and demanding, among the great Kuusamo river routes, the Oulankajoki gives you a chance to see mighty canyons from a canoe or kayak. You *must* carry your canoe at least four times – past parts of the Oulanka Canyon, and waterfalls at Taivalköngäs and Kiutaköngäs. Study a river map before starting out.

The first leg, an 18km trip, starts from road 5, north of Ristikallio. The first 7km or so is relatively calm paddling, until you reach the impressive Oulanka Canyon. The safe section extends for about 1km, after which you should pull aside and carry your canoe past the dangerous rapids. You can overnight at Savilampi hut.

Some 3km after Savilampi are the Taivalköngäs. You'll need to carry your canoe, and there's a hut here too. The next 6km are quiet until Kiutaköngäs, where you'll need to carry your canoe. The park visitor centre and camping sites are nearby.

The second leg of the journey, a full 20km long, starts on the other side of Kiutaköngäs. You pass through 500m of quiet waters, then there's another waterfall, and it's carrying-time again!

On the final leg, the river becomes smooth and there is little to worry about as far as rapids go. This leg is suitable for families with children.

JUUMA
☎ 08

The village of Juuma is a popular base for treks along the Karhunkierros route. It's a convenient place to stock up on supplies, has several accommodation options, and there's daily transport from Kuusamo.

If you have a little time for trekking, take the **Little Bear's Ring**, a 12km loop trail, to Myllykoski Rapids and Jyrävänjärvi. The trail (leaving from by the Lomakylä café) crosses varying terrain, and has several interesting sights, including the 12m Jyrävä waterfall. The walk can be done in five to six hours and takes in some of the best of the entire Bear's Ring. There are two wilderness huts on this trail – Myllykoski and Siilastupa (see opposite) – and a couple of swing bridges. It's well signposted, and fairly busy.

Kitkan Safarit (☎ 0400 280 569; www.kitkansafarit .fi; Juumantie 134), near the car park, arranges whitewater rafting along the Kitkajoki and Oulankajoki, and rents out canoes and kayaks. A short 'family' paddle costs €25 per person, the two-hour 'wild route' is €50, the four-hour complete route is €70, and canoeing on the Oulankajoki is €40.

Sleeping & Eating

There are several accommodation choices in Juuma from June to August, and some places stay open throughout September. The best accommodation and eating option is the Basecamp lodge (see p290). Cottages can be rented year-round; contact the Kuusamo tourist office or the FinFun (☎ 0203 70021; www.finfun.fi; Huoparintie 1, Kuusamo) agency.

Lomakylä Retki-Etappi (☎ 863 218; Juumantie 134; tent sites €10, 4-person cabins €25; ☺ Jun-Sep) This place, on the Karhunkierros trail and at the start of the Little Bear's Ring, is the most convenient place to stay. The café serves snacks and meals. It also has a sauna and rents out rowing boats and bicycles.

Juuman Leirintä (☎ 863 212; Riekamontie 1; tent sites €8, cabins €22, cottages €60) This place has a lakeside location, a sauna, laundry and a café-restaurant that's open until 9pm. It's just north of the centre of Juuma, on the Käylä road.

Getting There & Away
In summer, the **excursion bus** (☎ 851 1052; www.pohjolanturistiauto.fi) makes the 50km trip from Kuusamo to Juuma, via Ruka, once daily (except Sunday). A **taxi** (☎ 868 1222) from Ruka to Juuma costs €30 for up to four people, from Kuusamo to Juuma €50.

ISO-SYÖTE & PIKKU-SYÖTE
☎ 08

Just two decades ago, Syöte, the southernmost fell in Finland, was covered by virgin forest. Not any more. Syöte's twin peaks, Iso-Syöte and Pikku-Syöte ('Big Syöte' and 'Little Syöte', respectively), are now dotted with ski lifts, ski tracks, hotels and restaurants. The proximity to Oulu, about two hours by car, makes this a popular winter ski destination.

In addition to its winter sports facilities, the Syöte area offers the visitor access to the National Park north and southwest of Iso-Syöte, with a network of walking tracks and wilderness huts.

Pudasjärven Matkailu Oy (☎ 823 400; fax 823 421, Varsitie 7; ☺ 8am-5pm Mon-Fri), in Pudasjärvi, is a travel agency that provides tourist information and assistance for the Syöte region. For online accommodation bookings and detailed information go to **Syöte** (www.syote.net).

Activities
At Iso-Syöte, there are 21 downhill slopes and 11 lifts. The vertical drop is 192m and the longest run is 1200m. There are some 110km of cross-country trails, all clearly marked. You can rent skiing equipment and purchase lift passes at Romekievari station.

Relatively few trekkers take advantage of the excellent walking tracks and free wilderness huts around Syöte. The majority of trekkers use the Ahmatupa hut as a base, and do a loop around the northern part of the trekking area. Another route, indicated by yellow markings on trees, makes a loop around Iso-Syöte hill. Additionally, the UKK route crosses through Syöte; see p282.

Sleeping & Eating
Practically all accommodation in the Syöte region can and should be arranged through Pudasjärven Matkailu Oy. Daily, weekly and weekend rates are available and in summer the places that remain open offer bargain rates, from around €200 a week.

Hostel Syöte (☎ 838 172; www.syotekeskus.fi; dm €14) This is a five-bed HI Hostel and easily the cheapest accommodation in the region. It's in the village centre near Pikku-Syöte and has a café.

There are dozens of *kelo* (pine) log cabins on top of Syöte Hill, and the most luxurious are equipped with kitchenettes and TVs. In the spring high season (the weeks surrounding Easter), these cabins cost from €100/500 per night/week and accommodate six people.

There are three wilderness huts and several *kota* or *laavu* shelters around the Syöte area, all of which are free of charge.

Getting There & Away
There is a bus service from Oulu to Syöte (€18.60, 2½ hours) each weekday afternoon. The bus back to Oulu departs each weekday morning.

Lapland & Sápmi

Lapland has an irresistible romance that is a draw for visitors and Finns alike. While you won't see polar bears or rocky fjords, there is something intangible that makes it magical.

Part of the spell it casts is in the awesome latitudes that are reached here. At Nuorgam, the northernmost point, we have passed Iceland and nearly all of Canada and Alaska.

It's also linked inextricably with the midnight sun, the Sámi peoples, the northern lights, and the wandering reindeer. And, of course, Santa Claus, who 'officially' resides here!

Lapland has awesome wildernesses and is *the* place in Finland to get active. Exploring the tundra, forests and fells is unforgettable. Whether you drive or trek, set aside time to get off the main roads. The sense of space, pure air and big skies is what is memorable here, more than the towns, which, having been razed during WWII, are mainly dull service centres.

It's important to pick your time in Lapland carefully. In the far north there's no sun for fifty days of the year, and no night for seventy-odd days. There's thick snow cover from mid-October to May. In June it's very muddy, and in July insects can be hard to deal with! If you're here to walk, August is great and in September the *ruska* (autumn) colours can be seen.

The far northern part of Lapland is known as Sápmi, home of the Sámi people and their reindeer herds. The main Sámi communities are around Inari and Hetta. Rovaniemi is the most popular gateway to the north.

HIGHLIGHTS

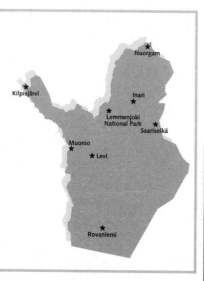

- Experiencing Finland's best wilderness fell walking in places like **Saariselkä** (p314), **Lemmenjoki National Park** (p322) and **Kilpisjärvi** (p310)
- Dashing through the snow in a sled pulled by a team of huskies in **Muonio (p307)**
- Seeing the awe-inspiring **aurora borealis** (p307) – nature's Arctic light show
- Skiing or snowboarding at **Levi** (p305), Finland's most happening resort
- Fishing for salmon on the **Tenojoki** (p326) at Nuorgam
- Shopping for handicrafts in **Inari** (p322), the Sámi capital of Finland
- Learning about the northern environments at Rovaniemi's superb **Arktikum** museum (p298)

History

When Sámi peoples were pushed north by migrating Finns, a gradual process that took place through the early first millennium AD, their traditions evolved and developed. Many legends remain, including those of miracle-working witches who could fly and transform themselves into strange creatures. Conspicuous lakes or rocks became *seita* (holy sites), the island of Ukko on Inarijärvi being the best known of these.

Inari was an important Sámi trading centre in the early 1500s, when there were Sámi settlements throughout the vast territory. During the 1600s, the Swedes increased their presence in northern Finland. In 1670 cult sites and religious objects of the Sámi were destroyed by Gabriel Tuderus (1638–1703), who represented the Lutheran Church. Wooden churches were built throughout Lapland, the oldest remaining in Sodankylä and Tervola, south of Rovaniemi.

During the following centuries, more Finns were attracted to the vast province, adopted reindeer-herding and were assimilated into the Sámi communities (or vice versa), especially in southern Lapland.

The area of Petsamo, northeast of Inari, was annexed to Finland in 1920 by the Treaty of Tartu and a nickel mine opened in 1937. Russians attacked the area during the Winter War (1939–40) and the area was evacuated on 4 September 1944. The Soviet Union annexed the mineral-rich area and has kept it

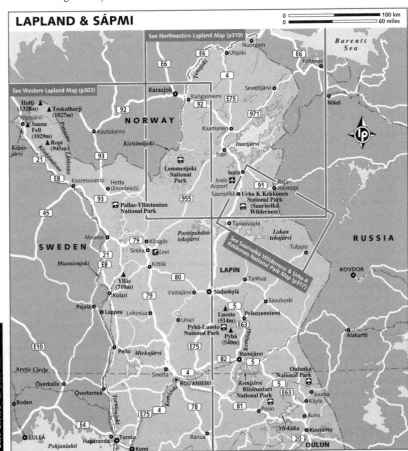

LAPLAND & SÁPMI

ever since. The Skolt Sámi from Petsamo were resettled in Sevettijärvi, Nellim and Virtaniemi in northeastern Lapland.

The peace agreement of 1944 between Finland and the Soviet Union meant the German army had to retreat. They did so in a scorched-earth manner, burning and destroying all buildings in their path to hold off pursuit. Only a few churches, villages and houses in Lapland date from the period before WWII.

Activities

The attraction of Lapland is the outdoors and the great range of exciting things to do almost year-round. There's good downhill skiing for almost six months of the year at several spots; Levi (p305) is Finland's most popular ski resort, while smaller Pyhä, Luosto and Ylläs are more family- than party-oriented. All these spots also have extensive cross-country trails too.

One of the most memorable activities in Lapland is sleigh safaris. Pulled by a team of huskies or reindeer, you cross the snowy wilderness, overnighting in log cabins with a relaxing wood sauna and eating meals cooked over a fire. You can organise trips of up to a week or more, or just head out for a jaunt of a couple of hours. Similar trips can be arranged on snowmobiles, too. Muonio and Saariselkä are particularly good places for these excursions.

Once the snow melts, there are some fabulous multiday treks and shorter walks in Lapland. The national parks network offers everything from wheelchair-accessible nature trails to demanding wilderness routes for experienced hikers, but there are good walks almost everywhere, including around Kilpisjärvi, in the far northwest, and Sevettijärvi, in the remote northeast.

Walking in Lapland is good from July until mid-October – there's snow cover from November to mid-May, and the ground is mushy from the thaw until late June. It's great in August, when most of the biting insects have disappeared, and beautiful in September, when the *ruska* colours paint the landscape in an incredible array of hues.

The rivers of Lapland are frisky indeed, and there are several excellent canoeing routes and spots for whitewater rafting. The Ounasjoki (p305) is probably the best of the canoeing routes. Fishing is popular year-round. Ice-fishing is a memorable and sociable experience, and the beautiful Teno Valley (p326) offers superb salmon-fishing.

All major settlements have plenty of tour operators, most of whom offer all these activities. Rovaniemi, the main town in Lapland, is a popular base, but Saariselkä, Levi and Muonio are equally good and have the advantage of being further out in the wilderness, with a more authentically Lapp feel.

National Parks

There are six national parks in Lapland, three of which – the country's three largest – offer particularly rewarding trekking.

In the northeast, Urho K Kekkonen National Park (p316) covers a huge wilderness area and is one of the country's most popular hiking destinations. Even larger is Lemmenjoki National Park (p322) near Inari,

The Ounasjoki (p305) is probably the best of the canoeing routes. Fishing is popular year-round. Ice-fishing is a memorable and sociable experience, and the beautiful Teno Valley (p326) offers superb salmon-fishing.

All major settlements have plenty of tour operators, most of whom offer all these activities. Rovaniemi, the main town in Lapland, is a popular base, but Saariselkä, Levi and Muonio are equally good and have the advantage of being further out in the wilderness, with a more authentically Lapp feel.

Self-Catering Accommodation

There is a huge quantity of self-catering apartments, wooden cottages and cabins throughout the region. Out of season, the ski resorts are particularly fertile ground; fully-furnished places with their own sauna can be great value in summer.

Local tourist offices often double as booking agents for these accommodation options; see the Information sections of the relevant towns. **Wild North** (☎ 020-564 7647; www.wildnorth.net), an arm of the Forest and Park Service, has a large selection of cabins available throughout the region.

Language

As well as Finnish, there are three Sámi languages spoken in the region, and signs in Sámi areas are bilingual. See boxed text, p325 for more details about Sámi language.

Dangers & Annoyances

Lapland is the coldest part of Finland; winter temperatures regularly fall to -30°C, and sometimes much lower. Even in summer, bad weather can descend rapidly, so be prepared for all conditions when climbing fells or hiking.

From mid-June to early August, Lapland is home to millions of biting insects, ranging from mosquitoes to blackflies, midges and various types of horsefly. At times there are quite literally clouds of them, and during this *räkkä* (biting insect) season, you'll need heavy-duty repellent. By early August, most of the 'squadrons' have dispersed.

Parts of Lapland are real wilderness zones, and trekkers/skiers should always speak to the excellent staff of the national parks information centres before attempting unmarked routes.

Driving in Lapland calls for particular caution due to the reindeer (see boxed text, p42).

Getting Around

Considering how remote some areas are, the bus connections are good, although there may only be one service a day, and none on Sundays. More remote villages may only be accessible by hitching or by postbus, where seats can be booked on the postman's daily round.

Lapland is a good place to hire a car, with Rovaniemi having the most choice. Petrol stations are sparsely spread, and some are automatic. Many of these don't accept foreign credit cards, so always have some cash handy.

ROVANIEMI

☎ 016 / pop 35,377

Rovaniemi is the capital of Lapland, and its major gateway and service centre. Most visitors to the area will find themselves passing through it at some point, and the Arktikum museum is an excellent introduction to the mysteries of these latitudes. That said, Rovaniemi isn't a particularly memorable place; use it as a launching pad for farther-flung parts of Lapland, or to arrange tours, of which there is a huge choice. It also has some of Lapland's better hotels, restaurants, and bars, and is a convenient place to hire a car.

Many of Rovaniemi's visitors come to cross the Arctic Circle, which lies some 8km north of town. This has also become the 'official' residence of everyone's favourite beardie-weirdie Santa Claus, who lives in a tacky complex of tourist shops and ho-ho-hos most cheerfully as the euros roll in!

The town itself is modern and relatively uninteresting, although it is memorably set on the fast-flowing Kemijoki, spanned by Jätkänkynttilä Bridge dubbed the 'Lumberjack's Candle' for its light-topped pylons. After the complete destruction of Rovaniemi by the Germans in 1944, it was rebuilt from a plan by Alvar Aalto, with the main streets radiating out from Hallituskatu in the shape of reindeer antlers – though this is a more than a little hard to actually to see on the ground.

Information

BOOKSHOPS

Suomalainen Kirjakauppa (☎ 342 3822; Rovakatu 24) Sells English-language paperbacks and maps of Lapland.

INTERNET ACCESS

Public library (☎ 322 2463; Hallituskatu 9; ☺ 11am-7pm Mon-Fri, 11am-5pm Sat) Aalto-designed; has free Internet access. There's also pricy (€2/15 minutes) access at the tourist office.

LEFT LUGGAGE

There are lockers (€2 to €3) at both train and bus stations, and a storage counter at the train station.

POST

Main post office (Postikatu 1) Near the train and bus stations. There's a more central branch at Koskikatu 9, but many visitors prefer to send their postcards from the busy Santa Claus post office at the Arctic Circle (see p302).

TOURIST INFORMATION

Etiäinen (☎ 020-564 7820; etiainen@metsa.fi; ☺ 9am-5pm Mon-Fri May & Oct, 9am-5pm Nov-Apr & Jun-Sep) This place at Napapiiri is the information centre for the national parks and trekking regions, with information on hiking and fishing in Lapland. The office also sells maps and fishing permits, and books cottages.

Santa Claus Tourist Centre (☎ 346 270; www .rovaniemi.fi; Rovakatu 21; ☺ 8am-5pm Mon-Fri Sep-May, 8am-6pm Mon-Fri, 10am-6pm Sat & Sun Jun-Aug) The tourist office shamelessly goes by this name, but is an excellent source of information for all of Lapland.

LAPLAND & SÁPMI

TRAVEL AGENCIES

In summer there are river cruises, whitewater rafting, fishing and trips to reindeer and husky farms. In winter, it's snowmobiling, sled safaris and skiing.

Arctic Safaris (☎ 340 0400; www.arcticsafaris.fi; Koskikatu 6) Has weekly tour programmes for winter and summer.

Eräsetti Safaris (☎ 362 811; www.erasetti.fi; Valtakatu) Specialists in this region with another office at Santa Claus Village, Napapiiri.

Lapland Safaris (☎ 331 1200; www.laplandsafaris.com; Koskikatu 1) The largest and best-established of Rovaniemi's tour operators.

Safartica (☎ 311 485; www.safartica.com; Valtakatu 20) Specialists in husky safaris.

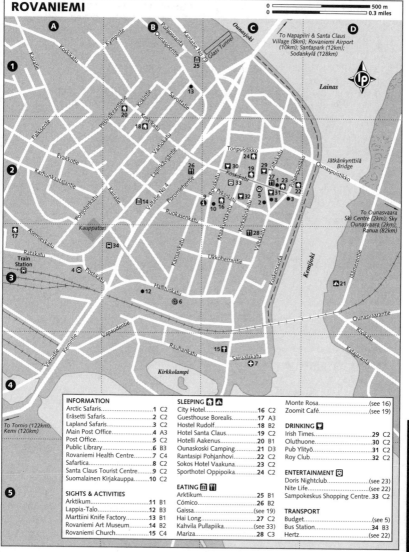

ROVANIEMI

LAPLAND & SÁPMI

Sights

ARKTIKUM

With its beautifully designed glass tunnel stretching out to the Ounasjoki, **Arktikum** (☎ 322 3260; www.arktikum.fi; Pohjoisranta 4; adult/student/child €11/8.50/5; 🕙 9am-7pm mid-Jun–mid-Aug, 10am-6pm daily early Jun, late Aug & Dec, 10am-5pm Tue-Sun Sep-Nov, 10am-6pm Tue-Sun Jan-May) is one of Finland's best museums, albeit with a hefty admission fee. Exhibition spaces include superb static and interactive displays focusing on Arctic flora and fauna, as well as on the peoples of Arctic Europe, Asia and North America. The level of information is very impressive; this is really a place to learn about the unique northern environments, and there is an excellent research library. There are also good displays of canoes, dwellings, fishing materials, and costumes of various northern peoples (including a good exhibition on the Sámi), as well as a room devoted to the history of Rovaniemi itself. A scale model shows the destruction wrought by the Axis retreat in 1944. There's also a multivision theatre and a good restaurant. You should allow yourself at least a couple of hours to get around it all.

LAPPIA-TALO

Rovaniemi's **concert hall** (☎ 322 2495; Hallituskatu 11; 🕙 11am-5pm Tue-Thu, 11am-7pm Fri, 11am-2pm Sat) is one of several buildings in Rovaniemi designed by architect Alvar Aalto (others include the adjacent library and town hall). The hall is used by the Rovaniemi Theatre Company, Lapland Music School and Chamber Orchestra of Lapland, and other organsiations.

ROVANIEMI ART MUSEUM

This **museum** (☎ 322 2822; Lapinkävijäntie 4; adult/child €4/free; 🕙 noon-5pm Tue-Sun) has changing temporary exhibitions of contemporary Finnish art. Admission is free on Saturdays.

ROVANIEMI CHURCH

Completed in 1950, this **church** (Rauhankatu 45; 🕙 9am-9pm mid-May–early Sep) replaces the one destroyed during WWII. The impressively large fresco behind the altar depicts a Christ figure emerging from Lappish scenery. A work of Lennart Segerstråle, it has two sides, one populated by the faithful, the other by brawling drunkards and ravening wolves.

MARTTIINI KNIFE FACTORY

This former **factory** (☎ 330 3396; Vartiokatu 32; 🕙 10am-6pm Mon-Fri, 10am-2pm Sat, noon-4pm Sun) of Finland's most famous knife manufacturer is open to visitors. It has a small knife and photo exhibition, and a shop where you can buy knives cheaper than elsewhere. It's across the road from the Arktikum

OUNASVAARA SKI CENTRE

This **winter ski centre** (☎ 369 045; www.ounasvaara .net), about 3km east of the town centre, has six downhill ski slopes and three ski jumps, plus 123km of cross-country skiing tracks. Skiing equipment can be rented here, and there's also a fun toboggan run alongside the Sky Ounasvaara hotel (opposite), open year-round if it's not raining.

Activities & Tours

Rovaniemi is a popular base from which to sample 'typically Lappish' activities. There's a greater number of tourists here than elsewhere, so tours go out daily during the summer and winter high seasons; the downside is the feeling that you're not quite in Lapland's remote wilderness.

Snowmobile and husky- or reindeer-sled **safaris** are popular in winter. Summer tours include **river cruises** (often combined with a visit to a reindeer farm), **white-water rafting** and **fishing** expeditions. Summer tours hover around the €65 mark for a three-hour trip; a short jaunt on the river is €20. Unsurprisingly, winter activities are more expensive: snowmobile safaris start at €95 per person and go up to €150, depending on what they're combined with, and there's a hefty supplement if you're only one person riding the snowmobile. Husky or reindeer sledding starts at around €100/150 for two/four hours. There are some good-value trips combining, for example, sledding, snowmobiling and ice-fishing.

For bookings contact one of the travel agencies in town (see p297) or the tourist office. All tours are in English, and most will pick up from hotels in town.

Bicycles can be rented from **Arctic Safaris** (Koskikatu 6) and from **Hertz** (Pohjanpuistikko 2).

Festivals & Events

Rovaniemi is as busy in winter as it is in summer, and there are festivals here year-round. With the Arctic Circle – and Santa

Claus – close by, Christmas is a big time of the year and there are plenty of festive activities in December. The **Northern Lights Festival** in February offers a variety of sports and arts events. In March, Rovaniemi hosts the **Ounasvaara Winter Games**, with skiing and ski-jumping competitions. **Jutajaiset** (www .jutajaiset.net), a Midsummer festival in late June, showcases folk music, dance and other Lappish traditions.

Sleeping

BUDGET

Hostel Rudolf (☎ 321 321; www.hotelsantaclaus.fi; Koskikatu 41; dm €23, s/d €34/46; P ✗ &) Currently Rovaniemi's only hostel, this is a handy HI-affiliated spot just west of the centre. The rooms are comfortable and well-equipped, with spick 'n' span beds, TV and bathroom. There's a good kitchen available and a sauna. The hostel is unstaffed and so run by the Hotel Santa Claus, which is, rather inconveniently, where you have to go to check in and get your keycard.

Ounaskoski Camping (☎ 345 304; Jäämerentie 1; tent sites €13 plus €4.50 per person; ☼ late May–mid-Sep) Beautifully situated on the bank of the river just across from the town centre, this place has tent and van sites only. There are great views of the bridge and fewer insects than in many Lapland campsites.

MIDRANGE

Hotel Santa Claus (☎ 321 321; www.hotelsantaclaus .fi; Korkalonkatu 29; s/d €121/137, Sat, Sun & summer r €82; P ✗ 🖳 &) We suppose it was unavoidable that something was named after him, but thankfully this excellent hotel is devoid of sleighbells and 'ho ho ho' kitsch. It's right in the heart of town and very new and busy, with helpful staff and a great bar and restaurant. The rooms have all the trimmings and are spacious, with a sofa and good-sized beds; a small supplement gets you a superior room, which is slightly bigger. The bathrooms are stylishly black-marbled. There are also suites with their own sauna and a couple of apartments available.

Hotelli Aakenus (☎ 342 2051; www.hotelliaakenus .net; Koskikatu 47; s/d €65/75, summer r €53; P ✗ 🖳) A short distance west of the centre, this hotel looks fairly unassuming from the outside but actually has very nice bright, comfortable rooms with a decent bathroom and a comfortable couch. The summer rate is

excellent, and is valid from mid-May right through to the end of August. The Arktikum is a short stroll away.

Guesthouse Borealis (☎ 342 0130; www.guesthouse borealis.com; Asemieskatu 1; s/d/tr €47/63/86; P ✗ 🖳) Very handy for the train station, this friendly family-run guesthouse is a good option, and slightly cheaper in summer. The simply decorated rooms are light and warm, with traditional woven mats and their own small bathroom; some also have a balcony. Downstairs is an apartment (€185) that sleeps up to seven people. Breakfast (with porridge) is included and there's a sauna.

City Hotel (☎ 330 0111; www.cityhotel.fi; Pekankatu 9; s/d €91/115, summer r from €65; P ✗ 🖳) This place near the tourist office is fairly stylish and has an intimate feel. The rooms are never going to be 'cat-swinging' venues but are nicely kitted out in dark wood. Summer rates are attractive, and there's a good restaurant and an excellent terraced café-bar, as well as a pub and live music venue downstairs.

Sporthotel Oppipoika (☎ 338 8111, 346 969; hotel .oppipoika@ramk.fi; Korkalonkatu 33; s/d €73/88, weekends €63/76; ☼ mid-Aug–May; ✗ 🍴) This unusual hotel, run by the hospitality school of the local polytechnic college, is very central and pretty good value: it has a pool and gym, and a very elegant restaurant run by the catering section. Reception is open from 7am to 11pm Monday to Saturday; call ☎ 310 445 at other times.

Rantasipi Pohjanhovi (☎ 33711; www.rantasipi.fi; Pohjanpuistikko 2; s/d €115/135, Sat & Sun €86, summer r €68; P ✗ 🍴 &) This is the oldest hotel in Rovaniemi, having been rebuilt in 1947 at the end of the war. There are two grades of rooms, some of which have nice views over the river or park. It has a legendary restaurant with live music.

Sky Ounasvaara (☎ 335 3311; www.laplandhotels .com; Ounasvaarantie; summer r from €67, Jan-May from €135; P ✗) This is 3km east of the town centre at the crest of Ounasvaara Hill. The main reason to stay here is to be on the doorstep of the Ounasvaara ski centre. In summer, the hotel is a peaceful spot away from the 'bustle' of Rovaniemi, and rooms are quite substantially discounted. Many of the rooms, which are smart, have polished floorboards and their own sauna. There are also apartments and ten luxurious log cabins, as well as a restaurant with great views.

WILL THE REAL SANTA CLAUS PLEASE STAND UP?

Finland, and particularly Lapland, has a strong claim to being the home of Santa Claus. This isn't the North Pole, but Lapland has the reindeer, the winter climate, the mystique and these days it has Santa's post office. But the historic St Nicholas – the real man behind the Santa myth – wouldn't have known a reindeer from a camel and would have melted in a typical Santa suit, as he lived in temperate present-day Turkey!

The story of the real St Nicholas goes something like this: many centuries ago, a poor peasant, father of three daughters, did not have enough money for their wedding dowries. To ensure that at least two of the daughters would have money enough to attract husbands, the man decided that he would have to sell the youngest daughter into slavery. The soon-to-be-sainted Nicholas got word of the terrible situation, crept into the family's house while they were sleeping and magically filled a sock with golden coins. The youngest daughter was saved, all three daughters were joyfully married and the whole family lived happily ever after.

Since then Santa Claus has been filling socks with presents every Christmas. In Finland, Uncle Markus, a legend of children's radio in the middle years of the twentieth century, established the Finnish legend that a gift-giving Santa Claus lived in Korvatunturi Hill, right at the Russian border. Long before that, in pagan times, Finns had believed in an evil male goat spirit that demanded gifts on the shortest day of the year. The two stories eventually blended, which is why the Finnish name for Santa is *Joulupukki*, which literally translates as 'Christmas stud goat'.

Sokos Hotel Vaakuna (☎ 020-1234 695; www.soko shotels.fi; Koskikatu 4; s/d €112/131, Sat & Sun €85, summer €80; P ⊠ ▣) This is one of the town's top hotels with elegant rooms, a big breakfast and free sauna. It can feel a little empty in summer, but the rates are good at this time, and last from May until September.

Eating

Gaissa (☎ 321 321; mains €12-25; ☽ 5.30-11pm Mon-Sat, Sun Dec & Jan) The restaurant of the Hotel Santa Claus is an elegantly candlelit upstairs dining room that serves a mix of Lappish and international food including tapas, pasta and curries. There is a set 'Rovaniemi menu' for €36.50, featuring whitefish roe and flambéed reindeer.

Zoomlt Café (☎ 321 321; Koskikatu; ☽ 11am-11pm, later at weekends) This large light, modern café is an excellent place to have a drink, breakfast or snack. Right in the heart of town, its terrace is the spot to be on a sunny afternoon. Service is good, and at lunchtimes on weekdays there are tasty stir fries, panini and wraps available. There's a minimum age of 20 after 8pm.

Monte Rosa (☎ 330 0111; Pekankatu 9; mains €9-12; ☽ 11am-11pm Mon-Fri, 1-11pm Sat & Sun) Monte Rosa, attached to the City Hotel, offers very tasty food in an intimate, warmly lit interior and great side terrace. The menu spans a variety of cuisines, with fajitas and pizzas lining up alongside some quality Finnish fare.

Arktikum (☎ 322 3263; Pohjoisranta; mains €10-19; ☽ 10am-4pm, 10am-5pm mid-Jun–mid-Aug) Located in the Arktikum museum, this restaurant is very good value. There's a lunch buffet (€10 including hot dish) and an à la carte menu that features good-value local food, such as reindeer fillet, and a selection of excellent soups.

Hai Long (☎ 313 133; Valtakatu 22; lunch buffet €7.50, mains €9-17; ☽ 11am-10pm) The best of Rovaniemi's Chinese restaurants, this has a very spacious interior and good service. It's popular at lunchtime, but also good value in the evenings, with several set menus, larger tables with lazy Susans, and plenty of choice.

Kahvila Pullapiika (☎ 318 189; Sampokeskus shopping centre; ☽ 8.30am-6pm Mon-Fri, 9am-4pm Sat) This café is a popular meeting place for locals of all ages. The glass counter shields a tempting array of savouries and cakes, including a tasty sachertorte. They also do a decent cappuccino.

Mariza (☎ 319 616; Ruokasenkatu 2; lunch buffet €5.90-6.50; ☽ 9.30am-3pm Mon-Fri) A simple but smartish workers' lunch place offering a fabulous lunch buffet of home-cooked Finnish food, including hot dishes, soup and salad.

Cómico (☎ 344 433; Koskikatu 25; mains €8-16; ☽ 11am-midnight, later at weekends) This offbeat American diner–type place serves burgers, steaks and Tex-Mex fare and screens old movies. It's not sophisticated, with a plastic feel, but the portions are generous.

LAPLAND & SÁPMI

Drinking & Entertainment

Excluding the winter ski resorts, Rovaniemi is the only place north of Oulu with a half-decent nightlife, and along with the partying locals and students there are always a few curious tourists.

Ylityö (☎ 318 755; Koskikatu 5) This self-styled 'minibar' is an independent, offbeat place and great for a drink. There are no seats, just tables to lean on, and the ceiling is festooned with ribbons of business cards. At €3.50, the pints are also reasonably priced.

Irish Times (☎ 319 925; Valtakatu 35; ⏲ 2pm-3am) This convivial Irish bar is a top choice for a good night of Finnish pubbing. It has an excellent heated terrace at the back, and regular live music and karaoke, while the downstairs bar has pool tables. There's a snug, friendly feel about the whole set-up. There's a €5 cover charge at weekends.

Oluthuone (☎ 313 715; Koskikatu; ⏲ 10am-1am Mon-Thu, 11am-3am Fri & Sat, noon-midnight Sun) In summer, it's hard to resist sitting out under the midnight sun in the open beer terrace of this place set up on the pedestrian part of Koskikatu.

Roy Club (☎ 313 705; Maakuntakatu 24; ⏲ 10pm-4am) Near the City Hotel, this basement venue is packed after 2am with a cheery student crowd a little the worse for wear. Cover charge is usually €5.

Rovaniemi's major business hotels all have nightclubs and dancing, with a minimum age of 20 to 24 and a cover charge of around €5 on weekends.

Doris Nightclub (Sokos Hotel Vaakuna; ⏲ to 4am) This is a popular choice, open late most nights.

Nite Life (☎ 33 711; Pohjanpuistikko 2; ⏲ to 4am Fri & Sat) For Finnish-style dancing (tango and *humppa*) try this place, located in the Hotel Rantasipi Pohjanhovi. There's a dancefloor and also a nightclub section, with an €8 cover.

Inside the Sampokeskus shopping centre you'll find a cinema offering recent American releases subtitled in Swedish and Finnish.

Shopping

Sámi handicrafts made from reindeer skin and horn, or Arctic birch, are popular souvenirs; trekkers may want to buy a *kuksa* (carved birch cup).

The traditional Sámi costume, which is very colourful, and handmade Sámi hats, mittens and shoes are also top sellers.

The widest selection of souvenirs (and decent prices) can be found in shops at Napapiiri (p302).

Getting There & Away

AIR

The Rovaniemi airport is Finland's most northerly major airport, and the 'official airport of Santa Claus' – does he hangar his sleigh here then? Finnair flies here daily from Helsinki, Kemi and Oulu. The budget carrier Blue1 also has almost-daily flights between Rovaniemi and Helsinki.

BUS

Rovaniemi is the main transport hub in Lapland. Frequent express buses go south to Kemi (€18.90, 1¾ to 2¼ hours) and Oulu (€32.30, 3¾ hours); also to Muonio (€33.60, 3½ hours), Hetta (Enontekiö; €39.20, five hours) and Kilpisjärvi (€53.50, eight hours) in the northwest; Kuusamo (€25.40, three hours) in the east; and to Sodankylä (€21.30, two hours), Ivalo (€42, five hours) and Inari (€44.50, 5½ hours) in the north, with some continuing on to Norway.

TRAIN

The train is the best way to travel between Helsinki and Rovaniemi (from €71.40, 10 to 12 hours) – it's considerably quicker and cheaper than the bus. There are four daily direct services (via Oulu), including overnight services. There's one train connection daily to Kemijärvi, further northeast (€12.80, 1½ hours).

Getting Around

The Rovaniemi airport is 10km north of the town centre. Buses meet each arriving Finnair flight (€5, 15 minutes). Airport buses leave the bus station 50 minutes before flight departures, picking up at several hotels in the centre. A shared airport taxi costs €9. These can be booked on ☎ 362 222 a day before departure.

Most major car-rental agencies are represented, and have outlets in the centre and at the airport. Try **Budget** (☎ 312 266; www .budget.fi; Koskikatu 9) beside the post office, or **Hertz** (☎ 313 300; www.hertz.fi; Pohjanpuistikko 2), at the Rantasipi Pohjanhovi hotel.

LAPLAND & SÁPMI

AROUND ROVANIEMI
Napapiiri (The Arctic Circle) & Santa Claus Village

The Arctic Circle is the southernmost line at which the midnight sun can be seen, at a latitude of roughly 66.5° north. In Finland the Arctic Circle is called **Napapiiri** and it crosses the main Rovaniemi–Sodankylä road about 8km north of Rovaniemi (although the Arctic Circle can actually shift several metres daily). From here on up the never truly sets in midsummer and never rises in midwinter.

Even though the Arctic Circle can be crossed by road at several points in Lapland, the official **Arctic Circle marker** is right here, conveniently painted on the roadside – and built right on top of it is the 'official' **Santa Claus Village** (www.santaclausvillage .info; admission free; 9am-7pm Dec-late Aug, 10am-5pm late Aug-Nov). Nowhere else in Finland is there such an unadulterated shrine to commercialism. The **Santa Claus Main Post Office** (FIN-96930 Arctic Circle) is here, and it receives half a million letters each year from children all over the world (with kids from the UK, Italy, Poland and France the biggest correspondents). As tacky and trite as this may sound, it's all good fun, and you can send a postcard home with an official Santa stamp (for €6 you can arrange to have it delivered at Christmas). In a nearby building is the home of the portly saint himself (www.santaclauslive .com); it's free to queue up to meet the jolly man (present during opening hours except 11am to noon and 3 to 4pm), who is quite a linguist, but check with the bank manager before promising the children photos – they are €17 each and you aren't allowed to take your own. Tour groups have great fun crossing the line painted on the asphalt (supposedly marking the circle) in order to be awarded their Arctic Circle certificates (€4.20).

If you're not interested in all the hype, the village still has some of the best souvenir and handicraft shops in Lapland, some good cafés and restaurants, a traditional salmon-smoking fire, and Etiäinen, the information centre for national parks and trekking regions (see p296).

The village is 8km north of Rovaniemi on the Sodankylä–Ivalo road. Bus 8 heads there from town.

Santapark

This Christmas-theme **amusement park** (333 0000; www.santapark.com; adult/child/family €20/15/50; 10am-6pm Tue-Sun late Nov–mid-Jan, 10am-4pm Easter holidays & Tue-Sat Midsummer–mid- Aug) at Syväsenvaara Mountain is 2km west of the Rovaniemi airport. Local buses connect the park with the city centre. Additionally, there is a free shuttle service between Santa Claus Village and Santapark, or in winter you can pay a fee to travel by snowmobile or reindeer sleigh between the two attractions. Santapark is built inside a cavern in the mountain and features an army of elves baking gingerbread, a magic sleigh ride, a Christmas carousel, an ice-bar, a theatre, a restaurant and, of course, Santa Claus himself. It's great fun for young kids but otherwise give it a miss. Discount ticket packages are available for families.

Ranua Zoo

The town of Ranua, 82km south of Rovaniemi, on Road 78, is home to the **Ranua Zoo** (355 1921; www.ranuazoo.com; adult/child Apr-Sep €12/8.50, Oct-Mar €10/8.50; 9am-7pm Jun-Aug, 10am-4pm Sep-May), the northernmost of all such parks and a popular day trip from Rovaniemi. Its 30 mammal and 30 bird species – including brown and polar bears, forest reindeer, owls, lynx, Arctic fox and wolverines – are native to Finland and the Arctic and are housed in spacious natural enclosures linked by a 3km circular path. Remember that the bears hibernate from November to March.

There are daily buses to Ranua from Oulu and Kajaani, and several daily connections from Rovaniemi (€22.90 return, 1¼ hours). There's a hotel, which also has dormitory accommodation, the **Ilveslinna** (355 1201; www.hotelliilveslinna.fi; dm from €15, r from €50;) within walking distance of the zoo.

WESTERN LAPLAND

YLLÄS
 016

Ylläs, 35km northeast of Kolari, is the highest fell in Finland to offer downhill skiing. On either side of the mountain are the villages Äkäslompolo and Ylläsjärvi. Both are typical ski-resort towns filled with top-end hotels and holiday cottages, although

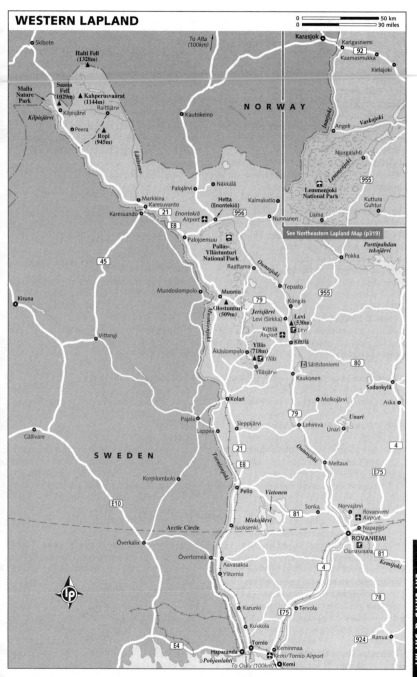

WESTERN LAPLAND

See Northeastern Lapland Map (p319)

LAPLAND & SÁPMI

Ylläsjärvi is smaller and virtually shuts down outside the ski season. Äkäslompolo is a nice place to be in summer: it sits by the edge of a lake and pretty river, and there are plenty of good walks around here. The village itself is mostly on the main road; the ski slopes are 5km up a side road. On the other side of the mountain, the centre of Ylläsjärvi is also about 5km from its slopes.

The ski area is at the southern boundary of Pallas-Yllästunturi National Park (see p308).

Kellokas Nature Centre (☎ 020-564 7039; kellokas@metsa.fi; Tunturintie 54) is a national parks visitor centre at the foot of the fell's western slopes, 4km from Äkäslompolo village. It has environmental and geological exhibits on the surrounding area and multimedia displays, as well as maps, information and advice on hiking in the park.

For tourist information in Äkäslompolo, contact **Ylläksen Matkailu Oy** (☎ 510 5100; www.yllaksenmatkailu.fi).

Activities

SKIING & SNOWBOARDING

Ylläs has 37 downhill slopes and 17 lifts, plus special areas for snowboarders. The vertical drop is 463m and the longest run is 3km. Cross-country skiing trails total 250km. Lift passes cost €26 per day and equipment rental and ski lessons are available. The ski season usually runs from November to May.

MOUNTAIN BIKING & HIKING

In summer Ylläs is popular with mountain-biking enthusiasts. **Ylläs Holiday Service** (☎ 569 666) rents bikes (from €11.80 a day) and has guided bike tours.

There are numerous nature trails and hiking possibilities in the region. A couple of long-distance treks head to Olos or Levi from Ylläs (50km to 55km); there are several shorter trails including the 3.5km **Varkaankuru** ('Thieves' Gorge') nature trail, and the 15km **Kiiruna Circuit**, both of which start from the Kellokas Nature Centre. For experienced hikers it's possible to walk all the way to Pallastunturi (72km) and from there on to Hetta beyond the park's northern boundary (see p309).

Sleeping

There are plenty of empty hotel rooms and cottages around Ylläs during summer. For accommodation bookings, contact **Ylläs Majoituspalvelut** (Ylläsjärvi ☎ 482 000, Äkäslompolo ☎ 0208-692 585).

Holiday Centre Seita (☎ 569 211; www.seitahotelli.fi; 2-4 person cottages May-Aug €52-67; P X R) On the main road in Äkäslompolo is a complex including a hotel, cottages, restaurant and smoke sauna, and it's one of the more reasonably priced places. In the winter high season rooms and cottages are let only by the week from €280 to €560 per person; in the summer the large grassy grounds are very pleasant.

Hotel Ylläshumina (☎ 569 501; www.yllashumina.com; Tiurajärventie; s/d €69/86; P X) In Äkäslompolo, near the lake, is this flamboyant complex that looks like a wooden peacock in a courtship display. It's got reasonably priced apartments for rent and a good restaurant-pub.

Getting There & Away

During the ski season, there is a shuttle service from Kittilä airport to Ylläsjärvi (€10) and Äkäslompolo (€13). Phone ☎ 0600 14919 for bookings.

The nearest train station is at Kolari and there are connecting buses to Ylläsjärvi and Äkäslompolo.

A few long-distance buses travel via Äkäslompolo each week. For Ylläsjärvi, catch one of the local buses that run Monday to Friday between Kolari and Kittilä.

KITTILÄ

☎ 016 / pop 5833

One of the main service centres for northwestern Lapland, Kittilä has little to recommend it to travellers except as a base or jumping-off point for the ski resort of Levi, 17km to the north. Although Kittilä is the regional centre, Levi is now, in fact, so big and trendy that roles have been effectively reversed, at least in winter time.

Gasthaus Kultaisen Ahman Majatalo (☎ 642 043; Valtatie 42; summer s/d €40/50, winter €50/76) a friendly B&B right in the village centre, with breakfast served in your room. **Hotelli Kittilä** (☎ 643 201; hotelli.kittila@levi.fi; Valtatie 49; s/d €51/59, high season €69/95; P X R), on the main road, is Kittilä's only real hotel. Rooms are spacious, and there's a sauna and a small pool. The restaurant serves a good buffet lunch (€8) and there's dancing and entertainment some evenings.

LAPLAND & SÁPMI

There are daily flights between Helsinki and Kittilä. The airport is 4km north of town. Four buses a day run between Rovaniemi and Kittilä (2½ hours). All stop at the K petrol station, and continue to Levi.

LEVI (SIRKKA)

☎ 016

Levi is a skiing centre that has experienced massive growth in recent years, and now attracts equivalent numbers of visitors to Ruka (p286), placing it at the top of the tree as far as Finnish skiing is concerned. There are several nightclubs, some fine restaurants and plenty of accommodation in a fairly compact area; most of the action is within a stone's throw of the lifts. For this reason, Levi hosts many high-profile skiing competitions. Levi is actually the name of the fell, while Sirkka is the village, but most people refer to the whole place as Levi.

The ski season usually runs from November to May, with the busiest period in March and April, when the snow is good, temperatures aren't extreme, and there's a bit of sun. In summer and autumn, trekking and mountain biking are the main outdoor activities.

The efficient and informative **Levin Matkailu Oy Keskusvaraamo** (☎ 639 3300; www.levi.fi; Myllyojantie 2; 🕑 9am-4.30pm Mon-Fri, 11am-4pm Sat & Sun, open weekends until 5.30pm at busy periods) is the tourist information centre and accommodation booking agency. It's behind the teepee-like building on the roundabout in the centre of the resort. Staff can book accommodation, including cottages, and activities such as snowmobile safaris, dog-sled treks and reindeer rides. Many independent tour operators are based in Sirkka/Levi, making it a good place to join organised tours – from canoeing in summer to dog-sledding in winter.

Activities

SKIING & SNOWBOARDING

Levi ski resort (☎ 641 246; leviskiresort@levi.fi) has 47 downhill slopes and 26 lifts (four are free children's lifts, one is a gondola). The vertical drop is approximately 325m, and the longest run is 2.5km. There are two half-pipes and a superpipe for snowboarders, a snow park, and several ski runs for children. Don't let the Arctic darkness put you off either; the main slope is well-lit and stays open until 8pm.

Opportunities for cross-country skiing are also good, with trails totalling 230km, 28km of that illuminated. On longer ski treks, you can stay overnight in wilderness huts, which have supplies of firewood.

In the high season (February to early May), lift tickets cost €4/3 per adult/child for a single ride, €16.50/10 for one hour, €30/19 for one day, and €144/86 for a week. Rates are lower in summer and midwinter. Downhill, telemark and cross-country skis, snowboards, sleds and snowshoes are all available for rental. Standard ski rental costs from €23/83 per day/week; snowboards and boots are €22/90 a day/week. Lessons are also available at Levi.

CANOEING

The long Ounasjoki is one of the best canoeing routes in Lapland. The river runs from Hetta in the north to Rovaniemi in the south, and passes through Raattama, Levi, Kittilä and Kaukonen. **PerheSafarit** (☎ 643 861, 040-504 7364) runs excursions and rents equipment.

DOG-SLEDDING

In winter, **Polar Speed Tours** (☎ 653 447; www .levi.fi/polarspeed) organises one- to five-day dog-sledding safaris, with accommodation in wilderness huts. The dogs are kennelled at a **husky farm** (☎ 040-570 6572; 🕑 10am-4pm) at Köngäs, 10km northeast of Levi. In summer you can tour the farm (adult/child €4/2) and meet the dogs.

OTHER ACTIVITIES

There are numerous other things you can turn your hand to in Levi and the surrounding area, demanding greater or lesser adrenalin levels: snowmobiling, fishing, horse-riding, moped safaris, reindeer races and hot-air ballooning! Due to be opened in summer 2006 is a much-hyped golf course; where else in the world do the greenkeepers get seven months' holiday?! Contact the tourist office for details.

Sleeping & Eating

Levi is one of Finland's most popular winter holiday centres and prices go through the roof in the peak season of February to May and in December, too.

For apartment/cottage rentals, head straight for the tourist information office, which is also an accommodation booking agency. There's a huge variety of apartments and cottages; in the height of the winter season, expect to pay €1000 to €2000 for a week right in the centre for an all-mod-cons apartment sleeping four to six. In summer, though, you can get a good cottage from €40 per night, sleeping four. Hotel prices are also heavily reduced at this time.

Hotelli K5 Levi (☎ 639 1100; www.k5levi.fi; Kätkän-rannantie 2; r Mar-Apr €169-180, May-Aug €74, rest of year €108-145; P ✗ ☐) Right opposite the tourist office, this sleek modern hotel is Levi's most stylish lodging option. The rooms are excellent; most come with sauna and glassed-in balcony, and those that don't have a Jacuzzi. There are also good family rooms and 16 classy holiday apartments. All rooms feature very comfortable new beds and DVD players (free movies at reception). Although the design is as classy as in any Helsinki hotel, they haven't forgotten where they are: there's a laundry, mountain bikes and sets of skis free for guests' use, and a drying cupboard in all the rooms. There are two good restaurants, one of them specialising in Lapp dishes.

Hullu Poro (Crazy Reindeer; ☎ 651 0100; www.hul luporo.fi; ski season d with sauna €90-160, d without sauna €80-110, summer from €56/66; P ✗) A bit off the main Sirkka–Levi road, this place has good rooms, a little more expensive with sauna, and some designed for families, as well as eight-person duplex apartments. There also are four very popular restaurants, and a venue, the Areena, with live music almost every night in ski season, DJs, and dancing on two floors. In winter, it also operates the Snow Guesthouse, in Köngäs, 10km north-east of Levi. It's made entirely of snow and ice, and has seven beautiful rooms.

Hotel Levitunturi Spa (☎ 646 301; www.hotel lilevitunturi.fi; high season s/d €140/165, May-Sep r €80; P ✗ ☐ ☚ ♿) Opposite the tourist office in the heart of the resort, this is a good hotel with spa facilities that are a blessing after a day on the slopes. It's very family-friendly – there's even a 'ball pool'. The complex has five restaurants (grouped together under the moniker 'Restaurant World': is 1500 covers really a selling point?) and also a lively nightlife in winter. Nonguests can use the spa facilities for €12 for 1½ hours.

Tiikun Tii Pii (☎ 0400 405 415; tiikuntiipii@levi.fi; Kätkäntie; €50 per head; ☚ evenings by arrangement) The most interesting eating option by far, this is a Lapp hut 2.5km from the centre which is bookable for two to 15 people. You get a drink on arrival and watch the traditional dishes being prepared (nettle soup, smoked reindeer steak or salmon, Lapp cheese), before enjoying them in the cosy interior. Drinks with the meal are included in the price (you can also bring your own), and there's plenty of entertainment, such as story-telling the Sámi way *(yoiks)*. It's a lot of fun. You must book ahead; there are normally two timeslots per night (6pm and 9pm).

For a meal or a drink with panoramic views, **Ravintola Tuikku** (☎ 640 601; mains €13-25) is perched right on top of the fell and looks over the surrounding hills and lakes. It's open year-round and can be reached by chairlift or by road. During the height of the ski-season it has theme nights: fondue, six-course specials, and more.

Getting There & Away

Sirkka/Levi is on road 79, 170km north of Rovaniemi. All buses from Rovaniemi to Kittilä continue on to here; some Muonio-bound buses also stop. A bus also meets all incoming flights at the Kittilä airport, 15km to the south. During the ski season, there are direct buses from Helsinki to Levi, leaving on Fridays at 7.45pm.

MUONIO
☎ 016
The village of Muonio is the last signifi-cant stop on road 21 before Kilpisjärvi and Norway. There are plenty of places to stay around here, and some low-key skiing in winter. The wooden **church** in Muonio dates from 1817. When the village was burned during WWII, the church was somehow spared. The local **open-air museum** (admission free; ☚ 10am-5pm Tue-Sat summer) is a collection of prewar buildings and local artefacts.

Sights & Activities

The large, modern **Kiela Naturium** (☎ 532 280; www.kielanaturium.fi; ☚ 10am-6pm Mon-Sat mid-Feb–mid-Apr & Jul-Sep, to 5pm Mon-Fri mid-Apr–Jun & Oct–mid-Feb) opened in 2002 and combines tourist information, a nifty 3D multi-media fells nature display controlled by touch-panel and joystick, an interesting planetarium with an aurora borealis show (adult/child €10/6; every 20 minutes),

---

THE NORTHERN LIGHTS

The northern lights, or aurora borealis, are an utterly haunting, exhilarating and memorable sight, and they are often visible to observers standing at or above the Arctic Circle (latitude 66º), which includes a large portion of Lapland. They're especially visible around the equinoxes (late September and March), and are particularly striking during the dark winter; in summer, the sun more or less renders them invisible.

The aurora appears as curtains of greenish-white light stretching east to west across the sky for thousands of kilometres. At its lower edge, the aurora typically shades to a crimson-red glow. Hues of blue and violet can also be seen. The lights seem to shift and swirl in the night sky – they can almost be said to dance.

The northern lights have a less famous southern counterpart, the aurora australis or southern lights, which encircles the South Pole. Both are oval in shape with a diameter of approximately 2000km.

These auroral storms, however eerie, are quite natural. They're created when charged particles (protons and electrons) from the sun bombard the earth. These are deflected towards the north and south poles by the Earth's magnetic field. There they hit the earth's outer atmosphere, 100km to 1000km above ground, causing highly charged electrons to collide with molecules of nitrogen and oxygen. The excess energy from these collisions creates the colourful lights we see in the sky.

The ancients had other explanations for the spectacle: the Greeks described it as 'blood rain'; the Inuit attributed the phenomenon to 'sky dwellers'; and the ancient inhabitants of Lapland believed it was caused by a giant fox swishing its tail above the Arctic tundra. The Finnish word for the northern lights is *revontulet* (literally 'foxfires').

---

restaurant and gift shop. Even if you're just passing through, it's worth pausing to look around in here.

Three kilometres south of the centre, the excellent **Harriniva Holiday Centre** (☎ 530 0300; www.harriniva.fi) has a vast programme of summer and winter activities for individuals or small groups. These range from a couple of hours to multiday adventures. It also rents canoes and kayaks for exploring the Muonionjoki, fishing equipment and mountain bikes, and it organises guided mountain-bike and hiking tours. In winter, there are excellent dog-sledding safaris from 1½ hours (€60) to two days (€440), or week-long trips combining dogs, reindeer and snowmobiling (€1390). In summer, the centre offers daily guided white-water rafting trips from €25 for a 1½-hour trip.

Harriniva has the **Arktinen Rekikoirakeskus** (Arctic sled-dog centre) with over 400 loveable dogs, all with names and personalities, and a great guided tour of their town (for that is what it is) is €7/4 per adult/child. This is the best tour in Lapland as far as learning about the different breeds of huskies and their characteristics. You should prebook it the day before; there are three departures daily.

Birdwatchers should get a canoe and head out on Muonionjärvi, which teems with life in early summer. There's a bird-watching tower on the shore and another on Rukomasaari.

Sleeping & Eating

Harriniva Holiday Centre (s/d summer €68/78, autumn €78/88, winter up to €120/140, cabin for 1-/3-persons from €20/36, apt from €95; (P) (X)) The Harriniva is also a good place to stay. There are simple cabins by the river (nice but plenty of mosquitoes), as well as good hotel rooms and apartments. There's also a good restaurant and bar here; the kitchen is open until 10.30pm, and the pub is about the liveliest in Muonio.

Lomamaja Pekonen (☎ 532 237; fax 532 236; Lahenrannantie 10; s/d €26/40, cottages €27-59) This place is near the centre of Muonio. It's friendly, and has rooms and a range of cottages in a slightly cramped area by the river, as well as canoes and bicycles for rent and guided trips of the Muonionjoki in summer.

Restaurant Kammari (www.kammari.com; mains €7.50-14.50; ⏰ 2pm-midnight) By the Hotel Olos, at the ski area 6km east of town, this restaurant is the best place for pizzas, steaks, hamburgers and kebabs. It's a friendly spot, with a cosy, intimate dining room.

Getting There & Away

Muonio is at the junction of Lapland's main two northwest-bound roads; the 21, which runs from Tornio to Kilpisjärvi, and the 79, which runs northwest from Rovaniemi via Kittilä.

There are three daily buses from Rovaniemi (€32.30, 3½ hours) via Kittilä, and services from Kemi/Tornio.

HETTA (ENONTEKIÖ)

☎ 016

Hetta (signposted and labelled on some maps as Enontekiö), is the centre of the municipality of Enontekiö, and a good place to start trekking and exploration of the area. This is the northern end of the popular Pallastunturi Trek (right), which brings many travellers to the village. Hetta has a large Sámi population, and although not a big place, with just a few dozen houses on either side of the road, it's very likeable and has some excellent spots to bed down for the night.

The **Tunturi-Lapin Luontokeskus** (☎ 0205-647 950; ☺ 9am-8pm Mon-Fri, 9am-5pm Sat & Sun in summer, Sep & Mar-Apr, 9am-4pm Mon-Fri at other times) at the eastern end of town provides information about Pallas-Yllästunturi National Park, and doubles as the **main tourist office** (☎ 556 211; www.enontekio.fi). There are interesting nature displays relating to the park and slide shows (on request) in English, as well as a café.

In the centre of Hetta is the slender-spired **Enontekiö church** (☺ summer), built in 1952 with the financial help of American churches. The organ was a gift from Germany. The church has an altar mosaic that pictures Christ blessing Lapland and its people.

A less permanent building is the annual **snow castle**, freezing from mid-December to mid-April.

The biggest festival in Hetta is Marianpäivä (feast day of the Annunciation), usually celebrated in March; there are Sámi dances and engagement parties, and the town buzzes with activity.

Sleeping & Eating

Hetan Majatalo (☎ 554 0400; www.hetan-majatalo.fi; s/d summer €57/76, rest of year €62/84; P ⊠ ⬚ ⬚) A great place to stay, this fine guesthouse

is of comfortable hotel standard and very friendly. Set back from the main road, it's quiet but in the centre of town, and has a peaceful garden. The rooms are good, with TV and bathroom; breakfast and use of the sauna are included. At busy periods they do a buffet lunch.

Hetan Lomakyla (☎ 521 521, 0400 205 408; tent sites €10-14, 2-person cabin €45, small/large cottages €60/80; ☺ Mar-Oct) This place has a very upmarket set of grey-painted wooden cottages with kitchen, sauna and a loft sleeping area, as well as simpler cabins. It's good-value and very friendly, and there are various discounts and activities on offer.

Lapland Hotels Hetta (☎ 521 361; www.lapland hotels.com; hostel s/d summer €52/64, peak €74/90, hotel s/d summer €74/90, peak €116/128; ☺ Feb-Apr, Jun-Sep, Nov & Dec; P ⊠ ⬚ ⬚) At the eastern end of town towards the visitor centre, this hotel has two classes of room: 'hostel' rooms that have their own toilet but shared shower and hotel rooms that are spacious, with large beds. There are also apartments for rental, and a good restaurant open for dinner only.

Hotelli Jussantupa (☎ 521 101; www.jussantupa.fi; ⬚) This is in the town centre and is a bit of a focal point. It has a good restaurant and the most popular bar in town, with dancing on weekends. The hotel has a sauna.

Ounasloma (☎ 521 055, 049-396 510; tent sites €8, cabins from €43, cottages with sauna from €68; ☺ Mar-Oct) This is a friendly place with a series of excellent cottages and camping facilities in a nice little area by the river. They have free boats and do skiing excursions.

Getting There & Away

Finnair flies to Enontekiö regularly, sometimes via Rovaniemi. The airport is 7km west of Hetta.

Buses to Hetta run daily from Rovaniemi (€42, five hours) via Kittilä and Muonio. One bus continues in summer to Kautokeino in Norway. To get to Kilpisjärvi from Hetta, you have to change buses at Palojoensuu. There are also buses to Hetta from Muonio.

PALLAS-YLLÄSTUNTURI NATIONAL PARK

☎ 016

Now the third-largest national park in Finland, it was created in 2005 from the previous Pallas-Ounastunturi Park, established in 1938, and the former Ylläs Nature Reserve. It now forms a long, thin area running from Hetta in the north to the Ylläs ski area in the south (see p302). The main attraction is the excellent 55km trekking route from the village of Hetta to Pallastunturi in the middle of the park, where there's a hotel, information centre and transport connections. Experienced trekkers can continue from here to Ylläs, although there are few facilities as yet on that section. In winter, Pallastunturi Fell is a small but popular place for both cross-country and downhill skiing. The longest slope is 2km.

Pallastunturi Nature Centre (☎ 0205-647 930; pallastunturi@metsa.fi; ☽ 9am-5pm daily Jun-Sep, 9am-4pm Mon-Fri Oct-May) at Pallastunturi Fell sells trekking maps (€18), makes reservations for locked huts (€9) and provides information and advice about the region, and its flora and fauna. It has slide presentations in several languages. You'll also find a **nature centre** in Hetta (opposite) and another one in Äkäslompolo (p302).

Trekking Route

The 55km trek from Hetta village to Pallastunturi (or vice versa) is one of the easiest in the country: pretty, flattish, light forest cover with sandy soil. It takes three to four days to complete. The route is well marked, with poles every 50m or so, and there are several wilderness huts along the way (see right).

The popularity and ease of this trek means that some huts get pretty crowded at peak times – at Hannukuru hut there may be up to 60 people staying at one time!

Day 1 Starting from Hetta village, you must cross a lake to get to the national park. There is a boat-taxi that costs €4. Walk 7km through a forest to Pyhäkero hut, then ascend to the high Pyhäkero (peak), which is part of Ounastunturi Fell. It's 7km to Sioskuru hut.

Day 2 This section of the trail is mostly treeless plateau with good visibility. You might want to take a detour to Tappuri hut for lunch before continuing to Pahakuru hut (10km). If it's full, continue 2km to Hannukuru, the 'capital' of the Pallastunturi Fell area.

Day 3 The first leg is 5km over relatively difficult terrain to a small *laavu* (simple shelter) where you can cook lunch. Another 9km takes you through pleasant mountains to the small hut of Montelli. If it is full, continue 1km on to Nammalankuru hut.

Day 4 The final day takes you through some magnificent high mountains. There is only one place to stop, a simple *laavu* and campfire place 2.5km from Nammalankuru. From here, it's a 10km uphill walk to Hotel Pallastunturi.

On to Ylläs It's about 70km from Pallastunturi to the park's southernmost border, by the ski resorts at Ylläs. It's about 21km to the village of Rauka from Pallastunturi, and then another 11km to the Pahtavuoma hut. Beyond here, there's a simple shelter at Kotamaja, and several fireplace points.

Sleeping

WILDERNESS HUTS

For trekkers in the national park, free accommodation is available in wilderness huts. Following is a list of huts from north to south.

Pyhäkero This hut is 7km from the lake. There is room for six people, and a gas stove and a toilet. In March and April there's also a café.

Sioskuru Sioskuru is 8km from Pyhäkero hut and accommodates up to 16 people. There are mattresses, a gas stove, a telephone and some dry firewood. There's a rental cabin here also, sleeping up to eight.

Tappuri This nice hut is 1km off the main path. It accommodates eight people, and has a gas stove and good drinking water from a nearby creek.

Pahakuru This hut is 11km from Sioskuru. It sleeps up to six people, and has a gas stove and a toilet. You'll need to walk a few hundred metres to get water.

Hannukuru Just 2km from Pahakuru, and at the halfway point on the route, this hut has room for 16 people, but it is often full. There are mattresses, a gas stove and a telephone here, plus plenty of firewood and a lakeside sauna. There's also a rental cabin sleeping up to eight.

Montelli This intimate little hut on the high fells has a fireplace and sleeps four people. It's 12km beyond Hannukuru and 15km from Pallastunturi.

Nammalankuru Just 2km beyond Montelli hut is this large hut that accommodates 16 people. There is a gas stove, a telephone and fine fell scenery. There's also a rental cabin sleeping up to eight.

Pahtavuoma This hut is 32km south of Pallastunturi on the route to Ylläs. It's low-roofed and sleeps up to four. It has a fireplace.

HOTELS

Hotel Pallas (☎ 532 441; www.laplandhotels.com; s/d winter €111/142, summer €52/64; P ⊠) This noble old wooden place is up in the fells, 50m from the national park information centre, and just what you want to see when you finish your trek from Hetta. The first hotel in Lapland was built on this site in 1938. There are cheaper rooms, which have their own toilet but share a shower. Rates include a good all-you-can-eat breakfast. It's overpriced during the ski season, but good value at other times; it's friendly and has a tame summer reindeer hanging around. There's a nice lakeside sauna and you can jump in the hole in the ice in winter!

Getting There & Away

In summer, there's a daily bus from Muonio to Pallastunturi (€5, 40 minutes). At other times, you'll have to hitch or call a local taxi on ☎ 538 582, or ☎ 0400 393 103.

KILPISJÄRVI

☎ 016

The remote village of Kilpisjärvi, the northernmost settlement in the 'arm' of Finland, is on the doorstep of both Norway and Sweden. At 480m above sea level, this small border post, wedged between the lake of Kilpisjärvi and the magnificent surrounding fells, is also the highest village in Finland. Unless you're just passing through on your way to Tromsøor Narvik in Norway, the main reason to venture out here is for summer trekking or spring cross-country skiing. There are popular walks to the joint border post of Finland, Norway and Sweden, up the spectacular Saana Fell, home to the rough-legged buzzard, and longer treks to Finland's highest fell, Halti (1328m).

Every Midsummer, the folk of Kilpisjärvi put on a ski race at Saana Fell, where the snow may not melt until mid-July. From Saana, you'll see pockets of snow in the mountains of Norway that almost never melt.

Kilpisjärvi consists of two small settlements 5km apart – the main (southern) centre has the information office, the hotel, petrol station and supermarket, as well as most of the accommodation. The northern knot, 2km shy of the border, has the Kilpisjärven Retkeilykeskus (Kilpisjärvi Hiking Centre) and a shop.

Information

Kilpisjärven Retkeilykeskus (Kilpisjärvi Hiking Centre; ☎ 537 771; www.kilpisjarvi.info) This is a central meeting place for all trekkers. They hire bikes and hiking and skiing equipment. There's also a café here and accommodation close to the main walking routes.

Luontotalo (☎ 020-564 7990; kilpisjarvi@metsa.fi; 9am-8pm Mon-Fri, 9am-5pm Sat & Sun Jun-Sep, 9am-4pm Mon-Fri Oct-May) At the southern end of the village, this new national parks centre is effectively the tourist information office. It has maps and advice on trekking and a nature display.

Activities

TREKKING

The area around Kilpisjärvi offers fantastic trekking. Routes range from easy day treks to demanding two-week treks into the mountains.

A marked loop route to slate-capped **Saana Fell** (1029m) starts at Kilpisjärven Retkeilykeskus and takes around three to four hours return if you walk to the summit. There's a longer loop trail that takes eight hours.

Another incredibly popular day trek is the 15km route through **Malla Nature Park** to the joint border crossing of Finland, Sweden and Norway. At the border crossing is a free wilderness hut, where you can stay overnight. Alternatively, there's a daily **boat service** (☎ 0400 669 392; one way/return €11/16; 1hr return) at 10am, 2pm and 6pm from May to August to a short distance from the border, allowing you to visit the easy way, or to walk only the return leg.

For experienced trekkers, a one- to two-week trip from Saana Fell to **Halti Fell** (1328m), the highest point in Finland (there is still snow in June), is a demanding but rewarding trip. All trekking routes and wilderness huts around the Kilpisjärvi area are clearly displayed on the 1:100,000 *Käsivarsi* map (€18). The 1:50,000 *Kilpisjärvi* topographical sheet (€6) covers a smaller area.

SCENIC FLIGHTS

There is a heliport at the southern end of Kilpisjärvi. Helicopter sightseeing flights cost around €100 per person with minimum numbers required. For information, call **Heliflite** (☎ 537 743; www.heliflite.fi).

Sleeping & Eating

There are heaps of campsites with cabins lining the main road. Many places are only open during the trekking season, which is June to September.

Hotel Kilpisjärven (☎ 537 761; www.kilpis-hotel .com; s/d €65/75, 3-/4-bed apt €105/123) This hotel is on the main road through Kilpisjärvi, opposite the supermarket. It's a comfortable place, and one of the centres of village life. It has two grades of room: the 'hostel' beds share showers. Its large restaurant (open 3.30 to 11pm; mains €13 to €24) serves some tasty Lapp dishes, including a 'Northern Union': tender reindeer fillet and salmon (€24). The bar is open until 2am and is about as lively as Kilpisjärvi can offer.

Kilpisjärven Retkeilykeskus (☎ 537 771; retkeily keskus@sunpoint.net; tent sites €12, s/d €50/60,4-person cottages €65; ⊙ Jun-Sep) This place, close to the border but 5km north of the village, is conveniently close to the trekking routes and is a centre for information. You'll find a range of rooms and cottages here all of them with a private bathroom. The restaurant dishes up a good all-you-can-eat buffet lunch daily in the high season (€10, open 2 to 7pm daily).

Kilpisjärven Lomakylä (☎ 537 801, 0400 396 684; www.kilpisjarvi.net; camping €10-14, cabins €90-150, apt €70-120) This is the best of the clutch of camping 'n' cabins sites in the centre of Kilpisjärvi. It's got a café, and some excellent wooden cottages and apartments with their own sauna, loft bedroom, fully-equipped kitchen, TV and video (films at reception). These are great value in summer.

As well as the restaurants at the hotel and Kilpisjärven Retkeilykeskus, there's a cheap grilli next door to the supermarket, and **Ida-Sofie Café** (☎ 539 229), serving yummy Lappish dishes and snacks.

Getting There & Away

There is a daily bus connection between Rovaniemi and Kilpisjärvi (€53.50, six to eight hours) via Kittilä and Muonio.

It's a spectacular drive on the excellent sealed road from Muonio to Kilpisjärvi (almost 200km). There are service stations at the small settlement of Kaaresuvanto (where there's a border crossing into Sweden) and in Kilpisjärvi itself. Two kilometres north of Kilpisjärvi, the road continues into Norway and a spectacular ascent through mountains before descending to the fjords.

EASTERN LAPLAND

KEMIJÄRVI

☎ 016 / pop 9,500

Kemijärvi is an alternative gateway to Lapland, situated on the important north–south highway 5, at the end of the northeastern railway line. It's a pleasant enough place on a spectacular lake, although the crisscross road network and sprawling suburbs diminish the appeal. The centre is compact, and there are a couple of good places to stay.

The **tourist office** (☎ 878 394; Vapaudenkatu 8; ⊙ 9am-4pm Mon-Fri year-round; 🖳) is in the centre of town and like the **public library** (Hietaniemenkatu 3) has free Internet access. Nearby is a bookshop to stock up on English paperbacks for the long Lapp nights.

Kemijärvi's biggest attraction apart from the lake are the fine wooden sculptures dotted throughout the town, legacies of the international wood-sculpting festivals.

Festivals & Events

The **Kemijärvi Sculpture Week**, a festival of woodcarving, is held in late June or early July every odd year. It attracts artists from many European countries and is an interesting event as all the woodcarvers work outside, in view of the public.

In mid-September, Kemijärvi hosts **Ruska Swing**, a festival of swing dancing and swing music. Participants come from around the world, and there is a special 'Swing Train' from Helsinki.

Sleeping & Eating

Mestarin Kievari (☎ 813 577; www.mestarinkievari .fi; Kirkkokatu 9; s/d €70/85, summer €68/78, mains €10-24, lunch buffet €10; Ⓟ ✕) This is the best place to sleep and dine in town. The rooms themselves are fairly simple with wooden floorboards and small beds; some of the single rooms have their own sauna. The restaurant has a menu ranging from pizza and salads to gourmet fish and game dishes.

Hostel Kemijärvi (☎ 040-581 2007; fax 813 342; Lohelankatu 1; dm from €16, s/d €32/45; Ⓟ ✕) This place on the lake, 300m west of the camping ground, is HI-affiliated, with a kitchen, sauna and boats for rent. The same owners have cottages for rent nearby.

Hietaniemi Camping (☎ 813 640; tent sites €8, 4-person cabin €30-40; ⊙ Mar-late Sep) Just 200m west of the town centre on Pöyliöjärvi, a secondary part of the main lake. There are good-value newly built cabins. You can rent boats and bikes here.

Getting There & Away

The bus terminal is in the centre of town. There are services to Pyhä (€7.50), Rovaniemi (€15.20), Sodankylä (€18.90) and elsewhere. There's one daily train to Helsinki, via Rovaniemi (€12.80, 1½ hours).

SODANKYLÄ

☎ 016 / pop 9336

The pleasant village of Sodankylä is a busy service centre for the expansive surrounding area, which has a population density of just 0.8 people per sq km! It's at the important junction of the main two southbound highways and makes a decent staging post on the way between Rovaniemi and the north; even if you're just passing through, stop to see the wooden church – humble but achingly beautiful. Sodankylä can also be used as a base for visiting the ski fields at Pyhä and Luosto and the amethyst mine at Lampivaara.

The **tourist office** (☎ 618 168; www.sodankyla.fi; Jäämerentie 7; 🕙 9am-5pm Mon-Fri) is at the intersection of the Kemijärvi and Rovaniemi roads on the main street. Opposite is the library, with Internet access. Nearby in a small park, the bronze **statue** of *The Reindeer and the Lapp* celebrates reindeer husbandry, one of Lapland's most important industries.

One of the few buildings in Lapland to survive the massive destruction of the Germans' scorched-earth retreat in WWII is the **old wooden church** (🕙 9am-6pm Jun–mid-Aug, 10am-6pm Fri-Mon rest of Aug) by the tourist office, near the Kitinen riverside. It is the region's oldest and dates back to 1689. The church stands in a graveyard encircled by a low wooden fence and is noteworthy for its decorative shingles and prominent prong-like standards. The interior is simple and charming, with gnarled wooden benches and pulpit, and a simple altar made from leftover beams. A painting of the Last Supper from the early eighteenth century is the only adornment. The stone church nearby was built in 1859.

Andreas Alariesto Art Gallery (☎ 618 643; adult/child €5/2; 🕙 10am-5pm Mon-Sat, noon-6pm Sun Jun–mid-Sep, 10am-5pm Mon-Fri, 10am-4pm Sat, noon-4pm Sun mid-Sep–May), in the same building as the tourist office, displays paintings by the famous Lapp artist Alariesto (1900–89), who favoured a primitive style. There are many images of Sámi life.

By now you've probably seen reindeer wandering the roads, but if you want to learn more about these vital livestock, **Mattila Reindeer Farm** (☎ 0400 187 877; Meltauksentie 975; adult/child €10/5; 🕙 10am-5pm Mon-Fri), at Riipi village 26km southwest of Sodankylä, is a family-run farm where you can meet and feed the reindeer. Phone ahead to arrange a visit; a minimum of four people may be required.

Sleeping & Eating

Majatalo Kolme Veljestä (☎ 611 216; www.majata lokolmeveljesta.fi; Ivalontie 1; s/d/tr €38/54/65; P ✗) This simple guesthouse about 500m north of the bus station has tidy rooms with attractive modern furniture but narrow beds. Guests get free tea and coffee and use of a kitchen; there's also a guest lounge and sauna.

Hotel Sodankylä (☎ 617 121; fax 613 545; Unarintie 15; s/d €85/104, Sat, Sun & summer €70/80; P ✗) This place is right across the road from the bus station. It's a standard brick-built hotel with comfortable rooms that aren't quite worth the price outside of summer. The staff is friendly, and there's a restaurant serving tasty salmon, pork and reindeer dishes, as well as a vegetable hot-pot.

Camping Sodankylä Nilimella (☎ 612 181; www .naturex-ventures.fi; tent sites €12, cabin €34-42; 🕙 Jun–mid-Aug) This camping ground is across the river from the village. It's a friendly place with a sauna and good facilities. The cabins are simple but have a campstove and fridge.

Cafe Kerttuli (☎ 624 383; Jäämerentie 11; mains €7-16; 🕙 10am-7pm Mon-Fri, 11am-4pm Sat) A lovely café with soups, quiches (try the reindeer-and-mushroom pie), cakes, full meals, good coffee and a terrace on the street. There's a lunch special on weekdays for €9. Behind it is the popular local bar, Rooperante.

Pizza-Paikka (☎ 612 990; Jäämerentie 25; pizzas €7-9; 🕙 11am-10pm, 11am-11pm at weekends) At the northern end of the main strip through town, this place has a nice terrace and is fully licensed. Pizzas – and only pizzas – are what they serve, and they are pretty tasty.

Seita Baari (☎ 611 386; Jäämerentie 20) A simple place, with plastic chairs and no frills, that offers good and inexpensive home-made food, including Lappish specialities such as *poronkäristys* (sautéed reindeer).

Getting There & Away

Sodankylä is on the main Rovaniemi–Ivalo road (No 4), and road 5 from Kemijärvi and Karelia ends here. There are regular Gold Line and Express buses from Rovaniemi, Ivalo and Kemijärvi. The bus terminal is just off the main road.

PYHÄ-LUOSTO REGION

☎ 016

The area between the fells of Luosto (514m) and Pyhä (540m) forms a popular winter sports centre, with a skiing season extending from February to May. Most of the area has recently been incorporated into the Pyhä-Luosto National Park, which is excellent for trekking. Pyhä and Luosto, 25km apart, both have ski slopes and are fully serviced resort 'villages'. They make an effort to keep things busy during the summer season as well, with plenty of activities.

Orientation & Information

Pyhä is about 14km from the main Kemijärvi to Sodankylä road, while Luosto is the same distance east of the Rovaniemi–Sodankylä road. A good road connects the two resorts. Luosto is very compact, while Pyhä is spread out: there are services along the road by Pyhäjärvi, but the main ski slope and accommodation is 3km further west (signposted Pyhätunturi).

For information on Pyhä-Luosto National Park and summer activities, such as hiking and fishing, drop by the park's **Pyhätunturi Visitor Centre** (☎ 020-564 7302; pyhatunturi@metsa.fi; ☑ 9am-6pm Jun-Sep & Mar-Apr, 9am-4pm Tue-Fri, Sat 9am-2pm Oct-Feb & May), adjacent to the Pyhä downhill ski centre; follow signs from the main Kemijärvi–Sodankylä road 5.

Just down the hill from here, the **Pyhähippu Reservation Centre** (☎ 882820; www.pyha.fi; ☑ 9am-8pm Nov-Apr & Jul-Sep, 9.30am-5pm at other times) offers tourist information and arranges excellent accommodation at 130 cottages and apartments.

In Luosto, the travel agency **Pyhä-Luosto Matkailu** (☎ 020-730 3020; www.pyha-luostomatkailu .fi; Pyhä-Luostontie 2) also has tourist information for the region, and books cottages. It's open office hours, but at other times head next door to Kerttuli restaurant.

Sights

LAMPIVAARA AMETHYST MINE

The **amethyst mine** (☎ 0400 523 924; www.amethyst mine.fi; Lampivaara Fell; adult/child €12/7; ☑ 11am-5pm Jun–mid-Aug, 11am-4pm mid-Aug–Sep, call for winter opening hours or ask in the amethyst shop in Luosto) 5km above Luosto is the only working amethyst mine in Europe. There are guided tours on the hour, and you get to have a dig around for your own piece of amethyst. The mine is accessible by forest road from Luosto; follow the signs. If you don't have a car, it's a pleasant hike, or €10 flat fare by **taxi** (☎ 106 425).

PYHÄ-LUOSTO NATIONAL PARK

Created in 2005, this 142-sq-km park was a long time in the making, and incorporates Pyhätunturi, previously the oldest national park in Finland, established in 1938. The core of the park is the long line of fells stretching 35km from Pyhä itself to north of Luosto. There are several peaks around the 530m mark, and winding gorges between them. The most notable sight is the 200m deep Isokuru Gorge by Pyhätunturi Fell.

There is a bird-watching tower at the southeastern corner of the park, about 2.5km from the Visitor Centre. A circular nature trail of 5km takes you there.

The small Aittokuru Gorge, just west of Pyhäjärvi, has a spectacular **gorge theatre**, with frequent performances in the summer months. It's well worth a look even if there's nothing on.

ARCTIC ANIMALS

More or less midway between Pyhä and Luosto, **Pyhä-Luosto Husky and Reindeer Park** (☎ 0400 272 714; www.huskysafaris.com; adult/child €12/8; ☑ noon-6pm Jun-Sep) has over a hundred dogs and some reindeer, used in the winter for sled trips. There's a guided visit and presentation at 2pm daily. There's also a café here.

Activities

SKIING

At Pyhä there are 10 ski runs and seven lifts. The longest run is 1.8km, with a vertical drop of 280m. At Luosto, there are seven runs and four lifts, plus a halfpipe and special slopes for snowboarders. The longest ski run is 1.5km, with a vertical drop of 230m.

Between them, Pyhä and Luosto have over 150km of trails for cross-country skiers, some 40km of which are lit. You can rent equipment from the ski centre at either location.

TREKKING

Within Pyhä-Luosto National Park there are several marked hiking trails, including a 10km loop trail to Pyhäkuru Gorge, and a 35km trail to Luosto; this involves plenty of ascents and descents as it climbs from fell to fell. Many of the trails are open in winter to cross-country skiers. These trails start at the Pyhätunturi Visitor Centre; others begin at Luosto, including a 14km circular nature trail crossing the fells to flatlands on the other side.

For an overnight trek, a good map is highly recommended, such as the 1:40,000 *Luosto-Pyhätunturi* map (€4), which can be purchased at the Visitor Centre and in local hotels and resorts. Shorter walks are possible without a map.

Tours
LuontoSafarit (☎ 624 336; www.luosto.fi; Orresokantie 1, Luosto) rents snowmobiles and also runs a series of excursions and safaris on the vehicles. As always, you need a valid drivers license to operate one. In summer, canoeing, quadbiking and hiking trips are offered.

Sleeping & Eating
By far the best places to sleep in Pyhä and Luosto are the cottages and apartments maintained by the agencies listed previously under Information. In summer, for example, €47 will get a luxury apartment or cottage for two, a great deal as most come complete with sofa, balcony, sauna, and fireplace with free firewood, not to mention a fully equipped kitchen and a drying cupboard. Rates increase sharply in winter; this is also true of the hotels.

Hotelli Pyhätunturi (☎ 856 111; www.pyha.fi; summer s/d €51/70; P ⊠ ⌨) This is the main hotel at the Pyhä ski slopes and has attractive rooms and excellent facilities, including gym and Jacuzzis. There is a great view from the hotel's restaurant, Racca – a spacious but fairly romantic place when candlelit. There are also self-contained chalets available.

Hotel Luostotunturi (☎ 620 400; www.luosto tunturi.com; summer r from €70, winter s/d to €116/144; P ⊠ ⌨ ⌨) This curious-looking hotel is in the centre of Luosto and is designed to resemble a reindeer's earmark: a series of distinctive notches cut into the ear. (This however isn't readily apparent.) As well as a range of log cabins for rental, the hotel has good rooms and a spa complex that's just what's needed after a day on the fells. It's open to nonguests (adult/child €11/7), too. The hotel also rents bikes and scooters.

Scandic Hotel Luosto (☎ 624 400; www.scandic -hotels.com; r summer €79; P ⊠) What, an attractive hotel at a ski resort? Indeed, for this long low building in Luosto is just a good old log cabin. Quite a smart one, mind you, and containing what claims to be the

world's 'largest log cabin restaurant'. There are just five rooms in the old cabin; the rest of the accommodation is in luxurious individual cabins, all with their own sauna and fireplace. There is also a site for caravans and campervans by the ski slope.

There are many designated camping areas within a short walk from the Pyhätunturi Visitor Centre.

There are several huts where you can stay overnight in the national park. The most useful is the Huttuloma wilderness hut that sleeps six people. On the Pyhä-Luosto trail, accommodation is possible at Kapusta and Rykimäkuru huts and there's another hut at Yli-Luosto, the end-point of the range of fells and the national park itself.

Getting There & Away
There's a daily bus from Rovaniemi to Luosto (€17, one hour 40 minutes) and Pyhä (€19, two hours), that stops at Rovaniemi airport en route. There's also a bus from Kemijärvi to Pyhä, which operates Monday to Saturday. There are buses between Luosto and Sodankylä on Monday to Friday, from mid-August until the end of May.

SAARISELKÄ REGION
☎ 016
The Saariselkä region includes villages and towns surrounding the Saariselkä Wilderness and Urho K Kekkonen National Park (UKK), the most popular wilderness trekking area in Lapland, if not all of Finland. These outposts have national park information centres, as well as shops and supermarkets where you can grab trekking supplies.

In winter, the region is popular for winter sports, with sleigh safaris, snowmobiling, cross-country and downhill skiing all available.

Saariselkä
Saariselkä village (Sámi: Suolocielgi) is a winter sports centre and also a base for trekkers heading into the Saariselkä Wilderness area. It feels more like a resort than a community, and prices are higher than in other towns in Lapland. All necessary trekking supplies are available in local sports shops and supermarkets, and there are good transport connections to and from town, and plenty of accommodation. It's a

great place to set yourself up for some typically Lappish activities, too.

For information, head for the glamorous new Siula Centre, just off the main road near the Neste petrol station. Saariselkä's increasing popularity with tour groups can be seen by the presence of Marimekko and Iittala design shops; here you will also find the office of **Pohjois-Lapin Matkailu** (North Lapland Tourism; ☎ 668 402; www.saariselka.fi; 🕙 10am-6pm Mon-Fri, 11am-5pm Sat Sep & Apr), the helpful tourist information point. There's Internet access here (€1 per 10 minutes). Next to it is **Metsähallitus Customer Service Point Kiehinen** (☎ 020-564 7200; www.outdoors.fi), an information point for the national parks, with hiking information, maps and a small nature display.

Activities & Tours

Saariselkä has plenty to offer the active traveller. For skiers, there are 12 downhill slopes served by six lifts. The longest run is 1300m and the vertical drop is 180m. There's also a sledge run that's a lot of fun. Cross-country trails in the area total 240km, some 35 of which are lit. Cross-country and downhill ski rentals are available in the village, as are sledges. A lift pass for one/five days costs €29/110 in the peak of the season.

There are many other activities that can be organised here, including dog- and reindeer-sledding (around €65 for two hours), gold-panning (€25), snowmobiling (€60/90 for one/three hours), fishing (€60 for three hours), rafting (€160/230 for one/two days) and mountain biking (€30 for four to five hours). Prices for all these vary according to the operator and the time of year. The big hotels all organise activities, and the tourist office can book them for you too. Other tour operators:

Eräsetti (☎ 668 345; www.erasetti.fi; Saariseläntie 14) Hiking, biking, canoeing, fishing, gold-panning, snowmobiling, dog- and reindeer-sledding, cross-country skiing.

Lapland Safaris(☎ 668 901; www.laplandsafaris .com; Siura Building) Snowmobile safaris, gold-panning and more.

LuontoLoma (☎ 668 706; www.saariselka.fi/luonto loma) Fishing, rafting, snowshoe treks, reindeer- and husky-sleighing, snowmobile rental.

SLEEPING & EATING

Prices in Saariselkä's hotels are highest during the ski season and *ruska* (late August

to mid-September). The **Saariselän Keskusvaraamo Booking Centre** (☎ 668 400; keskusvaraamo@ saariselka.fi) can organise most forms of accommodation in the village, from apartment rentals to log cabins and hotel rooms.

Here, as in other parts of Finland, Villi Pohjola, the accommodation division of the Forest and Park Service, has many rural cabins and cottages for rental. Ask at the Metsähallitus Customer Service Point, or contact **Villi Pohjola** (☎ 020-564 4333; www.villipo hjola.fi) directly.

Saariselän Tunturihotelli (☎ 681 501; www.saarise lantunturihotelli.fi; s/d €105/125, off-season from €85/100; P ✕ ⌨) This fine old hotel is spread over several buildings, including the flamboyant Dalmatian-like Paraspaikka annexe. The rooms and service are good, and there's also a bewildering range of apartments, all of which have their own sauna. They start at €125 for a two-person apartment off-season; an eight-person apartment costs €2210 per week during the high-season, and has a Jacuzzi, balcony, the works.

Holiday Club Saariselkä (☎ 6828; www.holiday club.fi; s/d from €100/126; P ✕ ⌨ 🐾 ♿) This is an enormous spa hotel in the centre of the village. In addition to hotel rooms, holiday chalets are available. There are plenty of leisure activities on offer here, and non-guests can use the spa facilities for €12. The restaurant has a big €14 dinner buffet.

Saariselän Panimo (☎ 6756 500; www.saariselan panimo.fi; s/d from €29/38; P ✕) This is the local village pub with some inexpensive huts for rent out the back. The huts, sleeping six to eight people, have their own kitchen, living room and sauna.

Pirkon Pirtti (☎ 668 050; Honkapolki 2; pizzas €7-9, mains €12-19; 🕙 lunch & dinner) Just up the hill from the tourist office building, this unassuming little place doesn't look much from the outside, but has a lovely cosy interior with a fireplace. As well as tasty pizzas, it serves delicious Lapp specialities – readers have extolled the virtues of the reindeer in pepper sauce – at very reasonable prices. It's also a good place for a beer.

Petronella (☎ 668 930; mains €13.50-28; 🕙 lunch & dinner Sep & Nov-May) This place serves lavish portions of Lappish food and is probably the finest restaurant in Saariselkä. It's closed in summer.

For lunch, the **Huippu** (☎ 668 803; 🕙 lunch & dinner) at nearby Kaunispää, 2km northeast, is no stranger to tour buses. It serves tasty food and has excellent views. The buffet is very extensive. You can walk (or ski) there easily from town.

GETTING THERE & AWAY

Each flight arriving at Ivalo airport is met by a shuttle bus to Saariselkä. Northbound buses from Rovaniemi stop on request at Saariselkä, and some buses make a loop through the village. During the ski season, there is an express bus from Helsinki, leaving at 7.45pm on Fridays.

Kiilopää

Kiilopää, 17km southeast of Saariselkä village, is another major trekking centre for the region, and is an excellent spot to start or finish your trek. Marked trails head directly into the wilderness from here.

Tunturikeskus Kiilopää (Fell Centre Kiilopää; ☎ 670 0700; www.kiilopaa.com; s/d summer from €65/74, high season to €90/120; P ☐) is an excellent and very professional facility that takes care of all accommodation and services. It rents mountain bikes, rucksacks, sleeping bags, skiing equipment and more. It also sells fishing permits and dispenses sound advice on trekking; guided treks are possible. There are hotel rooms and a café-restaurant (packed lunch €6, dinner €17), as well as a variety of cottages and apartments starting at €80 for a four-person apartment in summer, and the **Ahopää hostel** (dm from €22), a comfortable HI-affiliated facility with a kitchen, sauna, laundry and café.

Kiilopää is 6km from the main road 4; turn off at the Kakslauttanen hotel complex 11km south of Saariselkä. Several daily buses do the one-hour trip between Ivalo and Kiilopää; a bus meets every incoming flight to Ivalo airport. If you are travelling by bus from Rovaniemi, check whether the bus runs to Kiilopää: not all do.

Tankavaara

Tankavaara (www.tankavaara.fi), 32km south of Saariselkä, is locally famous as the 'Gold Village', a slightly kitsch reminder of the gold-rush days that once brought hundreds of hopeful diggers to the Saariselkä area.

Also here is the excellent **Koilliskaira Visitor Centre** (☎ 0205-647 251; ukpuisto@metsa.fi; ⏰ 9am-6pm Jun-Sep, 9am-4pm Mon-Fri Oct-May), with the best possible advice on activities and trekking in UKK. It also has top exhibitions on local wildlife, including a display on the raptor population upstairs, a slide-show, a shop and a good selection of maps. Three circular **nature trails** arc out from the centre (1km, 3km and 6km); a booklet available from the centre gives good extra information about these routes.

The **Kultamuseo** (Gold Prospector Museum; ☎ 626 171; adult/child €7/3.50; ⏰ 9am-6pm Jun-Aug, 9am-5pm Sep, 10am-4pm Mon-Fri Oct-May) displays tools and other paraphernalia from Lapland's crazy gold-fever years, minerals and gemstones, and extends its scope to gold rushes around the world. You can try your luck and pan for gold in summer (€3.50/20 per hour/day). Gold-related events and festivals are held in summer, the biggest being the **Goldpanners' Festival** in early August, which includes the Finnish Goldpanning Championships.

Korundi (☎ 626 158; fax 626 261; d/apt €50, 2-/4-bed cabin €37/47; P ☒) has doubles, apartments and rustic log cabins, as well as a café-bar and the atmospheric, timbered restaurant **Wanha Waskoolimies** (Ye Olde Goldpanner; mains €9-17), which serves steaks, reindeer, salmon, soup and Lapp Schnapps.

Tankavaara is on the main Rovaniemi–Ivalo road. All northbound buses pass the village, stopping on request.

SAARISELKÄ WILDERNESS & URHO K KEKKONEN NATIONAL PARK

The Saariselkä Wilderness – which includes the 2538-sq-km Urho K Kekkonen National Park and also large tracts of protected forestry lands – extends to the Russian border. It's a fabulous wilderness, home to bears, wolverines and golden eagles, as well as many thousands of free-grazing reindeer. This is a highly rated trekking area, partly because of the large network of wilderness huts, but also for the unspoilt beauty of the low *tunturi* hills. You certainly won't be alone in peak season on the most popular routes, but there are plenty of options in this huge and memorable expanse of forest, fell and marshland.

Orientation & Information

The park is divided into four zones, each with different rules. The basic zone is the area closest to main roads. Camping and fires are only allowed in designated places; to minimise

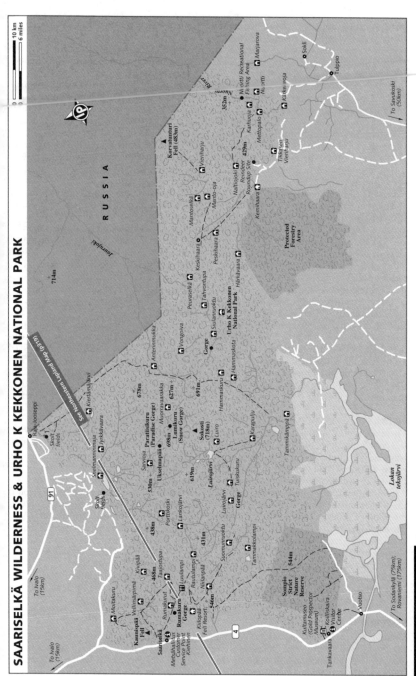

SAARISELKÄ WILDERNESS & URHO K KEKKONEN NATIONAL PARK

environmental impact it is recommended to make use of previously-used pitches. In the wilderness zones of Saariselkä (west) and Nuortti (southeast, between Tulppio and Kemihaara), camping is allowed everywhere except in certain gorges and on treeless areas. In the Kemi-Sompio wilderness zone (east), camping is allowed everywhere.

Although fires (using dead wood) are allowed in certain areas, you should take a camp stove, because fire bans are common in summer. In most areas, fires are only allowed at designated fireplace zones (these are supplied with firewood). The fire bans supersede all other regulations.

There are national park visitor centres in Saariselkä, Tankavaara (Koilliskaira) and Savukoski villages. The Koilliskaira centre is particularly good for practical trekking tips; you can also pick up information at Kiilopää, although it isn't an official information centre. A map and compass are *essential* for the most remote areas of the park.

There are three maps available for the area, published by Genimap. The western part of the park is shown on the 1:50,000 *Saariselkä-Kiilopää* map; the 1:50,000 *Sokosti-Suomujoki* map will take you beyond Luirojärvi; the entire park is shown on the 1:100,000 *Koilliskaira* map. Each map costs €14. The visitors' centres also sell a simpler map for day-trip walks (€3).

Sights

There are several natural attractions within the park boundaries, of which the **Rumakuru Gorge**, near the hut of the same name, is closest to the main road. **Luirojärvi** is the most popular destination for any trek, including a hike up the nearby **Sokosti summit** (718m), the highest in the park. **Paratiisikuru** (Paradise Gorge), a steep descent from the 698m **Ukselmapää summit**, and the nearby **Lumikuru** (Snow Gorge), are popular day trips between Sarvioja and Muorravaarakka huts.

There are two historical **Skolt fields**, with restored old houses, 2km south of Raja-Jooseppi, and 2km west of Snelmanninmaja hut, respectively.

Trekking

There are a large number of possible walking routes in the Saariselkä area. Use wilderness huts as bases and destinations, and create your own itinerary according to your ability:

an experienced, fit trekker can cover up to 4km per hour, and up to 25km per day. You will need to carry all food, as wilderness huts in the park are not stocked with supplies; water in rivers is drinkable.

The four- to six-day loop from the main road to Luirojärvi is the most popular, and can be extended beyond the lake. To reach areas where few have been, take a one-week walk from Kiilopää to Kemihaara.

The most remote route follows old roads and walking routes through the fells all the way from Raja-Jooseppi in the north to Kemihaara or Tulppio in the southeast.

Note that despite its popularity, Saariselkä can be tough going for the less experienced. Trails – particularly in the eastern part of the park – can be faint or almost nonexistent. Winter ski safaris can become especially dangerous during cold spells, and some areas are only suitable for expert ski-trekkers. Take advice from the park visitor centres on current conditions and route descriptions.

Sleeping

Within the park are 200 designated camping areas, all free. There are close to 30 wilderness huts in the park that may be used free of charge. Some of these have locked areas with beds and a few cabins within the park, which must both be booked in advance. The charge is €9 per bed per night; this is on a shared basis. Book beds at any of the park visitor centres.

A few wilderness huts close to the main road are for day use only – you can overnight at one of these in an emergency. You'll need a sleeping bag and mat for the wilderness huts; the bookable ones have mattresses. Some huts have gas or wood-burning stoves and sometimes telephones and saunas. Almost all are near water. The visitor centres can supply maps and details of the huts.

Getting There & Away

The easiest starting points for treks are Saariselkä or Kiilopää. From Savukoski you can catch a **post taxi** (☎ 040-730 6484; ✆ Wed & Fri) to Kemihaara village, 1km from the park's boundary.

The Raja-Jooseppi border station is another starting point for treks, as it takes you directly into the real wilderness; you can get there by taxi-bus from Ivalo.

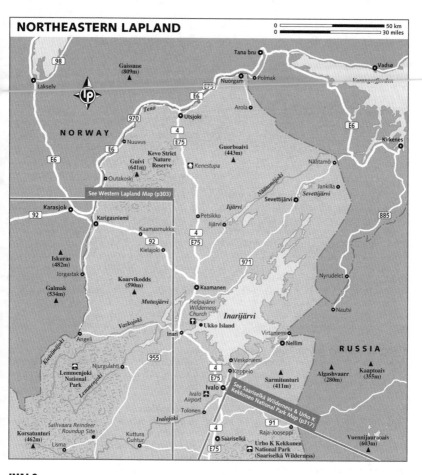

IVALO

☎ 016 / pop 3500

Ivalo (Sámi: Avvil) has all the shops and services you would expect in a small Finnish town, but it makes no pretence of being a tourist destination, apart from having an airport used mainly by incoming tour groups.

Ivalo does have a unique subculture though: gold-panners. This is the nearest 'big smoke' for hermits who spend their time panning the Ivalojoki for gold. Hotel Kultahippu is one place where any gold found is traded for booze, and where incredible tales are told before panners return to their solitary, secretive hunt for the mother lode.

Opposite the Spar supermarket on the main road, **Inarilainen** (☎ 663 311; Ivalontie 7;

9am-4.30pm, to 7pm in summer) is the local weekly news-magazine shop, but also serves as a tourist information point.

Activities
DOG-SLEDDING

There are several husky breeding farms around Ivalo, and in winter, a dog-sledding safari is a superb, though demanding (and expensive), way of experiencing the Lapland wilderness.

Kamisak (☎ 667 736; kamisak@hotmail.com), run by Eija and Reijo Järvinen, is about 5km south of Ivalo and open year-round. There's a good little café, plenty of knowledgeable chat about all things canine, and you can take an informal tour of the husky

LAPLAND & SÁPMI

enclosures and meet the dogs (adult/child €4/2); a boardwalk points out some of the area's typical berries and plants. In winter, from around November to April, they run safaris weekly. These range from a half-day trip with a two-person sled (€100, 10km) and full-day safaris (€135, 30km) to three- and five-day safaris, where participants get their own sleds and are taught how to drive and care for their own team of five to eight dogs. The price (around €1000 per person for five days) includes everything.

OTHER ACTIVITIES

If you've always fancied yourself as another Mikä Häkkinen, Kimi Räikkönen, or Marcus Grönholm, or are simply a bit short on confidence swerving around reindeer or negotiating those icy roads, pay the **Arctic Rally Team** (☎ 663 456; www.arcticrallyteam.fi; Ivalontie 25) a visit. They organise crash courses (so to speak) in winter driving, rallying and even navigating (left! I mean right! Oops!).

Based at the Hotel Ivalo, Club Nord arranges mainly winter activities, including husky-sledding and snowmobiling.

Sleeping, Eating & Drinking

Hotel Ivalo (☎ 688 111; www.hotelivalo.fi; Ivalontie 34; s/d with breakfast €75/95; meals from €9.50-22; P X 🖥 🛒 🕭) On the southern approach to town is this well-equipped hotel, with standard rooms, a sauna and a nice indoor pool. In quieter periods, you may be able to nab a 'walk-in' discount. The hotel hires bikes to guests; there's also a pool table and pub, as well as a tour agency on site. The restaurant is the best eating option in Ivalo.

Hotel Kultahippu (☎ 661 825; fax 662 510; Petsamontie 1; s/d from €57/70) Ivalo's other hotel, the 'speck of gold' is by the riverside at the north end of town. It has the town's main pub, and the nightclub Hipun Kellari (🕒 10pm-4am Fri & Sat) is where the community gathers for weekly drinking and dancing.

Getting There & Away

There are daily flights from Helsinki to Ivalo, and regular air services from many other Finnish towns. The airport is 12km south of Ivalo; a connecting bus to the centre meets each arriving flight.

Daily buses from Rovaniemi all stop in Ivalo. Car-rental companies with offices at Ivalo airport (and in town) include Avis,

Budget, Hertz and Europcar. Rates are the same as elsewhere in Finland.

A road runs east from Ivalo to the Russian city of Murmansk, 303 kilometres away. Three weekly buses (see p346) travel the distance. The border is crossed at Raja-Jooseppi, 53km from Ivalo. This is also a possible starting point for treks into the Saariselkä wilderness. For Raja-Jooseppi, catch the Murmansk bus, which leaves Ivalo at 3.30pm on Mondays, Wednesdays and Fridays (€9, 50 minutes).

INARI

☎ 016 / pop 550

If you blink behind the wheel or nod off in the bus you might miss the village of Inari (Sámi: Anár). It is the main Sámi community in the region and a centre for genuine Sámi handicrafts – although the galleries and boutique shops have an air of commercialism, this is the best place in Finland to shop for genuine Lappish and Sámi handmade textiles, jewellery, silverware and woodwork.

Inari is a good base for exploring Sápmi, but it has some fine attractions of its own. Spend a day or two here visiting the Siida museum, trekking to the Wilderness Church, and taking an afternoon cruise on Inarijärvi.

Information

Inari Info (☎ 661 666; www.inarilapland.org; 🕒 10am-5pm mid-Sep–May, 9am-7pm Jun–mid Sep) In the centre of the village, it has tourist information as well as Internet access and a post office. Fishing rods (€10/day) and bikes (€10/20 for 4/24hr) can be hired.

Sights

SIIDA – SÁMI MUSEUM & NORTHERN LAPLAND NATURE CENTRE

One of the finest museums in Finland, **Siida** (☎ 665 212, www.siida.fi; adult/student/child €8/6.50/4; 🕒 9am-8pm daily Jun-Sep, 10am-5pm Tue-Sun Oct-May) should not be missed. Overall, the exhibition successfully brings to life Sámi origins, culture, traditions, lifestyle and present-day struggles. There are diverse temporary exhibits, a good timeline introduction to the history of the area, and a superb, detailed display on the Arctic environment, flora, fauna and geology. Outside is a good open-air museum featuring Sámi buildings, handicrafts and artefacts, including several dastardly traps for bears, foxes and wolves. A theatrette shows pretty visuals of the northern lights and Inarijärvi; there's also a fine craft shop and top-value café, where €8.50 will get you a hot dish and free use of the salad bar (open 11am to 3pm).

PIELPAJÄRVI WILDERNESS CHURCH

The *erämaakirkko* (wilderness church) of Pielpajärvi is accessible from Inari by a marked walking track (7.5km one way) from the parking area at SIIDA. If you have a vehicle there's another car park 2.5km beyond here, up Sarviniementie, from where it's a 4.3km walk to the church. In winter, you'll need snowshoes and a keen attitude to do this. The church area has been an important marketplace for the Sámi over the centuries, with the first church erected here in 1646. The present church was built in 1760, and restored in the 1970s. It's always open.

SÁMI CHURCH

This **church** (🕒 mid-Jun–mid-Aug) was built in 1952 with American financing. The altar painting depicts a wandering Sámi family meeting Christ. Inari Sámi and Fell Sámi are spoken in this church, west of the main street on the road to Lemmenjoki National Park.

Festivals & Events

It doesn't get much more Lappish than **reindeer races** – they're held in Inari, sleds and all, over the last week of May on Inarijärvi. It's a local event with festivities, betting and a winner's cup. The reindeer are antlerless, and the sport looks a little like crazy water-skiing (with the reindeer as boats).

Tours

There are daily cruises run by **Lake & Snow** (☎ 0400 295 731) on Inarijärvi from mid-June (as soon as the ice melts) to late August (€13, two hours). Departures are at 2pm daily, with an additional departure in July at 6pm. Boats leave from the wharf at the Siida car park. The destination is **Ukko Island** (Sámi: Äjjih), sacred to the Sámi. During the brief (20-minute) stop, most people climb to the top of the island, but there are also cave formations at the island's northern end. The same company also organises fishing trips and snowmobile safaris.

There are two seaplanes parked in the lake that serve as air taxis. They also do 10-minute **scenic flights** (☎ 0400 879 628; €110 for 1-3 people) and chartered trips around Inarijärvi.

At the Kultahovi Hotel, **Koskenlaskua Rafting** (☎ 0400 453 234) runs one-hour trips on the rapids here (€25), or more involved three-hour excursions on the Juutua river (€87).

Sleeping & Eating

Hotel Inarin Kultahovi (☎ 671 221; inarin.kultahovi @co.inet.fi; Saarikoskentie 2; s/d €66/86; P ✗) This is tucked away just off the road to Lemmenjoki National Park and is a cosy place popular with tour groups. The rooms have been recently renovated and are pleasant but nothing special – unless, that is, you can get one overlooking the rapids. The riverside sauna is great, and there's a **restaurant** (mains €9.50-26; 🕒 11am-11pm) with a good-value à la carte menu of Lappish specialities and set three-course menus. The dining area looks over the beautiful Alakoski. Appetisers include crêpes filled with forest mushrooms (€5.80), while the local trout is tasty, as is the reindeer fillet with game sauce.

Hotel Inari (☎ 671 026; www.hotelliinari.fi; s/d €38/45, apt €79; P ✗) This place is the hub of the village and has decent rooms with private bathroom, a minibar and TV; it's worth paying a little extra to face the lake, rather than the road. It can get noisy on Friday and Saturday nights, when the bar downstairs kicks off. There are also mini-apartments with their own sauna and kitchenette. The hotel also has a **restaurant** (pizzas €4-8, mains €10-13) with all the Lappish dishes – plenty of reindeer and salmon prepared in a variety of ways. Pizzas include sautéed reindeer, peach and onion, and there are inexpensive burgers. There's also a grilli that claims to be open 24 hours, and a bar, which is the hub of village life and has a glassed-in terrace where you can watch the seaplanes and see the amazing things the sun can do at these latitudes.

Lomakylä Inari (☎ 671 108; fax 671 480; 2-/4- person cabin from €25/35, cottages with sauna €84-150; 🕒 Jun-late Sep) There are a couple of bungalow villages near the camping ground but closer to town is this place, within easy walking distance of the bus station. It's not particularly friendly but has a café and sauna, decent cabins with fridge and stove, and good facilities. Call ahead out of season as it sometimes opens if there are bookings.

Uruniemi Camping (☎ 671 331; www.uruniemi .com; tent sites €11, d cottages from €17, 4-person cottages €34-42; ⊗ Jun-late Sep) This place, 2km south of town, is a well-equipped lakeside camping ground with cottages, café, sauna, and boats and bikes for hire.

The Siida museum is a great spot to have lunch.

Shopping

Inari is the main centre for Sámi *duodji* (handicrafts) and there are several studios and boutique shops in the village. Among the items on sale here are bags, pouches and boots made from reindeer hide, knitted gloves and socks, traditional textiles, shawls and the strikingly colourful Sámi hats, bone-handle knives, carved wooden bowls, cups and other souvenir handicrafts, jewellery, and CDs and tapes of Sámi music.

Sámi Duodji Ry (☎ 671 254; Lehtolantie 1; ⊗ 10am-6pm daily Jul & Aug, 10am-5pm Mon-Fri, 10am-3pm Sat Sep-Jun) This place, next door to the library, is the main outlet representing Sámi products. It has a good range of Sámi books and CDs, as well as beautifully crafted silverware and clothing.

Samekki (☎ 671 086; ⊗ 10am-4pm Mon-Fri, also weekends mid-Jun–mid-Aug) Down a small lane behind the library is the studio of Petteri Laiti, a famous artisan among Finnish Sámi. The silverwork and handicrafts are very highly regarded; you'll often see the artist at work here.

Inarin Hopea (☎ 671 333; Sillankorva), opposite the Siida museum, sells hand-worked silver items.

Getting There & Away

Heading north on the much-travelled Arctic Rd 4, Inari is the next stop after Ivalo, 38km beyond it. At least two daily buses travel between Rovaniemi and Inari, and on to Utsjoki.

LEMMENJOKI NATIONAL PARK

At 2855 sq km, Lemmenjoki (Sámi: Leammi) is the largest national park in Finland. Saariselkä is much more popular with trekkers, but the Lemmenjoki experience is more diverse: slush through desolate wilderness rivers, explore the rough landscape and bump into gold-panners in the middle of nowhere. The Morgamjoki is the main gold-panning area, and there are several

old huts where gold-panners still sleep in summer.

The **Lemmenjoki Nature Centre** (☎ 0205-647 793; ⊗ 9am-5pm Jun-Sep) is just before the village of Njurgulahti (often just called Lemmenjoki), about 50km southwest of Inari. It has a small interpretative exhibition and a powerful set of binoculars, and you can purchase maps and fishing permits here. There is food and accommodation in the lakeside village.

Sights & Activities
SALLIVAARA REINDEER ROUNDUP SITE

The roundup site, 70km southwest of Inari, was built in 1933 (although some huts date back to the 1890s) and used by Sámi reindeer herders twice yearly until 1964. Roundups were an important social event for the people of northern Lapland, usually lasting several weeks and involving hundreds of people and animals. The Sallivaara reindeer corrals and cabins were reconstructed in 1997, and it's now possible to stay overnight in one of the Sallivaara huts. Many people come here in spring and summer for the top quality bird-watching on nearby wetlands. To reach the site, park at Repojoki parking area then follow the marked trail, 6km one way. Reindeer roundups are held in this area (although these corrals are no longer in use), but since the timing is dependent on many factors, to see one requires a great deal of luck or contact with a reindeer herder.

TREKKING

Almost all trails start from Njurgulahti, including a 4km marked nature trail suitable for families with children. The majority of the trekking routes are within the relatively small area between the rivers Lemmenjoki and Vaskojoki. An 18km loop between Kultala and Ravadasjärvi huts takes you to some of the most interesting gold-panning areas. As you can do this in two days, many trekkers head over Ladnjoaivi Fell to Vaskojoki hut and back, which extends the trek to four to five days. For any serious trekking, you will need the 1:100,000 *Lemmenjoki* map (€18), available at the Lemmenjoki Nature Centre.

Tours

In summer, a couple of local boat services cruise the Lemmenjoki valley, from Njurgulahti village to the Kultahamina wilderness hut at Kultasatama (Gold Harbour). A 20km marked trail also follows the course of the river, so you can take the boat one way, then hike back. You can also get on or off the boat at other jetties along the route. There are at least two departures a day from mid-June to mid-September (€14/27 one way/return).

Sleeping

There are two camping and cabin places at Njurgulahti, 12km from the main (a relative term in Lapland) Inari–Kittilä road. They both have cafés and operate boat trips on the river. The national park entrance and trailheads are 1.5km away.

Lemmenjoen Lomamajat (☎ /fax 016-673 435; ahkuntupa@hotmail.com; camping per person €2, 2-/4-person cabin from €31/43) This is a switched-on place with various packages including half and full board. The owner speaks good English and runs river cruises (from €8 for a run-about, to €21 for a trip up to the gold-panning areas), rents canoes (€17/100 per day/week) and makes transport arrangements. The café, Ahkun Tupa, does a great lunch for €8.50 and has buns with enough cinnamon to season a small nation.

Next door, **Lemmenjoki Travel Service** (☎ 016-673 430; tent sites €6, r per person €10, cottages €20), has a similar set-up.

Valkeaporo (☎ 016-673 001; www.valkeaporo.fi; tent sites per person/family €7/14, 4-/6-person cottages €40/56; ☼ Apr-Oct) Near the turn-off from the main Inari–Kittilä road, on the shores of Menes-järvi, this is another good base for river trips on the Lemmenjoki. In addition to good facilities and boat and canoe hire, it offers three-hour trips on the river for €22 and all-day gold-panning trips for €37. Both trips require a minimum of six people.

Inside the park, nine wilderness huts along the most popular trekking routes provide free accommodation (three can be booked in advance for a fee). Several are along the riverboat route.

Getting There & Away

There is one taxi-bus on weekdays between Inari and Njurgulahti village; it currently leaves Inari at 3pm and involves a change, but check with the tourist office in Inari. In summer, the afternoon bus waits in the village until the boat has made the return trip, then drives back to Inari. A local taxi service can be called on ☎ 0400 396 312.

KEVO STRICT NATURE RESERVE

The 712-sq-km Kevo Strict Nature Reserve, northwest of Inari, was established in 1956. Within its boundaries you'll find some of the most breathtaking scenery in Finland (although it's nothing spectacular if you've spent your life in Norway, or near the Grand Canyon) along the splendid 40km gorge of the Kevojoki (Sámi: Geävu), which also has some decent waterfalls.

Rules for visiting the Kevo reserve are stricter than those concerning national parks: hikers cannot hunt, fish or collect plants and berries, and *must* stay on marked trails. The gorge area is off-limits from April to mid-June.

The main trail is 63km long and runs through the canyon, from Ruktajärvi, near the Utsjoki–Kaamanen road, to the Karigasniemi–Kaamanen road. The trek is rough and takes about four days one way. Use the 1:100,000 *Kevo* topographical sheet.

Sleeping

You will need a tent if you plan to hike through the canyon, as there is only one wilderness hut on this route (although there are another two on the return leg). Camping is permitted within the reserve only at a dozen designated sites.

Kenestupa (☎ 678 531) On the Utsjoki–Kaamanen road, this place is an option for those who hike through. It rents cabins and has a sauna, so end your trek here and take advantage of that cleansing sweat!

There are three free wilderness huts along a northwestern path that does not descend into the gorge. From south to north, the huts are: Ruktajärvi, at the southern end of the gorge route (accommodates eight people and has a telephone and an oven); Njávgoaivi (10 people, telephone); and Kuivi, inside the park (10 people, oven). It's best to do these as a round-trip trek, from Sulaoja trailhead to Kuivi hut and back.

Getting There & Away

The preferred route is to start from the southwest; catch the Karigasniemi-bound bus from Inari and ask the driver to drop you off at the Sulaoja trailhead. From Kenestupa you can catch buses to Inari or Nuorgam.

Those with a car can leave it at Kenestupa, catch the afternoon bus to Kaamanen and change to the Karigasniemi-bound bus.

THE SÁMI OF FINLAND

Sámi (sápmelaš in their own language) are the indigenous inhabitants of Lapland and are today spread across four countries from the Kola peninsula in Russia to the southern Norwegian mountains. More than half of the 70,000 Sámi population are across the border in Norway, while Finland numbers around 8000, but there are close cultural ties across the borders. The Sámi region is called Sápmi. About half of Finnish Sámi live in the Finnish part of Sápmi.

According to stone carvings and archaeological evidence, this region was first settled soon after the last Ice Age around 10,000 years ago, but it wasn't until the beginning of the Christian era – the early Iron Age – that Finns and Sámi had become two distinct groups with diverging languages. The early inhabitants were nomadic people – hunters, fishers and food-gatherers – who migrated with the seasons. They hunted wild reindeer, fished and harvested berries in the summer months, and traded meat, clothing and handicrafts.

EARLY TRADITIONS & BELIEFS

Early Sámi society was based on the *siida*, small groups comprising a number of families who controlled particular hunting and fishing grounds. Families lived in a *kota*, a traditional dwelling resembling the tepee or wigwam of native North Americans. It could be easily set up as a temporary shelter while following the migrating reindeer herds, and more permanent *kota* were overlaid with turf to insulate the fabric and reindeer pelt covering. A 'winter village' system also developed, where groups would come together to help survive the harsh winter months.

The natural environment was essential to the Sámi existence: they worshipped the sun (father), earth (mother) and wind and believed all things in nature had a soul. The stars and constellations provided mythology – the North Star, the brightest in the night sky, was the Pillar of the World. The Sámi believed in many gods and their link with the gods was through the shaman, the most important member of the community. By beating a drum, the shaman could go into a trance and communicate with the gods, ask advice or determine their will. The drums featured in drawings depicting life, nature and the gods, usually with the sun as the central image. Forced conversion to Christianity in the 17th century spelt the end for the shamans and the traditional drums.

Traditional legends, rules of society and fairytales were handed down through the generations by storytelling. A unique form of storytelling was the *yoik*, a chant in which the singer would use words, or imitate the sounds of animals and nature to describe experiences. The *yoik* is still used by the Sámi today, sometimes accompanied by instruments.

ROLE OF THE REINDEER

Reindeer has always been central to the existence of the Sámi people. They ate the meat, took milk from the cows, used the fur for clothing and bedding, and made fish hooks and harpoons from the bones and antlers. Today around 40% of Sámi living in Sápmi are involved in reindeer husbandry; tourism is another big employer.

Originally the Sámi hunted wild reindeer, usually trapping them in pitfalls. Hunting continued until around the 16th century, when the Sámi began to domesticate entire herds and migrate with them. Towards the end of the 19th century, Finland's reindeer herders were organised into *paliskunta* (cooperatives), of which there are now around 56 in northern Finland. Reindeer wander free around the large natural areas within each *paliskunta*, which is bordered by enormous fences that cross the Lapland wilderness. Each herder is responsible for his stock and identifies them by earmarks – a series of distinctive notches cut into the ear of each animal.

The reindeer cycle follows a distinct pattern. Calves are born in May and June. At the end of June the herd is gathered and the calves earmarked. In summer, when not being driven mad by insects, the reindeer graze on fells and meadows, storing energy for winter. In September, before mating season, males are herded and separated for slaughter – up to 120,000 reindeer are slaughtered annually. By November the snow has come and the reindeer subsist by foraging for lichen. The animals are herded onto winter grazing grounds – these days herders use snowmobiles, mobile phones and even helicopters to control their herds, so they no longer need to continually migrate with them.

SÁMI CLOTHING & HANDICRAFTS

The Sámi have always used the material at their disposal – reindeer furs, antlers and bone, birch burl and wool – to make utensils, carvings, clothing and textiles. The colourful Sámi costumes, featuring jackets, pants or skirts embroidered with bright red, blue and yellow patterns, are now mostly worn on special occasions and during Sámi festivals.

Sámi handicrafts (including bags and boots made from reindeer hide, knitted gloves and socks, textiles, shawls, the strikingly colourful Sámi hats, jewellery and silverware) are recognised as indigenous art. Genuine Sámi handicrafts carry the name *Sámi duodji* (see p322 for more information).

SÁMI LANGUAGES

The cultural identity of Finland's Sámi population is closely linked to language, which has undergone a revival in recent years. Sámi languages are related to Finnish and other Finno-Ugric languages. There are three Sámi languages, not very mutually intelligible, used in Finland today, although there are under 2000 regular users. Sámi is taught in local schools, and legislation grants Sámis the right of Sámi usage in offices in Sápmi. In Utsjoki Sámi speakers constitute almost the majority of the population. You will find another seven Sámi languages in Norway, Sweden and Russia.

Fell Sámi

The most common of Sámi languages, Fell Sámi (also known as Northern Sámi or Mountain Sámi), is spoken by Utsjoki and Enontekiö Sámi, and thousands of Sámi in Norway. Fell Sámi is considered the standard Sámi, and there is plenty of literature, printed in Utsjoki and in Karasjok (Norway).

Written Fell Sámi includes several accented letters but does not directly correspond to spoken Sámi. In fact, many Sámi find written Sámi difficult to learn. For example, *giitu* (for 'thanks') is pronounced **gheech**-too, but the strongly aspirated 'h' is not written. Likewise, *dat* is pronounced as tah-ch. You can ask Sámis to read these words out loud to learn the correct pronunciation.

Inari Sámi

Although spoken by some people in the region around Inarijärvi, Inari Sámi is rarely written and seems to be heading for extinction.

Skolt Sámi

The rare Skolt Sámi language (Finnish: *kolttasaame*) is spoken by approximately 600 Sámi people who live in Sevettijärvi and Nellim villages. Being refugees from the Petsamo region (which was annexed by the Soviet Union), they maintain Russian Orthodox traditions and have close ties with Sámi groups who live on the Kola peninsula in Russia. Skolt Sámi contains some Russian loan words.

THE SÁMI TODAY

Sámis have been subjected to oppression in the past. They were forcibly converted to (Protestant) Christianity in the 17th century, and their religious traditions were made illegal. This has led to a situation where many Sámi define themselves not as Sámi but rather as ordinary Finns.

They were also heavily taxed by the Swedish state but were not officially recognised as landowners. Today Sámi rights are defended and their language is prominently displayed in Sámi regions in Finnish Lapland. Finland was the first country to inaugurate a popularly elected Sámi parliament in 1972 (Norway followed in 1989 and Sweden in 1993). The universal right to 'Sámi territory' (a somewhat blurry definition) is continuously disputed. No 'homeland' or 'reservation' has been created so far, and the parliament does not have power of self-government on issues relating to Sámi peoples.

However, the Sámi identity is gaining strength in Finland. There is a common Sámi flag, Sámi National Day is celebrated on 6 February, there is a Sámi radio station (101.9FM) and increased tourism is providing economic benefits through the sale of Sámi handicrafts. For more information on Sámi culture, visit the excellent Siida museum in Inari or the Arktikum in Rovaniemi.

LAPLAND & SÁPMI

INARI TO NORWAY
☎ 016

Since Norway stretches across the top of northern Finland, there are three main routes north from Inari into Norway: to the west via Karigasniemi (the most common route to Nordkapp); straight up to Utsjoki; and east to Kirkenes via Sevettijärvi. From Utsjoki, you can turn east along the fabulous Teno salmon river to Nuorgam, the northernmost village in the EU.

Kaamanen

Kaamanen, 25km north of Inari, is just the crossing point of the three northern roads. The Kotipuoti shop has postal services and a petrol station. All buses – and most locals for that matter – call at **Kaamasen Kievari** (☎ 672 713; mains €13-23; 😌 9am-midnight), a busy, legendary pub and roadhouse a few kilometres north of the Sevettijärvi turn-off and 5km south of the Karigasniemi crossing. It has a café, petrol station and hard-drinking bar, as well as an excellent restaurant serving local dishes such as salmon, whitefish, and a top reindeer steak with herb potatoes (€22.30). They also have rooms and cabins (HI-affiliated), but Jokitörmä, 1km to the south, is better.

Hostel Jokitörmä (☎ 672 725; fax 672 745; tent sites €13, dm cabin/room €16/19, s/d cabin €28/38; P ✕), on the Arctic Hwy about 24km north of Inari, is a great little HI-affiliated hostel. The cabins are small and cosy and look over the river, although mosquito repellent is in order in summer. They have a simple stove but no fridge. You can camp here with tents or vans, too. There are also good two- and four-person rooms, and a separate set of cottages, with full facilities.

Karigasniemi

The small village of Karigasniemi (Sámi: Gáregasnjárga) is the main crossing point from Finland to Norway, along the popular Nordkapp route. It has services such as a bank and a post office. Fell Sámi (see boxed text, p325), the language of the local people of Karigasniemi, is a dialect spoken across the border in Norway.

Camping Tenorinne (☎ 676 113; tent sites €14, 2-/4-person cabin €30/42; 😌 Jun–mid-Sep) has rustic log cabins and a pleasant location away from the main road.

Two buses a day travel from Ivalo to Karigasniemi, continuing on to the Norwegian town of Karasjok. A shared taxi travels to Sámi villages north of Karigasniemi along the Tenojoki on Tuesday and Friday.

Utsjoki

The border village of Utsjoki (Sámi: Ohcejohka) is not an attractive place by any means, straggling along the main road, but there's a crossing into Norway here and it's home to a fairly large Sámi population. There are two banks, a post office and several shops here, but little else to detain the visitor.

The tourist office, **Utsjoki Info** (☎ 686 234, 686 111; 😌 Jun-late Sep) is on the left just before the bridge to Norway and jointly run by the municipality and Metsähallitus (the Forest and Park Service). There's a small nature display, maps for sale and information specifically on Kevo Strict Nature Reserve.

There's a campsite, and **Hotelli Luossajohka** (☎ 321 2100; fax 677 126; Luossatie; s/d €55/73, with bath €73/93; P ✕), up the road by the Osuuspankki bank, is the only hotel in the town itself; it also has a restaurant and bar, but isn't particularly inviting. There are a couple of fast-food places on the main road, and Giisá, a café with Internet access that sells bus tickets.

Nuorgam & the Teno Valley

The 43km road from Utsjoki northeast to Nuorgam (Sámi: Njuorggan), the northernmost village of Finland (70 degrees and 4 minutes north of the equator), is one of Lapland's most spectacular. It follows the impressive and broad Tenojoki, one of Europe's best **salmon-fishing** destinations. Most anglers gather near Boratbokcankoski and Alaköngäs Rapids, 7km southwest of the village centre, but there are good spots right along this stretch (and also the other way from Utsjoki, towards Karigasniemi).

Apart from fishing, there's not a great deal to do in Nuorgam, but it's a relaxing spot, and much nicer than Utsjoki. The majority of the 200 residents are Sámi. There's a supermarket, petrol station, restaurant and pub in town, but the heart of village life is **Nuorgamin Lomakeskus** (☎ 678 312; tent sites €10-16, r €25-40, cabin €45-65; café 😌 10am-6pm Mon-Sat, noon-4pm Sun; P ✕ 💻), which has a range of accommodation options, including camping and log cabins, and a sauna. It sells fishing permits, has a café with good daily hot meals and an Internet terminal, and is a good source of local information. It also sells the souvenir T-shirt 'Nuorgam: Pieni mutta pohjoisin' (Nuorgam: Small but northernmost).

There are many campsites and cabin villages scattered along the narrow road on the Finnish side of the river; at least a dozen between Nuorgam and Utsjoki, and several more on the Karigasniemi road. They cater mainly to fishing parties and are good-value, costing from €35 for a basic cabin. The Utsjoki tourist office has a full list.

Nuorgam is the northern end of a trekking route from Sevettijärvi (see right).

A late-evening bus travels from Rovaniemi via Ivalo and Inari to Nuorgam; there's also an afternoon bus on weekdays. At weekends, an afternoon bus makes the journey from Ivalo. The late bus heads on to Tana bru in Norway, but otherwise it's 4km to the border, and a further 2km to the Norwegian border town of Polmak.

Sevettijärvi

The road east from Kaamanen heads along the shore of Inarijärvi to the village of Sevettijärvi (Skolt Sámi: Ce'vetjäu'rr), in the far northeast of Finland. This area is home to a distinctive Lappish group called Skolt Sámi; some of the Skolt speak Skoltish (see boxed text, p325), Finnish and Russian. There are 300 Skolt Sámi in and around Sevettijärvi. It's a peaceful wilderness drive along the shores of Inarijärvi up this way, but there's not a lot in the way of attractions except fishing on the Näätämöjoki and the Sevettijärvi, and the excellent trekking opportunities in the lake-filled, remote corner of Finland to the northeast and northwest.

Sevettijärven Lomamajat (☎ 672 215; cabin from €30) behind the church is a family-run place

with two- and four-bed cabins. Amazingly it's not on a lake, but there is a sauna.

Nilituvat (☎ 672 240; tent sites €10, s/d cabins €20/30), 3.5km south of Sevettijärvi, is right on the main road but also beside a lake. There are cabins, and a self-contained eight-person cottage with sauna for €70.

Sevetin Baari, by the lake in the centre of town, is the only place that offers meals, snacks and coffee, and is also the local post office. Its opening hours are somewhat erratic, so don't rely on it. There is a single supermarket in the village.

There is a bus connection between Ivalo and Sevettijärvi on weekdays. There is no petrol station in Sevettijärvi; the nearest services are in the border village of Näätämö, 30km northeast, or Kaamanen, 92km away. Näätämö (Skolt Sámi: Njauddam) has a seven-day supermarket as well.

Trekking Around Sevettijärvi

The Sevettijärvi region has more lakes per square kilometre than any other region in Finland. Very few trekkers explore this remote wilderness, yet it is worth the effort it takes to reach it.

The **Sevettijärvi to Nuorgam** trek is an established route, and the most popular from Sevettijärvi. You'll need the 1:50,000 trekking maps for the area, available at Karttakeskus in Helsinki.

There are two places to start the trek; the better one is just north of Sevettijärvi, at Saunaranta. You'll see a sign that reads 'Ahvenjärvi 5', and a trekking sign – 12km to Opukasjärvi, 69km to Pulmankijärvi. There are six mountain huts along the route; from the final wilderness hut you can walk to Nuorgam along a road, or make a phone call from a local home for a taxi to Nuorgam village.

There are several other possible routes in the area, all more or less waymarked.

Directory

CONTENTS

PRACTICALITIES

- Helsingin Sanomat (www.helsinginsano mat.fi/english) is the main daily paper in Finland. There's an English version online.

- Foreign newspapers and magazines are widely available

- The national radio broadcaster is YLE (www.yle.fi), which has a number of stations including the popular YLE X, formerly Radio Mafia, and devoted to nonmainstream music.

- Capital FM (94.5MHz) in Helsinki broadcasts 24-hour excerpts from world news stations.

- National TV networks broadcast plenty of English-language programs, subtitled in Finnish.

- Finland uses the VHS-PAL 525 system. V-8 videos are not commonly available in Finland.

- The electric current is 220V AC, 50Hz, and plugs are of the standard northern European type with two round pins that require no switch.

- Finland uses the metric system (see the conversion table in the inside front cover of this book). Decimals are indicated by commas.

ACCOMMODATION

Sleeping listings in this guide are mostly divided into three price categories, based on the cost of a standard double room at its most expensive; budget (up to €60), midrange (€60 to €150), and top end (€150 plus).

There's not a marvellous range of characterful accommodation in Finland. In towns, the norm is comfortable, functional hotels and hostels rather than whimsical converted castles or cosy cottages. There are many places that only open in summer.

As most hotels in Finland cater to business travellers, nearly all of them offer heavily discounted rates at weekends (normally Friday, Saturday, and Sunday nights) and during summer (usually late June to mid-August). The price for a double room is often halved at these times: good news for the visitor.

Helsinki has a hotel booking service; in other places your best bet is the tourist office, which will give you lists and might phone places on your behalf.

All hotels and hostels have a huge majority of nonsmoking rooms, and many don't allow smoking at all. Smokers should request a smoking room when booking.

Campgrounds

Finland's camping grounds are a delight, and have much to offer. Even if you're not a tent and campstove person, they can be an excellent choice, as many have cabins and cottages for rent on a nightly or weekly basis, some of which can be very luxurious.

There are over 200 official camping grounds in Finland, most situated in appealing lakeside or forested locations. The majority are only open in summer, say from late May to late August. Typical facilities include a kitchen area, laundry, sauna, playground, boat and bike rentals, a café and minigolf (a Finnish addiction!). Simple cabins usually have electric light, bunk beds and a fridge, while the larger cottages will come with fully equipped kitchen, TV, sauna, bathroom and separate bedrooms. These can be great value, particularly for families and groups.

In Finland the *jokamiehenoikeus* (right of public access) grants you legal permission to temporarily pitch your tent in a wide range of places. See p45 for more information.

Farmstays

Many farmhouses around Finland offer B&B accommodation, a unique opportunity to meet local people and experience their way of life. They offer plenty of activities, too, from horse riding to helping with a harvest. Some farmstays are independent, family-run affairs, while others are loosely gathered under an umbrella organization. In general, prices are good – from around €30 per person per night, country breakfast included. Your hosts may not speak much English, so it pays to arrange the booking through a local tourist office or **Lomarengas** (Map p64; ☎ 09-5766 3350; www.lomarengas.fi; Eteläesplanadi 22, 00130 Helsinki).

Guesthouses

A guesthouse in Finland, called a *matkakoti*, tends to be a slightly run-down establishment meant for travelling salespeople and dubious types. They're usually in town centres near the train station, are cheap and offer rooms with shared bathroom facilities.

However, there are a few guesthouses out there that just don't fit the category. These places are exceptionally clean and offer pleasant, homey accommodation in old wooden houses. Ask to see a room before paying – that's the best way to know what you're getting. Naantali and Hanko on the southwestern coast are particularly good places for guesthouses.

Most guesthouses offer a breakfast buffet, which is usually included in the price of accommodation.

Hostels

If you're travelling alone, hostels generally offer the best-value roof over your head, and can be good value for two people staying in a twin room. Finnish hostels are invariably clean, comfortable and very well-equipped, though most are in somewhat institutional buildings. From June to August, university accommodation is converted into summer hostels; these are usually great value, as you often get your own room, usually with a private kitchen and bathroom. These summer hostels are good for families, as they often have two interconnecting rooms.

Most Finnish hostels are run by the Finnish Youth Hostel Association (SRM) and are affiliated with Hostelling International (HI). The average cost is €15 to €20 per person per night. Most hostels offer private single/double rooms. If you have an HI card you'll receive a €2.50 discount per person on the rates quoted in this book. You can join HI in your own country – check the **International Youth Hostel Federation** (www.iyhf.org) for contact details of your home association – or you can join up at any HI-affiliated hostel, or at the **head office** (Suomen Retkeilymajajärjestö, SRM; ☎ 09-694 0377; www.srm.fi; Yrjönkatu 38B, 00100 Helsinki). In Finland the cost is €17 for a year's membership. You can stay at a hostel without an HI card, and there are no age restrictions.

You can also bring your own sheets (or sleeping sheet) and pillowcase; linen rentals cost €3 to €6. Sleeping bags are usually not considered acceptable substitutes, although some summer hostels will accept them (or at least turn a blind eye). Breakfast is generally not included in the price of a dorm bed (but may be with a private room), but is available for around €4 to €6. Most hostels have kitchen facilities, and many have a sauna.

The free publication *Hostellit* gives a full listing of all HI-affiliated Finnish hostels, as does the SRM website.

Hotels

Most big hotels in Finland cater to business travellers and most belong to one of a few major chains, including **Sokos** (www.sokoshotels.fi), **Scandic** (www.scandic-hotels.com) and **Cumulus** (www.cumulus.fi). **Finlandia** (www.finlandiahotels.fi) is an association of independent hotels, while many others belong to the **Best Western** (www.bestwestern.fi) franchise-style system. They can be quite luxurious, although standard rooms

DIRECTORY

are usually compact and functional. Service tends to be good and the restaurants and nightclubs are often the most popular in town. Hotels are mostly spotlessly clean, efficiently run and always have a sauna, which can be booked for private use. A shared sauna session is often included in the rate. Most hotels have suites with a private sauna.

Although full rack-rate prices are fairly high, hotels in Finland offer lower rates in summer (from late June to mid- or the end of August), and also at weekends (usually Friday, Saturday and Sunday nights). At that time you can usually get a double room in a reasonably fancy hotel from between €65 and €80. The discount for singles is marginal at all times, so you may prefer to pay extra for a double room, which are usually much larger. Similarly, many hotels have two classes of room, with a significantly better room available for a little extra money.

Most hotel rooms have tiny Nordic bathrooms; if you want a bathtub, this can usually be arranged. Many hotels have 'allergy rooms', which have no carpet and minimal fabric.

All Finnish hotels have a large, plentiful and invariably delicious buffet breakfast included in the rate.

FINNCHEQUES
The Finncheque plan, available in most chain hotels in Finland, allows accommodation in over 140 hotels at the discounted price of €36 or €45 per person in a double room. Each Finncheque is a 'coupon' good for one night's stay at a participating hotel, and any supplements are paid directly to the hotel. Single occupancy costs an extra €25, paid with a supplementary cheque. Finncheques are valid from June to September and at weekends throughout the year. In practice, as hotels offer discounts in summer and at weekends anyway, they are only really worth using in early June and September. They can be purchased at participating hotels or through a travel agency in your home country.

Self-Catering Accommodation
There are thousands of cabins and cottages for rent in Finland. They can be booked through tourist offices, mostly from €200 a week or more for four people. Rarely available on a nightly basis (but see Camping,

p328), weekend rentals are possible outside busy periods such as Midsummer.

Lakeside holiday cabins and cottages represent the classic Finnish vacation and are a terrific idea if you have a group (or family) and would like to settle down to enjoy a particular corner of the countryside. They are usually fully equipped with cooking utensils, sauna and a rowing boat, although the cheapest, most 'rustic' ones may not even have electricity and require that you fetch your own water at a well. However, this is considered a true holiday, Finnish style.

Prices are highest during Midsummer and the skiing holidays, when you'll need to book well in advance. Tax is not always included in quoted prices. Most websites and agencies specialize in a certain area: check the regional chapters. The following are a few companies that specialize in wider areas:

Ålandsresor (☎ 018-28000; www.alandsresor.fi; PO Box 62, 22101 Mariehamn) On the Åland islands.

Järvi-Savo (☎ 015-365 399; www.matka-miettinen .fi; Hallituskatu 2, 50100 Mikkeli) Shares a website with Saimaatours. Cottages in the lakes of eastern and central Finland.

Lomarengas (☎ 09-5766 3350; www.lomarengas.fi; Eteläesplanadi 22, 00130 Helsinki) The biggest selection.

Saimaatours (☎ 05-411 7722; www.matka-miettinen .fi; Kirkkokatu 10, 53100 Lappeenranta) Shares a website with Järvi-Savo. Cottages in the lakes of eastern and central Finland.

Villi Pohjola (☎ 020-344 122; www.wildnorth.net) This arm of the Forests and Parks Service has cottages and cabins for rent all over Finland, but especially in Lapland and the north.

Wilderness Huts
See p46 for details on huts, shelters and other options on trekking routes.

BUSINESS HOURS
Banks are open from 9am to 4.30pm Monday to Friday. Shops are generally open 9am to 6pm Monday to Friday, and to 3pm on Saturday. Post offices usually open from 9am to 6pm Monday to Friday. Alko stores (the state-owned network of liquor stores) are generally open 9am to 8pm Monday to Friday (sometimes until 9pm on Thursday or Friday), and until 6pm Saturday. Many supermarkets and Helsinki department stores stay open until 9pm or 10pm Monday to Friday and open all day on Saturday and Sunday.

Finns lunch early, so restaurants usually open at 11am, closing at around 10pm, earlier for simpler places. Lunch specials run until 2pm or 3pm. Bars tend to open from 4pm to midnight, later at weekends. Any variations are noted in the reviews.

CHILDREN

Finland is incredibly child-friendly, and is one of the best places to holiday with them. Domestic tourism is largely dictated by children's needs, and child-friendly attractions abound. Even potentially stuffy museums often make a real effort to appeal to kids, with simplified child-height information, hands-on activities, or activity sheets.

Practicalities

Local tourist information booklets and brochures usually highlight attractions with family appeal; the webpage www.visitfinland. com/family also lists attractions by region.

Lonely Planet's *Travel with Children* by Cathy Lanigan is a good source of general information.

Most Finnish hotels and hostels will put an extra bed in a room for little extra cost – and kids under 12 often sleep free. Many hotel rooms have sofas that can fold out into beds or family-suites, and hostels often have connecting rooms. Camp sites are especially good, with self-catering cabins good value for families. There are always things to do and other children in these places, and some of the larger ones offer child-minding services or activity programs.

Car-rental firms have children's safety seats for hire at a nominal cost, but it is essential that you book them in advance. The same goes for highchairs and cots (cribs); they're standard in many restaurants and hotels, but numbers may be limited.

Entrance fees and transport tickets for children tend to be around 60% of the adult charge in Finland. If this is not the case, child prices are included in the text.

Sights & Activities

All areas of Finland have plenty to offer, depending on what appeals. Activities like canoeing and fishing are available almost everywhere, and large towns all have a swimming complex that includes water-slides, Jacuzzis, saunas and table tennis; excellent for all ages and in both summer and winter.

Finland's best kid-friendly theme parks are Moominworld at Naantali (p212), Särkänniemi (p173) in Tampere, and Wasalandia and Tropiclandia (p250) in Vaasa. For attractions in and around Helsinki, see p70.

CLIMATE CHARTS

Finland is two different places in winter and summer. Summer is fairly reliably dry and hot, although by August things can already begin to get chilly. Of course, winters *are*

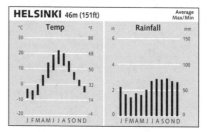

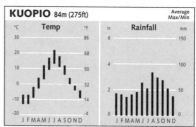

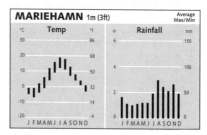

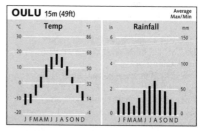

DIRECTORY

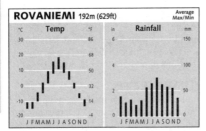

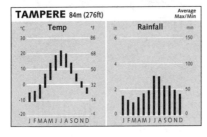

cold, but the cold is dry. In most parts snow first falls in October and clears by the end of March, but in Lapland snow can fall as early as September and stay until late May.

These graphs tell the statistical story; see p13 for a discussion of conditions at various times of year.

COURSES
Language

There are intensive courses in Finnish each summer (June to August) at the universities in Helsinki, Oulu, Lahti, Tampere, Turku, Kuopio and Jyväskylä. For more information contact **Suomen Kesäyliopistot** (☎ 03-214 7626; www.kesayliopistot.fi; Rautatienkatu 26, 33100 Tampere).

The following universities also teach basic courses in Finnish language and culture, with classes typically running either a full term or an intensive period in August. Course fees for nonstudents are typically €80 to €150.

University of Helsinki Language Centre (☎ 09-1912 3234; www.helsinki.fi/kksc/language.services; Yliopistonkatu 5, 00014 Helsinki) One-month classes €135. There's even an online course to get you started.

University of Jyväskylä Language Centre (☎ 014-260 3751; http://kielikompassi.jyu.fi; PO Box 35, 40014 Jyväskylän Yliopisto)

University of Oulu Language Centre (☎ 08-553 3203; www.oulu.fi/kielikeskus; PL 7200, 90014 Oulun Yliopisto)

University of Tampere Language Centre (☎ 03-355 111; www.uta.fi/laitokset/kielikeskus; Kielikeskus, 33014 Tampereen Yliopisto)

University of Turku Language Centre (☎ 02-333 5975; www.kielikeskus.utu.fi; Horttokuja 2, 20014 Turun Yliopisto)

CUSTOMS

Travellers should encounter few problems with Finnish customs. Travellers arriving from outside the EU can bring duty-free goods up to the value of €175 into Finland without declaration. You can also bring in up to 16L of beer, 2L of wine and 1L of spirits, 200 cigarettes or 250g of tobacco and 50g of perfume. If you're coming from another EU country, there is no restriction on the value of gifts or purchases for your own use, except for tobacco from new EU member states.

Although technically part of the EU, arriving on or from the Åland islands carries the same import restrictions as arriving from a non-EU country. Check the latest situation on the Finnish customs website www.tulli.fi, at the border crossing or on an international ferry.

DANGERS & ANNOYANCES

Finland is a very safe, nonthreatening country to travel in but there are some potential risks to consider.

Weather extremes, especially in Lapland, can cause unexpected danger at any time of the year. Extreme cold kills lone trekkers almost every winter in the wilderness, and cold rain can also be a problem in summer.

June and July are the worst months for mosquitoes, which are a major nuisance in the country, particularly in Lapland. Insect repellent or those beautiful hat-nets are essential.

In more remote places you may run across eccentric people, who you will have to accept as they are: sometimes suspicious of outsiders. The gloomy winter may lead to unpredictable behaviour and alcohol abuse.

In urban areas, violence mostly occurs in association with intoxicated local males, who are normally rowdy and intimidating rather than outright aggressive.

DISABLED TRAVELLERS

Finland may be the best-equipped country in the world for the disabled traveller. By law, most institutions must provide ramps, lifts and special toilets for disabled persons; all new hotels and restaurants must install disabled facilities. Trains and city buses are also accessible by wheelchair. Some national parks offer accessible nature trails.

In general, the majority of tourist brochures and information booklets give information about disabled facilities, but it's worth getting in touch with **Rullaten Ry** (☎ 09-805 7393; www.rullaten.fi, www.accessibletravelling.fi; Pajutie 7, 02770 Espoo) before leaving home. This, the Finnish disabled travellers organization, offers advice on 'friendly' places to visit, eat and stay, as well as activities. They publish two booklets, one for all of Finland, another on just Helsinki; these can be ordered from the website. You can order a booklet on accommodation and travel for disabled persons through its website. Another booklet, available at the Helsinki tourist office, focuses just on the capital, which has *Accessible Helsinki*, a program aiming to maximize disabled access in the capital by 2011.

Näkövammaisten Keskusliitto (☎ 09-396 041; www.nkl.fi; Marjaniementie 74, Iiris 00030) is the Finnish national association for the visually impaired. They can give advice on travel in the country, as well as provide details of dedicated holiday centres with a wide range of summer and winter activities on offer.

Kuurojen Liitto (☎ 09-5803 770; www.kl.deaf.fi; PO Box 57, Helsinki 00401) is the equivalent organization for the hearing impaired.

Before leaving home, get in touch with your national support organization – preferably the 'travel officer' if there is one. These places often have complete libraries devoted to travel, and can put you in touch with travel agencies which specialize in tours for the disabled.

DISCOUNT CARDS
Camping Cards
The **Camping Card International** (www.camping cardinternational.org) is basically a campingground ID. These cards are available from your local camping federation (the website has details) and incorporate third-party insurance for damage you may cause. Many camping grounds offer a discount if you sign in with one.

The **Camping Card Scandinavia** is a similar document, and brings a discount at most Finnish camp sites. It can be ordered (allow three weeks for delivery) from the website www.camping.fi, or a temporary version purchased in summer at most camping grounds; the cost is €6.

Hostelling Card
If you plan to stay in youth hostels in Finland, consider joining the International Youth Hostels Federation (IYHF), also called Hostelling International (HI). It's not mandatory to be a member to stay in Finnish hostels. The card also gives discounts on most lake ferries and some sea ones. See p329 for more information about becoming a member.

Seniors Cards
For a small fee, European nationals aged over 60 can get a Rail Europe Senior Card as an add-on to their national rail senior pass. It entitles the holder to reduced fares in some European countries, and percentage savings vary according to the route. Note that anyone aged 65 or over receives a 50% discount on Finnish trains and 30% on intercity buses. There are also rail passes available for travel within Scandinavia for nationals of any country who are aged over 55; inquire at your local travel agency for information. Seniors with proof of age can also receive discounts at many museums, tourist attractions and some public transport.

Student & Youth Cards
The most useful of these is the International Student Identity Card (ISIC), a plastic ID-style card with your photograph, which provides discounts on many forms of transport (including airlines, ferries and local public transport), reduced or free admission to museums and sights, and cheap meals in student cafeterias – a worthwhile way of cutting costs in expensive Finland. Because of the proliferation of fake ISIC cards, carry your home student ID or a letter from your university as a back-up. Some airlines won't give student discounts without it.

Some discounts are given on age rather than student status. If you're aged under 26, you can apply for the Euro26 card (www.eyca.org) or the International Youth Travel Card (IYTC). These cards are available through student unions, hostelling organizations or youth-oriented travel agencies. They don't automatically entitle you to discounts, and some companies and institutions refuse to recognize them altogether, but you won't find out until you flash the card.

If you are studying in Finland, a Finnish student card will get you discounts on transport and more.

EMBASSIES & CONSULATES
Finland's Embassies & Consulates
Visas and information can be obtained at Finnish diplomatic missions (full list at http://formin.finland.fi):

Australia (☎ 02 6273 3800; www.finland.org.au; 12 Darwin Ave, Yarralumla, ACT 2600)

Canada (☎ 613-288 2233; www.finland.ca; 55 Metcalfe St, Suite 850, Ottawa K1P 6L5)

Denmark (☎ 3313 4214; www.finamb.dk; Sankt Annae Plads 24, 1250 Copenhagen K)

Estonia (☎ 610 3200; www.finland.ee; Kohtu 4, EE-15180 Tallinn)

France (☎ 01 44 18 19 20; www.amb-finlande.fr; 1 Place de Finlande, 75007 Paris)

Germany (☎ 030-505030; www.finnland.de; Rauch-strasse 1, 10787 Berlin)

Ireland (☎ 01-478 1344; www.finland.ie; Russell House, Stokes Pl, St Stephen's Green, Dublin 2)

Japan (☎ 03-5447 6000; www.finland.or.jp; 3-5-39 Minami-Azabu, Minato-ku, Tokyo 106-8561)

Latvia (☎ 371-707 8800; www.finland.lv; Kalpaka bulv. 1, LV-1605 Riga)

Netherlands (☎ 070-346 9754; www.finlande.nl; Groot Hertoginnelaan 16, 2517 EG Den Haag)

New Zealand (Colin Beyer; ☎ 04-499 4599, tas@sglaw .co.nz; Simpson Grierson, Level 24, HSBC Towner, 195 Lambton Quay, Wellington) This is the Honorary Consulate General, otherwise contact the embassy in Australia.

Norway (☎ 2212 4900; www.finland.no; Thomas Heftyes gate 1, 0244 Oslo)

Russia (☎ 095-787 4174; www.finemb-moscow.fi; Kropotkinskij Pereulok 15-17, 119034 Moscow G-34)

Sweden (☎ 08-676 6700; www.finland.se; Gärdesgatan 11, 11527 Stockholm)

UK (☎ 020-7838 6200; www.finemb.org.uk; 38 Chesham Place, London SW1X 8HW)

USA (☎ 202-298 5800; www.finland.org; 3301 Massa-chusetts Ave NW, Washington, DC 20008)

Embassies & Consulates in Finland
The following is a list of foreign government representatives in Helsinki. Use the Helsinki area telephone code (☎ 09) if calling from elsewhere.

Australia (Map pp60-1; ☎ 4777 6640; australian. consulate@tradimex.fi; Museokatu 25B) This is the consu-late; the nearest embassy is in Stockholm (www.sweden .embassy.gov.au).

Canada (Map p64; ☎ 228 530; www.canada.fi; Pohjois-esplanadi 25B)

Denmark (Map p64; ☎ 684 1050; www.denmark.fi; Keskuskatu 1A)

Estonia (Map pp60-1; ☎ 622 0260; www.estemb.fi; Itäinen Puistotie 10)

France (Map pp60-1; ☎ 618 780; www.france.fi; Itäinen Puistotie 13)

Germany (☎ 458 580; www.germanembassy.fi; Krogiuksentie 4B)

Ireland (Map p64; ☎ 646 006; embassy.ireland@welho .com; Erottajankatu 7A)

Japan (Map p64; ☎ 686 0200; www.fi.emb-japan.go.jp; Eteläranta 8)

Latvia (Map pp60-1; ☎ 4764 7244; embassy.finland@ mfa.gov.lv; Armfeltintie 10)

Lithuania (Map p64; ☎ 608 210; www.lithuania.fi; Rauhankatu 13A)

Netherlands (Map p64; ☎ 228 920; www.netherlands .fi; Erottajankatu 19B)

New Zealand (☎ 470 1818; paddais@paddais.net; Jo-hanneksenrinne 2) This is the consulate-general; otherwise contact embassy in The Hague, Netherlands.

Norway (Map pp60-1; ☎ 686 0180; www.norge.fi; Rehbinderintie 17)

Russia (Map pp60-1; ☎ 661 876; rusembassy@co.inet .fi; Tehtaankatu 1B)

Sweden (Map p64; ☎ 687 7660; www.sverige.fi; Pohjoisesplanadi 7B)

UK (Map pp60-1; ☎ 2286 5100; www.britishembassy .gov.uk; Itäinen Puistotie 17)

USA (Map pp60-1; ☎ 616 250; www.usembassy.fi; Itäinen Puistotie 14B)

FESTIVALS & EVENTS
One of the great things about travelling in Finland in summer is the myriad festivals, concerts, competitions and events that take place around the country, some con-ventional, some seriously wacky. On any given trip you're sure to stumble across a few full-scale festivals, but you could eas-ily plan your trip around them, hopping from jazz to folk to dance to wife-carrying championships.

The biggest and best festivals are held between June and August, but there are events somewhere in Finland year-round. The following is a list of most of Finland's events – for more information see www .festivals.fi or pick up the free *Finland Fes-tivals* booklet in any tourist office.

February
Runeberg Day 5 February, nationwide. People eat 'Runeberg cakes', available in all shops, to commemorate the national poet.

Laskiainen Seven weeks before Easter, nationwide. Festival of downhill skiing and winter sports. People eat *laskiaispulla*, a wheat bun with whipped cream and hot milk.

March

Pääsiäinen Easter. On Sunday people go to church or paint eggs and eat *mämmi* (pudding made of rye and malt).

Hetan Musiikkipäivät (www.hetanmusiikkipaivat.fi) Hetta village, Enontekiö; chamber music. At Easter.

Tampereen Elokuvajuhlat (www.tamperefilmfestival .fi) Tampere; festival of international short films.

Oulu Music Festival (www.oulunmusiikkijuhlat.fi) Oulu; classical and chamber music.

Lahti Ski Games (www.lahtiskigames.com) Lahti; ski jumping.

Tar Ski Race Oulu; long-distance cross-country ski race.

Marathon Ice-Fishing Oulu; world's longest nonstop ice-fishing contest.

Maria's Day Festival (www.enontekio.fi) Hetta village, Enontekiö; Sámi festival of arts, sports contests.

April

Tampere Biennale (www.tampere.fi/festival/music) Tampere; new Finnish music. Held in even-numbered years only.

April Jazz Espoo (www.apriljazz.fi) Espoo; jazz.

Reindeer Champion Race Inari; reindeer-sleigh racing.

May

Vappu May Day. Traditionally a festival of students and workers, this also marks the beginning of summer, and is celebrated with plenty of alcohol and merrymaking. People drink *sima* mead and eat *tippaleipä* cookies.

Äitienpäivä Mothers' Day. Everyone takes their mother out for a buffet lunch.

Kemin Sarjakuvapäivät (www.kemi.fi/sarjis) Kemi; international comic-strip festival.

Kainuun Jazz Kevät Kajaani; international jazz, blues and rock acts.

Vaasa Choir Festival (www.vaasa.fi/choirfestival) Vaasa; European choirs.

June

Midsummer's Eve & Day Juhannus (Midsummer) is the most important annual event for Finns. Celebrated with bonfires and dancing. People head to summer cottages to celebrate the longest day of the year. It is also the day of the Finnish flag, as well as the day of John the Baptist.

Praasniekka These Orthodox celebrations are day-long religious and folk festivals held in North Karelia and other eastern provinces between May and September, most notably at the end of June.

Ilmajoen Music Festival (www.ilmajoenmusiikkijuhlat .fi) Ilmajoki; classical and folk music and folk operas.

Naantali Music Festival (www.naantalimusic.com) Naantali; chamber music.

Jutajaiset (www.jutajaiset.net) Rovaniemi; folk music and dance, Sámi traditions.

Midnight Sun Film Festival (www.msfilmfestival.fi) Sodankylä; international films.

Riihimäen kesäkonsertit (www.riihimaki.fi/kesakon sertit) Riihimäki; classical music.

Tampere Vocal Music Festival (www.tampere.fi/vocal) Choirs and ensemble singing.

Provinssirock (www.provinssirock.fi) Seinäjoki; rock music.

Nummirock (www.nummirock.fi) Kauhajoki; heavy metal music.

Åland Organ Festival Åland; organ music in medieval churches.

Korsholm Music Festival (www.korsholmmusicfestival .fi) Vaasa; chamber music.

Avanti! Summer Sounds (www.avantimusic.fi) Porvoo; eclectic music from baroque to rock.

International Kalottjazz and Blues Festival (www .kalottjazzblues.net) Tornio (Finland) and Haparanda (Sweden); jazz and blues.

Kuopio Tanssii ja Soi (www.kuopiodancefestival.fi) Kuopio; international dance.

Ruisrock (www.ruisrock.fi) Turku; oldest rock-music festival.

Sata-Häme Soi (www.satahamesoi.fi) Ikaalinen; accordion music.

Midnight Sun Golf Tournament (www.tornio.fi) Tornio (Finland) and Haparanda (Sweden); golf competition.

Helsinki Day Helsinki; celebrates the founding of Helsinki on 12 June.

Puistoblues (www.puistoblues.fi) Late Jun or early Jul, Järvenpää; blues and jazz.

Tar Burning Week Oulu; Midsummer festival.

Savonlinna Ballet Festival (www.savonlinnaballet .net) Savonlinna; often with top Russian troupes.

July

Mikkeli Music Festival (www.mikkelimusic.net) Mikkeli; classical music.

Imatra Big Band Festival (www.ibbf.fi) Imatra; big-band music.

Jyväskylän Kesä (www.jyvaskyla.fi/kesa) Jyväskylä; all the arts.

Rauma Lace Week (www.rauma.fi) Rauma; lace-making demonstrations, carnival.

Rauman Festivo (www.raumanfestivo.fi) Rauma; chamber music.

Savonlinna Opera Festival (www.operafestival.fi) Savonlinna; one of Finland's most notable festivals.

Tangomarkkinat (www.tangomarkkinat.fi) Seinäjoki; tango music.

Pori Jazz Festival (www.porijazz.fi) Pori; one of Finland's most notable festivals.

Kaustinen Folk Music Festival (www.kaustinen.fi) Kaustinen; folk music and dance.

DIRECTORY

Down by the Laituri (www.dbtl.fi) Turku; rock music.
Kuhmon Kamarimusiikki (www.kuhmofestival.fi)
Kuhmo; chamber music.
Joensuu Gospel Festival (www.suomengospel.org)
Joensuu; gospel music.
Lieksan Vaskiviikko (www.lieksabrass.com) Lieksa;
brass music.
Työväen Musiikkitapahtuma (www.valmu.com)
Valkeakoski; workers' music.
Joutsa Folk Festival (www.joutsa.fi/jouto) Joutsa;
traditional Finnish summer festival.
Wife-Carrying World Championships (www
.sonkajarvi.fi) Sonkajärvi; unusual husband-and-wife team
competition with international participants and beer prizes.
Evakon Pruasniekka Iisalmi; traditional festival of the
Orthodox church.
Kotka Maritime Festival (www.meripaivat.com)
Kotka; music, sailing races and cruises.
Sleepyhead Day Naantali; on 27 July the laziest person
in the town is thrown into the sea.
Kihaus Folk Music Festival (www.kihaus.fi) Rääkkylä;
widely acclaimed festival of modern and experimental
Finnish folk music and dancing.

August
Taiteiden Yö A night of art, held in Helsinki and other
towns in late August. Street performances, fringe art and
concerts – a good atmosphere and exciting.
Lappeenranta Music Festival (www.lemi.fi) Lappeen-
ranta and Lemi; festival of international music.
Tampere International Theatre Festival (www.
teatterikesa.fi) Tampere; international and Finnish theatre.
Katrina Festival (www.katrina.aland.fi) Åland, chamber
music.
Lahden Urkuviikko (www.lahtiorgan.net) Lahti; organ
music.
Hamina Tattoo (www.haminatattoo.com) Hamina;
military music. Even years only.
Turku Music Festival (www.turkumusicfestival.fi)
Turku; classical and contemporary music.
Lahti Jazz Festival (www.jazztori.com) Lahti; jazz.
Häme Castle Children's Festival (www.hippalot.net)
Hämeenlinna, dance, theatre and other performances.
Elojazz & Blues (www.welcome.to/jazz20) Oulu; jazz
and blues.
Helsinki Festival (www.helsinkifestival.fi) Helsinki;
all-arts festival.
Air Guitar World Championships (www.airguitar
worldchampionships.com) Oulu.
Neste Rally Finland (www.nesterallyfinland.fi) Jyväskylä.
Finnish round of the World Rally Championship. Lots of fun.

September
International Roma Music Festival (www.romani
taiteenkeskus.com) Porvoo; Romany concerts and carnival.

Lahti Sibelius Festival (www.lahti.fi/symphony) Lahti;
orchestral performances.

October
Oulaisten Musiikkiviikot (www.musiikkiviikot.fi)
Oulainen; eclectic music.
Baltic Herring Market Helsinki; traditional outdoor
herring market.

November
All Souls' Day The first Saturday of November sees
people visit the graves of deceased friends and relatives.
Oulu International Children's Film Festival (www
.oulu.fi) Oulu; international children's films.
Tampere Jazz Happening (www.tampere.fi/jazz) Jazz
and world music.

December
Itsenäisyyspäivä Finland celebrates independence on
6 December with torchlight processions, fireworks and
concerts.
Pikkujoulu 'Little Christmas'; parties are organized in the
weeks leading up to Christmas and much *glögi* (hot punch)
is consumed.
Joulu Christmas is a family celebration.

FOOD

The Food and Drink chapter (p52) dis-
cusses what to expect in restaurants and
bars in Finland. Restaurant reviews in the
book are divided into three price categories:
budget (most mains under €10), midrange
(most mains €10 to €20), and top end (most
mains over €20).

GAY & LESBIAN TRAVELLERS

Finland is one of the more tolerant of destinations for gay and lesbian travellers; fittingly enough for the nation that produced
the artist Tom of Finland. Although there
is no parallel to the lively and active gay
communities of Copenhagen or Stockholm,
Helsinki has a good selection of bars and
clubs (see p70). In smaller towns and in
rural areas attitudes lag behind a little.

In 2001, the Finnish government passed
a law allowing gay and lesbian couples official recognition and most of the rights of
married couples. Current information is
available from the Finnish organization for
gay and lesbian equality, **Seksuaalinen tasa-
vertaisus** (SETA; Map pp60-1; ☎ 09-681 2580; www
.seta.fi; Hietalahdenkatu 2B 16, Helsinki).

Other useful websites:
http://ranneliike.net Events, links, and information.

www.finnqueer.net Online journal discussing issues and news.

www.sappho.net Finnish lesbian site with information and links.

www.z-lehti.fi Finnish gay & lesbian magazine. Currently in Finnish but English content planned.

HOLIDAYS

Finland grinds to a halt twice a year: around Christmas (sometimes including the New Year) and during the Midsummer weekend at the end of June. Plan ahead and avoid travelling during those times. Most hotels and restaurants close over these periods too.

Every town and city in Finland puts on a barrage of festivals between mid-June and mid-August, so accommodation will be tight if you coincide. Anyone who has been in Finland on vappu (May Day) will know it's a big day for Finns and the breweries.

Public Holidays

The following are public holidays celebrated throughout Finland:

New Year's Day 1 January
Epiphany 6 January
Good Friday 14 April 2006, 6 April 2007
Easter Sunday & Monday 16–17 April 2006, 8–9 April 2007
May Day 1 May
Ascension Day May
Whitsunday Late May or early June
Midsummer's Eve & Day Weekend in June closest to the 24th
All Saints Day 1st Saturday in November
Independence Day 6 December
Christmas Eve 24 December
Christmas Day 25 December
Boxing Day 26 December

School Holidays

Schools are on holiday in summer from early June to mid August; they also are off for a week in late February, a week in late October, and two weeks over Christmas. It's traditional for classes to go on school trips in late May and the first few days of June, which can mean that budget accommodation is heavily booked out in some areas.

INSURANCE

Citizens of the European Economic Area (the EU plus Iceland, Norway and Liechtenstein) are entitled to free medical care in Finland (see p355).

For citizens of other countries, travel insurance is a good idea, as it is for anyone who wants to cover theft or loss. Read the fine print carefully as activities like canoeing, skiing, etc might not be included.

See p350 for car insurance.

INTERNET ACCESS

The good news is Internet access is free and widely available in Finland. Every public library in every town has at least one Internet terminal (big libraries have up to a dozen) that can be used free of charge. The downside is that there's a time limit – normally 15 to 30 minutes. If you want longer, you may have to book a slot. You're also restricted by library opening hours, which vary but are typically Monday to Friday only.

Many tourist offices have an Internet terminal that you can use for free (usually 15 minutes), as do a handful of businesses such as cafés in larger cities. Because of this free access, dedicated Internet cafés are not so common in Finland, but you can find a few in Helsinki, Turku, Tampere and a few other towns. They charge €2 to €5 per hour. Check at www.netcaféguide.com for a list.

If you are travelling with your own computer, things are fairly bright. Wireless Internet access is very widespread; most business hotels, and many restaurants, cafés and bars offer free access to customers and guests. You'll need a wireless LAN card for your laptop. Some hotels also offer cable modem access (usually for a fee); otherwise use a phone socket. See the websites www.kropla.com or www.teleadapt.com for help doing this. If your ISP doesn't have global access numbers (Compuserve, AOL and AT&T are examples of ISPs that do), it will be cheaper to use a roaming service such as **Netaway** (www.netaway.com) than make international calls to your home ISP.

LAUNDRY

Laundrettes are thin on the ground in Finland. Check the local telephone book – they are listed as *Pesuloita. Itsepalvelupesula* denotes self-service laundrettes. Most camping grounds and many hostels have self-service laundry facilities. Hotels typically offer (expensive) laundry and dry-cleaning services.

LEGAL AGE

- Voting: 18
- Driving: 18
- Sex: 16 for all
- Drinking: 18
- To buy spirits: 20
- Nightclub entry: varies, but can be up to 25

LEGAL MATTERS

Traffic laws are strict, as are drug laws. Fines for minor offences (such as speeding) are based on the offender's income and assets. This system has led to some well-documented and slightly absurd situations where high-flying Finns breaking the speed limit have been fined as much as €170,000! However, police usually treat bona fide tourists politely in less serious situations. Fishing without a permit is illegal.

MAPS

Almost all local tourist offices offer free city and regional maps that are adequate for finding your way around. Trekking, canoeing and road maps are available from **Karttakeskus Aleksi** (Map p64; ☎ 020-134 0460; www .karttakeskus.fi; Aleksanterinkatu 26, 00100 Helsinki) who produce and sell the largest variety of Finnish maps, and will also ship maps abroad.

Karttakeskus' 1:800,000 AT road map (*Autoilijan Tiekartta*; €11) of the entire country is sufficient for most basic road travel. There is also a series of 19 GT road maps at a scale of 1:200,000. These maps are very clear and show practically all the places that you might be interested in, including hostels and wilderness huts. For extensive driving you're best off with the GT road atlas (€45), updated annually.

Karttakeskus has produced approximately 40 titles for trekking areas, including walking-track presentations of town areas (in 1:25,000 to 1:50,000 scale) and national park maps (1:50,000 to 1:100,000). For the highest level of detail and accuracy, there are 1:20,000 maps available as well. Prices are around €12. Maps for lakes and waterways are also available.

MONEY

Finland uses the euro. Euro notes come in five, 10, 20, 100, 200 and 500 denominations and coins in five, 10, 20, 50 cents and €1 and €2. Euro coins from other countries are legal tender, but 1 and 2 cent coins aren't used.

Swedish krona (including coins) are accepted on Åland and in western Lapland, and Norwegian krona can be used in areas near the Norwegian border in northern Lapland.

ATMs

Using ATMs with a credit or debit card is by far the easiest way of getting cash in Finland. The ATMs have a name, Otto, and can be found even in small villages. Finnish ATMs accept foreign bank cards with Cirrus, Maestro, MasterCard, Visa, Visa Electron, Plus and Amex symbols. Withdrawals using a foreign ATM incur a transaction fee (contact your home bank for details) so it makes good sense to withdraw a reasonable amount each time. The exchange rate is usually better than that offered for travellers cheques or cash exchanges. Keep a copy of the international number to call if your cards are lost or stolen.

Credit Cards

Finns are dedicated users of plastic. Credit cards are accepted and used virtually everywhere – purchasing a beer in a bar with a credit card is not out of the question and it's a common way to pay for accommodation and restaurant meals. Credit cards such as MasterCard and Visa are accepted at most hotels, hostels, restaurants, shops and department stores, and you'll usually need one if you want to hire a car.

Many Finnish petrol stations are automatic. They accept cash (euro notes) and credit cards, but many accept only Finnish-issued credit and debit cards, so are useless to foreign travellers without cash. Don't rely on them.

Moneychangers

The best way to carry and obtain local currency is by using an ATM or credit card, just as most Finns do. Another option is travellers cheques and cash, which can be exchanged at banks. In the big cities independent exchange facilities such as **Forex** (www.forex.fi) usually offer better rates than banks. Finnish post offices also provide banking services and tend to keep longer hours than banks, particularly in remote villages. Airports and international ferries have exchange facilities. for more exchange rate information, see the Quick Reference page on the inside front cover.

Taxes & Refunds

The value-added tax (ALV), usually of 22%, is included in marked prices but may be deducted if you post goods from the point of sale. Alternatively, at stores showing the 'Tax Free for Tourists' sign, foreign visitors who are not EU citizens can get a 12% to 16% refund on items priced over €40. Present the tax-refund 'cheque' to the refund window at your departure point from the EU (eg, airport transit halls, aboard international ferries, at overland border crossings). For more information on VAT refunds contact **Global Refund Finland** (☎ 09-6132 9600; www.globalrefund .com; PO Box 460, 00101 Helsinki).

Tipping

Tipping is not is an essential part of the culture and Finns generally don't, unless rewarding exceptional service. In big cities hospitality staff at decent restaurants will expect it. You will pay service charges in restaurants as percentages; these are generally included in the quoted menu price. You might tell the taxi driver to *'pidä loput'* ('keep the change'). Doormen at fancy clubs and restaurants may also expect a small tip, but this is often a mandatory payment in the form of a 'coat charge'.

Travellers Cheques

Travellers cheques aren't nearly as convenient as using ATMs. Most banks in Finland will exchange travellers cheques but charge commission fees of up to €7. Exchange offices, such as Forex in Helsinki, Turku, Tampere and other big cities, exchange cheques quickly at good rates for a flat €2 fee. There are no American Express offices that change travellers cheques in Finland. Thomas Cook, represented by Travelex, has offices in Helsinki and Turku.

Cheques denominated in US dollars or pounds sterling are easily cashed but it makes sense to buy your cheques in euros so the currency doesn't have to be converted when you cash them in Finland.

PHOTOGRAPHY & VIDEO

Finland's seasonal extremes – snow and little sunlight in winter, followed by almost continuous daylight in summer – can pose challenges for the inexperienced photographer. In particular, the risk of underexposure is great when shooting snowy landscapes – you should know how your camera works, and whether you'll need to correct for this.

Print and slide film is readily available in Finnish cities, and film processing is speedy, fairly cheap and of high quality. A roll of standard 36-exposure print film costs around €5 to €7. Anttila department stores generally offer good prices on film. Any photo shop will happily burn digital photos onto CDs and many will include a CD in the cost of developing a regular film.

POST

Stamps can be bought at bus or train stations and R-kiosk newsstands as well as at the *posti* (post office; www.posti.fi). Post offices sell packing material of various sizes.

Postcards and letters weighing up to 20g cost €0.65 to anywhere in the world (including within Finland) by *lentoposti* (air mail).

Poste restante is located at main post offices in cities. Postcodes in Finland are five-digit numbers that follow this logic: the first two numbers indicate towns and areas, the next two identify the post office in the town or area, and the last number is always 0, except for a post office box or poste restante, in which case the last number is 1. The main post office is always 10 in all large towns, so the postcode for the main post office in Helsinki is 00101, for Turku 20101, for Tampere 33101, for Savonlinna 57101 and for Rovaniemi 96101.

International parcel post is expensive in Finland; a 5kg package to Europe, for example, will cost around €35.

SHOPPING

On the whole, prices in Finland are lower than in other Nordic countries – which isn't to say that there are any real bargains here, particularly on those items for which Finland is famous: glassware, pottery, woollens and various handicrafts made from pine or birch.

If you're heading to the Baltic countries such as Tallinn, Estonia – which can be visited on a day trip from Helsinki – you'll find that prices there are cheaper still, and for many of the same types of items of more or less the same quality.

Lappish, or Sámi, handicrafts include jewellery, clothing, textiles and hunting knives, as well as other items made from local wood, reindeer bone and hide, metals and semiprecious stones. Duodji are authentic handicrafts produced according to Sámi traditions. A genuine item, which can be expensive, will carry a special 'Duodji' token. Sámi handicrafts can be found at markets and shops in Helsinki and throughout Lapland, but for the widest selections visit the Sámi villages of Inari (p322) and Hetta (Enontekiö; p308).

Trekkers will want to purchase a *kuksa* (cup) made in traditional Sámi fashion from the burl of a birch tree. These are widely available throughout Finland, at markets and in handicraft or souvenir shops. Quality of workmanship varies, as does price, but the typical *kuksa* costs about €20.

Local markets are good places to purchase colourful *lapaset* (woollen mittens), *myssy* or *pipo* (hats) and *villapusero* (sweaters), necessary for surviving the cold Finnish winters, as well as *raanu* or *ryijy* (woven wall hangings). A good hand-knitted sweater sells for at least €200. Local folk – particularly in Åland – will often 'knit to order', taking your measurements and then posting the sweater to you in two or three months, once it's finished. It's possible to find cheaper, machine-knitted wool sweaters in Finnish markets, but check the labels – they probably were made in Norway.

If you DIY, contact the nearest Käsityöasema (a centre that preserves cottage industries) and create your own handicrafts. There are hundreds of these in Finland, and many are especially geared towards visitors. You pay only for the material, plus a small fee for equipment rental.

For decades, Finland has been world famous for its indigenous glass production. The Savoy vase designed by Alvar Aalto is a good 'souvenir of Finland', although expensive. Department stores and finer shops carry it as well as other stylish vases by Iittala, Nuutajärvi and Humppila. Big roadside discount shops also stock Finnish glassware, plus designer pottery and cooking utensils; most of this is schlock.

Hunting and carving knives made by the Marttiini company are well known internationally, as are fishing lures and flies made by Kuusamo.

It's possible to find bargains on trekking goods such as jackets and down sleeping bags. Chains such as Partio-Aitta and Lassen Retkiaitta specialize in outdoor equipment, but many sports shops, such as Intersport or Kesport, also have good selections.

SOLO TRAVELLERS

Finland is one of the world's safest places, so travelling alone poses little risk. In smaller hotels and guesthouses, expect to pay 60% to 70% of the double-room rate. Many business-class hotels, however, scandalously charge the same price for a single or double room (the company picks up the tab). If this is the case, make sure you get a decent double-sized room!

Many camp sites offer cheaper rates for solo campers, but normally charge the two-person rate for cottages and cabins.

TELEPHONE

Public telephones are reasonably common in Finland, although the high level of mobile phone usage is making them redundant. The vast majority accept plastic Telecards or credit cards, but a few older ones accept coins. Phonecards can be purchased at post offices, shops and R-kioski newsstands.

International calls are expensive, but are cheapest between 10pm and 8am Monday to Friday and all day Saturday and Sunday. Large cities have telecentres where you can make international calls from booths at much cheaper rates than from public phones. Similarly, you can buy cut-rate international phone cards from kiosks; there are several varieties, with rates clearly marked.

Mobile Phones

Finland has one of the world's highest rates of mobile-phone usage, which is not surprising since Nokia is Finnish. Getting on to the mobile network is easy with the prepaid system using **Sonera** (www.sonera.fi), **Telering** (www.telering.fi) or **DNA** (www.dnafinland.fi). Bring your own phone and simply buy a starter kit from a phone shop or any R-kiosk. At the time of writing, you could get a SIM card for €17, which included €10 of call credit. You can buy recharge cards from the same outlets.

If travelling with your own phone from America or Japan, check with your service provider that is will work in Europe's GSM 900/1800 network.

Phone Codes
The country code for Finland is ☎ 358. To dial abroad it's ☎ 00. The number for the international operator is ☎ 020208.

TIME
Finnish time is two hours ahead of GMT in winter. When it's noon in Finland it's 2am in Los Angeles, 5am in New York, 10am in London, 7pm or 9pm in Sydney and 11am in Sweden and Western Europe. Daylight Saving Time, when clocks go forward one hour, applies from late March or early April to the end of October.

The 24-hour clock is used commonly for transport times, opening hours, etc. If you see *Ma-Pe 9-20*, for example, it means that a place is open Monday to Friday from 9am to 8pm.

TOILETS
Ridiculously, toilets in train and bus stations require a fee of €1 or €2. Other public conveniences cost around €0.40.

TOURIST INFORMATION
All major Finnish towns have a tourist office with helpful, English-speaking staff, English-language brochures and excellent free maps. In summer, these offices are often staffed by university students on vacation. Most offices publish a miniguide to their town or region and all have a website (which is usually www .nameoftown.fi). Additionally, many offices stockpile brochures, maps and advice for lots of other towns and regions in Finland.

The main office of the **Finnish Tourist Board** (Matkailun Edistämiskeskus, MEK; Map p64; ☎ 4176 9300; www.visitfinland.com; Eteläesplanadi 4; 00100 Helsinki) is located near the kauppatori in the centre of Helsinki. Their website lists overseas branches that can also provide information.

VISAS
A valid passport or EU identity card is required to enter Finland. Most Western nationals don't need a tourist visa for stays of less than three months; South Africans need a Schengen visa. For more information contact the nearest Finnish embassy or consulate, or the **Directorate of Immigration** (☎ 09-4765 500; www.uvi.fi; Panimokatu 2A, 00580 Helsinki).

RUSSIAN & ESTONIAN VISAS
All foreigners require a visa to travel into Russia from Finland. Russian visas take about eight working days to process in Helsinki (you must leave your passport at the embassy) so you may want to get one before leaving home. Helsinki tour companies specializing in travel to Russia can usually expedite a visa much quicker, but for a fee.

European citizens and most Western nationals don't require a visa for a short stay in Estonia, but citizens of South Africa do (a valid Latvian or Lithuanian visa is valid). Check out the website of the **Estonian Foreign Ministry** (www.vm.ee).

WOMEN TRAVELLERS
Finland is one of the safest places to travel in the world. Women often travel alone or in pairs around the region, which should pose no problems. Outside of Helsinki, however, and especially in the north, bars can be fairly unreconstructed places, and solo women may well get a bit of hassle from drunk locals.

WORK
There is very little work open to foreigners because of high local unemployment. It's possible to get a job teaching English at a Finnish company, but standards are very high so previous experience and good references are essential. Students can apply for limited summer employment, and au pair arrangements are possible for up to 18 months.

Australian and New Zealand citizens aged between 18 and 30 can apply for a one year working holiday visa under a reciprocal arrangement.

For any serious career-oriented work, a work permit is required for all foreigners other than EU citizens. Employment must be secured before applying for the work permit, and the work permit must be filed in advance of arrival in Finland, together with a letter from the intended employer and other proof of employment. Work permits can be obtained from the Finnish embassy in your home country. A residence permit may also be required. For more information contact the **Directorate of Immigration** (☎ 09-476 5500; www.uvi.fi; PO Box 92, 00531 Helsinki).

Transport

TRANSPORT

THINGS CHANGE...

The information in this chapter is particularly vulnerable to change. Check directly with the airline or a travel agent to make sure you understand how a fare (and ticket you may buy) works and be aware of the security requirements for international travel. Shop carefully. The details given in this chapter should be regarded as pointers and are not a substitute for your own careful, up-to-date research.

GETTING THERE & AWAY

ENTERING THE COUNTRY
Passport
EU nationals, Schengen agreement countries, and citizens of Switzerland and small EU affiliates such as Andorra and Monaco can enter Finland with a valid passport or identity card. All other nationalities need a valid passport. Most Western nationals don't need a visa; South Africans are among those that do.

See http://formin.finland.fi for a full list of requirements.

AIR
Direct flights to Finland are not the cheapest in Europe, but it is served by various budget carriers, including Ryanair from London and Frankfurt, Germanwings from Cologne, and Blue1 from Copenhagen and Stockholm. Most other flights are with Finnair or Scandinavian Airlines (SAS).

Airports & Airlines
Nearly all flights to Finland land at **Helsinki-Vantaa airport** (HEL; ☎ 0200 14636; www.helsinki-vantaa.fi), situated 19km north of the capital.

Other international airports include Tampere (TMP), Turku (TKU), Oulu (OUL), Vaasa (VAA) and Rovaniemi (RVN), the transport hub of Lapland.

There are good flight connections to Finland from all over the world. Finnair, the Finnish national carrier, and SAS have scheduled flights to Helsinki from most major cities in Europe, as well as from New York, San Francisco, Cairo, Bangkok, Hong Kong, Singapore, Beijing, Shanghai, Guangzhou, Osaka and Tokyo.

To Turku, Vaasa, Oulu and Tampere there are several nonstop flights daily from Stockholm.

Airlines flying to and from Finland (all phone numbers in Helsinki with an 09 code unless otherwise stated):

Adria Airways (JP; ☎ 6151 4135; www.adria-airways.com)

Aer Lingus (EI; ☎ 6122 0260; www.aerlingus.ie)

Aeroflot Russian Airlines (SU; ☎ 659 655; www.aeroflot.com)

Air Baltic (BT; ☎ 020-386 000; www.airbaltic.com)

Air Finland (FIF; ☎ 251 200; www.airfinland.fi)

Air France (AF; ☎ 8568 0500; www.airfrance.com)

American Airlines (AA; ☎ 9800 14620; www.aa.com)

Austrian Airlines (OS; ☎ 020-386 000; www.aua.com)

Blue1 (KF; ☎ 06000 25831; www.blue1.com)

British Airways (BA; ☎ 6937 9538; www.ba.com)

Czech Airlines (OK; ☎ 681 2650; www.csa.cz)

European Executive Express (☎ 02 415 4957; www.european.se, in Sweden)

Finnair (AY; ☎ 81881; www.finnair.com)

FlyMe (FLY; ☎ 0100 30010; www.flyme.com)

Germanwings (4U; ☎ +49 1805 955 855; www.germanwings.com, in Germany)

Iberia (IB; ☎ 6877 8950; www.iberia.es)
Icelandair (FI; ☎ 6126 070; www.icelandair.com)
KLM (KL; ☎ 020-353 355; www.klm.com)
Lithuanian Airlines (TE; ☎ 6226 2299; www.lal.lt)
LOT Polish Airlines (LO; ☎ 6937 9036; www.lot.com)
Lufthansa (LH; ☎ 020-386 000; www.lufthansa.com)
Malev Hungarian Airlines (MA; ☎ 622 0922, www.malev.hu)
Ryanair (FR; ☎ 0600 16010; www.ryanair.com)
SAS Scandinavian Airlines (SK; ☎ 06000 53686; www.scandinavian.net)
SN Brussels Airlines (SN; ☎ 6937 9358; www.flysn.com)
Spanair (JK; ☎ 6151 4135; www.spanair.es)
Swiss International (LX; ☎ 6937 9034; www.swiss.com)

Tickets

As with most European destinations, flights are usually cheaper if they include a Saturday night stay. One-way flights are rarely good value.

Online ticket sales work well if you are doing a simple return trip on a specific date; however, online fare generators are no substitute for a travel agent who knows all about special deals, has strategies for avoiding stopovers and can offer advice.

The following are some useful websites for online purchases and price comparisons:

Ebookers (www.ebookers.com) Another good online flight booker.
Expedia (www.expedia.com) Reliable online flight agent run by Microsoft.
Flights.com (www.flights.com) A truly international site for flight-only tickets; cheap fares and easy-to-search database.
Kelkoo (www.kelkoo.com) Compares flight prices from several sources.
Opodo (www.opodo.com) Online sales from a confederation of world airlines.
Travelocity (www.travelocity.com) This US site allows you to search for fares (in US dollars) to and from practically anywhere.
WhichBudget (www.whichbudget.com) Up-to-date listings of routes flown by budget airlines.

INTERCONTINENTAL (RTW) TICKETS

Round-the-world (RTW) tickets are often real bargains. They are usually put together by a combination of airlines and allow you to fly anywhere you want on their route systems so long as you do not backtrack. There may be restrictions on how many stops you are permitted and usually the tickets are valid for 90 days up to a year. An alternative type of RTW ticket is one put together by a travel agency using a combination of discounted tickets.

Finnair is part of the OneWorld airline alliance with Qantas, British Airways, Cathay Pacific, American Airlines, Iberia, Aer Lingus and LanChile.

SAS AIR PASSES

If you're visiting more countries in Scandinavia and the Baltic, one of the airpasses offered by SAS might be right for you. They offer competitive pricing on internal and international flights in the region, bought as coupons. You must have a return ticket to Scandinavia on SAS (or partner airlines Spanair, Lufthansa, Icelandair or United) to qualify for purchase.

The Visit Scandinavia airpass is open to residents of European countries other than Scandinavia and Finland. You can buy domestic flights within Denmark, Norway and Sweden, as well as international legs between these three and Finland.

The Visit Baltic pass includes the option of flights to Estonia, Latvia, Lithuania, Russia and Ukraine. You must be a resident of a European country outside this area.

The Visit Europe pass includes flights to other European countries and is only open to non-European residents.

Asia

Most Asian countries offer fairly competitive deals, with Bangkok, Singapore and Hong Kong the best places to shop around for discount tickets. Flights from Asia to Europe tend to be cheaper in Asia than flights Europe, so it's worth purchasing the return flight while in Asia. Most airlines sell a standard European fare, regardless of the distance flown from the first stop.

Finnair flies direct from Helsinki to all three major travel hubs, as well as to Tokyo, Beijing, Shanghai, Guangzhou and Osaka.

STA Travel (www.statravel.com) is a recommended agent with branches in Hong Kong, Singapore, India, Malaysia, Thailand, Taiwan, China, Japan and South Korea among others.

Australia & New Zealand

Flying from Australia is a two-stage journey (at least), with likely stopovers in either Singapore or Bangkok, and cities in

TRANSPORT

Europe. It's also possible to go via Japan and/or Russia. Finnair flies to Sydney, in partnership with Qantas, British Airways and Cathay Pacific. KLM, Lufthansa, Austrian Airlines and a few other European airlines fly to Helsinki from Australia via London, Amsterdam, Frankfurt, Vienna and other cities.

You may want to consider a round-the-world option, which can work out not much more expensive. These are often the best value from New Zealand. Depending on which airline you choose, you may fly across Asia (Singapore Airlines, Thai Airlines, Air New Zealand), with possible stopovers in India, Bangkok or Singapore, or across the USA (United, American Airlines, Continental), with possible stopovers in Honolulu, Australia or one of the Pacific islands.

Useful agencies:

Flight Centre Australia (☎ 133 133; www.flightcentre .com.au); New Zealand (☎ 0800 243 544; www.flightcen tre.co.nz) has dozens of branches throughout Australia and New Zealand.

STA Travel Australia (☎ 1300 733 035; www.statravel .com.au); New Zealand (☎ 09 309 9723; www.statravel .co.nz) Offices in most major cities.

Trailfinders Australia (☎ 02 9247 7666, 03 9600 3022; www.trailfinders.com.au) Reliable travel agent.

Travel Online (www.travelonline.co.nz) Good New Zealand website for checking flights.

Travel.Com (www.travel.com.au) Good Australian online site that allows you to look up fares and flights into and out of the country.

Continental Europe

Helsinki is well connected to most European capitals and major cities by a number of airlines. Particularly good are the connections with Scandinavian and Baltic capitals. The websites listed under Tickets (see p343) offer good prices and comparisons for return fares to Helsinki.

The budget airlines Ryanair, Germanwings, and Blue1 offer the cheapest fares off-season (check www.whichbudget.com for the current situation in this rapidly-changing market), but in summer you may find that the regular carriers offer more competitive fares.

STA Travel (www.statravel.com) has branches in many European nations, while **Kilroy Travels** (www.kilroytravels.com) has branches in Nordic countries and the Netherlands. Other recommended agents:

France OTU Voyages (☎ 01 44 41 38 50; www.otu.fr); Voyageurs du Monde (☎ 01 40 15 11 15; www.vdm.com); Nouvelles Frontières (☎ 08 25 00 08 25 nationwide, www .nouvelles-frontieres.fr) Reliable travel agents with online booking.

Germany Just Travel (☎ 089 747 333; www.justtravel .de) English-speaking travel agent.

Italy CTS Viaggi (☎ 199 501150; www.cts.it) Specialists in student travel.

Netherlands Airfair (☎ 020 620 5121; www.airfair.nl) Useful flight agent.

Spain Edreams (www.edreams.es); Viajar.com (☎ 902 902 522; www.viajar.com) Two competitive online agents.

UK & Ireland

From Britain, the cheapest service to Finland is often Ryanair's daily flight from London Stansted to Tampere. There are also direct nonstop scheduled services run by Finnair and British Airways from Helsinki to London, Manchester, Dublin, and, as of April 2006, Edinburgh.

Discount air travel is big business in the UK – this is the discount centre of Europe. Advertisements for many travel agencies are in the travel pages of the weekend broadsheet newspapers, *Time Out*, the *Evening Standard* and the free *TNT* magazine. Shop around – many of the ultracheap fares you see advertised won't be available when you call, but something usually comes up.

As well as the websites mentioned above, some recommended travel agents are:

Ebookers (☎ 0870 814 0000; www.ebookers.com)

North South Travel (☎ 01245 608 291; www.north southtravel.co.uk) Profits go to the developing world.

Nortours (☎ 0870 7447 305; www.norvista.co.uk) Specialists in Nordic travel.

Scantours (☎ 020 7839 2927; www.scantours.co.uk) Specialists in the region.

STA Travel (☎ 0870 160 0599; www.statravel.co.uk) Branches across the UK and Ireland.

Trailfinders (www.trailfinders.co.uk) Check website for closest branch.

USIT (☎ 01 602 1904, 028 90 327 111; www.usit.ie) Ireland-wide specialists in youth travel.

USA & Canada

Finnair flies direct from Helsinki to New York and, in summer, to Toronto, but it's likely that you'll find cheaper fares involving a change of flight in another European city. You could fly to London, for example, and take advantage of the budget Ryanair service to Tampere.

Popular travel agents:

Flight Centre USA (☎ 1866 WORLD 51; www.flightcen tre.us); Canada (☎ 1877 478 8747; www.flightcentre.ca) Offices across the USA and Canada.

STA Travel (☎ 800 781 4040; www.statravel.com) Offices in major US cities.

Travel CUTS (☎ 800 667 2887; www.travelcuts.com) Canada's national student travel agency; offices in all major cities.

LAND
Border Crossings
There are ten border crossings from northern Sweden to northern Finland across Tornionjoki and Muonionjoki, and the main highway in both countries runs parallel to the border from Tornio/Haparanda to Kaaresuvanto/Karesuando. There are no passport or customs formalities, and if you're driving up along the border you can alternate between countries.

Between Norway and Finland, there are six road border crossings, plus a few legal crossings along wilderness tracks. The main Nordkapp (North Cape) route goes from Rovaniemi via Inari and Kaamanen to Karigasniemi; there's also a crossing further west at Kilpisjärvi.

There are eight border crossings between Finland and Russia. Along the popular Helsinki–Vyborg–St Petersburg corridor there are two Finland-Russia road crossings: Nuijamaa (Russian side: Brusnichnoe) and Vaalimaa (Russian side: Torfyanovka).

The Russian borders are serious affairs; you must already have a visa to cross into Russia (see p341).

Bus
It's a long way to Finland by bus from the UK and central Europe – you're unlikely to save too much money over a plane fare. **Eurolines** (www.eurolines.com) don't have direct services to Helsinki except from Russia (see p346), but they may be useful if you plan to visit other Nordic countries en route.

Car & Motorcycle
Motorists and motorcyclists will need the vehicle's registration papers, and liability insurance. You may have to contact your insurer to initiate Europe-wide 'Green Card' coverage. A home licence from most Western countries is valid. Contact your local automobile association for details about all documentation.

See p346 for information about driving in Finland.

Car Ride Services
Car pooling is a good way of sharing costs, especially when travelling long distances. Useful websites to search for drivers or to enter your details for prospective passengers are:

www.allostop.com Canadian site that lists a range of European links.

www.compartir.org Spanish site with Europe-wide lifts.

www.freewheelers.co.uk British site with worldwide lifts.

www.mitfahrzentrale.de In German and perhaps the most useful site. You pay a reservation fee.

Train
The typical route to Finland from any point in Europe goes via Denmark and Sweden. There are direct long-distance trains to Stockholm from various major cities in Europe. Train passes give discounts on most ferry routes across to Finland.

Asia
TRAIN
To and from central and eastern Asia, a train can work out at about the same price as flying, and it can be a lot more fun.

Helsinki is a good place to start your journey across Russia into Asia. Frequent trains run between Helsinki and Moscow (see p346), and there are three routes to/from Moscow across Siberia with connections to China, Japan and Korea: the Trans-Siberian to/from Vladivostok, and the Trans-Mongolian and Trans-Manchurian, both to/from Beijing. There's a fourth route south from Moscow and across Kazakhstan, following part of the old Silk Road to Beijing. These trips take several days, often involve stopovers, and prices vary according to the direction you are travelling, where you buy your ticket and what is included.

For details on Trans-Siberian options see Lonely Planet's *Trans-Siberian Railway*.

Norway
BUS
There's a wide range of buses from Finland to and from various points in Norway, many running in summer only. The main

TRANSPORT

operator is **Eskelisen Lapin Linjat** (www.eskelisen-lapinlinjat.com), whose website has detailed timetables.

Most crossings are in the northeast part of Finland; these routes often originate in Rovaniemi and continue via Sodankylä and Ivalo or Inari. They then proceed to Karasjok, Lakselv, Tanabru or Kirkenes. There is one daily bus in summer from Oulu to Nordkapp (North Cape) via Rovaniemi, Inari and Karasjok. On the western route, a daily bus runs from Oulu to Rovaniemi and Muonio; in summer this continues to Kilpisjärvi and Tromsø (12½ hours).

TRAIN
There is no train service between Finland and Norway.

Russia
BUS
There are two daily express buses to Vyborg and St Petersburg from Helsinki, one originating in Turku. There's also one daily from Tampere and three weekly from Lappeenranta. A visa is required to enter Russia. Check current timetables on www.matkahuolto.info and book tickets at the city bus station or a travel agency. The one-way fare from Helsinki to Vyborg is €34.70 (five to six hours) and to St Petersburg it's €53.50 (eight to nine hours).

Goldlines (www.goldline.fi) run three weekly buses from Rovaniemi (€90, 15 hours) via Ivalo (€50, 7½ hours) to Murmansk.

CAR & MOTORCYCLE
If you plan to drive into Russia, you'll need an international licence and certificate of registration, passport and visa, and insurance. **Ingonord** (☎ 09-251 0300; www.ingonord.com; Salomonkatu 5C, 00100 Helsinki) can arrange temporary Russian cover. Scandinavian car rental companies do not allow their cars to be taken into Russia.

TRAIN
Finland uses broad-gauge tracks, similar to those in Russia, so there are regular trains to/from Russia. Tickets for these trains are sold at the international ticket counter at Helsinki train station. The rail crossing is at Vainikkala (Russian side: Luzhayka).

There are three daily trains from Helsinki to Russia, travelling via the Finnish stations of Lahti, Kouvola and Vainikkala. You must have a valid Russian visa, but border formalities have been fast-tracked so that passport checks are now carried out on board the moving train.

The *Tolstoi* sleeper runs from Helsinki to Moscow (via St Petersburg), arriving at the Russian capital early in the morning. One way costs 2nd/1st class €85/127. The fare includes a sleeper berth in both classes.

The *Sibelius* and *Repin* run daily between Helsinki and St Petersburg (5½ hours) via Vyborg (3¾ hours). The *Sibelius* is a Finnish day train (2nd/1st class €50.80/80.40, seats only). The Russian *Repin* has 2nd-class seats (€50.80) or 1st-class sleeping berths (€89.10). Return fares are double. There are significant discounts for families and small groups. See www.vr.fi for details.

Sweden
BUS
The quickest route to Finland from southern Sweden is by ferry (see below opposite). In the north, there are buses from Sweden to the Finnish town of Tornio, which is just across the river from Haparanda in Sweden.

Tapanis Buss (www.tapanis.se) Stockholm (☎ 08-153 300); Haparanda (☎ 0922-12 955) runs express coaches from Stockholm to Tornio via Haparanda twice a week on the E4 Hwy (Skr480/€55, 14 hours).

Alternatively, pick a bus stop from where you can walk to Finland, although you can generally pick up a local bus to the station in the Finnish town or vice versa. Swedish trains travel as far north as Boden; from there take buses (train passes are valid) to Haparanda, and on to Tornio and Kemi. Inter-Rail passes cover bus travel all the way from Boden to Kemi.

TRAIN
There is no direct train service between Finland and Sweden, but train passes give discounts on ferry and bus connections.

SEA
Arriving in Finland by ferry is a memorable way to begin your visit, especially if you dock in Helsinki. Baltic ferries are some of the world's most impressive sea-going craft, especially considering they are passenger ferries rather than cruise ships.

The big ferries are floating hotels-cum-shopping plazas, with duty-free shopping, restaurants, bars, karaoke, nightclubs and saunas. Many Scandinavians use them simply for boozy overnight cruises, so they can get pretty rowdy on Friday and Saturday nights, when you may need to book in advance.

Services are year-round between major cities; book ahead in summer and if travelling with a vehicle. The boats are amazingly cheap if you travel deck class (without a cabin): they make their money from duty-free purchases. Many ferry lines offer 50% discounts for holders of Eurail, Scanrail and Inter-Rail passes. Some offer discounts for seniors, and for ISIC and youth card-holders; inquire when purchasing your ticket. There are usually discounts for families and small groups travelling together.

Ferry companies have detailed timetables and fares on their websites. Fares vary according to season. Here is a list of operators with their Finnish contact numbers:

Birka Line (☎ 018-27330; www.birkaline.com)
Eckerö Line (☎ 09-2288 544; www.eckeroline.fi; www.eckerolinjen.fi)
Finnlines (☎ 010-34350; www.finnlines.fi)
Linda Line (☎ 09-668 9700; www.lindaliini.ee)
Nordic Jet Line (☎ 09-681 770; www-eng.njl.fi)
RG Line (☎ 06-3200 300; www.rgline.com)
SeaWind Line (☎ 0800 16800; www.seawind.fi)
Silja Line (☎ 09-18041; www.silja.fi)
Superfast Ferries (☎ 09-2534 0640; www.superfast.com)
Tallink (☎ 09-228 311; www.tallink.fi)
Viking Line (☎ 09-12351; www.vikingline.fi)

Estonia

Several ferry companies ply the Gulf of Finland between Helsinki and Tallinn in Estonia. Since most nationalities (except Canadians) don't require a visa and the trip is so quick and cheap, it's a very popular day trip from Helsinki (see boxed text, p83). Competition between the companies keeps the prices low, and if you're heading to Estonia for onward travel it can be cheaper to get a same-day return ticket than a one-way ticket. Car ferries cross in 3½ hours, catamarans and hydrofoils in about 1½ hours. Service is heavy year-round, although in winter there are fewer departures, and the traffic is also slower because of ice. Cancellations occur if the sea is rough; the express boats are more prone to this. Phone the day before to check on sailings in winter.

Ferries are cheapest: Eckerö Line has only one departure daily but is the cheapest with a return fare of €25 in high season. Tallink, Viking Line and Silja Line have several daily departures (€17 to €25, one way). Vehicle space costs around €17.

Catamarans and hydrofoils cost between €22 and €28 one way depending on the company, time of year, time of day and the day of the week. Linda Line, Nordic Jet Line and Tallink offer these routes. Tallink are somewhat pricier, at €34 to €39 for adults in summer, but have vehicle space on their fast ferry (€23 to €27 one-way for standard-sized cars).

Tickets can be booked online, at the ferry company offices in central Helsinki, from the ferry terminal, or from the Helsinki city tourist office (for a hefty booking fee).

See Visas (p341) for details of Estonian entry requirements.

Germany

Finnlines has year-round service from Helsinki to Travemünde (from €302 September to May, from €408 June to August one way plus €100 per vehicle, 34 to 36 hours) with a connecting bus service to Hamburg.

Superfast Ferries has a speedy ferry running service between Rostock and Hanko on the south coast of Finland (21 hours), Tuesday to Sunday, and daily late May to late August. The ferries all depart in the evening and the minimum one-way fare is €75 in 'airline seats', or €155 in a cabin. Vehicles cost from €116.

Sweden

Stockholm is the main gateway to Finland, due to the incredibly luxurious passenger ferries that travel regularly between Stockholm and Turku or Helsinki. There are two main competing operators, Silja Line (blue-and-white ferries) and Viking Line (red-and-white ferries), with smaller companies operating on certain routes.

The major source of income for these ferry companies is duty-free shopping. Because the ferries stop at the Åland islands, tax-free shopping is possible on board, even though Sweden and Finland are both in the European Union. Thus

TRANSPORT

Swedes and Finns can avoid the high sales taxes in both countries, especially for alcohol and cigarettes. For the traveller, this means ferry companies can afford to keep fares unusually low. Whether you choose to blow the rest of your cash on board on a megabuffet, disco dancing or a case of aquavit – well, that's up to you.

There are cabins, but you can buy a passenger ticket and sleep in the salons or any spare patch of inside deck (or just not sleep at all, as many partying passengers do). There are luggage lockers on board. Viking Line is the cheapest, but note that Friday-night departures are more expensive than departures on other days of the week. Silja line also does regular special prices.

In summer, overnight crossings (passenger ticket only) from Stockholm start at €25 to Turku (11 to 12 hours) and €46 to Helsinki (16 hours). Note that Åbo is Swedish for Turku.

All Viking and Silja ferries travelling between Stockholm and Turku call in at Mariehamn in Åland. The SeaWind Line runs the same route (11 hours, from €58 per vehicle, including one to four passengers), but stops in Långnäs. Additionally, Birka Cruises travels between Mariehamn and Stockholm, and both Viking and Silja Lines offers service between Mariehamn/Turku and Kapellskär, Sweden, a small harbour in the northern part of Stockholm province. This cuts the journey considerably; a connecting bus to Stockholm is included in the price of the ferry.

Eckerö Linjen sails from Grisslehamn, north of Stockholm, to Eckerö in Åland. It's by far the quickest, at just two hours, and, with prices starting from €5.50 return, it's a bargain, especially as the connecting bus from Stockholm, Uppsala or Gävle (Sweden) is free.

From the main Åland island group it's possible to island-hop across the archipelago to mainland Finland (or vice versa) on free ferries. See p232 for details.

RG Lines sails from Vaasa in Finland, to Umeå, Sweden (€50 to €60/SEK450 to SEK540, four hours) one or two times daily (and once weekly to Sundsvall) in summer. Finnlines run a simpler cargo ferry, which connects Naantali, near Turku, with Kapellskär three times daily.

GETTING AROUND

A thick book of timetables for all domestic buses and trains is published every year by Edita (www.turisti.fi), based in Helsinki. While all of this information is on the Internet, if you like having it at your fingertips, the tome costs €28.

A great journey planner for Finland's public transport network is online at www .matka.fi.

AIR
Airlines in Finland
Finnair is the principal domestic carrier, and runs a comprehensive network from Helsinki, and from a couple of regional hubs. Standard prices are fairly expensive, but Happy Hour rates, which can be booked up to a week in advance, offer significant savings. Also check the www .finnair.fi website for *äkkilähdot* (quick getaway) offers. Children under 12 and seniors receive a 70% discount. If you're between 17 and 24 the youth discount is 50%, but even better value is the youth stand-by fare. Available to those aged between 17 and 24, you need to arrive at the airport one hour before the flight of your choice and wait to see if there are any seats. Under this plan, any one-way direct flight costs €64 to €79 – a huge saving from, say, Helsinki to Rovaniemi (cheaper than the train). If you don't get on your desired flight, your money is refunded.

Special discounts are offered on some routes in summer, and 'snow fares' give discounts of 50% to 70% on selected flights between Helsinki and Lapland during non-holiday periods from January to May.

If you book in advance, the budget carrier Blue1 offers the sharpest rates on routes from Helsinki to a range of Finnish cities, with prices as low as €33 one way.

Airlines flying domestically:

Blue1 (☎ 06000 25831; www.blue1.com) Budget flights from Helsinki to Kuopio, Oulu, Rovaniemi and Vaasa.

European Executive Express (☎ 02 415 4957; www .european.se) Flights between Åland and Turku, as well as summer ones between Helsinki-Savonlinna/Mikkeli.

Finnair (☎ 81881; www.finnair.com) Extensive domestic network includes flights by subsidiaries FinnComm and Golden Air.

BICYCLE

Finland is largely a flat country and as bicycle-friendly as any country you'll find, with plenty of bike paths that cyclists share with inline skaters in summer. The only drawback to an extensive tour is distance, but bikes can be taken on most trains, buses and ferries. Åland is particularly good for cycling. Helmets are required by law.

For more information about cycling in Finland see p47.

BOAT
Lake & River Crossings

Lake and river ferries operate during summer. Departures tend to be sporadic from May to mid-June and during August, but are very steady from mid-June to the end of July. These ferries are more than mere transport – a lake cruise, particularly from one town to another, is a bona fide Finnish experience.

Apart from two-hour cruises starting from towns such as Jyväskylä, Kuopio, Savonlinna, Tampere, Mikkeli, you can actually cover half of Finland on scheduled boat routes. The most popular routes are Tampere–Hämeenlinna, Savonlinna–Kuopio, Lahti–Jyväskylä and Joensuu–Koli–Nurmes. See Getting There & Away in the relevant town sections for details.

Sea Ferries

Several kinds of ferries operate between various islands and coastal towns, especially near Turku and in the province of Åland. See p232 and p212 for specific information.

Several cruise companies run express boats to interesting islands off the coast, particularly along the south coast. From Helsinki the foremost tour is the short trip to Suomenlinna. Likewise, there are summer cruises aboard historic steamships to mainland towns that may be reached more by car, bus or train. Popular sea routes are Turku–Naantali and Helsinki–Porvoo.

For ferries, www.liikkujat.com is a useful timetable website.

BUS

Long-distance buses in Finland are efficient and run on schedule. They're comfortable, and the service is comprehensive, covering 90% of Finland's roads.

Compared with Finnish trains, buses are better for travelling from village to village, while trains are more convenient and cheaper for fast travel between the big centres. There are two kinds of intercity bus services: *vakiovuorot* (regular buses) stopping frequently at towns and villages, and *pikavuorot* (express buses) travelling swiftly between cities. Because there are few motorways in Finland, even express buses aren't that fast, covering 100km in less than two hours and 400km in about six hours.

Long-distance and express bus travel ticketing is handled by **Matkahuolto** (☎ 0200-4000; www.matkahuolto.fi), whose excellent website has all timetables.

Each town and municipal centre has a *linja-autoasema* (bus terminal), with local timetables displayed (*lähtevät* is departures, *saapuvat* arrivals). Bus schedules change often so *always* double-check – particularly in rural areas where there may be only one weekly bus on some routes.

Most buses run hourly Monday to Friday between major towns. Restricted services operate on Saturday and public holidays. During summer, when school services are suspended, buses are dramatically reduced. The Matkahuolto offices work normal business hours, but you can always buy tickets on the buses.

Costs

Prices in this guide refer to express services if they are available, or local services if not. Ticket prices are fixed and depend on the number of kilometres travelled; return tickets are 10% cheaper than two one-way fares, provided the trip is at least 80km in one direction. Express buses cost up to €3 more than regular buses. The one-way fare for a 100km trip is normal/express €13.70/16.20. Children aged four to 11 always pay half fare, while children between 12 and 16 get a 30% to 50% reduction. For student discounts, you need to buy a student coach discount card (€5.80) from any bus station. Proper student ID and a passport photo is required, and the card entitles you to a 50% discount on journeys more than 80km.

If booking three or more adult tickets together, a 25% discount applies, meaning good news for groups.

Following are some sample one-way fares from Helsinki:

Destination	Express (€)
Hämeenlinna	18.90
Hanko	21.30
Inari	124.00
Joensuu	63.40
Jyväskylä	39.20
Kuopio	58.50
Lappeenranta	34.70
Oulu	72.50
Pori	39.20
Rovaniemi	96.20
Savonlinna	44.50
Tampere	28.10
Turku	25.60

CAR & MOTORCYCLE

Driving around Finland is hassle-free. Finnish drivers are remarkably considerate and polite – rarely will you hear a horn blast in anger and 'road rage' is almost an unknown phenomenon. Finland's road network is excellent and well signposted between centres, although there are only a few motorways around major cities. When approaching a town or city, look for signs saying *keskusta* (town centre), where you can usually find parking. Only in remote forests and rural areas will you find unsurfaced roads or dirt tracks. There are no road tolls.

Petrol is much more expensive than in the USA and generally above average compared with other European countries.

Driving Licence & Insurance

An international licence is not required to drive in Finland. However, you'll need the driving licence from your home country to bring a car into Finland, or if you plan to rent a car – a passport alone won't suffice. A Green Card (insurance card) is recommended but not required for visitors from most countries that subscribe to this European insurance system. Those who are from countries who do belong to the Green Card plan will need to arrange insurance on arrival. Insurance is included with car rental.

The Finnish national motoring organisation, **Autoliitto** (☎ 09-774 761; www.autoliitto.fi;

ROAD DISTANCES (km)

	Helsinki	Jyväskylä	Kuopio	Kuusamo	Lappeenranta	Oulu	Rovaniemi	Savonlinna	Tampere	Turku
Jyväskylä	272									
Kuopio	383	144								
Kuusamo	804	553	419							
Lappeenranta	223	219	264	684						
Oulu	612	339	286	215	551					
Rovaniemi	837	563	511	191	776	224				
Savonlinna	338	206	160	579	155	446	671			
Tampere	174	148	293	702	275	491	712	355		
Turku	166	304	448	848	361	633	858	446	155	
Vaasa	419	282	377	533	501	318	543	488	241	348

DRIVING IN WINTER

Snow and ice on the roads, potentially from September to April, and as late as June in Lapland, make driving a serious undertaking. Snow chains are illegal: instead, people use snow tyres, which have metal studs. Cars hired at these times will be properly equipped; you can also hire snow tyres from garages and car hire agencies.

The cooling system of the car must have enough antifreeze to cope with the temperatures, and windscreen washer water must also have a high proportion of detergent.

Most cars in Finland have a block heater, which electrically heats the engine prior to starting it. Most public carparks have an outlet pole. In really cold weather, you should start heating the engine at least an hour before leaving: many garages have a timing mechanism. Make sure you carry jump leads just in case!

The website www.tiehallinto.fi has a fantastic system of webcams on most main roads in Finland, so you can check what condition the roads are in on your prospective route!

During winter, there are various 'ice roads' that are short-cuts across frozen lakes. Once every decade or so, you can even drive to Åland!

Hämeentie 105A, 00550 Helsinki), can also answer questions.

Hire

Car rental in Finland is more expensive than elsewhere in Europe, but between a group of three or four it can work out at a reasonable cost. From the major rental companies a small car, such as a VW Polo or Renault Clio, costs from €60 per day with 100km free, and €0.35 per kilometre thereafter, or €75 to €90 with unlimited kilometres. As ever, there are much cheaper deals online. At the time of writing, www.webcarhire.com was a reliable operator offering excellent rates.

Car-rental companies with offices in many Finnish cities include **Budget** (☎ 09-686 6500; www.budget.fi), **Hertz** (☎ 0800 112 233; www.hertz.fi), **Europcar** (Helsinki ☎ 09-7515 5444; www.europcar.fi) and **Avis** (Helsinki ☎ 09-441 155; www.avis.fi). There are also local operators, especially in Helsinki (p84).

Road Rules

Most Finnish roads are only two lanes wide, and traffic keeps to the right. Use extreme caution when passing on these narrow roads. The speed limit is 50km/h in built-up areas and from 80km/h to 100km/h on highways. *All* motor vehicles must use headlights at *all* times, and wearing seat belts is compulsory for *all* passengers. The blood alcohol limit is 0.05%.

Foreign cars must display a nationality sticker and foreign visitors must be fully insured – see opposite). Foreign drivers should keep in mind that in Finland, cars entering an intersection from the right *always* have right of way, even when that car is on a minor road. Those who are used to driving in the USA and other countries where stop signs regulate every intersection will find that it takes some time to adjust to this system. Again, Finnish drivers are unexpectedly considerate and usually approach intersections with care.

See boxed text, p42 for the significant hazards posed by reindeer and elk. This may sound comical, but they are a deadly danger.

Many Finnish petrol stations are automatic. They accept euros and credit cards, but many accept only Finnish-issued credit and debit cards, so are useless to foreign travellers without cash. Don't rely on them. If the instructions are in Finnish and Swedish only, insert banknotes and press *setelikuittaus* after the last note, then choose the pump and select the petrol type. Change is not given.

HITCHING

Relatively few Finns like picking up hitch-hikers but the few friendly ones do it with enthusiasm. Drivers will ask, *Minne matka?* (Where are you going?), so you just tell them your destination. It's fairly common in remote areas where there may only be one bus a day.

Hitching between Lapland and Sweden or Norway is only really recommended from June to August. Carry waterproof gear and expect long waits. Being positive also

TRANSPORT

helps; getting stranded on an Artic Sea fjord is a unique experience that you will probably never forget. There's the midnight sun, fresh winds and abundant birdlife to enjoy while you wait…and wait…and wait…

LOCAL TRANSPORT

The only tram and metro networks are in Helsinki. There is a bus service in all Finnish cities and towns, with departures every 10 to 15 minutes in Helsinki and other large towns, and every 30 minutes in smaller towns. Fares are usually around €2.50, payable to the driver. See individual towns for details of local public transport.

Taxi

Hail taxis at bus and train stations or pick up the phone; they are listed in the phone book under 'Taksi'. Like anywhere, taxis in Finland are expensive – typically the fare is €4 plus a per-kilometre charge. There's a surcharge for night and weekend service.

Shared taxis often cover airport routes, and are a common mode of transport in Karelia, and, to a lesser extent, Lapland.

TRAIN

Trains of the State Railways of Finland (Valtion Rautatiet or VR) are clean, reliable and usually on schedule. They are fast, efficient and the best form of public transport for covering major routes such as Helsinki to Tampere, Kuopio, Oulu or Rovaniemi. On longer routes there are two- and three-bed sleepers and special car-carriers.

There are three main train lines: the Pohjanmaa (West) line runs between Helsinki and Oulu, and continues to Kemijärvi in Lapland; the Karelian route runs from Helsinki to Nurmes via Joensuu; and the Savonian route runs from Kouvola in the south to Kajaani, via Kuopio and Iisalmi.

VR Ltd Finnish Railways (☎ 0600-41902; www .vr.fi) has its own travel bureau at main stations and can advise on all schedules and tickets. Prices, timetables and other information can be found on VR's website.

Classes

VR has passenger trains in two classes – 1st and 2nd. Most carriages are open 2nd-class carriages with soft chairs. Many trains have just one 1st-class carriage, containing small compartments, each seating six passengers.

On longer routes there are night trains with single, two- and three-bed sleeping berths.

The main classes of trains are the high-speed Pendolino (the fastest and most expensive class), fast Intercity (IC), Express, and Regional trains. Regional trains are the cheapest and slowest services. They have only 2nd-class carriages, do not require seat reservations and stop frequently.

Costs

Different classes of trains are priced differently (Regional being the cheapest, Pendolino the most expensive), and a supplement is charged for travel on IC and Pendolino trains. A one-way ticket for a 100km express train journey costs approximately €13/19 in 2nd/1st class.

Children under 17 pay half fare and children aged under six travel free (but without a seat). A child travels free with every adult on long-distance trips, and there are also discounts for seniors, local students, and any group of three or more adults travelling together.

If you purchase your ticket from the conductor after boarding from a station where the ticket office was open, a €3 'penalty' is charged (€6 on Pendolino). The 1st-class fare is 1½ times the price of a 2nd-class ticket, and a return fare is about 10% less than two one-way tickets. Sample one-way fares for 2nd-class Inter-City travel from Helsinki:

Destination	Cost (€)	Duration (hrs)
Joensuu	52.70	5¼
Kuopio	47.00	5
Oulu	68.00	6
Rovaniemi	71.40	10-12
Savonlinna	47.90	5
Tampere	24.90	2
Turku	24.90	2

SLEEPING BERTHS

These are available on overnight trains in one-/two-/three-bed cabins, and cost a flat rate of €43 for a single berth (with a 1st-class ticket), and €21/11 per person for double/triple berths, in addition to the cost of an ordinary ticket. These prices rise to €60/31/16 at Christmas time. The main night train routes are Helsinki, Tampere or Turku to Oulu, Rovaniemi and Kolari.

MAJOR RAILWAY ROUTES

Map labels: Kolari, Kemijärvi, ROVANIEMI, Kemi, OULU, Vihanti, Kontiomaki, Kajaani, Ylivieska, Kokkola, Iisalmi, Nurmes, Lieksa, Vaasa, Seinäjoki, Kuopio, Joensuu, Häapamäki, Pieksämäki, Parkano, Jyväskylä, Varkaus, Jämsä, Savonlinna, MIKKELI, Parikkala, Pori, Orivesi, Tampere, Kokemäki, Toijala, HÄMEENLINNA, Imatra, Loimaa, Kouvola, Lappeenranta, Riihimäki, Lahti, Vainikkala, TURKU, Salo, Kerava, Kotka, Karjaa, HELSINKI, Hanko

BICYCLES
See p47 for details on transporting bikes.

CAR
Some trains transport cars from the south to Oulu, Rovaniemi and Kolari – which is handy if you've brought your own vehicle and are keen on exploring Lapland. From Helsinki to Rovaniemi, the cost (except during the Christmas period) is €215 for a car plus a cabin that accommodates one to three people.

Reservations
Seat reservations are included in the ticket price on all trains except regional services. Advance reservations are mandatory on IC and the high-speed Pendolino trains,

and are advised for travel on Express trains during summer.

Train Passes

International train passes accepted for travel on trains in Finland include the Eurailpass, Eurail Flexipass and Inter-Rail Ticket, but these are only worth having if you're doing a lot of rail travel in Europe.

Eurail passes (www.eurail.com) can only be bought by residents of non-European countries and are supposed to be purchased before arriving in Europe. These are valid for unlimited travel in most western and some eastern European countries, as well as Silja Line ferries between Sweden and Finland. If you've lived in Europe for more than six months, you're eligible for an Inter-Rail pass (www.interrailnet.com), which is a better buy. The Inter-Rail pass is split into eight zones, with zone B covering Sweden, Norway and Finland. The price for any one zone is UK£145/215 (up to/over 26) for 16 days and UK£205/295 for 22 days. See your local travel agency for more information about these rail passes.

SCANRAIL PASS

Scanrail (www.scanrail.com) is the best-value international rail pass to use when travelling in Finland. It's a flexible rail pass covering travel in Denmark, Norway, Sweden and Finland. The pass can be purchased in Scandinavia, but there are restrictions on its use in the country of purchase. For instance, if you buy the pass in Finland, you can only use it to travel for three days in Finland. It's far better to buy the pass outside the Nordic countries.

There are three versions. For travel on any five days within a two-month period, the pass costs €160/204/230 for under 26/senior/adult 2nd class travel. For travel on any 10 days within a two-month period, the pass costs €215/274/308. For unlimited travel over 21 consecutive days, it's €249/316/358.

FINNRAIL PASS

A national rail pass, the Finnrail Pass, is available to travellers residing outside Finland, and it is the best-value pass if you're not planning on travelling elsewhere in Scandinavia. The pass is good for three, five or 10 days of travel within a one-month period. The Finnrail Pass may be purchased from the VR travel agency Matkapalvelu, at major train stations in Finland, or from your local travel agency before arrival in Finland. The cost for 2nd-/1st-class travel is €122/182 for three days; €163/24 for five days; €220/331 for 10 days. As with any pass, you need to plan your trips wisely to make it pay.

Health

CONTENTS

Health-wise, there's very little to worry about while travelling in Finland. Your main risks are likely to be viral infections in winter, sunburn and mosquito bites in summer, plus typical travellers complaints like foot blisters and an upset stomach.

BEFORE YOU GO

INSURANCE

EU, EEA and Swiss citizens are entitled to free medical care in Finland, but you should carry proof of this entitlement. This comes in the form of the EHIC, the European Health Insurance Card, which has replaced the E111 form in most EU countries.

If you don't fall into this category, a travel-insurance policy is a good idea. Some policies offer a range of medical-expense options; the higher ones are chiefly for countries such as the USA, which have extremely high medical costs. There is a wide variety of policies available, so check the small print.

Some policies specifically exclude 'dangerous activities', which can include skiing, snowmobiling, even trekking. You may prefer a policy that pays doctors or hospitals directly rather than you having to pay on the spot and claim later. If you have to claim later make sure you keep all documentation. Some policies ask you to call back (reverse charges) to a centre in your home country where an immediate assessment of your problem is made.

Although EU citizens are covered for medical care, you may want to consider travel insurance to cover loss/theft.

IN FINLAND

AVAILABILITY & COST OF HEALTH CARE

Apteekki (local pharmacies) – of which there are many in all Finnish cities and towns – and neighbourhood health care centres are good places to visit if you have a minor medical problem and can explain what it is. Visitors whose home countries have reciprocal medical-care agreements with Finland and who can produce a passport (or sickness insurance card or EHIC for those from EU countries) are charged the same as Finns for medical assistance: €8 to visit a doctor, €21 per day for hospitalisation. Those from other countries are charged the full cost of treatment. Tourist offices and hotels can put you in touch with a doctor or dentist; in Helsinki your embassy will probably know one who speaks your language.

TRAVELLER'S DIARRHOEA

Simple things like a change of water, food or climate can all cause a mild bout of diarrhoea, but a few rushed toilet trips with no other symptoms is not indicative of a major problem.

Dehydration is the main danger with any diarrhoea, particularly in children or the elderly as it can occur quite quickly. Under all circumstances *fluid replacement* (at least equal to the volume being lost) is the most important thing to remember. Weak black tea with a little sugar, soda water, or soft drinks allowed to go flat and diluted 50% with clean water are all good.

ENVIRONMENTAL HAZARDS
Cuts & Scratches

Wash well and treat any cut with an antiseptic such as povidone-iodine. Where possible avoid bandages and Band-Aids, which can keep wounds wet.

Food

Finnish food is of a very high hygiene standard. Mushroom and berry-picking is a favourite pastime in this part of the world, but make sure you don't eat any that haven't been positively identified as safe.

HEALTH

Hypothermia

If you are trekking in Lapland or simply staying outdoors for long periods, particularly in winter, be prepared for the cold. In fact, if you are out walking or hitching, be prepared for cold, wet or windy conditions even in summer.

Hypothermia occurs when the body loses heat faster than it can produce it and the core temperature of the body falls. It is surprisingly easy to progress from very cold to dangerously cold due to a combination of wind, wet clothing, fatigue and hunger, even if the air temperature is above freezing. It is best to dress in layers; silk, wool and some of the new artificial fibres are all good insulating materials. A hat is important, as a lot of heat is lost through the head. A strong, waterproof outer layer (and a 'space' blanket for emergencies) is essential. Carry basic supplies, including food containing simple sugars to generate heat quickly and fluid to drink.

Symptoms of hypothermia are exhaustion, numb skin (particularly toes and fingers), shivering, slurred speech, irrational or violent behaviour, lethargy, stumbling, dizzy spells, muscle cramps and violent bursts of energy. Irrationality may take the form of sufferers claiming they are warm and trying to take off their clothes.

To treat mild hypothermia, first get the person out of the wind and/or rain, remove their clothing if it's wet and replace it with dry, warm clothing. Give them hot liquids – not alcohol – and some high-kilojoule, easily digestible food. Do not rub victims, but instead allow them to slowly warm themselves. This should be enough to treat the early stages of hypothermia. The early recognition and treatment of mild hypothermia is the only way to prevent severe hypothermia, which is a critical condition.

Insect Bites & Stings

In Finland, the mosquito breeding season is very short (about six weeks in July and August), but the mosquitoes make good use of the time. They are a major nuisance in most parts of Finland, and those in Lapland are particularly large, fierce and persistent.

The best way to handle the mosquito problem is through prevention. From June to August, travellers are advised to wear light-coloured clothing, particularly long pants and long sleeved shirts, and avoid highly scented perfumes or aftershave. Use *ohvi* (mosquito repellent) liberally; the 'Off' brand seems to be particularly effective. If you have a mosquito net, use this too. There are net hats available in sports shops; if you don't mind how absurd they look these are useful for treks and outdoor activities.

When all else fails and the pesky suckers have had their piece of you, look for Etono, a concentrated antihistamine salve that is sold in stick form, for relief from bites. It is available at most pharmacies.

Parasites

TICKS

You should always check all over your body if you have been walking through a potentially tick-infested area – this would include rural areas of the Åland islands and in any forested areas – as ticks can cause skin infections and other more serious diseases. If a tick is found attached, press down around the tick's head with tweezers, grab the head and gently pull upwards. Avoid pulling the rear of the body as this may squeeze the tick's gut contents through the attached mouth parts into the skin, increasing the risk of infection and disease. Smearing chemicals on the tick will not make it let go and is not recommended.

Snakes

The only venomous snake in Finland is the common viper, and human deaths from viper bites are extremely rare. All snakes hibernate from autumn to spring. To minimise your chances of being bitten always wear boots, socks and long trousers when walking through undergrowth where snakes may be present.

Sunburn

You can get sunburnt surprisingly quickly, even through cloud, or in sub-zero temperatures. Use sunscreen, hat and barrier cream for your nose and lips. Calamine lotion or Stingose are good for mild sunburn. Protect your eyes with good-quality sunglasses, particularly if you are going near water, sand or snow.

HEALTH

Water

You can drink the tap water in all Finnish towns and villages, and it's usually delicious. Always be wary of drinking natural water; a recent survey ranked Finland's lakes and rivers among some of the most polluted in Europe. A burbling stream may look crystal clear and very inviting, but there may be pulp factories, people or sheep lurking upstream. Many trekkers in the wilderness of eastern Lapland claim that springs there are safe to drink from without purifying – use your own best judgment as to whether you'd care to follow that advice. The simplest way to purify water is to boil it, use a water filter, or add purification tablets.

HEALTH

Language

CONTENTS

The Finnish language is a distinct national icon that sets Finland apart from all its Western European neighbours. It is not a Scandinavian language, nor is it related to any of the Indo-European languages. There are, however, many loan words from Baltic, Slavic and Germanic languages, and many words are derived from English. It is a Uralic language belonging to the Finno-Ugric family, and is closely related to Estonian It also shares common origins with Samoyed and languages spoken in the Volga basin of Russia. Linguists have even recognised similarities between Finnish and Korean grammar. The most widely spoken Finno-Ugric language is Hungarian, but its similarities with Finnish are few.

There are some six million Finnish speakers in Finland, Sweden, Norway and Russian Karelia. In Finnish, Finland itself is known as *Suomi*, and the language as *suomi*. With 15 cases for nouns, and at least 160 conjugations and personal forms for verbs, it is not an easy language to learn. There are no articles (a, the) and no genders, but the word for 'no' *(ei)* also conjugates.

Fortunately, staff at most tourist offices and hotels are fluent English speakers; bus drivers and staff at guesthouses, hostels and restaurants may not be – though they'll often fetch someone who can help. Finns who speak Finnish to a foreigner usually do so extremely clearly and 'according to the book'. Mistakes made by visitors are kindly tolerated, and even your most bumbling attempts will be warmly appreciated. A

final note: in Finnish, **ä** is pronounced as in 'bat', and **ö** is pronounced 'er', as in 'her' (with no 'r' sound). These letters are the last two in the Finnish alphabet. Lonely Planet's *Scandinavian Phrasebook* is a handy pocket-sized introduction to Finnish, Swedish and other languages of the region.

ACCOMMODATION

I'm looking for ...	Etsin ...
the youth hostel	retkeilymajaa
the campground	leirintäaluetta
a hotel	hotellia
a guesthouse	matkustajakotia
What's the address?	Mikä on osoite?
Do you have a ...?	Onko teillä ...?
bed	sänkyä
cheap room	halpaa huonetta
single room	yhden hengen huonetta
double room	kahden hengen huonetta
for one night	yhdeksi yöksi
for two nights	kahdeksi yöksi
How much is it ...?	Paljonko maksaa ...?
per night	vuorokausi
per person	yhdeltä henkilöltä
Does it include	Sisältyykö hintaan
breakfast/sheets?	aamiainen/lakanat?
Can I see the room?	Voinko nähdä huoneen?
Where is the toilet?	Missä on vessa?
I'm/we're leaving now.	Olen/olemme lähdössä nyt.
Do you have ...?	Onko teillä ...?
a clean sheet	puhtaat lakanat
hot water	kuumaa vettä
a key	avain
a shower	suihku
sauna	sauna

CONVERSATION & ESSENTIALS

Good day.	Hyvää päivää
Hi!	Hei/Moi/Terve! (less formal)
Goodbye.	Näkemiin.
Bye!	Hei hei! or Moi moi! (less formal)
Good morning.	Hyvää huomenta.

Good evening.	*Hyvää Iltaa*
Thank you (very much).	*Kiitos (paljon).*
You're welcome.	*Ole hyvä.*
Yes.	*Kyllä/Joo.*
No.	*Ei.*
Maybe.	*Ehkä.*
Excuse me.	*Anteeksi.*
I'm sorry. (forgive me)	*Olen pahoillani (anna anteeksi).*
How are you?	*Mitä kuuluu?*
I'm fine, thanks.	*Kiitos hyvää.*
Where are you from?	*Mistä olet kotoisin?*
I'm from ...	*Olen ... -sta*
What's your name?	*Mikä sinun nimi on?*
My name is ...	*Minun nimeni on ...*
I'm a tourist/student.	*Olen turisti/opiskelija.*
Are you married?	*Oletko naimisissa?*
Do you like ...?	*Pidätkö ...?*
I like it very much.	*Pidän siitä paljon.*
I don't like ...	*En pidä ...*
May I?	*Saisinko?*
I understand.	*Ymmärrän.*
I don't understand.	*En ymmärrä.*
Does anyone speak English?	*Puhuuko kukaan englantia?*
How do you say ... (in Finnish)?	*Miten sanotaan ... (suomeksi)?*
Please write it down.	*Voitko kirjoittaa sen.*

EMERGENCIES

Help!	*Apua!*
Go away!	*Mene pois!*
Call a doctor!	*Kutsu lääkäri!*
Call the police!	*Kutsu poliisi!*
I'm allergic to ...	*Olen allerginen ...*
penicillin	*penisilliinille*
antibiotics	*antibiooteille*

NUMBERS

½	*puoli*
1	*yksi*
2	*kaksi*
3	*kolme*
4	*neljä*
5	*viisi*
6	*kuusi*
7	*seitsemän*
8	*kahdeksan*
9	*yhdeksän*
10	*kymmenen*
11	*yksitoista*
12	*kaksitoista*

100	*sata*
1000	*tuhat*
1,000,000	*miljoona*

PAPERWORK

Surname	*Sukunimi*
Given names	*Etunimet*
Date of birth	*Syntymäaika*
Place of birth	*Syntymäpaikka*
Nationality	*Kansallisuus*
Male/Female	*Mies/Nainen*
Passport	*Passi*

SHOPPING & SERVICES

Where is the/a ...?	*Missä on ...?*
bank	*pankki*
town centre	*keskusta*
embassy	*suurlähetystö*
entrance	*sisäänkäynti*
exit	*uloskäynti*
hospital	*sairaala*
market	*tori*
police	*poliisi*
post office	*posti*
public toilet	*yleinen vessa*
restaurant	*ravintola*
telephone office	*Tele-toimisto*
tourist office	*matkailutoimisto*

I'd like to change ...	*Haluaisin vaihtaa ...*
some money	*rahaa*
travellers cheques	*matkashekkejä*

| I want to make a telephone call. | *Haluaisin soittaa puhelun* |

I'm looking for ...	*Etsin ...*
the chemist	*apteekkia*
clothing	*vaatteita*
souvenirs	*matkamuistoja*

How much is it?	*Mitä se maksaa?*
I'd like to buy it.	*Haluan ostaa sen.*
It's too expensive for me.	*Se on liian kallis minulle.*
Can I look at it?	*Voinko katsoa sitä?*
I'm just looking.	*Minä vain katselen.*

Do you have ...?	*Onko ...?*
another colour	*muuta väriä*
another size	*muuta kokoa*

| big/bigger | *iso/isompi* |
| small/smaller | *pieni/pienempi* |

more/less	enemmän/vähemmän
cheap/cheaper	halpa/halvempi

TIME & DATES

When?	Milloin?
today	tänään
tonight	tänä iltana
tomorrow	huomenna
yesterday	eilen
all day	koko päivän
every day	joka päivä

Monday	maanantai
Tuesday	tiistai
Wednesday	keskiviikko
Thursday	torstai
Friday	perjantai
Saturday	lauantai
Sunday	sunnuntai

January	tammikuu
February	helmikuu
March	maaliskuu
April	huhtikuu
May	toukokuu
June	kesäkuu
July	heinäkuu
August	elokuu
September	syyskuu
October	lokakuu
November	marraskuu
December	joulukuu

What time is it?	Mitä kello on?
It's ... o'clock	Kello on ...
in the morning	aamulla
in the evening	illalla
1.15	vartin yli yksi
1.30	puoli kaksi
1.45	varttia vaille kaksi

TRANSPORT

I want to go to ...	Haluan mennä ...
How long does the trip take?	Kauanko matka kestää?
Do I need to change?	Täytyykö minun vaihtaa?

Where does ... leave from?	Mistä ... lähtee?
What time does ... leave/arrive?	Mihin aikaan lähtee/saapuu ...?
it	se
the boat/ferry	vene/lautta
the bus/tram	bussi/raitiovaunu
the train	juna
the plane	lentokone

The train is ...	Juna on ...
delayed	myöhässä
cancelled	peruutettu

airport	lentoasema
bus station	linja-autoasema
left-luggage locker	säilytyslokero
one-way	yhdensuuntainen
platform	laituri
return (ticket)	menopaluu (lippu)
station	asema
ticket	lippu
ticket office	lipputoimisto
ticket machine	lippuautomaatti
timetable	aikataulu

I'd like to hire a ...	Haluaisin vuokrata ...
bicycle	polkupyörän
car	auton
canoe	kanootin
rowing boat	soutuveneen
guide	oppaan

Directions

How do I get to ...?	Miten pääsen ...?
Where is ...?	Missä on ...?
Please show me (on the map).	Näyttäisitkö minulle (kartalta).
Is it near?	Onko se lähellä?
Is it far?	Onko se kaukana?
(Go) straight ahead.	(Kulje) suoraan eteenpäin.
(Turn) left.	(Käänny) vasempaan.
(Turn) right.	(Käänny) oikeaan.
at the traffic lights	liikennevaloissa
at the next/second/ third corner	seuraavassa/toisessa/ kolmannessa risteyksessä
here/there	täällä/siellä
up/down	ylös/alas
behind/opposite	takana/vastapäätä
north/south	pohjoinen/etelä
east/west	itä/länsi

SIGNS	
Sisään	Entrance
Ulos	Exit
Avoinna	Open
Suljettu	Closed
Kielletty	Prohibited
WC	Toilet

LANGUAGE

Glossary

Throughout Finland you will often hear the words *järvi* (lake), *lampi* (pond), *saari* (island), *ranta* (shore), *niemi* (cape), *lahti* (bay), *koski* (rapids), *virta* (stream) and *joki* (river).

You may meet many of the following terms and abbreviations during your travels in Finland. Unless otherwise noted, all entries are Finnish. See also p358.

aamianen – breakfast
aamu – morning
aapa – open bog
aatto – eve, usually the afternoon/evening before a holiday
Ahvenanmaa – Finnish for Åland (the Swedish, official and locally preferred name)
aikataulu – timetable
aikuinen – adult (plural: *aikuiset*)
aitta – small wooden storage shed in a traditional farmhouse, used for guests
ala- – lower, eg in place names; see also *yli, ylä-*
apotek – pharmacy (Swedish)
apteekki – pharmacy
asema – station, eg *linja-autoasema* (bus station), *rauta-tieasema* (train station) or *lentoasema* (airport terminal)
avoinna – open, eg a shop or museum

baari – simple restaurant serving light lager and some snacks (also called *kapakka*)
barn – child (Swedish)
bensa – petrol
bibliotek – library (Swedish)
bruk – early ironworks precinct (Swedish)
bussi – bus (informal); 'properly' called *linja-auto*
-by – village (Swedish); as in Godby (in Åland) or Nykarleby (in Pohjanmaa)

eläkeläinen – pensioner, senior (plural: *eläkeläiset*; abbreviation: *eläk*)
erämaa – wilderness (also called *kaira* or *korpi*)
etelä – south

feresi – traditional Karelian dress for women, formerly worn daily but now worn only on festival days

gamla – old (Swedish)
gatan – street (Swedish)
grilli – stand or kiosk selling burgers, grilled sausages and other greasy snacks

halla – typically a night frost in early summer that often destroys crops or berries
hämärä – twilight
hamn – harbour (Swedish)
hautausmaa – cemetery; see also *kalmisto*
henkilö – person, as in 'per person' (abbreviation: *hlö* or *h*)
hilla – highly appreciated orange Arctic cloudberry, which grows on marshlands (also *lakka* or *suomuurain*)
hinnasto – price list
hinta – cost or price
huone – room
hytty – cabin, eg a train or ship

ikäraja – age limit, eg in bars and clubs
ilta – evening
iltapäivä – afternoon
istumapaikka – seat, eg on a train
itä – east; *itään* means 'to the east'
itikkä – mosquito; also called *sääski*

jää – ice
jääkiekko – ice hockey, the unofficial national religion; also informally called *lätkä*
jäätie – ice road; road over a lake in winter
jäkälä – lichen
järvi – lake
joiku – sung lyric poem, also called *yoik* among the Sámi
jokamiehenoikeus – 'everyman's right', every person's right to wilderness access
joki – river
joulu – Christmas
joulupukki – Santa Claus
juhannus – see Midsummer
juna – train

kaamos – twilight time, the period of eerie half-light above the Arctic Circle when the sun doesn't rise above the horizon
kahvila – café
kahvio – cafeteria-style café, usually more basic than a *kahvila*
kaira – see *erämaa*
kala – fish; *kalastus* means 'fishing'
Kalevala – the national epic of Finland; *Kalevala* is a 19th-century literary creation combining old poetry, runes and folk tales with creation myths and ethical teaching
kalmisto – old graveyard, especially pre-Medieval or Orthodox
kämppä – wilderness hut, cabin

känykkä – usual term for a *matkapuhelin* (mobile phone)
kansallispuisto – national park
kantele – Karelian stringed instrument similar to a zither; its music is hauntingly beautiful
kapakka – see *baari*
karhu – bear
Karjala – Karelia
kartano – manor
kasvis- – vegetarian, eg *kasvisruoka* (vegetarian food)
katu – street
kauppa – shop
kauppahalli – market hall
kauppatori – market square (usually just referred to as *tori*)
kaupungintalo – city hall
kaupunki – city (plenty of rather small towns have 'city' status in Finland)
kävelyreitti – walking track; usually well signposted and marked
kelirikko – season of bad roads after the snow has melted
kelkka – sled or sledge; see also *moottorikelkka*
kello – watch, time (abbreviation: *klo*)
kelo – dead, standing, barkless tree, usually pine
kesä – summer
keskus – centre (eg, of a town)
kevät – spring (season)
kioski – small stand that sells sweets, newspapers, phonecards, food items and beer
kirjakauppa – bookshop
kirjasto – library
kirkko – church
kirkonkylä – any village that has a church
kiuas – sauna oven
kokko – bonfire, lit during Midsummer festivals
köngäs – rapids, waterfall
korpi – see *erämaa*
koski – rapids
kota – Sámi hut, resembling a teepee or wigwam (from the Finnish word *koti*)
koti – home
kotimaa – 'home country'
koulu – school
kruunu – crown, krone (Norway's currency)
kuja – lane
kuksa – Sámi cup, carved from the burl of a birch tree
kunta – commune or municipality, the smallest administrative unit in Finland
kuntopolku – 'fitness path'; jogging track in summer, skiing track in winter
kuusi – spruce
kylä – village
kypylä – spa

lääkäri – doctor
laakso – valley

lääni – province
laavu – Sámi permanent or temporary open-air shelter, also used by trekkers
lahti – bay
laituri – platform (for buses or trains); wharf or pier
lakka – cloudberry, see also *hilla*
lampi – pond, small lake
lähtevät – departures
länsi – west; *länteen* means 'to the east'
laiva – ship
lappalainen – Finnish or indigenous person from Lapland; this is a contentious term in some parts of the north, and many indigenous people will only refer to themselves as Sámi
Lappi – Lapland, a province and a popular term, usually applied to the land north of Oulu; it's better understood as roughly the area between Rovaniemi and Sodankylä; north of this is the Sámi region called Sápmi, which many consider the 'true Lapland'; see also Sápmi
lapsi – child (plural: *lapset*; abbreviation: *l*); *lasten* means 'children's'
lasku – bill; receipt
leirintäalue – camping ground
lentokenttä – airstrip or airport (terminal: *lentoasema*)
liiteri – shelter for firewood
linja-auto – bus (informally called *bussi*)
linna – castle
linnoitus – fortification
lintu – bird
lippu – ticket
lossi – a small ferry for travel across a strait
lounas – lunch
lumi – snow; often in the generic form *lunta*
luontopolku – nature trail
lupa – permit or permission

maa – country, earth, land
maatila – farm
mäki – hill
mänty – pine tree, most common and distinctive of Finnish trees; upper trunk and branches are barkless and almost orange
majoitus – accommodation
maksu – payment, charge, fare
makuu – sleep, as in *makuupaikka* (berth on a train or ship), *makuuvaunu* (sleeping car on a train) and *makuupussi* (sleeping bag)
marja – berry
Matkahuolto – national umbrella company managing the long-distance bus system
matkakoti – guesthouse, inn; also called *matkustajakoti* (traveller home)
matkatoimisto – travel agency
meri – sea
metsä – forest

Midsummer – (or *juhannus*) longest day of the year, celebrated at the end of June, beginning on Friday evening *(juhannusaatto)*. Saturday, Sunday and Monday following are also serious holidays when Finland is basically closed.

mies – man (plural: *miehet*)
mökki – cottage
moottorikelkka – snowmobile (Finns often call these 'snow scooters' in English)
muikku – vendace, or whitefish, a common lake fish
museo – museum
mustamakkara – mild sausage made with cow's blood, black-pudding style
mustikka – bilberry, resembles a blueberry

nähtävyys – tourist attraction
Napapiiri – Arctic Circle
nainen – woman (plural: *naiset*)
niemi – cape
nuoska – wet snow
nuotio – campfire
Norja – Norway

öljy – oil
olut – beer
opas – guide
opastuskeskus – information centre, usually of a national park
opiskelija – (high-school) student; see also *ylioppilas*
Oy – abbreviation for Osakeyhtiö, a joint-stock company; in Swedish it's Ab, short for Aktiebolag

pää – head, end
pääsymaksu – entry fee
päivä – day; *pävittäin* means 'daily'
pakkanen – frost; below-freezing weather
pankki – bank
pelto – cultivated field
peura – deer
pikkujoulu – 'Little Christmas', an informal party arranged by companies or schools leading up to Christmas
pirtti – the living area of a Finnish farmhouse; a word often affixed to a rustic restaurant or tourist attraction
pitkospuu – boardwalk constructed over wetlands or swamps
pitopöytä – major pig-out buffet table
pohjoinen – north; also *pohjois-*
polku – path
polkupyörä – bicycle
polttopuu – firewood
poro – reindeer, a generic term for the common, domesticated variety
poroerotus – reindeer roundup, held annually in designated places in Sápmi
poronhoitoalue – reindeer herding area

poronkusema – a handy Lappish unit of distance: how far a reindeer walks before relieving itself
posti – post office, mail
Praasniekka – also *Prazniek*; Orthodox religious festival that sometimes includes a *ristinsaatto* to a lake, where a sermon takes place
pubi – pub serving strong alcohol and very little food
puhelin – telephone; a mobile phone is formally called *matkapuhelin* – see also *känykkä*
puisto – park
pulkka – boat sledge
puro – stream
puu – tree, wood
puukko – Finnish-style sheath knife

raatihuone – town hall; see also *kaupungintalo*
rådhus – town hall (Swedish)
raja – border
ranta – shore
räntä – wet snow (snowing)
rauhoitettu – protected
rautatie – railway
ravintola – restaurant, but also a bar
reppu – backpack
retkeilymaja – hostel
retki – excursion
revontulet – Northern Lights, literally 'fires of the fox'
ristinsaatto – an annual Orthodox festival to commemorate a regional saint, involving a procession of the cross
roskakori – rubbish bin
rotko – gorge
ruoka – food
ruokalista – menu
ruokaravintola – a food restaurant
runo – poem
Ruotsi – Sweden
rupla – Russian rouble
ruska – gorgeous but brief period in autumn (fall) when leaves turn red and yellow

sää – weather
Sámi – the term for most indigenous people in the north of Finland; see also *lappalainen*
saari – island
saapuvat – arrivals
sääski – mosquito (in Lapland and Sápmi)
sähkö – electricity
sähköposti – email
sairaala – hospital
Saksa – Germany
salmi – strait
Sápmi – the area where Sámi culture and customs are still active; it is a quasi-legal territory covering parts of northern Sweden, Norway and Russia as well as the far north of Finland
satama – harbour

savusauna – 'smoke sauna'; these have no chimney but a small outlet for smoke
savuton – nonsmoking
seisopöytä – buffet; see also *pitopöytä*
sieni – mushroom
silta – bridge
sora – gravel
sota – war
sotilasalue – military area
SRM – Suomen Retkeilymajajärjesto, or Youth Hostel Association of Finland
stad – city or town (Swedish)
suihku – shower
sukset – skiis
suljettu – closed
suo – swamp, bog, marsh
suomalainen – Finnish, Finn
Suomi – Finland
susi – wolf

taide – art or skill
taival – track, trail
talo – house or building
talvi – winter
tanssi – dance
tanssilava – dance floor or stage
Tapaninpäivä – Boxing Day
tavarasäilytys – left-luggage counter
teltta – tent
tervas – old pine tree stump with a high tar content and a distinctive smell. It burns well, so Finnish trekkers use it to light fires, even in wet weather (also *tervaskanto*).
tie – road
torget – market square (Swedish)
tori – market square; also called *kauppatori*
tsasouna – small chapel or prayer hall used by the Orthodox faith
tukki – log
tulva – flood
tunturi – a northern fell, or large hill, that is treeless on top (as opposed to the less dramatic, tree-covered *vaara*); most of Finland's fells are in the Sápmi area, where many are sacred to the Sámi

tuohi – birch bark
tuomiokirkko – cathedral
tuoppi – beer-glass
tupa – hut
turve – peat

uimahalli – indoor swimming pool
uimaranta – swimming beach
uistin – lure (in fishing)
uitto – log floating
uusi – new

vaara – danger; low, broad hill (typical in Lapland Province and North Karelia)
vaellus – trek (verb *vaeltaa*)
vägen – road (Swedish)
vaivaisukko – a pauper statue outside many of the old wooden churches used as a receptacle for church donations
valaistu latu – illuminated skiing track
valtio – State or government
vandrarhem – hostel (Swedish)
vanha – old
vappaa – free, available (basic form: *vappa*)
varattu – reserved
vaunu – train carriage or wagon
Venäjä – Russia
vene – boat
vero – tax
vesi – water (generic form: *vettä*)
virasto – state or local government office building
Viro – Estonia
viisumi – visa
vuode – bed
vuori – mountain
vuorokausi – 24 hours (abbreviation: *vrk*), eg for rentals
vyöhyke – zone

WC – toilet

yli, ylä- – upper; see also *ala-*
yliopisto – university
ylioppilas – university student
yö – night

Behind the Scenes

THIS BOOK

This 5th edition was updated by Andy Symington. The 1st edition of Finland was researched and written by Virpi Mäkelä. Markus Lehtipuu and Jennifer Brewer updated the 2nd and 3rd editions respectively. Paul Harding updated the 4th edition. This edition of *Finland* was commissioned in Lonely Planet's London office, and produced by the following:

Commissioning Editors Amanda Canning, Sam Trafford
Coordinating Editor Craig Kilburn
Coordinating Cartographers David Connolly, Jody Whiteoak
Coordinating Layout Designer Cara Smith
Assisting Layout Designer Wibowo Rusli
Managing Cartographers Alison Lyall, Mark Griffiths
Assisting Editors Lutie Clark, Maryanne Netto, Helen Koehne
Cover Designer Annika Roojun
Colour Designer John Shippick
Project Manager Brigitte Ellemor
Indexer Nancy Ianni
Language Content Coordinator Quentin Frayne

Thanks to Adrian Persoglia, Adriana Mammarella, Sally Darmody, Celia Wood

THANKS
ANDY SYMINGTON

I am indebted to numerous helpful people that I met in tourist offices, bus stations, bars and cafés along the road in Finland. More specifically, I owe a great deal to Riika Åkerlind, who first instilled in me a great love of her country and selflessly contributed advice, time, Finnish grammar and good company to this update.

Gustav and Marja Schulman, not for the first time, laid on a warm and generous Finnish welcome for me. For various kindnesses I also thank Auli Åkerlind, Iain, Teija and Jonah Campbell, Riku Åkerlind and Benita Auvinen, David Jackson and Menchu Hevia, Kile Flink and Krisse Lundqvist, Colum, Elina and Sara Gaynor, Mirjam Schulman and Rami Eskelinen, Tiina Mikkonen and Becca Worledge. Further afield, I thank my parents for their support and Begoña García de León for following the map and more.

OUR READERS

Many thanks to the hundreds of travellers who used the last edition and wrote to us with helpful hints, useful advice and interesting anecdotes:

A Annabel Battersby **B** David Bell, Mariano Berkenwald, Derek Blackburn, John Blom, Carmen Boudreau-Kiviaho, Danilo Bracco, Vanessa Burgess **C** Gordon Campbell McMillan, John Carmody, Maria Castillo-Stone, Therese Catanzariti, Alessandra Cingi, Rich Clare **D** Karsten Dax, Jeroen de Graaf, Stephan Dorrenberg **E** Jorge Enero, Nick Eskelinen **F** Wayne Forester **G** Peter Garvey, Krista Goff, Sam Golledge, Michael Gowen **H** Tuukka Härkönen, Annette Harris, Frank Higbie, Alistair Holford, Kevin Hubbard, Hannele Huhtala, Veikko Huhtinen, Brendon Hyde **J** Markus Jokipaltio **K** Matias Käld **L** Tero Lahtinen, Lotta Lehikoinen, Michael Lienemann, Steven Lim, Philip Lowe **M** Sami Makelainen, Mike Mimirinis, Thomas Misersky, Jordan Mitchell **N** Danny Nguyen, Matti Niskanen **O** Paul Offermanns **P** Palava Pensas, Mika Perkiomaki, Wilga

---

THE LONELY PLANET STORY

The story begins with a classic travel adventure: Tony and Maureen Wheeler's 1972 journey across Europe and Asia to Australia. There was no useful information about the overland trail then, so Tony and Maureen published the first Lonely Planet guidebook to meet a growing need.

From a kitchen table, Lonely Planet has grown to become the largest independent travel publisher in the world, with offices in Melbourne (Australia), Oakland (USA) and London (UK). Today Lonely Planet guidebooks cover the globe. There is an ever-growing list of books and information in a variety of media. Some things haven't changed. The main aim is still to make it possible for adventurous travellers to get out there – to explore and better understand the world.

At Lonely Planet we believe travellers can make a positive contribution to the countries they visit – if they respect their host communities and spend their money wisely. Every year 5% of company profit is donated to charities around the world.

Pruden **R** Arndt Riester, Tiina Rinne, Bruce Rumage **S** Thomas Siepert, David Szylit **T** Tomi Tenetz, Malla Tennila, Adine Thoresen, Alicia Trezise **V** Thomas Vikberg, Teya Vitu **W** Sandra Wessels, Bronson Whitford, Lawrie Williams, Mark and Ulrike Wilson, Tuula and Richard Wright **Z** Nico Zila

ACKNOWLEDGMENTS

Many thanks to the following for the use of their content:

Globe on back cover ©Mountain High Maps 1993 Digital Wisdom, Inc.

SEND US YOUR FEEDBACK

We love to hear from travellers – your comments keep us on our toes and help make our books better. Our well-travelled team reads every word on what you loved or loathed about this book. Although we cannot reply individually to postal submissions, we always guarantee that your feedback goes straight to the appropriate authors, in time for the next edition. Each person who sends us information is thanked in the next edition – and the most useful submissions are rewarded with a free book.

To send us your updates – and find out about Lonely Planet events, newsletters and travel news – visit our award-winning website: **www.lonelyplanet.com/feedback**.

Note: We may edit, reproduce and incorporate your comments in Lonely Planet products such as guidebooks, websites and digital products, so let us know if you don't want your comments reproduced or your name acknowledged. For a copy of our privacy policy visit www.lonelyplanet.com/privacy.

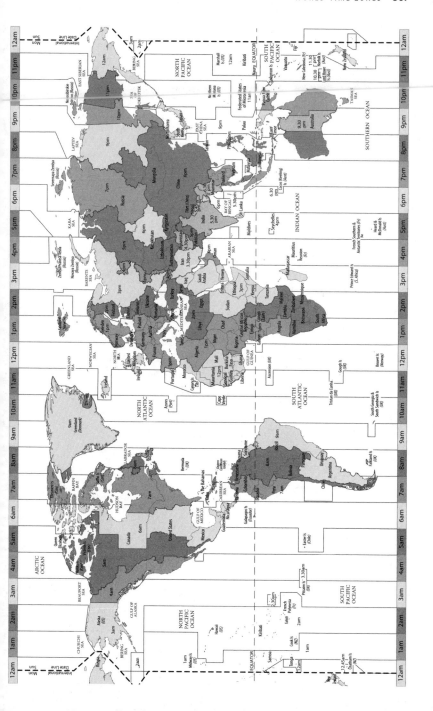

376

Index

000 Map pages
000 Photograph pages

000 Map pages
000 Photograph pages

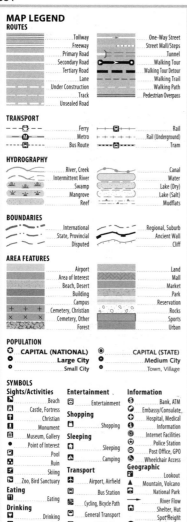

MAP LEGEND

ROUTES

Tollway	One-Way Street
Freeway	Street Mall/Steps
Primary Road	Tunnel
Secondary Road	Walking Tour
Tertiary Road	Walking Tour Detour
Lane	Walking Trail
Under Construction	Walking Path
Track	Pedestrian Overpass
Unsealed Road	

TRANSPORT

Ferry	Rail
Metro	Rail (Underground)
Bus Route	Tram

HYDROGRAPHY

River, Creek	Canal
Intermittent River	Water
Swamp	Lake (Dry)
Mangrove	Lake (Salt)
Reef	Mudflats

BOUNDARIES

International	Regional, Suburb
State, Provincial	Ancient Wall
Disputed	Cliff

AREA FEATURES

Airport	Land
Area of Interest	Mall
Beach, Desert	Market
Building	Park
Campus	Reservation
Cemetery, Christian	Rocks
Cemetery, Other	Sports
Forest	Urban

POPULATION

○ CAPITAL (NATIONAL)	◉ CAPITAL (STATE)
● Large City	● Medium City
○ Small City	○ Town, Village

SYMBOLS

Sights/Activities
- Beach
- Castle, Fortress
- Christian
- Monument
- Museum, Gallery
- Point of Interest
- Pool
- Ruin
- Skiing
- Zoo, Bird Sanctuary

Eating
- Eating

Drinking
- Drinking
- Café

Entertainment
- Entertainment

Shopping
- Shopping

Sleeping
- Sleeping
- Camping

Transport
- Airport, Airfield
- Bus Station
- Cycling, Bicycle Path
- General Transport
- Parking Area

Information
- Bank, ATM
- Embassy/Consulate
- Hospital, Medical
- Information
- Internet Facilities
- Police Station
- Post Office, GPO
- Wheelchair Access

Geographic
- Lookout
- Mountain, Volcano
- National Park
- River Flow
- Shelter, Hut
- Spot Height
- Waterfall

LONELY PLANET OFFICES

Australia
Head Office
Locked Bag 1, Footscray, Victoria 3011
☎ 03 8379 8000, fax 03 8379 8111
talk2us@lonelyplanet.com.au

USA
150 Linden St, Oakland, CA 94607
☎ 510 893 8555, toll free 800 275 8555
fax 510 893 8572
info@lonelyplanet.com

UK
72-82 Rosebery Ave,
Clerkenwell, London EC1R 4RW
☎ 020 7841 9000, fax 020 7841 9001
go@lonelyplanet.co.uk

Published by Lonely Planet Publications Pty Ltd
ABN 36 005 607 983

© Lonely Planet Publications Pty Ltd 2006

© photographers as indicated 2006

Cover photographs: Two legs wearing skin shoes in the snow, Lapland, by Gorilla / NordicPhotos, Ullamaija Hänninen (front); Reindeer wandering the streets of Vuotso, Craig Pershouse, Lonely Planet Images (back). Many of the images in this guide are available for licensing from Lonely Planet Images: www.lonelyplanetimages.com.

Printed through Colorcraft Ltd, Hong Kong.
Printed in China